AF540502

Structure and Growth of Mega City

An Inter-Industry Analysis

About the Author

Poonam Sharma is presently a lecturer in Geography at Shaheed Bhagat Singh College, University of Delhi. She completed her Ph.D. in Geography from University of Delhi in 2006. She has participated in several seminars and conferences. Also she has contributed a good number of research papers in journals of national repute and books.

Structure and Growth of Mega City

An Inter-Industry Analysis

Poonam Sharma

CONCEPT PUBLISHING COMPANY PVT. LTD.
NEW DELHI-110059

ISBN-13-978-81-8069-675-6 **ISBN-10-81-8069-675-8**

First Published 2010

Published and Printed by

Concept Publishing Company Pvt. Ltd.
Regd. Office:
A/15-16, Commercial Block, Mohan Garden
New Delhi-110059 (India)
Phones : 25351460, 25351794, *Fax* : 091-11-25357109
Email : publishing@conceptpub.com
Website: www.conceptpub.com

Editorial Office:
H-13, Bali Nagar, New Delhi-110 015, India

Cataloging in Publication Data-- *Courtesy:* D.K. Agencies (P) Ltd. <docinfo@dkagencies.com>

Sharma, Poonam, *Dr.*
Structure and growth of mega city: an inter-industry analysis / Poonam Sharma.
p. cm.
Originally presented as the author's thesis (Ph. D.)--University of Delhi, 2006.
Study conducted in Delhi, India.
Includes bibliographical references (p.).
Includes index.
ISBN 13: 9788180696756 ISBN 10: 8180696758

1. Delhi (India : Union Territory)--Economic conditions. 2. Industrialization--India--Delhi (Union Territory) 3. Industrial policy--India--Delhi (Union Territory) 4. Input-output analysis--India--Delhi (Union Territory) 5. Industries--Environmental aspects--India--Delhi (Union Territory) 6. City planning--India--Delhi (Union Territory) I. Title.

DDC 330.95456 22

Preface

The urban environment constitutes a complex of social phenomena in which economic and non-economic factors are intricately related. A myriad of economic and historical factors explain the location of cities, industries within them, the relationships and inter-dependence within the economy, and outside the economy. Besides the economic aspects of agglomeration, there also exist household economies, which include opportunities for earning higher incomes, wide variety of jobs, public services, leisure and cultural amenities. Then, there are more nebulous social agglomeration economies, which refer to the functions performed by cities as center of innovation through the urban hierarchy and to urban hinterlands. The centralizing pull of urbanization economies creates clusters of differentiated influence zones. Cities exist for specific economic reasons; economies obtained from urban location and the consumption benefits help to explain the pattern of cities and towns through space.

Metropolitan cities play a major role in the modern national as well as global economy by virtue of their functions as the agglomerated growth centers of the world capitalism, continually reinforcing their practical importance. In the present research an attempt has been made to study Delhi's economic structure to analyze the spatial, temporal and horizontal structure of industries. The spatial structure has been studied through various economic and environmental aspects in twenty-eight approved industrial areas of Delhi. The temporal structure of industries has been studied for the period of three decades from 1971-2001. Horizontal structure, *i.e.* linkage and inter-dependence of the economy has been explained through backward and forward linkages. Since, industries are functionally related, the analysis has highlighted the demand by one industry for the product of other, *i.e.* backward and forward linkages. The strength of an economy of a region can be measured in terms of the extent of inter-feeding among the industrial sectors comprising the total complex. Output multiplier have been computed to measures impact of one unit of increase or decrease on a particular sector, *i.e.* direct output multiplier and impact on the whole economy, *i.e.* indirect output multiplier. Another aspect of rapid industrialization is its environmental repercussions. Frequently unnoticed and too often disregarded, undesirable by product are linked directly to the network of physical relationship that govern day-to-day operation of our economic system. The technical inter-dependence between the levels of desirable and undesirable outputs is described in terms of structural coefficients similar to those among all the regular branches of production and consumption. This research makes an endeavour to explain how such externalities (pollution) are associated with modern technology and uncontrolled and unplanned economic growth. The work is the first application of input-output analysis to the economy of Delhi conceived in a geographic perspective.

The present research is completely based on secondary data source. The required data is collected from different Government departments, Ministries and bodies, as Central Statistical Organization, Planning Commission, National Sample Survey Organization, Central Pollution Control Board, Delhi Pollution Control Committee, Delhi Development Authority, Directorate of Economics and Statistics, Directorate of Industries, and reports of various Departments of Delhi Administration. The secondary data used in the entire research work has been obtained from the most authentic, reliable and the only source of data generation in the particular field.

Acknowledgements

I would like to take this opportunity to acknowledge my deepest gratitude to many persons and institutions for their cooperation in terms of time, efforts and guidance without which this research would not have been accomplished.

I am indebted to my supervisor, Prof. B. Thakur of the Department of Geography, University of Delhi for his interest, encouragement and guidance in completing the work.

I also equally owe a debt of gratitude to Prof. R.P. Misra, Department of Geography, University of Delhi under whose supervision and inspiration I began this research work. I express my gratitude to Prof. S.K. Aggarwal, Head, Department of Geography, University of Delhi, for his full cooperation in allowing me to use facilities of the department. I am thankful to Prof. Noor Mohammad and Dr. R.B. Singh, members of advisory committee for their critical comments in preparing the research proposal.

I wish to record my sincere appreciation and thanks to Mr. Rakesh Kohli, Deputy Director-General, National Accounts Division and Mr. A.C. Sharma, Joint Director, National Accounts Division, Central Statistical Organization, Ministry of Statistics and Plan Implementation, New Delhi, for their guidance and help in preparation of input-output transaction tables in the present work. Thanks are also due to Mrs. Renuka Ravindran, Deputy Director, Directorate of Census Operations, Delhi for her suggestions and observations in the present work. I owe a token of thanks to Mr. Joginder Singh, Joint Director, Industrial Statistics Wing, Central Statistical Organisation, New Delhi and Mr. S. Ray, Director, Industrial Statistics Wing, Central Statistical Organisation, Kolkata for providing relevant Annual Survey of Industries data for this research. I wish to thank Dr. Chandra Prakash, Senior Environmental Engineer, Mr. Y.P. Bhatti and Mr. Dinesh Jindal, Delhi Pollution Control Committee and Mr. S. Sharma, Assistant Director, Department of Industries, for their help in data accessibility.

I am thankful to library staff of Ratan Tata Library, Jawaharlal Nehru University Library, School of Planning and Architecture Library, Central Statistical Organisation Library, Planning Commission Library and Udyog Bhawan Library, for allowing me to use required literature. I am estremely thankful to Concept Publishing Company for publishing the book.

I wish to thank Mr. Luv Sharma of Cosmic Technographics, Mr. Debatosh Biswas and Mr. Subhash Sharma for their cooperation in map preparation. I am also thankful to my younger brother Pradeep Sharma, Chartered Accountant for helping in processing huge data involved in preparing input-output transaction table and making me learn computer skills.

I am thankful to Dr. Anu Kapur, Reader, Department of Geography, University of Delhi for being a friend and source of encouragement. Thanks are also due to my friends Dr. V.A.V. Raman from Shaheed Bhagat Singh College, Dr. Punyatoya Patra from Aditi College and Ms. Anupma Hasija, Ms. Rakhi Parijat and Ms. Ritu Ahlawat from Miranda House.

Last but not least, my sincere thanks goes to my husband, Rajeev Sharma, who has been a great support and strength for me. I would equally like to acknowledge my daughter, Saumya for her patience and bearing my non-availability to her for longer hours. I am indebted to my parent-in-laws, parents, Bhaisaheb, Bhabi and family members for their blessings, tolerance and constant encouragement during my work. My gratitude to the almighty God is beyond words to express that enabled me to do the work.

It is my responsibility to acknowledge authors and researchers whose views have been referred in this research work.

Poonam Sharma

Contents

List of Tables

List of Appendices

List of Abbreviations

ASI	Annual Survey of Industries
Cd	Cadmium
CETP	Common Effluent Treatment Plants
CIS	Change in Stocks
Cr	Chromium
CSO	Central Statistical Organization
Cu	Copper
DCB	Delhi Cantonment Board
DDA	Delhi Development Authority
DFC	Delhi Financial Corporation
DIT	Delhi Improvement Trust
DSIDC	Delhi State Industrial Development Corporation
EXP	Export
Fe	Ferrous
GDP	Gross Domestic Product
GFCE	Government Final Consumption Expenditure
GFCF	Gross Fixed Capital Formation
GVA	Gross Value Added
II Use	Intermediate Use
IMP	Import
IOTT	Input-Output Transactions Tables
ISI	Indian Statistical Institute
ITM	Indirect Tax Matrix
Kl	Kiloliter
M U	Million Units
MCD	Municipal Corporation of Delhi
Mg/d	Million Gallons per Day
Mn	Manganese
MPD	Master Plan of Delhi
MRTS	Mass Rapid Transmit System

NAS	National Accounts Statistics
NCR	National Capital Region
NCTD	National Capital Territory of Delhi
NDMC	New Delhi Municipal Corporation
NEERI	National Environment Engineering Research Institute
Ni	Nickel
NIC	National Industrial Classification
NSSO	National Sample Survey Organization
Pb	Lead
PFCE	Private Final Consumption Expenditure
Ph	Phosphorous
S.M.A	Small and Medium Industries Area
S.S.I.	Small Scale Industries
TTM	Trade and Transport Margin Matrix
Zn	Zinc

Chapter - 1

Introduction

The city is akin to an organism in the process of evolution. Its internal structure, circulation and metabolism changes as it grows or declines, expands or contracts, and its links with the outside world undergo quantitative or qualitative change. The economy of the city, thus, continues in flux, it changes its location within the city in response to changes in different city functions, on the one hand, and changes in social, demographic, economic, and technological settings, on the other hand. City is marked by functional changes through time in response to its role in the regional system of cities. All these changes are often accompanied by changes in structure and form[1]. To understand this temporal and spatial dynamics of the city, one has to analyze its internal structure and external relations as economic functions of the city, the process of production and consumption. The urban environment constitutes a complex of social phenomena in which economic and non-economic factors are intricately related[2].

The urban agglomeration is a significant economic factor of production, which includes economies of scale, localization economies and urbanization economies,[3] (although urban and industrial growth beyond the optimum scale of functions and operation will result in diseconomies of scale, which generate many of the critical urban problems that characterize metropolitan areas). Increasing urban size provides markets and complementary industries that expanding industries use to take advantage of potential economies of large-scale operations. A variety of economic factors are operative in creating economies for firms engaged in widely differentiated activities within urban areas. The sum of these benefits is designated as urbanization economies. The centralizing pull of these economies creates clusters of differentiated industries or influence zones. The external economies exist in many facets of the urban economy interactions.[4] The specific economic factors of urban economies that are obtained from urban location and the consumption benefits help to explain the pattern of cities and towns through space.[5] A myriad of economic and historical factors explain the location of cities, industries within them, the relationships and inter-dependence within the economy, and outside the economy.[6] Besides the economic aspects of agglomeration, there also exist household economies, which include opportunities for earning higher incomes, wide variety of jobs, public services, leisure and cultural amenities. Then, there are more nebulous social agglomeration economies, which refer to the functions performed by cities as center of innovation through the urban hierarchy and urban hinterlands[7].

The complexity of urban economy has enhanced with the transformation of mode of production from simple self-contained to more complex processes leading to specialization, mass production and globalization[8]. The need to investigate the web of economic inter-dependence, both theoretically and empirically, has become important for planning and forecasting purposes. While investigating the economic structure of an economy, one can visualize the importance of five factors that determine the kind and amount of economic activity in the region. These include location *i.e.* market, raw material, labour, skill and capital; the second is cost of production, and the third is technology of production which usually stimulates its citizens to search out new developments and adopt the feasible ones; the fourth is the supply of factors of production and the extent to which they are responsible to prices and opportunities, the fifth is the demand side of the equation. All these factors are closely inter-linked that give character to an economy. A change in any of these factors results in concurrent change in other factors.

Metropolitan City, Economy and Ecology

Delhi has witnessed rapid industrial growth in the last decade and half. During the period 1981-2001 there has been an increase of about 65 per cent in the number of industrial units from 42000 in 1981 it has reached to 1.29 lakhs in 2001. The investment rose from 700 crore rupees in 1981 to 1659 crores rupees in 1991, and has reached to 2524 crores in 2001. The production in terms of rupees has increased by about 73 per cent from 1700 crore rupees in 1981 to 6310 crore rupees in 2001. The industries employed about 5.68 lakhs persons in 1981, this rose to 7.3 lakhs in 1991, and 14.4 lakhs in 2001. Industries in Delhi region form a complex group, comprising manufacturing plants, textile, chemical, leather, metal and alloys, machinery and equipment, transport equipment, food products and activities associated with or related to manufacturing process, repair services, personal services and sanitary, generation and transmission of electricity, gas and cold storage etc. Industrial sector occupies an important position in Delhi's economy and plays a pivotal role in its rapid urban and economic development.

Metropolitan cities and city systems play a major role in the modern national as well as global economy. They do so by virtue of their functions as the agglomerated growth centers of the world capitalism, continually reinforcing their practical importance[9]. In this manner, metropolitan cities tend to deepen and widen their competitive advantages over time. A steep rise in the role of knowledge as a factor of production and enhanced by information technology, production, distribution and exchange became important element in the economic system[10]. Largely these economic dynamics of cities[11] and city systems can be understood in relation to the logic and dynamics of urban enterprises, which deploy themselves across space, consume resources, enter into different forms of co-operation or competition and transact with one another intra and inter-regionally[12].

There are several approaches and techniques, which are used by regional scientists to analyze the underlying inter-dependence among the sectors of a regional economy. Input-output analysis is one of them. It is a technique of looking at the existing inter-firm, inter-industry and inter-regional transactions and of determining the impact of various sectoral and regional changes in an economy.

The nature of linkage among different sectors of economy plays an important role in the economic development. The linkage arising through technological inter-connection between various sectors of economy led to the exploration of key sectors. Sectors having strong linkage effects are in a favourable position to induce expansion and the inducement mechanism that may encourage production activities. The linkages are two-fold: one, that uses significant amount of intermediate inputs from others are termed as backward linkage effects, the other, that induces attempts at utilization of its outputs as inputs in some other or new activities are known as forward linkage effects. Thus, a pattern of push and pull can be worked out by identifying the sectors with higher technological linkages.

This technique can be fruitfully used in preparing the economic base study of a region and in planning and forecasting. The present study is designed to analyse the structure of the economy of Delhi using input-output analysis with a view to find out the ensuing changes and future directions.

Environmental stresses and strains are now ubiquitous phenomena appearing in all economic systems, regardless of political ideology and level of economic development. Continual growth in production, perceived set of finite resources, emergence of new technologies, discovery of new pollutants and increasing recognition of the trans-national nature and values of some environmental resources, are just some factors generating concerns for environment.

Most of the environmental problems have stemmed from the universal phenomena of rapid urbanization, migration of population into cities and industrial development without ecological norms[13]. The cities and urban areas with high concentration of industries as well as massive motor vehicle flows are beset by environmental problems particularly, deteriorating air, water quality, noise pollution and resultant health hazards. The problems that persist in urban areas are most acutely felt in large cities. Given the rate with which cities are growing and with the general absence of pollution control measures in many of them, pollution problems are getting worse.

Besides looking to the economic web of Delhi, the present work also makes an endeavour to analyse the interdependence between environmental degradation and economic structure. Since, pollution is the by-product or say an integral part of production process[14], it has its own implications for the economy. For example, pollution abatement itself became a sector of the economy, which costs money both directly and indirectly. In each of its many forms pollution is related in a measurable way to some particular consumption or production process. The quality of carbon monoxide in the air, for example, bears a definite relationship to the amount of fuel burnt by various types of automotive engines, the discharge of polluted water into streams or lakes is linked directly to the level of output of steel, paper, textile etc., and its amount depend, in each instance, on the technological characteristics of the particular industry.

In the present book an attempt is made to study Delhi's economic structure at three levels:

1. The spatial structure of industries. For measuring

spatial structure of industries in the city, various economic and environmental aspects have been studied in twenty-eight approved industrial areas of Delhi.

2. The temporal structure of industries. The temporal study includes the period of three decades from 1971-2001.
3. Horizontal structure, *i.e.* their linkage and inter-dependence explained through (a) backward and forward linkages. Since, industries are functionally related, the analysis highlights the demand by one industry for the product of other, *i.e.* backward and forward linkages. The strength of an economy of a region is measured in terms of the extent of inter-feeding among the industrial sectors comprising the total complex. (b) output multipliers these are indices of impact which measures impact of one unit of increase or decrease on a particular sector, i.*e.* direct output multiplier and impact on the whole economy, i.e. indirect output multiplier.

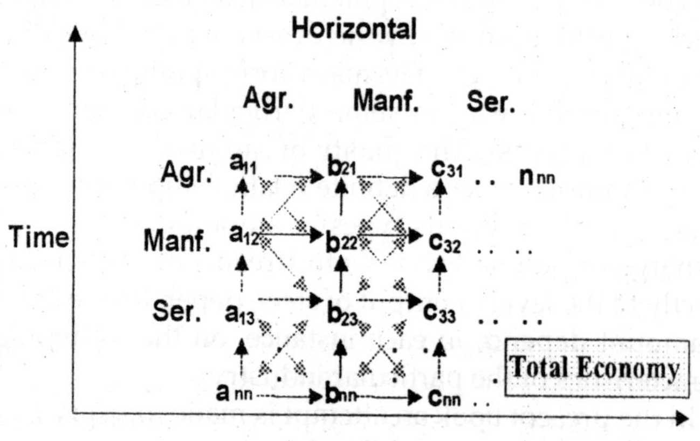

Fig. 1.1 : Level of Analysis

Another aspect of rapid industrialization is its environmental repercussions. Frequently unnoticed and too often disregarded, undesirable by-product are linked directly to the network of physical relationship that govern day-to-day operation of our economic system. The technical inter-dependence between the levels of desirable and undesirable outputs can be described in terms of structural coefficients similar to those among all the regular branches of production and consumption. This research makes an endeavour to explain how such externalities (pollution) are associated with modern technology and uncontrolled and unplanned economic growth. Since, pollution is the dark side of this production and consumption process and also very much in-built in the system, it needs careful attention.

Urban Economy and Inter-Industry Analysis : A Critical Review

To trace the works on variety of urban issues as economic structure, distribution of income, industries, social, demographic, environmental and energy problem, and applications of input-output economics in different urban, regional and ecological analysis, the present literature survey has been classified into following sub-heads: (1) the background, (2) construction of input-output tables, (3) regional studies, (4) ecological analysis, (5) impact studies, (6) studies on technical aspect on input-output economics, and (7) works on trade.

The Background

Theoretical explorations in economic structural analysis began more than two centuries ago with the construction of 'Tableau Economic' (1766) by the French Economist Francois Quesnay, in which notion of compartmentalized treatment of necessarily inter-dependent productive activities was perhaps first formally advanced (discussed by Phillips[15] and

Barna[16]). At this time, another French Economist, Leon Walras employed a somewhat similar approach in his examination of the conditions for economic equilibrium. Walras[17] model contains set of equations for consumer income and expenditure, production cost in each sector and total demand and supply of commodities and factors of production.

Leontief in his 1930s work for which he received the Nobel Prize in Economics in 1973, provided inter-industry analysis as form of a tool or practical instrument. Leontief presented the theoretical framework of United States input-output tables for the year 1919 and 1929 in 1936[18]. Somewhat later, he came with book on the input-output structures of the U.S. economy in 1941[19], this book was revised in 1951[20] in an enlarged and expanded edition that presented the U.S. input-output table for 1939. Progress in the development of national input-output model proceeded in the 1940s and 1950s and work continued at Bureau of Labour Statistics. In 1944, first practical application was made with an exercise for estimating effects of war on employment. By 1950s and 1960s, input-output analysis as a technique became part of national income accounting programme and fully integrated with national income and product accounts. Dorfman[21] pointed out that Leontief's approach was to simplify the Walrasian system to the extent necessary to derive a set of parameters for his model from a single observation of each of the inter-industry transactions in the economy and omitted the effects of limited factor suppliers from the systems. Leontief model precludes many of the adjustments characterizing the Walrasian concept of general equilibrium.

Construction of Input-Output Tables

The second edition of Leontief (1941) was published in 1951[22] in which a 1939 table was added for United States; and in the same year the documentation for the first official table for the country was done, which was constructed by Bureau of Labour Statistics for the year 1947. It was probably the most extensive documented set of analysis that gave details of 500 sectors. The other examples of early constructions include efforts of USSR Central Statistical Board to prepare balance-sheet of national economy for 1923 that was published in 1926[23] (considered one of the earliest attempts), that was later stopped by Stalin. During 1970s, tables were constructed for all Republics for 1966 and 1972. In Britain, Barna[24] in 1952 and Stewart[25] in 1958 made the efforts for construction of national input-output accounts. In Denmark[26] Department of Statistics prepared input-output transaction tables in 1948 and 1951. In the Netherlands, Boer[27] and Tilanus[28] were pioneers. Chenery and Clark[29] prepared input-output accounts for Italy in 1953. Hoglund and Werin[30] prepared the first input-output tables for Sweden in 1957, and Rasul[31] for Pakistan.

In India, a beginning was made in this field at the Indian Statistical Institute (ISI) Calcutta in 1954 in connection with various studies on planning taken up by the Institute. Goodwin and Chowdhary[32] were associated with first twelve-sector table for 1950-51 released by ISI in the form of a mimeographed paper in 1955. Datta's[33] work on inter-industry relations in India included a sixteen-sector table for the year 1949-50 with details on national income, which was released as a working paper by ISI in 1954. Malenbaum[34] also prepared a small input-output table for 1951-52. By this time the work on the subject in Indian Statistical Institute was put on a systematic basis, and a standard 36-sector classification was adopted. A 36-sector table was prepared for 1951-52, 1953-54 and 1955-56[35] and later this table was enlarged to 50-sector table.

In 1959, the Central Statistical Organization of Government of India consisting of economists and statisticians set up a committee to look into the work of Indian Statistical Institute. This committee realized increasing use of input-output tables for the purpose of planning. The inter-industry unit's work was shifted from ISI Calcutta to ISI Delhi, so that it can work in close coordination with Planning Commission and Central Statistical Organization. The Perspective Planning Division of the Planning Commission has worked out a table for 1960-61, 1965, which was later updated to 1973-74. The first Input-Output Transactions Tables (IOTT) consistent with the National Accounts Statistics (NAS) for the year 1968-69[36] was published by Central Statistical Organization (CSO), which was prepared jointly by CSO and Planning Commission. Subsequent to its completion, the CSO undertook the preparation of IOTT for the year 1973-74[37] at its own and descended to continue the work for the preparation of IOTT's on regular bases and publish them every five years. Since then, the CSO brought out the reports on IOTT for the reference years 1978-79, [38] 1983-84, [39] 1980-90[40] and 1993-94[41] in June 1989, September 1990, November 1997 and July 2000, respectively.

More and more countries followed the suit and at a later stage, lists of tables and their main characteristics were set out in United Nations Statistical office reports[42], work on the construction of table gave rise to discussions on questions of classifications, definitions and treatments. The United Nations published the main issues relating to input-output analysis in 1966[43] and 1973. [44]

Regional Studies

From an early stage input-output has been used as a method of regional analysis. Isard[45] proposed the original regional analysis in 1951 when he empirically studied United States economy by dividing it into three regions each with twenty industries. Leontief[46] described a different kind of a model, making use of the distinction between locally and nationally balanced commodities in 1953. Moses[47] provided a model complementary to proceeding ones, in which he connected pair-wise regions for each commodities trade pattern. These theoretical developments proved a good foundation for further application of input-output analysis at local, regional and national level.

Evan and Hoffenberg[48] worked out the transaction table for American economy for the year 1947 for five hundred sectors. Moore and Peterson[49] prepared input-output tables for Utah economy for the year 1947. Isard and Kuenne[50] studied impact of steel upon the New York-Philadelphia industrial region. Tiebout[51] prepared input-output table for Washington State for fifty-four sectors. Artle[52] studied the economy of Stockholm. Watanabe[53] analyzed economic systems of Japan. Weisskoff[54] studied development and trade dependence of Puerto Rico economy. Hirsch[55] prepared input-output for St. Louise metropolitan economy. Simpson and Tsukui[56] have demonstrated that economic structure of United States of America and Japan, although superficially dissimilar; contain almost identical patterns of industries, which are strongly interrelated through input-output tables for the two countries. Polenske[57] prepared a comprehensive multi-region input-output model for the United States for forty-four regions. Kurtzweg[58] made structural comparisons of the US and USSR economies through input-output method. Carter and Ireri[59] prepared two state models for studying Arizona and California. Torii and Fukasaku[60] studied the evolution process of industrial structure and changes in the linkage structure of Japan and Korea. Forsell[61] used input-output model for the analysis of growth of industries in Finland economy in 1960 and 1970 for projecting increase in output of industries. Urata[62] studied the effect of changes in production structure, final demand, labour requirements and capital requirement for Soviet economy. Nyhus,[63] Rampa and Lanza,[64] Granberg,[65] Costa,[66] Waelbraeck and Gupta[67] have made an attempt towards generating multinational input-output tables, synthesizing regional and national models and experimenting with variety of model building across nations for analyzing the international macro economic systems.

Day[68] studied industrial development and technological change of iron and steel industries of both United States and Japan. Rieffer and Tiebout[69] developed inter-regional input-output model for California-Washington region for testing trade coefficients. Staglin and Wessels[70] computed inter-temporal analysis of structural change in general economy based on input-output tables with fifty-six sectors. Augustinovics[71] designated a long-term planning model for Hungary, which is a multi-sectoral linear model based on input-output tables.

Bedzek and Wendling[72] studied the disaggregated structural change between three time periods in American economy. Selvaldon[73] prepared time-series aspect of input-output accounting on the bases of annual input-output accounts for Norway for eighty-nine sectors. Jensen and Hewings[74] worked on regional economic structure of Queensland (Australia) using input-output analysis at three-sector level of aggregation alongwith regression analysis to assess the strength of relationship between the corresponding cells of regional transaction table. Wolff and Howell[75] developed a growth accounting framework from a standard input-output system to analyze sources of overall productivity growth in the economy through sectoral technical change, change in consumption of final output and change in the skill composition of labour force. Hewings[76] prepared input-output table for Indonesia. Pfaijfar and Dolinar[77] prepared input-output table for Slovenian economy, Piispalla[78] for Finland economy, Masakova and Sokolin[79] prepared input-output table for Russia.

Dhar[80] prepared one of the first input-output tables for India, through static open type inter-regional tables. Chakravorti[81] presented features of inter-industry table and aspects of structural characteristics of Turkish economy in thirty-seven sectors. Hazari[82] and Saluja[83] also constructed input-output tables for India. Alagh and Kashyap[84] prepared input-output model for Gujarat for analyzing sectoral output levels and, consequently employment generation potentials were projected. Paithankar[85] worked out thirty two-sector inter-industry flow trades for Marathwada region at purchasers' price to suggest expansion of industries for further economic growth. Saxena and Bhatnagar [86] compared the regional input-output models for Rajasthan, Punjab and Haryana to examine the technological differences between the industrial sectors of the three states and dominance of a particular sector in a state. Singh and Joshi[87] assessed magnitude of linkages and identified key sectors in favourable position to induce expansion of other sectors of the economy of Uttar Pradesh. Dhar[88] prepared regional input-output table for West Bengal and Calcutta metropolitan city. Koti and Santanam[89] prepared input-output table for Maharashtra at purchasers' prices. Sri Prakash and Patnaik[90] constructed input-output transaction tables for Madhya Pradesh, Mehta[91] prepared inter-industry flows for Rajasthan, Panchmukhi[92] did production analysis for Karnataka economy, Bhalla[93] studied the economies of Punjab and Haryana and Singh[94] studied industries of West Bengal.

Ecological Studies

Leontief,[95, 96] has designed a model to evaluate policy decisions covering industrial pollution regulation and the impact of the increase in pollution abatement capital costs on the cost of pollution control. He incorporated input-output model with undesirable environmental effects of modern technology and uncontrolled economic growth. Ayres and Kneese[97] accounted for the flow of materials in the environmental sector, they termed to the concept of material balance, which is based upon the physical law of conservation of mass. Victor[98] has focused on economic-ecological linkage. His approach allows the extension of the basic input-output table directly to the ecological sector.

Daly and Isard[99] attempted to incorporate the environment directly into their respective input-output structure. Both models tried to explain interactions within the economic sector, between the economic sector and the environmental sector, and within the environment sector. Giarratani[100] has examined the impact of meeting air pollution abatement standards on manpower requirements in West Virginia within a regional input-output framework. The effect of technological change and the capital requirements of several statement alternatives were compared. Lesuis and Nijkamp[101] attempted to deal with conflicts between energy, pollution and economic issues in an international framework. On the basis of inter-regional input-output model extended with pollution and energy sectors. The input-output structure was adjusted by incorporating price effects of inputs *via* demand relationships. Lee[102] presented a complementary formulation of economic system with anti-pollution measures that overcomes the problem of determining the existence and uniqueness of a feasible solution. Johnson and Bennett[103] developed a regional input-output model that dealt with both environmental sector and traditional treatment of economy. Given a specific industrial mix and location, the model permits the determination of variable effluent discharge on a firm-by-firm basis, which could be internalized for environmental cost efficiently.

Liews[104] developed a pollution related input-output model responding both income and substitution effects which allows policy-makers to evaluate economic effects of shortages in resources such as water, energy and other mineral products on regional and national economies. Forsund[105] used input-output model of the Norwegian economy for empirical analysis of discharge coefficients related to the production sectors. Carter[106] gave a quantitative appraisal of the implications of some specific pollution statement and energy technologies that tend to reduce the rate of economic growth. Nestor and Pasurka[107] have defined environmental protection activities in the context of input-output framework. Isard, Choghuill, and Kissin[108] developed model for analyzing input-output coefficient table besides supplemented with air, water, and solid waste pollution coefficients for comprehensive planning purpose. Isard[109] also gave insight on linkages of socio-economic and ecological systems. Cumberland and Korbach[110] described inter-industry model with techniques of tracing waste flow, material balance concept for measuring economic environmental relationship. Cumberland and Stram[111] developed a model subsequently to study radioactive waste produced in United States for non-military purposes. Costanza[112] worked out input-output analysis of energy-economy linkages extended by incorporating the energy, cost of labour, government services and dollar energy inputs. Miller and Blair[113] discussed various models relating to input-output analysis and their environmental aspect.

Hammada[114] attempted to predict industrial activity and its environmental effects in the central area of Hokkaido by an input-output model linked with small-scale economic model of the region in terms of pollution emitted from industrial activity and residents alongwith demand of space, water, and power. Kogiku and D'Arge[115] developed model of waste generation and with consumption behaviour of the economy's inhabitants. Lipnowski's[116] study attempted to gauge growth potentials in the presence of complete environmental preservation, Stone[117] discussed pollution in terms of an evaluation approach, Allen and Reid[118] applied ecological input-output to analyze material flow in industries and Machado[119] studied the impact of foreign trade on energy use and emissions. Lange[120] prepared natural resource accounts and Alcantara and Radilla[121] used input-output approach for identifying main sectors that are responsible for CO_2 emission in the country.

Impact Studies

Selvlic and Gradic[122] worked on to capture numerous direct and indirect effects of mutual interactions of the radical structural changes induced by economic reforms in Yugoslavia within input-output framework. Hadded[123] attempted input-output analysis to study reference to the role of propulsive firms in the development process of a growth pole in Brazil and concluded that it was possible to operationalise some of Perroux's ideas. Riedel[124] examined empirically resource allocation consequences of a foot-loose industrial structure to find imported inputs and manufacturing output. Evan and Baxter[125] worked on multi-regional economic-demographic model for projecting final demands, technical coefficients alongwith demographic considerations. Fujita[126] evaluated the potential effects of a policy to decrease the gross output of the agricultural sector in the economy of Hokkaido region using an input-output model. Batey and Weeks[127] attempted to establish an economic input analysis to be influenced by the choice of household disaggregation by focusing on four specific input-output models. Baumol and Wolff[128] empirically demonstrated input-output analysis as a tool for policy design to reduce petroleum use through subsidies for other energy sources, to reduce the polluting emission of production process and stimulate employment ratio. Staglin[129] studied information economy as catalyst for structural changes in advanced economies. He found impact of new information technology on employment and economic development alongwith the relevance of information activities and information occupations.

Prasad[130] assessed the role of natural resources in India's international trade together with labour and capital within the input-output framework. Nath[131] worked on the coefficients of manpower requirements per unit of output in private sector of manufacturing industries in India. Hashim and Dadi,[132] Venkatramaih and Argade[133] worked on industries. Mahajan[134] and Bhalla[135] studied various impacts as regional or temporal, direct, indirect and induced. Paithankar[136] studied the change in the pattern of the government expenditure and generation of repercussions on the national economy among different states and different industries. Rangarajan and Reddy[137] studied impact of prices on commodities, when price of a commodity increases through the inter-industry dynamics. The model was applied to forecast the impact of increase in the prices of coal and petroleum products. Chandel[138] worked on inter-temporal linkages. Solo,[139] Stanley,[140] Krishnamurty,[141] Louiseek,[142] Beckmann,[143] Eskelinen,[144] Reed,[145] Veena,[146] Sastry,[147] Scherer[148], Sawyer[149], and Saenz[150] have made impact studies of different kinds.

Studies on Technical Aspects of Input-Output Economics

Leontief[151] designed an open dynamic system for long range projection of economic system which would enable a planner to determine and to display in a compact manageable term, the limitations imposed on the possible path of a particular economic system by given sets of input-output coefficients describing its changing structural properties over the period of time concerned. Almon and Atkinson[152] discussed within the framework of dynamic input-output system in which investment by an industry was determined by past and present growth of output. Byrd[153] also used dynamic inverse to study crude oil industry cost over time among nine regions of United States. Nijkamp and Reggiani[154] analyzed a dynamic spatial interaction model with optimum control for studying technological changes on demand side and indirect implications for the spatial allocation of commodities. Los[155] worked out a simple dynamic input-output model integrating the issues like technology, investment, trade and education. Kalmbach and Kurz,[156] Jorgenson,[157] Raa[158] and Johonsen[159] worked on variety of dynamic models. Mathur[160] worked on importance and application of dynamic input-output model for planning in developing countries. Koti[161] studied elements of dynamic inverse for Indian economy for insight into the process of economic system.

Morrison and Smith[162] integrated non-survey input-output methods in consistent way with an empirically derived input-output model. McMenamin and Haring[163] presented a new non-survey method for building a regional input-output table and performed some accuracy comparisons among several of non-survey methods. Roepke and Adams[164] applied factor analysis to an input-output table as means of identifying functionally related groups of industries or industrial complexes. Hewings[165] discussed problems encountered in utilizing a state input-output table for sub-regional inter-regional analysis. Sebald and Bulbard[166] demonstrated a method for restructuring input-output models so that parameters more accurately reflect real technological options. Algera and Tuinen[167] dealt with the problems of input-output tables as improvement of results in relation to the demand for consistency over time, comparability with previous years. Bedzek[168] examined three hypotheses central to the Leontief input-output model, namely, constant price coefficients are more stable than current ones; intermediate coefficients are more stable than final demand ones and aggregate coefficients are more stable than disaggregate coefficients. Lynch[169] performed updating procedure of a flow matrix both with and without exogenous information, *i.e.* modified and standard methods. Bon[170] introduced a new class of supply-side multi-regional input-output model with sufficient conditions on regional trade matrices that ensure a generalized supply-side model will be convergent. Gigantes and Hoffman[171] described an input-output model that solves simultaneously for prices, outputs, intermediate and primary inputs including profits, imports, external prices and final expenditures.

Dietzenbacher[172] derived analytical expressions of the sensitivity of input-output multiplier to errors in the data.

Buford[173] described a new procedure for computing approximate inter-industry multipliers that could be used for specific industries. Garhart[174] involved both additive components and multiplicative components and concluded that depending on the nature of the error and the type of multiplier being considered, errors in the technical coefficients could cause even greater errors in multipliers than can regional purchase coefficient errors. Phibbs and Holsman[175] attempted to estimate the multipliers for an input-output table. Pigozzi and Hinojosa[176] found out regional coefficients from national tables. West,[177] Richardson,[178] Jensen,[179] Isserman,[180] Latham,[181] Wurtele[182] Karaska,[183] and Hewings[184] worked on coefficients. Park,[185] Stevens and Glynnis,[186] Dwyer and Waugh,[187] Evans[188] have discussed generations of errors in input-output tables.

Matuszewski[189] worked on input-output models with modifiable coefficients, which provided a relatively convenient framework for organizing the data relevant to certain special purpose as large corporation and regional data. Chakravorti and Raa[190] worked on the aggregation problems in input-output analysis, which arises in two cases, the construction of the input-output tables and application of the model for forecasting sectoral output. Morimoto,[191] Ara,[192] Blin[193] and Theil[194] analyzed aggregation issues. Mukherjee[195] discussed in detail the construction and uses of input-output transaction tables in India. Bawa and Gupta[196] stated about the use of producer's prices and purchaser's prices in the preparation of flow matrices. Mathur[197] demonstrated the use of shadow prices in a developing economy for resource allocation. Das and Sardesai[198] attempted an exercise to test a methodology based on input-output analysis and linear programming for determining the optional location of industries in various regions from the point of view of transport cost. Prasad[199] carried out price-proportionality and aggregations, inverse element and aggregation in input-output analysis.

Bharadwaj[200] made an exhaustive survey of methodological problems in applications of input-output analysis in developing countries. Sarkar[201] proposed a method to correct individual coefficient with aggregative approach. Ghosh[202] presented a review of different models proposed for correction of input-output forecasts.

Cohen[203] examined the use of social accounting matrix multipliers as a framework for gaining insight into development policy on issues of growth and distribution. Pyatt and Round[204] used social accounting matrices for studying development planning. Keuning[205] and Bon[206] discussed fundamentals of qualitative algebra, qualitative input-output and qualitative multi-regional input-output models. Holub and Schnabl[207] and Czayka[208] have also talked about qualitative input-output models. Strassert[209] worked into new domain of national and regional input-output accounting as physical input-output analysis. Pan[210] prepared a socio and ecological integrated input-output table for China.

Studies on Trade

Barker[211] attempted to measure the magnitude and direction of reciprocating effects of trade in an input-output framework. McGilvary and Simpson[212] studied pattern of international trade and predominant factors influencing the trade between two countries of Ireland and United Kingdom. Torii and Akayama[213] studied the effect of tariff reduction as an instrument of regional cooperation among the major Pacific countries through combined multi-sectoral, linear programming model with an international regional input-output model.

Moses[214] worked on the inter-regional trade patterns through input-output analysis. Lecomber[215] used input-output analysis for treatment of foreign trade in an economy. Kol[216] examined trade between developing and industrial countries in relation to key sectors on the basis of linkage effect on employment, income or output. Petri[217] developed a multi-lateral model using input-output approach for analyzing the trade and patterns of trade between two countries. Thorbecke[218] has worked on multi-country trade model and its impact on economies. Tokoyama[219] analyzed the relationship of trade and its effect on product and development of a country. Weisskoff and Wolff[220] studied net effect of the industrialization process of the structure of import flows and resulting changes in import dependence. Veduras[221] prepared a multi-regional, multi-setoral model for the Spanish economy with special attribute of analyzing inter-regional trade flows. Hewings and Munroe[222] studied inter-industry trade among different regions within the country. Sakurai and Moriizumi[223] investigated trade linkages and trade position in terms of division of labour. Sonis and Hewings[224] examined the hierarchy of intra and inter-regional trade flow to analyze the phenomena of horizontal and vertical trade specifications. Bulmer-Thomas[225-26] David,[227] Greytak,[228] Kuyenhoven,[229] John,[230] Suzuki,[231] Morley and Smith[232] Emerson,[233] Linnemann,[234] Round,[235] Peschal,[236] Frankel and Stein,[237] Proops[238] Bruno[239] have also studied various aspects of trade through input-output model.

Panchmukhi. [240-42] discussed import substitution aspect through inter-linkages in an input-output model. Sastry[243] examined resource cost of import substitution to the economy in terms of domestic resources due to the establishment of indigenous manufacturing in India.

Scope of Study

As per nature of problem discussed above, investigation into the economic web of the metropolitan city seems very significant. In order to assess the economic structure the main objectives of the study are to:

1. identify spatial economic structure of industries in Delhi.
2. analyze spatial environmental structure of industries in Delhi.
3. prepare inter-industry transaction tables of Delhi for the years 1970-71 and 2000-01.
4. identify sectors or industries loosing or gaining ground.
5. explore temporal and horizontal structure, i.e. linkages and inter-dependence of industries in Delhi.
6. internalize the pollution levels (production externalities) into the input- output transaction table.

Hypothesis(es)

1. Inter-industry linkages of Delhi have undergone substantial changes during the last three decades.
2. Basic component (export orientation) of production has increased in Delhi.
3. The economic liberalization leads to technological obsolescence of traditional firms and plants.
4. Rapid industrialization increases the output of externalities (pollution).

Metropolitan Economy : Delhi at a Glance

Delhi is spread over an area of 1483 sq kms of land consisting of Delhi Municipal Corporation (Urban), NDMC, Delhi Cantonment, 29 Census Town and two rural Tehsils. Delhi had grown at rapid pace during the past few decades. From mere 14.5 lakhs populations in 1951, it reached to 93.7 lakhs in 1991, and has reached to 137 lakhs in 2001. Each year approximately 2 lakh people migrate to Delhi from neighbouring states. The impact of in-migration is immediately reflected in changing ratios of rural and urban population. Rural component was 10.30 per cent in 1971 which has further decreased to 7.21 per cent in 1981. But in 1991, the rural population to the total population increased to 10.07 per cent, mainly due to the urbanization of rural settlements and in 2001 it is 6.9 per cent. Shortage of housing facilities in Delhi has forced people to settle in rural areas where land prices and rent are comparatively lower.

The industrial growth of Delhi can be traced to the later half of the nineteenth century when three iron foundries and engineering works were established, textile industry's foundation was laid as mentioned in Gazetteer of Rural Delhi[244]. According to Fourth Economic Census (1998) [245], Delhi ranked 12th in India in terms of number of enterprises with total 6.86 lakh enterprises which were 4.49 lakh in 1988, which are engaged in various economic activities except crop production and plantation. In these enterprises about 35 lakhs persons are working, which were 20.23 lakhs in 1988. The detailed employment classification reveals that manufacturing activity is the largest employer as it provides employment to 41.4 per cent persons, social community and personal services employed 17.89 per cent employment and retail trade 15.41 per cent. In this, 90 per cent of workers are male. Of the total enterprises 97.45 per cent of the enterprises are located in urban areas and the remaining 2.45 per cent in rural areas. Besides these, the unregistered component of industrial activity in Delhi is also substantial.

With such a broad and rapidly expanding industrial base over the years and also with globalization and liberalization of economy, several multinational companies have entered into the web, making Delhi an integral part of the global economy. Delhi's industrial and commercial structure is undergoing rapid change. New technologies, management techniques and products are generating new inter-sectoral and inter-regional relations. The present study is designed to examine emerging inter-industry relations and their implications.

Data Source and Methodology

The present research is completely based on secondary data source. The required data is collected from different Government departments, Ministries and bodies as Central Statistical Organization, Planning Commission, National Sample Survey Organization, Central Pollution Control Board, Delhi Development Authority, Directorate of Economics and Statistics, Directorate of Industries, Delhi Pollution Control Committee, and reports of various Departments of Delhi Administration.

The Chapter 4 and 5, where spatial, economic and environmental structure of industries of Delhi have been analyzed, is based on the data from the Census of Industries published from Delhi Pollution Control Committee, Profile of Industries published from Department of Industries, unpublished information on industrial areas/estate, investment, production and employment from Department of Industries. Master Plan Document of 1962, 1981, 2001 and Master Plan 2021 under preparation (partial information) is used. Economic Survey of Delhi from Department of Planning, Statistical Handbook of Delhi, Quarterly Digest of Delhi, Economic Census of Delhi from Directorate of Economics and Statistics, different Census reports on Delhi, Census on Hazardous Industries in Delhi from Delhi Pollution Control Committee and various Supreme Court orders regarding industrial pollution in Delhi are referred.

Chapter 6, 7 and 8 are based on input-output transaction tables prepared as a part of study of the present research work. For the preparation of these input-output tables for two points of time, *i.e.* 1970-71 and 2000-01, data has been collected from Annual Survey of Industries (ASI) which provides data for item-wise inputs and outputs for respective years at three digit level alongwith data on fuel use for registered manufacturing. As regards the unregistered manufacturing concerned data has been obtained from

National Sample Survey Organization (NSSO) survey on unregistered manufacturing for the required years. Primary sector and tertiary data have been obtained from State Accounts Division. Data for demand vectors have been taken from report on Household Consumer Expenditure, Economic Purpose Classification Report and Delhi Budget Document. Also reports from Central Statistical Organization on National Industrial Classification, report on Concordance Tables, and National Input-output Transaction tables for the years 1973-74 and 1993-94 have been used.

The secondary data used in the entire research work has been taken from the most authentic, reliable and the only source of data generation in the field.

In the present research work secondary data has been tabulated as per requirement. Average, percentage and graphical techniques like line graph, bar graph, pie chart, connectivity graph alongwith cartographic techniques and other map representations for various types of data have been used in the entire work.

The present study analyses the inter-dependence among different sectors of economy of Delhi at disaggregated levels, *i.e.* three-digit level classification of industries for the period 1971 and 2001. The base year of the study is 1971, as secondary data of quality from census and other sources are not available for previous years. For analysis, inter-industry transaction table is prepared and Leontief input-output static model[246] is used. Attempts are also made to internalize the aspects of pollution in the model for investigation of pollution as the part of production process, its relationship with various sectors of the economy. The technique is discussed in detail in Chapter three.

Chapterisation

The book is organized into nine chapters. The first chapter introduces the study and deals with metropolitan city its economy and ecology alongwith review of earlier studies, data source methodology scope of this work, data source and research methodology. The second chapter deals with physico-cultural and economic environment of the study area in relevance to present research. This consists of discussion on geology, physiography, drainage, soil types, population and other socio-cultural aspects. The third chapter discusses theoretical and mathematical issues of input-output model used in the present research. The fourth chapter illustrates economic parameters of industries in approved industrial areas of Delhi. This includes growth, nature, type of ownership, size of plots, type of industrial activities and establishments other than industries in these areas. The fifth chapter describes environmental aspects related to industrial activity in conformed industrial areas. The discussion includes air pollution, wastewater generation and hazardous wastes caused in these areas. The sixth chapter explains approaches and procedures used for compilation of input-output transaction table and deals with structural relations of economy emerging from input-output analysis, linkages, multiplier and connectivity study in 1970-71. The seventh chapter analyses the structure of economy as regards inter-industry relations, linkages, multipliers and connectivity relations in 2000-01. The eighth chapter discusses the comparative analysis of input-output structure of the economy in 1970-71 and 2000-01. The last chapter summarizes the results, presents conclusions and suggests directions for further research.

References

1. Nijkamp, P. and Chatterjee, L. (1981) *Urban Problems and Economic Development,* Berlin: Springer-Verlag.
2. Mills, E.S. (1972) Studies in the *Structure of Urban Economy,* Baltimore: Johns Hopkins University Press.
3. Perloff, H.S. (1968) *Issues in Urban Economics, Baltimore:* Johns Hopkins University Press.
4. Roberts, P. (ed.) (1993) *Managing the Metropolis: Metropolitan Renaissance,* Aveburg: Aidrshot.
5. Alfred, L.E. and Graham, A.K. (1976) *Introduction to Urban Dynamics,* Cambridge: Wright Hillen Press.

6. Lawrence, H. (1996) *The Good City*, Bloomington: Indiana University Press.
7. Leahy, W.H. (1970) *Urban Economics: Theory, Development and Planning*, New York: Free Press.
8. Lakshmanan, T.R. and Nijkamp, P. (1993) *Structure and Change in the Space Economy*, Berlin: Springer-Verlag.
9. Hansen, N.M. (1975) *Challenges of Urban Growth: The Basic Economic Size of City Size and Structure*, London: Lexington Books.
10. Edel, M. and Rothenbergi, J. (1972) *Readings in Urban Economics*, New York: McMillan.
11. Miyao, T. and Kanenato, Y. (1987) *Urban Dynamics and Urban Externalities*, London: Harwood Academic Publishers.
12. Duer, F. (1976) *Urban Economy*, Scarton: Intext Educational Publications.
13. Berry, B.J.L. and Horton, F.E. (1974) *Urban Environmental Management: Planning for Pollution Control*, Englewood Cliffs, N. J. : Prentice-Hall.
14. Norton, G.A. and Parlour, J.W. (1972) "The economic philosophy of pollution: A critique", *Environment Planning*, 4: 3-11.
15. Phillips, A. (1955) "The tableau economique as a simple Leontief model", *Quarterly Journal of Economics*, 69(1): 137-44.
16. Barna, T. (1975) "Quesnay's tableau in modern guise", *The Economic Journal*, 85: 485-496.
17. Walras, L. (1954) *Elements of Pure Economics, 1874*, Translated in English by W.J. Homewood, London: Allen and Unwin Inc.
18. Leontief, W.W. (1936) "Quantitative input and output relations in the economic system of the United States", *Review of Economics and Statistics*, 18: 93-115.
19. Leontief, W.W. (1941) *The Structure of United States Economy, 1919-39*, Harvard: Harvard University Press.
20. *Ibid*, Second Edition, 1951.
21. Dorfman, R. (1954) "The nature and significance of input-output technique", *Review of Economics and Statistics*, 36:121-33.
22. Leontief, W.W. (1941) *The Structure of United States Economy, Op.cit.*, Second Edition 1951.
23. U.S.S.R, Central Statistical Board, Balance Sheet of the National Economy of USSR 1923-24, transaction of the Board, 26, Moscow, discussed in G.T.Vladimir (1977) *Studies in Soviet Input-Output Analysis*, New York: Praeger Publishers, 4-12
24. Barna, T. (1952) "The interdependence of the British economy", *Journal of the Royal Statistical Society*, 115(A): 29-81.
25. Stewart, I.G. (1958) "Input-output tables for the United Kingdom, 1948", *The Review of Industry*, 28: 7-15.
26. Mentioned by Richard, S. (1986) "Where are we now" in I. Sohn (ed.) *Readings in Input-Output Analysis*, New York: Oxford University Press, 13-31.

27. Boer, P.M.C. (1982) *Input-Output Relations: A Theoretical and Empirical Study for the Netherlands 1949-67,* Berlin: Springer-Verlag.
28. Tilanus, C.B. (1966) *Input-Output Experiments: The Netherlands 1948-61,* Rotterdavis: Rotterdam University Press.
29. Chenery, H.B and Clark, P.G. (1958) "Structure and growth of Italian economy", *Econometrics,* 26 (4): 481-521.
30. Hoglund, B. and Werin, L. (1964) *The Production System of the Swedish Economy: An Input-Output Study,* Uppsala: Almquist and Wiksells.
31. Rasul, G. (1964) *Input-Output Relationship in Pakistan in 1954,* Rotterdam: Rotterdam University Press.
32. Goodwin, R.R. and Chowdhary, T.P. (1955) *Transaction Matrices for the Indian Union, 1950-51,* Indian Statistical Institute (Mimeographed Paper), No. 17.
33. Dutta, U. (1954) *A Preliminary Study of Inter-Industry Relations in India,* Indian Statistical Institute, Working Paper, No. 7.
34. Malenbaum, W. (1955) "India's domestic product, 1951-52 to 1953-54", *Indian Economic Journal,* 11(3): 247-253.
35. Mukherjee, M. (1967) "On the construction of inter-industry transaction tables in India", in P.N. Mathur, and R. Bharadwaj (eds.) *Economic Analysis in Input-Output Framework,* Poona: Gokhale Institute of Political Economy, 15-26.
36. Central Statistical Organisation (1978) *Input-Output Transaction Table-1968-69,* Ministry of Statistics and Programme Implementation, Government of India, Delhi.
37. Central Statistical Organisation (1981) *Input-Output Transaction Table-1973-74,* Ministry of Statistics and Programme Implementation, Government of India, Delhi.
38. Central Statistical Organisation (1989) *Input-Output Transaction Table-1978-79,* Ministry of Statistics and Programme Implementation, Government of India, Delhi.
39. Central Statistical Organisation (1990) *Input-Output Transaction Table-1983-84,* Ministry of Statistics and Programme Implementation, Government of India, Delhi.
40. Central Statistical Organisation (1997) *Input-Output Transaction Table-1989-90,* Ministry of Statistics and Programme Implementation, Government of India, Delhi.
41. Central Statistical Organisation (2000) *Input-Output Transaction Table-1993-94,* Ministry of Statistics and Programme Implementation, Government of India, Delhi.
42. United Nations (1968) *Directory for National Studies Concerned Urban-Regional Research,* New York: U.N.
43. United Nations Statistical Office (1966) *Problems in Input-Output Tables and Analysis, Studies in Methods,* Series F, No. 14, New York: U.N.

44. United Nations Statistical Office (1973) Problems in Input-Output Tables and Analysis, Studies in Methods, Series F, No. 14, New York: U.N.
45. Israd, W. (1951) "Regional input-output analysis: A model of space economy", *Review of Economics and Statistics,* 34:318-28.
46. Leontief, W. (1986) Studies of the Structure of American Economy, New York: Oxford University Press, 94-129.
47. Moses, L.N. (1955) "The stability of inter-regional trading patterns and input-output analysis", *The American Economic Review,* 45: 808-32.
48. Evan, W.D. and Hoffenberg, P.M. (1952) "Inter-industry relations study", *Review of Economics and Statistics,* 34:74 -89.
49. Moore, F. T. and Peterson, W. (1955) "Regional analysis: an inter-industry model of Utah", *Review of Economics and Statistics,* 37: 368-83.
50. Isard, W. and Kuenne, R. E. (1953) "The impact of steel upon the Greater New York—Philadelphia industrial region", *Review of Economics and Statistics,* 35: 289-301.
51. Tiebout, C.M. (1969) "An empirical regional input-output projection model: The State of Washington", *Review of Economics and Statistics,* 51: 334 -40.
52. Artle, R. (1959) *Studies in the Structure of Stockholm Economy,* Stockholm: Stockholm School of Economics.
53. Watanabe, T. (1970) "Planning application of Leontief model in Japan", in A.P. Carter, and A. Brody (eds.) *Contributions to Input-Output Analysis,* Amsterdam: North Holland, Publishing Company, 9-23.
54. Weisskoff, R. (1975) "Development and trade dependence: The case of Puerto Rico, 1948-63", *Review of Economics and Statistics,* 57: 470-77.
55. Hirsch, W.Z. (1959) "Inter-industry relations of a metropolitan area", *Review of Economics and Statistics,* 41: 360-67.
56. Simpson, D. and Tsukui, J. (1965) "The development structures of input-output tables", *Review of Economics and Statistics,* 47: 434-46.
57. Polenske, K.R (1986) "The implementation of a multi-regional input-output model for United States", in I. Sohn (ed.) *Readings in Input-Output Analysis,* New York: Oxford University Press, 93-106.
58. Kurtzweg, L.R (1977) "A comparison of the US and USSR economies", in V.G. Treml (ed.) *Studies in Soviet Input-Output Analysis,* New York: Praeger Publishers, 369-412.
59. Carter, H.O. and Ireri, D. (1970) "Linkage of California-Arizona input-output models to analyze water transfer patterns", in A. P. Carter and A. Brody (eds.) *Applications of Input-Output Analysis,* Amsterdam: North-Holland Publishing Company, 119-137.

60. Torii, Y. and Fukasaku, K. (1984) "Economic development: An input-output analysis of Republic of Korea and Japan", in *U.N. Proceedings of the Seventh International Conference on Input-Output Techniques,* New York, 333-366.
61. Forsell, O. (1988) "Growth and change in finish economy", in M. Giaschini (ed.) *Input-Output Analysis,* New York: Chapman and Hall Ltd., 287-302.
62. Urata, S. (1988) "Economic growth and structural change in Soviet economy: 1959-72", in M. Giaschini (ed.) *Input-Output Analysis,* New York: Chapman and Hal Ltd., 303-324.
63. Nyhus, D. (1988) "The international system of macro economic input-output model", in M.Giaschini (ed.) *Input-Output Analysis,* New York: Chapman and Hall Ltd., 391-410.
64. Rampa, G. and Lanza, A. (1988) "A model for assessing the growth opportunities of EEC countries", in M. Giaschini (ed.) *Input-Output Analysis,* New York: Chapman and Hall Ltd., 367-390.
65. Granberg, A.G. (1991) "The SYRENA (synthesis of regional and national model) complex", in W. Peterson, (ed.) *Advances in Input-Output Analysis,* New York: Oxford University Press, 161-172.
66. Costa, A.M. (1984) "U.N. global modeling: experimental projection on the bases of alternative procedures", in Proceedings of the *Seventh International Conference on Input-Output Techniques,* New York, 7-32.
67. Waelbraeck, J. and Gupta, S. P. (1984) "World Bank global modelling research", in Proceedings of *the Seventh International Conference on Input-Output Techniques,* New York, 102-112.
68. Day, R.H. (1970) "Recursive programming model of industrial development and technological change", in A. P. Carter and A. Brody (eds.) *Contribution to Input-Output Analysis,* Amsterdam: North Holland Publishing Economy, 99-118.
69. Rieffer, R. and Tiebout, C.M. (1970) "Inter-regional input-output: An empirical California-Washington model", *Journal of Regional Science,* 10:135-152.
70. Staglin, P. and Wessels, H. (1971) "Inter-temporal analysis of structural change in the German economy", in A.P. Carter and A. Brody (eds.) *Input-Output Techniques,* Amsterdam: North Holland Publishing Company, 370-393.
71. Augustinovics, M. (1971) "A twin pair of model of long-term planning", in A. P. Carter and A. Brody (eds.) *Input-Output Techniques,* Amsterdam: North Holland Publishing Company, 1971, 502-578.
72. Bedzek, R.H. and Wendling, R.M. (1976) "Disaggregation of structure change in the American economy: 1947-1966", *Review of Income and Wealth,* 22: 167-182.
73. Selvaldon, P. (1986) "The stability of input-output coefficients", in

I. Sohn, (ed.) *Reading in Input-Output Analysis*, Oxford: Oxford University Press, 226-52.

74. Jensen, R.C. and Hewings, G.J.D. (1987) "The study of regional economic structure: using input-output tables", *Urban Studies*, 22: 207-220.
75. Wolff, E.W. and Howell, D.R. (1989) "Labour quality and productivity growth in United States: an input-output growth accounting frameworks", in R.E. Miller and K.R. Polenske (eds.) *Frontiers in Input-Output Analysis*, New York: Oxford University Press, 148-164.
76. Hewings, G.H. (1993) "The development and use of inter-regional models for Indonesia", *Review of Urban and Regional Development Studies*, 5:135-153.
77. Pfaijfar, L. and Dolinar, L. (2000) "Inter-sectoral linkages in the Slovenian economy for the years 1990, 1992, 1993 and 1995", Paper in *13th International Conference on Input-Output Techniques*, Italy.
78. Piispala, J. (2000) "On regionalizing input-output tables: regional tables in Finland", Paper in *13th International Conference on Input-Output Techniques*, Italy.
79. Masakova, I.D. and Sokolin, V. L. (1988) "Experience of input-output tables for Russia", Paper in *12th International Conference on Input-Output Techniques*, New York, 18-22.
80. Dhar, R. (1967) "The study of inter-regional relations of the Indian economy 1953-54", in P.N. Mathur (ed.) *Economic Analysis in Input-Output Framework*, Poona: Gokhale Institute.
81. Chakravorti, A.K. (1969) "Some aspects of the structural characteristics of the Turkish economy", *Vijnana*, 11: 236-255.
82. Hazari, B.R. (1970) "Empirical identification of key sectors in Indian economy", *Review of Economics and Statistics*, 53: 301-305.
83. Saluja, M.R. (1968) "Structure of Indian economy: inter-industry flows", *Sankhya*, 30:97-122.
84. Alagh, Y.K. and Kashyap, S.P. (1972) "A consistent forecasting model of Gujarat's economy", *Anvesak*, 2:127-37.
85. Paithankar, R.G. (1976) "Inter-industry study of Marathwada region", in P.N.Mathur (ed.) *Economic Analysis in Input-Output Framework*, Poona: Gokhale Institute of Political Economy, 187-208.
86. Saxena, K.K. and Bhatnagar, E. (1987) "Comparison of regional input-output tables", *Anvesak*, 17: 77-113.
87. Singh, S. and Joshi, M. (1991) "Structural linkages and key sectors in the Economy of Uttar Pradesh", *Indian Journal of Regional Science*, 23: 89-94.
88. Dhar, R. (1967) "The study of inter-regional relations of the Indian economy-1953-54", in P.N. Mathur (ed.) *Economic Analysis in Input-Output Framework*, Poona: Gokhale Institute of Political Economy, 155-166.

89. Koti, R.K. and Santanam, K.V. (1967) "Capital coefficient matrix", in P.N. Mathur and R. Bhardwaj (eds.) *Economic Analysis in Input-Output Framework,* Poona: Gokhale Institute of Political Economy, 65-87.
90. Prakash, S. and Patnaik, P.K. (1975) "Inter-industry structure of the economy of Madhya Pradesh", *Anvesak,* 5:141-186.
91. Mehta, B.C. (1971) "Structure of Rajasthan economy", *Anvesak,* 1: 274-80.
92. Panchmukhi, V.R. (1967) "Planning for import substitution: Some methodological and empirical results", in P.N. Mathur (ed.) *Economic Analysis in Input-Output Framework,* Poona: Gokhale Institute of Political Economy, 184-219.
93. Bhalla, G.S. (1971) "Sectoral income multipliers in Punjab and India", *Anvesak,* 1: 210-229.
94. Singh, B. (1972) "West Bengal's industrial economy: An analysis in input-output framework", *Anvesak,* 2: 216-18.
95. Leontief, W. (1970) "Environmental repercussions and the economic structure: An input-output approach", *Review of Economics and Statistics,* 52: 262-71.
96. Leontief, W. (1986) *Input-Output Economics,* New York: Oxford University Press, 279-94.
97. Ayres, R. and Knees, A. (1969) "Production, consumption and externalities", *American Economic Review,* 59:282-97.
98. Victor, R. (1968) *Pollution: Economy and Environment,* London: Allen and Unwin.
99. Isard, W. and Daly, H.E. (1968) "On economics of life science", *Journal of Political Economy,* 76: 392-406.
100. Giarratani, F. (1974) "Air pollution abatement: Output and relative price effects", *Environment and Planning,* 6: 307-12.
101. Lesuis, P. and Nijkamp, P. (1980) "An inter-regional policy model for energy-economic-environmental interactions", *Regional Science and Urban Economics,* 10: 343-70.
102. Lee, K.S. (1981) "A generalized model of an economy with environmental protection", *Review of Economics and Statistics,* 64: 466-73.
103. Johnson, M.H. and Bennett, J.T. (1981) "Regional environmental and economic impact evaluation", *Regional Science and Urban Economics,* 11: 215-230.
104. Liews, C. J. (1984) "Pollution related variable input-output model", *Urban Economics,* 15: 327-49.
105. Forsund, F.R. (1985) "Input-output model and the environment", in A.V. Kneese and J.L. Sweeney (eds.) *Handbook of Natural Resources and Energy Economics,* Vol.1, New York: Economics Science Publishers, 325-41.

106. Carter, A.P. (1986) "Energy, environment and economic growth", *Journal of Economics and Management,* 5: 587-92.
107. Nester, D.V. and Pasurka, C.A. (1995) "Environmental economic accounting and indicators of economic importance of environmental protection activities", *Review of Income and Wealth,* 41: 46-87.
108. Isard, W., Choghuill C. and Kissin, J. (eds.) (1971) *Ecological and Economic Analysis for Regional Planning,* New York: Free Press.
109. Isard, W. (1967) "On linkages of socio-economic and ecological systems", *Papers and Proceedings of Regional Science Association,* 21: 79-99.
110. Cumberland, J.H. and Korbach, J.K. (1973) "A regional inter-industry environmental model", *Papers and Proceedings of Regional Science Association,* 30: 61-75.
111. Cumberland, J.H. and Stram, B.M. (1974) "Empirical application of input-output models to environmental problems", in K.R. Polenske and J.U. Skolka (eds.) *Advances in Input-Output Analysis,* Cambridge: Ballinger Publishing Company, 365-383.
112. Costanza, R. (1986) "Embodied energy and economic valuation", in I. Sohn (ed.) *Readings in Input-Output Analysis,* New York: Oxford University Press, 432-444.
113. Miller, R.E. and Blair, P.D. (1986) *Input-Output Analysis: Foundations and Extensions,* New Jersey: Prentice-Hall, 236-265.
114. Hammada, F. (1991) "A long-term projection of the industrial and environment aspects of the Hokkaido economy: 1985-2005", in W. Peterson (eds.) *Advances in Input-Output Analysis,* New York: Oxford University Press, 223-235.
115. Kogiku, K.C. and D'Arge, R.C. (1973) "Economic Growth and Environment", *Review of Economic Studies,* 4: 61-76.
116. Lipnowski, I.F. (1976) "An input-output analysis of environmental preservation", *Journal of Environmental Economics and Management,* 3:205-14.
117. Stone, R. (1972) "The evaluation of pollution balancing gains and losses", *Minerva,* 10: 412-25.
118. Allen, J.K. and Reid, B. (2004) "Material flow analysis in industrial system", *Journal of Industrial Ecology,* 8: 69-91.
119. Machado, G.V. (2000) "Ecology use and CO_2 emission: An input-output approach applied to Brazilian case", Paper in *13th International Conference on Input-Output Techniques,* Italy.
120. Lange, G.M. (1998) "Applying integrated environment natural resource accounts and input-output model for development planning in Indonesia", *Economic Systems Research,* 10: 113-34.
121. Alcantara, V. and Radilla E. (2000) "CO_2 emission from production perspective in Spain", Paper in *13th International Conference on Input-Output Techniques,* Italy.

122. Selvlic, M. and Gradic, G. (1972) "Using input-output analysis for Yugoslavia price and currency reforms", in A.P. Carter and A. Brody (eds.) *Input-Output Techniques,* Amsterdam: North Holland Publishing Company, 233-241.

123. Hadded, P.R. (1973) "Experiments with input-output analysis at regional and local level", *Annals of Regional Science,* 7: 23-46.

124. Riedel, J. (1975) "Factor proportions, linkages and open developing economy", *The Review of Economics and Statistics,* 57: 484-94.

125. Evans, M. and Baxter, J. (1980) "Regionalizing national projections with a multi-regional input-output model linked to demographic model", *Annals of Regional Science,* 14: 57-71.

126. Fujita, N. (1989) "Input-output analysis of agricultural production quotas", *Annals of Regional Science,* 23: 40-50.

127. Batey, P.W.J. and Weeks, M.J. (1989) "The effects of household disaggregation in extended input-output models", in R.E. Miller and K.R. Polenske (eds.) *Frontiers in Input-Output Analysis,* New York: Oxford University Press, 1989.

128. Baumol, W.S. and Wolff, E.N. (1994) "A key role of input-output analysis in policy design", *Regional Science and Urban Economics,* 24: 93-113.

129. Staglin, R. (1989) "Towards an input-output sub-system for information sector", in R.E. Miller, K R. Polenske, and A.Z. Rose (eds.) *Frontiers in Input-Output, Analysis,* New York: Oxford University Press, 65-78.

130. Prasad, K.N. (1967) "Structure of India's trade explorations with natural resources", in P.N. Mathur (ed.) *Economic Analysis and Input-Output Framework,* Vol. 3, Poona: Gokhale Institute of Political Economy, 220-229.

131. Nath, R. (1967) "Skill-cost input coefficients in Indian manufacturing", in P.N. Mathur (ed.) *Economic Analysis and Input-Output Framework,* Vol. 3, Poona: Gokhale Institute of Political Economy, 54-66.

132. Hashim, S.R. and Dadi, M. (1967) "Leontief capital-output ratio for large-scale manufacturing industries", in P.N. Mathur (ed.) *Economic Analysis and Input-Output Framework,* Vol. 3, Poona: Gokhale Institute of Political Economy, 220-229.

133. Venkatramaih, P. and Argade, L. (1979) "Input-output coefficients and their impact on production level", Artha *Vijnana,* 21: 479-56.

134. Mahajan, B.M. (1970) "Why regional input-output analysis ?", *Artha Vijnana,* 12: 507-522.

135. Bhalla, G.S. (1971) "Sectoral income multipliers in India and Punjab", *Anvesak,* 1:20-9.

136. Paithankar, R.V. (1976) "Economic impact of the indigenous purchase by the Government of India during 1961-66", *Anvesak,* 6: 83-92.

137. Rangarajan, C. and Reddy, K.S. (1981) "Impact of hike in prices of coal and petroleum products on the other sector of the economy", *Artha Vijnana*, 28: 176-181.
138. Chandel, H. (1991) "Inter-temporal, inter-industry linkage pattern of Gujarat manufacturing industries", *Anvesak*, 21:19-40.
139. Solo, R. (1953) "Industrial capacity as a concept in input-output analysis", *Review of Economics and Statistics*, 35: 354-57.
140. Stanley, H.M. (1967) "An inter-industry analysis of wages and plant size", *Review of Economics and Statistics*, 51: 341-45.
141. Krishnamurty, J. and Hazari, B.R. (1970) "Employment implications of India's industrialization: An input-output approach", *Review of Economics and Statistics*, 52: 262-71.
142. Louiseek, A.C. (1982) "Industrial cluster analysis: Backward and forward linkages", *Annals of Regional Science*, 165: 36-47.
143. Beckmann, M.J. (1971) "An input-output model of a von-thunen economy", *Annals of Regional Science*, 5: 6-10.
144. Eskelinen, H. (1983) "Core and periphery in a three region input-output framework", *Annals of Regional Science*, 17: 41-56.
145. Reed, J.D. (1971) "The impact of a dominant industry on a metropolitan area", *Annals of Regional Science*, 5: 62-83.
146. Veena, D.R. (1974) "Input-output model for manpower projection and occupation and educational level in Gujarat", *Anvesak*, 4: 119-144.
147. Sastry, M.L. (1992) "Estimating the economic impact of elderly migration: an input-output analysis", *Growth and Change*, 54-65.
148. Scherer, F. M. (1982) "Inter-industry technology flows and productivity measurement", Review *of Economics and Statistics*, 64: 627-34.
149. Sawyer, J.A. (1991) "Forecasting with input-output matrices", *Economic System Research*, 4: 325-47.
150. Saenz, G.M. (2000) "A hybrid input-output model of water", Paper of *13th International Conference on Input-output Techniques*, Italy.
151. Leontief, W. (1986) *Input-Output Economics*, New York: Oxford University Press, 294-320.
152. Almon, C. and Atkinson, L.C. (1972) "Dynamic inter-industry forecasting for business planning", in A.P. Carter and A. Brody (eds.) *Input-Output Techniques*, Amsterdam: North Holland Publishing Company, 518-530.
153. Byrd, B. (1972) "The crude oil industry in USA and Leontief dynamic inverse", in A.P. Carter and A. Brody (eds.), *Input-Output Techniques*, Amsterdam: North Holland Publishing Company, 531-561.
154. Nijkamp, P. and Reggiani, A. (1988) "Analysis of dynamic spatial interaction models", *Geographical Analysis*, 20: 18-30.
155. Los, B. (2000) "Endogenous growth and structural change in a dynamic input-output model', Paper of *13th International Conference on Input-Output Techniques*, Italy.

156. Kalmbach, P. and Kurz, H.D. (1990) "A dynàmic input-output study of West Germany", *Structural Change and Economic Dynamics*, 1: 371-86.
157. Jorgenson, D.W. (1960) "Dynamic input-output system", *Review of Economic Studies*, 28: 105-116.
158. Raa, T. (1986) "Dynamic input-output analysis", *Review of Economics and Statistics*, 68: 300-10.
159. Johonsen, L. (1978) "On the theory of dynamic input-output models with different time profiles of capital construction", *Journal of Economic Theory*, 19: 573-33.
160. Mathur, P.N. (1975) ".Input-output Economics", *Anvesak*, 5:1-18.
161. Koti, R.K. (1967) "Dynamic inverse for the Indian Economy-1963", in P.N. Mathur (ed.) *Economic Analysis in Input-Output Framework*, Poona: Gokhale Institute of Political Economy, 65-86.
162. Morrison, W. and Smith, P. (1974) "Non-survey input-output techniques at the small area level", *Journal of Regional Science*, 14:1-29.
163. McMenamin, D.G. and Haring, S.E. (1974) "An appraisal of non-survey techniques for estimating regional input-output models", *Journal of Regional Science*, 14: 191-205.
164. Roepke, H. and Adams, D. (1974) "A new approach to the identification of industrial complexes using input-output data", *Journal of Regional Science*, 14: 15-29.
165. Hewings, G.J.D. (1984) "Updating regional input-output tables", *Socio-Economic Planning Sciences*, 18: 319-336.
166. Sebald, A. V. and Bulbard, C.W. (1977) "Effects of parametric uncertainty and technological change in input-output models", *Review of Economics and Statistics*, 59:75-81.
167. Algera, S.B. and Tuinen, H.K.V.C. (1983) "Problems in the compilation of input-output tables in the Netherlands", *Review of Income and Wealth*, 89: 67-87.
168. Bedzek, R.H. (1984) "Test of three hypothesis relating to the Leontief input-output model', *Journal of Royal Statistical Society*, 147:499-509.
169. Lynch, R.G. (1986) "An assessment of methods for updating input-output tables", in I. Sohn (ed.) *Readings in Input-Output Analysis*, Oxford: Oxford University Press, 271-284.
170. Bon, R. (1988) "Supply-side multi-regional input-output models", *Journal of Regional Science*, 29: 41-52.
171. Gigantes, T. and Hoffman, R. (1972) "A price output nucleus for simulation models", in A.P. Carter and A. Brody (eds.) *Input-Output Techniques*, Amsterdam: North Holland Publishing Company, 319-342.
172. Dietzenbacher, E. (1990) "The sensitivity of input-output multipliers", *Journal of Regional Science*, 30: 239-58.

173. Buford, R.L. (1977) "Regional input -output multipliers within a full input- output table", *Annals of Regional Science,* 11: 21-38.
174. Garhart, R.E. Jr. (1985) "The role of error structure in simulations on regional input-output analysis", *Journal of Regional Science,* 25: 353-366.
175. Phibbs, P.J. and Holsman, A.J. (1982) "Estimating input-output multipliers: A hybrid approach", *Environment and Planning,* 14: 335-342.
176. Pigozzi, B.W. and Hinojosa, R.C. (1985) "Regional input-output inverse coefficients", *Growth and Change,* 16: 8-12.
177. West, G. (1981) "An efficient approach to the estimation of regional input-output multipliers", *Environment and Planning,* 13: 857-867.
178. Richardson, H.R. (1985) "Input-output and economic base multipliers", *Journal of Regional Science,* 25: 647-661.
179. Jensen, R.C. (1980) "The effect of relative coefficient size on input-output multipliers", *Environment and Planning,* 12: 654-670.
180. Isserman, A.M. (1977) "A bracketing approach for estimating regional economic impact multipliers", *Environment and Planning,* 9: 1003-11.
181. Latham, W.R. III and Montgomery M. (1979) "Method for calculating regional industry impact multiplier", *Growth and Change,* 10: 2-9.
182. Wurtele, W.C. (1958) "A problem encountered in the comparison of technical coefficients", *Review of Economic Studies,* 26:148-152.
183. Karaska, G. (1968) "Variation of input-output coefficients for different levels of aggregation", *Journal of Regional Science,* 8: 215-27.
184. Hewings, G. (1977) "Evaluating the possibilities for exchanging regional input-output coefficients", *Environment and Planning,* 9: 927-44.
185. Park, S. (1973) "On input-output multipliers with errors in input-output coefficients", *Journal of Economic Theory,* 6: 399-403.
186. Stevens, B. and Glynnis, A.T. (1980) "Error generation in regional input-output analysis", in P. Saul (ed.) *Economic Impact Analysis: Methodology and Application,* Boston: Martinus Nijhoff, 68-84.
187. Dwyer, P.S. and Waugh, F.U. (1953) "On errors in matrix inversion", *Journal of American Statistical Association,* 6 8: 289-319.
188. Evans, W.D. (1954) "The effect of structural matrix errors on inter-industry relations estimate", *Econometrica,* 22: 461-480.
189. Matuszewski, T. (1972) "Partly disaggregated rectangular input-output models and their use for purpose of a large corporation", in A.P. Carter and A. Brody (eds.) *Input-Output Techniques,* Amsterdam: North Holland Publishing Company, 301-318.
190. Chakravorti, D. and Raa, T. (1981) "Aggregation problem in input-output analysis: A survey", *Artha Vijnana,* 23: 326-344.
191. Morimoto, Y. (1970) "On aggregation in input-output analysis", *Review of Economic Studies,* 37: 119-26.
192. Ara, K. (1959) "The aggregation problem in input-output analysis", *Econometrica,* 27: 257-262.

193. Blin, J.M. (1977) "Technological similarity and aggregation in input-output system", *Review of Economics and Statistics*, 59: 82-91.
194. Theil, H. (1967) "The information approach to the aggregation of input-output tables", *Review of Economics and Statistics*, 53: 451-61.
195. Mukherjee, M. (1967) "On the construction and use of inter-industry transactions table in India", in P.N. Mathur (ed.) *Economic Analysis in Input-Output Framework*, Poona: Gokhale Institute of Political Economy, 15-26.
196. Bawa, U.S. and Gupta, T.R. (1967) "Purchasers prices, producers prices and margins in the organized industries in India", in P.N. Mathur (ed.) *Economic Analysis in Input-Output Framework*, Poona: Gokhale Institute of Political Economy, 34-41.
197. Mathur, P.N. (1969) "Input-output flow table 1963", *Artha Vijnana*, 11:181-199.
198. Das, N. and Sardesai, D.D. (1976) "Location of industries in India and transport cost minimization", in P.N. Mathur (ed.) *Economic Analysis in Input-Output Framework*, Poona: Gokhale Institute of Political Economy, 177-183.
199. Prasad, K.N. (1969) "Aggregation in input-output analysis", *Artha Vijnana*, 11: 167-179.
200. Bharadwaj, R. (1969) "Methodological survey of the application of input-output in developing countries", *Artha Vijnana*, 11:148-165.
201. Sarkar, H. (1975) "A model for forecasting of input-output coefficient: An aggregate approach", *Anvesak*, 5: 45-48.
202. Ghosh, A. (1967) "An inter-regional model for production and transportation of commodities for different regions of India", *Artha Vijnana*, 9: 210-227.
203. Cohen, S.I. (1989) "Multipliers analysis in social accounting and input-output framework", in R.E. Miller and K.R. Polenske (eds.) *Frontiers in Input-Output Analysis*, New York: Oxford University Press, 79-102.
204. Pyatt, G. and Round, J.I. (1988) "Social accounting matrices for development planning", *Review of Income and Wealth*, 23: 339-64.
205. Keuning, S. (1988) "Guidelines for the construction of a social accounting matrix", *Review of Income and Wealth*, 34: 71-100.
206. Bon, R. (1988) "Qualitative input-output analysis", *Journal of Regional Science*, 28:41-50.
207. Holub, H.W. and Schnabl, H. (1985) "Qualitative input-output analysis and structural information", *Economic Modelling*, 2: 67-73.
208. Czayka, L. (1972) *Qualitative Input-Output Analysis*, Berlin: Verlag Anton Hain.
209. Strassert, G. (2001) "The flow network of a physical input-output table: Theory and applications", in M. Lahr and E. Dietzenbaher, (eds.) *Input-Output Analysis: Frontiers and Extensions*, London: Macmillan.

210. Pan, X. (2000) "Social and ecological accounting matrix: an empirical study for China", Papers of *13th International Conference on Input-Output Techniques,* Italy.
211. Barker, T.S. (1973) "Foreign trade in multi-sectoral models", in A.P. Carter and A. Brody, (eds.) *Input-Output Techniques,* Amsterdam: North Holland Publishing Company, 111-126.
212. McGilvary, J. and Simpson, D.C. (1972) "The pattern of Irish trade", in A.P. Carter and A. Brody, (eds.) *Input-Output Techniques,* Amsterdam: North Holland Publishing Company, 1972.
213. Torii, Y. and Akayama, Y. (1989) "Effects of tariff reductions on trade in the Asia-Pacific Region", in R.E. Miller, K.R. Polenske and A. Z. Rose (eds.) *Frontiers of Input-Output Analysis,* New York: Oxford University Press, 165-179.
214. Moses, L.N. (1955) "The stability of inter-regional trading patterns and input-output analysis", *American Economic Review,* 45: 803-832.
215.. Lecomber, J.R.C. (1973) "Input-output and the trading economy", in W.F. Gossling (ed.) *Input-Output in United Kingdom,* London: Frank Cass and Company Ltd., 124-148.
216. Kol, J. (1991) "Comparative advantage and international shifts in employment and trade relation", in W. Peterson (ed.) *Advances in Input-Output Analysis,* New York: Oxford University Press, 199-210.
217. Petri, P. (1976) "A multi-lateral model for Japanese-American trade", in K.R. Polenske, and J. V. Skolka (eds.) *Advances in Input-Output Analysis,* Cambridge: Ballinger, 481-497.
218. Thorbecke, E. and Alfred, J.F. (1974) "A ten-region model of world trade", in W. Sellekaerts (ed.) *International Trade and Finance,* London: Macmillan, 91-112.
219. Tokoyama, K. (1976) "Structure of trade, production and development", in K. R. Polenske, and J.V. Skolka (eds.) *Advances in Input-Output Analysis,* Cambridge: Ballinger, 463-478.
220. Weisskoff, R. and Wolff, E. (1975) "Development and trade dependence: The case of Puerto Rico", *Review of Economics and Statistics,* 57: 470-77.
221. Verduras, C.A. (2000) "The estimation of the inter-regional trade in the context of an inter-regional input-output model", Paper, *13th International Conference on Input-Output Techniques,* Italy.
222. Hewings, G.J.D. and Munroe, D.K. (2000) "The role of inter-industry trade in inter-regional trade in Midwest of US", Papers, *13th International Conference on Input-Output Techniques,* Italy.
223. Sakurai N. and Moriizumi, Y. (2000) "Trade pattern and factor use: Evidence for Asia-Pacific countries", Papers, *13th International Conference on Input-Output Techniques,* Italy.
224. Sonis, M. and Hewings, G.J.D. (1995) "The structure of multi-regional trade flows: Hierarchy, feedbacks and spatial linkages", *Annals of Regional Science,* 29: 409-430.

225. Bulmer-Thomas, V. (1978) "Trade, structure and linkages in Costa Rica", *Journal of Development Economics*, 5: 73-86.
226. Bulmer-Thomas, V. (1979) "Export promotion *vs*. Import substitution in Central American common market", *Journal of Economic Studies*, 6:182-203.
227. David, G. (1970) "Regional impact of inter-regional trade in input-output analysis", Papers *of the Regional Science Association*, 25:203-220.
228. Greytak, D. (1970) "Regional impact of inter-regional trade", *Papers of the Regional Science Association*, 25: 203-17.
229. Kuyenhoven, A. (1974) "Sectoral appraisal where trade opportunities are limited", in K. Polenske and J.V. Skolka (eds.) *Advances in Input-Output Analysis*, Cambridge: Ballinger, 279-293.
230. John, A.S. (1972) "Import forecasts for input-output models", *Review of Income and Wealth*, 18: 303-12.
231. Suzuki, K. (1971) "Stability of the structure of the inter-regional flow of goods", *Journal of Regional Science*, 11:187-209.
232. Morley, S. and Smith, G. (1970) "On the measurement of import substitution", *American Economic Review*, 60: 728-735.
233. Emerson, M.J. (1969) "Towards dynamic regional export model", *Annals of Regional Science*, 3: 127-138.
234. Linnemann, A. (1966) *An Economic Study of International Trade Flows*, Amsterdam: North Holland Publishing Company.
235. Round, J. I. (1978) "On estimating trade flows in inter-regional input-output models", *Regional Science and Urban Economics*, 7: 289-302.
236. Peschal, K. (1981) "On the impact of geographic distance on factors of production and trade", *Environment and Planning*, 13: 605-622.
237. Frankel, J.A. and Stein, E. (1998), "Continental trading blocks: Are they natural or supernatural?" in J. A. Frankel (ed.) *The Rationalization of the World Economy*, Chicago: University of Chicago Press.
238. Proops, J.L. (1999) "International trade and sustainability footprints", *Ecological Economics*, 28: 75-97.
239. Bruno, M. (1971) "Optimal pattern of trade and development", in H. Chenery (ed.) *Studies in Development Planning*, Cambridge: Harvard University Press.
240. Panchmukhi, V.R. (1967) "Planning for import substitution: Some mythological and empirical results", in P. N. Mathur (ed.) *Economic Analysis in Input-Output Framework*, Poona: Gokhale Institute of Political Economy.
241. Panchmukhi, V.R. (1973) "Revealed comparative advantage: Indian trade with East Asian countries", *Economic and Political Weekly*, 7: 65-74.
242. Panchmukhi, V.R. (1974) "A multi-sectoral and multi-country planning model for production and trade", in K. R. Polenske and

J. V. Skolka (eds.) *Advances in Input-Output Analysis*, Cambridge: Ballinger, 499-527.

243. Stastry, D.V. (1976) "Import substitution in Indian economy: A case of automobiles", in P. N. Mathur (ed.) *Economic Analysis in Input-Output Framework*, Poona: Gokhale Institute of Political Economy.
244. Gazetteer of Rural Delhi (1976) Delhi Administration, Delhi.
245. Report on Fourth Economic Census (1998) Directorate of Economics and Statistics, National Capital Territory of Delhi, Delhi.
246. For theoretical and mathematical aspect of the technique refer chapter 3.

Chapter - 2

Delhi : Its Cultural-Economic Scenario

Introduction

The previous chapter introduced the conceptual framework, literature review, nature of problem, scope of the study, data sources and research methodology. The present chapter deals with physico-cultural and economic environment relevant to present research. This consists of understanding geology, relief, drainage, soil types, population growth and development of the city and other socio-cultural aspects.

The city of Delhi has a distinct personality of its own with centuries of glorious history. Being the capital of the largest democracy and prime metropolis of India, it is gaining importance among the largest metropolitan cities of the world. Often described as the capital for conquerors, and the capital for centuries, the city has been a focal point in Indian history[1]. Delhi, developed at various sites during different times by several Sultans, Kings and Emperors, was abandoned subsequently. They have left their imprints on its internal physical structure, space relations, social configuration, values and ethos. From Indraprastha to the walled city of Shahjahanabad, hailed as cradle of empires, and alternatively given up as graveyard of dynasties, even the British could not overlook the geographical and strategic importance of Delhi[2]. There has been a constellation of many Delhi's, of which today three alive remains are Shahja-hanabad, the walled city built by the Mughal Emperor; New Delhi, the masterpiece of Sir Edwin Lutyens in the last phase of British Raj; and the post-independence (1947) Master Plan (1962) Delhi, which is growing and sprawling horizontally and vertically.

Delhi with its chequered history has been shaped by a set of extremely complex forces. It is a city with unique blend of old and new[3]. Its deep rooted traditions, fast growing population, expanding administrative and economic functions in the global economic, political and strategic context, modern technological imperatives, strong economic base reflected in a high participation rate, high proportion of total workers engaged in manufacturing, trade and commerce make the city distinctive. It is a major center of income and wealth with highest per capita income (Rs.24450, 2000-01, at current prices) amongst the states and union territories of India, and a number of other forces that the city epitomizes historically, physically and socio-economically.

The present day Delhi after evolving through various successions represents a typical society. It shows true metropolitan character with people from all regions and religions of India and abroad. Being a large metropolitan city it faces the urban problems as well. Due to the unprecedented growth of population with huge migration from neighbouring states, a large number of people reside in slums and squatter settlements, with other problems of water supply, sewerage disposal, housing, electricity, health, transportation and pollution.

Location

The Union Territory of Delhi comprises of an area of 1483 km^2 and ranks 26th in size among states/union territories. It has maximum length of 51.90 km and maximum width is 48.48 km. It is situated in the heart of the Indian subcontinent between 28° 24' 17" N and 28° 53' 00" N latitudes and 75° 50' 24" E and 77° 20' 37" E longitudes. Haryana borders it on northwest and south, on the east by U.P. with the river Yamuna flowing on its eastern border in a north-south direction. Delhi's altitude ranges between 213 and 305 meters above sea level with a general slope of the land from northwest to southeast. The Yamuna river and terminal part of Aravallis hill range are the two main geographical features of the city. The parts of Aravallis range are covered with forests and are called ridges; they are city's lungs and help maintain its environment (Fig. 2.1).

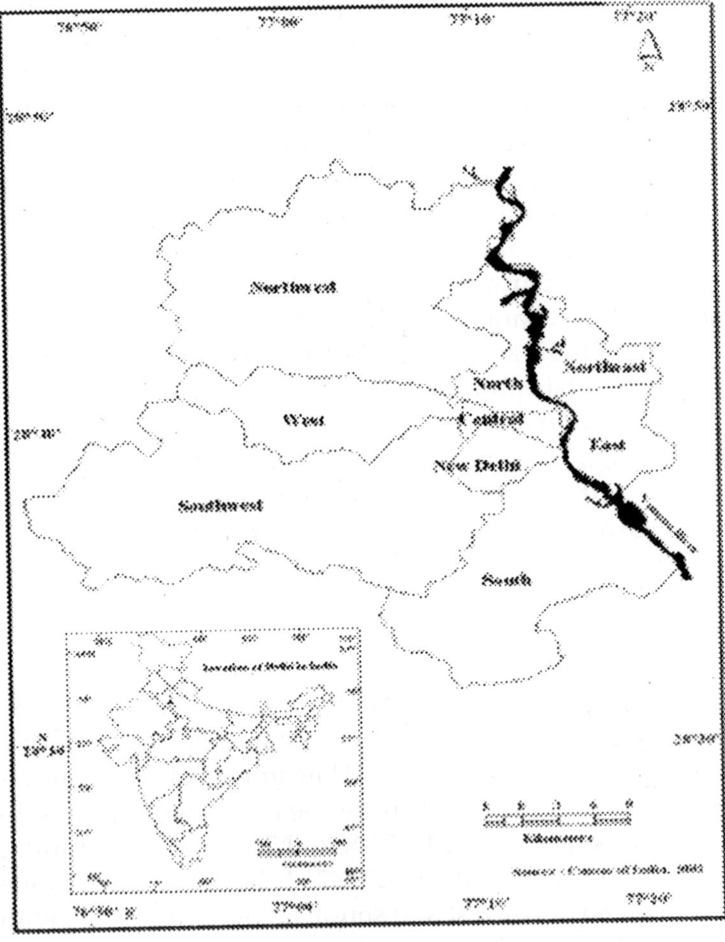

Fig. 2.1 : Location of NCT : Administrative Divisions–Districts 2001

History of Delhi

Delhi is one of the most ancient and historic cities of India. While several cities have risen and decayed, and have been the capitals of the mighty empires and kingdoms.

Delhi remained historically and politically important[4]. Its political importance can be judged from the existence of mausoleums of at least eleven well-known emperors of India, and tombs of about half a dozen minor ones. Generally, only seven cities of Delhi are mentioned, but, if the smaller towns and strongholds are taken into account, the number goes to fifteen[5].

The city has been described as the Indian Rome. It has been the imperial city of India for over 700 years, and Seven Hills of Rome are represented by seven cities of Delhi. In modern Rome, the hills are difficult to be distinguished because of the buildings; modern Delhi exhibits only scattered monuments of its former greatness, and the abandoned cities are difficult to be distinguished[6]. Delhi is said to have derived its name from Raja Dilu or Dhilo a member of the Mauryan dynasty who ruled in the period earlier to the beginning of Christian era. An inscription (1328 A.D.) in village Sarban in Delhi mentions that Tomras founded Dilli. Delhi as a place name seems to have been referred to, for the first time during first and second centuries A.D. Ptolemy, the celebrated Roman geographer, who visited India during second century A.D., has marked in his map 'Daidala' close to Indraprastha[7]. However, there is no mention of any city like Indraprastha in any of the works of Greek writers; even Chinese pilgrim, Huien Tsang has not made any mention about this city in his memoirs.

Indraprastha, the renowned city of Pandavas was probably founded in the 10th century B.C. After its decay, nothing is known for centuries thereafter, and again after Mauryan king Raja Dilu[8], the city fell into oblivion for about 750 years. The account of some important cities, which have risen after Indraprastha and Raja Dilu are:

(i) *Lal Kot* —It is known as city of Anangpals of Kanauj belonging to Tumar or Tomara or Tunwar dynasty, founded by Bilan Deo, better known as Anang Pal in 736 A.D. Anang Pal restored Delhi and he and probably several of his successors made it their capital. In the middle of the 11th Century, Anang Pal II expelled from Kanauj by Chandra Deva, rebuilt and adorned the city, surrounding it with a massive Fort named Lal Kot. The remains of those walls are still believed to exist in a line of grand old ruins that circle the site of the Qutub Minar.

(ii) *Raipithora*—Prithvi Raj, who succeeded his father Anang Pal III in the last quarter of the 12th century, was known as Raipithora. He built the walled city of Raipithora, five miles in circumference. Qutub-ud-Din Aibek, a slave king extended the city beyond the old Lal Kot to plains in the northwest. Raipithora was a border city of Chauhan Kingdom and King Prithvi Raj.

(iii) *Fort of Siri*—In 1290 A.D. Jalal-ud-din Khilji founded a new dynasty. Ala-ud-din Khilji, after repelling the attack of Mangols, built a fort called Siri that was about two miles north of Lal Kot and, later turned it into a city. He constructed a capacious tank called Hauzkhas. The place is now known as Shahpur.

(iv) *Tughlakabad*—Gias-ud-din founded the Tughlak dynasty in Delhi in 1321 A.D. They built a new city called Tughlakabad on a rocky out-crop of hills at a distance of about five km. to southeast of Raipithora, city of Chauhan. He built his city in order to protect himself from the repeated attacks of Mangols. It was never fully occupied for want of adequate water supply. Later it was abandoned.

(v) *Firozabad of Feroze Shah Tughlak* — After succeeding the throne in 1354 A.D., Feroze Shah abandoned Old

Delhi near Qutub Minar and built a new city in 1360 A.D., at a site near the ancient city of Indraprastha. Firozabad was an open city without a wall around it and occupied all the ground from Old Indraprastha to ridge including the site of Shahajahanabad, which was later, built by Shah Jahan. Later, Timur invaded and occupied Delhi for a period of two weeks only but left it in a state of desolation.

(vi) *Din Panah of Indraprastha of Humayun and Sher Shah*— Humayun, Babar's son, re-occupied the old state of Indraprastha between 1530 and 1540 A.D. and rebuilt it under the name 'Din Panah'. He was expelled by Sher Shah who named his city as Shergarh on the site of Firozabad and Indraprastha. His city was 9 km^2 in circumference,

(vii) *Shahjahanabad of Shah Jahan*— After Jahangir's death in 1627 A.D., his eldest son Khurrom succeeded him assuming the title of Shahjahan and transferred his capital from Agra to Delhi. He built imperial city of Shahajahanabad between the years 1636 and 1658 A.D. that is presently known as Red Fort. Shah Jahan, the great builder, built this walled city to accommodate a population of 60,000, having magnificent and great mosque, called the Jama Masjid.

Delhi maintained its importance during the reign of Aurangzeb, but after his death, began the rapid decline of Mughal Empire. In subsequent years, when Delhi was facing an upheaval, Nadir Shah a Persian took over the possession of Delhi, forcing Emperor Mohammad Shah, the then ruler of Delhi to surrender in 1739. He played havoc by ordering massacre in Delhi for fifty-eight days and, finally, rode out of Delhi on May 16, 1739. After Mughal rule, the British conquered Delhi in 1803. In 1829, the British constituted the district of Delhi, which included two Parganas in the north and south of Shahjahanabad. After 1857, Delhi started growing faster. In 1861, Delhi district comprised of three tehsils, *i.e.* Delhi, Ballabgarh and Sonepat. In the later half of 19th century, it saw the coming of railways, postal services and metalled roads. In 1911, King George-V announced shifting of the capital of British India from Calcutta to Delhi. Delhi was reconstituted and Sonepat tehsil was transferred to Rohtak district and a greater part of Ballabgarh tehsil was transferred to Gurgaon district. Thus, Delhi district comprised of the, then, Delhi tehsil and the remaining portion of Ballabgarh tehsil. In 1915, Shahadara town and some villages across the river Yamuna, which at that time were parts of Meerut district in Uttar Pradesh, were added to Delhi

As a result of shifting of capital of India from Calcutta to Delhi in 1911, Civil Lines on the western slopes of ridge and a entirely new city at Raisina, south of Shahjahanabad and east of ancient city of Indraprastha and corresponds by and large with present New Delhi, was built as the capital of British India. The city was developed on a garden city pattern with wide annexes with double rows of trees. The Cantonment at that time located to the west of Viceroy Lodge was shifted to southwest of the new capital, where it is presently located.

Physiography

Relief and Drainage

Physiographically, the Delhi Union Territory can be divided into five types of terrain (Gazetteer of Delhi, 1976):

(i) *Rocky Relief :* The rocky stretch running through the central part of the territory in a northeast and southwest direction from Wazirabad to Mahipalpur is also known as a Delhi Ridge.

(ii) *Badland :* Lying in the vicinity of the rocky relief, it stretches from present day Anand Parbat to Harcharanpur. The rocky area, which is highly jointed has resulted in the percolation of rainwater and gave rise to a fine textured dendritic drainage leading to the formation of these badlands. The entire zone is an area of intense soil erosion.

(iii) *Undulating Surface :* This surface, which is separated by riverine stretch of about 3 meters from the Yamuna floodplains, as observed at Wazirabad Barrage has a centripetal drainage system in its western and southern part through the Nangloi, Sahibi and Palam drains.

(iv) *Najafgarh Drain :* The only escape from the depressions of undulating surface is the Najafgarh Drain which flows in a north-east direction and joins Yamuna near Wazirabad. The course of this link channel has two main stretches with a combined capacity of 3000 cusecs for drainage. However, this proves inadequate during heavy rains causing spillage and flooding.

(v) *Floodplains of Yamuna :* It comprises of an area of 161 km^2 extending up to a maximum of 14 km, from the river in the north. It includes, northern and eastern parts of the territory of Delhi (Fig.2.2).

The drainage network of Delhi is controlled by river Yamuna. On eastern sides of Yamuna there are two drains called Eastern Yamuna Canal and Hindon Canal. The Agra Canal originates from river Yamuna in the southeastern part of Delhi and flows towards Haryana. The Bangar area of Delhi has a major Najafgarh Drain that almost divides the main territory in northern and southern parts. Several smaller drains join the Najafgarh Drain at various stages. The Western Yamuna Canal flowing from north to south supports drinking water requirements (Fig.2.2).

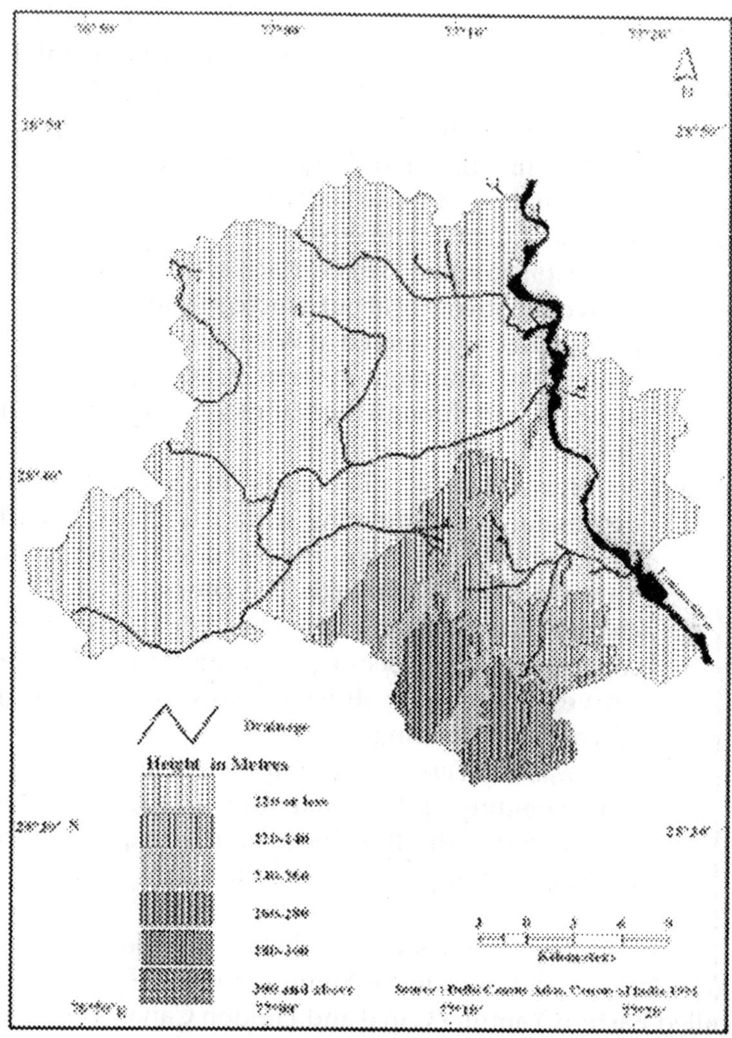

Fig. 2.2 : NCT : Relief and Drainage

Geology

The rocks of Delhi belong to the earliest and latest chapters of geological history of the Earth: the Pre-Cambrian and the Quaternary. The intervening records are missing here, as the region has been lying exposed to sub-aerial erosion since it rose from beneath the sea in late Pre-Cambrian times referred to as the Alwar series of Delhi system in the nomenclature of Indian geology. The Alwar series of rocks occur in small hills, ridges and plateaus, which are probably vestiges of a major folded structure.

They are surrounded by the alluvium and wind blown sand of the Quaternary period. The Quaternary deposits cover all the plains occupying over three-fourths of the area of Delhi[9] (Fig. 2.3).

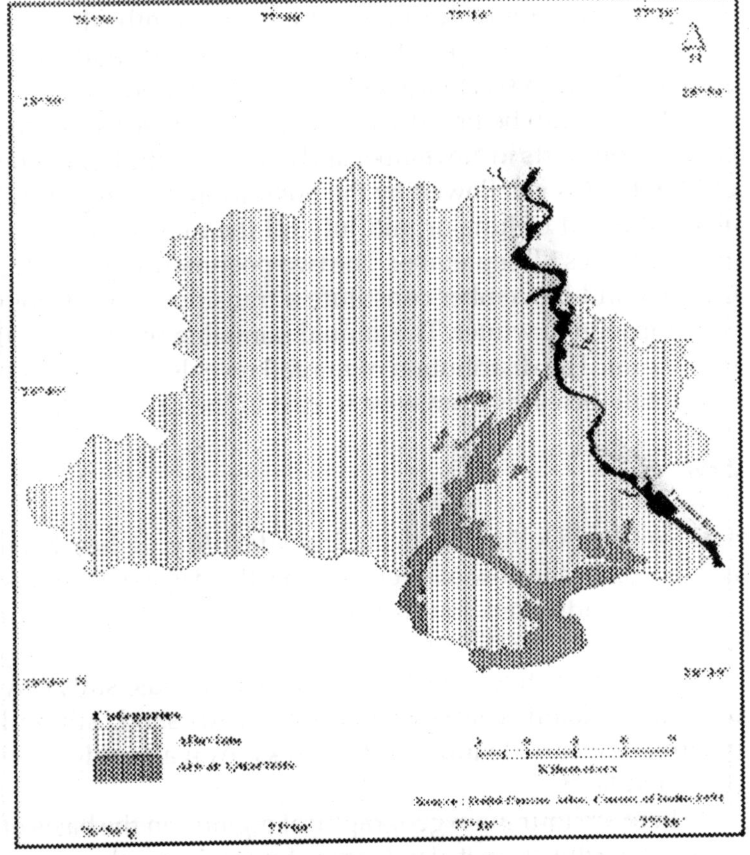

Fig. 2.3 : NCT : Geology

Climate

The Delhi Ridge and river Yamuna are the two main geographical features that influence the climate of Delhi. Due to its geographical location between the Indo-Gangetic plain (in the east), the Thar desert (in the west) the Aravallis (in the southwest) and the Himalayas (in the north), Delhi is characterized by a unique semi-arid climate with extremes of summer and winter[10]. During summer months of April to June, temperatures rise to 40-45 degree Celsius; winter months are typically cold with temperatures falling to 4-5 degree Celsius. Only during the monsoon months does the air of oceanic origin penetrate into this district and cause increased humidity, cloudiness and precipitation.

The year can be broadly divided into four seasons. The cold season starts in November and extends to the beginning of March. This is followed by the hot season, which lasts till about the end of June or mid July till the monsoon arrives and continues till September. The two post-monsoon months October and November constitute a transition period from the monsoon to winter. The annual rainfall ranges from 300 to 700 mm. The distribution of rainfall reveals that intensity of rainfall increases from west to east in the city (Fig. 2.4).

Soil

The soils of Delhi are of medium fertility. It has been influenced by the flow of river Yamuna, flood water, the ridge and the winds from southwestern direction. Five types of soils are found in the city: (a) sandy loam, (b) calcareous, silty clay loam (fine loam), (c) mixed calcareous, silty, clay and sandy loam (coarse to fine loam), (d) sand, silt and calcareous (coarse loamy), and (e) rocky, Aravallis ridge and dissected land.

There are four main geographical regions on the basis of soils. In northwest, silt clay loam is found. In southern part

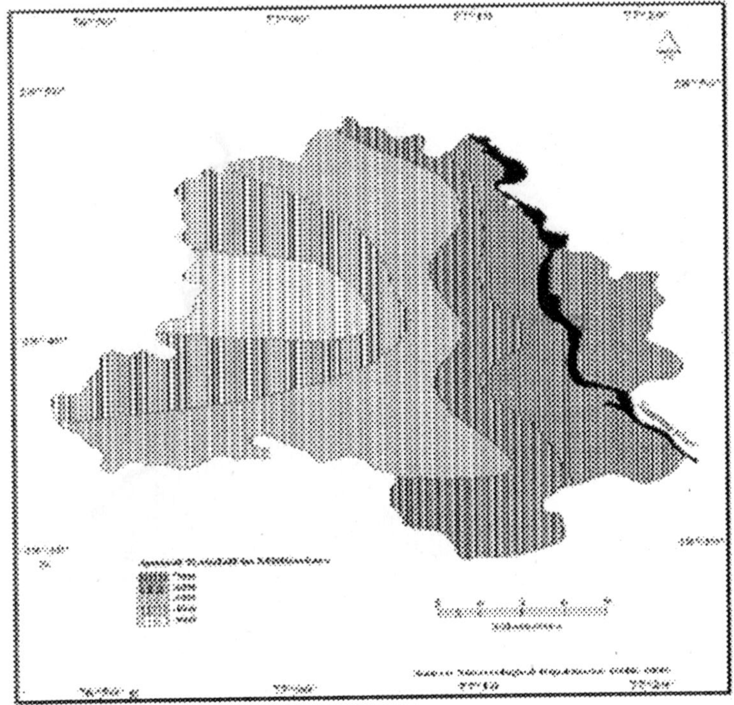

Fig. 2.4 : NCT : Rainfall

rocky ridge and dissected land spreads, while sandy loam is found in southwestern and northeastern has mixed calcareous, silty, clay and sandy loam is found. The sandy loam found in southwest is deficient in nitrogen elements and also has a high salinity; therefore, this soil is not very good for cultivation. The coarse to fine loamy soil as found in northeast, mostly along river Yamuna is good for growing crops and vegetables. The rocky Aravallis ridge and dissected land are found in southern part (Fig. 2.5).

Vegetation

Delhi is characterized by semi-arid, open scrub forest type commonly referred to as 'Rakhs' or broadly classified under

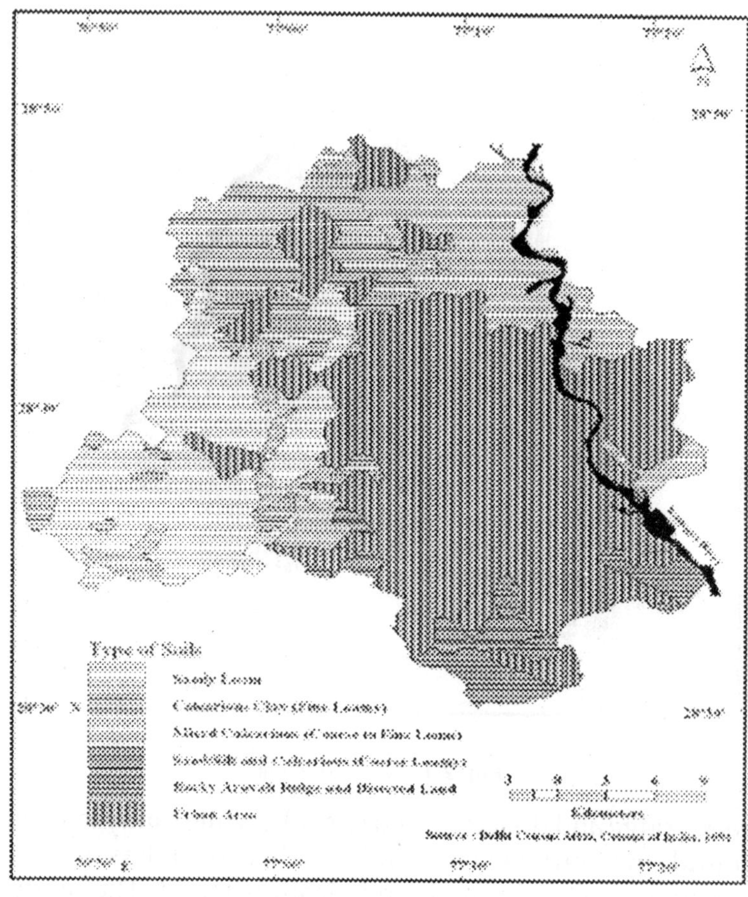

Fig. 2.5 : NCT : Soils

tropical thorny secondary forest. The physiognomic aspects of such vegetation type are the presence of open canopy, absence of distinct stories, abundance of low, stunted, nakedness of the ground (except in monsoon months) and total absence of woody climbers and epiphytes. The overall climate is, however, unfavourable for the growth of any luxuriant vegetation. The forest cover has increased from 0.76 per cent of the total area in 1981 to 1.75 percent in 1994 to 5.93 per cent in 2000-01[11] (Fig. 2.6).

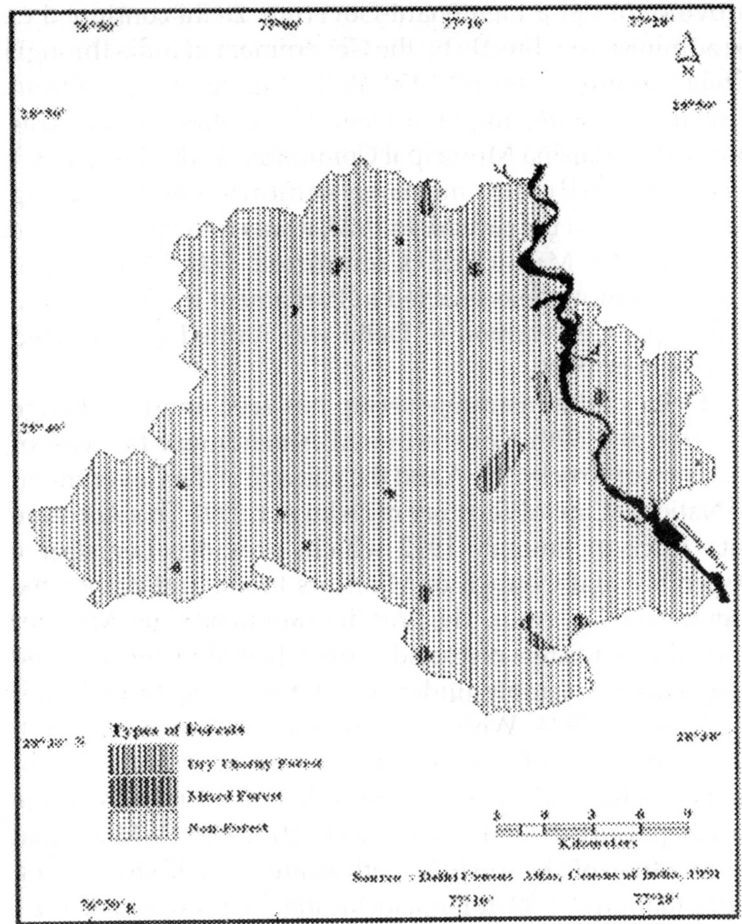

Fig. 2.6 : NCT : Forests

Administrative System

The British began their rule in Delhi in 1805 with the operation of general regulations made by them under the charge of the Resident and Chief Commissioner of Delhi. The system continued with periodic modifications till 1857. In 1858, British made Delhi a provincial town of the Frontier Province and later transferred it to newly formed Punjab province under a Lieutenant-Governor. Delhi continued to be administered directly by the Government of India through Chief Commissioner till 1950. With shifting of capital from Calcutta to Delhi, Imperial Delhi Committee of 1913 was notified as Raisina Municipal Committee under Punjab Act 1911 primarily for meeting sanitary needs during construction of the capital. In 1927, it was re-designed as the New Delhi Municipal Committee. The Municipal Corporation Act was enacted in Parliament in 1957 and the Municipal Corporation of Delhi was formed with elected members in 1958.

Delhi's administrative set-up has seen another change through the 69th Constitutional Amendment by way of insertion of Article 239–A and the passage of the Government of National Capital Territory of Delhi Act, 1991.This Act came into force in January 1992 which, provides Legislative Assembly and Council of Ministers to aid and advice the Lieutenant-Governor. The President appoints Chief Minister and other Ministers on the advice of Chief Minister. The first Legislative Assembly under this Act was constituted after elections in 1993. With the new administrative set-up in Delhi, in place of single district, 9 districts and 27 sub-divisions have been created since January 1997. The three municipal jurisdictions exist as well. The largest is Municipal Corporation of Delhi (MCD) with an area of 1397 km^2 serving a population of 8.89 million, including the rural area of 891.1 km^2 with the population of 0.95 million, and 599.6 km^2 of urban area with its population of 8.04 million. The rest of the Union Territory area is wholly urban shared between two small authorities: New Delhi Municipal Committee (NDMC) with an area of 42.7 km^2 accommodating 0.29 million people, and Delhi Cantonment Board (DCB) with an area of 43 km^2 serving 0.09 million people (Table 2.1).

The National Capital Territory of Delhi was a uni-district territory with two tehsils, *i.e.* Delhi, Mehrauli, and 32 towns

Table 2.1: Area and Population of Municipal Authorities

Municipal Administrative Unit	Area (km^2)					Population (in million)				
	1961	*1971*	*1981*	*1991*	*2001*	*1961*	*1971*	*1981*	*1991*	*2001*
1. Municipal Corporation of Delhi (Urban)	240.84	360.55	431.09	699.60	805.38	2.3	3.6	4.8	8.04	12.81
2. New Delhi Municipal Committee	42.74	42.74	42.74	42.74	42.74	0.26	0.30	0.27	0.29	0.31
3. Delhi Cantonment Board	42.97	42.97	42.97	42.97	42.97	0.04	0.06	0.08	0.09	1.24
4. National Capital Territory of Delhi	1483.0	1483.0	1483.0	1483.0	1483.0	2.6	4.0	6.2	9.4	13.80
(A) Urban	326.54	446.3	591.9	685.35	891.09	2.35	3.64	5.76	8.42	12.81
(B) Rural	1157.1	1033.7	891.1	797.66	591.91	0.29	0.41	0.45	0.95	0.97

Source : Statistical Handbook, Directorate of Statistics and Economics, Government of National Capital Territory, Delhi, 1981,1985,1992, 2002.

till 1997. During the Census of 1901 and 1911 there were only two towns, namely, Delhi Municipal Committee and Shahdara. Later, in 1921, Shahdara was merged with Delhi Municipal Committee to form one town. However, in 1931, the number of towns rose to three, *i.e.* Old Delhi, New Delhi and Shahdara. With the consequent urban change in the administration set-up in 1941 the area of Delhi was reorganized into nine towns, with further erection of new town, namely, West Delhi. Thereafter, the picture entirely changed and Delhi Municipal Corporation came into being in 1958. At the time of 1961 Census, there were only three towns, *i.e.* MCD (Urban), NDMC and Delhi Cantonment. The position remained same till 1971. At the time of 1981 Census, 27 villages were declared as census towns, thereby raising the number of towns from 3 to 30. In 1991 Census, towns again underwent changes raising the number to 32. Thus, since 1961 the area under the zone of MCD has witnessed considerable increase of about 149 per cent in its urban area. At the time of 1971 Census, forty villages were added in the jurisdiction of MCD, thereby increasing its area from 240.84 km^2 in 1961 to 360.55 km^2 in 1971; further, in 1981, it increased to 431.09 km^2, and again rose to 699.6 $km.^2$ by 1991 Census (Table 2.2).

In 1961, the numbers of villages were 300 covering 1157.5 km^2 area accommodating 2.9 lakh persons. The number of villages declined to 258 in 1971 with the reduction in area to 1033.7 $km.^2$ and population of 4.19 lakhs. In 1981, the villages further came down to 231 with the total rural area of 891.1 km^2 and population to 4.52 lakhs, *i.e.* 7.27 per cent of the total population. The entire rural area of Delhi is divided into two tehsils, namely, Delhi and Mehrauli. As per 1991 Census, out of 209 villages, 10 villages are uninhabited. The total rural area is spread over 797.6 km^2 with supporting population of 9.43 lakhs. In 2001, there were 56 census towns and 165 villages and whole city has been divided into 9 districts and 27 tehsils (Fig. 2.7).

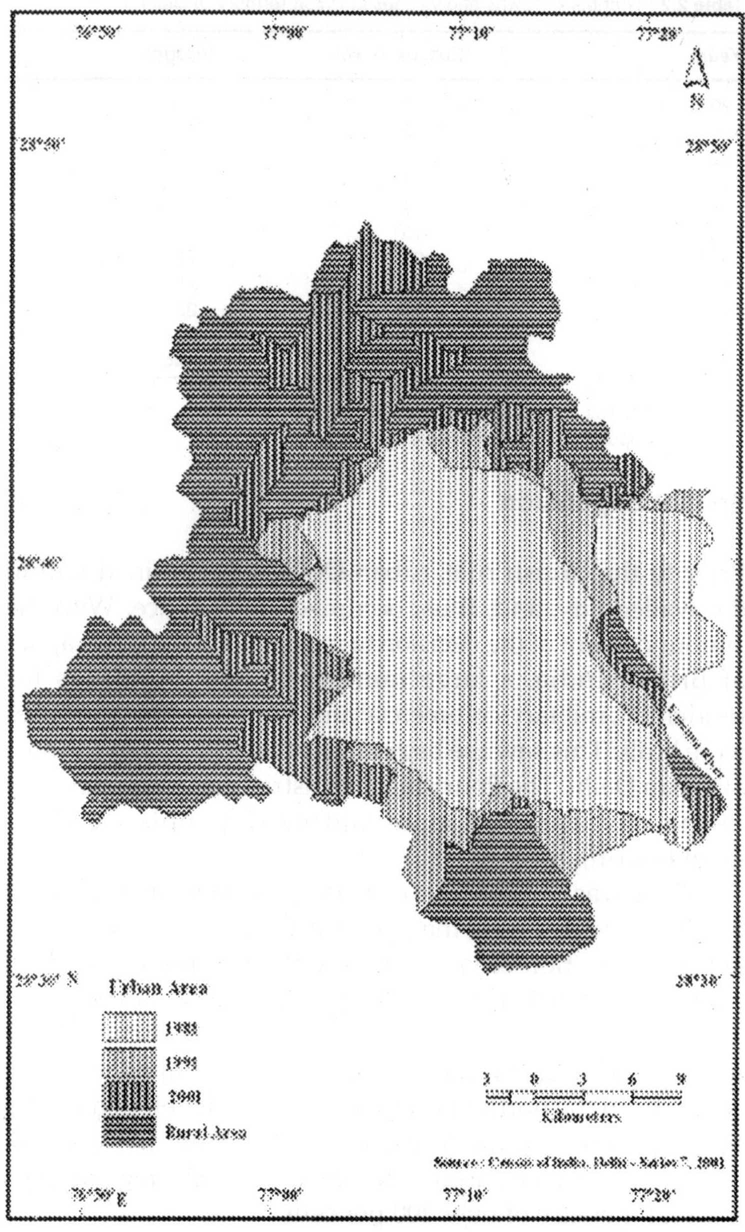

Fig. 2.7 : NCT : Extent of Urban Area (1981-2001)

Table 2.2 : Number of Towns and Villages in Union Territory of Delhi

Years	*Census Towns*	*Villages*
1901	02	N.A.
1911	02	N.A.
1921	01	357
1931	03	359
1941	09	359
1957	10	341
1961	03	300
1971	03	258
1981	27	231
1991	29	209
2001	59	165

Source : Census of India, 1981,Series-28 and Census of India, 2001,Rural-Urban Population Totals, Paper-2, Series 8.

Spatial Expansion

Prior to the British rule, urban Delhi was confined within the walled city, and, thus, occupied small space. With the announcement of the decision to make Delhi, the new capital of British India, a large number of new buildings for residential, military, commercial and administrative purposes were built. This saw the beginning of an increase in the area of urban Delhi. The flourishing industrial and trade activities in the city attracted more and more people from the neighbouring areas.

There was considerable increase in the land area occupied by urban Delhi during the period 1911-21. Shifting of capital led to acquisition of land for New Delhi complex south of walled city. Further, 10,000 acres of land were notified and acquired to the southwest of the site of the new capital city for relocation of the cantonment from civil lines. Another 100 acres to the north of cantonment were developed for the Imperial Agricultural Research Institute (now IARI, Pusa). The urban area increased to 168.09 km^2 in 1921, registering a decadal increase of over 200 per cent.

In the following decades, the physical expansion of the city was slow as the urban area of Delhi increased by 0.80 per cent in 1921-31, 2.7 and 12.17 per cent in 1931-41 and 1941-51, respectively. Another major expansion in the urban area of Delhi took place after partition of India in 1947. Agricultural lands in south and west Delhi were acquired to provide residences to these displaced people. Hence, 1951-61 experienced 66 per cent increase in urban area. Independence saw spurt in developmental activities, and a process of encroachment on adjacent rural land to meet the rising demands of residences, infrastructure facilities etc.

For development of the city, the Delhi Improvement Trust (DIT) was constituted in 1937.In addition to manage the acquired land, it was also assigned the job of rehabilitation of the households to be shifted from slums. Delhi Development Authority (DDA) was set-up in December 1957 under Delhi Development Act 1957, as a successor to DIT for planned development. DDA prepared Master Plan in 1962, which envisaged development of 44,770 hectares of urban area by 1981 for urban population of 46 lakhs. Subsequently, development of additional 4,000 hectares of urban area at Patparganj, Sarita Vihar and Vasant Kunj was added in the target of the first Master Plan. The first Master Plan (1961-81) was reviewed and amended for its extension for another 20 years in 1990. The amended Master Plan (second Master Plan 2001) envisaged acquisition of 20,000 hectares of land for urban area extension of Delhi by 2001 making a target for development of 68,770 hectares urban area. DDA has subsequently proposed to develop 83,804 hectares of land as urban area within the framework of MPD 2001.This includes 3,360 hectares area for urban development along National Highways, 1,996 hectares of Dwarka Phase II and 9,700 hectares of Yamuna bed. DDA has reviewed the provisions of the Master Plan 2001 and actual development of urban area in Delhi to date with a view to revise the Master Plan with reference to the target period for 2021.

Demographic Structure

Growth of Population

Delhi, like any other metropolitan cities in the developing world, is one of the fastest growing cities with an annual growth rate of 4.3 per cent per annum. Being capital of India, it has a special attraction to migrants. A relatively strong diversified economy, high levels of per capita income, a hub of educational institutions, a well developed road network, and a large share of funding from the Government of India, have kept on-going streams of migration active. As a result of this, population of the capital is growing at a tremendous pace. The decennial growth rate between the last two censuses was 46.1 per cent for urban Delhi and 108.6 per cent for rural Delhi. This is causing excessive clustering, haphazard urban growth and spilling over of the urban activities into the countryside, transforming its character. The need for urban land, housing, and provision of infrastructure and civic amenities is also increasing rapidly.

Delhi experienced accelerated growth mainly after the Partition of India with influx of refugees from Pakistan. The medieval and early British period Delhi was wholly or partly enclosed area. In the 20th century, first proclamation of Delhi as the capital of the British empire, and later the refugee influx led to the encroachment of the peripheral areas by the urban people. Ever since, centrifugal forces working within the capital have created a dynamic fringe zone that grows as the city expands. Multiplication and intensification of services in the post-Independence period, expansion of commerce and trade, and growing industrialization and globalization of the economy are main factors responsible for unabated growth of population of Delhi.

There was not much change in Delhi's population during 1901-11 when it grew by just 1.98 per cent. In 1901, the population of the city was 4.05 lakhs that increased to 4.14 lakhs by 1941, with the decadal growth of 18 per cent in

1911-21, 30 per cent in 1921-31 and 44.3 per cent in 1931-41. The major spurt of growth in population occurred in the wake of Partition, when Delhi gained 8.2 lakhs people, and an increase of 90 per cent over 1941 figures was obtained. Delhi, which was sixth largest city in India in 1941, became the third ranking city in 1951. In the following decades, the decennial growth of population has been 52.4 per cent in 1951-61, 50.9 per cent in 1961-71, and 50.6 per cent in 1981-91 and in 2001 it is 46.3 per cent. The annual growth rate of 4.24 per cent during 1981-91 was almost double to that of national average growth rate. In 2001, annual growthrate was 3.86 per cent, which, has reduced from previous decade (Table 2.3).

Table 2.3 : Growth of Population in Delhi

Years	*Population (in lakh)*			*Per cent Variation*		
	Total	*Urban*	*Rural*	*Total*	*Urban*	*Rural*
1901	4.06	2.09	1.97	-	-	-
1911	4.14	2.33	1.81	2.0	11.7	-8.10
1921	4.88	3.04	1.84	18.0	30.7	1.70
1931	6.36	4.47	1.89	30.3	47.0	2.70
1941	12.18	9.96	2.22	44.3	55.5	17.50
1951	17.44	14.37	3.07	90.0	106.6	38.30
1961	26.59	23.59	2.99	52.4	64.2	-2.6
1971	40.66	36.47	4.19	50.9	54.6	40.10
1981	62.20	57.68	4.52	54.0	58.16	8.00
1991	94.20	84.27	9.43	50.64	46.10	108.63
2001	137.82	128.19	9.63	46.30	52.11	2.12

Source : Obtained from Census of India, Population Totals, 1981,1991 and 2001.

Urban population accounts for a very large proportion of population in Delhi. Its share in population has been more than 50 per cent since 1901, but in recent decades it has been increasing steadily. According to 1991 Census, about 90 per cent of the population of the National Capital Territory resides in urban areas, which is 92 per cent in 2001. In 1901, the urban population of the city was 2.1 lakhs. By 1941, it was 6.9 lakhs, with the decadal growth of 11.7 per cent during the period 1901-11, 27.9 per cent in 1911-21, 47 per cent in 1921-31 and 55 per cent in 1931-41. Partition saw exchange of population between India and Pakistan, resulting into a major spurt in population of urban Delhi, thus, witnessed a decadal growth of 106.58 per cent during 1941-51 (Table 2.3).

As compared to the urban population, the growth in rural population has been small. In 1901, the rural population of Delhi was 1.9 lakhs, after registering a negative growth in the decade 1901-11 due to epidemic of plague. The rural population grew by 4.6 per cent in 1911-21, 2.5 per cent in 1921-31, 17.7 per cent and 38.1 per cent in 1931-41 and 1941-51, respectively. In 1951-61, a negative growth of 2.5 per cent was witnessed; it was because 48 villages were declared urbanized by the time of next Census. Steady migration into Delhi also saw an increase in its rural population in 1971, which reached the level of 4.1 lakhs. The decade of 1981-91 saw an increase of about 110 per cent in rural population from 4.5 lakhs to 9.5 lakhs in 1991. This increase may be attributed to large-scale immigration of people from urban areas to villages of Delhi. Besides, the expanding city is increasingly encroaching rural areas without a formal declaration of these areas as urban. The *de facto* city limit now lies far outwards than its *dejure* limit (Table 2.3).

Density of Population

The density of population is closely related to urbanization; the higher the rate of urbanization the greater becomes the human occupancy of land per km^2. The intensity with which a km^2 of land is used increases with the rising demands of an ever increasing population. Although, over the years, both rural and urban density of population has increased steadily, there is greater difference between the two. Urban density of population, according to Table 2.4 has always been more than rural density of population.

Before the British era and with the construction of the walled city, majority of the population residing in Delhi were confined within the walled city. Hence, the density of population in urban areas was as high as 10568 in 1901 and 11798 in 1911. During 1911-21, the city of New Delhi came into existence with large area and sparse population. The urban land areas recorded a decadal growth of 288.6 per cent. It was during this decade that the urban density of population registered a negative growth rate of 84.64 per cent and density was 1812 per km^2. With Delhi becoming the capital city of imperial India, new opportunity's opened up for workers, professionals, traders, administrators. Hence, people started moving into the city; thus, urban population registered an increase of 46.9 per cent and 55.4 per cent in 1921-31 and 1931-41. As a result, the density of urban areas in 1931 and 1941 reached to 2639 and 3470 persons per km^2, respectively. The decadal growth for these periods was 45.64 per cent and 31.48 per cent, respectively (Table 2.4).

Table 2.4 : Density of Population

Years	*Total Density*	*Rural Density*	*Urban Density*	*Decadal Growth in Urban Density (per cent)*
1901	271	135	10568	–
1911	245	123	11798	11.63
1921	326	140	1812	-84.64
1931	426	144	2639	45.64
1941	613	171	3470	31.48
1951	1174	243	7169	10.59
1961	1792	258	7225	0.78
1971	2738	403	8175	13.10
1981	4194	507	9745	19.24
1991	6352	1190	12361	26.84
2001	9294	1627	14387	16.39

Source : Census of India, District Census Handbook 1981, 1991 and Provisional Population Totals, Series 1, 2001.

Partition brought 80 per cent increase in Delhi's population. Therefore, the density of population for the decade 1941-51 reached to 7169 that was double the previous decade. The 1951-61 witnessed small increase in the urban density. This was due to the fact that, urban area increased from 196 km^2 to 326 km^2 *i.e.* an increase of 66 per cent. The decade of 1961-71 registered an increase of 13.10 per cent and 19.24 per cent in 1971-81; the 1981-91 witnessed the decennial growth of 26.8 per cent in the urban density of the city by reaching the figure of 12361 per km^2 and in 2001 urban density has been 14387 persons/km^2 (Table 2.4).

In contrast to the urban density of population, rural density of population has always been low. In 1901, the density of population in rural areas was 135 and did not register much change till 1931-41 when it was 171. After the Partition when a large number of people flocked to Delhi, the rural areas registered 38 per cent increase in its population and 10 per cent decrease in its area. Thus, in 1941-51, the rural density increased by 42 per cent and reached to 243; by 1951-51 it grew to 258 indicating a small increase. Ever since 1961, the rural density of population has increased growing by 56 per cent in 1961-71 and 134.7 per cent in 1981-91. In 2001 it reached to 1627 persons/km^2. Growing population and steady encroachment of rural areas by the expanding city for various residential, industrial, trade, recreational, educational and other purposes is putting pressure on the available land, causing intensity of land use and density to increase in coming decades (Table 2.4).

Delhi was considered as a single district for population Census 1991. In 1996, the Government of National Capital Territory of Delhi has been divided in 9 districts and 27 sub-divisions, *i.e.* tehsils. The distribution of population in tehsils as demonstrated in Fig. 2.8 reflects that Parliament Street, Cannaught Place and Chanakya Puri of New Delhi district; Karol Bagh, Paharganj and Sadar Bazar tehsils of Central district, and Vivek Vihar of East district have lowest population, *i.e.* less than 2.11 lakhs. Shahdara tehsil of northeast district, Daryaganj of Central district and Delhi Cantonment of Southwest district follows with 2.11 to 3.67 lakhs population. In addition to this, Narela and Model Town in northwest, Civil Lines in Civil Lines district have population concentration between 3.67 to 6.31 lakhs. In this category, the other tehsils include Seema Puri in Northwest, Gandhi Nagar in East, Punjabi Bagh and Rajouri Garden in West, Vasant Vihar in Southwest and Kalkaji in South district. It is also shown that Seelam Pur in Northeast, Preet Vihar in East, Najafgarh in Southwest and Defence Colony in South district have population ranging between 6.31 to 10.6 lakhs. Interestingly, Saraswati Vihar in Northwest district has highest concentration of population, *i.e.* 18 lakhs. As is apparently observed from Fig. 2.8 that the proportion of rural population is very small. The tehsils with more than 90 per cent urban population includes Saraswati Vihar, Civil Lines, Seelam Pur, Seema Puri, Preet Vihar, Patel Nagar, Delhi Cantonment, Vasant Vihar, Defence Colony, Hauz Khas and Kalkaji. Added to it, there are tehsils with complete urban population, these include Model Town, Sadar Bazar, Kotwali, Shahdara, Vivek Vihar, Cannaught Place, Chanakya Puri, Karol Bagh and Rajouri Garden. Surprisingly, Narela has maximum rural population, *i.e.* 30 per cent followed by 20 per cent in Gandhi Nagar (Fig. 2.8).

Sex ratio is an important demographic indicator. The sex ratio of Delhi has declined from 827 in 1991 to 821 in the year 2001. The low sex ratio also reflects heavy in-migration (as one of the factors) to the city that mainly includes men population. The sex ratio pattern in tehsils reveals least sex ratio in Delhi Cantonment, *i.e.* 692; this low ratio may be explained by the fact that it is an army area. The tehsils of Narela, Kotwali, Cannaught Place and Kalkaji fall in the sex ratio category of 694 to 786. Added to it, Model Town, Parliament Street, Chanakya Puri, Paharganj, Rajouri Garden, Najafgarh, Defence Colony and Hauz Khas have sex ratio ranging from 787 to 819. Conversely, Saraswati Vihar, Civil Lines, Sadar Bazar, Seelam Pur, Gandhi Nagar, Preet Vihar, Punjabi Bagh and Patel Nagar fall in the category of 819 to 848. It is interesting to note that sex ratio of more

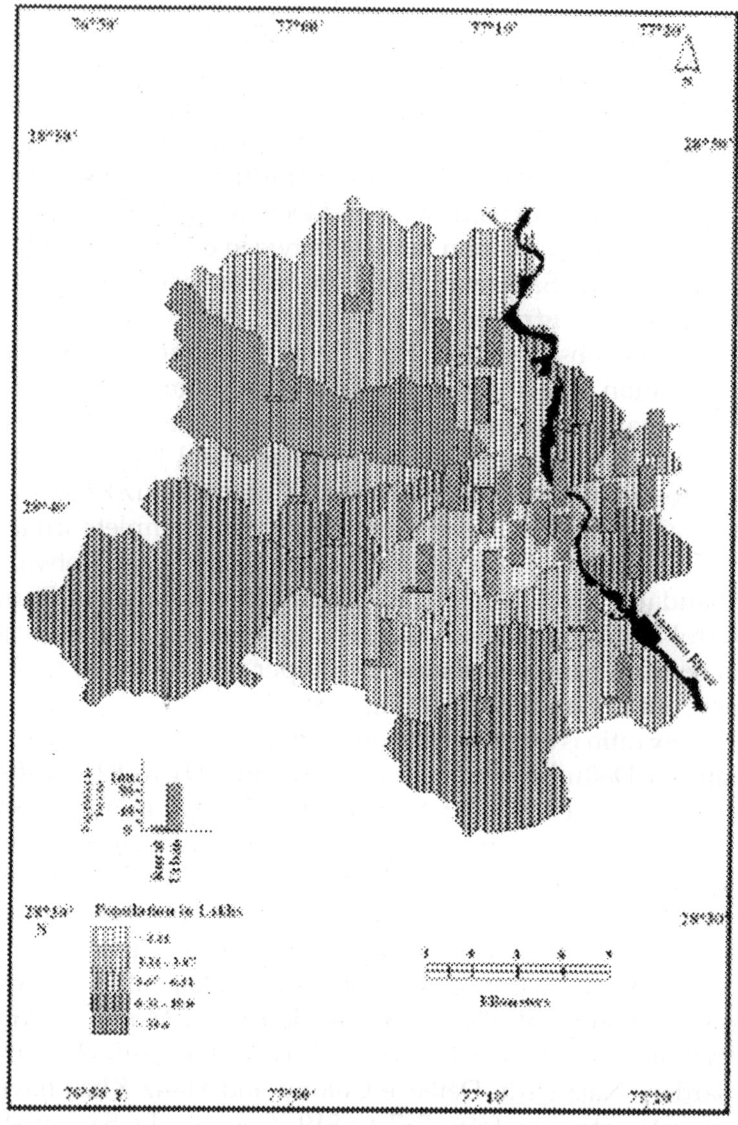

Fig. 2.8 : NCT : Distribution of Population: 2001

than 848 is observed in Shahdara, Seema Puri, Vivek Vihar, Karol Bagh and Daryaganj tehsils (Fig. 2.9).

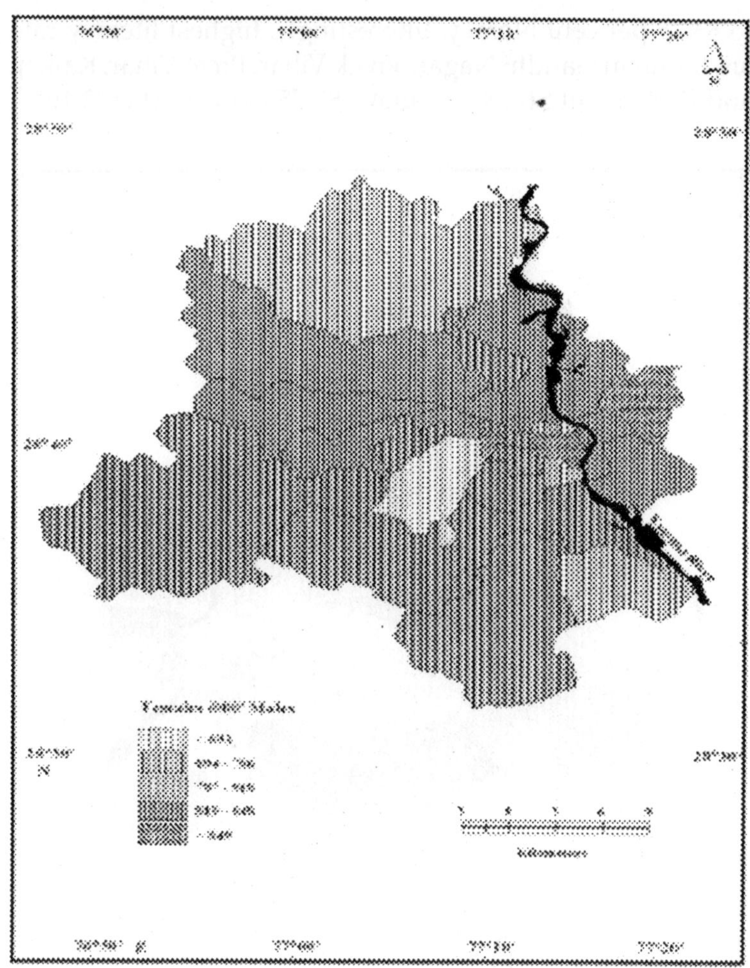

Fig. 2.9 : NCT : Sex Ratio : 2001

The literacy rate pattern as exhibited in Fig. 2.10 demonstrates that less than 77.31 per cent literacy is seen in Kotwali Daryaganj and Rajouri Garden. In addition to this, Narela, Model Town, Sadar Bazar, Seelam Pur, Seema Puri, Chanakya Puri, Paharganj and Patel Nagar fall in the category of 77.31 to 80.6 per cent literacy. Conversely, Saraswati Vihar, Civil Lines, Shahdara, Hauz Khas have 80.6

to 83.75 per cent literacy. Interestingly, highest literacy rate are found in Gandhi Nagar, Vivek Vihar, Preet Vihar, Kalkaji and Parliament Street, *i.e.* above 83.75 per cent (Fig. 2.10).

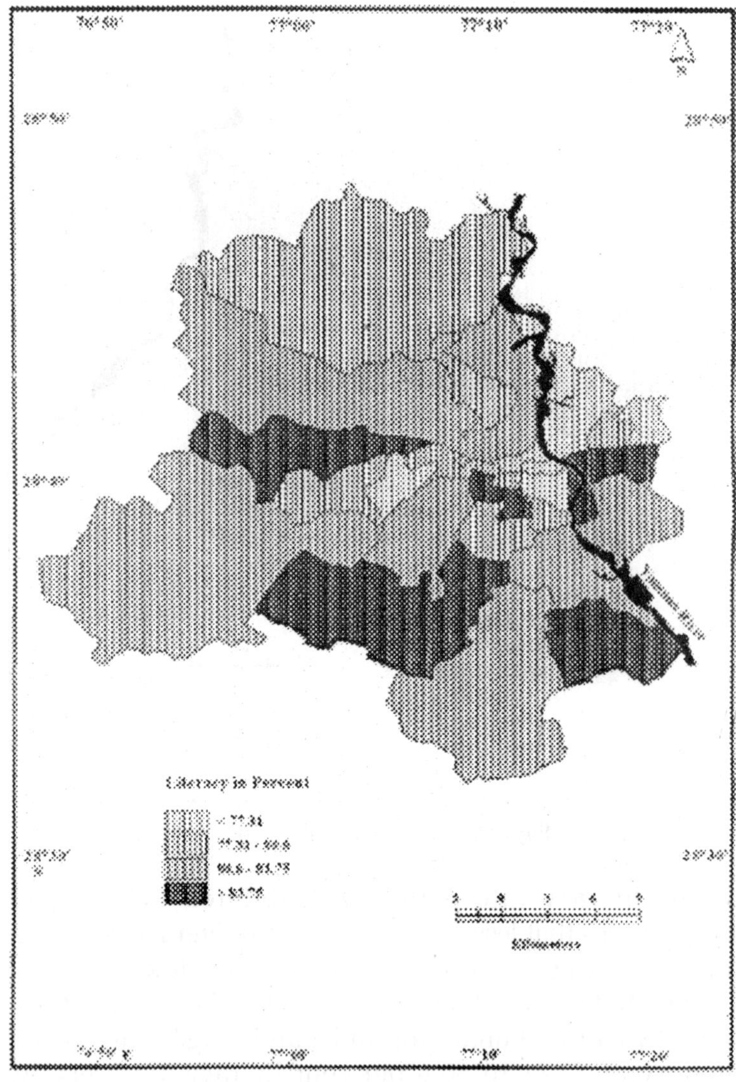

Fig. 2.10 : NCT : Literacy Rate: 2001

Migration

Migration, in recent years, has largely increased on account of development plans, education, industrialization, improved transportation and communication. Delhi is largely a city of migrants. Migration has always been a potent factor in its growth and form. Migration from various states accounts for more than 50 per cent share in the total increase in city's population. Before 1961, migration constituted 48.65 per cent of increase in population. There was a decrease in 1961-71 to 37.3 per cent, but in 1971-81 migrants comprised 57 per cent of the total increase.

Among the States, Uttar Pradesh remains the largest contributor to migration in Delhi accounting for 48 per cent, followed by Haryana, Punjab, and Rajasthan. Besides, these, Delhi draws job seekers form all-over the country. Even the totally unskilled people have been drawn to the capital in search of a better life, such people find employment in lower rung of the workforce in Government and private establishments, a sizeable proportion becomes domestic servants. Migrant workers dominate the construction business; these migrants are the chief constituents of the slum and squatter settlements in Delhi. Employment by far is an important reason behind the movement of people. According to 1981 Census, 27.83 per cent of migration was because of employment reasons followed by marriages, education and others.

As Delhi continues to seek people from all-over the country the trends of migration are bound to accelerate in the near future creating demand on its resources (Table 2.5).

Industrial Progress

Having been the seat of various emperors, Delhi has been attracting skilled craftsmen who found the courts and the attending nobility, ready-made market for the articles

Table 2.5 : Migration of Population in Delhi (in lakh)

Period	*Total Increase in Population*	*Natural Growth*	*Migrants*
1951-61	9.14	4.69 (51.31)	4.45 (48.68)
1961-71	14.07	8.82 (62.69)	5.25 (37.31)
1971-81	21.55	9.26 (42.97)	12.29 (57.03)
1981-91	32.35	13.91 (42.99)	18.44 (57.01)
1991-2001	43.62	19.02 (43.76)	24.53 (56.23)

Source : Conceptual Plan, Delhi Urban Arts Commission 1986.The 1981-91 and 1991- 2001 data has been referred from Economic Survey, Department of Planning, Government of National Capital Territory, Delhi, 2001-2002.Figures in bracket indicate per cent.

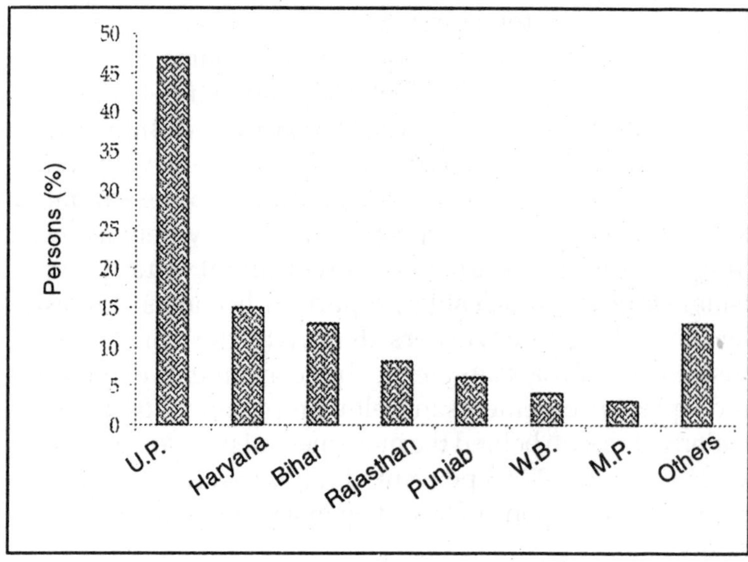

Fig. 2.11 : Origins of Migration to Delhi

manufactured by them. It gained importance in arts, crafts and industries like jewellery, embroidery, silver vases etc. Delhi has been well known for its master craftsman and quality of products but was never considered an industrial town. The present industrial growth can be traced back to the later half of the 19th century when three iron foundries and engineering workers were established in Delhi. And by 1951, the number of registered factories in Delhi increased to 431 as against 227 in 1945. After Independence, the Five-Year Plans were chalked out for the planned development of the country; this also gave a boost to industrial growth in Delhi. The period 1951-61 witnessed 100 per cent increase in the number of units with 60 crores of investment. Production in terms of rupees increased by about 242 per cent and employment in this sector rose to 187,000 persons. Economic reforms and change in industrial policy further gave a push to this sector. Hence industries grew by 120 per cent in the period 1981-91 and 481 per cent in 1991-2001. Besides these, the unregistered component of industrial activity in Delhi is also sizable.

At present, Delhi has 1.29 lakhs industries with a capital investment of Rs.3000 crores and production of over Rs.6310 crores, employing 14.4 lakhs persons (30 per cent of the total workforce in Delhi). The industries contribute one-fourth of the Municipal Corporation's revenue, Rs.800 crores as sales tax and Rs.5000 crores as central excise. This growth is primarily in small-scale sector as only a small number of industries account for large and medium scale. As per the sample survey conducted by DDA in 1981 for comprehensive amendments in the Master Plan of Delhi 1962, about 92 per cent of the then existing 46000 industrial units employed only 20 workers or less. The average employment in these units was 9.3 workers. The textile products, perhaps, because of a few large units had the highest average employment (17.7) worker, while personal and repair services had the lowest (5.2) workers. It is, therefore, clear that bulk of the industries in Delhi are small in character (Table 2.6).

The 1981 sample survey also revealed that about 80 per cent of the industrial units were in other than the planned industrial location. A substantial portion of them is highly

Table 2.6 : Industrial Progress in Delhi

Years	*No. of Industrial Units*	*Investment (Rs. in crore)*	*Production (Rs. in crore)*	*Employment (number)*
1951	8,000	18.13	35.35	95,000
1961	17,000	60.00	121.00	1,87,034
1971	26,000	190.00	388.00	2,91,585
1981	45,000	700.00	1700.00	5,68,910
1991	85,000	1659.00	4462.00	7,30,951
2001	1,29,000	3000.00	6310.00	14,35,962

Source : Profile of Industries, Directorate of Industries, and Government of NCT of Delhi, 2002.

hazardous and noxious, like plastic products and steel polishing, which has penetrated deep into residential areas. In the decade 1981-91, 39000 industrial units have sprung up, but no industrial estate has been developed in Delhi, except the DSIDC's (Delhi State Industrial Development Corporation) Narela Complex for 1800 units. So, 90 per cent of the industrial units in Delhi are located where they should not be.

Manufacturing sector, the main constituent of industrial sector, has an important role in Delhi's economy. It makes a significant contribution of about 23 per cent in the gross state domestic product of Delhi. In the total value of output of organized industrial sector in Delhi, the units engaged in the manufacturing activities contribute about 80 per cent. The number of registered factories engaged in manufacturing has increased from 1096 in 1961 to 1868 in 1971 and rose to 5647 in 1991, further increased to 6682 in 2000, thus, registering more than three times increase during the 1971-2000 period. The zone-wise distribution of number of factories engaged in manufacturing activities (1991 Census) reveals that 1115 factories (20.5 per cent of the total factories) are located in the west zone followed by 965 (17.8 per cent) in the south zone and 780 factories (14.4 per cent) located in Rohini zone. It must be stated that 53 per cent of the total factories in Delhi are located in these three zones. It is seen that 22 per cent of the total factories are engaged in the activities of manufacturing of electrical machinery, apparatus, appliances and machines tool, followed by 16 per cent in manufacturing of textile product, 10 per cent in the manufacturing of metal products and 9 per cent in chemical and chemical products.

The Union Territory of Delhi is predominantly an urban area without much hinterland. As the rate of growth of population of Delhi is high and Delhi being the National Capital, an industrial policy statement for Delhi was prepared and announced in 1982. This policy lays special emphasis on promotion of industries which can achieve optional level of production with less space and power; can generate maximum employment to local skilled persons; sophisticated industries producing high value added items, cover areas of new technology; do not cause congestion and transportation bottlenecks; and are of non-pollutant and non-hazardous nature. Apart from this, the policy statement also laid emphasis on traditional industries, *viz.*, handicrafts, handlooms, and khadi and household industries.

Since 1987, Delhi Administration has adopted a policy of encouraging only small-scale industrial units and only non-polluting and non-hazardous type. The Master Plan of Delhi (MDP-2001) statutorily puts an embargo on further growth of hazardous and noxious large and extensive industries. Industrial areas proposed in MPD-1962 were mainly in the categories of flatted factories, light industries and extensive industries, i.e. at a density of about 500-600 workers per hectare, 100 workers per hectare and 70 workers per hectare, respectively. Large manufacturing units were proposed in ring towns; and small and medium industries were identified at different locations for estimated employment generation, based on zoning regulations provided for different types of industries. Counting upon the unsavory experience of the sixties under MPD 1982, a number of non-conforming industrial units took alternative plots in new industrial estates, but failed to wind up at old sites. To meet the requirements of shifting industries from non-conforming areas and to accommodate new industrial units, MPD-2001 lays down development within a time framework of 20 years for two locations in urban extension and 16 light industrial areas for specific group of industries. The industrial policy of Delhi has been comprehensively elaborated and provided in the Master Plan of Delhi and National Capital Region Plan in respect of permissibility, location, development, control, environmental guidelines and relocation. These policies have been quite effective in planned industrial estates, but have not been very successful in respect of relocation of industries from non-conforming areas.

Workers

A person is defined as a worker or as employed provided he/she participates in any economically productive activity. The rate of increase of the workforce in Delhi during 1951-61 was 51.95 per cent which decreased to 43.79 per cent in the decade of 1961-71, it has been 61.72 per cent in 1971-81 decade which again declined in the next decade of 1981-91 to 49.47 per cent and in 1991-2001 it is 49.62 per cent. The Census results of 2001 shows that the population of Delhi has increased from 94.21 lakhs in 1991 to 137.83 lakhs in 2001 showing an increase of 46.30 per cent over 1991. The workers constituted 31.51 per cent of Delhi's population in 1991 and 32.23 per cent in 2001 (Table 2.7).

The shift in the occupational structure in broad categories resulted that the proportion of workers in primary sector has declined in past decades from 7.68 per cent in 1951 to 2 per cent in 2001. Secondary sector has witnessed an increase in the workforce from 16.94 per cent in 1951 to 41.4 per cent in 2001. The tertiary sector workforce has also declined marginally from 75.38 per cent in 1951 to 58.6 per cent in 2001 (Table 2.7).

Table 2.7 : Main Workers (per cent)

Sectors	*1951*	*1961*	*1971*	*1981*	*1991*	*2001*
Primary	7.68	8.36	4.75	3.81	2.85	2.00
Secondary	16.94	26.03	29.04	34.87	32.43	41.40
Tertiary	75.38	65.61	66.01	61.32	64.72	58.6
Total worker	100	100	100	100	100	100
Total population (in lakhs)	17.44	26.58	40.65	62.20	94.20	137.8
Per cent of workers to total population	32.21	32.14	30.21	31.93	31.51	32.23

Source : Economic Survey (2001-02) Department of Planning, Government of National Capital Territory of Delhi, Delhi.

The proportion of different category of workers in Delhi in year 2001 indicates that cultivator worker's proportion have been highest in Southwest district, *i.e.* 2.34 per cent followed by Northwest with 1.58 per cent and North while least per cent of this category of workers in New Delhi and Central district. Agricultural workers are also highest in Northwest and Southwest, least in New Delhi and Central districts. Household industry workers are witnessed maximum in Central district, closely followed by Northeast district with least 1.57 per cent in New Delhi district. In the category of other workers, highest proportions are evident in New Delhi district with 98.38 per cent followed by South with 97.17 per cent, West and East district with 95 per cent. In most district it is above 94 per cent of the total workers (Fig. 2.12).

Infrastructure

The quality of life depends very much on the level of availability, accessibility and quality of infrastructure. The rapid growth of population necessitates augmentation of water supply, power supply, sewerage, drainage and solid waste management. Analyzing the present state of affairs, infrastructure problems have become a cause of crisis in the metropolitan life.

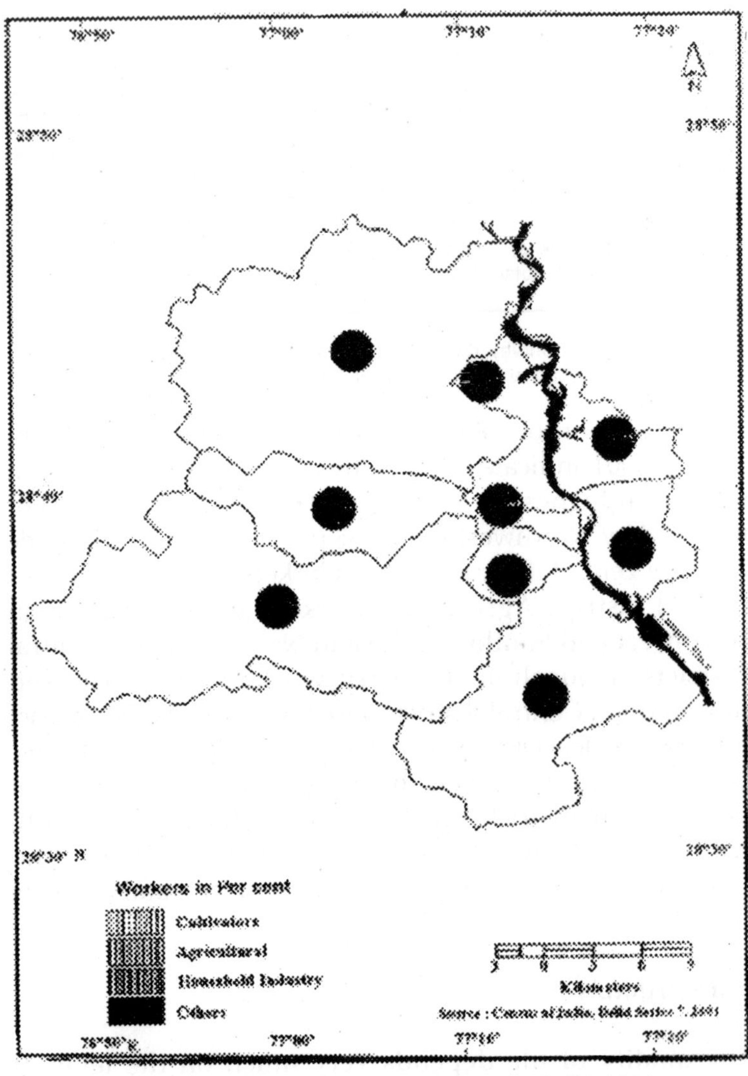

Fig. 2.12 : NCT : Category of Workers in Delhi: 2001

Water

Delhi has to depend on the Yamuna River for raw water though partial supply of water in trans-Yamuna areas is being provided from the Tehri Dam in U.P. and Kishav Lahwar and Giri dam in Himachal Pradesh. They can provide major share of water requirements when completed. To provide additional water supply the existing water treatment of 671 mg/d. would require augmentation and also construction of a new water treatment plants. Water treatment capacity in 1981 was 247 mg/d (million gallons per day) which has increased to 620 in 1981 and 650 by 2001 (Table 2.8).

Table 2.8 : Status of Water Treatment Plants

Water Treatment Plant	*Capacity in mg/d*		
	1981	*1991*	*2001*
Chandrawal 1st & 2nd	90	90	90
Wazirabad	80	120	120
Haiderpur 1st & 2nd	50	200	200
Shahdara	-	100	100
New plants (2) in northwest Delhi	-	40	40
Okhla	6	-	-
Renney wells, local tubewell	27	70	119
Total	247	620	650

Source: Economic Survey (2001-02) Department of Planning, Government of National Capital Territory of Delhi, Delhi.

The consumption trends of water as evident from the Table 2.9 reveals that total consumption has increased from 1561 lakhs liters in 1975-76 to 10770 lakhs liters in 2001, *i.e.* an increase of 590 per cent. This has increased by 127 per cent from 1995-96 to 2001. The per capita consumption has increased from 31 kiloliters to 50 in the same period. The domestic consumption of water has registered an increase of 250 per cent from 1174 kiloliters in 1975 to 9296 in 2001, whereas the commercial and industrial use of water rose from 387 in 1975-76 to 1475 lakhs liters in 2001 (Table 2.9).

As far as the supply of water is concerned, it is far from uniform distribution. The New Delhi Municipal Corporation and Cantonment area gets average supply above 450 liters per capita per day while Narela/Najafgarh zone gets less

Table 2.9 : Consumption of Water in Delhi

Years	*1975-76*	*1980-81*	*1985-86*	*1990-91*	*1995-96*	*2000-01*
Total water consumption (lakh k. liter)	1561	1953	2436	4540	4741	10770
Domestic	1174	1542	1929	4013	4114	9296
Industrial	387	411	507	527	627	1475
Per capita consumption (k. liters)	31.0	33.0	34.9	43.7	49.0	50

Source : Statistical Handbook, Directorate of Economics and Statistics, Government of National Capital Territory of Delhi, 1981,1991,2002.

than 80 liters per capita on an average, that is, 18 times higher than Mehrauli. Mehrauli area has the lowest water supply. Some parts of the city are getting less than 35 liters per capita per day water supply. Moderate supplies are seen in West, Civil Lines and Karol Bagh zones, while low supplies are found in South Delhi and Shahdara area (Fig. 2.13).

The demand-supply gap of water has caused the groundwater withdrawal in Delhi, which has resulted in the fall of groundwater levels in the range of 20-30 meters below land surface in south and southwestern parts of Delhi. Groundwater availability has been seen up to 10 meters in northwestern parts of the city. Over-exploitation of groundwater has disturbed hydrological balance leading to decline in productivity of wells, increasing pumping costs and more energy requirements (Fig. 2.14).

Besides quantity, the quality of potable water is another serious problem as it directly affects the health of people. The quality of groundwater is also variable in space and depth. In some areas, west of ridge the salinity of groundwater generally increases toward southwest and northwest direction. Occurrences of high nitrate concentration are seen at several locations, *i.e.* parts of Shahdara and Kanjhawala have nitrate above 1000 mg/liter in groundwater. Such high nitrate concentration in shallow

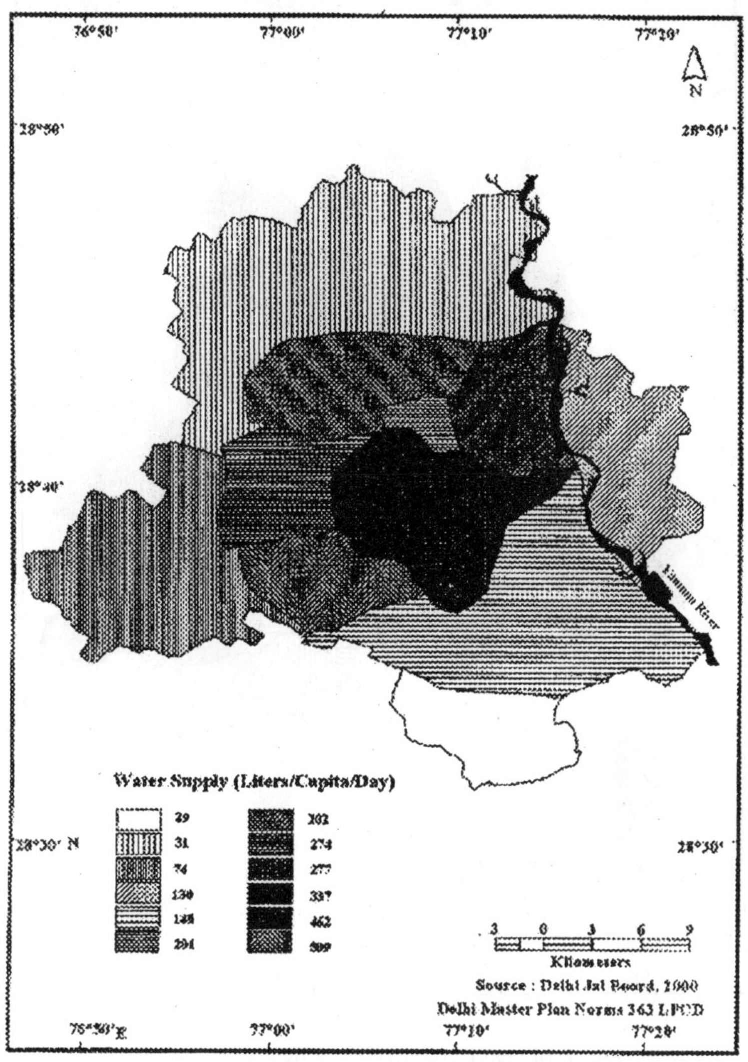

Fig. 2.13 : NTC : Level of Water Supply

groundwater could be due to leaching from solid waste, discharge from sewerage etc. The groundwater in vicinity of landfills in Yamuna floodplains also has high nitrate concentration (Fig. 2.15).

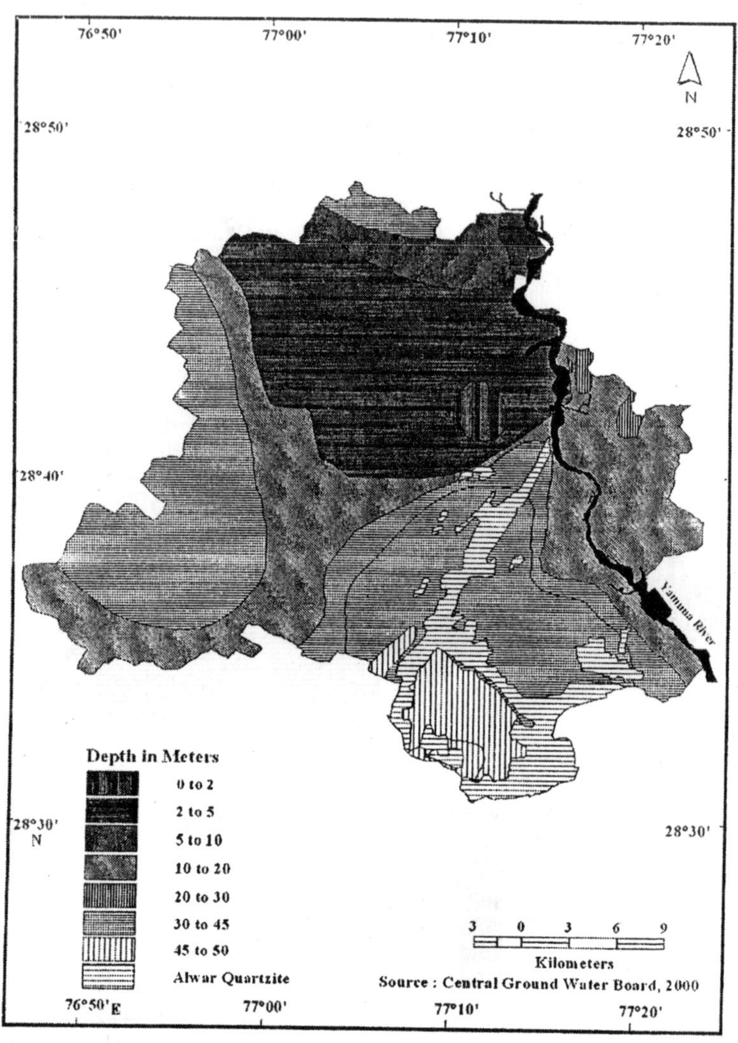

Fig. 2.14 : NCT : Groundwater Availability, 2000

Sewage

Existing capacity of sewerage system in Delhi is grossly inadequate, as about 70 per cent of present population does

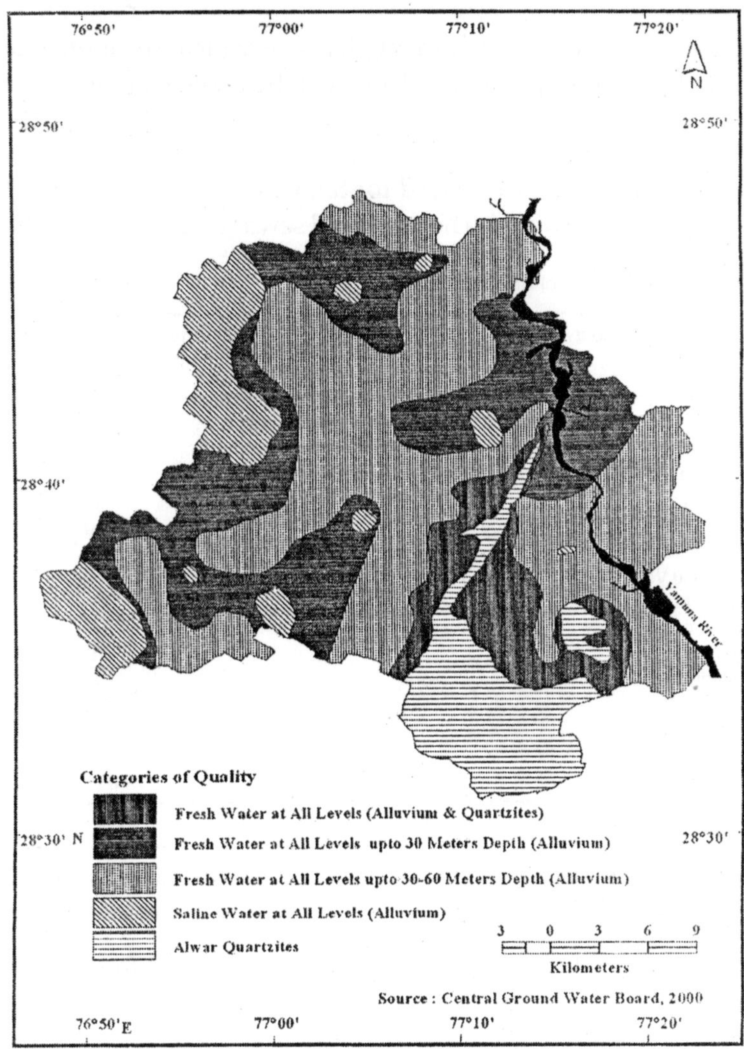

Fig. 2.15 : NCT : Groundwater Quality, 2000

not have access to regular municipal sewerage. The increasing pollution in River Yamuna is also a major indicator of lack of sewerage treatment facilities. By augmenting the capacity of existing treatment plants, as well as through new plants, the liquid waste in Delhi can be taken care of.

The capacity of existing plant includes, 140mg/d for Okhla, 72 mg/d for Keshopur, 40 mg/d each for Coronation Pillar, Rithala and 10 mg/d for Shahdara. This gives a total capacity of 302 mg/d. The proposed sewage treatment plants'

Table 2.10 : Status of Sewage Treatment in Delhi

Sewage Treatment Plant	*Existing Capacity in mg/d*		
	1981	*1991*	*2001*
Okhla	66	140	140
Keshopur	32	72	72
Coronation Pillar	20	40	40
Rithala	-	40	40
Shahdara	-	10	10
Kondli	-	-	45
Yamuna Vihar	-	-	10
Ghitorni	-	-	5
Vasant Kunj	-	-	5
Narela	-	-	10
Najafgarh	-	-	5
Delhi Gate	-	-	2.2
Timarpur	-	-	6
Rohini	-	-	15 (P)
Nilothi	-	-	40 (P)
Total	118	302	335.2

Source : Delhi Master Plan, Revised 2001, Delhi Development Authority. (P)-denotes proposed.

capacity would be 45 mg/d for Kondli, 10 mg/d for Narela and Yamuna Vihar. Vasant Kunj, Ghitorni, Najafgarh, Pappankala and Nilothi with 20-40 mg/d. Timarpur with 5 mg/d each, while Delhi Gate with 2.2 mg/d (Table 2.10 and Fig. 2.16).

Power

The availability of power is one of the important factors for the development of any place. The Delhi Vidyut Board used

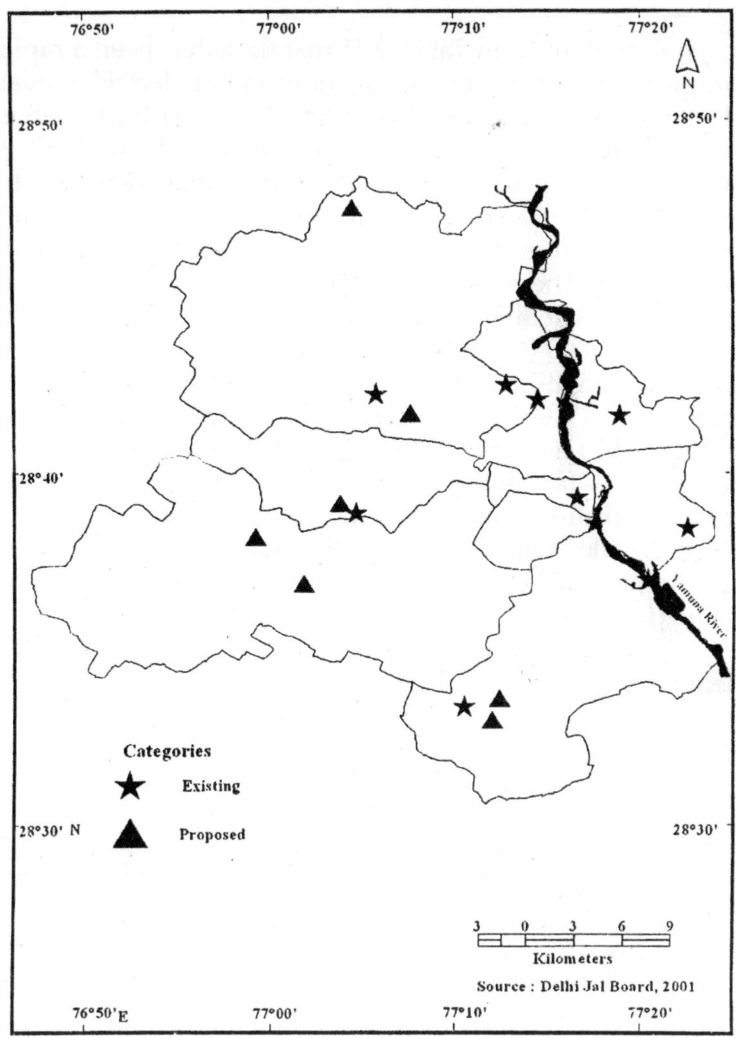

Fig. 2.16 : Sewage Treatment Plants - 2001

to be the only agency responsible for distribution and supply of electricity throughout the city, now after privatization it is with private companies.

It is evident from Table 2.11 that there has been a rapid progressive increase in the consumption of electricity over the last three decades. The domestic consumption has increased by about 1515 per cent from 1970-71 to 2001. It was 233 million units (m.u.) in 1970-71 that increased to 701(m.u.) in 1980-81, 2316 (m.u.) in 1990-91 and 3873 (m.u.) in 2000-01, thus, increase of 201, 230 and 62 per cent, respectively. The consumption of commercial and industrial categories has enhanced by about 450 and 1318 per cent in 1970-71 to 2000-01, respectively. Commercial use rose from 210 (m.u.) in 1971 to 453, 1093 and 1501 (m.u.) in 1980-81, 1990-91 and 2001, respectively. Similarly, industrial use witnessed a rise from 208 (m.u.) in 1970-71 to 2949 (m.u.) in 2000-01. As far as the generation is concerned, the local generation shows a marginal increase of 150 per cent in the three decades while the shortfall is made by the purchases from other states, which rose by about 4043 per cent in the same period (Table 2.11).

Transportation

From the point of view of transport, Delhi constitutes a center

Table 2.11: Generation and Consumption of Electricity (in million units)

Sl.No.	*Items*	*1970-71*	*1980-81*	*1990-91*	*2000-01*
1.	Electricity generated and purchased				
	(a) Locally generated	1027	1313	2351	2553
	(b) Purchased from Nangal and other states	362	1613	6378	14997
2.	Electricity consumption				
	(a) Domestic	233	701	2316	3762
	(b) Commercial	210	453	1093	1156
	(c) Industrial	208	590	1952	2949
	(d) Public Water Works	107	175	347	527
	(e) Licensed (NDMC and MES)	272	453	707	944
	Total	1030	2372	6415	9713

Source : Statistical Handbook, Directorate of Statistics and Economics, Government of National Capital Territory, Delhi, 1981,1985,1992, and 2002.

of both national as well as international importance. Delhi is having road links with different parts of the country from its olden days. The Grand Trunk Road, which is a national highway of great importance, passes through Delhi. The transport system was greatly developed by Mughals and later East India Company took steps to bring improvements. Transportation planning in Delhi under Master Plans has aimed at minimizing the gap between demand and supply by increasing the capacity of the urban transport plan involving projection of past trends which has been snowballing towards increased supply of roads for automobile traffic, public mass transport system, mass rapid transit system and improvement in pedestrian movement.

The total number of vehicles has increased from 37375 in 1961 to 3456579 in 2001. Thus, registering an increase of 446 per cent from 1961 to 1971, 175 per cent increase from 1971 to 1981, 242 per cent from 1981 to 1991 and 80 per cent from 1991 to 2001. The number of cars and jeeps has increased from 15084 in 1961 to 968894 in 2001. The rise in two wheelers is from 12081 in 1961 to 364010 in 1981 and 2265955 in 2001 (Table 2.12).

The road network in Delhi is being developed and maintained by Public Works Department. The road network in Delhi has been seen 28508 kms (including 388 kms of national highways) in 2001. Delhi had 1749 kms of road length per 100 sq.kms area as compared to national average

Table 2.12 : Number of Registered Vehicles in Delhi

Years	*Total*	*Cars/ Jeeps*	*Motor Cycles/ Scooters*	*Autos*	*Taxi*	*Buses*	*Goods Vehicles*
1961	37375	15084	12081	2757	1977	1342	4134
1971	204078	61521	109112	10812	4105	3266	15262
1981	561768	123655	364010	20920	6583	8528	38071
1991	1923787	427743	1294066	65829	10426	19671	106052
2001	3456579	968894	2265955	86985	20628	47578	161650

Source : Statistical Handbook, Directorate of Economics and Statistics, Government of National Capital Territory of Delhi, 1981,1991,2002.

of 73 km per100 sq.kms area in 2001. The road network has increased from 380 kms in 1970-71 to 28508 kms in 2001, *i.e.* a three-fold increase, while the number of vehicles has increased from 2.04 lakhs in 1970-71 to 34.56 lakhs in 2001, *i.e.* a sixteen-time increase.

The Mass Rapid Transmit System (MRTS), an ambitious project that aimed at providing a non-polluting, efficient rail-based transport system, properly integrated with road transport system, has already completed its first phase of connectivity and other phases are progressively towards completion.

Utilization of Land

The rural area of Delhi has reduced from 1314 km^2 in 1921 to 591 km^2 in 2001, *i.e.* from 88 per cent to 40 per cent during the last eight decades. The total number of inhabited villages in Delhi has also gone down from 314 in 1921 to 165 in 2001. This shows the effect of metropolitan growth on the rural areas of Delhi. Increasing urban activities are putting pressure on the surrounding rural lands; further, in recent years phenomenon of land to be treated essentially as an economic commodity and increase in rural land value has added a new dimension by introducing land speculation on a large-scale.

Urban land accounts for 60 per cent of the total land area. This increasing trend points towards the gradual encroachment of land by steadily increasing urbanization trend. These trends indicate that a sizable part of rural Delhi is being swallowed up by the metropolitan expansion with basic amenities and services falling short of requirements. The rural land, thus, is constantly under threat. The pattern of utilization of land has also changed significantly and now the land is being used for other commercial purposes instead of agricultural purposes.

It would be apparent from Table 2.13 that area not available for cultivation has increased considerably over the years and has increased more double during 1961-2001. Within this category land put to non-agricultural use alone accounts for more than 70 per cent and the pace at which the expansion of the city is taking place to accommodate the population growth and the intensification of the existing and addition to newer functions of the city, it will continue to increase rapidly. As compared to this, net sown area in Delhi has reduced to half during the last four decades. The total cropped area has considerably decreased from 113482 hectares in 1960-61 to 52816 hectares in 2001 (Table 2.13).

Table 2.13 : Utilisation of Land in Delhi (in hectares)

Land Uses	*1960-61*	*1970-71*	*1980-81*	*1990-91*	*2000-01*
Area according to village papers	147952	147612	147488	147488	147488
Forests	1415	1143	1434	1561	-
Area not available for cultivation	34496	47314	50277	74248	89689
(a) Land put to non-agricultural uses	33469	34207	34248	64562	76597
(b) Barren and uncultivable land	1027	13107	17829	9687	13092
Other uncultivated land excluding fallow land	18138	3602	2719	12864	11143
Permanent pastures and grazing land	4863	402	864	176	61
Land under miscellaneous tree crops (net sown area not included)	-	41	1064	1267	1189
Cultivable waste land	13275	3159	791	10850	9893
Fallow land	6497	15043	32707	13864	11544
Net sown area	87406	80510	58551	48357	34034
Area more than once	26076	36057	29048	27882	18782
Total cropped area	113482	116585	87599	76239	52816

Source: Statistical Handbook, Directorate of Economics and Statistics, Government of National Capital Territory of Delhi, 1981,1991, 2002.

Size of Land Holdings

From the above discussion it is clear that in the last fifty years the rural area has been reduced by more than fifty per cent. It implies that the continuous increase in population, lack of open space within the urban area, more demand of land for using transportation, industrial and commercial uses have resulted in large conversion of land in the rural-urban fringe. The sizes of agricultural land holdings are decreasing over the years and the number of smallholdings is gradually increasing in rural Delhi.

Table 2.14 shows change in percentage area under different sizes of land holdings over the years. Rapidly increasing smaller land holdings highlight the fragmentation of land holdings, change in farmland uses and land increasingly used as an economic asset. Accounting for only 1 per cent in 1964-65, smaller land holdings of 1 hectare by 1976-77 reached 45.72 per cent. This indicates that nearly 46 per cent of the rural land area was divided into one-hectare small units. As against this, the bigger land holdings of above eight hectares, which accounted for 46 per cent in 1964-65, decreased a little by 1968-69. It registered a decrease of 85 per cent over a period of 8-9 years, reaching 6 per cent in 1976-77. The increase was five times in between 12 hectares for the time period 1965-77. Not much change is discernible in the medium category of 2 to 4 hectares in the same time period. Large land category of 4 to 8 hectares has decreased by 75 per cent reaching six per cent in 1976-77. The number of landholdings belonging to less than one hectare of land increased from 51 per cent in 1985-86 to 61.5 per cent in 1990-91. The number of land holdings above eight hectares has gone down from 1.7 to 1.1 per cent in the five year period from 1985-86 to 1990-90. Gradually, these land holdings found their way into the open market for land speculation and conversion of agricultural land into non-agricultural uses continued. Thus, the areas surrounding the city are witnessing transformation on a large scale (Table 2.14).

Table 2.14 : Size of Land Holdings

Land Area (hectare)	*1964-65*	*1970-71*	*1976-77*	*1985-86*	*1990-91*	*2000-01*
1	1.14	43.32	45.72	51	61.5	60.62
1-2	3.48	18.03	17.15	17.15	17.15	17.98
2-4	17.6	18.23	18.49	17.0	11.8	12.33
4-8	31.62	10.84	12.50	12.3	7.6	8.16
Above 8	46.13	9.58	6.14	1.7	1.1	0.88
Total	100	100	100	100	100	100

Source : Gazetteer Unit, National Capital Territory of Delhi, Delhi.

Land Policy

In Delhi, since 1962, a policy of large-scale acquisition and development of land has been pursued. Under this policy, Delhi Development Authority (DDA) set-up under the Delhi Development Act, 1957 has been the organization for land planning, disposal and development. It has acquired and developed land to meet the rising housing, institutional, industrial, and commercial demands. But there has been a widening gap in the acquisition and development of land needed to meet the rising demands of urbanization. This imbalance has resulted into unauthorized sub-division of rural land in the areas adjoining the existing urban land in the construction of urban residential building on the acquired agricultural land, and an increase in land speculations.

With population of Delhi increasing at a rapid rate, acquired land has not been developed at a desired pace. For a projected population of about 12.8 million by 2001, Master Plan for Delhi had envisaged additional development of about 24,000 hectares of land, but population growth revealed an increase of nearly 14 million in 2001, and so far, only 10,000 hectares have been added to the urban area.

Conclusion

This chapter is of special significance in the study as it

provides comprehensive picture of the study area. This includes description of historical background of the city, relief, drainage, geology, climate, soils and rainfall. The administrative, demographic and socio-cultural structure including industries, workers, infrastructure, and land use are illustrated in detail. The growth and development of the city in many respects are covered. Most of the parameters are discussed with reference to data pertaining to three decades.

References

1. Forrest, G. W. (1977) *Delhi: Cities of India,* New Delhi: Metropolitan Book Co. Pvt. Ltd., 136-60.
2. Nagpaul, H. (1988) "Delhi", in M. Dogan and J.D. Kasarda (eds.) *The Metropolitan Era,* London: Sage Publications, 2: 184-211.
3. Jain, A.K. (1990) *The Making of a Metropolis: Planning and Growth of Delhi,* New Delhi: National Book Organization.
4. Hearn, G. R. (1974) *Seven Cities of Delhi,* New Delhi: S.B.W. Publishers.
5. Frykenberg, R.E. (1986) *Delhi Through the Ages: Essays in Urban History, Culture and Society,* Delhi: Oxford University Press.
6. Delhi Gazetteer (1976) Delhi Administration, Delhi, 41-58.
7. District Census Handbook, Delhi (1981) Series 27, Census of India, Delhi.
8. Immanuel, N. (1999) "Delhi", *Encyclopedia of World Cities,* Chicago: Fitzroy Dearborn Publishers, 198-199.
9. Delhi Gazetteer (1976) Delhi Administration, Delhi.
10. Bhatia, S.S. (1957) "Historical geography of Delhi", *The Indian Geographer,* 2:17-43.
11. Economic Survey (2001-02) Department of Planning, Government of National Capital Territory Delhi, p. 12.

Chapter - 3

Theory and Methods of Input Industry Analysis

Introduction

The previous chapter dealt with some aspects of physico-cultural and economic environments of the city covering geology, physiography, drainage, soil types, population and other socio-cultural aspects. The present chapter describes the concept and methodology of input-output technique used in this research. It discusses historical development, basic input-output model, input-output table and its fundamental relationships, applications of the model and extensions of this technique.

Historical Development

Input-output analysis is the name given to an analytical framework developed by Leontief in the late 1930s, when he published an input-output system of the United States economy in 1936[1], work for which he received the Nobel Prize in Economic Sciences in 1973. In fact, the origin of the idea of detailed accounting of inter-industry flows may be traced back to Quesnay, a French economist, who published 'Tableau Economique' in 1758[2], which was a diagrammatic representation of how expenditure can be traced through an economy in a systematic way. In his later work, he placed information in the form of a table resembling the socalled 'transaction table'. More than a century after Quesnay,

Walras,[3] a French economist applied the concepts of Newtonian mechanics for developing a theory of general equilibrium in economics. Walras in 1874 used a set of production coefficients with the related quantities of factors of production per unit of a particular product to the level of total production of that product. All new ideas have ancient roots, but they take fresh forms as they are developed and applied in new ways; this is true for input-output analysis. Leontief used elements from previous studies on economic inter-dependence and made a unique contribution by simplifying the Walrasian system of equations, thus, he created a new system for which statistical information could be compiled and which brought many new insights into the interdependence of prices, outputs, and incomes in different sectors of the economy.

Leontief presented the theoretical framework of United States input-output tables for 1919 and 1929 in 1936[4]. Somewhat later, followed this he came with book on the input-output structures of the U.S. economy in 1941.[5] This book was revised in 1951[6] in an enlarged and expanded edition that presented the U.S. input-output table for 1939. Progress in the development of national input-output model proceeded in the 1940s and 1950s and work continued at Bureau of Labour Statistics in U.S. In 1944, first practical application was made with an exercise for estimating effects of war on employment. By 1950s and 1960s, input-output analysis as a technique became part of national income accounting programme and fully integrated with national income and product accounts. As Dorfman[7] pointed out that Leontief's approach was to simplify the Walrasian system to the extent necessary to derive a set of parameters for his model from a single observation of each of the inter-industry transactions in the economy and omitted the effects of limited factor suppliers from the systems. Leontief model precludes many of the adjustments characterizing the Walrasian concept of general equilibrium.

The other examples of early constructions include efforts of USSR Central Statistical Board to prepare balance sheet of national economy for 1923, which was published in 1926[8] (considered one of the earliest attempts), which was later stopped by Stalin. During 1970s, transaction tables were constructed for all Republics for 1966 and 1972. In Britain, Barna[9] in 1953 and Stewart[10] in 1958 made the efforts for the construction of national input-output accounts. In Denmark[11], the Department of Statistics prepared transaction tables in 1948 and 1951. In the Netherlands, Boer[12] and Tilanus[13] worked for transaction tables. Chenery and Clark[14] prepared input-output accounts for Italy in 1953. Hogland and Werin[15] prepared the first input-output tables for Sweden in 1957 and Rasul[16] prepared for Pakistan.

The development of regional input-output analysis also dates from early 1950s. There were a number of studies constructing regional transaction tables, which were rather crude operations by today's standards, since unadjusted national coefficients were used, and even the format of the tables produced was a miniature version of national tables with highly aggregated import and export flows. It was later in 1951, that Isard outlined the structure of his 'ideal interregional model', an ideal in the sense, since it required treating a regional industry as entirely different industry from the same industry in another region; thus, a forty-regional, eighty-industry model became equivalent to an input-output table containing 3200 sectors. Moses[17] provided a model, in which he connected pair-wise regions for each commodities trade pattern. Evan and Hoffenberg[18] worked out the transaction table for American economy for 1947 for five hundred sectors. Moore and Peterson[19] prepared input-output tables for Utah economy for 1947. Isard and Kuenne[20] studied impact of steel upon the New York-Philadelphia industrial region. Tiebout[21] prepared input-output table for Washington State for fifty-four sectors. Artle[22] studied the economy of Stockholm. Watanabe[23] analyzed economic systems of Japan. Weisskoff[24] studied development and trade dependence of Puerto Rico economy. Hirsch[25] prepared input-output for St. Louise metropolitan economy. Simpson and Tsukui[26] have demonstrated that economic structure of United States of America and Japan, although superficially dissimilar; contain almost identical patterns of industries, which are strongly interrelated through input-output tables. A comprehensive multi-region input-output model was prepared by Polenske[27] for United States for forty-four regions. Kurtzweg[28] made structural comparisons of the US and USSR economies through input-output methodology. Carter and Ireri[29] prepared two state models for studying Arizona and California. Torii and Fukasaku[30] studied the evolution process of industrial structure and changes in the linkage structure of Japan and Korea. Forsell[31] used input-output model for analyzing the growth of industries in Finland economy in 1960 and 1970s for projecting increase in output of industries. Urata[32] studied the effect of changes in production structure, in sectional composition of final demand, level of final demand, labour requirements and capital requirement for Soviet economy. Nyhus,[33] Rampa,[34] Granberg,[35] Costa,[36] Waelbraeck and Gupta [37] have attempted towards generating multinational input-output tables, synthesizing regional and national models and experimenting with variety of model building across nations for analyzing the international macro economic systems.

With the rapid spread of input-output analysis, there emerged theoretical and practical problems that indicated a pressing need for practitioners in this field to exchange their experiences, and so the first international input-output conference was convened in 1950 in the Netherlands with fifteen participants. The second conference in 1954 in Vienna, Italy, the third, was held in 1961, the fourth in 1968, and the fifth in 1971 in Geneva. Besides, these international conferences, regional conferences also complemented the development of the technique

In recent years, the input-output framework has been extended to deal explicitly with such topics as inter-regional flows of products, energy consumption, environmental pollution and employment associated with industrial production and other complex analysis because of the advances in computer technology. Leontief reported that 'a generalized solution of a complete set of thirty-eight simultaneous linear equations took fifty six hours on Harvard make calculator'. And by 1967, the time was reduced drastically to about 36 seconds to invert a hundred sector table and now just ten seconds for handing a 360 by 65 sector table.

Input-Output Table and Fundamental Relationships

An input-output table describes the flow of goods and services between all individual sectors of an economy over a specified period of time. It is a descriptive framework for showing the relationship between industries and sectors, and between inputs and outputs under certain economic assumptions about the nature of production function. It is an analytical tool for measuring the impact of autonomous disturbances on an economy's output and income.[38]

An input-output table is constructed from observed data for an economic area a nation, a region or a state. The economic activity in the area must be divisible into a number of segments or producing sectors. These may be industries in usual sense (*e.g.* steel) or they may be much smaller categories (*e.g.* steel nails) or much larger ones (*e.g.* manufacturing). The necessary data are flows of products from each of the sectors (as a producer) to each of the sectors (as a purchaser). These inter-industry flows or inter-sectoral flows are measured for a particular time period, usually a year, in monetary terms. In accounting for transactions between and among all sectors, it is possible in principle to record all exchanges either in physical or in monetary terms. While the physical measure is perhaps a better reflection of one sector's use of another sector's product, there are enormous measurement problems when sectors actually sell more than one good. For these and other reasons, accounts are generally kept in monetary terms (Table 3.1).

Table 3.1: Input-Output Transactions Table (Sample Framework)

		Producers								*Final Demand*			
		Agriculture	*Mining*	*Construction*	*Manufacturing*	*Trade*	*Transportation*	*Services*	*Other*	*Personal Consumption Expenditure*	*Gross Private Domestic Investment*	*Net Exports of Good and Services*	*Government Purchases of Goods and Services*
Producers	Agriculture												
	Mining												
	Construction												
	Manufacturing												
	Trade												
	Transportation												
	Services												
	Other												
Value added										Gross National Product			

The basic information from which an input-output model is developed is contained in an inter-industry transaction table. The row of each table describes the distribution of a producer's output throughout the economy. The column describes the composition of inputs required by a particular industry to produce its output. In addition, in any economy there are sales or purchases that are more external or exogenous to the industrial sectors that constitute the producers in the economy, for *e.g.* households, governments and foreign trade. The demand of these units, and hence, magnitudes of their purchases from each of the industrial sectors are generally determined by considerations that are relatively unrelated to the amount being produced in each of the units. For example, government demands for defence aircraft is related to broad changes in national policy or budget levels; consumer demand for cars has different impact, and so on. The demand for such external units, since it tends to be much more for goods to be used as such and not to be used as an input to an industrial production process, is generally, referred to as 'final demand column'. The additional rows labeled as value added, account for other (non-industrial) inputs to production, such as labour, capital and inventory items. The flows of import and export are also entered.

Input-Output Model

The input-output model has enabled regional analysts to handle quantitatively, economy-wide system rather than particular parts thereof and, thus, illuminates the nature of economic structure. The simple Leontief system can be described in terms of a set of simultaneous linear equation in which the levels of production of different sectors are unknown, and can be estimated on the basis of the information contained in input-output table provided there is final demand vector. The input-output model is based on the premise that it is possible to divide all productive activities in an economy in sectors, whose inter-relations can be meaningfully expressed in a set of simple input functions. The criteria for establishing sectors must be derived from knowledge of the characteristics of the productive activities being aggregated as well as the use of the outputs. The Leontief model includes some type of interdependence among economic units and excludes other types. It specifically includes the interdependence resulting from the sales of commodities from one sector to another and from the use of the same primary factors. It specifically excludes substitution among the outputs of different sectors, either in final users or as input to other sectors, and non-market inter-dependence in the form of external economies and diseconomies and of different sectors exogenously determined.

The model is based on certain assumptions that includes :

(a) each sector produces a single homogeneous output with a single input structure and there is no substitution between the outputs of different sectors.
(b) there is fixed proportion of Leontief type production function. In other words, the quantity of each input used by any sector is a constant proportion only of the level of output of that sector or the account of the input used directly proportional to its output.
(c) the input-output table must satisfy the viability condition. The condition ensures that the level of gross output in each sector is adequate to meet the intermediate and final demand for that sector or alternatively the output X_i, should not be less than direct and indirect requirement of the output of this sector for producing the output X_i.

The structure of the model can be described through the set of equations. Assuming the economy consists of n sectors, then, the total distribution of the physical output of each sector can be described by the following equations.

$$X_i = \sum_j X_{ij} + Y_i \text{ (i = 1.2...n)} \qquad \dots \quad (1)$$

Where, $\sum_j X_{ij}$ is total intermediate demand for output of sector i,

X_i is total output of sector *i* and Y_j denotes the output of industry *i* available for outside consumption or final demand. Equation system (1) known as the balance equation, says that, the total gross output of sector is equal to inter-industrial requirement (including self sector) and different components of final demand. On the bases of proportionality assumption, it can be written as:

$$X_i = a_{ij} X_j \qquad \dots \qquad \dots \quad (2)$$

a_{ij} is the requirement of output of sector I used as input for a unit level production of sector j. a $_{ij}$'s are known as the structural or technical coefficients. The above balanced equation can be written as:

$$X_i = \sum a_{ij} X_j + Y_i \text{ or} \qquad \dots \qquad \dots \quad (3)$$
$$(I-A) X = -Y \qquad \dots \qquad \dots \quad (4)$$

Where A (n, n) is the input-output coefficient matrix, X is the vector of outputs and Y is the vector comprising of the total final demand. The matrix A is obtained by dividing each column of the flow matrix by the total output of the purchasing sector. If the coefficient matrix A is given and the level of final demand is estimated, it is possible to solve the equations $(I-A)$ $X = Y$ and estimate the levels of gross outputs of various sectors.

The input coefficients a_{ij} are direct input requirements and they not provide indirect requirements. For instance, production of one unit of car requires the direct inputs of steel, component and tyres, which in turn require inputs from the output of other sectors for their production and so on in the chain. Through the input-output technique the direct as well as indirect requirements of producing an additional unit of any sector can be estimated.

The equations $(I–A)\ X=Y$ on solving gives :

$$X = (I-A)^{-1}\ Y \qquad \dots \qquad \dots \qquad (5)$$
$$= R * Y$$
$$R = [\ r_{ij}\ ]$$

Where, the matrix R is known as Leontief matrix. In this, each r_{ij} explains the amount of output of sector i required directly and indirectly for one unit of final demand for sector j. This consists of fundamental relationship of a Leontief system. Through the input-output system the direct as well as indirect requirements of producing an additional unit of any sector can be estimated by Leontief inverse, which explain full impact of the final demand for the output of each sector on all other sectors of the economy.

These equations serve to make explicit the dependence of inter-industry flows on the total outputs of each sector. This is actually the structural matrix that enables to make predictions and forecasts for the economy under various possible circumstances. The equation (3) may be written in the form of matrix terms as well in the following form.

$$A = \begin{bmatrix} a_{11} & a_{12} & \dots & a_{1i} & \dots & a_{1n} \\ a_{21} & a_{22} & \dots & a_{2i} & \dots & a_{2n} \\ a_{n1} & a_{n2} & \dots & a_{ni} & \dots & a_{nn} \end{bmatrix}$$

$$X = \begin{bmatrix} X_1 \\ X_2 \\ \vdots \\ X_n \end{bmatrix} \qquad Y = \begin{bmatrix} Y_1 \\ Y_2 \\ \vdots \\ Y_n \end{bmatrix}$$

Here, the first subscript on a coefficient determines its row and the second its column. As there are n rows and columns in this matrix, it is square of type of matrix $(n \times n)$, with the output of each sector into a column vector (X) and the final demand of each sector into a column vector (V). This means that equation (3) can now be rewritten in matrix terms as :

$$X = AX + Y \quad \text{or} \quad \ldots \quad \ldots \quad (3)$$

$$(I - A)\, X\, Y \quad \ldots \quad \ldots \quad (4)$$

Where, I is the unit or identity matrix. The matrix $(I–A)$ will have $(1–a_{11})$, $(1–a_{22})$, $(1– a_{ij})$, ..., $(1 – a_{nn})$ on its main diagonals and, since the identity matrix contains zeros everywhereelse, (I – A) will simply contain $–a_{ij}$ terms elsewhere. Then, the complete $n \times n$ system is just equation (5). The matrix A is known as the matrix of technical input-output coefficient or direct input coefficient. If $(I–A) \neq 0$, than $(I–A)^{-1}$ can be found and unique solution is given by

$$X = (I - A^{-1}Y \quad \ldots \quad \ldots \quad (5)$$

Where, $(I–A)^{-1}$ is often referred to as the Leontief inverse, which is the most useful and powerful tool to capture both direct and indirect effects of any change in exogenous vector *Y*. This equation (5) translates a given final bill of goods into vector gross outputs. If, however, there were any negative entries in the matrix $(I–A)^{-1}$, the Leontief inverse, as it is usually called, there would be an economically meaningless result implying that some final demands have negative impact on gross output. Therefore, restrictions need to be put on the input-output coefficients to ensure sensible interpretations are significant. The important restrictions known as the Hawkins-Simon conditions, the restrictions are : first, that the diagonal of the $(I–A)^{-1}$ matrix should strictly be positive (*i.e.*, $1-a_{ij} > 0$) and, secondly, that all principal minors of the $(I-A)$ matrix be positive.

Each entry in the inverse matrix is called 'interdependency coefficient'. The coefficient represents the direct and indirect requirements of sector *i*'s per unit of final demand for the output of a sector *j*. This inverse matrix can be multiplied by any size and composition of final demand in order to obtain the levels of gross output of each industry. This provides with a powerful tool of analysis since it enables to measure the total impact on the economy of exogenous disturbance, *i.e.* change in final demand.

Applications of Input-Output Model

Multipliers

One of the major uses of information in the format of an input-output model is to assess the effect on an economy with changing elements that are exogenous to the model of that economy. When the exogenous changes occur because of the action of one impacting agent, and when the changes are expected to occur in the short-run, the term 'impact analysis' is usually employed. On the other hand, when longer-term and broader changes are examined, the outputs from all regional sectors will be needed to satisfy this demand; this is an exercise in 'regional forecasting'. As the period of projection gets longer, the accuracy of such an exercise tends to decrease. Whether using the input-output model for impact analysis or for forecasting, the general form is $X = [I-A]^{-1}Y$. Thus, the usefulness of the result, X, will depend on the correctness of both $[I-A]^{-1}$ and Y.

The three most frequently used types of multipliers are those that estimate the effects of the exogenous changes in (a) outputs of sectors in the economy, (b) income earned by households because of the new outputs, and (c) employment that is expected to be generated because of the new outputs.

The notion of multipliers rests upon the difference between the initial effect of an exogenous (final demand) change and the total effect of that change. The total effects can be defined, in two ways—as the direct and indirect effects or as direct, indirect and induced effects. The multipliers that are found by using direct and indirect effects are also known as simple or direct multipliers. When, direct, indirect and induced effects are used, they are called total multipliers.

Output Multipliers

An output multiplier for sector *j* is defined as the total value of production in all sectors of the economy that is necessary in order to satisfy a rupee's worth of final demand for sector *j*'s output. For simple output multipliers, this total production is the direct and indirect output effect, obtained from a model in which households are exogenous. The output multiplier is the ratio of direct and indirect effects to the initial effect alone. It is an indicator of the degree of structural inter-dependence between each sector and rest of the economy.

Output multiplier of a commodity-producing sector is the factor by which a unit increases in the demand for and, consequently, production of the commodity in that sector leads to expansion of, output in the whole economy. This multiplier is the sum of the factors by which individual sectors of the economy get expanded for unit increase in the demand for product in one sector. In fact, the direct output multipliers for various sectors of the economy are simply the column sums of the Leontief inverse. This can be mathematically explained as follows: Let X is the column vector with elements $X_1, X_2, X_3 \ldots X_n$ and F the column vector with elements $F_1, F_2,$ and $F_3 \ldots F_n$ and A_{ij} are the elements of the Leontief inverse, where X_i is the output of sector *i* and F_i is the demand for the product of sector *i*. Suppose these there the incremental final demand for sector *i* is 1 and for other sector is 0, which means that vector $F = (0, 0.0 ... 1, 0.0 ...)$ with 1 in the ith placed 0 elsewhere. The equation $X = (I-A)^{-A}F$ will give generated demand of A_{ij} in the ith sector and of

$\sum_{i=1}^{n} A_{ij}$ in the entire economy. Thus, the column sums of Leontief inverse are output coefficients. They measure only the direct and indirect impact. A_{ij} gives direct impact and

$\sum_{i=1}^{n} A_{ij}$ indirect impact is computed by the Leontief inverse matrix.

If final demand for the product of any sector increases, the output required of that sector would no doubt increase but would also call for increased output from almost all other sectors because of the linkages. Input-output analysis facilitates the assessment of the impact of increased final demand in a sector on the output of various other sectors and in the economy as a whole. In fact, for any sector, the elements in the column corresponding to that sector in the Leontief inverse gives the factors known as the output coefficients or multipliers, by which the output in different sectors of the economy would get multiplied for a unit increase in the demand in the given sector. The sum of the elements in column, therefore would give the factor, called the output coefficient or multiplier, by which the output of the entire economy would increase for a unit increase in the final demand for the product of a given sector. The impact of an increase in the final demand for the output of any sector would be (a) directly on the output of that sector alone, (b) indirectly on the output of several other sectors because of linkages, and (c) through ripple effects caused by increased income and expenditure among households. Output coefficients are correspondingly of three types, one measuring only the direct the second the sum of the direct and indirect impacts and third the total (including the induced effect) of an increase in the final demand. If, in input-output analysis the open model is used (in open model household are kept as endogenous sector, *i.e.* technologically is related with productive sector) one gets the direct and indirect impacts, while using the closed model (in closed model household sector is considered as exogenous sector which is not technologically interconnected with productive sectors) would indicate the total impact (including the induced impact as well).

Income Multipliers

As the name implies, income multipliers attempt to translate, in one way or another, the impact of final demand changes into changes in income received by households, rather than translating the final demand changes into total value of sectoral output. Household income multipliers is straight forward approach to simply convert each element in a particular column of $(I-A)^{-1}$, which measures the direct and indirect output effects, into rupees' worth of household income via household input coefficients. Thus, the direct plus indirect effects for sector *j* would be in terms of rupees' worth of new household income, and the initial effect is in terms of (one) rupee worth of final demand, and hence, output of sector *j*. They translate an initial output estimate into an expanded estimate of the value of resulting household income. Again, simple refers to the fact that multipliers are found using elements in the $(I-A)^{-1}$ matrix, with household exogenous.

Employment Multiplier

Regional impact analyses are frequently pre-occupied with the employment creating effects of industrial expansion, because regional policy-makers may be primarily concerned with forecasting employment in a particular area. For this reason, it is often useful to be able to derive employment multipliers as well as income multipliers from the input-output model. It is possible to estimate relationship between the value of output of a sector and employment in that sector (in physical terms), then one can calculate employment multipliers, rather than income multipliers, for each sector. Employment effects or household employment multiplier measures parallel to the income effects and household income multipliers. The major difference is that of the use of physical labour coefficients instead of the monetary labour input coefficients.

Regional Multipliers

It is often in the case that impact analysis is needed at regional level. For example, central or state or regional government may wish to allocate funds for labour skill training in one or more industries among several districts and so on. The various kind of multipliers discussed above would acquire a spatial dimension by using elements of A^R (Matrix A for region R) and its Leontief inverse. If estimates of household inputs, household consumption and income earned in the region are available, the model can be closed with respect to households, allowing calculation of regional total output multipliers. Similarly, with the information on regional labour inputs (in monetary forms) and household consumption coefficients, various income multipliers can be found for the region. With the estimates on regional employment (in physical terms) per rupee's worth of output of the two sectors, various regional employment multipliers can be calculated.

For inter-regional input-output models, also a wider variety of multiplier measures are possible, essentially, output, income and employment effects can be calculated for a single region (region L) for each of the other regions, for the rest of the economy (aggregated over all regions outside of L) and for the total many-region economy.

Linkages

Backward and Forward Linkages

The linkage analysis helps in identifying the sectors of high backward and forward linkages for further expansion and industrial planning in the economy. The input-output table provides an excellent opportunity to measure the linkage. First, backward linkage aims to measure the potential stimulus to other activities from investment in sector *j*. Almost every industry producing goods or services takes inputs from other sector of the economy and, in turn, provides inputs to the latter in the respective production process. These relationships define an industry's backward and forward linkage, respectively— backward linkage refers to relative purchases of inputs by a sector, while forward linkage refers to the downstream industries using the output of the specified industry or commodity as input in producing their own goods and services or, in other words, relative sales by a sector to other sectors.

The strong backward linkage reflects that each new industrial investment will offer opportunities for suppliers. In terms of selecting 'key sectors' of an economy, backward linkages are very useful. High backward linkage occurs when a sector uses output of many other sectors as an input, thus, by expanding capacity in such a sector 'inducement' or stimuli are provided to supplier industries; which will have an incentive to expand output to take advantage of the increased demand of its output by that sector. The basic idea of backward linkage is to trace the output increase that occurs in supplying sectors when there is change in the sector using their output as inputs. In mathematical terms it can be defined as follows :

Backward linkage of sector '*j*' with sector '*i*', $B_{ji} = \frac{X_{ij}}{\sum_{i=1}^{n} X_{ij}}$

The high forward linkage occur when a sector's output is or could be used by many other sectors as an input; by expanding capacity such a sector, 'inducements' are provided to using industries that now have an incentive to expand output to take advantage of the increased availability of inputs. The strong forward linkage explain that each new industrial investment will offer inducement to user industries by providing more inputs. Forward linkages are also significant in terms of selecting key sectors of an economy, *i.e.* higher the forward linkage stronger the impact area or the stronger the chain effect of linkages. The basic idea of forward linkage is to trace the output increase that occurs or might occur in using industries when there is change in the sector supplying inputs. A measure of the overall strength of the backward or forward linkages is what is called the linkage coefficient. This coefficient measures the strength of the linkages of the sector under consideration compared to other sectors of the economy as defined by Rasmussen.[39]

Forward linkage of sector '*i*' with sector '*j*', $$F_{ij} = \frac{X_{ij}}{\sum_{j=1}^{n} X_{ij}}$$

The higher these coefficients, the stronger are the linkages between two sectors.

High forward linkages occur when a sector's output is or could be used by many other sectors as an input; by expanding capacity in such a sector, inducement is provided to using industries which now have an incentive to expand output, to take advantage of the increased availability of inputs. Given the interpretation of the *i*, *j*th element of the Leontief inverse, a measure of forward linkage might, therefore, be the row sum of this inverse, which (when normalized as for all sectors increases by unity). If the impact is large, it suggests that increased investment in sector *i* would induce output increase in all using sectors, as users take advantage of the increased availability of inputs.

With a large input-output table, a small sector *j* which relies heavily on sector *i* for input, will lead to a biased index of forward linkage for sector *i*. Capacity expansion in sector *i* based on high forward linkage might therefore, have a disappointing impact on the overall rate of growth of the economy, because of the small size of the using sector *j*. Thus, coefficient of linkages is used. A measure of the overall strength of the backward or forward linkages is what is called the linkage coefficient. This coefficient measures the strength of the linkages of the sector under consideration compared to other sectors of the economy as defined by Rasmussen.

The Backward Linkage Coefficient of sector '*j*'

$$\overline{L}_j = \frac{\sum_{j=1}^{n} L_{ij} / n}{\sum_{i=1}^{n}\sum_{j=1}^{n} L_{ij} / n^2}$$

The Forward Linkage Coefficient of sector '*i*' is similarly defined as :

$$\overline{L}_i = \frac{\sum_{i=1}^{n} L_{ij} / n}{\sum_{i=1}^{n}\sum_{j=1}^{n} L_{ij} / n^2}$$

Where L_{ij} are the elements of the Leontief inverse, which are the output multipliers that measure the requirements from various sectors for producing one unit of output of *j*th sector. The above formula can be interpreted easily. In this case, the numerator gives the direct and indirect requirements of input from sector '*i*' required to meet one unit of final demand for the output of sector '*j*', and the denominator gives the direct and indirect increase in demand for an average industry in the economy. In case, it means that the average direct and indirect input requirement for unit demand increase in *j*th industry is greater than the average for the whole economy, or that the backward linkage of sector '*j*' is strong.

Open and Closed Models

The model that has been dealt with so far, is an open model, $X = (I - A)^{-1}Y$, depends on the existence of exogenous sector, disconnected from the technologically interrelated productive sector, since it is here that the important final demands for output originate. The basic kinds of transactions that constitute the activity of this sector are consumption purchases by households, sales to governments, and net exports. Households (consumers) earn incomes in payment for their labour inputs to production processes, and as consumers, they spend their income in rather well patterned ways. And, in particular, a change in the amount of labour needed for production in one or more sectors will lead to a change in the amount spent by households as a group for consumption. In other words, although households tend to purchase goods for 'final' consumption, to their income, which depends on the outputs of each of the sectors.

Thus, one could move the household sector from the final demand column and place it inside the technically interrelated table, that is, make it one of the 'endogenous' sectors. This is known as closing the model with respect to households. This requires a row and a column for the new household sector, the former showing how its output (labour services) is used as an input by the various sectors and the latter showing the structure of its purchases (consumption) distributed among the sectors. It is customary to add the household row and column at the bottom and to the right of the coefficient table, respectively. Flows to consumers, representing wages and salaries, would fill an $(n+1)$st row. Flows from consumers, representing the values of household purchases of the goods of the n sectors, would fill a column. Finally, an element in the $(n+1)$st row and the $(n+1)$st column would represent household purchases of labour services. Thus, all equations would be modified.

Household input coefficients are found in the same manner as any other element in an input-output coefficient table. The value of sector j's purchases of labour (for a given period), divided by the value of total output of sector j, X_j, gives the values of household services (labour) used per rupees' worth of j's output. For the elements of household purchases (consumption) column, the value of vector i's sale to households is divided by the total output of the household sector.

Some Extensions of Basic Input-Output Analysis

Input-Output Model at Regional Level

Originally, the application of input-output model was carried out at national level to assess the impact on individual sector of the economy with a change in production. Later, interest in economic analysis at the regional level whether for a group of states, an individual state or a metropolitan area – has led to modifications of input-output model, which attempt to reflect the peculiarities of a regional problem. Such regional input-output models deal with a single region or with two or more regions with their interconnections. Such case is termed as inter-regional or multi-regional input-output analysis. Some of the earliest regional applications are found in Moore and Peterson[40], Isard and Kuenne[41] and Hirsch.[42]

In inter-regional input-output analysis in the economic system is described not only in terms of interdependent industries, but also in several interrelated regions. The output of each region is defined as a combination of outputs of economic activities carried on within its geographic boundaries, its inputs accordingly comprise the direct inputs of these industries and the goods and services absorbed directly by the final demand sectors of that region. The movement of commodities or services from one region to another reflects the existence of a direct input-output relationship between the industries or an industry and the final demand sector located within their respective boundaries. Indirect regional interdependence gives rise to what is commonly called multi-regional patterns.

A complete inter-industry matrix is specified for each, and in addition inter-industry flows in each direction between regions are recorded in a set of inter-regional matrices, with one matrix for each pair of regions. Thus, a complete four region inter-regional model would contain a total of sixteen sub-matrices, four intra-regional matrices on the diagonal and twelve inter-regional matrices. This enables each economic activity to be identified by industrial group and by location, *i.e.* by region. Each region has an $n \times n$ matrix representing its own industrial structure and other $n \times n$ matrices illustrating the inter-industry. The inter-regional inter-industry coefficients are bound with the same assumptions as the regional inter-industry coefficients; both are treated as the standard input coefficients of Leontief model. Thus, any change in final demand directly calls for a proportional change in each of the inputs, not only each local industry input but also in each industry input from the other regions of the system. The assumption of fixed and constant production coefficients has repercussions on inter-regional inter-industry relations.

Isard's[43] inter-regional model is useful study as a reference norm for theory; another empirical approximation to full inter-regional model is a two-region model for California-Washington developed by Rieffer and Tiebout.[44]

Dynamic Input-Output Analysis

In using an input-output framework for long-run regional forecasting, it is necessary to employ a dynamic model. For short-run projections, the standard static model is used by deriving forecasts for regional gross outputs by using the original inverse matrix and by projecting changes in final demand. For medium-run forecasts the inter-industry matrix would be adjusted by allowing the changes in the input coefficients and possibility for shifts in regional trade coefficients. A truly dynamic model must allow the structural relations between stocks (capital) and flows (output) and take explicit account of the fact that substantial increase in output will create additional capacity requirements so that projected changes in final demand will not only require more intermediate goods but also investment goods from all appropriate sectors in the economy.

The theoretical development of dynamic input-output models owes most to Leontief[45] and refinements by Dorfman.[46] Almon and Atkinson[47] have taken empirical implementation at the national level. The problems of making a dynamic input-output model operation at the regional level relies a great deal on the work of Jorgenson,[48] and Johonsen.[49] One of the analytically and operationally most useful properties of open input-output system is the linear additivity of their solutions with respect to changes in final demand. Each element of the final bill of goods generates a separate chain of direct and indirect input requirements. The total requirements generated by any given vector of final demand are, thus, represented by the sum of such chains, each corresponding to one particular component of that vector. This remains true even if some of the separable sets have negative elements provided the others contain corresponding positive elements large enough to yield a positive or at least a non-negative sum total. The use of dynamic inverse brings the obvious advantage of separatability and additivity into the empirical analysis of economic change. The presence of negative elements in any of the separate input chains imposes limits on the strict use of additive assumptions. It is feasible to determine sequence of total input requirements on the basis of a given dynamic inverse only for those time-phased bills of goods that generate larger positive than negative output requirements for the products of each industry in each period of time.

Price Models

In simple input-output model, prices play the most marginal parts; all price elasticity of substitution is assumed zero and money plays no more than an accommodating role. The price models can be computed from input-output tables that are useful in two contexts: (i) the study of efficiency, and (ii) the study of price determination. Efficiency price models have been developed primarily by East European economists in order to provide a rational basis for reforming the price systems of their countries; price determination models, on the other hand, have been developed mainly in the context of western economies in an effort to understand the process of inter-sectoral price transmission and wage price spiral etc.

The reason why the input-output tables can be used to compute price model is because the basic assumption of the input-output model concerns fixed coefficients of production and constant returns to scale. It follows that the long-run (supply) price of any commodity (sector) is not determined by the scale of output but by the invariant unit cost of production. Thus, quantities do not appear in price model and it is possible to compute set of prices without simultaneously determining a set of quantities. Some input-output economists have tried to partition the input-output matrix so as to conform to the division of commodities between those where demand considerations affect prices (flex prices) and those where prices are determined by supply price alone (fix price) and have then used the input-output model to reflect this division.

Optimization Models

In simple input-output models, there is nothing to optimize.

In the quantity model, a given bill of final goods yields one and only one feasible set of output while in the price model a given set of primary input coefficients providers only one possible vector of prices, with only one consistent and feasible solution. There is no room for choice and, therefore, nothing to optimize.

It is because of its thorough going linearity that linear programming can be introduced into input-output model. In terms of linear programming semantics, the input-output quality circuit is known as the primal and the price circuit as the dual. Optimization models based on input-output techniques enjoy enormous popularity and have become sophisticated, including their extension to a dynamic framework.

Supply-Side Input-Output Models

The standard input-output model is a demand side model or a demand driven model. Once a set of demands on outputs is established, the model assumes that all the necessary inputs to satisfy the needs for production to meet that demand will be supplied.

In standard input-output model, the Leontief inverse relates sectoral gross outputs to the amount of final product. Several economists, for example, Gosh[50] and Augustinovics[51] have suggested that an alternative point of view can be taken with the basic input-output data. This alternative interpretation relates sectoral production to the primary inputs, *i.e.* a unit of value entering the inter-industry system at the beginning of the process. This approach is made operational by essentially rotating or transposing vertical (column) view of the model to a horizontal (row) one. Instead of dividing each column of *b* by the gross output of the sector associated with that column is divide each row of *b* of the gross output of the sector associated with that row. *A* is used to denote the direct resulting input-output coefficients matrix.

The basic assumption of the supply-side approach is that

output distribution pattern stable in an economic system, *i.e.* if output of sector is doubled, then one might expect that, the sales from i to each of the sectors that purchase from i will also be doubled. That is, instead of fixed input coefficients, fixed output coefficients are assumed in supply-side model.

Environment Input-Output Analysis

Many researchers dealing with environmental pollution generation and abatement associated with industry activity have extended the input-output framework. The principle problem to be resolved in environmental model is the appropriate unit of measurement of environment (or ecological) quantities, many of the relationships between the ecological and economic system are non-linear. Moreover, ecological inputs and outputs — the use of common property resources, for *e.g.* streams and rivers as inputs, use of environmental media or sinks in which to dispose of wastes, and the output of pollutants from the production process — have no market price because they can neither be made subject to the laws of property rights nor exchanged in a market. Although most of these environmental inputs and outputs can be measured in physical terms, they can only be assigned monetary values by allocating shadow prices to them. This makes it difficult to incorporate them in an input-output framework. Despite these difficulties, an input-output approach is helpful in the analysis of environmental resources and waste creation problems. Much of the studies treat environmental problems within general input-output model that could well refer to a national economy or even a closed economy. Few pioneering environmental models are: Cumberland model,[52] he was the first economist to include environmental effects in an extended inter-industry model, and his work is the only study to be concerned with regional analysis, Isard-Daly[53] model have developed similar approach to the problem of how to incorporate the environment within input-output framework. The main feature of the analysis is a general input-output flows matrix that includes both economic activities and environmental processes, Leontief model is the one has described a model in which environmental pollution is integrated in a standard type of input-output table. In Leontief's words 'the technical interdependence between the levels of desirable and undesirable outputs can be described in terms of structural coefficients similar to those used to trace the structural interdependence between all the regular branches of production and consumption' and the approach of Victor Model[54] is more general than Leontief in keeping with traditional input-output accounting conventions than Cumberland's and Isard-Daly's. Accordingly, the model includes only flows of free goods from the environment into the economy and of waste products from the economy to the environment, but the benefits accruing from it is that the model can be implemented. He used a forty-commodity sixteen-industry model for the economic system as his basic framework. His input-output table was divided into two sectors; the economic, which is a standard commodity-industry table expressed in monetary values and the ecological expressed in weight terms. The later was broken into sub-sectors reflecting land, air and water, respectively. Among others, Ayres and Knees[55] used more precisely in a closed economy when there is no change in the mass of capital equipments, inventories of finished and semi-finished products, and consumable durable. The mass of ecological inputs to an economy must equal the mass of its ecological outputs. It is the material balance equation. Nine matrices, eight vectors and one scalar vector describe the model. The role of input- output models in the analysis of environmental and ecological problem has been put-forth through the main pioneering alternative input-output framework.

Conclusion

This chapter is of special significance as it provides comprehensive details of the input-output technique used in present research giving details of historical development, mathematical and theoretical structure, alongwith extensions of the technique and applied aspects of it. This chapter is foundation for basic objective of this study, *i.e.* preparation of input-output transaction table for the year 1970-71 and 2000-01. This discussion helps in understanding chapter 6th, 7th and 8th in the present work.

References

1. Leontief, W.W. (1936) "Quantitative input and output relations, in the economic system of the United States", *op. cit.*
2. Phillips, A. (1955) "The tableau economique as a simple Leontief model", op.cit.
3. Walras, L. (1954) "Elements of pure economics, 1874", *op.cit.*
4. Leontief, W.W. (1936) "Quantitative input and output relations, in the economic system of the United States", *op.cit.*
5. Leontief, W.W. (1941) The Structure of United States Economy, 1919-39, *op.cit.*,
6. *Ibid*, Second Edition, 1951.
7. Dorfman, R. (1954) "The nature and significance of input-output", *op. cit.*
8. U.S.S.R, Central Statistical Board, Balance-Sheet of the National Economy of USSR 1923-24, *op. cit.*
9. Barna, T. (1952) "The interdependence of the British Economy", *op. cit.*
10. Stewart, I.G. (1958) "Input-output tables for the United Kingdom 1948", *op. cit.*
11. Mentioned by Richard, S. (1986) "Where are we now", *op. cit.*
12. Boer, P.M.C. (1982) Input-Output Relations: A Theoretical and Empirical Study for Netherlands 1949-67, *op. cit.*
13. Tilanus, C.B. (1966) Input-Output Experiments: The Netherlands 1948-61, *op. cit.*
14. Chenery, H.B and Clark, P.G. (1958) "Structure and Growth of Italian Economy", *op. cit.*
15. Hoglund, B. and Werin, L. (1964) The Production System of the Swedish Economy: An Input-Output Study, *op. cit.*
16. Rasul, G. (1964) Input-output Relationship in Pakistan in 1954, *op. cit.*
17. Moses, L.N. (1955) "The stability of inter-regional trading patterns and input-output analysis", *op. cit.*
18. Evan, W.D. and Hoffenberg D. (1952) "Inter-industry relations study", *op. cit.*

19. Moore, F. T. and Peterson, W. (1955) "Regional analysis: An inter-industry model of Utah", *op. cit.*
20. Isard, W. and Kuenne, R. E. (1953) "The impact of steel upon the Greater New York -Philadelphia industrial region", *op. cit.*
21. Tiebout, C.M. (1969) "An empirical regional input-output projection model: The state of Washington", *op. cit.*
22. Artle, R. (1959) Studies in the Structure of Stockholm Economy, *op. cit.*
23. Watanabe, T. (1970) "Planning application of Leontief model in Japan", *op. cit.*
24. Weisskoff, R. (1975) "Development and trade dependence, the Case of Puerto Rico: 1948-63", *op. cit.*
25. Hirsch, W.Z. (1959) "Inter-industry relations of a metropolitan area", *op. cit.*
26. Simpson, D. and Tsukui, J. (1965) "The development structures of input-output tables", *op. cit.*
27. Polenske, K.R. (1986) "The implementation of a multi-regional input-output model for United States", *op. cit.*
28. Kurtzweg, L.R. (1977) "A comparison of the US and USSR economies", *op. cit.*
29. Carter, H.O. and Ireri, D. (1970) "Linkage of California-Arizona input-output models to analyze water transfer patterns", *op. cit.*
30. Torii, Y. and Fukasaku, K. (1984) "Economic development: An input-output analysis of Republic of Korea and Japan, in United Nations", *op. cit.*
31. Forsell, O. (1988) "Growth and change in Finish Economy", *op. cit.*
32. Urata, S. (1988) "Economic growth and structural change in Soviet Economy: 1959-72", *op. cit.*
33. Nyhus, D. (1988) "The international system of macro economic Input-Output Model", *op. cit.*
34. Rampa, G. and Lanza, A. (1988) "A model for assessing the growth opportunities of EEC countries", *op. cit.*
35. Granberg, A.G. (1991) "Synthesis of regional and national model complex", *op. cit.*
36. Costa, A.M. (1984) "U.N. global modeling: experimental projection on the bases of alternative procedures", *op. cit.*
37. Waelbraeck, J. and Gupta, S.P. (1984) "World Bank global modelling research", *op. cit.*
38. Heppel, L. (2000) "Input-output analysis" in R.J. Johnston, D. Gregory, G. Pratt and M. Watts (eds.) *Dictionary of Human Geography,* Oxford: Blackwell Publishers Ltd., p. 397.
39. Rasmussen, P.N. (1956) *Studies in Inter-sectoral Relations,* Amsterdam : North-Holland.
40. Moore, F. T. and Peterson, W. (1955) "Regional analysis: An inter-industry model of Utah", *op. cit.*

41. Isard, W. and Kuenne, R. E. (1953) "The impact of steel upon the Greater New York -Philadelphia industrial region", *op. cit.*
42. Hirsch, W.Z. (1959) "Inter-industry relations of a metropolitan area", *op. cit.*
43. Isard, W. (1951) "Regional input-output analysis: A model of space economy", *op. cit.*
44. Rieffer, R. and Tiebout, C.M. (1970) "Inter-regional Input-Output: An Empirical California-Washington Model", *Journal of Regional Science*, Vol. 10, 1970,135-152.
45. Leontief, W. (1986) *Input-Output Economics*, New York: Oxford University Press, 294-320.
46. Dorfman, R. (1954) "The nature and significance of input-output", *op. cit.*
47. Almon, C. and Atkinson, L.C. (1972) "Dynamic inter-industry forecasting for business planning", *op. cit.*
48. Jorgenson, D.W. (1960) "Dynamic input-output system", *Review of Economic Studies*, 28:105-116.
49. Johonsen, L. (1978) "On the theory of dynamic input-output models with different time profiles", *op. cit.*
50. Ghosh, A. (1964) *Experiments with Input-Output Model*, Cambridge: Cambridge University Press.
51. Augustinovics, M. (1971) "A twin pair of model of long-term planning", *op. cit.*
52. Cumberland, J.H. and Korbach, J.K. (1973) "A regional inter-industry environmental model", *op. cit.*
53. Isard, W. and Daly, H.E. (1968) "On economics of life science", *op. cit.*
54. Victor, R. (1972) *Pollution: Economy and Environment, op. cit.*
55. Ayres, R. and Knees, A. (1969) "Production, consumption and externalities", *op. cit.*

Chapter-4

Structure of Industries

Introduction

The detailed description about input-output technique has been given in the previous Chapter. It gave details of its historical development, mathematical and theoretical foundations, alongwith extensions of the technique and its applied aspects. The present chapter discusses economic structure of industries in approved industrial areas of Delhi. This chapter mainly consists of three sections: (a) Master Plans and industrial growth and development, (b) analysis of different economic parameters regarding industries, and (c) analyses of economic aspects of industries in twenty-eight industrial areas.

Delhi, till recently, considered as unifunctional (administrative) city, is no longer true. As revealed by the Economic Census[1] conducted by the Government of National Capital Territory of Delhi, it has emerged as a multifunctional city. Industries have played a vital role in the economic growth of Delhi. They contribute to about 21 per cent of the gross state domestic product. The proportion of workers in primary sector has gone down from 7.68 per cent in 1951 to 2 per cent in 2001, tertiary sector has also gone down from 75.38 per cent in 1951 to 58.60 per cent in 2001, whereas the proportion of workers in secondary sector has substantially increased from 16.94 per cent in 1951 to 41.4 per cent in 2001 (Fig. 4.1). Today, Delhi has over 1.37 lakh manufacturing enterprises and majority of them are located in non-conforming zones.

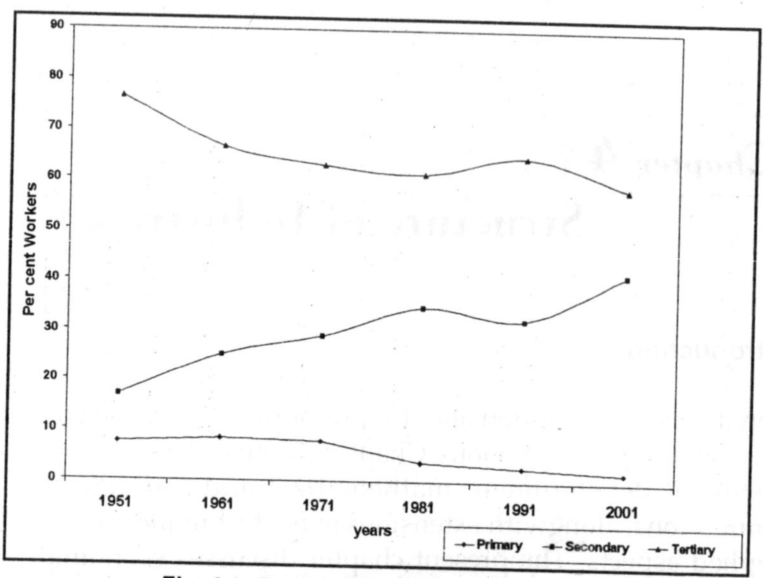

Fig. 4.1: Sectoral Workforce Participation

They are major components of Delhi's vibrant economy with Rs.3000 crores investment producing goods and material worth Rs.6310 crores and providing employment to a large workforce of 14.40 lakhs people with an average of nine persons per unit. Where 30 per cent of such enterprises employ less than four workers indicating that majority of the industries are very small units as per Economic Survey[2] of Government of National Capital Territory of Delhi 2001-2002. These enterprises use a large number of municipal and other services and, thus, keep Delhi city as an engine of growth running to its capacity. Many of these have been in existence for almost 30 to 40 years [Figs. 4.2 (a), (b), (c), (d)].

The recent Economic Census shows that Delhi has ranked twelfth in all-India ranking in number of enterprises contributing about 2.88 per cent of the total. The secondary sector enterprises, *i.e.* the manufacturing sector are growing fast providing employment to 14.4 lakhs persons (41.4 per cent) with a growth rate of 15.78 per cent as compared to the overall growth rate of 8.7 per cent. Thus, manufacturing has

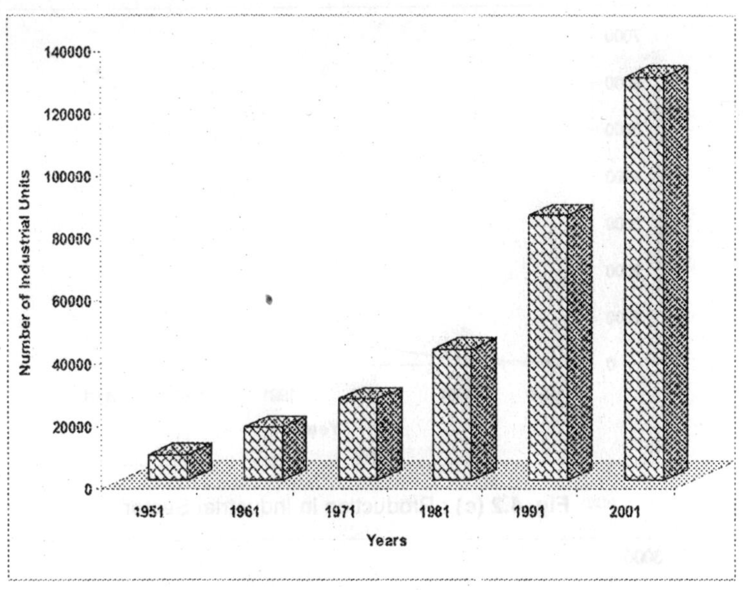

Fig. 4.2(a) : Number of Industrial Units

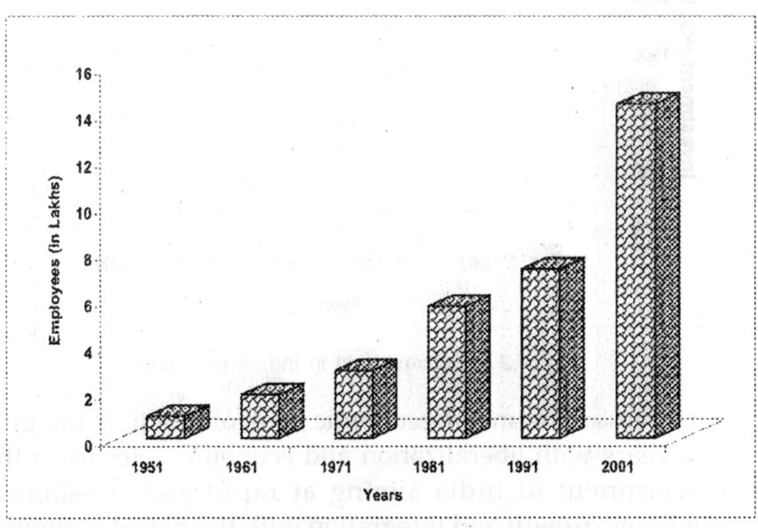

Fig. 4.2 (b) : Employment in Industrial Sector

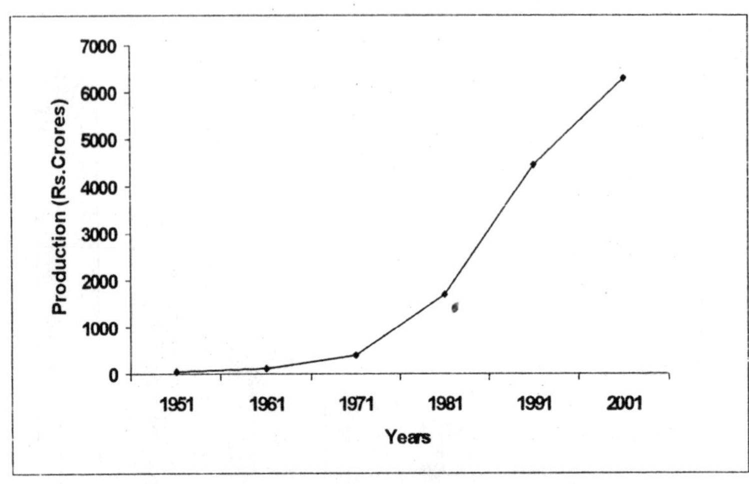

Fig. 4.2 (c) : Production in Industrial Sector

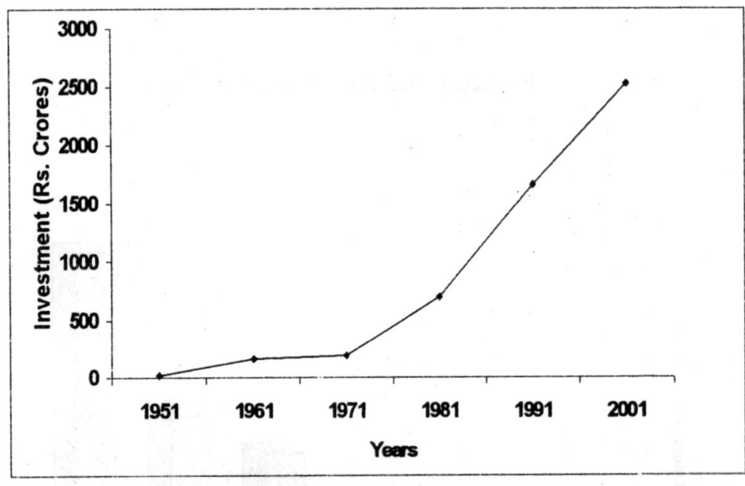

Fig. 4.2 (d): Investment in Industrial Sector

emerged as the major economic base of Delhi in the past few years with liberalization and economic reforms of the Government of India aiming at rapid and substantial economic growth and integration with the global economy. The industrial policy reforms have reduced the industrial licensing requirement, removed restrictions on investment and have facilitated easy access to foreign technology and foreign direct investment, besides liberalization policy for spectacular growth of industries. Other significant factors are availability of good quality infrastructures like road transport, tele-communications, water, power, linkage with rest of the country and overseas countries, availability of technically skilled manpower, existence of number of technical, financial research and development institutions.

The concentration of different industrial activities reveals that the other categories, which comprises miscellaneous manufacturing industries, repair of capital goods, repair and services are the highest order, followed by food products, beverages and tobacco products, 12 per cent of the total. Fabricated metal products and manufacturing of wearing apparel are next in order. The other moderately significant industrial activities are paper and publishing, chemical and chemical products, manufacture of electrical and electronic equipments, leather products and footwear. The sectors of less importance are manufacture of textiles, manufacture of rubber and plastic and manufacture of transport equipment and motor vehicles [Fig. 4.2(e)].

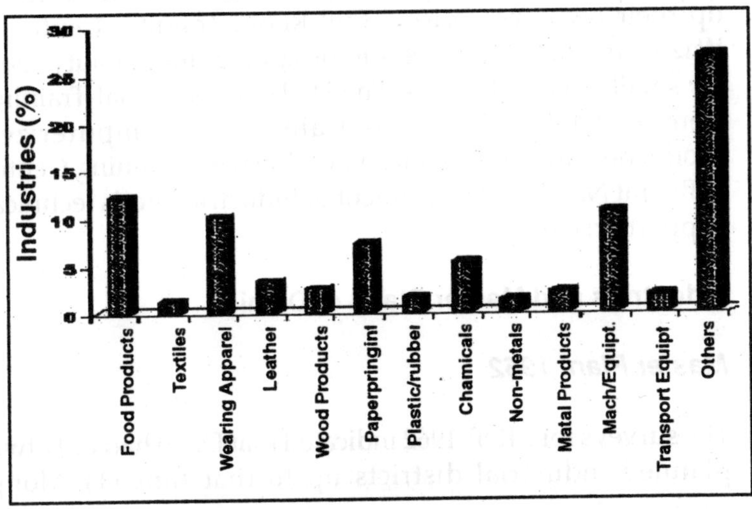

Fig. 4.2(e): Types of Industrial Activity

In order to make the National Capital Territory of Delhi a world class cyber state, Delhi Government has planned to set up 'Hi-tech city for information technology' on about 100 acres of land with the best communication links, uninterrupted and clean water supply with back up power generation and other advanced facilities. A world trade center is also planned to provide instant information flow and interaction amongst various countries in international trade and commerce. A 'Bio-Technology Park' is planned in collaboration with the University of Delhi that will help in the up-gradation of technology of existing industries and non-polluting industries in Delhi. The Delhi Financial Corporation (DFC) caters to the financial needs of industries located in National Capital Territory of Delhi besides also provides financial assistance to service sectors. The Delhi State Industrial Development Corporation (DSIDC) was set up in 1971 that assists, finances and promotes the interest of small-scale industries in Delhi. The Delhi Khadi and Village Industries Board provides financial assistance for setting up village industries unit and marketing outlets. The Delhi Scheduled Caste Financial and Development Corporation provides loan to Scheduled Caste families who want to set up their own enterprises. Tool Room Training Center at Wazirpur since 1978 assists in designing high quality tools for small-scale industries. The Hi-Tech Vocational Training Center at Okhla provides training for computerized production and control machines. Weavers Training Center at Bharat Nagar by Department of Industries etc. is technical support systems.

Industries and Master Plans of Delhi

Master Plan: 1962

The surveys for MDP-1962 indicated that Delhi had only two planned industrial districts up to that time:(1) Along

Najafgarh Road in zone 'H' by erstwhile Delhi Improvement Trust (DIT), and (2) at Okhla in Zone 'F', by now disbanded Rehabilitation Ministry. After Partition, small entrepreneurial units got accelerated in scattered form all-over the city. A few tiny units also came up within several 'Lal Dora' areas of revenue villages and where till that time no urban rules and regulations were applied as they were outside the urban fence. They all added up to 18 per cent of workforce (primarily through 6372 licensed units and several unlicensed ones). MDP-1962 opted for the orderly industrial growth in Delhi through a promotional framework in order to ensure that at least 25 per cent of the workforce was in secondary sector by 1981. Orderly industrial growth was envisaged through:

(a) Flatted factories—192 acres in central and intermediate locations.
(b) Industrial-*cum*-work centres—108 acres for very small plots in extended city as part of community/district centers.
(c) Special industries—103 acres for clean research based units or plots in zone F.
(d) Light and service industries—1583 acres for small and medium-sized plots near built-up areas for non-nuisance activities.
(e) Extensive industries—3600 acres for medium to large plots in extended city.
(f) Extractive and allied industries (in rural Delhi beyond the green belt and mainly for the building industry).
(g) Large-scale and heavy industries were excluded in the Union Territory but accepted in the Delhi Metropolitan Area (Ring Towns on Delhi's doorsteps). The Master Plan land use component of industrial use zones was a little over 5 per cent (6006 acres).

It has been proposed in MPD-1962 that the industrial policy in Delhi and the pattern of growth and development need to be stipulated in accordance with the national policy to invite investment in industry. The availability of the adequate land for industrial expansion, associated provision to decentralize industry from its concentration around the large population in central Delhi, more rigorous enforcement of existing factory regulations like light and safety and the possible promulgation of new regulations were planned.The provision of water, electricity, streets and other utilities as an important incentive for the development of land for the industrial purpose was provided. Heavy industries requiring huge demand for water supply, sewerage disposal were planned to be located in the metropolitan area and even in the National Capital Region. In locating the industries outside Delhi, factors such as inter-state transportation, octroi tax and relation with mother city are to be considered. The industrial redevelopment and location policy are worked out considering the cost of property and the rental value of different locations and different conditions of occupancy. NCR member states were required to take up full responsibility for providing adequate industrial land and the co-operation of concerned agencies so that the land is made available alongwith utility services for the industries. No large new industries be allowed, preference be given to industries, which were essential for feeding, servicing or maintaining Delhi's population.

The policy largely opened guarded avenues for the manufacturing sector in Delhi and gave impetus to the Union Territory Directorate of Industries and the Delhi State Industrial Development Corporation (DSIDC), which is its main implementation arm, for industrial promotional growth. In retrospect, the industrial sector has not grown the way envisaged in MPD-1962. This is also true of other sectors, but the dynamism of manufacturing in economic accretion (but in locations of their choice) has largely skewed the multi-functional planned development process of the NCTD. Table 4.1 shows the MPD-62 zone-wise allocation of land for industries and the actual achievements (in acres). Less than 50 per cent of the land as earmarked for this activity

Table 4.1: Zone-wise Allocation of Land

Zones	*Types of Land*	*Area Proposed (in acres)*	*Area Developed (in acres)*
A	Flatted Factories	43	Nil
B	Light Manufacturing Industries	54	54
	Flatted Factories	42	26
	Extensive Industries	Nil	70
C	Light Manufacturing Industries	113	119
	Flatted Factories	18	18
	Extensive Industries	919	Nil
D	Light Manufacturing Industries	341	315
	Flatted Factories	45	Nil
	Extensive Industries	1014	500
	Special Industries	103	Nil
	Extractive	357	Nil
E	Light Manufacturing Industries	89	119
	Service Industries	118	Nil
	Flatted Factories	16	Nil
	Extensive Industries	89	Nil
F	Light Manufacturing Industries	383	393
	Service Industries	27	29
	Flatted Factories	10	10
	Extensive Industries	469	Nil
G	Service Industries	179	179
	Light Manufacturing Industries	112	112
	Flatted Factories	38	38
H	Service Industries	11	11
	Light Manufacturing Industries	46	146
	Flatted Factories	55	55
	Extensive Industries	410	88
	Total	6006	2914

Source : Base Study on Industries (2001) Delhi Urban Environment and Infrastructure Improvement Project, Government of National Capital Territory of Delhi, Delhi.

(about 6000 Ac.) has been so utilized. Yet the percentage of the workforce was about 25 per cent (as envisaged in the plan but for organized activities). This has been through about 46000 registered units (8000 in approved industrial areas, 15000 household types and 23000 in non-conforming areas) and an estimated 37000 unregistered units. An industrial workforce that increased from 1.87 lakhs in 1961 to 4.63 lakhs in 1981, Economic Census of 1988 indicates that there were 83167 manufacturing enterprises at that time. It indicates that over 37000 units were unregistered.

Table 4.1 also shows that there has not been much enthusiasm for plots in pockets earmarked for extensive industries (zones C, D, E, G, and about 50 per cent in zone F). The special industrial zone has not taken off and flatted factories were not built in zones A, F and G. Though, there has been success in zones C and E and there were partial achievements in zone D (Fig.4.3). Pockets earmarked for service industries and light manufacturing have generally been utilized, though some have been taken at cheaper industrial rate and developed for housing and other uses (*e.g.* Kirti Nagar). The trend has been towards small units and which is less capital intensive and also need less space. Such units can also change production according to consumer market demands. Accordingly, units employing 20 or more workers have steadily declined and units between 5 to 9 workers have increased. In fact, nearly 4 out of 5 units in Delhi employed less than 10 workers each. The mega city has moved towards an industrial mixed land use climate and which make monitoring of power usage, effluent discharge and other hazards difficult to address though statistically they contributes substantially to economic accretion and employment. Unregistered units also participate in this process but their use of electricity and other services and their uncontrolled environmental damage has been a cause of concern, even before 1981.

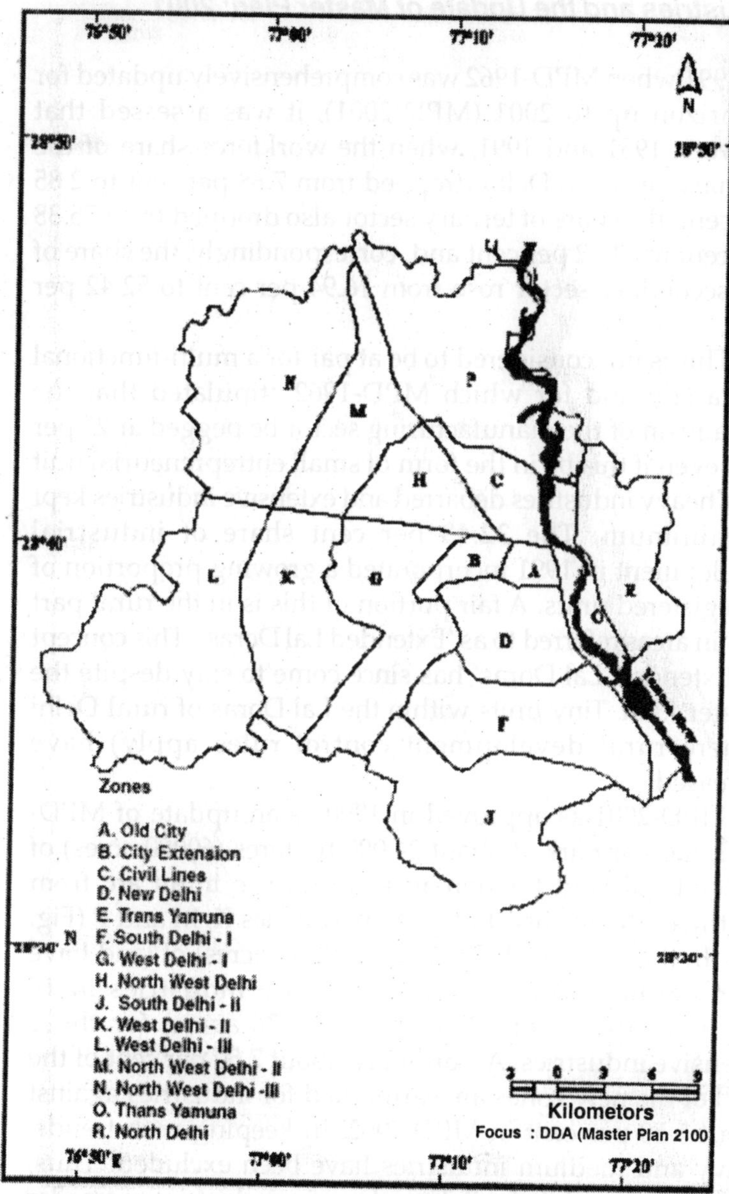

Fig. 4.3 : Planning Zones (DDA)

Industries and the Update of Master Plan: 2001

By 1991,when MPD-1962 was comprehensively updated for a horizon up to 2001 (MPD-2001), it was assessed that between 1951 and 1991, when the workforce share of the primary sector in Delhi dropped from 7.68 per cent to 2.85 per cent, the share of tertiary sector also dropped from 75.38 per cent to 64.72 per cent and, correspondingly, the share of the secondary sector rose from 16.94 per cent to 52.42 per cent.

This is not considered to be at par for a multi-functional mega city and for which MPD-1962 stipulated that the dynamism of the manufacturing sector be pegged at 25 per cent even if this be in the form of small entrepreneurial unit with heavy industries debarred and extensive industries kept to minimum. The 32.43 per cent share of industrial employment in 1991 incorporated a growing proportion of unregistered units. A fair portion of this is in the rural part within areas referred to as 'Extended Lal Doras'. This concept of 'Extended Lal Doras' has since come to stay despite the Master Plan. Tiny units within the Lal Doras of rural Delhi (where rural development control rules apply) have increased.

MPD-2001 as approved in 1990 as an update of MPD-1962, has earmarked about 24,000 hectares (60000 acres) of agricultural land for non-agricultural use in an arc from southwest to northeast Delhi in new zones K, M and P (Fig. 4.3). In these zones, 1553 hectares (3727 acres) of land have been earmarked for light and service industries in 16 locations apart from 265 hectares (636 acres) for those extensive industries. Accordingly, about 7.50 per cent of the total of the new zones are earmarked for industries against about 5.50 per cent in MPD-1962. In keeping with trends, heavy and medium industries have been excluded. Thus, locations are mainly for light and service industries of smaller plot sizes than MPD-1962.

MPD-2001 has also offered a platform for relocation of non-conforming units and approved new activities in organized areas. Specifically, no new units employing more than 50 persons are to be permitted. At the same time, the Plan caters to conforming household and non-polluting units in residential, commercial and mixed land use areas. Industries have been grouped into eight exhaustive categories (A to H)[3] and specifically group H (hazardous/noxious) is prohibited within Delhi. Group 'F' industries are also being re-looked for relocation within the city. The industrial location proposals and their maximum permissible power loads, plot-sizes and workers are shown in Table 4.2. Typically, the Plan is for clean small-scale units in organized environment with all environmental safeguards. MPD -2001 was proposed for an urban population of about 128 lakhs by

Table 4.2 : Maximum Permissible Power Load, Plot Size and Workers (MPD-2001)

Use Zones	*Industry Group Permitted*	*Max. Workers*	*Max. Power Load (kW)*	*Max. Plot Size (sq. m) (in case of development)*
Residential	A	5	1	30
Local Shopping	A, *B*	5	3	
Community Center	A, *B, C*	9	3	
District Center	A, *B, C*	19	5	
Service Center				
	Repair & service industries for automobile electric appliances, building		To provide essential services to neighbouring residential areas	50
Service Industries	A, *B, B, D, E*	6	30	1000
Flatted Industries	A, *B, C, D, E*		30	1000
Light Industries	Food industries*G, I*	6	30	3000
Extensive Industries	A, *B, C, D, E, F,*			3000
Industrial Estimates in Rural use Zones	G		30	2000

Source : MPD-2001, Delhi Development Authority. For industry groups refer Appendix I.

2001, while actual population of 2001 is 138 lakhs. The Plan has taken cognizance of the fact that about 30 per cent of the workforce is in secondary sector. Even so, this entails slowing down of the industrial workforce and which as per the 1998 Economic Census[4] showed a workforce of 41.4 per cent of the total. This was through 1.29 lakh units offering employment to around 14.40 lakh people. This unprecedented growth in units, employment, investment and production is already highlighted in the beginning of this chapter.

The Plan document supported the mixed land use concept to small entrepreneurs, professionals, artisans, mechanics and the like to carry on their locations in their homes, without having to compete in the 'commercial land markets' as also to "cut down unnecessary commuting to work centers". It is reported that there could be around 1.2 lakh such household units in Delhi at present (a growing number of them are unregistered). In alarming levels of environmental degradation in city, the highly visible industrial sector is high on the list of closure/removal/relocation and otherwise strict controls. From February 1996, the Supreme Court has stepped into the scene. This calls for immediate time bound corrective and long-term provisions as now offered in the second comprehensive update of MPD-1962 within the year 2021 as a horizon (MPD-2021).

Current Industrial Policy and Relocation

A rapidly deteriorating environment all round led to the Supreme Court issuing time bound directives and even selective strictures. This was a decade after the 1985 petition. A survey in 1995 by the Delhi Pollution Control Committee led to a notice to 9164 'polluting units' followed by Supreme Court in 1996 ordering that 1333 hazardous units be closed and moved out of city. This list was later expanded to cover 2245 units. Among its corrective action-albeit long-term was to restate its industrial policy largely in line with MPD-2001. Accordingly, the Ninth Five Year Plan of Delhi now stipulates the following for the industrial sector :

(a) Only non-polluting small-scale industries with low power consumption and less space requirements, generating employment for skilled personnel, would be encouraged.
(b) New industrial estates/flatted factory complexes would be developed only for relocating those polluting industrial units which are to be shifted from non-conforming areas in compliance with orders from Hon'ble Supreme Court.
(c) Industry department will work for the achievement of the objective "Pollution Free Delhi" by constructing single/combined effluent treatment plants in the industrial areas.
(d) Industrial units using high technology and producing high value added goods would be encouraged.
(e) Effective measures will be undertaken for quality control.
(f) Effective steps would be undertaken to increase export promotion activities.
(g) Schemes would implement for women entrepreneurs and other weaker sections of society; electronic, light engineering, garments, handlooms and leather industries other than tanneries would be encouraged.

The 1996 Supreme Court order was interpreted as the shifting of all industries not confirming to MPD-2001. Accordingly, based on action by Delhi State Industrial Corporation, 51,846 applications for shifting were accepted for relocation of which it was estimated that less than half were hazardous or polluting. The first effort in relocation was for about 16,000 units in the Bawana-Holambi Kalan area. Some units were also to be accommodated within existing industrial estates and flatted factories. For the balance (Over 35,000 units), it is a joint exercise between Delhi Administration and the DDA (Table 4.3).

Table 4.3 : Industrial Units Relocated Upto 2000

Category	*Location*	*No. of Units*
Water Polluting	Narela	967
General Category	Bawana	5596
General Category	Bawana	9326
	Jhilmil	96
	Badli	23
	Patparganj	78
Total		16086

Source: Annual Plan Document (2002), Government of National Capital Territory of Delhi, Delhi.

Out of the total 51851 applicants, who had applied for allotment of industrial plots under relocation scheme, about 26,500 applicants have been found eligible for allotment, 16086 applicants have been allotted industrial plots in different areas as mentioned above. Structural Plan of 1865 acres of land acquired in village Bawana, Holambi Kalan, Holambi Khurd has been approved by DDA and also changes in land use from agricultural to industrial has been done by DDA and Ministry of Urban Development.

It is evident from Table 4.4 that there are approximately 1.29 lakh industrial units. Nearly, 22000 units are operating in conformed industrial areas. There are 24000 industrial units in non-conformed areas, 16000 units are such that are in non-conformed areas but have applied for plot in conformed areas and 5000 in local commercial centers in residential areas. There are 25000 cottage industrial units and 31363 units are scattered in various other areas. The Government of Delhi has requested Delhi Development Authority (DDA) for certain amendments in the Master Plan like '*in situ* regularization' of various areas of industrial concentration where more than seventy per cent residential premises have already been converted to industrial use, making parameters governing household industries board based and to allow service sector industry which caters to the day-to-day needs of the residents of Delhi such as atta chakkies, dry cleaners, scooter repair shop etc., to run from local commercial/residential areas. The proposal for amendment to the master Plan' *in-situ* regularization' of industrial concentration areas has since been approved by the DDA who, in turn, has referred it to Ministry of Urban Development under Section 11 (A) of Delhi Development Act, 1957 (Table 4.4).

Table 4.4 : Status of Industrial Areas and Regularization

Type of Industrial Units	*Approximate Number*
(i) Units in conforming zones	22,000
(ii) Units in 15 areas proposed for regularization	12,000
(iii) Units in 40 other selected areas with similar characteristics that may be considered for regularization if non-polluting and satisfy conditions	12,000
(iv) Units in local commercial areas which can be regularized without much difficulty	5,000
(v) Units working as single hand like cottage industry considered as allowable household units as per master plan regulations with revised norms as recommended in the policy	25,000
(vi) Units from present non-conforming zones which have applied for space in new industrial estate being developed	16,000
Total of (i) to (vi) above	92,000
Remaining units scattered in various places which either should find place in regular industrial zones in Delhi or shift outside the city in NCR (129363-92000)	31,363

Source : Base Study on Industries (2001) Delhi Urban Environment and Infrastructure Improvement Project, Government of National Capital Territory of Delhi, Delhi.

The lists of areas of industrial concentration in non-conforming zones, which have been recommended by DDA for regularization, are mentioned in Table 4.5. These areas comprise manufacturing activities like, plastic goods, packaging, engineering items, metal casting, auto parts, wire drawing, footwear, crockery, rubber, recycling of plastic etc. Among the 15 areas Vishwas Nagar, Khyala, Trinagar are the areas with 4000 units in first two and 2000 units in the third one. Other areas like Peeragarhi, Basai Dharapur, Libaspur, Karawal Nagar, Dabri, Mundka etc., have industrial units ranging from 100 to 800 in number. It is in the above context that the regularization of industrial areas or incorporation of such areas in the MPD-2021 has been viewed. Table 4.5 gives details regarding the areas of industrial concentration.

Master Plan of Delhi: 2021

The National Capital Territory of Delhi has a non-expandable area of 1483 sq.km and a projected population of 230 lakhs by 2021. Therefore, as densities for work and living increase, space for recreation and urban agriculture (market gardens) would correspondingly decrease and environmental problems would escalate. In this process and due to globalization the mega city of Delhi would be a favoured location for international and national business houses and quality information exchange, research and culture. As a seat of federal governance, its role in protocol and ceremonial would also grow; all this not only need appropriate urban spaces but also sanitized environs.

Towards a goal of an environmentally balanced mega city of Delhi 2021, trends are crystallizing towards: (a) the regulated growth of the secondary sector, (b) the *in-situ* up-gradation of existing units that are environmentally compatible, (c) the relocation of units within city at appropriate locations to the extent possible–provided they are not noxious or hazardous, (d) the continued debarring of heavy/large and other land intensive units, (e) new light

Table 4.5: Industrial Areas for Regularization

Name of the Area	*Approx. No. of Units*	*Nature of Items Manufactured*
Shahzada Bagh Extension	300	Plastic goods, packaging engineering items footwear etc.
Nangli Sakrawati	100	Plastic goods, engineering goods, aluminum casting, rubber/foam mattresses, auto-parts, melamine crockery
Mundka	200	Footwear fabrication, foundry, casting, machinery etc.
Vishwas Nagar	4,000	About 80% of the industries are engaged in the copper wire drawing and plastic wires and cables. The remaining 20% are allied industries, *e.g.* packaging, printing, plastic compound etc.
Khyala 1.Narsing Garden 2.Khyala Village 3.Vishnu Garden	4,000	Light engineering injection molding, plastic, pressure cookers electronic goods, and dyeing.
Tri Nagar	2000	About 75% of industries are engaged in the manufacturing of footwear and plastic goods. The remaining 25% are allied industries *e.g.* packaging printing dies and moulds etc.
Shalimar Village	250	Plastic, engineering items, auto parts, bread etc.
Hastsal	200	Foam/plastic goods packaging melamine crockery, scooter parts, dal mill, adhesive, engineering items and bread etc.
Karawal Nagar	200	Auto parts packaging, engineering items, plastic
Peeragarhi	500	Auto parts, battery packaging, ice factory, plastic goods, reprocessing of plastic.
Basai Dharapur	800	Motor parts, engineering goods, electric motor, fans, electric bulb, boundary, molding, and electrical items, fans parts and accessories.
Dabri	200	Engineering goods, plastic products, packaging, auto parts, steel fabrications etc.,
Libaspur	375	Packaging, auto parts, dyeing and bleaching plastic goods, rubbers products, washing soap, recycling of plastics.
Haiderpur	200	Plastic, wires and cables, engineering goods, electrical goods, plastic products, cable, tin metal boxes, steel fabrications, wire drawing etc.
G.T.Karnal Road (behind 'O' block industrial areas and adjoining the flyover of Ashok Vihar)	50	Packaging, leather workshop, electrical goods etc.

Source : Base Study on Industries (2001) Delhi Urban Environment and Infrastructure Improvement Project, Government of National Capital Territory of Delhi, Delhi.

and service industries to be in well developed sites next to housing/shelter and air, road and rail transport and other services; and (f) a workable lateral partnership with states that have land within the NCR, primarily for the deflection of new units that eye Delhi as a destination. The policies of MPD-2021 have recognized that environmental actions will shape than follow economic trends. According to MPD-2021, the industrial location policy should emphasize the following points:

(a) Compulsory registration of all industrial units with the industries department and the development of a database showing industrial unit location and/or expansion. Applications for new units or expansion should accompany an environmental clearance certificate.
(b) High-tech, high-skill industrial units.
(c) Household/cottage units may be regularized/ permitted within prescribed norms, to take care of changes in industrial products and processing.
(d) Some of the units in non-conforming zones as per MPD-2001 may be allowed to remain, providing they take anti-pollution measures. No hazardous units to be allowed.
(e) 'One window' approach to be strengthened for processing cases relating to industrial development.
(f) Industries department to be strengthened by adequate training in environmental matters and for registration of units, building the database, processing applications for environmental considerations.

Structure and Distribution of Industrial Activity in Approved Industrial Areas

There are twenty-eight approved or confirmed industrial

areas in Delhi apart from a few new locations coming up as developed industrial areas to relocate industries from residential areas. Industries are also functioning in a large number of non-conforming areas and number of units in such areas is many times higher than the units are in approved areas. In these twenty-eight industrial areas, a total of 21627 industrial units exist, about one-fifth of the units are either closed or their allocated plot is lying vacant. For instance, about 20 per cent of the total industrial units have yet not started construction on the site in the Narela Industrial Area. Similarly, 40 per cent industrial units are either closed or have not yet started construction work at Patparganj Industrial Area. In almost all industrial areas of Delhi, the nature and type of manufacturing and trading includes variety of activities as manufacturing of basic iron and steel, other fabricated metal products, metal working service activities, general purpose machinery, special purpose machinery, wearing apparel, basic chemicals, other chemical products, plastic products, insulate wire and cables, maintenance and repair of motor vehicles, printing and other business activities (Fig. 4.4).

Of the twenty-eight industrial areas, six are large industrial areas, namely, Okhla Industrial Area, Mayapuri Industrial Area, Wazirpur Industrial Area, Anand Parbat Industrial Estate, Kirti Nagar Industrial Estate and Narela Industrial Area. The Narela Industrial Area is newly developed where only 18 per cent of the allotted plots are functioning units and other are either under construction or lying vacant. About two-thirds of all industrial units (*i.e.* 21627) are located in these six larger industrial areas. Anand Parbat area is accommodating 17.23 per cent of industrial units, followed by Mayapuri 15.10 per cent of industrial units, Wazirpur and Kirti Nagar industrial areas 7.7 per cent and 6.82 per cent industrial units, respectively. Besides the newly developed Narela Industrial Area, the other approved industrial estates having large number of industrial units that are either closed or plots lying vacant or under

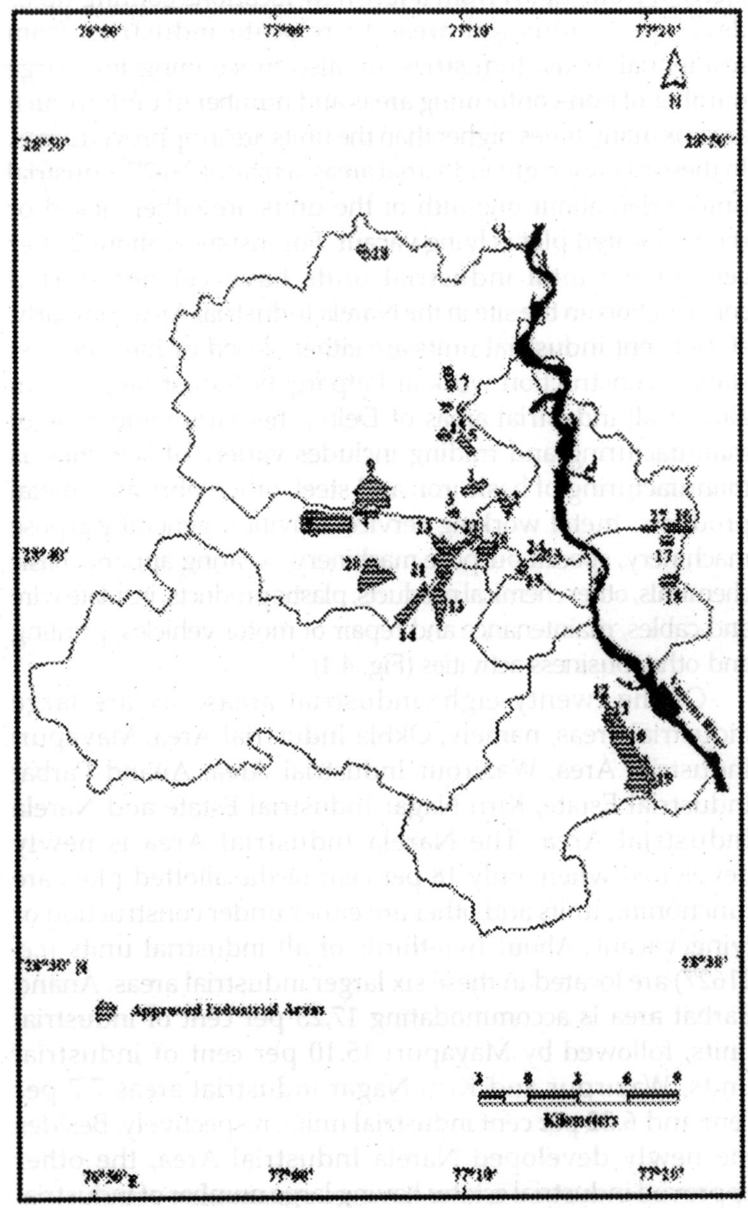

Fig. 4.4 : Location of Industrial Areas

construction is Patparganj with 50 per cent, Jhilmil 28 per cent, Rajasthan Udyog Nagar Industrial Area 28 per cent, Mangolpuri Area and Small-Scale Industrial Area (SSI) area with 21 per cent (Fig.4.5).

Another six approved industrial areas account for having less than one per cent of total industrial unit. The Okhla Industrial Estate, Rajasthan Udyog Nagar Industrial Estate, SMA Industrial Area, SSI Industrial Area, Tilak Nagar Industrial Area and Mohan Co-operative Industrial Area together accommodate 3.5 per cent of the total units in Delhi. About one-third of total industrial units exist in the rest sixteen industrial areas, which include Naraina with 3.5 per cent units, G.T.Karnal Road, Lawrence Road Area, Patparganj area 2.1 per cent, 2.6 per cent and 2.3 per cent of the total industrial units, respectively. Udyog Nagar, Nangloi and Jhandewalan flatted factories follows 1.8 per cent units in each of them. Okhla flatted factory, Badli and Jhilmil accommodate 1.4 per cent units in each of them. Najafgarh Road Industrial Area accounts for 1.7 per cent, whereas Moti Nagar, Shahdara and Friends Colony industrial areas have only about 1.1 per cent industrial units (Fig. 4.5).

Establishments other than industrial enterprises are found in almost all industrial areas. The total number of such establishments are 3972, which are mainly concentrated in eight industrial areas of Delhi. Wazirpur has highest number of such establishments, i.e. 961 followed by 494 and 425 establishments in Mangolpuri and Okhla, respectively, and also equally highly, i.e., 433 in Mangolpuri and 311 in Kirti Nagar. In the industrial areas of Lawrence Road, Naraina and Anand Parbat such establishments are 200 to 300. In the other industrial areas, the number of such establishments ranges from zero in Okhla flatted factory to 30-40 in Jhilmil, Patparganj, Mohan Co-operative, Jhandewalan and Mangolpuri. Najafgarh, Moti Nagar and Shahdara industrial area account for 70-80 such establishments (Fig. 4.6).

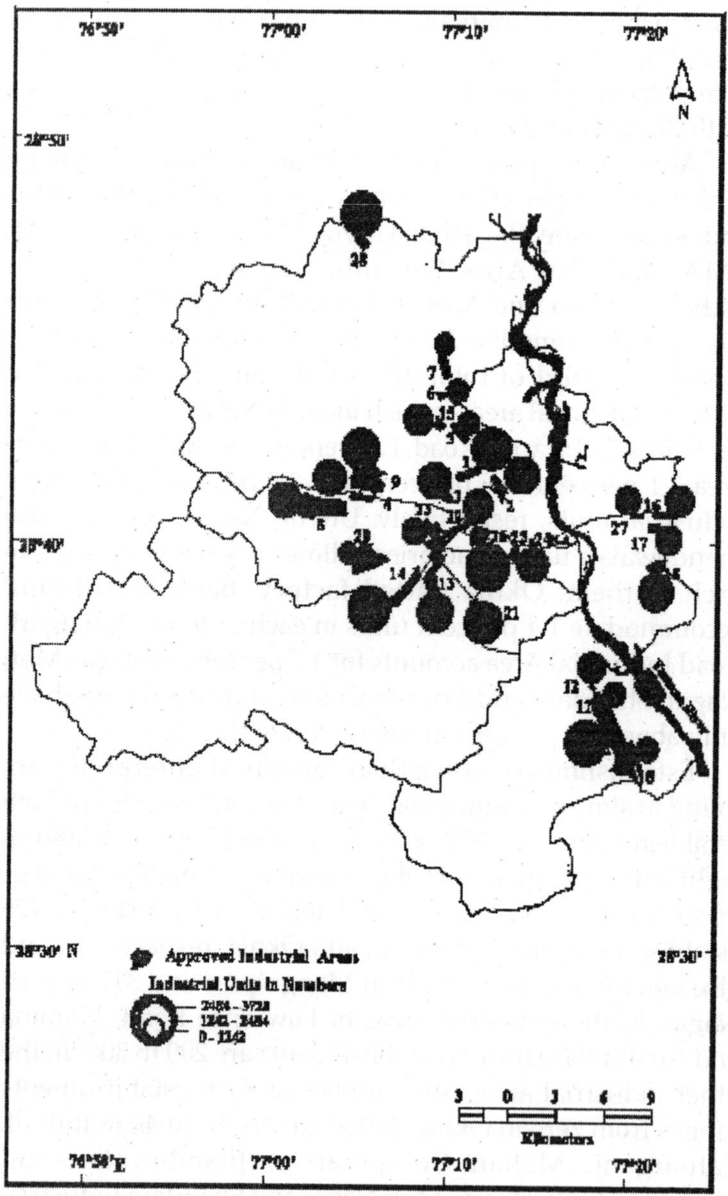

Fig. 4.5 : Number of Industrial Units

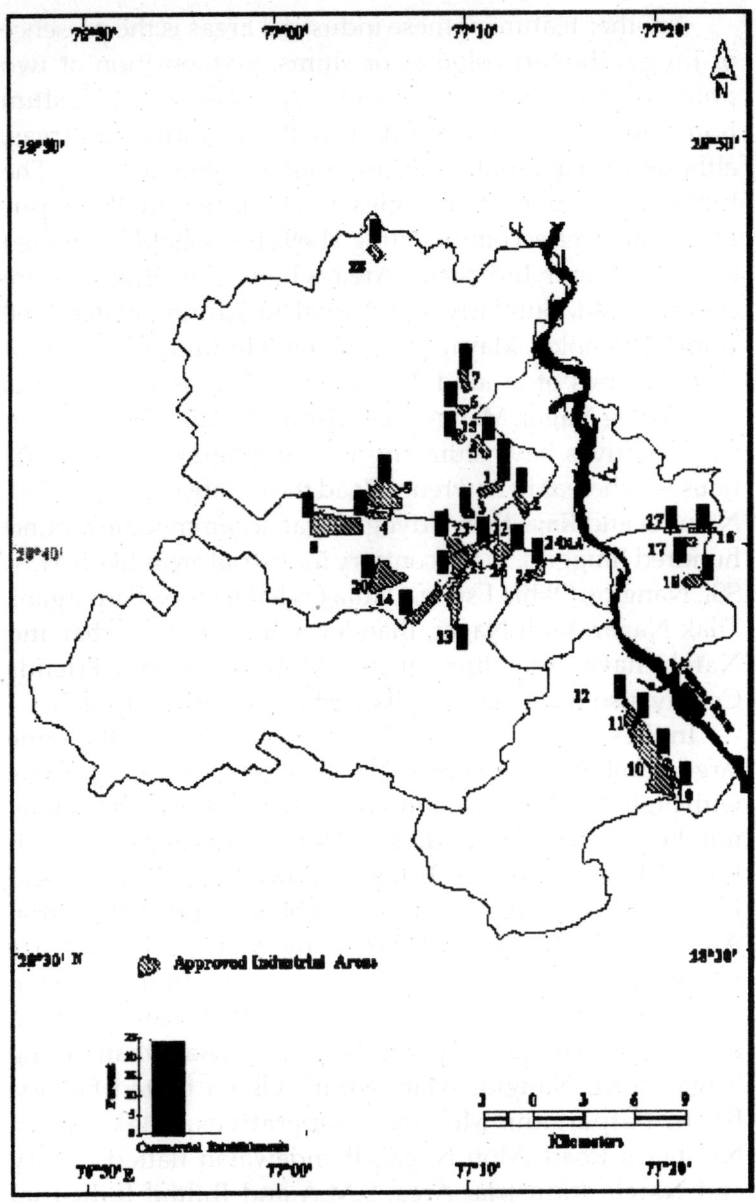

Fig. 4.6 : Other Commercial Establishments

Another feature of these industrial areas is the presence of Jhuggi-Jhopari colonies or slums, juxtaposition of two poles of economy and society. A total of 29257 slum households are concentrated in these industrial areas, although their number varies among different areas. The highest number of Jhuggies is clustered in Wazirpur Industrial Area accommodating 11,692 households, followed by Kirti Nagar Industrial Area where 5310 Jhuggies are concentrated. Similarly, G.T.Karnal Road inhabitates 4200 slum households. Mayapuri and Jhilmil Industrial areas have slum clusters of around 2000 houses. The industrial areas like Udyog Nagar, Mangolpuri, Badli, Shahdara and Mohan Co-operatives have slum clusters ranging from 250 to 500 houses, whereas in Lawrence Road the number is about 1500. Naraina and Rajasthan Udyog Nagar accommodate around hundred Jhuggies. In the contrary industrial areas like S.M.A, SSI, Nangloi, Okhla Estate, Okhla flatted factory, Patparganj, Tilak Nagar, Moti Nagar, Jhandewalan, Anand Parbat and Narela have zero slum cluster. Moti Nagar and Friends Colony also have very small number of slums (Fig. 4.7).

In these industrial areas, residences are not in the same large number as the slums. The Wazirpur Industrial Estate with highest number of slums has zero residence. Of the total number of 816 such residences, 500 residences exist in G.T. Karnal Road Industrial Estate, followed by 125 in Anand Parbat Industrial Area and 69 in Okhla. The other Industrial Areas as Kirti Nagar, Friends Colony, Mayapuri, Lawrence Road and Naraina have residences ranging from 6 to 50 in number. There are also industrial areas which are free from residences such as Wazirpur, Udyog Nagar, Rajasthan Udyog Nagar, S.S.I, Nangloi, Mangolpuri, Okhla flatted factory, Badli, Patparganj, Mohan Co-operatives, Tilak Nagar, Najafgarh Road, Moti Nagar, Jhandewalan flatted factory and Narela Industrial Area. S.M.A and Jhilmil Industrial Areas have almost negligible residences. The industrial areas with zero or almost negligible residences are mostly those

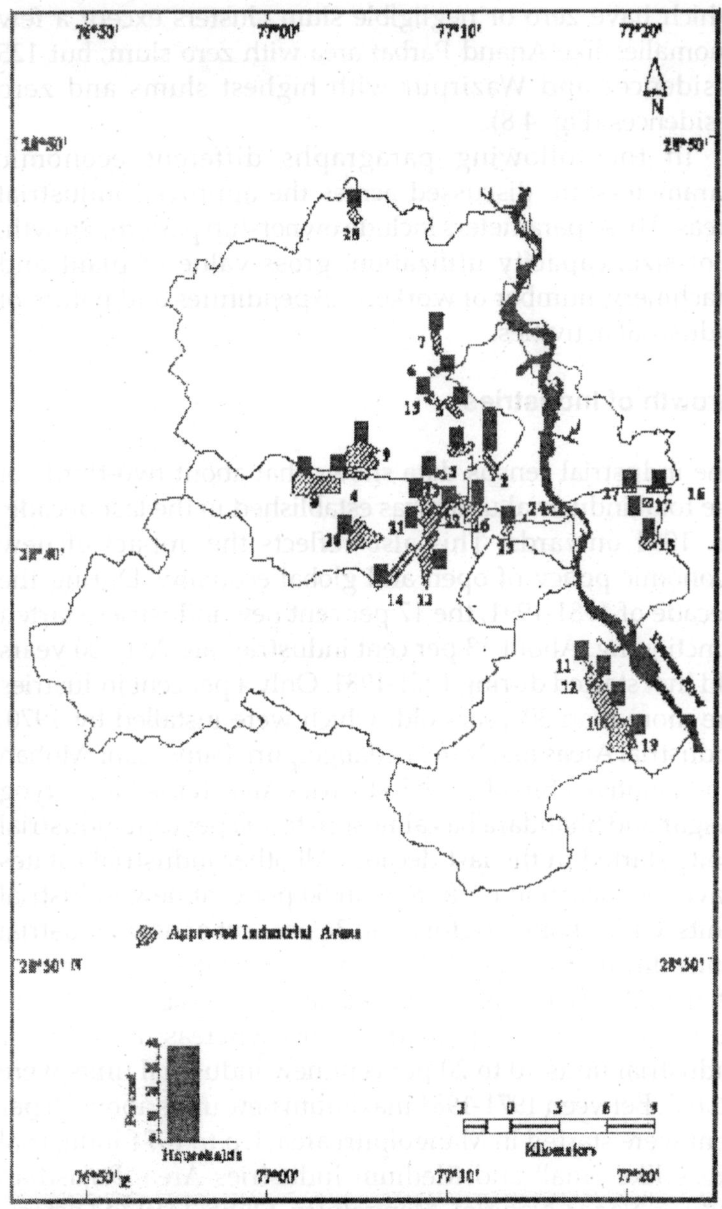

Fig. 4.7 : Slum Households

which have zero or negligible slum clusters except a few anomalies like Anand Parbat area with zero slum, but 125 residences and Wazirpur with highest slums and zero residences (Fig. 4.8).

In the following paragraphs different economic parameters are discussed across the approved industrial areas. These parameters include ownership pattern, growth, plot size, capacity utilization, gross value of plant and machinery, number of workers, expenditures and nature of industrial activities.

Growth of Industries

The industrial census data shows that about two-thirds of the total industrial units was established in the last decade, *i.e.* 1991 onwards. This also reflects the impact of new economic policy of open and global economy. During the decade of 1981-1991, the 17 per cent new industries started functioning. About 13 per cent industries are 20 to 30 years old that started during 1971-1981. Only 4 per cent industries are more than 30 years old, which were installed by 1970. Industrial Areas like Narela, Mangolpuri, Patparganj, Mohan Co-operatives, Small-Scale Industries Area, Rajasthan Udyog Nagar and Shahdara has almost 80 to 100 per cent industrial units started in the last decade. All other industrial estates have the inclusion of more than 50 per cent new industrial units. Okhla flatted factory had 36 per cent of new industrial units during this decade. Another four industrial estates of Shahadara, Tilak Nagar, Nangloi and Mangolpuri had 50 to 80 per cent of new industrial units whereas; in all other industrial units 10 to 20 per cent new industrial units were stated. Between 1971-1981 maximum new units about 30 per cent were started in Mangolpuri area. Up to 1971 industrial areas like Small and Medium Industries Area, Rajasthan Udyog Nagar, Nangloi, Mangolpuri, Okhla Flatted Factory, Shahdara, Mohan Co-operatives had very few or nil

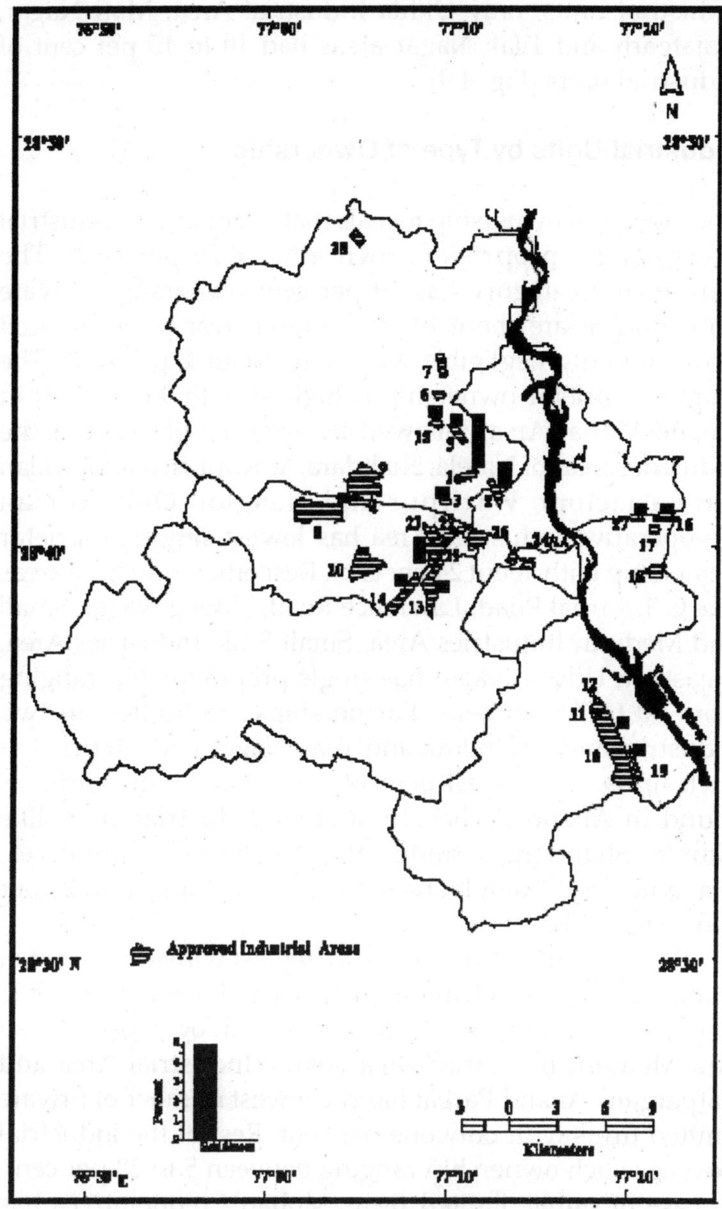

Fig. 4.8 : Residences Other than Slums, 2001

industrial units, only Okhla Industrial Area, Moti Nagar, Najafgarh and Tilak Nagar areas had 10 to 15 per cent of industrial units (Fig. 4.9).

Industrial Units by Type of Ownership

The pattern of ownership reveals that out of 21,627 industrial units, single proprietors own almost 70 per cent. The partnership category has 19 per cent ownership. Private limited firms are about 10 per cent, whereas public limited firms are only negligible with only about 2 per cent. The single proprietor ownership is highest with 90 per cent in Anand Parbat Area, followed by 70 to 80 per cent in the industrial areas of Narela, Shahdara, Mayapuri, Jhandewalan flatted factory, Wazirpur and Nangloi. Only Mohan Co-operative Industrial Area has lowest single proprietor ownership with about 24 per cent. Rest other industrial areas like G.T.Karnal Road, Lawrence Road, Udyog Nagar, Small and Medium Industries Area, Small-Scale Industries Area, Rajasthan Udyog Nagar has single proprietorship ranging from 30 to 70 per cent. Partnerships are highest in two industrial areas of Jhilmil and Tilak Nagar with 40 per cent such firms. The lowest percentage of partnership firms is found in Anand Parbat. In another industrial areas like Narela, Shahdara, Jhandewalan, Mohan Co-operatives, Mayapuri, SSI, Nangloi have the partnerships up to 20 per cent (Fig. 4.10).

Private limited firms are seen highest with 44 per cent in Mangolpuri and Mohan Co-operative followed by about 30 per cent in Udyog Nagar, Rajasthan Udyog Nagar, Small and Medium Industries Area, Okhla Industrial Area and Patparganj. Anand Parbat has the lowest number of private limited firms with only one per cent. Rest of the industrial area has such ownership ranging between 5 to 20 per cent. In case of public limited firms Mohan Co-operatives has highest of 14 per cent followed by 11 per cent in Okhla Industrial Area, 8 per cent in Rajasthan Udyog Nagar and

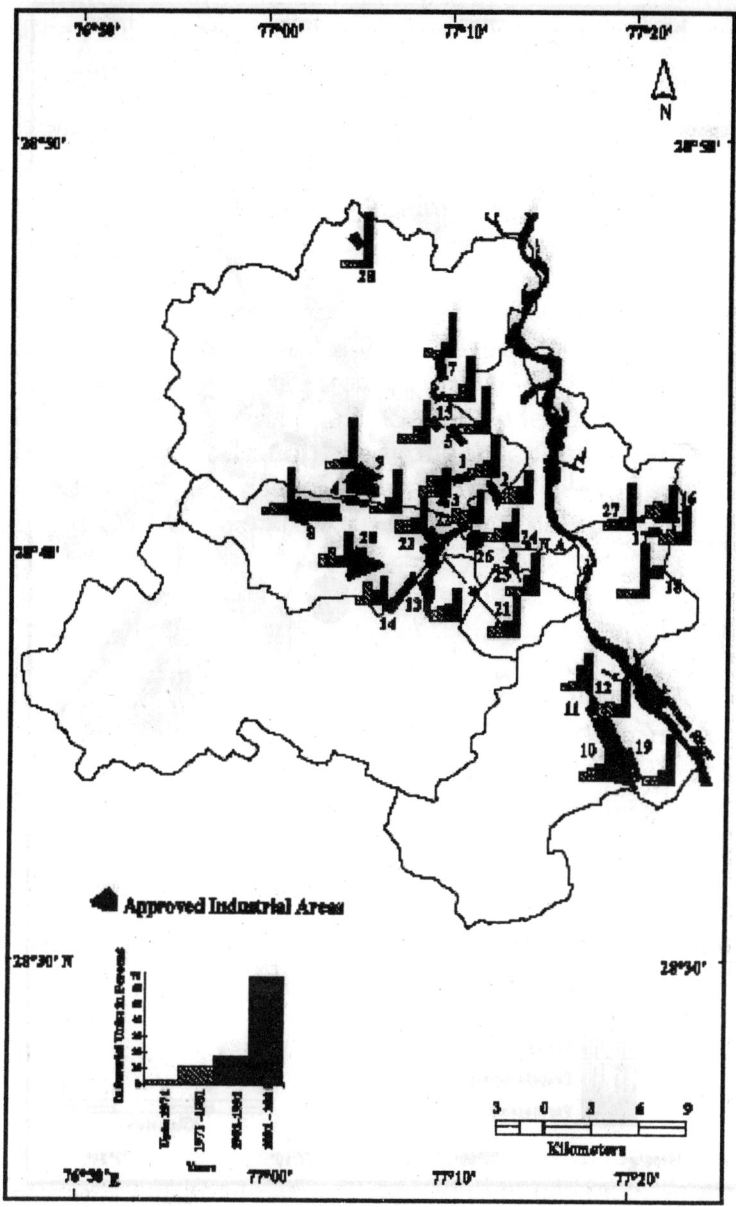

Fig. 4.9 : Growth of Industries, 1971-2001

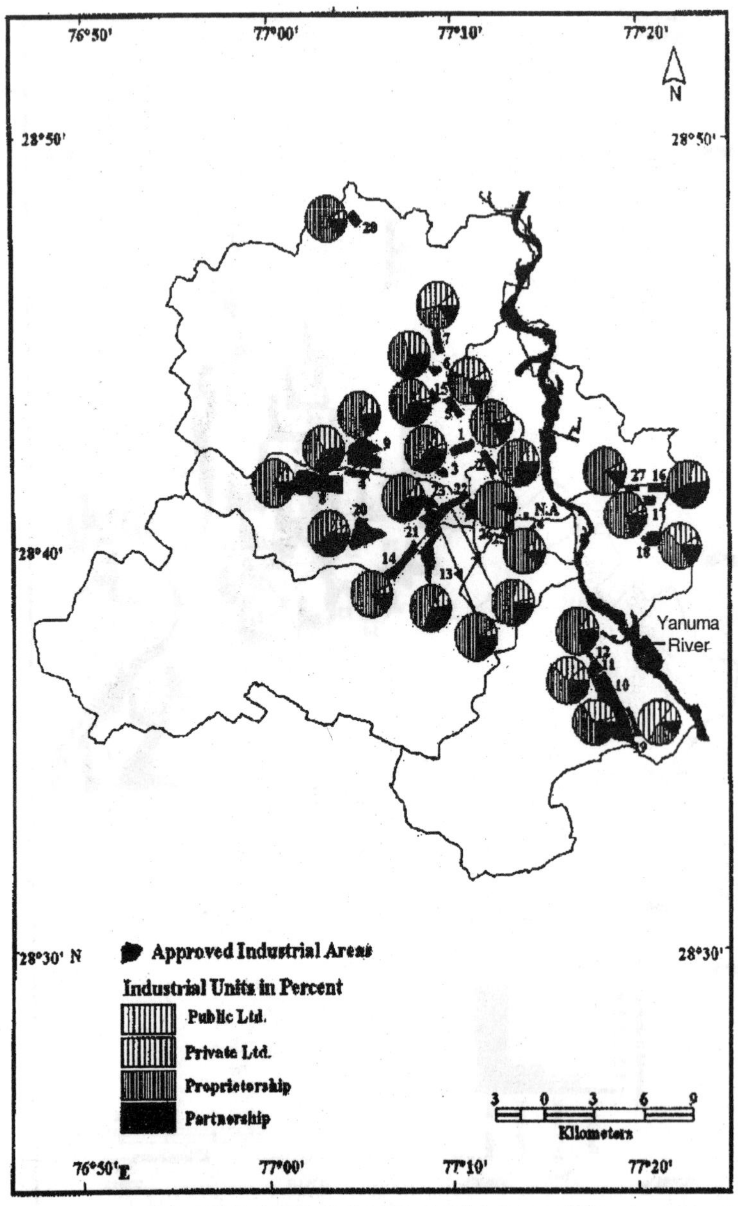

Fig. 4.10 : Ownership Pattern of Industries, 2001

7 per cent in Tilak Nagar Industrial Area. In other industrial areas it is very small percentage and zero in Shahdara Industrial Area (Fig. 4.10).

Ownership and Size of Plots

About 60 per cent industrial units are functioning in owned plots, whereas 40 per cent are operating in rented industrial plots. In the owned industrial plots nearly 27 per cent are operating in the plots of 200 to 500 sq. m area, about 20 per cent each units are functioning in plots of 100 to 200 sq. m, and above 500 sq.m. In 50 to 100 sq. m size plots about 20 per cent units are functioning whereas; only 13 per cent units have a plots size of less than 50 sq. m (Fig. 4.11).

In the owned plots Mohan Co-operative Industrial Area has most of the units, *i.e.* 84 per cent operating in the plot area of above 500 sq. m followed by Small-Scale Industries Area with 75 per cent units are of this size. Other industrial areas like Udyog Nagar, Small and Medium Industries Area, Rajasthan Udyog Nagar and Patparganj also have 50 to 60 per cent units in above 500 sq. m size. In the plot size of 200 to 500 sq. m Badli and Jhilmil have about 50 per cent of units operating, followed by 42 per cent units in Naraina. About 20 to 30 per cent units are functioning in Wazirpur, G.T, Karnal Road, Patparganj and Kirti Nagar areas. The plot sizes of 100 to 200 sq. m are highest in Mangolpuri (23 %). In less than 100 sq. m plots Mangolpuri, Kirti Nagar, Anand Parbat areas have about 20 per cent units operating and only Mangolpuri has 72 per cent units in this plot size (Fig. 4.11).

In the rented category, industrial plots of above 500 sq. m about 85 per cent units are in Narela, followed by more than 40 per cent units in Okhla Industrial Area. Industrial Areas like Udyog Nagar, Small and Medium Industries Area, Moti Nagar, Rajasthan Udyog Nagar have 10 per cent units of this size, rest other industrial areas have less than seven per cent units functioning in such big plots. Whereas Tilak

Nagar, Okhla flatted factory, Anand Parbat have almost no plots of this size, 20 to 30 per cent units functions in Moti Nagar, Kirti Nagar, and Patparganj in plots of 200 to 500 sq.m Udyog Nagar, G.T. Karnal Road, Badli, Najafgarh Road and Jhandewalan flatted factory have 8 to 12 per cent units. The rest all industrial areas less than 7 per cent plots belongs to this category. In category of less than 100 sq. m of plots industrial areas of Udyog Nagar, Small and Medium Industries Area, Small-Scale Industries Area, Rajasthan Udyog Nagar, Badli, Jhilmil, Patparganj and Narela have negligible plots. Maximum plots about 84 per cent of this size are accommodating industrial units in Okhla flatted factory (Fig. 4.11).

Capacity Utilization of Plants and Machine

Most of the industries have the installed capacity of plant and machinery of production of 500 units (kg/liter/numbers) per shift upon a single shift basis. Nearly, one-fourth unit of 21627 is utilizing only 50 per cent of their installed capacity, another 30 per cent industrial units the capacity utilization is up to three-quarter. Only 47 per cent industrial unit could manage to use more than three-quarter of their installed capacity while not a single unit is using its hundred per centinstalled capacity. The capacity utilization of more than 75 per cent is highest in Kirti Nagar (84%) per cent units fall in this category, followed by 40 to 60 per cent units in Mayapuri, Najafgarh, Moti Nagar, Jhandewalan, Shahdara, Narela, G.T. Karnal Road, Udyog Nagar, Okhla Industrial Area and Friends Colony. In rest other industrial areas about 30 per cent units fall in this category. The capacity utilization of upto three-quarter is highest in Okhla flatted factory (50 %), in other industrial areas 20 to 30 per cent units fall in this category, whereas Kirti Nagar has lowest (11 %) (Fig. 4.12).

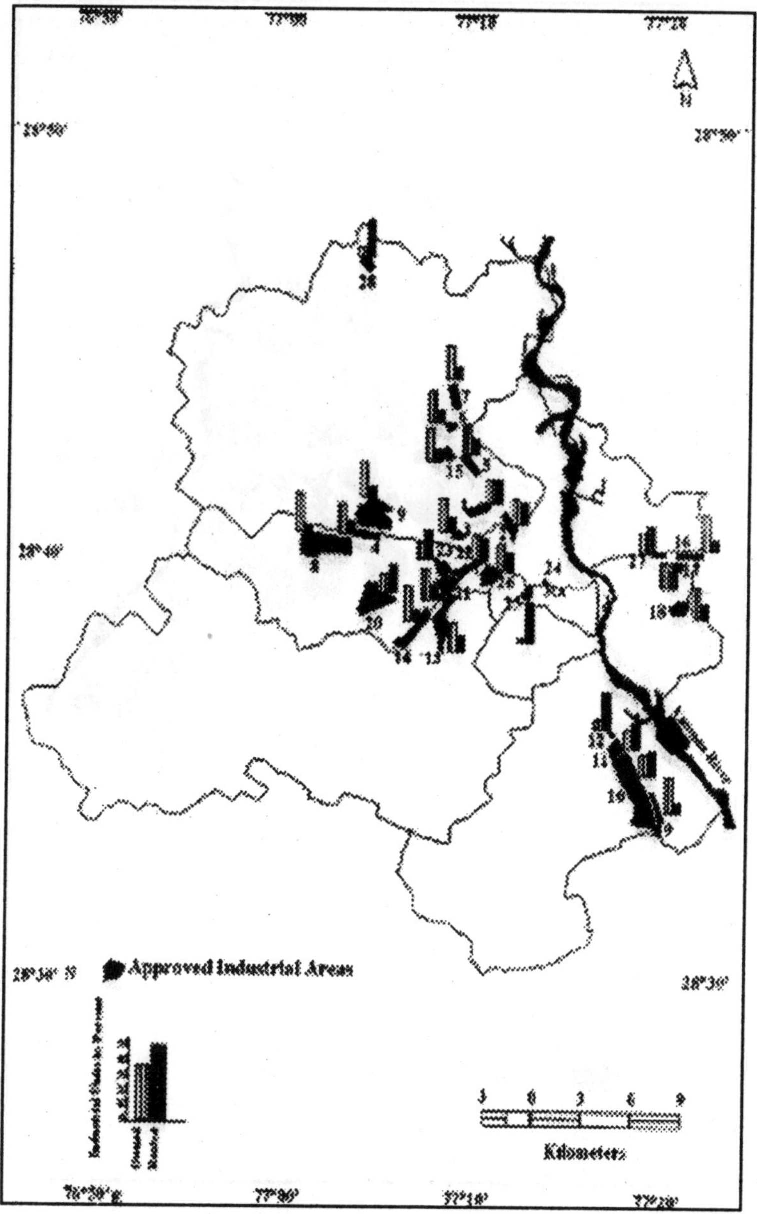

Fig. 4.11 : Ownership of Plots, 2001

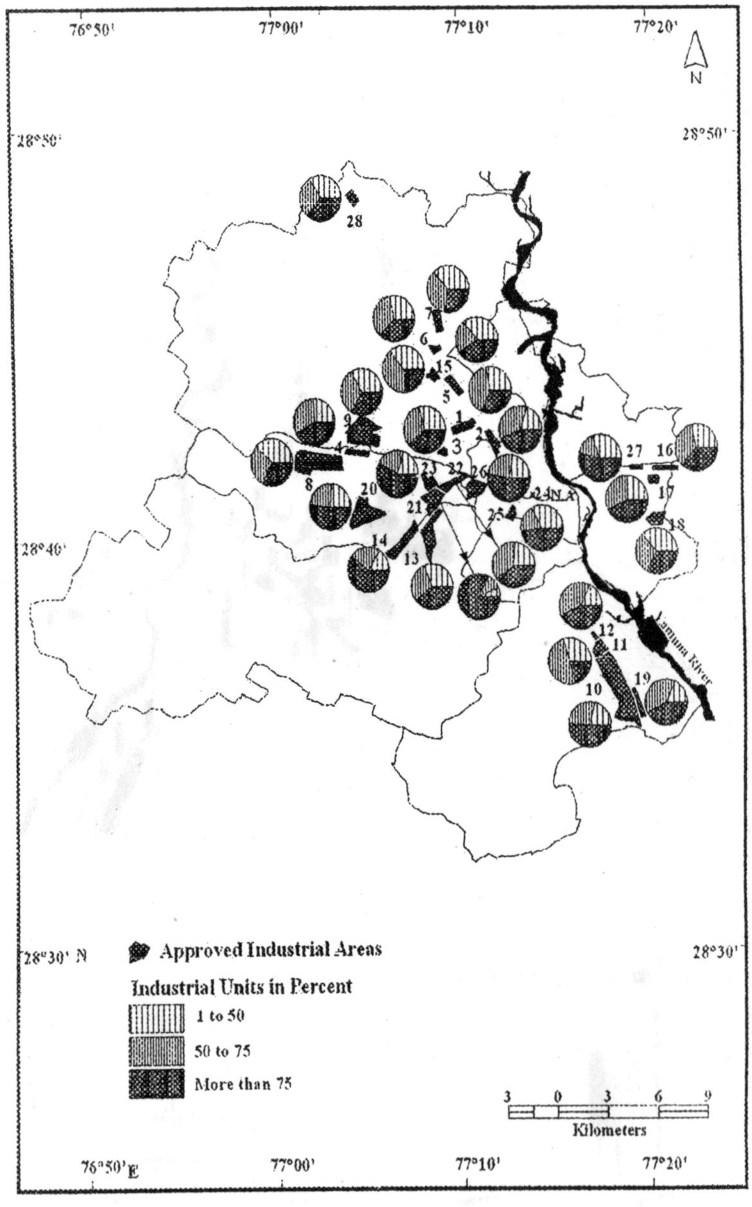

Fig. 4.12 : Capacity Utilization of Plant and Machinery, 2001

Gross Value of Plant and Machinery

In terms of gross value of plant and machinery, 43 per cent industrial units in Delhi have the investment of up to Rs. one lakh, about 33 per cent units lie in the category of Rs.1 to 5 lakhs investments in their plants and machineries. The investment of Rs. 5 to 10 lakhs made in setting up the operations by nearly 9 per cent industrial units. Another 8 per cent units fall in the category of investment ranging between Rs.10 to 25 lakhs. The investment of Rs. 25 to 100 lakhs is made by small number of industrial units (5%). Similarly, another small fraction of only about 3 per cent industrial units have investment of one crore and more in their plant and machinery (Fig. 4.13).

In terms of definition of industrial sectors based on investment in plant and machinery, about 92 per cent units in Delhi belong to the category of tiny units with their investment of up to Rs. 25 lakhs, and almost 97(cumulative) per cent units are small scale industrial units with the investment of Rs. 25 to 100 lakhs in their plant and machinery. Only nearly 3 per cent units fall in the medium category units, which have the investment of more than Rs. one crore (Fig. 4.13).

Gross value of investment in plant and machinery reveals different pattern among different industrial areas. In the first category of investment of up to Rs. one lakh, it is found that Anand Parbat has 73 per cent units belonging to this category, followed by industrial areas of Shahdara, Jhandewalan flatted factory, Kirti Nagar, Wazirpur, Lawrence Road, Moti Nagar, Okhla flatted factory and Friends Colony with about 40 to 50 per cent units. The rest of industrial areas have 10 to 20 per cent units, Mohan Co-operative Industrial Area has 5 per cent of its units belonging to this slab of investment.

In the investment category of Rs. one to five lakhs rupees, in most of the industrial areas nearly 30 to 40 per cent units fall, except Narela where nearly 60 per cent units fall in this

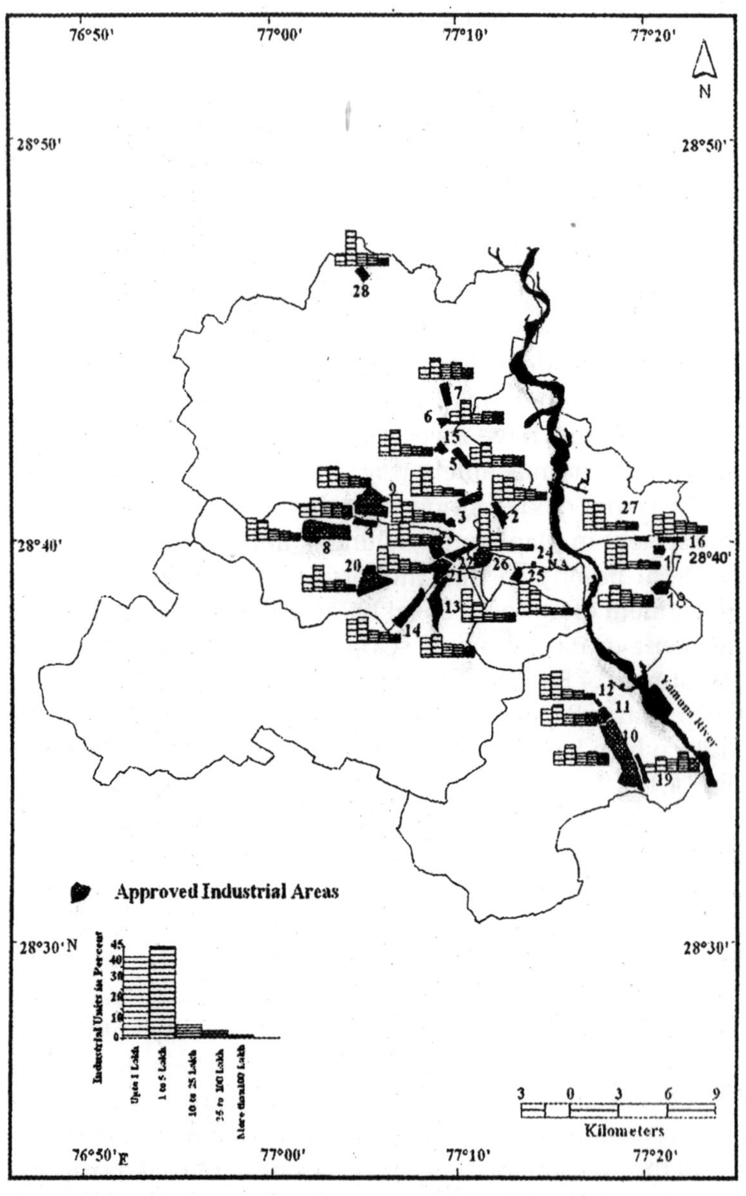

Fig. 4.13 : Gross Value of Plant and Machinery, 2001

category of investment. The investment of Rs. 5 to 10 lakhs is made by 10 to 20 per cent industrial units in many of the industrial areas, less than 10 per cent units of Wazirpur, Rajasthan Udyog Nagar, Okhla flatted factory, Tilak Nagar, Kirti Nagar, and Friends Colony lie in this investment range, and only nearly 2 per cent units of Anand Parbat and Shahdara have this much of investment in their plant and machinery (Fig. 4.13).

The industrial areas of G.T. Karnal Road, Udyog Nagar, Small and Medium Industries Area, Small-Scale Industries Area, Okhla, Naraina, Patparganj, Tilak Nagar and Najafgarh have 10 to 20 per cent of their unit with investment of 10 to 25 lakhs in plant and machinery. Less than 10 per cent units, of Okhla flatted factory, Moti Nagar and Shahdara fall in this category. Jhandewalan and Anand Parbat have nearly one per cent units belonging to this investment range. The investment of Rs. 25 to 100 lakhs is made by nearly 10 to 15 per cent units in Udyog Nagar, Small and Medium Industries Area, Small-Scale Industries Area, Okhla and Patparganj and Naraina. Mohan Co-operative Industrial Area has 20 per cent units with this investment, rest other industrial areas have 5 per cent of units' falls in this investment category. The investment of more than Rs. 1 crore is highest in Mohan Co-operative Industrial Area with 11 per cent unit, followed by Okhla, Tilak Nagar, Udyog Nagar, Small-Scale Industries Area, and Mangolpuri with 7 to 9 per cent units. The other areas have less than 5 per cent unit of this category. Industrial areas like Shahdara, Okhla flatted factory and G.T.Karnal Road have no industrial units with such investment (Fig. 4.13).

Number of Workers

In terms of number of workers employed, nearly 88 per cent industrial units in Delhi employ upto 20 workers. As demonstrated from (Fig. 4.14) 37 per cent of the total industrial units employ between 1 to 5 workers. Similarly, another 37 per cent units have 5 to 10 workers employed with them. Fifteen per cent of the total industrial units have the strength of workers ranging between 10 to 20, whereas only 8 per cent units employ between 20 to 50, merely 4 per cent of the total industrial units give employment to more than 50 workers (Fig. 4.14).

Employment pattern among different industrial areas of Delhi shows that industrial areas, namely, Anand Parbat, Kirti Nagar and Mayapuri have 60 per cent of industrial units employing 1 to 5 workers and other areas like Wazirpur, Lawrence Road, Nangloi, Moti Nagar, Jhandewalan, Shahdara and Najafgarh Road have 20 to 35 per cent industrial units. Industrial areas of Udyog Nagar, Small and Medium Industries Area, Okhla, Patparganj and Narela have less than 10 per cent units with this employment range. In the next category of 5 to 10 workers in all industrial areas have more than 20 per cent units. Wazirpur, Mangolpuri, Okhla flatted factory, Badli, Jhandewalan flatted factory, Shahdara and Narela Industrial Areas have more than 50 per cent units employing 5 to 10 workers. In rest of other industrial areas about 20 to 40 per cent units fall in this category of workers (Fig. 4.14).

In industrial areas of Small and Medium Industries Area, Small-Scale Industries Area and Kirti Nagar have more than 40 per cent enterprises employing in the range of 10 to 20 workers, followed by Udyog Nagar, G.T.Karnal Road, Okhla Industrial Area, Patparganj and Narela with more than 30 per cent units. Only three industrial areas viz. Jhandewalan flatted factory, Anand Parbat and Kirti Nagar have less than 10 per cent units in this employment range. In the next category of 20 to 50 workers only Small-Scale Industries Area has 30 per cent industrial unit, followed by 10 to 20 per cent unit in Udyog Nagar, Small-Scale Industries Area, Okhla, Naraina, Mohan Co-operative and Najafgarh Road. In the category of more than 50 employees, only Mohan Co-operative has more than 40 per cent enterprises, followed by Rajasthan Udyog Nagar, Okhla Industrial Area and Patparganj have 10 to 15 per cent units, whereas in rest all

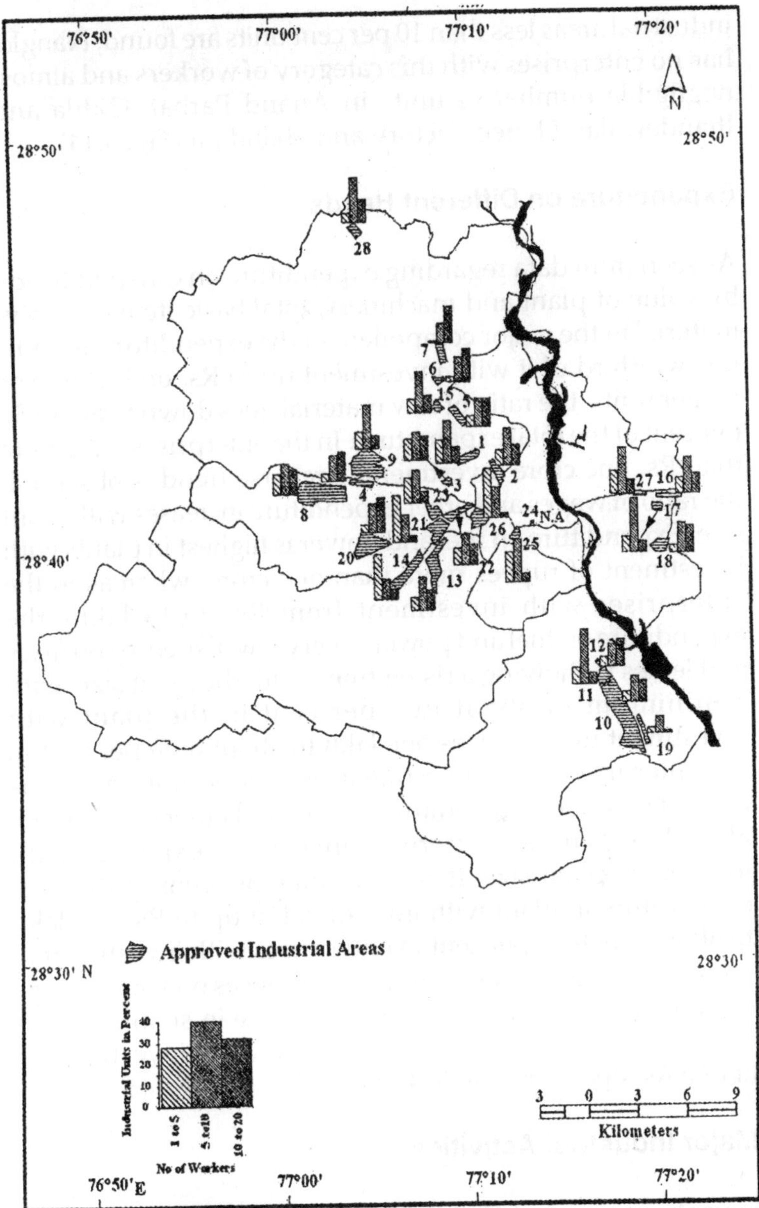

Fig. 4.14 : Number of Workers, 2001

industrial areas less than 10 per cent units are found. Nangloi has no enterprises with this category of workers and almost negligible number of units in Anand Parbat, Okhla and Jhandewalan Flatted Factory and Shahdara (Fig. 4.14).

Expenditure on Different Heads

As seen from data regarding expenditure on different heads by value of plant and machinery, total basic items, i.e. raw material in the major component of the expenditure account for two-third of it with investment up to Rs. one crore. For bigger units, the ratio of raw material goes down to about 50 per cent of the total expenditure. In the enterprises with more than Rs. one crore investment, a reverse trend is observed; the ratio of wages and other expenditure increases with plant size. Expenditure on fuel and power is highest in plants with investment of rupees more than one crore, whereas in the enterprises with investment from Rs. 25 to lakhs the expenditure on fuel and power is very low. Expenses on taxes and levies is showing a rising trend with the plant size, with a minimum of about two per cent in the plant with investment up to rupees one lakh to about nine per cent in the enterprises with investment of rupees more than one crore of their total expenditure. Wages and other expenditure also show similar pattern of increasing expenses with increase in plant size. It is about nine per cent of the total expenditure in plant with investment of up to Rs. one lakh to about nineteen per cent in enterprises with investment of more than Rs. one crore. Similarly, expenses on wages range between ten per cent of total expenditure in smaller plants to 17 per cent in industrial units that have an investment of above Rs. one crore (Table 4.6).

Major Industrial Activities

Seventy per cent of Delhi's industries are engaged mainly in eighteen industrial activities. Manufacture of fabricated metal products and metal working service activities being

Table 4.6 : Expenditure on Different Heads by Value of Plant and Machinery

Value (Rs. Lakh)	*Raw Material*	*Fuel/ Power*	*Taxes/ Levies*	*Other Expenditure*	*Wages*	*Total*
Up to 1	69.34	9.41	2.36	8.69	10.2	100
1 to 5	68.44	8.24	3.92	9.21	10.19	100
5 to 10	67.63	6.78	4.25	12.13	9.21	100
10 to 25	68.36	5.08	3.32	12.32	10.93	100
25 to 100	67.06	3.62	4.3	13.84	11.18	100
Above 100	48.28	8.08	8.56	18.7	16.38	100
Total	63.83	6.85	4.57	12.33	12.41	100

Source : Prepared from Census of Industries (2001) Delhi Pollution Control Committee, Delhi.

pursued by 15 per cent units, appears the largest industrial activity. 50 per cent units of this activity are located in Anand Parbat Industrial Area, followed by twenty-one per cent in Wazirpur, Badli and SMA. Second important industrial activity in Delhi is retail sale of second hand goods in stores. This activity is fully concentrated in Mayapuri Industrial Area. Wholesale of household goods, manufacture of plastic goods and manufacture of parts and accessories for motor vehicles and their engines each have 5 per cent of industrial units engaged in them. Wholesale of household goods is mainly located in Wazirpur, Mayapuri, Anand Parbat and Kirti Nagar. The manufacture of plastic goods is located mainly in Narela followed by Tilak Nagar and Rajasthan Udyog Nagar but in small percentage it is scattered in most of the industrial areas. Manufacture of parts and accessories of motor is concentrated in the industrial areas of G.T.Karnal Road, Badli and Anand Parbat. Manufacture of general purpose machinery and furniture accounts for about 4 per cent industrial enterprises in Delhi. The industrial activity has high concentration in Moti Nagar followed by G.T.Karnal Road, Okhla flatted factory and Jhilmil. Manufacture of furniture is highest in Kirti Nagar Industrial Area followed by Okhla (Table 4.7).

Manufacture of special purpose machinery, basic iron

and steel, wearing apparel, printing and maintenance and repair of motor vehicles accounts for nearly 3 per cent industrial units in Delhi. Special purpose machinery is located in the industrial areas of Nangloi (with highest) followed by Najafgarh Road, Patparganj and Anand Parbat. Basic iron and steel is highest in Small-Scale Industries Industrial Area followed by Small and Medium Industries Area and Narela. It is shown that wearing apparel is mainly concentrated in both Okhla areas followed by Patparganj, Jhandewalan flatted factory and Nangloi. Printing has high concentration in Naraina followed by Nangloi, G.T.Karnal Road and Patparganj. In case of maintenance and repair of motor vehicles, Mangolpuri has maximum number of enterprises, then, comes Lawrence Road, Mayapuri and Shahdara.

The other industrial activities *viz.* manufacture of basic precious and non-ferrous metal, manufacture of footwear, supporting and auxiliary transport activities, and retail trade of new goods in specialized stores, manufacture of other chemical products, other business activities etc., are about 2 per cent of the total industrial activities in Delhi. Manufacture of basic precious and non-ferrous metal is highest in Friends Colony, Badli and Jhilmil followed by Shahdara. As far as manufacture of footwear is concerned, this is scattered in many industrial areas with maximum number of enterprises in Udyog Nagar, Mangolpuri, Tilak Nagar, Najafgarh Road and Narela. In supporting and auxiliary transport activities, Lawrence Road has first rank followed by Mohan Co-operative, Rajasthan Udyog Nagar, Small and Medium Industries Area. The other retail trade of new goods in specialized stores is mainly found in Kirti Nagar and Wazirpur. Manufacture of chemical products is found in industrial areas of Udyog Nagar, Badli, Jhilmil, Friends Colony, Jhandewalan Flatted Factory, Moti Nagar and Mohan Co-operative, Rajasthan Udyog Nagar, Small-Scale Industries Industrial Area, Mangolpuri, Najafgarh Road and Narela. Other business activities are mainly concentrated in both Okhla (Table 4.7).

Manufacture of grain mill products, starch products and

Table 4.7 : Nature of Industrial Activities

Industrial Activity	*Industrial Units (%)*	*Areas of Concentration*
Manufacture of fabricated metal products, other metal prod.	15	Anand Parbat (50%), Wazirpur, Badli, small/medium industrial area (21%).
Retail sale of second hand goods	12	Mayapuri.
Manufacture of plastic goods	9	Narela followed by Tilak Nagar and Rajasthan Udyog Nagar.
Parts and accessories of motor vehicles	8	G.T.Karnal Road, Badli and Anand Parbat.
Wholesale of household goods	7	Wazirpur, Mayapuri, Anand Parbat and Kirti Nagar.
Manufacture of general purpose machinery	7	Moti Nagar, G.T.Karnal Road, Okhla flatted factory and Jhilmil.
Furniture	5	Kirti Nagar, Okhla.
Manufacture of special purpose machinery	4	Nangloi (with highest), Najafgarh Road, Patparganj and Anand Parbat.
Basic iron and steel	4	Small Scale Industries Industrial Area (Highest), Small and Medium Industries Area, Narela.
Wearing apparel	4	Okhla areas, Patparganj, Jhandewalan flatted factory and Nangloi.
Printing	4	Naraina (highest), Nangloi, G.T.Karnal Road and Patparganj.
Maintenance and repair of motor vehicles	4	Mangolpuri (Highest), Lawrence Road, Mayapuri and Shahdara.
Manufacture of basic precious and non-ferrous metal	3	Friends Colony (Highest), Badli, Jhilmil Shahdara.
Manufacture of footwear	3	Udyog Nagar (maximum), Mangolpuri, Tilak Nagar, Najafgarh Road, Narela
Supporting and auxiliary transport activities	2	Lawrence Road (Highest) Mohan Co-operative, Rajasthan Udyog Nagar, Small and Medium Industries area.
Manufacture of other chemical products	2	Udyog Nagar, Badli, Jhilmil, Friends Colony, Jhandewalan flatted factory, Moti Nagar and Mohan Co-operative, Rajasthan Udyog Nagar, Small-Scale Industries industrial area, Mangolpuri, Najafgarh Road and Narela.
Retail trade of new goods in specialized stores	2	Kirti Nagar and Wazirpur.
Manufacture of grain mill products	Less than 1	Lawrence Road and Narela.

(Contd...)

Table 4.7 : *(Contd...)*

Manufacture of other food products, processing and preservation oil, meat, fish, fruits, vegetables oil	Less than 1	Lawrence Road Industrial Area.
Tanning and dressing of leather, manufacture of luggage handbags	Less than 1	Jhandewalan flatted factory and Small-Scale Industries Area.
Manufacture of structural metal products, tanks, reservoirs	Less than 1	Okhla Industrial Area
Manufacture of electric/ electronic goods, wires, cables	Less than 1	Okhla flatted factory, Friends Colony, Jhilmil and Shahdara.
Manufacture of paper and paper products	Less than 1	Naraina and Tilak Nagar.
Software consultancy and supply	Less than 1	Jhandewalan flatted factory.

Source : Prepared from Census of Industries (2001) Delhi Pollution Control Committee, Delhi.

prepared animal feed is mainly found in Lawrence Road and Narela. Manufacture of other food products, processing and preservation oil, meat, fish, fruits, vegetables oil are only concentrating in Lawrence Road Industrial Area. Tanning and dressing of leather, manufacture of luggage handbags, is done only at two places Jhandewalan flatted factory and Small-scale Industries Industrial Area. Manufacture of structural metal products, tanks, reservoirs and steam engines is concentrated only at Okhla Industrial Area. Okhla flatted factory is the main area for manufacture of electric motors, generators and transformers and manufacture of other electrical equipment. As far as manufacture of insulated wires and cables is concerned it is located in Friends Colony, Jhilmil and Shahdara. Manufacture of paper and paper products is found only at Naraina and Tilak Nagar. Software consultancy and supply which is a new industrial activity added in the list of National Industrial Classification (NIC-1998) is mainly concentrated in Jhandewalan flatted factory (Table 4.7).

Structure of Approved Industrial Areas

The National Capital Territory of Delhi has twenty-eight industrial estates or areas approved as conform areas for carrying out the permitted industrial activities. All these industrial areas are different in terms of number of industries, number of plots, size of plots, nature of industry, investment in plant and machinery. The following paragraphs highlight the nature and structure of each of these twenty-eight industrial areas of Delhi.

Wazirpur Industrial Area

The Wazirpur Industrial Area located in Northwest district of Delhi accommodates 1665 industrial plots. This accounts for nearly 8 per cent of Delhi's industrial units. This area has establishments other than industrial units that are about more than nine hundred, highest in comparison to other industrial estates. The slum clusters in this area are biggest, housing nearly 11000 households, but interestingly, residences other than slums are nil.

In Wazirpur Industrial Area single proprietors own 75 per cent industrial units followed by nearly 20 per cent partnership ownership. About 5 per cent units are of private limited nature and only 1 per cent is public limited firm. The growth of industrial activity in this area reveals that around two-third numbers of units out of the total of 1665 started after 1991,which also reflects the impact of open and globalization of economy. In the previous years during the decade of 1981-1991 about 18 per cent units started, some 11 per cent new units were added during the decade of 1971 to 1981 and only 2 per cent industrial units were functioning upto the year 1971. As seen from Table 4.8 there are varieties of plot sizes ranging from 100 sq. m to above 500 sq. m that are owned as well as rented. Of the total 1665, plots 50 per cent units function in owned premises and about the same number on rent bases. In addition there are about 35 per cent plots of 100 sq. m. Of that, more than half are functioning in rented premises. It also to be added that in the category of 100 to 200 sq. m rented premises are more than owned. Interestingly, in the plot size of 100 to 500 sq. m maximum units are owned and about 7 per cent units functions in rented ones. In the category of above 500 sq. m eight per cent units are owned and only two per cent are on rent basis. In terms of gross value of plant and machinery it is revealed that 40 per cent units have upto Rs. one lakh and another 40 per cent have the gross value of about Rs.1 to 5 lakhs. About 10 per cent of industrial units have the value of plant and machinery worth Rs. 5 to 25 lakhs followed by 2 per cent units with Rs. 25 lakhs to one crore value and nearly two per cent industrial units have the gross worth of plant and machinery of more than Rs. one crore. Capacity utilization of plant and machinery indicates that about 30 per cent industrial units could use only half the capacity of their plant and machinery and only another one-third units could use more than seventy-five per cent. The information on number of workers explains that about 50 per cent industrial units in Wazirpur have 5 to 10 workers employed with them and one-fourth units are such that are employ 1 to 5 workers. One-fifth units have 10 to 20 workers and 20 to 50 workers are with nearly 5 per cent units. It is only one per cent industrial units that have more than 50 workers on their role (Table 4.8).

In Wazirpur Industrial Area, major industrial activities include manufacture of other fabricated metal products which account for one-third of the total units, next is basic iron and steel which is 12 per cent, retail trade of new goods in specialized stores about 5 per cent. Manufacture of plastic products and wholesale of non-agricultural intermediate products account for 4 per cent each of them, rest other activities are less than 4 per cent of the total.

G.T.Karnal Road Industrial Area

This industrial area located near Wazirpur Industrial Area

Table 4.8 : Wazirpur Industrial Area

1. General Attributes

Total number of units	1665
Establishment other than industrial units	961
Total number of slum households	11692
Residence other than slums	0

2. Type of Ownership

Type	*Proprietor*	*Partnership*	*Private Ltd.*	*Public Ltd.*	*Total*
Industrial Units (%)	74.88	17.93	5.50	1.34	100

3. Growth Pattern of Industries

Years	*Up to 1971*	*1971-81*	*1981-91*	*1991 -2001*	*Total*
Industrial Units (%)	2.52	11.47	18.14	67.87	100

4. Size of Industrial Units (sq. m)

Plot size	*1 -100*		*100 - 200*		*200- 500*		*500 +*		*Total*
Category	Own	Rented	Own	Rented	Own	Rented	Own	Rented	
Industrial Units (%)	3.90	27.75	11.83	13.39	21.74	7.51	8.05	2.82	100

5. Gross Value of Plant and Machinery

Value in Lakhs	*Upto1 lakh*	*1-5*	*5-10*	*10-25*	*25-100*	*More than 100*	*Total*
Per cent Units	40.06	45.13	7.02	3.51	2.34	1.95	100

6. Capacity Utilization of Plant and Machinery

Per cent Utilization	*1-50*	*50-75*	*More than 75*	*Total*
Industrial Units (%)	28.00	39.87	32.12	100

7. Number of Workers Employed

No. of Workers	*1-5*	*6-10*	*11-20*	*21-50*	*More than 50*	*Total*
Industrial Units (%)	26.07	50.81	17.08	4.79	1.25	100

Source : Prepared from Census of Industries (2001) Delhi Pollution Control Committee, Delhi.

in Northwest district accommodates 473 industrial units. This accounts for nearly 2 per cent of Delhi's total industries. There are 54 establishments that are other than industrial units, 500 residences other than slums and about 4000 slum households.

The type of ownership pattern shows that more than half of total units are single proprietors followed by 30 per cent partnership firms, with 12 per cent private limited firms and two per cent of public limited ownerships. Upto 1971, there were only 6 per cent of the total units, during the decade of 1971 to 1981, 20 per cent industrial units were added also followed similar growth in the next decade. It is also shown that more than 50 per cent industrial units started 1991 onwards. As seen from Table 4.9, size of industrial units and their ownership of premises reveals that almost equal number of plants are owned as well as rented. In the size plots of upto 100 sq. m 5 per cent units are owned, whereas 28 per cent units are on rent basis. In 100-200 sq. m plots almost the same numbers of units are run on owned as well as rented. Interestingly, maximum units in owned plots are found in the plot size of 200-500 sq. m rented premises are used by 8 per cent of units. The bigger plots of more than 500 sq. m have 12 per cent owned units and nearly half of it is on rented plots.

The gross value of plant and machinery reveals that more than one-third units have the gross value of upto Rs. one lakh and another one-third with Rs. 1 to 5 lakhs. Nearly one-fourth of the units have the gross value of Rs.10 to 25 lakhs and 5 per cent enterprises have Rs. 25 lakhs to one crore. Surprisingly, there is no industrial unit in the category of more than Rs. one crore. The capacity-utilization of plants and machinery indicates that 20 per cent industrial units could use half capacity of their plant and machinery; one-third plants use half to three-fourth capacity. While 44 per cent enterprises are able to utilize more than three-fourth capacity of their plant and machinery. In terms of number of workers employed, *i.e.* about 45 per cent have 6 to10 workers, almost one-fourth unit with 10 to 20 workers, and 1 to 5 workers are employed by nearly 16 per cent units. Another 10 per cent units have 20 to 50 workers, and three per cent with more than 50 workers (Table 4.9).

Table 4.9 : G.T.Karnal Road Industrial Area

1. General Attributes

Total number of units	473
Establishment other than industrial unit	54
Total number of slum households	4200
Residence other than slums	500

2. Type of Ownership

Type	*Proprietor*	*Partnership*	*Private Ltd.*	*Public Ltd.*	*Total*
Industrial Units (%)	55.63	29.85	13.76	1.04	100

3. Growth Pattern of Industries

Years	*Up to 1971*	*1971-81*	*1981-91*	*1991-2001*	*Total*
Industrial Units (%)	6.13	18.60	22.41	52.85	100

4. Size of Industrial Units (sq. m)

Plot Size	*1 -100*		*100 - 200*		*200- 500*		*500 +*		*Total*
Category	Own	Rented	Own	Rented	Own	Rented	Own	Rented	
Industrial Units (%)	6.55	24.1	77.61	8.46	28.33	8.34	12.26	6.35	100

5. Gross Value of Plant and Machinery

Value in Lakhs	*Upto1 lakh*	*1-5*	*5-10*	*10-25*	*25-100*	*More than 100*	*Total*
Per cent Units	36.94	33.12	33.12	11.15	5.41	0.00	100

6. Capacity Utilization of Plant and Machinery

Per cent Utilization	*1-50*	*50-75*	*More than 75*	*Total*
Industrial Units (%)	19.53	35.94	44.53	100

7. Number of Workers Employed

No. of Workers	*1-5*	*6-10*	*11-20*	*21-50*	*More than 50*	*Total*
Industrial Units (%)	16.67	45.08	23.50	11.75	3.01	100

Source : Prepared from Census of Industries (2001) Delhi Pollution Control Committee, Delhi.

Nature of industrial activity in G.T.Karnal Road Industrial Area includes a variety of industries with maximum of 12 per cent units of manufacture of parts and accessories for motor vehicles and their engines, followed by other fabricated metal products and metal working service activities accounting for about 9 per cent. Plastic product is another important activity with 8 per cent units engaged in it, followed by general purpose machinery and printing by nearly 5 per cent units.

Lawrence Road Industrial Area

The Lawrence Road Industrial Area is located in North Delhi on Ring Road comprising 446 industrial units accounting for about 2 per cent of the total industrial concentration of Delhi. The establishments other than industrial units are 291, nearly, 1500 slums besides accommodating only 10 households other than slums. This area is mainly a center for food products industries.

The ownership pattern of firms demonstrates that 50 per cent units are of partnership nature, followed by one-third private limited, 10 per cent public limited and only 3 per cent proprietor firms. Growth of industries as reflected from Table 4.10 reveals that upto 1971 only 4 per cent units came up, followed by the installation of one-fifth units in the next decade, same trend in 1981-91 and recording more than 40 per cent units in 1991-2001. The size of factory area shows that in plots of upto 100 sq. m 12 per cent units are in their own plots and 5 per cent in rented premises. In plot sizes of 100 to 200 and in 200 to 300 sq. m plots, more units are in own premises. Interestingly, more than 30 per cent industrial units are operating in own bigger plots of 500 sq. m. Expenditure on different heads by value of plant and machinery suggests that in tiny plants as well as the small-scale plants nearly 60 per cent of the total expense is on raw material followed by expenditure on wages and others category. The gross value of plant and machinery indicates that nearly 40 per cent units belong to very small investment, i.e. upto Rs. one lakh, one-fourth units have the worth between Rs. 1 to 5 lakhs, only 6 per cent units fall in the category of more than Rs. one crore. Eight per cent units are with value between Rs. 5 to 10 lakhs (Table 4.10)

Table 4.10 : Lawrence Road Industrial Area

1. General Attributes

Total number of units	446
Establishment other than industrial units	291
Total number of slum households	1471
Residence other than slums	10

2. Type of Ownership

Type	*Proprietor*	*Partnership*	*Private Ltd.*	*Public Ltd.*	*Total*
Industrial Units (%)	3.85	52.40	33.65	10.10	100

3. Growth Pattern of Industries

Years	*Upto 1971*	*1971-81*	*1981-91*	*1991 -2001*	*Total*
Industrial Units (%)	4.71	25.34	24.66	45.29	100

4. Size of Industrial Units (sq. m)

Plot Size	*1 -100*		*100 - 200*		*200-500*		*500 +*		*Total*
Category	Own	Rented	Own	Rented	Own	Rented	Own	Rented	
Industrial Units (%)	12.11	5.17	10.99	4.71	19.51	3.81	34.53	9.19	100

5. Gross Value of Plant and Machinery

Value in Lakhs	*Upto1 lakh*	*1-5*	*5-10*	*10-25*	*25-100*	*More than 100*	*Total*
Per cent Units	43.03	27.88	12.42	8.48	5.15	6.03	100

6. Capacity Utilization of Plant and Machinery

Per cent Utilization	*1-50*	*50-75*	*More than 75*	*Total*
Industrial Units (%)	29.43	32.17	38.40	100

7. Number of Workers Employed

No. of Workers	*1-5*	*6-10*	*11-20*	*21-50*	*More than 50*	*Total*
Industrial Units (%)	24.87	33.77	28.53	8.90	3.93	100

Source : Prepared from Census of Industries (2001) Delhi Pollution Control Committee, Delhi.

So far as the capacity-utilization of this plant and machinery is concerned, nearly 40 per cent units are able to harness more than three-fourths of their capacity, one-third units could use between 50 to 75 per cent and almost the similar number of firms could use only upto half capacity. In this industrial area almost 30 per cent units have 10 to 20 workers on their role, more than one-third firms employ 5 to 10 workers and another one-quarter units work with 1 to 5 people. Small number of firms employs more than 20 workers. It may also be noted that 10 per cent units have 20 to 50 workers and in more than 50 workers category there are only 3 per cent units (Table 4.10).

Udyog Nagar Industrial Area

Udyog Nagar Industrial Area is located in West district, which is comparatively newly developed area, accommodates nearly 400 industrial units. This accounts for about 2 per cent industrial concentration of Delhi. In this area establishment other than industrial units are 15 but accommodates more than 400 slum households. Surprisingly, there are no residences other than slums.

In terms of type of ownership almost two-third units are handled by single proprietors and partners, another 30 per cent firms are of private limited nature with only 1 per cent enterprises which are public limited. As seen from Table 4.11, it is clear that more than three-quarter enterprises started after 1991 with nearly 20 per cent industrial units began their production between 1981 and 1991. It is added that only 4 per cent units started during the decade 1971 to 1981 while less than 1 per cent units were present upto the year 1971. The size of industrial units reflects that the plot sizes are ranging between 100 to more 500 sq. m that are owned as well as rented premises. There are almost negligible numbers of plots, which are 100 sq. m in size and between 100-200 sq. m two per cent each are owned and rented. In plots of

200-500 sq.m 7 per cent units operates in owned plots while more than 10 per cent are functioning in rented plots. Added to it in more than 500 sq. m plots nearly two-third units are in owned premises and only 10 per cent units are using rented ones. The gross value of plant and machinery reflects that nearly 8 per cent industrial units are of medium size with more than Rs. one crore value of their plant and machinery followed by more than 10 per cent units with the value between Rs. 25 lakhs to one crore. Sixty per cent industrial units are with the gross value of their plant and machinery upto Rs. 10 lakhs and nearly 20 per cent enterprises between Rs. 10 to 25 lakhs (Table 4.11).

As far as the capacity-utilization in terms of plants and machinery is concerned around 40 per cent plants are using more than three-fourth capacity, 30 per cent units use between half to three-fourth, whereas nearly one-quarter of industrial units able to utilize 50 per cent capacity of their plant and machinery. In this industrial area, one-third industrial units employ worker, between 10 to 20, nearly same proportion of enterprises employ workers between 5 to 10 and one-fifth units have 20 to 50 workers. It is seen that more than 50 workers are employed with only less than ten per cent units (Table 4.11).

The nature of industrial activities in Udyog Nagar shows that 40 per cent units are engaged in manufacturing of footwear, 6 per cent in wearing apparel, 5 per cent enterprises each in plastic, other fabricated metal products and other chemical products. Rest other industrial activities are prevailing in very small or negligible proportion.

Rajasthan Udyog Nagar Industrial Area

This industrial estate is located in Northwest district where more than 100 industrial units are operating accounts for about 0.5 per cent of the total industrial units of the state. This estate also comprises establishments other than

Table 4.11 : Udyog Nagar Industrial Area

1. General Attributes

Total number of units	391
Establishment other than industrial units	15
Total number of slum households	428
Residence other than slums	0

2. Type of Ownership

Type	*Proprietor*	*Partnership*	*Private Ltd.*	*Public Ltd.*	*Total*
Industrial Units (%)	32.85	32.85	30.92	3.44	100

3. Growth Pattern of Industries

Years	*Upto 1971*	*1971-81*	*1981-91*	*1991 -2001*	*Total*
Industrial Units (%)	0.77	3.58	17.90	77.50	100

4. Size of Industrial Units (sq. m)

Plot Size	*1 -100*		*100 - 200*		*200- 500*		*500 +*		*Total*
Category	Own	Rented	Own	Rented	Own	Rented	Cwn	Rented	
Industrial Units (%)	0.51	1.28	2.30	2.05	7.16	11.0	64.45	11.0	100

5. Gross Value of Plant and Machinery

Value in Lakhs	*Upto 1lakh*	*1-5*	*5-10*	*10-25*	*25-100*	*More than 100*	*Total*
Per cent Units	14.95	27.84	19.07	18.566	11.86	7.73	100

6. Capacity, Utilization of Plant and Machinery

Per cent Utilization	*1-50*	*50-75*	*More than 75*	*Total*
Industrial Units (%)	25.73	31.55	42.72	100

7. Number of Workers Employed

No. of Workers	*1-5*	*6-10*	*11-20*	*21-50*	*More than 50*	*Total*
Industrial Units (%)	25.73	29.85	33.83	21.39	8.46	100

Source : Prepared from Census of Industries (2001) Delhi Pollution Control Committee, Delhi.

industrial units, which are 41. The total number of slum households is 137 and residences other than slums are nil.

As regards ownership, proprietorship firms are largest with 37 per cent units, partnership-run-enterprises accounts for 20 per cent and 7 per cent industrial units are of public limited nature. The growth of industrial activity in this area reveals that around 85 per cent of the industrial units started in 1991 onwards, whereas in the previous decades of 1981 to 1991 some 12 per cent units started their production. During 1971 to 1981, only three per cent enterprises started and nearly one per cent of the total units were operating upto 1971. The plot size as seen from Table 4.11 elucidates that there are no plots either in owned or rented category in plot size of upto 100 sq. m. It is also seen that in plots of 100 to 200 sq. m three per cent are owned plots and 15 per cent are in rented premises. In the plots of size of 200 to 500 sq. m, more than eight per cent units are operating in owned as well as rented category. Nearly 60 per cent industrial units are operating in own plots of more the 500 sq. m size with five per cent rented plots of this size (Table 4.12).

The pattern of gross value of plant and machinery manifests that maximum number of industrial units, *i.e.* 37 per cent units have upto Rs. 1 to 5 lakhs gross values of their plant and machinery, followed by one-fourth of enterprises with upto Rs. one lakh. Twelve per cent units are with the gross value of Rs. 10 to 25 lakhs and with another 10 per cent firms have the gross value of their plant and machinery ranging between Rs. 25 to 100 lakhs. Only 5 per cent enterprises are with the gross value of more than Rs. one crore. The capacity-utilization of the plant and machinery reveals that 40 per cent of the total industrial units are functioning at more than three-fourth capacity of their plant and machinery followed by 35 per cent of firms that are able to extract half capacity, and some nearly 23 per cent units are working within the one-fourth capacity utilization (Table 4.12).

The employment pattern explains that about two-third industrial units are working with 5 to 20 workers, whereas more than 50 workers are employed with 13 per cent industrial units. There are 11 per cent firms giving employment to workers between 1 to 5 and more than 7 per cent

Table 4.12 : Rajasthan Udyog Nagar Industrial Area

1. General Attributes

Total number of units	109
Establishment other than industrial units	41
Total number of slum households	137
Residence other than slums	Nil

2. Type of Ownership

Type	*Proprietor*	*Partnership*	*Private Ltd.*	*Public Ltd.*	*Total*
Industrial Units (%)	36.92	20.00	33.85	7.69	100

3. Growth Pattern of Industries

Years	Upto 1971	1971-81	1981-91	1991 -2001	Total
Industrial Units (%)	0.92	2.75	11.93	84.40	100

4. Size of Industrial Units (sq. m)

Plot Size	1 -100		100-200		200-500		500 +		Total
Category	Own	Rented	Own	Rented	Own	Rented	Own	Rented	
Industrial Units (%)	0.0	0.0	3.67	5.60	8.26	9.17	58.72	4.59	100

5. Gross Value of Plant and Machinery

Value in Lakhs	*Upto 1lakh*	*1-5*	*5-10*	*10-25*	*25-100*	*More than 100*	*Total*
Per cent Units	26.83	36.59	9.76	12.20	9.75	4.88	100

6. Capacity-Utilization of Plant and Machinery

Per cent Utilization	*1-50*	*50-75*	*More than 75*	*Total*
Industrial Units (%)	25.73	31.55	42.72	100

7. Number of Workers Employed

No. of Workers	*1-5*	*6-10*	*11-20*	*21-50*	*More than 50*	*Total*
Industrial Units (%)	11.32	33.96	33.96	7.55	13.21	100

Source : Prepared from Census of Industries (2001) Delhi Pollution Control Committee, Delhi.

enterprises have workers 20 to 50. In Rajasthan Udyog Nagar, industries include major activities such as manufacture of plastic products that account for nearly 20 per cent industrial units, followed by 12 per cent firms in other fabricated metal product and metal working service activities. Nearly, 9 per cent units each in parts and accessories for motor vehicles and their motor engines and supporting and auxiliary transport activities of travel agencies. In basic chemicals, 7 per cent industrial units are engaged and rest of other industrial activities also exists here but less in number.

Small and Medium Industrial Area

This industrial area is situated near Small-Scale Industries Area in Northwest district with a total of 174 industrial units accounting for approximately one per cent industries of Delhi. There are 13 establishments other than industrial units, 2 residences and no slums.

The ownership pattern reflects that a maximum of 37 per cent industrial units are under proprietorship, followed by one-third with partnership firms and more than one-fourth enterprises are private limited in nature with only 2 per cent of public limited. In terms of initiation of production, upto 1971, there were no industrial units in this area; even in the next decade of 1971 to 1981 merely 1 per cent industrial units began with their production. Nearly, 20 per cent firms were established during the decade of 1981 to 1991 but it is only in the last decade, *i.e.* 1991 to 2001, approximately 80 per cent enterprises installed their productions. The size or area of industrial units has been seen in terms of owned as well as rented premises. Upto 100 sq. m plot nearly 5 per cent units are functioned in owned premises and 2 per cent in rented ones. Whereas in 100 to 200 sq. m size, only 1 per cent firms have their owned plots and 5 per cent enterprises are in rented plots. In plots of 200 to 500 sq. m size, more industrial units are operating in rented premises than owned. It is also to be added that plots of 500 and more sq. m have two-third enterprises with own plots and 10 per cent works in rented premises. The industrial units assessed in terms of gross value of plant and machinery reflects that a maximum of more than one-third enterprises have the gross value of their plant and machinery ranging between Rs.1 to 5 lakhs, followed by 15 per cent of enterprises in each category of upto Rs. 1 to 5 lakhs and Rs. 10 to 25 lakhs and also same number of firms with Rs. 25 lakhs to one crore. There are 8 per cent industrial units with the gross value of their plant and machinery worth more than Rs. one crore. So far as the capacity-utilization of plant and machinery concerned, 27 of the firms are able to utilize only upto half capacity of their plant and machinery and one-third use capacity between 50 to 75 per cent. Interestingly, more than one-third firms utilize more than 75 per cent of capacity and none with complete capacity-utilization (Table 4.13).

The employment of workers exhibits that 40 per cent industrial units work with 10 to 20 workers, followed by more than one-fourth enterprises employing 5 to 10 workers. Twenty per cent enterprises have 20 to 50 workers, whereas in more than 50 workers' category only small numbers of industrial units fall. The nature of industrial activities in Small and Medium Industrial Area includes a variety from iron and steel, plastic products to travel agencies and manufacturing of basic iron and steel. Basic iron/steel and fabricated metal engage 40 per cent industrial units. Plastic products engage 7 per cent of the firms, followed by structural metal products, tanks, reservoirs and steam generators by 4 per cent enterprises and supporting and auxiliary transport activities by another four per cent industrial units.

Small Scale Industrial Area

It is located between Rajasthan Udyog Nagar Industrial Area and Small and Medium Industrial Area in Northwest district,

Table 4.13 : S.M.A. Industrial Area

1. General Attributes

Total number of units	174
Establishment other than industrial units	13
Total number of slum households	0
Residence other than slums	2

2. Type of Ownership

Type	*Proprietor*	*Partnership*	*Private Ltd.*	*Public Ltd.*	*Total*
Industrial Units (%)	36.78	33.33	27.59	2.15	100

3. Growth Pattern of Industries

Years	*Upto 1971*	*1971-81*	*1981-91*	*1991-2001*	*Total*
Industrial Units (%)	0.00	1.15	19.54	79.31	100

4. Size of Industrial Units (sq. m)

Plot Size	*1 -100*		*100 -200*		*200-500*		*500 +*		*Total*
Category	Own	Rented	Own	Rented	Own	Rented	Own	Rented	
Industrial Units (%)	4.59	3.27	1.15	4.60	6.32	6.90	64.37	9.77	100

5. Gross Value of Plant and Machinery

Value in Lakhs	*Upto 1lakh*	*1-5*	*5-10*	*10-25*	*25-100*	*More than 100*	*Total*
Per cent Units	15.38	37.18	10.26	15.38	14.10	7.69	100

6. Capacity-Utilization of Plant and Machinery

Per cent Utilization	*1-50*	*50-75*	*More than 75*	*Total*
Industrial Units (%)	27.91	34.88	37.21	100

7. Number of Workers Employed

No. of Workers	*1-5*	*6-10*	*11-20*	*21-50*	*More than 50*	*Total*
Industrial Units (%)	3.57	28.57	40.48	21.43	5.95	100

Source : Prepared from Census of Industries (2001) Delhi Pollution Control Committee, Delhi.

accommodating 81 industrial units that accounting only 0.4 per cent industrial activity of Delhi. This area also comprises 18 establishments other than industrial units and surprisingly, zero slum households and other residence.

Ownership pattern of industrial units reveals that maximum of 4 per cent industrial units are of private limited in nature followed by one-third owned by proprietors. Twelve per cent firms are under partnership and nearly 10 per cent with public limited ownership. The growth of industrial activity elucidates that only 3 per cent of total industrial units were established upto 1971 and in the following decade of 1971 to 1981 no industrial units were started, although in 1981 to 1991, 16 per cent firms began with their production. The decade 1991 to 2001 accounts for installation of 80 per cent of its enterprises. The factory size of industrial units shows plot size upto more than 500 sq. m with both rented and owned in nature. There is no plot in the category of upto 100 sq. m. In plots of 100 to 200 sq. m 1 per cent firms functions in each of rented and owned category. In 200 to 500 sq. m plots 4 per cent firms operates in owned and 5 per cent in rented premises. It is seen that maximum of three-fourth industrial units are working in owned plots of more than 500 sq. m. Added to it, highest numbers of firms in rented premises are seen in this category (Table 4.14).

The gross value of plant and machinery reveals that 30 per cent industrial units are with the value of Rs.1 to 5 lakhs, followed by more than 20 per cent in the slab of Rs.10 to 25 lakhs. Only 6 per cent of the enterprises are with the value of their plant and machinery more than Rs. one crore rupees. The capacity utilization of plant and machinery indicates that more than one-third firms work only on half of their capacity, another one-third utilizes only 50 to 75 per cent capacity. Surprisingly, one-quarter enterprises are using more than 75 per cent of the capacity of their plant and machinery. Employment of the workers in the industrial units exhibits that there are no firms with workers between 1 to 5 and also very small number of firms, *i.e.* 4 per cent employing more than 50 workers. Maximum of 44 per cent industrial units work with 10 to 20 workers on their roll, followed by 30 per

Table 4.14 : S.S.I. Industrial Area

1. General Attributes

Total number of units	81
Establishment other than industrial units	18
Total number of slum households	0
Residence other than slums	0

2. Type of Ownership

Type	*Proprietor*	*Partnership*	*Private Ltd.*	*Public Ltd.*	*Total*
Industrial Units (%)	*33.33*	*12.96*	*44.44*	*9.26*	*100*

3. Growth Pattern of Industries

Years	*Upto 1971*	*1971-81*	*1981-91*	*1991 -2001*	*Total*
Industrial Units (%)	2.47	0.00	16.05	81.48	100

4. Size of Industrial Units (sq. m)

Plot Size	1 -100		100 - 200		200- 500		500 +		Total
Category	Own	Rented	Own	Rented	Own	Rented	Own	Rented	
Industrial Units (%)	0.00	0.00	1.23	1.23	3.70	4.94	75.31	13.11	100

5. Gross Value of Plant and Machinery

Value in Lakhs	*Upto1lakh*	*1-5*	*5-10*	*10-25*	*25-100*	*More than 100*	*Total*
Per cent Units	12.00	30.00	18.00	22.00	12.00	6.00	100

6. Capacity Utilization of Plant and Machinery

Per cent Utilization	*1-50*	*50-75*	*More than 75*	*Total*
Industrial Units (%)	37.04	35.19	27.789	100

7. Number of Workers Employed

No. of Workers	*1-5*	*6-10*	*11-20*	*21-50*	*More than 50*	*Total*
Industrial Units (%)	0.00	22.00	44.00	30.00	4.00	100

Source : Prepared from Census of Industries (2001) Delhi Pollution Control Committee, Delhi.

cent enterprises employ workers between 20 to 30, and 22 per cent firms with 5 to 10 workers.

The nature of industrial activities explains that there is highest concentration of manufacture of basic iron and steel that engages nearly 30 per cent industrial units, followed by other fabricated metal products by 11 per cent firm. Tanning and dressing of leather, manufacture of luggage bags by 5 per cent firms and basic chemicals are pursued by nearly 4 per cent units. Besides, a host of other industrial activities in smaller fractions exist.

Nangloi Industrial Area

This industrial area is located in Northwest district accommodating nearly 400 industrial units, besides 38 establishments other than industrial units. There are no slum households and residences other than slum householders.

Ownership pattern exhibits that most of the establishments are smaller in investment. As it is evident from Table 4.15 that almost three-fourths of the total industrial units are proprietorship firms, followed by partnership enterprises they account for 13 per cent, private limited are only 10 per cent and merely 1 per cent is public limited type. The growth of industries demonstrates that upto 1971 only 0.26 per cent of the total of 400 industrial units were under operation. Even in following decade of 1971 to 1981 there were only 8 per cent firms. In the decade of 1981 to 1991 it was a negative growth with five firms under production, might be because of closure of certain units. It is only after 1991 that more than 85 per cent firms have started their production (Table 4.15).

In terms of size of factory area, more than three-quarter of the industrial units operate in plot size of upto100 sq. m in the owned category with nil in the rented premises. Twelve per cent firms own plots of 100 to 200 sq. m and 3 per cent in rented ones. In case of more than 500 sq. m plots, less than 1 per cent enterprises own and no one in rented plots of this size. The gross value of plant and machinery indicates that small investment enterprises as more than one-third of the

Table 4.15 : Nangloi Industrial Area

1. General Attributes

Total number of units	391
Establishment other than industrial units	38
Total number of slum households	0
Residence other than slums	0

2. Type of Ownership

Type	*Proprietor*	*Partnership*	*Private Ltd.*	*Public Ltd.*	*Total*
Industrial Units (%)	73.64	13.64	10.91	1.82	100

3. Growth Pattern of Industries

Years	*Upto 1971*	*1971-81*	*1981-91*	*1991 -2001*	*Total*
Industrial Units (%)	0.26	8.18	5.63	85.93	100

4. Size of Industrial Units (sq. m)

Plot Size	*1 -100*		*100-200*		*200-500*		*500 +*		*Total*
Category	Own	Rented	Own	Rented	Own	Rented	Own	Rented	
Industrial Units (%)	77.73	1.28	12.53	2.81	3.84	10.75	1.02	0.00	100

5. Gross Value of Plant and Machinery

Value in Lakhs	*Upto 1lakh*	*1-5*	*5-0*	*10-25*	*25-100*	*More than 100*	*Total*
Per cent Units	35.48	30.11	12.90	9.68	5.38	6.45	100

6. Capacity Utilization of Plant and Machinery

Per cent Utilization	*1-50*	*50-75*	*More than 75*	*Total*
Industrial Units (%)	38.53	28.44	33.03	100

7. Number of Workers Employed

No. of Workers	*1-5*	*6-10*	*11-20*	*21-50*	*More than 50*	*Total*
Industrial Units (%)	23.00	37.00	29.00	11.00	0.00	100

Source : Prepared from Census of Industries (2001) Delhi Pollution Control Committee, Delhi.

total industrial units are with the plant and machinery value of upto Rs. one lakh, followed by another nearly one-third with the investment of Rs.1 to 5 lakhs. It is also to be added that 20 per cent of enterprises are in the slab of Rs. 5 to 25 lakhs, 6 per cent of firms in each slab of Rs. 25 lakhs to one crore and more than Rs. one crore, respectively. The capacity utilization of this plant and machinery indicates that nearly 40 per cent of the firms use half of their capacity, another 30 per cent use upto three-fourth of the capacity and only one-third industrial units utilize more than 75 per cent of the capacity of their plant and machinery (Table 4.15).

The employment pattern shows that nearly 40 per cent of the industrial units work with 5 to 10 workers, followed by 30 per cent firms employing 10 to 20. Another 20 per cent units work with upto 5 workers, 20 to 50 workers work with 10 per cent industrial units. In Nangloi there is no enterprise with more than 50 workers on their roll.

Nangloi Industrial Area covers a variety of industrial activities. Manufacture of plastic products is a major activity accounting for one-fourth of its enterprises, followed by other fabricated metal products by 12 per cent of the firms and 8 per cent units does printing. Special purpose machinery engages 7 per cent units. Another 5 per cent enterprises are in manufacture of wearing apparel.

Mangolpuri Industrial Area

This industrial area is located in western Delhi beyond Nangloi Industrial Estate comprising nearly 900 industrial units accounting for 4 per cent industrial units of Delhi. Besides, nearly 500 establishments other than industrial units with no slum households and residences are found here.

The ownership pattern reveals that most of the firms are of small structure as two-third of the total industrial units are under proprietorship, followed by 20 per cent firms of partnership nature, private limited units are 15 per cent and public limited 1 per cent. The progress of industrial growth indicates almost negligible industrial units (0.35%) by 1971. Even following decade of 1971 to 1981 does not register noticeable change. Although during 1981 to 1991 began production with 5 per cent firms and it actually happened only after 1991 that more than 90 per cent enterprises came into existence. Industrial units with a varied size of their factory area are seen in Mangolpuri, with a maximum of 45 percent firms own plots upto 100 sq. m. this is followed by nearly one-fourth units functioning in owned plots of 100 to 200 sq. m. Besides 8 per cent on rented basis. In the category of 200 to 500 sq. m plots 12 per cent firms own while 4 per cent are in rented premises. There are 2 per cent industrial units in each of the owned and rented category in the plot size of more than 500 sq. m (Table 4.16).

The gross value of plant and machinery suggests that most units are of smaller nature, as 60 per cent of the industrial units have values of Rs. 5 lakhs. One-fourth of the firms falls in category of Rs. 5 to 25 lakhs, 7 per cent enterprises each in the group of Rs. 25 lakhs to one crore and more than Rs. one crore. In terms of the capacity-utilization of this plant and machinery almost 40 per cent utilize half of their capacity, another 28 per cent harness less than two-third. One-third firms use more than 75 per cent capacity each of their plant and machinery. The employment of workers shows that more than 50 per cent of the total industrial units work with 5 to 10 workers on their roll, 20 per cent firms employ upto 5 workers and 10 to 20 workers are with 15 per cent units. Another 10 per cent firms have 20 to 50 workers and more than 50 workers are employed by only three per cent of the total units (Table 4.16).

Mangolpuri industrial area has the main concentration of firms in maintenance and repair of motor vehicle that account for 20 per cent of total units, followed by 15 per cent firms engaged in manufacture of footwear. Plastic products are produced by 12 per cent enterprises, 5 per cent of units manufacture basic chemicals, 4 per cent plants manufacture other fabricated metal products and also small proportions of variety of other industrial activities.

Table 4.16 : Mangolpuri Industrial Area

1. General Attributes

Total number of units	866
Establishment other than industrial units	494
Total number of slum households	0
Residence other than slums	0

2. Type of Ownership

Type	*Proprietor*	*Partnership*	*Private Ltd.*	*Public Ltd.*	*Total*
Industrial Units (%)	64.16	20.34	14.04	0:97	100

3. Growth Pattern of Industries

Years	*Upto 1971*	*1971-81*	*1981-91*	*1991 -2001*	*Total*
Industrial Units (%)	0.35	1.04	5.20	93.42	100

4. Size of Industrial Units (sq. m)

Plot Size	*1 -100*		*100 - 200*		*200- 500*		*500 +*		*Total*
Category	Own	Rented	Own	Rented	Own	Rented	Own	Rented	
Industrial Units (%)	44.85	4.75	23.67	8.43	12.70	3.70	1.96	1.62	100

5. Gross Value of Plant and Machinery

Value in Lakhs	*Upto 1lakh*	*1-5*	*5-10*	*10-25*	*25-100*	*More than 100*	*Total*
Per cent Units	29.39	31.14	15.35	9.65	7.46	7.02	100

6. Capacity-Utilization of Plant and Machinery

Per cent Utilization	*1-50*	*50-75*	*More than 75*	*Total*
Industrial Units (%)	32.51	32.51	34.99	100

7. Number of Workers Employed

No. of Workers	*1-5*	*6-10*	*11-20*	*21-50*	*More than 50*	*Total*
Industrial Units (%)	19.44	52.78	14.44	9.72	3.61	100

Source : Prepared from Census of Industries (2001) Delhi Pollution Control Committee, Delhi.

Okhla Industrial Area

It is the third largest industrial area located in South district, housing nearly 2500 industrial units. This accounts for 20 per cent industrial units of Delhi. Besides, it also accommodates more than 400 other commercial establishments, more than 500 slum households and nearly 70 residences other than slum households. The nature of ownership manifests a mix pattern with more than 40 per cent industrial units under proprietorship and nearly one-fourth in partnership. In addition to this more than 30 per cent are of private limited nature and only 4 per cent of the total industrial units are in public limited sector. The industrial growth in this area shows very low profile of industries with less than 2 per cent of the total units upto 1971. The decade of 1971 to 1981 had 9 per cent industries. In the following 10 years of 1981 to 1991 the number of enterprises reached to nearly 20 per cent, but, mainly, 70 per cent of industrial units started their production only after 1991 (Table 4.17).

The size of the factory shows a variety of plot sizes. There are 6 per cent units in 100 sq. m, half of them in owned premises. In the category of 100 to 200 sq. m size, 10 per cent firms are in owned premises and 5 per cent in rented ones. Almost 16 per cent plants operate in owned plots and 7 per cent in rented plots in the category of 200 to 500 sq. m. In more than 500 sq. m plots only 15 per cent firms owned, whereas 40 per cent operate in rented premises. The gross value of plant and machinery elucidates that almost one-third industrial units have the gross value of their plant and machinery in the slabs of Rs. 1 to 5 lakhs. There are 13 per cent firms in the category of Rs. 5 to 10 lakhs and similar number of units fall in the slab of Rs. 25 lakhs to one crore. Added to it, 16 per cent enterprises are in the slab of upto Rs. one lakh and also same number of units belong to the slab of more than Rs. one crore. The capacity utilization of this plant and machinery exhibits a good picture where more than 50 per cent industrial units could use more than three-fourths of the capacity of their plant and machinery and

Table 4.17 : Okhla Industrial Area

1. General Attributes

Total number of units	2452
Establishment other than industrial units	425
Total nomber of slum households	520
Residence other than slums	69

2. Type of Ownership

Type	*Proprietor*	*Partnership*	*Private Ltd.*	*Public Ltd.*	*Total*
Industrial Units (%)	41.71	25.71	28.35	3.91	100

3. Growth Pattern of Industries

Years	*Upto 1971*	*1971-81*	*1981-91*	*1991-2001*	*Total*
Industrial Units (%)	1.80	9.18	18.11	70.92	100

4. Size of Industrial Units (sq. m)

Plot Size	*1 -100*		*100 - 200*		*200- 500*		*500 +*		*Total*
Category	Own	Rented	Own	Rented	Own	Rented	Own	Rented	
Industrial Units (%)	3.52	3.44	9.79	4.81	16.72	6.69	14.64	40.49	100

5. Gross Value of Plant and Machinery

Value in Lakhs	*Upto 1lakh*	*1-5*	*5-10*	*10-25*	*25-100*	*More than 100*	*Total*
Per cent Units	16.20	32.49	13.13	16.46	13.92	7.79	100

6. Capacity Utilization of Plant and Machinery

Per cent Utilization	*1-50*	*50-75*	*More than 75*	*Total*
Industrial Units (%)	20.72	28.30	50.97	100

7. Number of Workers Employed

No. of Workers	*1-5*	*6-10*	*11-20*	*21-50*	*More than 50*	*Total*
Industrial Units (%)	10.74	29.88	25.52	22.72	13.15	100

Source : Prepared from Census of Industries (2001) Delhi Pollution Control Committee, Delhi.

nearly 30 per cent firms use upto three-fourth of the capacity and 20 per cent units work on half capacity of their machinery (Table 4.17).

The employment of workers reveals that 30 per cent of the industrial units are with 5 to 10 workers, more than 20 per cent firms employ of 10 to 20 workers and similar number of units have 20 to 50 workers. Upto 5 workers are employed by nearly 10 per cent of units. Further, more than 13 per cent enterprises have employed above 50 workers. The nature of industrial activities shows manufacture of wearing apparels as activity by maximum number of plants, followed by printing, other fabricated metal products, plastic products and business activities.

Okhla Industrial Estate

It is a small estate located in South district near Okhla Industrial Area. It accommodates nearly 200 industrial units that contributes less than 1 per cent in the total industries of Delhi, besides, 15 other commercial establishments with no slum households and residences.

The nature of ownership indicates that proprietors run more than one-third industrial units, followed by nearly one-quarter in each, *i.e.* partnership and private limited. More than 10 per cent are of public limited nature. The progress of industries as evident from Table 4.18 shows maximum number of industries operating upto 1971 as compared to all other industrial areas of Delhi. In the next decade of 1971 to 1981 the number reached to 16 per cent, and after 1991 nearly 60 per cent enterprises started their production. As regards the size of factories is concerned, in 100 sq. m plots, equal numbers of enterprises, *i.e.* 9 per cent are seen in own as well as rented premises. In the plots of 100 to 200 sq. m, 6 per cent enterprises are in owned premises and 4 per cent in rented ones. It is also to be added that in more than 500 sq. m plots, only 20 per cent units own, whereas 43 per cent units operate from rented accommodation. The gross value of plant and machinery pattern shows more than 50 per cent of the industrial units are with the investment of upto Rs. 5 lakhs in their plant and machinery, followed by 15 per cent enterprises in the slab of Rs.25 lakhs to one crore. It is also evident that more than 10 per cent firms are slab of Rs.5 to 10 lakhs and same number of units are in slab of Rs. 10 to 25 lakhs. And nearly 10 per cent units belong to the category of more than Rs. one crore. The capacity-utilization of plant and machinery reveals that 40 per cent industrial units utilize more than three-fourth capacity; followed by another 40 per cent firms using upto three-fourth capacity and 20 per cent harness only half of their capacity (Table 4.18).

The employment of workers exhibits that 30 per cent of the total industrial units in this estate employ 10 to 20 workers, followed by one-fourth of firms with 5 to 10 workers on their roll, another 20 per cent enterprises in category employing 20 to 50 workers. Added to it, 20 per cent units have more than 50 workers and upto 5 workers work with 10 per cent of the plants. The main industrial activities in Okhla Industrial Estate are manufacture of other fabricated metal products, followed by wearing apparels, furniture, structural metal products, business activities, besides variety of other industrial activities of different nature.

Okhla Flatted Factory

The Okhla flatted factory complex is a small area situated near Okhla Industrial Estate in South district. It accommodates 300 industrial units that accounts for little more than 1 per cent industrial units of Delhi. There are no establishments other than industrial unit, slum household and residence.

In terms of nature of ownership nearly two-thirds of the total industrial units are of proprietorship type which indicate that Okhla Flatted Factory Complex has large segment of small stature units. These are followed by 20 per cent firms with partnership, more than 10 per cent enterprises of private limited nature and only 2 per cent of public limited type. The industrial growth in this area registered almost negligible

Table 4.18 : Okhla Industrial Estate

1. General Attributes

Total number of units	175
Establishment other than industrial units	15
Total number of slum households	0
Residence other than slums	0

2. T ype of Ownership

Type	*Proprietor*	*Partnership*	*Private Ltd.*	*Public Ltd.*	*Total*
Industrial Units (%)	36.51	24.60	23.02	11.11	100

3. Growth Pattern of Industries

Years	*Upto 1971*	*1971-81*	*1981-91*	*1991-2001*	*Total*
Industrial Units (%)	12.57	16.00	12.57	58.86	100

4. Size of Industrial Units (sq. m)

Plot Size	*1 -100*		*100 - 200*		*200- 500*		*500 +*		*Total*
Category	Own	Rented	Own	Rented	Own	Rented	Own	Rented	
Industrial Units (%)	9.22	9.71	6.29	3.43	4.47	5.14	18.29	43.43	100

5. Gross Value of Plant and Machinery

Value in Lakhs	*Upto 1lakh*	*1-5*	*5-10*	*10-25*	*25-100*	*More than 100*	*Total*
Per cent Units	22.08	31.17	11.69	11.69	14.29	9.09	100

6. Capacity Utilization of Plant and Machinery

Per cent Utilization	*1-50*	*50-75*	*More than 75*	*Total*
Industrial Units (%)	17.86	37.50	44.60	100

7. Number of Workers Employed

No. of Workers	*1-5*	*6-10*	*11-20*	*21-50*	*More than 50*	*Total*
Industrial Units (%)	9.09	24.55	30.91	18.18	17.27	100

Source : Prepared from Census of Industries (2001) Delhi Pollution Control Committee, Delhi.

upto 1971, which reached very small during 1971 to 1981. During 1981 to 1991 more than one-third of the total firms began and it is only after 1991 that more than 60 per cent enterprises came into existence. The total factory area of different industrial plot shows that there is no plot of the size of 100 to 200 sq. m, and more than 500 sq. m. In 100 sq. m nearly 3 per cent firms are in own premises and a majority of (80%) firms operate in rented premises. Added to it, in the category of 200 to 500 sq. m nearly 7 per cent of plants own and 3 per cent are on rent (Table 4.19).

The gross value of plant and machinery pattern reveals that 45 per cent industrial units have the worth of their plant and machinery between Rs. 1 to 5 lakhs, nearly 40 per cent firm are with Rs. 1 lakh. Nearly, 15 per cent of firms are with the value between Rs. 5 to 25 lakhs. Interestingly, there are no enterprises in slabs of Rs. 25 lakhs to one crore and more than Rs. one crore. The capacity-utilization of this plant and machinery indicate nearly 50 per cent of the industrial units use upto three-fourth of their capacity, 30 per cent of firms utilize only upto half of the capacity. Only 20 per cent enterprises harness more than three-fourth of their capacity. The employment of workers clearly shows two-third of the total industrial units work with 5 to 10 workers on their roll, 20 per cent of firms have upto 5 workers and little more than 10 per cent units work with 10 to 20 workers. A small fractions of firms employ 20 to 50 workers and more than 50 workers (Table 4.19).

The nature of industrial activity in Okhla Flatted Factory complex is highest in manufacture of other electrical equipments, followed by plastic products, electronic motors, generators, general-purpose machinery, other fabricated metal products, besides variety of other industrial activities in different proportions.

Naraina Industrial Area

This is a medium size industrial area in terms of number of industrial units, located in West district near Mayapuri and Kirti Nagar Industrial Areas. It accommodates nearly 800 industrial units. This contributes to more than 3 per cent of

Table 4.19 : Okhla Flatted Factory Complex

1. General Attributes

Total number of units	281
Establishment other than industrial units	0
Total number of slum households	0
Residence other than slums	0

2. Type of Ownership

Type	*Proprietor*	*Partnership*	*Private Ltd.*	*Public Ltd.*	*Total*
Industrial Units (%)	65.07	20.96	10.04	3.94	100

3. Growth Pattern of Industries

Years	*Upto 1971*	*1971-81*	*1981-91*	*1991 -2001*	*Total*
Industrial Units (%)	0.71	2.14	35.59	61.57	100

4. Size of Industrial Units (sq. m)

Plot Size	*1 -100*		*100 - 200*		*200- 500*		*500 +*		*Total*
Category	Own	Rented	Own	Rented	Own	Rented	Own	Rented	
Industrial Units (%)	2.46	86.83	0.00	0.00	7.47	2.14	0.00	0.00	100

5. Gross Value of Plant and Machinery

Value in Lakhs	*Upto 1lakh*	*1-5*	*5-10*	*10-25*	*25-100*	*More than 100*	*Total*
Per cent Units	38.76	46.63	8.43	6.18	0.00	0.00	100

6. Capacity-Utilization of Plant and Machinery

Per cent Utilization	*1-50*	*50-75*	*More than 75*	*Total*
Industrial Units (%)	29.68	48.86	21.46	100

7. Number of Workers Employed

No. of Workers	*1-5*	*6-10*	*11-20*	*21-50*	*More than 50*	*Total*
Industrial Units (%)	19.14	67.46	11.96	0.96	0.48	100

Source : Prepared from Census of Industries (2001) Delhi Pollution Control Committee, Delhi.

the total industries of Delhi. Besides, more than 200 establishments other than industrial units, nearly 100 slum households and 6 residences other than slum exist.

The nature of ownership shows that more than half of the total industrial units are under proprietorship, followed by 30 per cent firms of partnership nature. Private limited enterprises are more than 10 per cent and public limited firms are nearly 3 per cent. The growth of industries in this estate indicates that 10 per cent of the total industrial units were operating upto 1971, which reached to 16 per cent by 1981. More than 20 per cent firms began their production during the decade 1981 to 1991 and after 1991, 53 per cent enterprises started their production. The size of the factory area of industrial units in Naraina is mainly of 200 to 500 sq. m, which accounts for 42 per cent firms in owned plots and 6 per cent in the rented premises. Followed by 20 per cent enterprises operates in own plots of more than 500 sq. m and 6 per cent units in the rented ones. In the category of 100 sq. m, there are 5 per cent firms in own premises and 11 per cent in rented ones. Similarly, in 100 to 200 sq. m plot, there are more firms in rented premises than the owned plots (Table 4.20).

The pattern of gross value of plant and machinery reveals that most of the industrial units are of small nature as more than 30 per cent firms are with the value of Rs. 1 to 5 lakhs, followed by one-fourth enterprises in the category of upto Rs. one lakh. There are 13 per cent each in the slab of Rs. 5 to 10 lakhs and Rs.10 to 25 lakhs. In the category of upto one crore only less than 10 per cent firms fall and 4 per cent units with more than one crore worth of plant and machinery. The capacity-utilization of this plant and machinery exhibits that only 40 per cent of the industrial units utilize more than three-fourth of their capacity, whereas 30 per cent plants are working only on half capacity and another 30 per cent firms utilizes upto three-quarter of their capacity. The employment of workers indicates that 40 per cent of the industrial units have 5 to 10 workers on their roll, 20 per cent of the firms work with 10 to 20 workers and upto 5 workers are employed by 15 per cent enterprises. It is also shown that

15 per cent firms employ 20 to 50 workers and only 8 per cent enterprises works with more than 50 workers (Table 4.20).

Table 4.20 : Naraina Industrial Area

1. General Attributes

Total number of units	760
Establishment other than industrial units	207
Total number of slum households	96
Residence other than slums	6

2. Type of Ownership

Type	*Proprietor*	*Partnership*	*Private Ltd.*	*Public Ltd.*	*Total*
Industrial Units (%)	52.60	31.96	12.75	2.71	100

3. Growth Pattern of Industries

Years	*Upto 1971*	*1971-81*	*1981-91*	*1991 -2001*	*Total*
Industrial Units (%)	8.55	16.18	21.97	53.29	100

4. Size of Industrial Units (sq. m)

Plot Size	*1 -100*		*100 - 200*		*200- 500*		*500 +*		*Total*
Category	Own	Rented	Own	Rented	Own	Rented	Own	Rented	
Industrial Units (%)	6.15	10.93	3.95	6.71	42.50	5.92	17.50	6.56	100

5. Gross Value of Plant and Machinery

Value in Lakhs	*Upto 1Lakh*	*1-5*	*5-10*	*10-25*	*25-100*	*More than 100*	*Total*
Per cent Units	26.82	32.50	13.86	13.18	9.77	3.86	100

6. Capacity-Utilization of Plant and Machinery

Per cent Utilization	*1-50*	*50-75*	*More than 75*	*Total*
Industrial Units (%)	31.43	29.23	39.34	100

7. Number of Workers Employed

No. of Workers	*1-5*	*6-10*	*11-20*	*21-50*	*More than 50*	*Total*
Industrial Units (%)	14.12	39.50	22.90	15.08	8.40	100

Source : Prepared from Census of Industries (2001) Delhi Pollution Control Committee, Delhi.

The nature of industrial activity in Naraina clearly exhibits printing and service activities related to printing by maximum number of industrial units, followed by manufacture of other fabricated metal products, plastic products, paper and paper products and special purpose machinery, besides variety of other industrial activities.

Mayapuri Industrial Area

It is the second largest area located in West district near Naraina Industrial Area comprising more than 3000 industrial units that account for more than 15 per cent industrial activity of the city. Besides, more than 400 establishments other than industrial units, huge cluster of slums and 16 residences are also seen.

The ownership structure of these industrial units exhibits that majority of them are tiny industries as more than three-fourths of the units are with single proprietors, followed by 15 per cent of firms in partnership. In addition to 6 per cent private limited enterprises and 1 per cent public limited firms. The industrial growth profile of Mayapuri registered 4 per cent units upto 1971, with major increase (30%) during decade of 1971 to 1981. Whereas, the next decade did not register much growth, then, again after 1991 more than 40 per cent enterprises came into existence. Total factory area of industrial units shows that most of the industrial units operates in smaller plot sizes. Nearly, 40 per cent of the units own plot upto 100 sq. m followed by more than 20 per cent own plot of 200 to 500 sq. m. In the category of 100 to 200 sq. m, 15 per cent firms function in own premises. And only 7 per cent own plots in more than 500 sq. m size. Surprisingly, very small fractions of enterprises operate from rented plots in various categories (Table 4.21).

The gross value of plant and machinery indicates that most industrial units are of smaller type as more than one-third units fall in the category of upto Rs. one lakh. Nearly,

Table 4.21 : Mayapuri Industrial Area

1. General Attributes

Total number of units	3265
Establishment other than industrial units	433
Total number of slum households	2245
Residence other than slums	10

2. Type of Ownership

Type	*Proprietor*	*Partnership*	*Private Ltd.*	*Public Ltd.*	*Total*
Industrial Units (%)	77.89	15.19	5.72	1.20	100

3. Growth Pattern of Industries

Years	*Upto 1971*	*1971-81*	*1981-91*	*1991 -2001*	*Total*
Industrial Units (%)	4.01	32.13	16.97	46.89	100

4. Size of Industrial Units (sq. m)

Plot Size	*1 -100*		*100 - 200*		*200- 500*		*500 +*		*Total*
Category	Own	Rented	Own	Rented	Own	Rented	Own	Rented	
Industrial Units (%)	41.26	8.14	14.30	2.42	23.22	1.62	6.77	2.32	100

5. Gross Value of Plant and Machinery

Value in Lakhs	*Upto 1lakh*	*1-5*	*5-10*	*10-25*	*25-100*	*More than 100*	*Total*
Per cent Units	34.17	38.81	11.39	9.48	4.30	1.84	100

6. Capacity Utilization of Plant and Machinery

Per cent Utilization	*1-50*	*50-75*	*More than 75*	*Total*
Industrial Units (%)	15.73	24.21	60.07	100

7. Number of Workers Employed

No. of Workers	*1-5*	*6-10*	*11-20*	*21-50*	*More than 50*	*Total*
Industrial Units (%)	56.11	23.21	10.91	7.10	2.66	100

Source : Prepared from Census of Industries (2001) Delhi Pollution Control Committee, Delhi.

40 per cent units are with the value of Rs. 1 to 5 lakhs. In the category of Rs. 5 to 25 lakhs, 20 per cent enterprises fall, 4 per cent firm with upto Rs. one crore, nearly 2 per cent

units worth the plant and machinery of more than Rs.100 crores. The capacity-utilization of this plant and machinery shows a little better picture as compared to other industrial areas, with 60 per cent of its industrial units utilize more than three-quarter of their capacity, followed by one-fourth enterprises the capacity upto 75 per cent and only 15 per cent firm use upto half of their capacity. The number of workers employed, too, indicates small structure of industrial units as more than half of the total industrial units employ up to 5 workers, nearly one-fourth firms employ 5 to 10 workers and 10 to 20 workers in 10 per cent enterprises. Furthermore than 50 workers are employed in 3 per cent firms. The expenditure pattern on different heads by value of plant and machinery reveals that industrial units are with smaller worth of plant and machinery. These units spend more than 70 per cent on basic raw materials, which decreases upto 50 per cent in plants with slab of more than Rs.one crore where the expenses are more on other expenditures (Table 4.21).

The type of industrial activities in Mayapuri shows that more than one-third industrial units are engaged in retail sale of second-hand goods in stores followed by wholesale of non-agricultural intermediate products waste, manufacture of other fabricated metal products, sale of motor vehicle parts and accessories, maintenance and repair of motor vehicles, and variety of other industrial activities.

Badli Industrial Area

Badli is a medium order industrial area located in Northwest district, which accommodates 298 industrial units. Besides, 39 establishments other than industrial units, there are more than 500 slum households without other residences. After the relocation scheme many of the industrial units from non-approved areas are allotted plots here.

The ownership structure manifests that more than half of the total industrial units are smaller, handled by single proprietors, followed by one-third of firms under partnership. Ten per cent enterprises are private limited and nearly 3 per cent are of public limited type. The Badli area had very negligible industrial units upto 1971, in the next decade 4 per cent firm came up. During 1981-1991 decade, 20 per cent units began and after 1991 majority (70%) enterprises started their production. The total area of factory of these industrial units is mainly between 200 to 500 sq. m, as evident from Table 4.22, more than 45 per cent units own plot of this size and 10 per cent firms are in rented premises. In the category of more than 500 sq. m, 15 per cent plants own their plots. Similar number of firms own plots in the size of upto 100 sq. m. There are negligible plots in the category of 100 to 200 sq. m (Table 4.22).

The gross value of plant and machinery exhibits smaller structure of industrial units, with 70 per cent of firms worth upto Rs. 5 lakhs, 6 per cent of enterprises upto Rs. one crore value and five per cent of units with more than Rs. one crore. The capacity-utilization of this plant and machinery reveals that more than one-third of the total industrial units use half of their capacity, 40 per cent firms use upto three-fourths capacity and 20 per cent units harness more than three-fourths of their capacity. The number of workers employed indicates that 50 per cent of the firms have 5 to 10 workers on their roll followed by 20 per cent enterprises with 10 to 20 workers. It is also seen that upto 5 workers are employed in 15 per cent units and 3 per cent of firms have more than 50 workers (Table 4.22).

The type of industrial activities shows that more than one-fourth of industrial units are engaged in manufacture of other fabricated metal products, followed by plastic products, parts and accessories of motor vehicle, basic precious and semi-precious metal, other chemical products besides other industrial activities in various properties.

Table 4.22 : Badli Industrial Area

1. General Attributes

Total number of units	298
Establishment other than industrial units	39
Total number of slum households	508
Residence other than slums	0

2. Type of Ownership

Type	*Proprietor*	*Partnership*	*Private Ltd.*	*Public Ltd.*	*Total*
Industrial Units (%)	53.18	33.18	10.00	3.73	100

3. Growth Pattern of Industries

Years	*Upto 1971*	*1971-81*	*1981-91*	*1991-2001*	*Total*
Industrial Units (%)	1.68	4.63	20.47	73.49	100

4. Size of Industrial Units (sq. m)

Plot Size	*1 -100*		*100 - 200*		*200- 500*		*500 +*		*Total*
Category	Own	Rented	Own	Rented	Own	Rented	Own	Rented	
Industrial Units (%)	16.01	1.34	2.68	2.35	45.97	11.07	19.78	3.70	100

5. Gross Value of Plant and Machinery

Value in Lakhs	*Upto 1lakh*	*1-5*	*5-10*	*10-25*	*25-100*	*More than 100*	*Total*
Per cent Units	29.71	41.14	10.29	8.00	5.71	5.14	100

6. Capacity Utilization of Plant and Machinery

Per cent Utilization	*1-50*	*50-75*	*More than 75*	*Total*
Industrial Units (%)	35.58	41.35	23.08	100

7. Number of Workers Employed

No. of Workers	*1-5*	*6-10*	*11-20*	*21-50*	*More than 50*	*Total*
Industrial Units (%)	14.93	50.75	19.90	11.94	2.49	100

Source : Prepared from. Census of Industries (2001) Delhi Pollution Control Committee, Delhi.

Jhilmil Industrial Area

This is a middle order industrial area located in East district comprising of 300 industrial units, besides 45 establishments other than industrial units. Huge cluster of slum households also coexist.

The ownership structure of industrial units reflects that 80 per cent of the firms are under single proprietors and partnership. Private limited firms are 20 per cent and public limited firms are only 3 per cent. The industrial progress in this area shows that 10 per cent of the total industrial units were in operation upto 1971, in the next two-decades nearly 20 per cent firms were registered in each decade, whereas, 54 per cent of the enterprises began their production in 1991 to 2001. The total factory area of the industrial units reflects that maximum plots belong to the size of 200 to 500 sq. m. It is found that 50 per cent firms own premises and 6 per cent are on rent. Added to it, one-fourth firms own plots of more than 500 sq. m, and three per cent are on rent. In the plot size of plots of 100 to 200 sq. m, 10 per cent enterprises have own premises (Table 4.23).

So far as gross value of plant and machinery is concerned, 60 per cent of the industrial units worth upto Rs. 5 lakhs, 16 per cent firms belong to the slab of Rs. 5 to 10 lakhs, and 5 per cent enterprises fall in the category of upto Rs. one crore and more than Rs. one crore. The capacity-utilization of the plant and machinery shows that 29 per cent of the industrial units are working on half capacity of their plant and machinery, one-third enterprises are using upto 75 per cent and 37 per cent firms harness more than three-fourth of their plant capacity. Table 4.23 demonstrates that more than 43 per cent of the total industrial units works with 5 to 10 workers, nearly one-fourth enterprises have 10 to 20 workers on their roll and upto 5 workers are employed in 17 per cent of the firms. It is also to be added that 20 to 50 workers are employed with 12 per cent units and nearly 4 per cent of units have more than 50 workers (Table 4.23).

The Jhilmil Industrial Area covers variety of industrial activities, 30 per cent of the total of its industrial units are

Table 4.23 : Jhilmil Industrial Area

1. General Attributes

Total number of units	300
Establishment other than industrial units	45
Total number of slum households	2025
Residence other than slums	1

2. Type of Ownership

Type	*Proprietor*	*Partnership*	*Private Ltd.*	*Public Ltd.*	*Total*
Industrial Units (%)	37.73	41.82	17.27	3.12	100

3. Growth Pattern of Industries

Years	*Upto 1971*	*1971-81*	*1981-91*	*1991 -2001*	*Total*
Industrial Units (%)	10.34	18.33	17.33	54.00	100

4. Size of Industrial Units (sq. m)

Plot Size	*1 -100*		*100 - 200*		*200- 500*		*500 +*		*Total*
Category	Own	Rented	Own	Rented	Own	Rented	Own	Rented	
Industrial Units (%)	1.67	1.66	10.00	3.33	49.00	5.67	25.00	3.66	100

5. Gross Value of Plant and Machinery

Value in Lakhs	*Upto 1lakh*	*1-5*	*5-10*	*10-25*	*25-100*	*More than 100*	*Total*
Per cent Units	27.66	34.04	16.49	11.70	4.26	5.85	100

6. Capacity-Utilization of Plant and Machinery

Per cent Utilization	*1-50*	*50-75*	*More than 75*	*Total*
Industrial Units (%)	28.85	34.13	37.02	100

7. Number of Workers Employed

No. of Workers	*1-5*	*6-10*	*11-20*	*21-50*	*More than 50*	*Total*
Industrial Units (%)	17.35	43.37	23.47	12.24	3.57	100

Source : Prepared from Census of Industries (2001) Delhi Pollution Control Committee, Delhi.

engaged in basic precious and non-ferrous metals, followed by insulated wire and cable, other fabricated metal products, general purpose machinery, other chemicals products besides many other kinds of industries.

Friends Colony Industrial Area

It is a small industrial area comprising 261 industrial units located in East district. Besides 22 establishments other than industrial unit, 7 slum households and 17 other residences are seen.

The nature of ownership demonstrates that most of the industrial units are of smaller stature as 70 per cent of the enterprises are run under single proprietorship, followed by partnership in 20 per cent firms. Private limited firms are 7 per cent and 4 per cent enterprises are of public limited type. The industrial progress happened in different phases with 6 per cent industrial units upto 1971, in the next two decades almost one-fourth of firms came into existence, whereas nearly 70 per cent of the units began their production during the decade 1991-2001. The total factory area of the industrial units shows that nearly one-third of the firms own the plots of more than 500 sq. m. In the plot size of 100 to 200 sq. m, 10 per cent enterprises are operating in owned and 8 per cent in rented premises. In the category of 200 to 500 sq. m, and upto 100 sq. m, firms on rent are more than own premises. The gross value of plant and machinery reflects that majority of industrial units are of small nature as 84 per cent units worth upto Rs. 5 lakhs, only 9 per cent in the slab of Rs. 5 to 25 lakhs and only 5 per cent firms fall in the next higher categories. The capacity utilization of the plant and machinery indicates that 43 per cent industrial units harness more than three-fourths capacity, nearly one-quarter use half of its capacity and 30 per cent of the firms are using upto three-fourth of the capacity of their plant and machinery (Table 4.24).

The employment pattern, too, reveals that majority of the industrial units are of small stature as more than two-third of the units have 5 to 10 workers on their roll, 15 per cent work with upto 5 workers and only 10 per cent firm employ 10 to 20 workers. In addition to it small fractions of

Table 4.24 : Friends Colony Industrial Area

1. General Attributes

Total number of units	261
Establishment other than industrial units	22
Total number of slum households	7
Residence other than slums	17

2. Type of Ownership

Type	*Proprietor*	*Partnership*	*Private Ltd.*	*Public Ltd.*	*Total*
Industrial Units (%)	69.14	20.37	7.41	3.09	100

3. Growth Pattern of Industries

Years	*Upto 1971*	*1971-81*	*1981-91*	*1991 -2001*	*Total*
Industrial Units (%)	6.13	15.33	11.11	67.43	100

4. Size of Industrial Units (sq. m)

Plot Size	*1 -100*		*100 - 200*		*200- 500*		*500 +*		*Total*
Category	Own	Rented	Own	Rented	Own	Rented	Own	Rented	
Industrial Units (%)	10.24	15.70	10.34	8.43	4.21	10.73	34.48	5.72	100

5. Gross Value of Plant and Machinery

Value in Lakhs	*Upto 1lakh*	*1-5*	*5-10*	*10-25*	*25-100*	*More than 100*	*Total*
Per cent Units	42.37	42.37	4.24	5.93	2.54	2.54	100

6. Capacity-Utilization of Plant and Machinery

Per cent Utilization	*1-50*	*50-75*	*More than 75*	*Total*
Industrial Units (%)	24.84	31.85	43.31	100

7. Number of Workers Employed

No. of Workers	*1-5*	*6-10*	*11-20*	*21-50*	*More than 50*	*Total*
Industrial Units (%)	16.67	67.33	10.67	4.00	1.33	100

Source : Prepared from Census of Industries (2001) Delhi Pollution Control Committee, Delhi.

enterprises employ more than 50 workers. In Friends Colony Industrial Area, 40 per cent of the total industrial units are engaged in manufacture of basic precious and non-ferrous metals, followed by plastic products, insulated wire and cable, special purpose machinery, other chemical products, and variety of other industrial activities.

Patparganj Industrial Area

This is a middle level industrial area located in East district comprising more than 504 industrial units. It accounts 2.3 per cent share to total industries of city. It is also shown that there are 44 other commercial establishments, no slums households and other residences.

The ownership pattern manifests a mix one with 44 per cent of the total industrial units under single proprietorship, followed by 29 per cent firms of private limited in nature. As a result, 20 per cent are partnership firms and public limited units are more than 6 per cent. The establishment of industries shows that in the two decades during 1971-1991 the number of firms were almost negligible, 98 per cent industrial units have came into existence during 1991- 2001. The factory area of industrial units is mainly the bigger plot. It is seen that more than 50 per cent of the total industrial units operates in their own plots of more than 500 sq. m and very small number of firms are on rent in this category. In the plot size of 200 to 500 sq. m equal number (22%) of enterprises are in owned premises as well as in rented. In other categories of plots there are small fractions of units (Table 4.25).

In terms of gross value of plant and machinery, one-third of the total industrial units worth Rs. 1 to 5 lakhs followed by nearly one-quarter of firms with the value of Rs.5 to 10 lakhs. It is also to be added that in the slabs of up to Rs. one lakh, 12 per cent enterprises fall. In category Rs. 10 to 25 lakhs and Rs.25 lakhs to one crore, 14 per cent units fall in each, respectively. Interestingly, there are 4 per cent in the slab of more than Rs. one crore. The capacity utilization of the plant and machinery shows 37 per cent of the total

Table 4.25 : Patparganj Industrial Area

1. General Attributes

Total number of units	504
Establishment other than industrial units	44
Total number of slum households	0
Residence other than slums	0

2. Type of Ownership

Type	*Proprietor*	*Partnership*	*Private Ltd.*	*Public Ltd.*	*Total*
Industrial Units (%)	44.97	18.34	28.99	7.79	100

3. Growth Pattern of Industries

Years	*Up to 1971*	*1971-81*	*1981-91*	*1991 -2001*	*Total*
Industrial Units (%)	0.20	0.40	0.60	98.81	100

4. Size of Industrial Units (sq. m)

Plot Size	*1 -100*		*100 - 200*		*200- 500*		*500 +*		*Total*
Category	Own	Rented	Own	Rented	Own	Rented	Own	Rented	
Industrial Units (%)	0.00	0.40	0.40	0.79	22.02	22.02	53.17	1.19	100

5. Gross Value of Plant and Machinery

Value in Lakhs	*Upto 1lakh*	*1-5*	*5-10*	*10-25*	*25-100*	*More than 100*	*Total*
Per cent Units	12.12	33.33	23.24	14.12	13.11	4.06	100

6. Capacity-Utilization of Plant and Machinery

Per cent Utilization	*1-50*	*50-75*	*More than 75*	*Total*
Industrial Units (%)	37.04	30.25	30.71	100

7. Number of Workers Employed

No. of Workers	*1-5*	*6-10*	*11-20*	*21-50*	*More than 50*	*Total*
Industrial Units (%)	6.34	35.92	32.92	13.38	11.97	100

Source : Prepared from Census of Industries (2001) Delhi Pollution Control Committee, Delhi.

industrial units work only at half of their capacity, 30 per cent of enterprises use upto three-fourth of the capacity and more. The employment details exhibit a mix pattern where more than one-third of the total industrial units employ 5 to 10 workers, another nearly one-third firms worth with 10 to 20 workers and 13 per cent of enterprises have 20 to 50 workers. Added to it, more than 50 workers are employed in nearly 12 per cent of firms (Table 4.25).

In Patparganj Industrial Area manufacture of wearing apparel engages maximum number of industrial units, which is followed by other fabricated metal products, plastic products, printing and services activities related to printing, special purpose machinery alongwith variety of other industrial activities.

Mohan Co-operative Industrial Area

This industrial area is located in South district near Okhla Industrial Area comprising 185 industrial units alongwith more than 40 establishments other than industrial units. Slum households are 264 with no residences other than slum households.

The ownership of industrial units in Mohan Co-operative area has a different scenario as compared to other industrial areas of Delhi. It has second largest number of firms of private limited nature, followed by nearly a quarter of single proprietorship enterprises and 14 per cent of public limited nature besides a good number of partnership units. Establishment of industrial units shows a trend with almost negligible number of firms in the two decades of upto 1971 and 1971-1981. It also to be shown that 10 per cent of the total industrial units started during 1981-1991 and after 1991, 86 per cent of the enterprises came into existence. The size of the factory of the industrial units exhibits that there is almost no plot in size of upto 200 sq. m in owned as well as rented category. Even in the 200 to 500 sq. m size, very small number of plots are available. Interestingly, 84 per cent plots are owned and 7 per cent firms are on rent in the plot size of more than 500 sq. m (Table 4.26).

The gross value of plant and machinery shows a scattered pattern with 30 per cent of the total industrial units in the slab of Rs. 10 to 25 lakhs, followed by 20 per cent in the slab of upto Rs. 5 lakh and nearly the same number of firms in the category of Rs. 25 lakhs to one crore. It is also shown that 11 per cent enterprises belong to the slab of more than Rs. one crore. As regards capacity utilization of the plant and machinery, 42 per cent of the industrial units utilize more than three-fourth of their capacity of their plant and machinery, 40 per cent firms use between half to three-fourth capacity and 17 per cent enterprises work on less the half of their capacity. The employment of workers indicates that most of the industrial units are of bigger scale as 41 per cent of the enterprises have more than 50 workers on their roll, followed by 20 per cent in the category of 20 to 50 and same in the category of 10 to 20 workers (Table 4.26).

The nature of industrial activities in Mohan Co-operative is of varied nature, ranging from supporting and auxiliary transport activities, manufacture of wearing apparel, maintenance and repair of motor vehicles, other chemical products and plastic products.

Tilak Nagar Industrial Area

This is the smallest industrial area of Delhi comprising of only 36 industrial units. It is located in West district. Besides two other commercial establishments there are no slum households and other residences.

The ownership structure of industrial units elucidates that most of the units are of small size, as evident from Table 4.27 that single proprietors own 43 per cent of the industrial units, followed by another 40 per cent of firms with partnership. Private limited enterprises are 10 per cent and public limited are only 6 per cent of the total number of industries. The trend of establishment of industries manifests that upto 1971, 11 per cent of the total industrial units existed and in following decade one-fourth of firms was started.

Table 4.26 : Mohan Co-operative Industrial Area

1. General Attributes

Total number of units	185
Establishment other than industrial units	42
Total number of slum households	264
Residence other than slums	0

2. Type of Ownership

Type	*Proprietor*	*Partnership*	*Private Ltd.*	*Public Ltd.*	*Total*
Industrial Units (%)	23.44	10.94	43.75	21.87	100

3. Growth Pattern of Industries

Years	*Up to 1971*	*1971-81*	*1981-91*	*1991 -2001*	*Total*
Industrial Units (%)	0.54	1.08	10.81	87.57	100

4. Size of Industrial Units (sq. m)

Plot Size	*1 -100*		*100 - 200*		*200- 500*		*500 +*		*Total*
Category	Own	Rented	Own	Rented	Own	Rented	Own	Rented	
Industrial Units (%)	0.54	2.16	0.00	0.00	2.70	1.08	84.32	7.57	100

5. Gross Value of Plant and Machinery

Value in Lakhs	*Upto 1lakh*	*1-5*	*5-10*	*10-25*	*25-100*	*More than 100*	*Total*
Per cent Units	4.55	20.45	15.91	29.55	18.18	11.36	100

6. Capacity-Utilization of Plant and Machinery

Per cent Utilization	*1-50*	*50-75*	*More than 75*	*Total*
Industrial Units (%)	17.86	39.29	42.86	100

7. Number of Workers Employed

No. of Workers	*1-5*	*6-10*	*11-20*	*21-50*	*More than 50*	*Total*
Industrial Units (%)	3.64	18.18	18.19	18.18	41.82	100

Source : Prepared from Census of Industries (2001) Delhi Pollution Control Committee, Delhi.

Whereas during 1981-1991 only 5 per cent new enterprises started and nearly 60 per cent began after the year 1991 to 2001 (Table 4.27).

The size of factories varies from upto 100 sq. m to more than 500 sq. m. Nearly, one-fourth of the firms operates in each own and rented plots of upto 100 sq. m. Whereas in the category of 200 to 500 sq. m, 2 per cent enterprises own plots and 22 per cent on rent. In the category of more than 500 sq.m, 8 per cent industrial units own and 5 per cent are on rent. The gross value of plant and machinery indicates towards smaller enterprises in with 43 per cent of the firms worth their plant and machinery between Rs. 1 to 5 lakhs, 13 per cent belong to the group of Rs. 10 to 25 lakhs. It is also shown that very less number of firms are in the slab of upto Rs. one crore, though, nearly 9 per cent of the industrial units worth more than Rs. one crore. In terms of capacity utilization of this plant and machinery, one-quarter of the total industrial units works on half of their capacity, another one-fourth use up to 75 per cent of the capacity and nearly half of the firms harness more than three-fourth capacity of their plant and machinery. The pattern of workers employed with industrial units indicates that one-third of the enterprises employ 5 to 10 workers, 40 per cent of firms work with 10 to 20 workers and 10 per cent of them employ 20 to 50 workers. Surprisingly, more than 50 workers are with 7 per cent firms (Table 4.27).

In Tilak Nagar Industrial Area majority of the industrial units are engaged in manufacture of plastic products followed by other fabricated metal products, footwear, manufacture of paper and paper products, general purpose machinery alongwith variety of other industrial activities.

Kirti Nagar Industrial Area

Kirti Nagar is the fifth largest industrial area of Delhi accommodating nearly 1476 industrial units. It is located in West district near Moti Nagar Industrial Area. Alongwith more than 311 establishments other than industrial units, there is also second largest slum cluster with more than 5310 households and nearly 50 residences.

Table 4.27 : Tilak Nagar Industrial Area

1. General Attributes

Total number of units	36
Establishment other than industrial units	2
Total number of slum households	0
Residence other than slums	0

2. Type of Ownership

Type	*Proprietor*	*Partnership*	*Private Ltd.*	*Public Ltd.*	*Total*
Industrial Units (%)	43.33	40.00	10.00	6.67	100

3. Growth Pattern of Industries

Years	*Upto 1971*	*1971-81*	*1981-91*	*1991 -2001*	*Total*
Industrial Units (%)	11.11	25.00	5.56	58.33	100

4. Size of Industrial Units (sq. m)

Plot Size	*1 -100*		*100 - 200*		*200- 500*		*500 +*		*Total*
Category	Own	Rented	Own	Rented	Own	Rented	Own	Rented	
Indusirial Units (%)	22.32	27.77	5.56	5.57	2.78	22.22	8.33	5.56	100

5. Gross Value of Plant and Machinery

Value in Lakhs	*Upto 1lakh*	*1-5*	*5-10*	*10-25*	*25-100*	*More than 100*	*Total*
Per cent Units	21.47	43.48	8.70	13.04	4.35	8.70	100

6. Capacity-Utilization of Plant and Machinery

Per cent Utilization	*1-50*	*50-75*	*More than 75*	*Total*
Industrial Units (%)	25.93	25.93	48.15	100

7. Number of Workers Employed

No. of Workers	*1-5*	*6-10*	*11-20*	*21-50*	*More than 50*	*Total*
Industrial Units (%)	7.41	33.33	40.74	11.11	7.41	100

Source : Prepared from Census of Industries (2001) Delhi Pollution Control Committee, Delhi.

The nature of ownership pattern indicates majority of the industrial units are of tiny nature, as 70 per cent of the total enterprises are owned by single proprietors, followed by one-fourth of the firms with partnership. It is also to be noted that only 5 per cent of the units are private limited and public limited firms are almost negligible. The process of growth of industries in this area shows that only four per cent of firms upto 1971, 10 per cent establishment came up during 1971-1981 and 16 per cent units started during 1981 to 1991. Added to it nearly 70 per cent firms came into existence during 1990-2000. The size of factory area of the industrial units reveals that 31 per cent units own plots of the size of upto 100 sq. m and 8 per cent on rent. This is followed by 22 per cent firms in own plots of 200 to 500 sq. m and 10 per cent firms are on rent. In the category of 100 to 200 sq. m, more firms own plots than rented. Surprisingly, very small fraction of enterprises has bigger plots of more than 500 sq. m (Table 4.28).

The gross value of plant and machinery reveals that majority of the industrial units (80%) fall into the category of worth upto Rs. 5 lakhs. In other categories, 3 to 6 per cent of the firms fall and there are 1 per cent enterprises with more than Rs. one crore worth. In terms of capacity utilization of plant and machinery situation seems comparatively good as 83 per cent of the industrial units could use more than three-quarter of the capacity of their plant, followed by 10 per cent of firms who utilize upto three-quarter of the capacity and 5 per cent of the enterprises are working only at half of their capacity. The employment of workers exhibits that 56 per cent of the total industrial units work with upto 5 workers on their roll, followed by 31 per cent firms employing 5 to 10 workers. Typically, there are smaller number of firms which employ upto 50 and more than 50 workers (Table 4.28).

In Kirti Nagar Industrial Area nearly 40 per cent of the total industrial units are engaged in manufacture of furniture followed by wholesale of non-agricultural intermediate products, other retail trade of new goods in specialized stores, products of wood and cork and other fabricated metal products besides variety of other industrial activities.

Table 4.28 : Kirti Nagar Industrial Area

1. General Attributes

Total number of units	1476
Establishment other than industrial units	311
Total number of slum households	5310
Residence other than slums	49

2. Type of Ownership

Type	Proprietor	Partnership	Private Ltd.	Public Ltd.	Total
Industrial Units (%)	69.12	24.15	5.60	1.14	100

3. Growth Pattern of Industries

Years	*Upto 1971*	*1971-81*	*1981-91*	*1991 -2001*	*Total*
Industrial Units (%)	4.54	11.04	16.33	68.09	100

4. Size of Industrial Units (Sq. m)

Plot Size	*1 -100*		*100 - 200*		*200- 500*		*500 +*		*Total*
Category	Own	Rented	Own	Rented	Own	Rented	Own	Rented	
Industrial Units (%)	31.64	8.01	15.92	6.37	22.63	10.70	3.05	1.70	100

5. Gross Value of Plant and Machinery

Value in Lakhs	*Upto 1lakh*	*1-5*	*5-10*	*10-25*	*25-100*	*More than 100*	*Total*
Per cent Units	55.13	27.56	6.09	3.85	5.77	1.60	100

6. Capacity-Utilization of Plant and Machinery

Per cent Utilization	*1-50*	*50-75*	*More than 75*	*Total*
Industrial Units (%)	5.60	11.19	83.21	100

7. Number of Workers Employed

No. of Workers	*1-5*	*6-10*	*11-20*	*21-50*	*More than 50*	*Total*
Industrial Units (%)	56.58	31.81	6.36	3.68	1.56	100

Source : Prepared from Census of Industries (2001) Delhi Pollution Control Committee, Delhi.

Najafgarh Road Industrial Area

This is a medium category of industrial area comprising of

377 industrial units. It is located in West district. This area has 71 establishments other than industrial units with no slum households and other residences.

The ownership structure of the industrial units reveals that 52 per cent of the total units are with single proprietors indicating towards smaller units, followed by one-fourth of the firms with partnership and 15 per cent of private limited type. In addition, small fraction of units are of public limited nature. The establishment of industrial units in this area shows a good number of industries functioning upto 1971 (13%), registered 11 per cent new firms during 1971-1981. The next decade added 20 per cent new enterprises and after 1991, 55 per cent of the total industrial units came into existence. The factory area of the industrial units exhibits more of the bigger plots of more than 500 sq. m, *i.e.* 31 per cent units own plots and 7 per cent on rent. It is also seen that 12 per cent firms own plots in the size of 200 to 500 sq. m and 10 per cent on rent. In the category of 100 to 200 sq. m and upto 100 sq. m plots more number of enterprises are on rent than owned. The gross value of plant and machinery suggests that major units are small. It is shown that more than two-third of the total industrial units worth their plant and machinery upto Rs. 5 lakh. In the slab of upto Rs. 5 to 25 lakhs, there are 20 per cent of the firms and small proportion of firms worth the value of more than Rs. one crore (Table 4.29).

The capacity utilization of this plant and machinery indicates that 22 per cent of the firms utilize half of their capacity, 53 per cent total industrial units harness more than three-fourth capacity of their plant and machinery. The employment of workers reflects a mix pattern with a maximum one-third industrial units working with 5 to 10 workers, one-fourth of the firms employ 10 to 20 workers and nearly one-fifth enterprises with 5 workers on their roll. Added to it, 20 to 50 workers are employed by 13 per cent units and more than 50 workers are with 7 per cent

Table 4.29 : Najafgarh Industrial Area

1. General Attributes

Total number of units	377
Establishment other than industrial units	71
Total number of slum households	0
Residence other than slums	0

2. Type of Ownership

Type	*Proprietor*	*Partnership*	*Private Ltd.*	*Public Ltd.*	*Total*
Industrial Units (%)	52.82	25.00	16.55	5.63	100

3. Growth Pattern of Industries

Years	*Upto 1971*	*1971-81*	*1981-91*	*1991 -2001*	*Total*
Industrial Units (%)	13.79	11.14	19.89	55.17	100

4. Size of Industrial Units (Sq. m)

Plot Size	*1 -100*		*100 - 200*		*200- 500*		*500 +*		*Total*
Category	Own	Rented	Own	Rented	Own	Rented	Own	Rented	
Industrial Units (%)	4.25	14.33	8.22	10.88	12.47	10.88	31.83	7.96	100

5. Gross Value of Plant and Machinery

Value in Lakhs	*Upto 1lakh*	*1-5*	*5-10*	*10-25*	*25-100*	*More than 100*	*Total*
Per cent units	31.22	33.76	10.97	10.97	8.02	5.06	100

6. Capacity-Utilization of Plant and Machinery

Per cent Utilization	*1-50*	*50-75*	*More than 75*	*Total*
Industrial Units (%)	22.14	24.64	53.12	100

7. Number of Workers Employed

No. of Workers	*1-5*	*6-10*	*11-20*	*21-50*	*More than 50*	*Total*
Industrial Units (%)	19.33	35.69	23.79	13.75	7.43	100

Source : Prepared from Census of Industries (2001) Delhi Pollution Control Committee, Delhi.

enterprises. The Najafgarh Industrial Area has majority of industrial units engaged in manufacture of footwear, followed by other fabricated metal products, plastic products, basic chemicals, special purpose machinery and a variety of other industrial activities.

Moti Nagar Industrial Area

This is the small industrial area located in West district near Kirti Nagar Industrial Area comprising of 231 industrial units. Besides, 82 establishments other than industrial units, there exist two slum households and no residence.

The ownership structure of industrial units reflects that 60 per cent of the firms are owned by single proprietors, followed by 30 per cent enterprises with proprietorship and 10 per cent are private limited. It should also be noted that very negligible units are of public limited type. The progress of the industries shows highest number of the industrial units in Delhi upto the year 1971, registered one-fourth of new industries during the following two decades, although majority, *i.e.* (60%) of the enterprises began during 1991-2001.In addition, the size of industrial plots demonstrates a mix pattern, where 10 per cent units are in owned as well as rented plots of 100 sq. m. It is also shown that maximum industrial units function in the plot size of 200 to 500 sq. m (36%), of this 30 per cent units are on rent. Further, even in the plot size of more than 500 sq. m more firms are on rent than the owned ones. Grossly, more than half of the total units are in rented plots of various plot sizes (Table 4.30).

The gross value of plant and machinery indicates that there are nearly 70 per cent of the total industrial units worth up to Rs. 5 lakhs, more than one-fifth of the enterprises worth between Rs. 5 to 25 lakhs, small proportion of the units falling in the slab of upto Rs. one crore and more than that. In terms of capacity utilization, 57 per cent of the industrial units use more than three-fourth of the capacity of their plant and machinery, 20 per cent enterprises work on half and same number of units harness more than half of their capacity of plant. The pattern of employment of workers indicates that

Table 4.30 : Moti Nagar Industrial Area

1. General Attributes

Total number of units	231
Establishment other than industrial units	82
Total number of slum households	2
Residence other than slums	0

2. Type of Ownership

Type	*Proprietor*	*Partnership*	*Private Ltd.*	*Public Ltd.*	*Total*
Industrial Units (%)	59.18	30.61	9.52	0.68	100

3. Growth Pattern of Industries

Years	*Upto 1971*	*1971-81*	*1981-91*	*1991 -2001*	*Total*
Industrial Units (%)	14.28	10.39	14.72	60.61	100

4. Size of Industrial Units (Sq. m)

Plot Size	*1 -100*		*100 - 200*		*200- 500*		*500 +*		*Total*
Category	Own	Rented	Own	Rented	Own	Rented	Own	Rented	
Industrial Units (%)	12.55	15.15	5.63	9.09	6.49	30.30	7.79	12.99	100

5. Gross Value of Plant and Machinery

Value in Lakhs	*Upto 1Lakh*	*1-5*	*5-10*	*10-25*	*25-100*	*More than 100*	*Total*
Per cent Units	42.11	26.32	15.79	7.89	4.39	3.81	100

6. Capacity-Utilization of Plant and Machinery

Per cent Utilization	*1-50*	*50-75*	*More than 75*	*Total*
Industrial Units (%)	20.41	21.77	57.83	100

7. Number of Workers Employed

No. of Workers	*1-5*	*6-10*	*11-20*	*21-50*	*More than 50*	*Total*
Industrial Units (%)	29.77	40.46	12.21	13.74	3.82	100

Source : Prepared from Census of Industries (2001) Delhi Pollution Control Committee, Delhi.

40 per cent of the total industrial units work with 5 to 10 workers, followed by 30 per cent of firms with upto 5 workers. Similarly, 10 to 20 workers work with 12 per cent

units, 20 to 50 workers are employed with similar number of enterprises and small fraction of units also employs more than 50 workers (Table 4.30).

In Moti Nagar Industrial Area main industrial activities are manufacture of plastic product, followed by general-purpose machinery, other fabricated metal products, parts and accessories for motor vehicles, other chemical products besides a host of other industrial activities in different proportions.

Jhandewalan Flatted Factories Complex

This is a small industrial area located in Central district, comprising 389 industrial units. Besides 32 establishments other than industrial units, there is no slum household and other residence.

The structure of ownership of industrial units shows tiny set-ups, as more than three-fourths of the industrial units are owned by single proprietors, followed by 12 per cent partnership firms and 10 per cent of private limited enterprises with almost negligible public limited units. The progress of industries in this complex was almost negligible upto 1971 and during the decade of 1971-1981, one-quarter of the total industrial units began during 1981-1991. It is also to add that 73 per cent of the firms started during 1990- 2000. The size of factory area exhibits that there are mostly small size of plots and mainly on rent. In the plots of upto 100 sq. m, 83 per cent of the total industrial units operate on rent and very small fraction on own plots. In the rest other plot sizes, no firm own plots, whereas 12 per cent of the enterprises are in rented premises in 200 to 500 sq.m (Table 4.31).

The gross value of plant and machinery reflects that more than half of the total industrial units have the worth only upto Rs. one lakh. Thus, majority of them are very small units.

Table 4.31 : Jhandewalan Flatted Factory Complex

1. General Attributes

Total number of units	389
Establishment other than industrial units	32
Total number of slum households	0
Residence other than slums	0

2. Type of Ownership

Type	*Proprietor*	*Partnership*	*Private Ltd.*	*Public Ltd.*	*Total*
Industrial Units (%)	76.06	11.74	10.80	1.14	100

3. Growth Pattern of Industries

Years	*Up to 1971*	*1971-81*	*1981-91*	*1991 -2001*	*Total*
Industrial Units (%)	0.52	1.80	24.68	73.01	100

4. Size of Industrial Units (Sq.m)

Plot Size	*1 -100*		*100 - 200*		*200- 500*		*500 +*		*Total*
Category	Own	Rented	Own	Rented	Own	Rented	Own	Rented	
Industrial Units (%)	1.29	83.03	0.00	2.57	0.00	12.85	0.00	0.26	100

5. Gross Value of Plant and Machinery

Value in Lakhs	*Upto 1lakh*	*1-5*	*5-10*	*10-25*	*25-100*	*More than 100*	*Total*
Per cent Units	55.85	37.23	3.19	1.06	1.06	1.60	100

6. Capacity-Utilization of Plant and Machinery

Per cent Utilization	*1-50*	*50-75*	*More than 75*	*Total*
Industrial Units (%)	32.70	19.43	47.87	100

7. Number of Workers Employed

No. of Workers	*1-5*	*6-10*	*11-20*	*21-50*	*More than 50*	*Total*
Industrial Units (%)	36.67	53.33	8.57	9.95	0.48	100

Source : Prepared from Census of Industries (2001) Delhi Pollution Control Committee, Delhi.

This is followed by 37 per cent of the enterprises with the worth of Rs. 1 to 5 lakh. In terms of capacity utilization of plant and machinery, 48 per cent of the industrial units utilize more than three-fourth of the capacity of their plant and machinery, 30 per cent of enterprises work only half of their capacity and nearly one-fifth of units work between half to three-fourths capacity of their plant and machinery. The number of workers employed indicates that 50 per cent of the industrial units work with 5 to 10 workers, followed by 37 firms employing upto 5 workers, and 8 per cent enterprises employing upto 20 workers. Typically, small fraction of units work with upto 50 and more than 50 number of workers (Table 4.31).

In Jhandewalan flatted factories complex, major industrial activities are manufacture of wearing apparel, followed by software consultancy (which is not found in any other industrial area), other chemical products, domestic appliances, tanning and dressing of leather, besides a lot of other industrial activities.

Anand Parbat Industrial Area

This is the largest industrial area located in Central district near Jhandewalan flatted factory complex, comprising of 3727 industrial units. Alongwith 180 establishments other than industrial units, there are also 125 other residences. Surprisingly, no slum households are seen.

The ownership structure reflects that majority of the industrial units are small in size as 90 cent of the firms are owned by single proprietors, 8 per cent are partnership firms. Added to it, private limited are only one per cent and public limited are almost negligible. The growth of industries in this area reveals a slow progress; 5 per cent of the industrial units functioning upto 1971, in the next decade 13 per cent new firms came up. It is shown that during 1981-1991 one-fourth of the total enterprises began, while, 56 per cent firms came into existence after the year 1991. The size of the factory area of the industrial units shows that plots of more than 500 sq. m are negligibly small in number. Even in the plot size of 200 to 500 sq. m only 5 per cent units are seen and more than 70 per cent units operate in the plot of upto 100 sq. m, where 40 per cent own the plots and 30 per cent enterprises are in rented premises. In addition, in 100 to 200 sq. m, most of units are in own plots (Table 4.32).

The gross value of plant and machinery demonstrates that almost all the industrial units are small in nature as 72 per cent of the total industrial units have the worth of their plant and machinery upto Rs. 1 lakh, one-fourth enterprises upto Rs. 5 lakhs and nearly two per cent firms fall in the category of Rs. 5 to 10 lakhs. Whereas, in all other categories very small fraction of enterprises fall. The capacity utilization of the plant and machinery data suggests that 40 per cent of the total industrial units are using more than three-fourths of the capacity of their plant and machinery, nearly one-fourth plants works only on half of their capacity and more than one-third firms use its three-fourth capacity (Table 4.32).

The number of workers employed shows small size of industrial units where 60 per cent of the units work only with 5 workers, more than one-third of the firms have 5 to 10 workers on their roll and 10 to 20 workers are with 3 per cent enterprises. The other categories of workers are in very small fraction. In Anand Parbat Industrial Area majority of the industrial units are engaged in manufacture of other fabricated metal products, followed by parts and accessories for motor vehicles, wholesale of non-agricultural intermediate products, general purpose machinery, special purpose and machinery alongwith a variety of other industrial activities.

Shahdara Industrial Area

This is a small industrial area located in East district accommodating 241 industrial units alongwith 88 establishments other than industrial units. There are more than 352 slum households and 20 residences.

Table 4.32 : Anand Parbat Industrial Area

1. General Attributes

Total number of units	3727
Establishment other than industrial units	180
Total number of slum households	0
Residence other than slums	125

2. Type of Ownership

Type	*Proprietor*	*Partnership*	*Private Ltd.*	*Public Ltd.*	*Total*
Industrial Units (%)	89.80	8.26	1.258	6.60	100

3. Growth Pattern of Industries

Years	*Up to 1971*	*1971-81*	*1981-91*	*1991 -2001*	*Total*
Industrial Units (%)	5.37	13.17	25.03	56.43	100

4. Size of Industrial Units (Sq. m)

Plot Size	*1 -100*		*100 - 200*		*200- 500*		*500 +*		*Total*
Category	Own	Rented	Own	Rented	Own	Rented	Own	Rented	
Industrial Units (%)	38.87	31.82	18.14	3.49	5.21	1.69	0.38	0.41	100

5. Gross Value of Plant and Machinery

Value in Lakhs	*Upto 1lakh*	*1-5*	*5-10*	*10-25*	*25-100*	*More than 100*	*Total*
Per cent Units	72.56	24.23	1.66	0.72	0.35	0.48	100

6. Capacity-Utilization of Plant and Machinery

Per cent Utilization	*1-50*	*50-75*	*More than 75*	*Total*
Industrial Units (%)	24.12	36.39	39.49	100

7. Number of Workers Employed

No. of Workers	*1-5*	*6-10*	*11-20*	*21-50*	*More than 50*	*Total*
Industrial Units (%)	59.95	35.70	3.41	0.81	0.13	100

Source : Prepared from Census of Industries (2001) Delhi Pollution Control Committee, Delhi.

The ownership pattern of the industrial units shows that most of the units are of small structure as 79 per cent of the total firms are owned by single proprietors, followed by 13 per cent of enterprises with partnership and 7 per cent private limited. It should also be noted that no firm is of public limited nature. The progress of industries reflects that upto 1971 there were only 4 per cent of the total industries, in the next two decades 6 per cent new firms came up in each of the two periods, while 82 per cent of the industrial units started during the year 1991-2001. The size of factory of the industrial units exhibits a mixed pattern where in the plot size of upto 100 sq.m, 43 per cent firms are operating in rented premises with 10 per cent in owned plots. In the category of 100 to 200 sq.m, 16 per cent enterprises have own plots and 10 per cent are on rent. It is also shown that 7 per cent firms own plots of each category, *i.e.* 200 to 500 sq.m and more than 500 sq.m (Table 4.33).

The pattern of gross value of plant and machinery demonstrates that half of the total industrial units have the worth of their plant and machinery upto Rs. one lakh, more than one-third of the firms worth upto Rs. 5 lakhs and 5 per cent of the enterprises fall in slab of Rs.10 to 25 lakhs.

The capacity utilization of the plant and machinery shows that 53 per cent of the industrial units use more than three-fourth capacity of their plant and machinery, 30 per cent units work on half of their capacity and 15 per cent of the firms use its three-fourth of their capacity. The number of workers employed in the industrial units indicate smaller structure of firms where one-fourth firms work with upto 5 workers, 55 per cent enterprises have 5 to 10 workers with them and 15 per cent of the units employ 10 to 20 workers. In Shahdara industrial area the main industrial activities engaging maximum firms are manufacture of basic precious and non-ferrous metal, followed by insulated wires and cables, other fabricated metal products, wholesale of non-agriculture intermediate products, maintenance and repair of motor vehicle and others.

Narela Industrial Area

This is the fourth largest industrial area located in Northwest

Table 4.33 : Shahdara Industrial Area

1. General Attributes

Total number of units	241
Establishment other than industrial units	88
Total number of slum households	352
Residence other than slums	21

2. Type of Ownership

Type	*Proprietor*	*Partnership*	*Private Ltd.*	*Public Ltd.*	*Total*
Industrial Units (%)	79.27	13.41	6.71	0.61	100

3. Growth Pattern of Industries

Years	*Up to 1971*	*1971-81*	*1981-91*	*1991 -2001*	*Total*
Industrial Units (%)	4.14	6.64	6.22	82.99	100

4. Size of Industrial Units (Sq. m)

Plot Size	*1 -100*		*100 - 200*		*200- 500*		*500 +*		*Total*
Category	Own	Rented	Own	Rented	Own	Rented	Own	Rented	
Industrial Units (%)	9.54	43.15	16.18	9.96	7.47	4.15	7.47	2.07	100

5. Gross Value of Plant and Machinery

Value in Lakhs	*Upto 1lakh*	*1-5*	*5-10*	*10-25*	*25-100*	*More than 100*	*Total*
Per cent Units	50.00	38.75	2.50	5.00	3.75	0.00	100

6. Capacity-Utilization of Plant and Machinery

Per cent Utilization	*1-50*	*50-75*	*More than 75*	*Total*
Industrial Units (%)	31.21	15.03	53.76	100

7. Number of Workers Employed

No. of Workers	*1-5*	*6-10*	*11-20*	*21-50*	*More than 50*	*Total*
Industrial Units (%)	25.74	55.58	14.71	2.94	0.74	100

Source : Prepared from Census of Industries (2001) Delhi Pollution Control Committee, Delhi.

Delhi, comprising of more than 2073 industrial units. There are 9 other commercial establishments and slum households and other residences do not exist.

The structure of ownership reveals that there are small sizes of the firms where 78 per cent of the industrial units are with single proprietors, followed by 14 enterprises are of partnership nature. Private limited firms are 7 per cent but public limited are almost negligible. The progress of industries reflects that this area has developed only after 1991. It has been seen that during 1971 to 1991, there were no industrial units, almost hundred per cent of the total number of industrial units began during the decade 1991 to 2001. The size of the factory area shows mainly the plot of bigger size in rented category. In plot size of upto 100 sq. m, there are almost nil units. In the category of 100 to 200 sq. m, very small fraction of firms operates. The 200 to 500 sq. m plots accommodates 10 per cent unit in owned category with 2 per cent on rent. In addition to it, in more than 500 sq.m plots, 80 per cent of the enterprises are in rented premises and only 3 per cent in own plots (Table 4.34).

The gross value of plant and machinery indicates 60 per cent of the industrial units have the worth upto Rs. 1 to 5 lakhs. In the slab of Rs. 10 to 25 lakhs there are 10 per cent of the firms, whereas in the next two categories there are very small proportion of units. The capacity utilization of plant and machinery reflects one-third of the industrial units work on half of their capacity, 28 per cent firm use upto three-fourth of their capacity and more than one-third of the enterprises uses more than three-fourth capacity of their plant and machinery. The details on employment of workers elucidates that 56 per cent of the industrial units employ 5 to 10 workers, more than one-fourth of the firms work with 10 to 20 workers and 10 per cent of the enterprises have upto 5 workers with them. In addition, small number of firms employ upto 50 and more than 50 workers (Table 4.34).

In Narela Industrial Area majority of the industrial units are engaged in manufacturing of plastic products, followed by basic chemicals, grain mill products, footwear, the manufacture of basic iron and steel alongwith a variety of other industrial activities.

Table 4.34 : Narela Industrial Area

1. General Attributes

Total number of units	2073
Establishment other than industrial units	9
Total number of slum households	0
Residence other than slums	0

2. Type of Ownership

Type	*Proprietor*	*Partnership*	*Private Ltd.*	*Public Ltd.*	*Total*
Industrial Units (%)	78.53	14.11	7.06	0.31	100

3. Growth Pattern of Industries

Years	*Up to 1971*	*1971-81*	*1981-91*	*1991 -2001*	*Total*
Industrial Units (%)	0.00	0.00	0.05	99.95	100

4. Size of Industrial Units (Sq. m)

Plot Size	*1 -100*		*100 - 200*		*200- 500*		*500 +*		*Total*
Category	Own	Rented	Own	Rented	Own	Rented	Own	Rented	
Industrial Units (%)	0.05	0.10	0.14	0.14	9.36	2.75	2.94	84.52	100

5. Gross Value of Plant and Machinery

Value in Lakhs	*Upto 1lakh*	*1-5*	*5-10*	*10-25*	*25-100*	*More than 100*	*Total*
Per cent Units	11.97	59.86	13.38	9.86	3.52	1.41	100

6. Capacity Utilization of Plant and Machinery

Per cent Utilization	*1-50*	*50-75*	*More than 75*	*Total*
Industrial Units (%)	34.48	28.84	36.68	100

7. Number of Workers Employed

No. of Workers	*1-5*	*6-10*	*11-20*	*21-50*	*More than 50*	*Total*
Industrial Units (%)	9.31	56.28	28.34	5.26	0.81	100

Source : Prepared from Census of Industries (2001) Delhi Pollution Control Committee, Delhi.

Conclusion

The illustration of industries of Delhi in detail at different levels provides a clear picture of economic structure of industries. The secondary sector has a significant role to play in economy of city, as it has been elucidated from analyses in the chapter. The discussion on economic parameters at systematic level has provided insight into inter-industrial areas scenario. The analysis with regional approach analyzing each industrial area in detail reflects upon intra-industrial area picture.

It has been indicated that in most of the industrial areas maximum industrial units came up only in last decade, *i.e.* 1991-2001 as compared to the previous two decades between 1971-1991. This clearly indicated the relevance of open economy and globalization, thus, indicates towards impact of policies. It has been found that nearly, two-third of all industrial units are located in six large industrial areas, namely, Anand Parbat (17.23 per cent), Mayapuri (15.10 per cent), Okhla Industrial Area (11.34 per cent), Narela (9.59 per cent), Wazirpur (7.7 per cent) and Kirti Nagar (6.82 per cent). Only one-third of the units are located in remaining 22 industrial areas. On the other hand, another six areas each accounting for having less than 1 per cent of the total industrial units, includes Tilak Nagar, Small-scale Industries Area, Rajasthan Udyog Nagar, Small and Medium Industries Area, Okhla Industrial Estate and Mohan Co-operative Industrial Area. In terms of expenditures it has been seen that in the industrial unit of small investment expenses on raw material are more while as the investment range increase the expenditure of wage and others also significant. On an average, 8.8 per cent of the units' employ upto 20 workers, 37 per cent units employ between 1-5 workers, and 37 per cent industrial units employ between 6 to 10 workers. Maximum firms of Mohan Co-operative employ more than 50 workers. The main industrial activities are manufacture of fabricated metal products being pursued by more than 15 per cent industrial units, plastic products, parts and accessories of motor vehicle accounts for five per cent each. While furniture, general purpose machinery, special purpose machinery, iron steel, weaving apparel counts for more than 3 per cent each. Others like, printing, manufacture of footwears, business activities, transport activities, wholesale of household goods, retail of goods in specialized stores and chemical products engaged less than 3 per cent each. In terms of value of plant and machinery 92 per cent of industrial units fall in the category of tiny sectors, 5 per cent belong to small scale. Industries having plant and machinery over Rs. one crore comprise 3 per cent of the total units. The ownership pattern reveals that single proprietors own 69 per cent industrial units and partnership accounts for 19 per cent of units. Added to it private limited firms are 10 per cent while public limited units are 2 per cent. Maximum public limited firms are seen in Mohan Co-operative and Okhla Industrial Estate while maximum private limited are found in Small-Scale Industries Area. The capacity utilization reveals that one-fourth of the units have been utilizing less than 50 per cent of their installed capacity and 30 per cent unit work on upto 75 per cent of their capacity. Interestingly, only in Kirti Nagar Industrial Area more than 80 per cent units use more than 75 per cent capacity.

As regard the size and plot ownership it has been found that 60 per cent of the industrial units have owned industrial plots, and other operating on rented plots. Nearly 57 per cent of the total industrial units have been operating in plot size of less than 200 sq. m. It has been seen that Okhla and Jhandewalan flattered factories have more than 90 per cent units in rented premises. Surprisingly, highest owned plots are seen in Nangloi (95 %). Plot of biggest size, *i.e.* more than 500 sq. m are owned maximum in Mohan Co-operative Industrial Area while rented plots of the size are seen in Okhla Industrial Estate. In almost all-industrial areas, there are establishments other than industrial enterprises. The total number of such establishments are 3972, of which maximum are concentrated in Wazirpur, Mangolpuri and Okhla Industrial Area. While, Okhla flatted factories has no such establishment. As regards slums, maximum dwelling are seen in Wazirpur. Residence other than slums has been found maximum in G.T.Karnal Road Industrial Area.

References

1. Economic Census (1998) Directorate of Economics and Statistics, Government of National Capital Territory of Delhi, Delhi.
2. Economic Survey (2001-02) Department of Planning, Government of National Capital Territory of Delhi, Delhi.
3. For groups refer Appendix I.
4. Economic Census (1998) Directorate of Economics and Statistics, Government of National Capital Territory of Delhi, Delhi.

Chapter - 5

Industries and Environmental Pollution

Introduction

The previous chapter presented an analysis on role of industries in the economy of Delhi. The discussion included growth and development of industries and Master Plan, spatial distribution of industrial areas, analysis on different economic parameters among approved industrial areas, and detailed analysis of each industrial area with reference to economic structure. The present chapter deals with an analysis of environmental role of industries in urban economy. This chapter includes spatial distribution of polluting industries, non-polluting industries, air pollution, wastewater generation and hazardous waste generation. The pollution is also analyzed at industrial sector level alongwith illustration of existing pollution management practices.

Industrial sector, which plays a vital role in the economic growth of National Capital Territory of Delhi by contributing nearly 21 per cent to the state income and providing employment to about 41.4 per cent workers, also plays an environmental role. The manufacturing sector, besides acting as a vibrant source of creating growth in other sectors like transport, services etc., causes pollution of various nature to the system of the city. The main manufacturing process that contributes towards negative aspect of production chain are pickling, electroplating, anodizing, textile washing/dying, automobile service station, grinding mills, thermal power plants etc. Industries are causing as well as adding to the air, water, noise and solid (waste) pollution. It has been estimated that of the total, 20 per cent of air pollution is caused by industries in Delhi; it has been estimated that of the total 2082 ml/d wastewater, industrial discharge is 81.4 ml/d[1] . In terms of solid waste generation that is nearly 6000 tonnes per day of municipal solid waste, 200 tonnes per day hazardous industrial wastes[2] . The industrial pollutions are more toxic, hazardous, varied in nature and highly concentrated in terms of space and time. Thus, in case of pollution caused by manufacturing sector it is not proportion share in total pollution is important rather the significant aspect is nature, content and impact of these highly concentrated nature of pollution. In this chapter polluting industries in Delhi are analyzed at two levels : (a) spatial distribution of non-polluting and polluting industries in approved industrial areas; (b) spatial distribution of air pollution, wastewater generation and hazardous waste; and (c) levels of pollution in different industrial sectors and existing pollution practices.

Spatial Distribution of Non-Polluting and Polluting Industries

It has been seen that of the total 21627 industrial units, 59 per cent units are non-polluting, *i.e.* these industries are not causing any environmental concern. Rest of 41 per cent industrial units are polluting ones that are playing economic role alongwith embedded environmental pollution. These 41 per cent units include 19 per cent industries that are responsible for causing hazardous waste, 13 per cent units generating wastewater and 9 per cent industrial units are air polluting (Fig. 5.1).

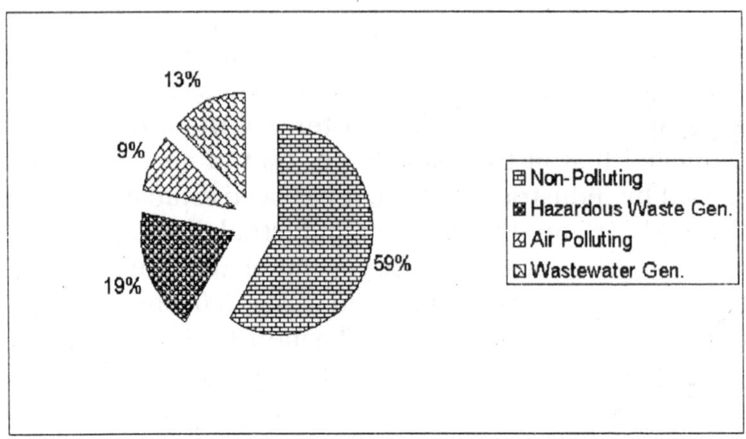

Fig. 5.1 : Types of Polluting Industrial Units

Non-Polluting Industries

Of the total 21627 industrial units, more than 70 per cent of them are found dry units or non-polluting which are not causing any kind of environmental concerns, thus, not adding negative externalities in the industrial production chain. The distribution of these non-polluting industrial units indicates that Kirti Nagar Industrial Area has maximum number of non-polluting units, *i.e.* more than 95 per cent, because more than 40 per cent units in this area are engaged in trading followed. This is followed by Okhla and Jhandewalan flatted factories complex where more than 90 per cent of industrial units are non-polluting ones where assembly of electronic components and dry textile processing are significant industrial sectors. Other areas are Udyog Nagar, Nangloi and Mangolpuri where more than 80 per cent of the industrial units are of non-polluting nature, dealing mainly with plastic products and dry textiles processing activity (Fig. 5.2).

The distribution of non-polluting industrial units as seen from Fig. 5.2 shows that 70 to 80 per cent of the industrial

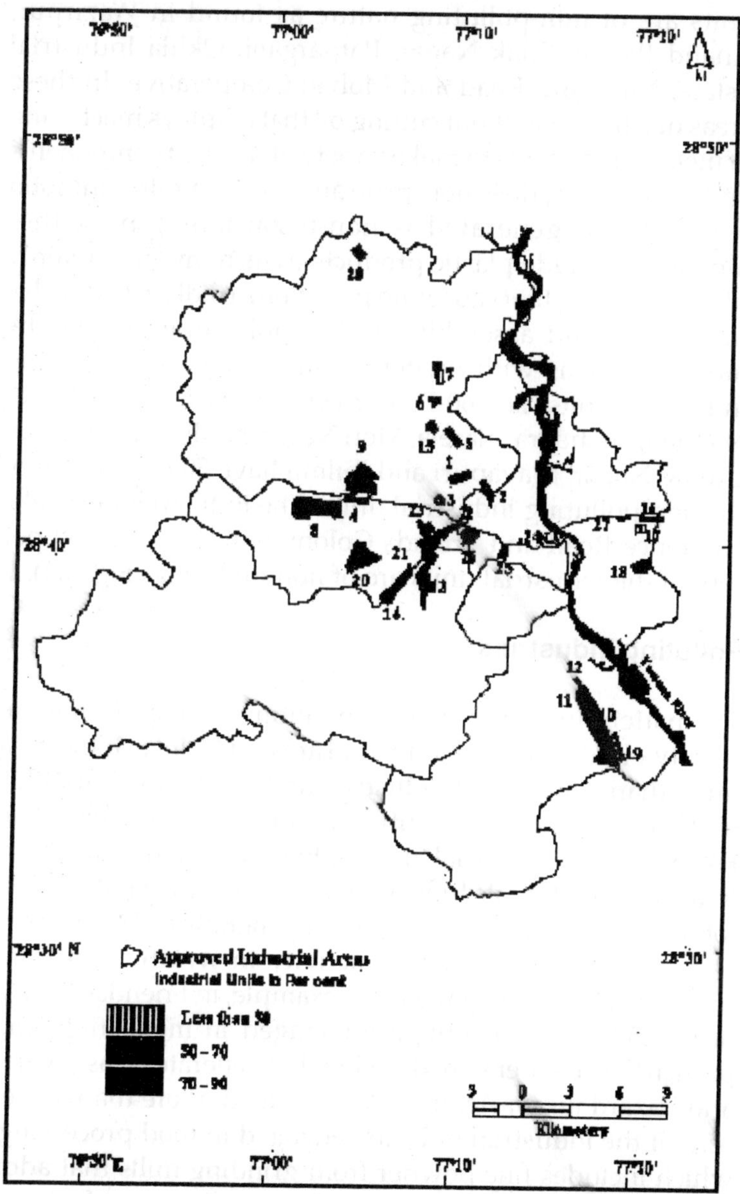

Fig. 5.2 : Distribution of Non-Polluting Industries, 2001

units are of non-polluting nature as found in Wazirpur, Anand Parbat, Tilak Nagar, Patparganj, Okhla Industrial Estate, Najafgarh Road and Mohan Co-operative. In these areas machining without cutting oil that employs machining of metal components to make variety of finished components and goods, thus, does not create any kind of pollution; solid waste that is generated is non-hazardous type. Other industries include plastic products (which involves mainly plastic molding that causes no pollution), trading, textile dry processing and assembly of electronic components.The industrial areas with moderate number of non-polluting industrial units, *i.e.*, 60-70 per cent are G.T.Karnal Road, Naraina, Shahdara, Narela, Moti Nagar, Badli and Rajasthan Udyog Nagar. Mayapuri and Jhilmil have 50-60 per cent of the non-polluting industrial units. The industrial areas like Lawrence Road and Friends Colony with less than 50 per cent of the industrial units are of non-polluting (Fig. 5.2).

Polluting Industries

The pattern of distribution of polluting industrial units in twenty-eight approved industrial areas of Delhi exhibits that more than a quarter of industrial units of the total of 21627 units in Delhi are of polluting nature. As is evident from Fig. 5.3, in the industrial areas of Friends Colony, Lawrence Road and Small-Scale Industries Area, more than half of their total industrial units are pollution generating. This is clear from the kind of industrial activity in which significant number of units is engaged. For example, in Friends Colony, nearly 50 per cent units are engaged in metal finishing particularly copper wire drawing that generates wastewater and hazardous waste. In Lawrence Road, more than 50 per cent of the industrial units are engaged in food processing, which includes fine powder from grinding mills that adds to particulate matter in the air, fruits and vegetables/meat processing, confectioneries and bakeries also causes wastewater. In Small-Scale Industries Area, metal finishing is a significant sector contributing towards pollution in the form of air, water and hazardous waste.

There are two industrial areas with 40-50 per cent of their industrial units causing environmental problems, *i.e.* Jhilmil and Mayapuri. In Jhilmil, metal finishing particularly copper wire drawing and chemicals are engaging more than 40 per cent of its units. Both of these activities create pollution of the above three types. The upper moderate category industrial areas, where 30-40 per cent of the industrial units are pollution generating, these areas are Rajasthan Udyog Nagar, Moti Nagar, Shahdara, Narela, Naraina and G.T. Karnal Road where metal finishing, rubber and food processing are significant industrial activities (Fig. 5.3).

The lower middle category is the industrial areas where 20-30 per cent of the industrial units contribute towards some or other kinds of pollution. These industrial areas include Mohan Cooperatives, Okhla, Small and Medium Industrial Areas, Wazirpur, Patparganj, Tilak Nagar, Najafgarh Road and Anand Parbat, where printing, machinery, rubber, paper products, and metal finishing are significant industrial sectors. The industrial areas where only 10-20 per cent of the industrial units are polluting and the rest are non-polluting include Jhandewalan and Okhla Flatted Factories, Mangolpuri, Nangloi and Udyog Nagar where most of the industrial activities are non-polluting. These comprise assembly of electronic components and textile dry processing. The only industrial area, i.e. Kirti Nagar that has lowest per cent of its industries causing pollution problems because more than 40 per cent of the units are engaged in trading (Fig. 5.3).

Of the total 21,627 industrial units in the twenty-eight approved industrial areas, more than a quarter of them is pollution-oriented. Of those, more than 5,000 polluting industrial units, 12 per cent are causing air pollution, 16 per cent are generating wastewater and one-third of them are

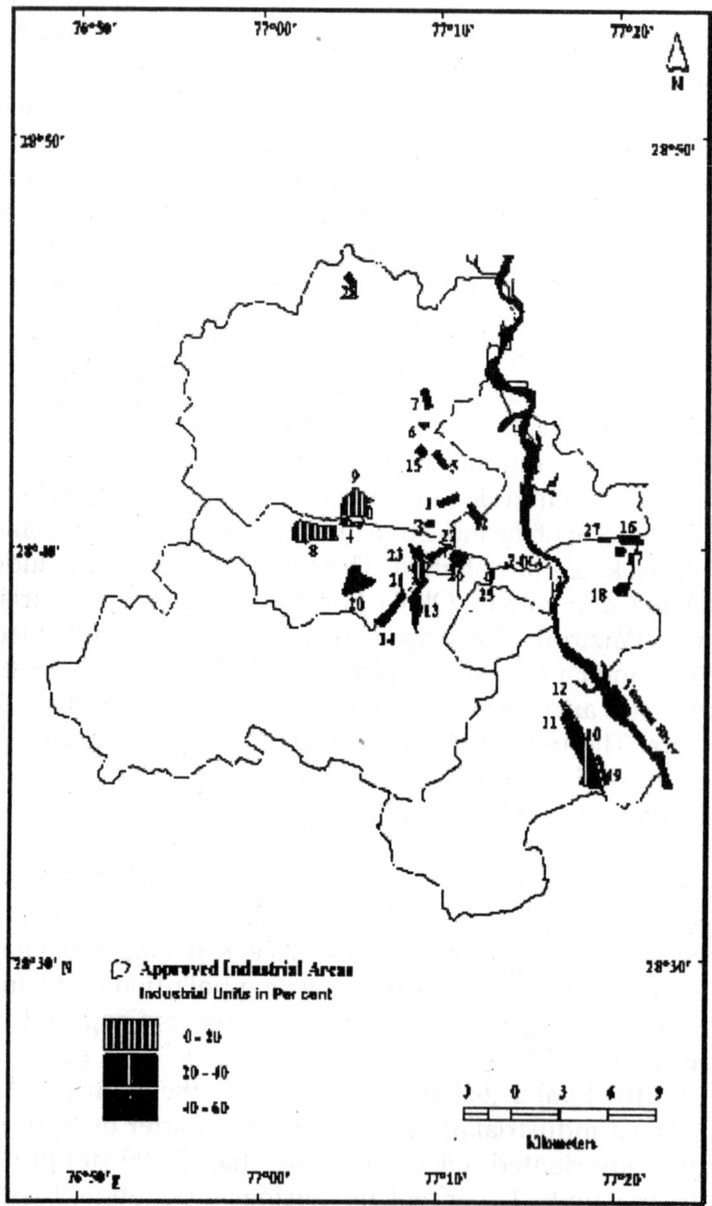

Fig. 5.3 : Distribution of Polluting Industries, 2001

creating hazardous wastes. The industrial units that are causing air pollution as well as hazardous wastes are more than 3 per cent; similarly, industrial units causing wastewater alongwith hazardous waste are more than 13 per cent. Industrial units with all the above three kinds of production externalities, *i.e.* air pollution, wastewater and hazardous wastes are nearly one-fifth of the total polluting industrial wastes (Fig. 5.3).

Air Polluting Industrial Units

The total polluting industrial units are 5773, of which 717 (12%) industrial units are causing air pollution. The distribution of these air polluting industrial units among different industrial areas reveals that air pollution is virtually not happening in the industrial areas of Jhandewalan, Okhla Flatted Factories, Okhla Industrial Estate and Mohan Co-operatives. The Industrial Areas of Lawrence Road, and Tilak Nagar have more than half of their units causing air pollution. Food products processing at Lawrence Road causes air pollution in terms of particular matter from mills and boilers; rubber industries at Tilak Nagar cause steam from furnaces. Narela, Najafgarh Road and Moti Nagar Industrial Areas have 30-40 per cent of their industrial units are polluting. In these areas also food products and rubber are important sector. Anand Parbat, Mangolpuri, and Rajasthan Udyog Nagar areas have 20-30 per cent of their industrial units of this kind. In these areas rubber, metal finishing and casting are responsible for air pollution. Kirti Nagar, Patparganj, Badli, Small and Medium Industrial Area and Udyog Nagar accommodate 10-20 per cent units contributing towards air pollution. In more than ten industrial areas, namely, Shahdara, Friends Colony, Jhilmil, Mangolpuri, Naraina, Okhla, S.S.I, Wazirpur, G.T Karnal Road and a small number of other industrial areas (Fig. 5.4).

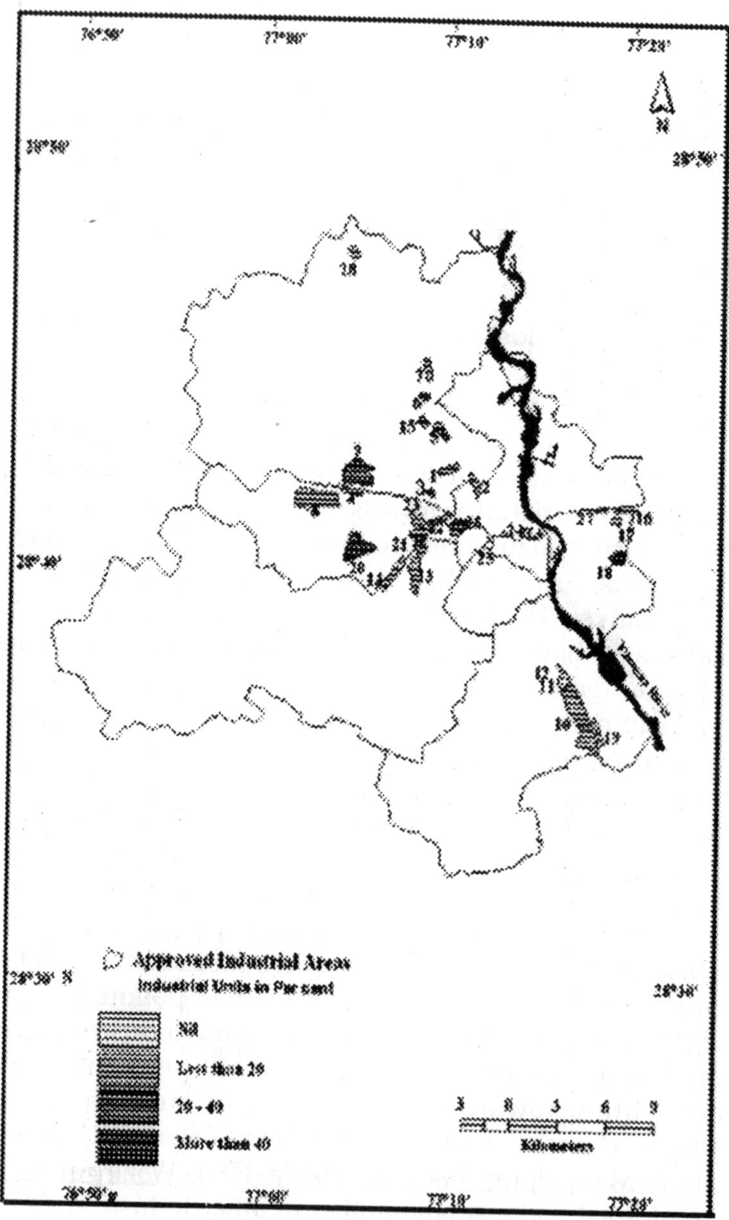

Fig. 5.4 : Air Polluting Industries

Wastewater Generating Industrial Units

Out of the total 5773 polluting industrial units, more than 900 are polluting in terms of wastewater-generation. The distribution of these wastewater-generating units indicates that maximum of more than 40 per cent of the industrial units are in Mohan Co-operatives. Electroplating (cause wastewater containing copper and other heavy metal), machinery with cutting oil, service stations etc. are significant activities. Anand Parbat and Narela have 30-40 per cent of the industrial units generating wastewater from metal finishing and machining activities (Fig. 5.5).

The industrial areas like Jhandewalan, Okhla flatted factories, Mangolpuri, Rajasthan Udyog Nagar, Moti Nagar and G.T Karnal Road contain 20-30 per cent of industrial units that are of this nature. The main responsible sectors are electronic component, rubber, printing, metal finishing. Eight industrial areas belong to the category of 10-20 per cent polluting units, *i.e.* Shahdara, Kirti Nagar, Patparganj, Okhla area, Nangloi, Wazirpur, Lawrence Road and Udyog Nagar. The industries related to wastewater are metal finishing, food processing, and chemicals. In Najafgarh Road, Badli, Jhilmil, Friends Colony, Mayapuri, Naraina, Small and Medium Industrial Area, 10 per cent of the units cause pollution. Tilak Nagar is the only industrial area where no water polluting industrial unit exits (Fig. 5.5).

Hazardous Waste Generating Industrial Units

Total hazardous waste generating industrial units are more than one-third of the total 5773 polluting units, which is higher than the number of air and water polluting industrial units. Among the different industrial areas it is found that more than 70 per cent industrial units of Jhandewalan flatted factories and Mayapuri are causing hazardous wastes, as reflected from the prevalent kind of industrial activities.

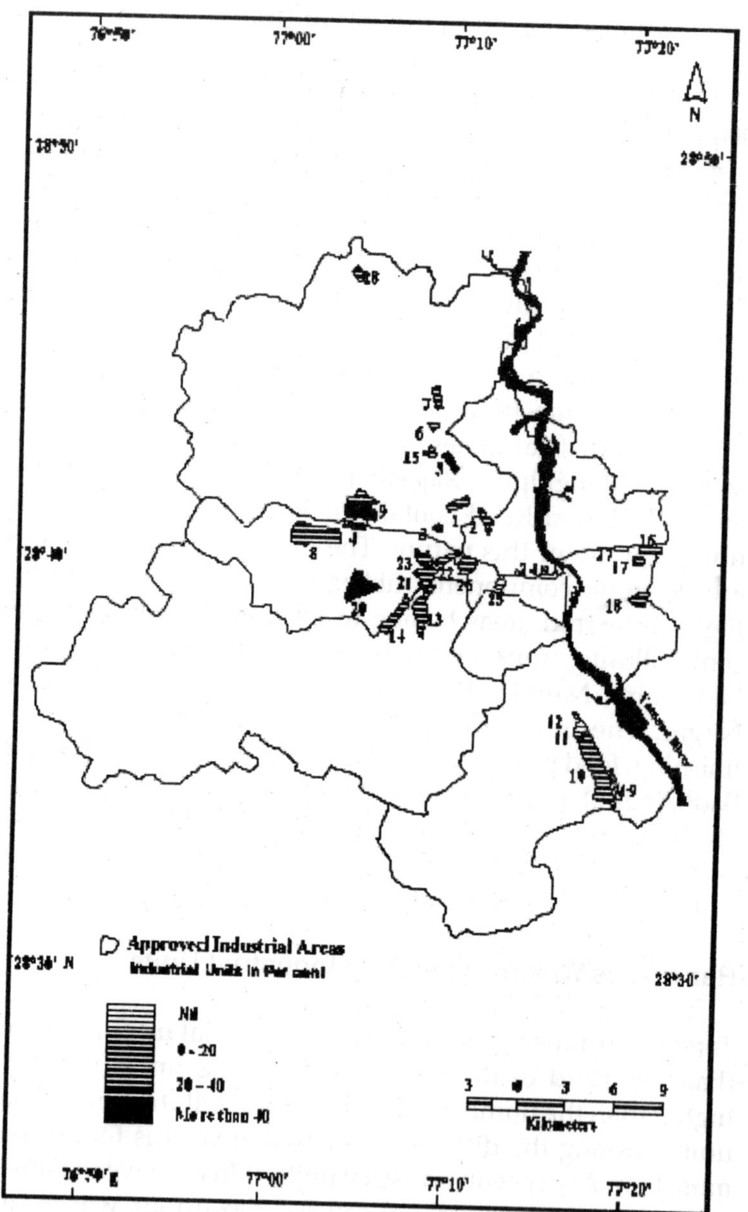

Fig. 5.5 : Wastewater Generating Industries, 2001

These include electronic components, printing, service stations in which treatment of wastewater generates hazardous waste. Okhla flatted factories follow this, with 60-70 per cent of the industrial units of this nature where electronic components, machining and printing are important sectors. In the three industrial areas of Naraina, Kirti Nagar and G.T Karnal Road 50-60, 40-50 and 30-40 per cent units, respectively, create hazardous waste. In the areas of Najafgarh Road, Mohan Co-operative, Patparganj, Okhla, Mangolpuri and Nangloi 20-30 per cent are hazardous waste generating units. These include mainly printing, electronic components, service stations and machining. Anand Parbat, Moti Nagar, Friends Colony and Lawrence Road areas have 10-20 per cent of the industrial units responsible for such waste. In many areas like Narela, Shahdara, Jhilmil, Badli, Small-Scale Industries Area, Rajasthan Udyog Nagar, Wazirpur and Small and Medium Industrial area have less than 10 per cent units are of this nature. Whereas, the only area without hazardous waste generating industrial units is Tilak Nagar (Fig. 5.6).

Air and Hazardous Waste Generating Units

Only 3 per cent of the total polluting units are responsible for this kind of double pollution, simultaneously. Wazirpur has maximum (25%) number of this type of industries followed by Mayapuri, Anand Parbat and Lawrence Road with 12 to 20 per cent of these units. In addition to it, the other areas that include G.T. Karnal Road, Rajasthan Udyog Nagar, Small-Scale Industries Area, Nangloi, Badli, Jhilmil, Friends Colony, Patparganj, Najafgarh Road, Moti Nagar and Shahdara have upto 5 per cent of these units. The major polluting activities include metal finishing and metal treatment (Table 5.1). It is seen from Table 5.1 that there are ten industrial areas, where such industries are not found which are responsible for both air pollution and hazardous

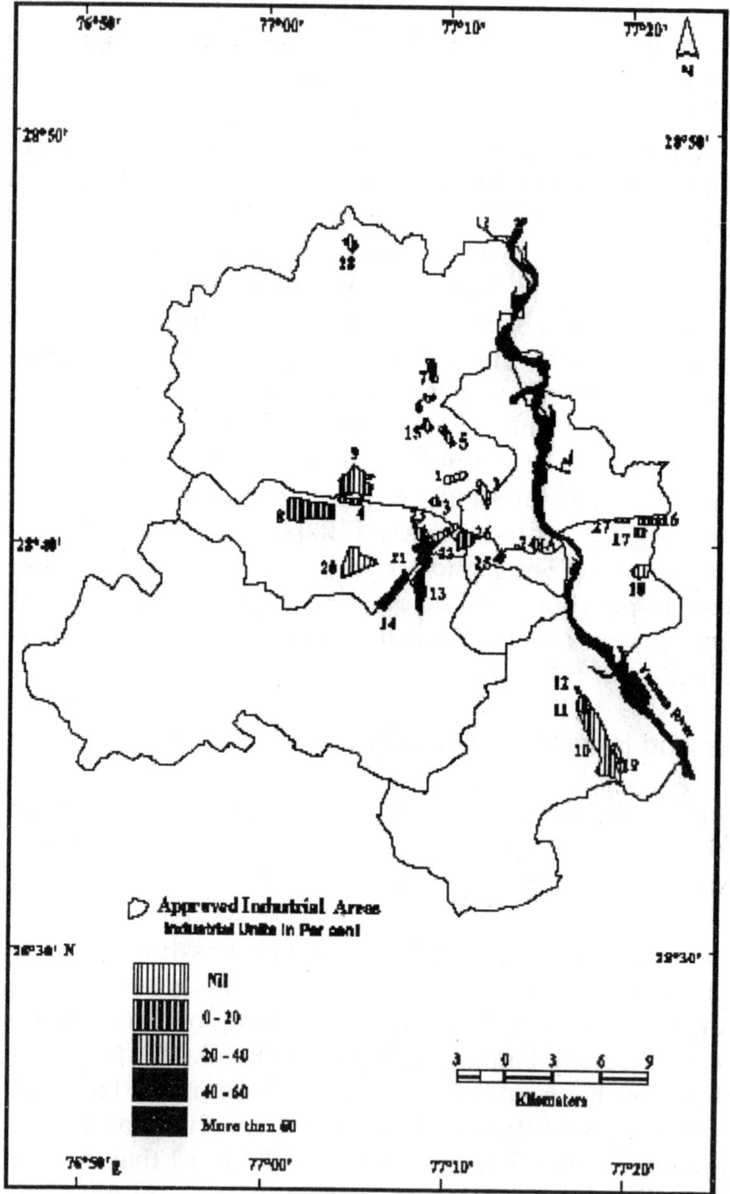

Fig. 5.6 : Hazardous Waste Generating Industries, 2001

waste together. These include Small and Medium Industries Area, Mangolpuri, Okhla Estate, Okhla flatted factories, Naraina, Mohan Co-operatives, Tilak Nagar, Kirti Nagar, Jhandewalan flatted factories and Narela.

Wastewater and Hazardous Waste Generating Units

Thirteen per cent of the total 5,773 polluting units are such that generate wastewater as well as hazardous waste together. The activities of such nature are metal finishing, casting and chemicals. As reflected from Table 5.1 Okhla Industrial Area, Mayapuri, Jhilmil and Friends Colony have maximum number of such units ranging from 10 to 13 per cent. It is also shown that Naraina, Wazirpur, Anand Parbat and Shahdara follow with 5 to 8 per cent such units. Added to it, the other areas including G.T Karnal Road, Lawrence Road, Udyog Nagar, Small-Scale Industries Area, Nangloi, Mangolpuri, Okhla Estate, Naraina, Badli, Patparganj, Najafgarh Road, Mohan Cooperatives, Tilak Nagar, Moti Nagar and Narela have less than five per cent of these units. Interestingly, there are very few areas as Rajasthan Udyog Nagar and Jhandewalan flatted factories, which has no such units that causes above two pollutions together (Table 5.1).

Air Pollution, Wastewater and Hazardous Waste Generating Units

Nearly one-fifth of the total polluting industrial units are such that generate all the above kinds of pollution in their production process, simultaneously. The industrial activities mainly include metal finishing, castings, and chemicals. As is evident from Table 5.1, Wazirpur has maximum number of these types of industrial activities, *i.e.* 23.75 per cent of them are located there. It is also to be added that Anand Parbat, Okhla Industrial Area and Mayapuri follow with 11 to 17 per cent of these units. In addition to it, there are areas with less than 7 per cent of these units, which include G.T

Table 5.1: Industrial Units by Types of Pollutions (in per cent)

Industrial Areas	*A/HW*	*WW/HW*	*A/WW/HW*
Wazirpur	25.00	6.38	23.75
G.T. Karnal Road	0.81	2.67	4.69
Lawrence Road	13.71	4.12	0.73
Udyog Nagar	1.61	1.03	1.03
Rajasthan Udyog Nagar	1.61	0.00	1.03
Small and Medium Industries	0.00	0.21	2.35
Small-Scale Industries	4.03	1.85	1.32
Nangloi	0.81	1.03	0.29
Mangolpuri	0.00	1.65	1.47
Okhla	2.42	10.91	12.61
Okhla Estate	0.00	1.85	0.88
Okhla Flatted Factory	0.00	0.21	0.15
Naraina	0.00	8.44	3.37
Mayapuri	17.74	11.93	11.58
Badli	2.42	0.82	6.74
Jhilmil	5.65	11.32	3.52
Friends Colony	0.81	13.17	0.73
Patparganj	0.81	1.65	1.03
Mohan Cooperative	0.00	0.82	0.15
Tilak Nagar	0.00	0.41	0.15
Kirti Nagar	0.00	0.41	1.17
Najafgarh	3.23	3.09	1.03
Moti Nagar	3.23	0.82	1.17
Birla Mills Site	N.A.	N.A.	N.A.
Jhandewalan Flatted Factory	0.00	0.00	0.00
Anand Parbat	15.32	7.61	17.30
Shahadara	0.81	5.35	0.88
Narela	0.00	2.26	0.88
Total	100.00	100.00	100.00

Source : Prepared from Census on Hazardous Industries (2001) Delhi Pollution Control Committee, Delhi.

Note : A-air pollution, WW—wastewater generation, HW-hazardous waste.

Karnal Road, Lawrence Road, Udyog Nagar, Small-Scale Industries Area, Nangloi, Mangolpuri, Okhla Estate, Okhla flatted factories, Naraina, Badli, Jhilmil, Patparganj, Najafgarh Road, Mohan Co-operatives, Najafgarh, Tilak Nagar, Moti Nagar, Shahdara and Narela. Surprisingly, Jhandewalan flatted factories is the only area that does not have such industries (Table 5.1).

Distribution of Non-Polluting Industries According to Industrial Sectors

In Delhi's 28 approved industrial areas, 73 per cent are non-polluting industries that play economic role and do not cause environmental problems. The number and distribution of non-polluting industries among industrial areas and industrial sectors is different. Some sectors are absolutely pollution free, whereas some have few pollution free processes. In others, few are generating only water or air pollution and some processes are responsible for combination of different types of pollution. The pattern of non-polluting industrial units is illustrated in the following paragraphs (Table 5.2 and Appendix XI-A).

Assembly

This sector includes most of non-polluting industrial units as seen from Table 5.2 that out of more than 900 units in this field close to 95 per cent are non-polluting. These units are spread most of industrial areas, with maximum of 160 in Okhla Industrial Area, followed by 100 units in Anand Parbat, also same number of units in Mayapuri and Okhla flatted factories. It is also to be added that more than 50 per cent units are seen each in Naraina and Wazirpur. In Shahdara, Rajasthan Udyog Nagar, Small and Medium Industrial Area Small-Scale Industrial Area this sector is found almost negligible.

Chemical

More than 300 industrial units, out of nearly 450 industrial units, are of non-polluting nature. These include wax products and polyester, which are non-polluting processes. These non-polluting chemical units are located in maximum number, *i.e.* 60 units in Mayapuri, followed by 43 units in Wazirpur, 30 in Okhla area, 20 in G.T. Karnal Road and Jhilmil each. More than ten units are seen in many areas like Narela, Jhandewalan flatted factories, Najafgarh Road, Badli and Naraina (Table 5.2).

Glass

Of the total 50 units engaged in glass process, more than 40 units are non-polluting, which handle glass-cutting, painting, blowing, beveling etc. These non-polluting units are scattered in small numbers in Wazirpur, G.T. Karnal Road, Okhla area, Mayapuri, Badli, Anand Parbat, and Kirti Nagar.

Leather

The sub-sector of leather stitching is non-polluting. It is seen (Table 5.2) that of 116 industrial units, 97 per cent are non-polluting. The Okhla Industrial Area has 30 units, 20 units are found in each Mayapuri and Jhandewalan Flatted Factories. Udyog Nagar has ten units and less than ten units are spread in Anand Parbat, Najafgarh, Moti Nagar, Naraina and Badli.

Machining

Among the various processes, machining without cutting oil is pollution free process, in which more than 6000, out of the total of nearly 7000 industrial units, are engaged. The distribution of these non-polluting industrial units in different industrial areas shows 700 units in Okhla Industrial Area. It is shown that 100-200 units are found in G.T. Karnal Road, Badli, Kirti Nagar, Najafgarh Road and Naraina. This activity is found in all industrial areas in smaller or larger proportions (Table 5.2).

Textile

Textile dry processing industrial units are non-polluting which includes the processes of spinning, weaving, knitting, twisting. They count nearly 1000 units of the total of little more than 1200 units. These non-polluting units are located in maximum number, *i.e.* more than 300 in Okhla Industrial Area, followed by Wazirpur, Anand Parbat, Jhandewalan flatted factories, Mayapuri, Naraina, Patparganj, Mangolpuri, Udyog Nagar and G.T Karnal Road. This activity is seen in every industrial area in some or other proportions except Tilak Nagar (Table 5.2).

Wood

Of the total of more than 600 industrial units, almost 99 per cent units are of non-polluting nature. Maximum concentration of these units is seen in Kirti Nagar followed by small numbers in Anand Parbat, Okhla area, Okhla Estate, Mayapuri, G.T. Karnal Road, Naraina and a few units in Badli, Jhilmil and Mangolpuri.

Food

In food sector, the sub-sectors of confectionery and cold storage are non-polluting which count for 100 units, out of a total of more than 400 units. These non-polluting food units are also located maximum in Lawrence Road and in very small number in Rajasthan Udyog Nagar, Okhla area, Kirti Nagar, Mangolpuri, Naraina, Mayapuri and Anand Parbat (Table 5.2).

Recycling

Only eight out of the total of nearly 150 units are non-polluting which mainly belong to rubber recycling. These non-polluting units are located in Mayapuri and Anand Parbat Industrial Areas.

Plastic Molding

This sector includes all pollution free process in which more than 2000 industrial units are engaged, maximum number of units, *i.e.* nearly 300 are located in Mayapuri followed by Mangolpuri, Narela, Wazirpur, Anand Parbat, Okhla area, Udyog Nagar, G.T.Karnal Road, Najafgarh, Nangloi and Kirti Nagar (Table 5.2).

Paper

Paper product sector includes non-polluting processes, which account for more than 400 non-polluting industrial units. This sector is spread in all industrial areas except Jhandewalan Flatted Factories. Maximum units are located in Okhla Industrial Area, followed by Anand Parbat, Wazirpur, G.T. Karnal Road, Kirti Nagar, and Najafgarh Road (Table 5.2).

Trading

This is obviously a non-polluting sector, which comprises nearly 3000 units. Maximum trading establishments are located in Mayapuri followed by Wazirpur, Okhla Industrial Area, Anand Parbat, Mayapuri, Jhandewalan Flatted Factories, Mangolpuri and G.T. Karnal Road. Trading units are not found in Lawrence Road, Udyog Nagar, Small-Scale Industrial Area, Nangloi and Badli (Table 5.2).

Service

Varieties of service establishments are also found in industrial areas. These are more than 800 units. Nearly 200 are located in Okhla area, followed by Mayapuri, Anand Parbat, Jhandewalan flatted factories, Naraina, Lawrence Road, and Najafgarh. Such units are absent in Rajasthan Udyog Nagar, Small-Scale Industrial Area, Badli and Jhilmil (Table 5.2).

Table 5.2 : Number of Polluting and Non-Polluting Industrial Units According to Sectors

Industrial Sector	*A*	*W*	*H*	*A/H*	*W/H*	*AWH*	*Non-polluting*	*Total*
Assembly			18				888	908(4.2)
Battery			10			6	18	34(0.15)
Casting						244	-	244(1.13)
Chemical	21	14	14		9	78	311	447(2.06)
Electronic Component					9		-	9(0.043)
Glass			6				44	50(0.23)
Heat Treatment	11			144		37	-	192(0.89)
Leather					3		113	116(0.53)
Machining		612	9				6369	990(32.32)
Metal Finishing		24	21		422	568	-	1035(4.7)
Printing			716		121		-	837(3.8)
Rubber	419			6			-	425(1.96)
Service Station			1244		202		-	1446(6.69)
Textile Wet Processing		68				113	-	181(0.84)
Wood					2		623	625(2.89)
Food	257	85			5		100	447(2.6)
Tobacco Products		21						214(0.10)
Restaurant/Banquets		73						73(0.34)
Recycling		117				22	8	147(0.68)
Plastic Molding							2213	2223(10.23)
Paper								420(1.94)
Textile (dry processing)								1028(4.74)
Trading								2785(12.68)
Services								849(3.90)
Miscellaneous.								70(0.36)
Vegetable Oil	17							17 (0.08)
Total	1008	1025	2038	200	773	1068	10695	21627(100)

Source : Prepared from Census on Hazardous Industries (2001) Delhi Pollution Control Committee, Delhi.

Note : A-air pollution W- wastewater, H-hazardous waste. Figure in parentheses are in per cent.

Distribution of Polluting Industries According to Industrial Sectors

Total of 21627 industrial units are engaged in variety of industrial sectors and sub-sectors in the twenty-eight approved industrial areas of Delhi. The distribution of various industrial units in terms of different industrial sectors indicates that machining is one major sector where nearly 7000 industrial units are engaged, of which more than 90 per cent is non-polluting. Another important sectors are plastic molding and trading where two to three thousand industrial units are engaged which are mainly non-polluting. Service stations are also in significant numbers, nearly 1500. Then, comes metal finishing and textiles that count for more than 2000 industrial units. Assembly sector has 500 to 1000 industrial units. Less than 500 units are seen in rubber, food products, paper, recycling, chemicals, casting, heat treatment and leather. Less than 100 units are found in glass, battery, restaurants/banquets and miscellaneous category. Details of the sector-wise pollution are examined in the following paragraphs (Table 5.2 and Appendix XI-B).

Assembly

This industrial sector includes the sub-sectors like electrical components and goods, electrical transformers, electronic components and goods, which mainly generates pollution in terms of hazardous waste. This sector has a total of more than 900 industrial units in Delhi, of which more than 800 belong to non-polluting category and nearly 20 units cause hazardous wastes. These polluting units are located in Jhandewalan flatted factories and Mayapuri area.

Battery

Assembly of battery, manufacture of lead and battery, reconditioning and recharging comprises this sector which is a comparatively smaller sector with a total of 34 units in Delhi. Of which 50 per cent are polluting units, hazardous waste is generated by 10 units and six units are such that cause all the three type of pollutions (air, water and hazardous waste). The distribution of these polluting units in different industrial areas reflects that hazardous waste is caused by seven units in Mayapuri area and by three units in Lawrence Road. The non-polluting industrial units indicate that more number of units are located in Mayapuri than in Anand Parbat, Mangolpuri, Okhla, Patparganj and Narela, whereas in rest other areas this activity is absent.

Casting

This involves casting of aluminium, brass, copper, iron, lead, zinc etc. It has some 244 industrial units and they cause all three types of pollution (air pollution, wastewater and hazardous waste). Nearly 90 units are located in Anand Parbat alone followed by more than 40 in Mayapuri, Jhilmil, Badli, Wazirpur and G.T. Road. Small numbers of units are seen in Small-Scale Industries Area, Okhla, Kirti Nagar and Najafgarh Road.

Chemical

This is a very wide sector comprising manufacture of soap, shampoos, cosmetics, wax products, thermocol, paints, pesticides and pharmaceutical formulation. A total of nearly 450 industrial units are engaged in chemical sector, which is a cause of variety of pollution in varied combinations. Of these 450 industrial units, more than 300 are non-polluting, whereas 21 are air polluting and 14 water polluting. Another 14 per cent of units are hazardous waste generating, 9 units cause wastewater as well as hazardous waste and nearly 80 units are such that are responsible for all the three kinds of production externalities. The distribution of polluting industrial units indicates that air-polluting units are located mainly in Wazirpur, Udyog Nagar, Mangolpuri, Patparganj and Najafgarh Road. Wastewater generating units are found in Okhla Industrial Area, Mayapuri and Wazirpur. Hazardous-waste oriented units are in G.T. Karnal Road, Kirti Nagar and Anand Parbat. The industrial units causing wastewater and hazardous wastes are seen in Mayapuri, Udyog Nagar, Okhla area and Anand Parbat. Maximum number of units, *i.e.* 80 contributing to three kinds of pollution are located in Okhla Industrial Area, besides small number of units in many areas like Wazirpur, G.T. Karnal Road, Lawrence Road, Badli, Mayapuri, Patparganj, Mohan Cooperatives, Najafgarh Road, Moti Nagar and Narela.

Electronic Components

This industrial sector comprises electroplating processes. This is responsible for generating wastewater and hazardous waste. This is extremely small sector with only nine industrial units, which are located in Okhla Industrial Area, Mayapuri and Okhla Flatted Factories.

Glass

Glass processing and glass etching with acid comprise this industrial sector. The former process is non-polluting and the latter one is polluting which causes hazardous waste. Total of 50 industrial units belong to this industrial sector of which only six units are polluting and more than 40 are non-polluting. These polluting units are located in Okhla industrial area, Jhilmil and Jhandewalan Flatted Factories.

Heat Treatment

Case hardening, hot rolling, forging and tempering are sub-sectors of heart treatment with nearly 200 industrial units engaged in this sector, causing pollutions of different nature. Air pollution and wastewater are generated maximum in Wazirpur by more than 50 units followed by Mayapuri with 30 units. Anand Parbat, Jhilmil, Najafgarh Road, Small-Scale Industries Area has less than 30 units. All the three types of pollution are caused in industrial areas of Wazirpur, G.T. Karnal Road, Okhla area, Naraina, Mayapuri, Jhilmil, Anand Parbat, and Kirti Nagar.

Leather

Dyeing, fat liquoring (post tanning) and stitching comprise the leather sector where former processes are pollution-oriented and later is non-polluting. In Delhi, more than 100 industrial units are engaged in leather works, of which only three units generate wastewater and hazardous waste. These polluting units are located in Moti Nagar and Okhla Industrial Estate.

Machining

This industrial sector comprises machining with cutting oil, without cutting oil and shot blasting, the first process generates wastewater and the last process causes air pollution. A total of nearly 7000 industrial units are related to machining, of which 90 per cent are non-polluting and 10 per cent are polluting. More than 600 industrial units are air and water polluting. The air polluting units are in small number found in G.T. Karnal Road, Mayapuri and Anand Parbat. Wastewater generating units are located maximum in Mayapuri, *i.e.* 60. It is also to be added that more than 40 units are found in areas of Okhla Industrial Area,G.T. Karnal Road, Wazirpur and Moti Nagar. Less than 10 units are scattered in many areas like Udyog Nagar, Rajasthan Udyog Nagar, Mangolpuri, Naraina, Patparganj, Mohan Cooperatives and Jhandewalan Flatted Factory.

Metal Finishing

This is a wider industrial sector covering copper/aluminium wire drawing, annealing, pickling, anodizing, galvanizing (hot dip coating), nickel chrome, zinc, gold, silver plating and powder coating. These varied processes cause a variety of pollutions from more than 1000 industrial units. Of these, 500 units are responsible for all three kinds of pollution together. More than 400 units contributing towards wastewater and hazardous waste together, 25 units cause wastewater and similar number generate hazardous waste. The distribution of industrial units responsible for all three kinds of pollutions together are found maximum in Wazirpur

(200 units), followed by 80 units in Anand Parbat and 50 units each in Mayapuri and Okhla Industrial Area. In G.T. Karnal Road, Naraina, Badli, Udyog Nagar, Small Medium industries areas and Shahdara 10 per cent units exist. The industrial units causing wastewater and hazardous waste together are seen maximum in Friends Colony (120 units), followed by Jhilmil (80 units), and Anand Parbat and Shahdara with almost 50 units, Mayapuri 30 units and Wazirpur 20 units. Whereas in other areas like Patparganj, Najafgarh Road, Moti Nagar less than 10 units are found. Only hazardous wastes generating metal finishing units are found maximum of 10 in Okhla Industrial Area and other areas are Mangolpuri, Friends Colony, and Mohan Co-operatives, Kirti Nagar and Najafgarh Road. The industrial units responsible for wastewater are located in Wazirpur, Mayapuri, G.T. Karnal Road, Okhla area, Jhilmil and Mohan Co-operatives.

Printing

The processes involved are plate making and printing. The former process causes wastewater and hazardous waste together and the latter process causes hazardous waste alone. There are more than 800 industrial units. Hazardous waste alone is generated by maximum of more than 200 units in Okhla Industrial Area, followed by Naraina with 100 units, Mayapuri with 92 units and Anand Parbat nearly 60 units. G.T. Karnal Road, Wazirpur, Najafgarh Road, Narela, Patparganj areas have less than10 per cent each. This activity is absent in Tilak Nagar. The industrial units that are generating wastewater and hazardous waste together are located maximum in Naraina (50 units), Okhla area (30 units) and 8 units in Anand Parbat. Whereas less than 5 units are seen in Wazirpur, G.T.Karnal Road, Nangloi, Jhilmil and Patparganj.

Rubber

This involves two processes, first using latex that causes air pollution and wastewater together and second using synthetic that generates only air pollution. More than 400 industrial units operate in this sector where only six units use latex and the rest use synthetic. Units in G.T.Karnal Road, Mayapuri, Badli and Anand Parbat use the latex technique. Maximum air pollution through synthetic use is seen in Anand Parbat in more than 200 units, followed by nearly 50 units in Mayapuri, 40 units in Najafgarh Road, Moti Nagar, Mangolpuri, Okhla area, Badli, and Narela. Less than 5 units are in Wazirpur, G.T. Karnal Road, Rajasthan Udyog Nagar, Small and Medium industries area, Small-Scale Industries Area and Naraina.

Service Stations

Total of 1446 service stations are operating in the approved industrial areas, which cause wastewater and hazardous waste together and hazardous waste alone from auto repairing. There are 40 units each in Mayapuri and Najafgarh Road. Nearly 30 units in Lawrence Road and more than 20 units in Wazirpur, G.T Karnal Road, Okhla Industrial Area, Okhla estate, Patparganj contribute towards wastewater and hazardous waste together. Whereas only hazardous waste is generated from more than 1100 units in Mayapuri, 50 units in Anand Parbat, 15 units in each G.T. Karnal Road, Lawrence Road and Kirti Nagar.

Textile (Wet Processing)

This industrial sector comprises of bleaching, dyeing, printing, washing of cotton synthetic fabric and yarn. These processes cause all three pollutions together. A total of 181 industrial units in the approved industrial areas are operating in this sector. Only wastewater is generated from washing process that is highest at Okhla industrial area with more than 40 units, besides 20 to 40 units in Wazirpur, Mayapuri, Patparganj and Kirti Nagar. Air pollution and wastewater together are generated from bleaching process that is found in Wazirpur and Mayapuri. All three types of pollutions have contributed maximum by 30 units in Okhla Industrial Area, followed by more than 20 units in Wazirpur, Mayapuri, Udyog Nagar, Small and Medium industries area, Small-Scale Industries Area, Naraina, Kirti Nagar and Najafgarh Road.

Wood

This industrial sector comprises of wood products and timber processing that generates wastewater from former and hazardous waste from the latter process. Out of more than 600 industrial units, only two units are engaged in timber processing which are located in Okhla Industrial Area and the rest are non-polluting units.

Food

Grinding mills, fruits and vegetables processing, meat processing, milk products, confectionery, bakery and mineral water comprise the food sector. There are more than 400 industrial units, of which more than 200 are air polluting, that is, mainly generated from grinding mills. More than 80 units cause wastewater and 5 units generate wastewater and hazardous wastes together. The distribution of polluting industrial units indicates maximum concentration of food processing units in Lawrence Road, where nearly 300 units are located. Narela has 60 units, 20 units in Okhla area, and 5-10 units in Mayapuri, Badli and Patparganj. Food industries are absent in G.T Karnal Road, Small and Medium Industries Area, Small-Scale Industries Area, Nangloi, Okhla Flatted Factories and many other areas.

Tobacco Blending

Total of about 20 units are engaged in tobacco blending that cause wastewater in the process. These are mainly located in Lawrence Road, Naraina, Patparganj, Najafgarh Road, Shahdara and Small and Medium Industrial Area.

Restaurants and Banquet Halls

There are 73 such establishments that mainly generate wastewater. Ten establishments of this nature are seen in Lawrence Road, Okhla area, Mayapuri, Anand Parbat, followed by Mohan Co-operatives, Mangolpuri, and few units in Moti Nagar, Kirti Nagar and Shahdara.

Recycling

The recycling sector comprises the recycling of ferrous, non-ferrous, rubber and plastic, where first two processes generate all three types of pollution, the third causes no pollution. More than 100 units are of plastic recycling that generates wastewater. There are 60 units in Narela, followed by Mangolpuri, Najafgarh Road, Wazirpur and Anand Parbat. Ferrous and non-ferrous recycling are done in 22 units in Anand Parbat, Mayapuri, Mangolpuri and Rajasthan Udyog Nagar.

Vegetable Oil

Expelling of vegetable oil is the main process for causing wastewater. Total 17 units are found, of which maximum of eight are located in Lawrence Road followed by Narela and Badli. This activity is absent in other industrial areas.

Wastewater Generation

The industrial units generating wastewater in the 28

Industrial Areas of Delhi are 12 per cent of the total industrial units of Delhi, which are generating 10867 kilolitres (kl) per day of wastewater. Different industrial areas contribute in various quantities to this total wastewater, highest amount of wastewater, *i.e.* more than 2000 kl/day is generated from Lawrence Road Industrial Area where majority of industrial units are engaged in food products processing. Next following areas are Rajasthan Udyog Nagar, Wazirpur and Okhla Industrial Area generating wastewater between 1000 to 2000 kl/d. In these areas, machining, plastic products and printing are main activities that involve lot of washing. Moderate amount of wastewater, *i.e.* 500 to 1000 kl/d is generated from Okhla Industrial Estate and Mohan Co-operatives where, too, machining is main activity. In many of the Industrial Areas like G.T. Karnal Road, Udyog Nagar, Small and Medium Industrial Area, Small-Scale Industrial Area, Naraina, Mayapuri, lower amount of wastewater, *i.e.* 100 to 500 kl/d is caused. Very low quantities of wastewater are generated in Jhilmil, Friends Colony, Jhandewalan and Okhla Flatted Factories, where assembly of electronic components and dry textiles are main activities, which do not require water. Tilak Nagar has no such units.

The generation of wastewater from various industrial sectors reveals that a maximum of 3535 kl/d is generated from textiles (wet processing) alone, which is followed by food products sector with 2704 kl/d, and then comes metal finishing with 2014.5 kl/d. Recycling, chemicals and service stations also cause good amount of wastewater. Although the industrial sectors like heat treatment, machining, rubber, leather-electronic components and battery generate smaller quantities of wastewater (Fig. 5.7).

The wastewater generation from different industrial areas as evidenced from (Fig.5.7) exhibits highest kilolitre per day, *i.e.* 2190 kl/d from Lawrence Road industrial area, followed by 1527 kl/d wastewater generated from a variety of industrial activities at Rajasthan Udyog Nagar, 1474 kl/d from

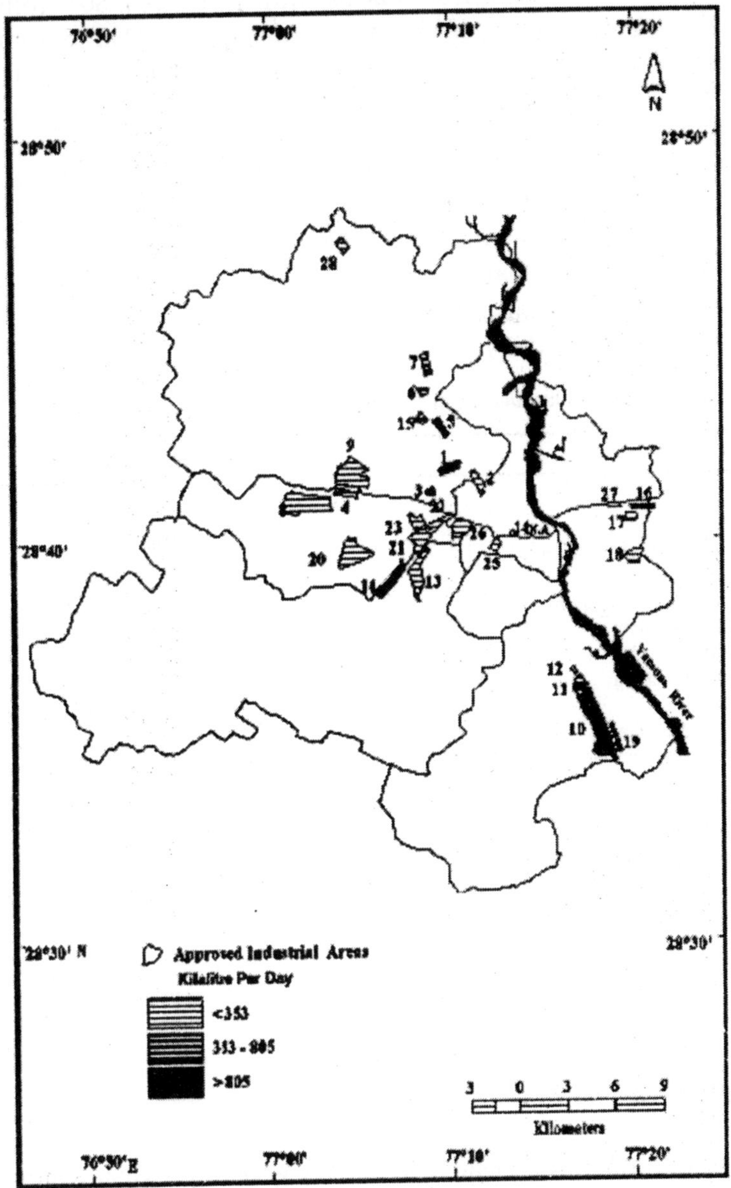

Fig. 5.7 : Wastewater Generation, 2001

Wazirpur, 1353 kl/d from Okhla Industrial Area, 805 from Mohan Co-operative, 483 kl/d from Mayapuri, 312 kl/d from Narela and less than 200 kl/d from Anand Parbat, Najafgarh, Kirti Nagar, Patparganj, Mangolpuri Industrial Areas. The lowest amount of wastewater is caused at Jhandewalan and Okhla flatted factories whereas Tilak Nagar contributes no wastewater. The industries causing wastewater are 13 per cent of the total contributing 10867 kiloliters per day of wastewater. The analysis of wastewater generation according to industrial sector and sub-sectors is as follows (Table 5.3 and Appendix XI-A).

Table 5.3 : Wastewater Generation from Industrial Sectors

Industrial Sectors	*Wastewater Generation kl/d*
Battery	0.1
Casting	N.A
Machining (with cutting oil)	79.4
Chemicals	445.1
Electronic Component	3
Heat Treatment	86
Leather	14
Metal Finishing	2095
Rubber	170
Service Station	616
Textile (wet processing)	4017
Wood	1
Food2707	
Tobacco Blending	2
Restaurants & Banquet Halls	51
Recycling	584
Vegetable Oil	Zero
Total	10867

Source : Obtained from Census on Hazardous Industries (2001) Delhi Pollution Control Committee, Delhi.

Battery

The manufacture of lead acid battery generates wastewater that is noticed in Naraina and Mayapuri, generating wastewater of 0.01 kiloliter per day (kl/d) at Naraina, 0.04

kl/d at Mayapuri industrial area. Whereas in the rest, the other twenty-six industrial areas it is nil which indicates the absence of this activity in those areas.

Casting, Machining and Metal Finishing

This includes the sub-sectors of brass cutting, machining without cutting oil, nickel and copper plating, powder coating and pickling. Wastewater generated in the process of above activities is very high in Small-Scale Industrial Area, i.e. 27 kl/d, 8 kl/d is generated at Mayapuri, 3 kl/d is contributed by each Wazirpur and Friends Colony. Jhilmil generates one kl/d wastewater in the casting and metal finishing process.

Chemical

This includes the industrial sub-sectors of shampoo, detergent, food colours and dyes and pharmaceutical formulations. The generation of wastewater from these activities reflects that wastewater from shampoo and detergent is at the rate of 4 kl/d and 3 kl/d at Okhla industrial area and Mayapuri, respectively. Food colours and dye wastewater are evident at Mayapuri that is 11 kl/d; the pharmaceutical formulations contribute 1 kl/d wastewater from each of Lawrence Road, Badli and Najafgarh Road. A very high, i.e. 362 kl/d is generated alone by Okhla Industrial Area and 62 kl/d from Kirti Nagar.

Electronic Component

This mainly includes Printed Circuit Board (PCB) manufacturing, which causes 2 kl/d wastewater at Okhla Industrial Area, 1kl/d each at Okhla Flatted Factory and Mayapuri.

Heat Treatment

This includes case hardening, forging, tempering, hot rolling etc. The wastewater generated in case hardening is highest at Badli and Jhilmil at the rate of 14-15 kl/d, followed by 7-8 kl/d at Kirti Nagar and Wazirpur, 5-6 kl/d at Anand Parbat and Najafgarh Road Industrial Area and G.T. Karnal Road Area. In case of hot rolling highest of 13 kl/d is seen at Wazirpur, 1-2 kl/d is wastewater is generated at Rajasthan Udyog Nagar, Small-Scale Industrial Area and Jhilmil Industrial Area.

Leather

This includes dyeing and fat liquoring (post-tanning). Wastewater generation from this process is seen only at Okhla Industrial Estate and Naraina at the rate of 6 k/ld and 2kl/d from Moti Nagar Industrial Area.

Machining

This comprises machining with cutting oil. High rates of wastewater generation are evident in Okhla Industrial Area and Anand Parbat at the rate of 12-13 kl/d 1 to 4 kl/d. Wastewater is also generated from Mayapuri, G.T.Karnal Road, Moti Nagar, Jhandewalan Flatted Factories, Rajasthan Udyog Nagar and Udyog Nagar. Very small quantity of 0.4 kl/d is noticed at Wazirpur.

Metal Finishing

The sub-sector includes copper wire drawing, annealing, pickling, cold rolling of stainless steel plates, anodizing gold, silver plating, nickel/chrome plating, metal powder coating and zinc plating. Copper wire drawing and pickling are generating 1 kl/d wastewater in the industrial areas of Wazirpur, Small-Scale Industrial Area, Mayapuri, Anand

Parbat and 6-7 kl/d is seen at Jhilmil and Badli. Annealing, pickling and cold rolling of stainless steel sheets are causing highest of 418 kl/d wastewater generation in Wazirpur, followed by 235 kl/d in Badli, 88 kl/d in Udyog Nagar, 50-60 kl/d in Small and Medium Industrial Area Small-Scale Industrial Area. Anodizing is generating wastewater 2 kl/d in Wazirpur, Okhla, and Shahdara, and 4-7 kl/d in Anand Parbat, Friends Colony and Mayapuri. Gold/Silver plating is causing very negligible quantity only in Mayapuri. Nickel/chrome plating wastewater generation is 87 kl/d in Mangolpuri, 50-60 kl/d in Wazirpur and Okhla, 20-26 kl/d in Anand Parbat and G.T.Karnal Road. Naraina and Mayapuri cause 13-19 kl/d, 1 to 6 kl/d is seen in Narela, Moti Nagar, Patparganj and Udyog Nagar. Pickling causes highest wastewater at the rate of 361 kl/d in Wazirpur, 77 kl/d in G.T.Karnal Road, 47 kl/d in Mayapuri and 25 kl/d in Anand Parbat areas. Powder coating is mainly generating wastewater in Anand Parbat at the rate of 97 kl/d. Zinc plating wastewater is highest in Okhla Industrial Area followed by Anand Parbat and Mayapuri area.

Rubber

Water pollution is generated in the process where latex is used. Highest generation of wastewater is seen in Mayapuri and Badli at the rate of 63 kl/d followed by Anand Parbat with 31 kl/d, G.T.Karnal Road contributes 13 kl/d, whereas in the rest other industrial areas this process is absent.

Service Station

Wastewater generation from heavy vehicles servicing is mainly produced in Lawrence Road, *i.e.* 179 kl/d, even for other vehicles also this area contributes highest, *i.e.* 107 kl/d. 94 kl/d in Mayapuri, 49 kl/d in Najafgarh Road, 47 kl/d in Okhla, 20 kl/d in Patparganj, Udyog Nagar and Friends

Colony follow this. Small quantities of polluted water are also generated at Kirti Nagar, Moti Nagar, Small and Medium Industrial Area, Anand Parbat, and Narela.

Textiles (Wet Processing)

Highest generation of wastewater is at Rajasthan Udyog Nagar through bleaching and dying of cotton fabrics, *i.e.*, 1388 kl/d, followed by Okhla industrial area with 689 kl/d, Okhla estate with 566 kl/d, Wazirpur with 566 kl/d. Smaller quantities of wastewater are generated in Friends Colony, Mayapuri and Kirti Nagar.

Food

Generation of wastewater from fruits, vegetables, meat, milk, bakery is highest in Lawrence Road with 1900 kl/d, followed by Mohan Co-operative with 778 kl/d, whereas, in the rest other industrial areas the activity is absent or negligible.

Recycling (Plastic)

Wastewater generation through plastic recycling is highest at Narela, *i.e.* 291 kl/d, followed by 69 kl/d in Mangolpuri. The other industrial areas are Najafgarh Road with 63 kl/d, Rajasthan Udyog Nagar with 49 kl/d and smaller quantities from Wazirpur, Nangloi, Mayapuri, Badli and Moti Nagar Industrial Area.

Hazardous Waste Generation

The industries generating hazardous wastes are 19 per cent of total industrial units in the approved industrial areas of Delhi, which contribute 1,51,584 Kilogram of hazardous wastes per day. Metal finishing, pharmaceutical formulations and printing mainly cause these hazardous wastes. The industrial sector-wise hazardous waste generation indicates that of the total 1,51,584 kg/d waste, highest amount of hazardous wastes is caused by the sector of metal finishing which includes, copper, gold, silver, nickel, zinc plating, anodizing, enameling pickling and metal powder coating. These processes cause hazardous wastes in terms of varnish residue and mainly effluent treatment plant sludge. They generate more than 101291 kg/d of wastes followed by textiles (wet processing) with 24076 kg/d of hazardous waste. Casting generates 7344 kg/d, service stations and recycling create wastes more than 1700 kg/d. Chemicals cause 859.2 kg/d of hazardous wastes and other industrial sectors like battery, electronic components, leather and glass contribute lesser quantities. Assembly sector causes least hazardous wastes (Table 5.4 and Appendix XI-D).

Table 5.4 : Hazardous Waste Generation

Industrial Sectors	*Hazardous Waste Generation kg/d*
Assembly	16
Battery	137
Casting	7464
Chemicals	446
Electronic Components	35
Glass	25
Heat Treatment	110
Leather	19
Metal Finishing	101336
Printing	14393
Service Station	1708
Textile (wet processing)	24098
Recycling	1797
Total	151584

Source : Obtained from Census on Hazardous Industries (2001) Delhi Pollution Control Committee, Delhi.

The Wazirpur industrial area contributes maximum amount of hazardous wastes, which are 44330 kl/d, followed by 8129 kg/d in Small-Scale Industrial Area, Mayapuri, and

Rajasthan Udyog Nagar. Narela causes hazardous waste of 12000 to 15000 kg/d. The industrial areas like Badli, Narela, Anand Parbat, Okhla estate and G.T.Karnal Road fall in the category of 5000 to 10000 kg/d followed by Udyog Nagar, Small and Medium industrial area, Naraina, Jhilmil, causing 2000 to 4000 kg/d. Lawrence Road, Mangolpuri, Kirti Nagar, Patparganj, Najafgarh Road, Shahdara contribute between 100 to 1000 kg/d. There are industrial areas like Nangloi and Moti Nagar generating upto 100 kg/d, whereas Tilak Nagar, Okhla and Jhandewalan Flatted Factories contribute negligible quantities of hazardous waste (Fig. 5.8). The pattern of hazardous waste generation according to industrial sectors and sub-sectors in different industrial areas of Delhi is discussed in the following paragraphs:

Assembly

In the process of assembly of electrical transformers, varnish residue remains as hazardous waste. A maximum of 9.6 kg/d of hazardous waste is generated at Mayapuri followed by 6.1 kg/d from Jhandewalan flatted factories, whereas in other areas this activity is absent.

Battery

In the manufacture of lead and battery and reconditioning or recharging battery causes hazardous waste. Mayapuri generates maximum hazardous waste of this kind, *i.e.* 236.3 kg/d followed by Lawrence Road with kg/d with 20 kg/d and 17.6 kg/d of waste from Naraina.

Casting

In the process of casting aluminium, brass, copper, iron, fuel cleaning residue and various metal slag are left as hazardous waste. These industrial processes generates 7464 kg/d of

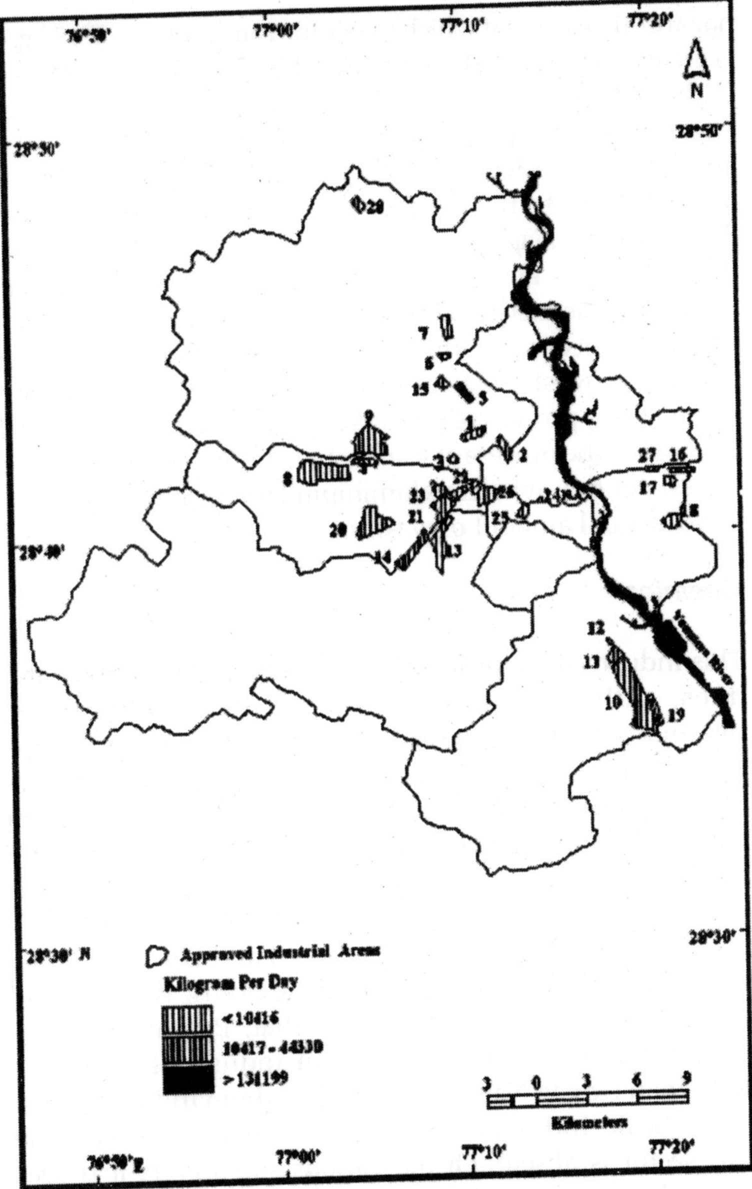

Fig. 5.8 : Hazardous Waste Generation, 2001

hazardous waste, of which maximum amount, *i.e.*, 2713 kg/d is created at Jhilmil alone, followed by 2022 kg/d at Anand Parbat. Mayapuri generates 1036 kg/d and Okhla Industrial Area with 673.7 kg/d. Small and Medium Industrial Area and Badli cause 300 kg/d whereas most of other industrial areas contribute 100 kg/d of waste, and negligibly low at Shahdara and Najafgarh Road. In the rest of industrial areas, this activity is absent. Most of this hazardous waste has resulted as the fuel gas-cleaning residue during various metal casting process. Of the total 7464 kg/d generation of hazardous waste, maximum of 4547 kg/d is contributed alone by the process of iron casting, followed by 2030 kg/d of waste in the process of lead casting, brass casting is caused lowest per day, whereas aluminium and copper are causing almost equal amount of wastes.

Chemical

This industrial sector includes cosmetics, food colours and dyes, adhesive products, pesticide formulations, pharmaceutical formulations and paint etc. In this process hazardous waste occurs as residue of various types, spillage of semi-finished products and effluent treatment plant sludge. This industrial sector causes a total of 446 kg/d of hazardous waste, of which highest of 189.3 kg/d of waste is contributed by Okhla Industrial Area, followed by Badli with 35.7 kg/d, Kirti Nagar with 29.1 kg/d and Lawrence Road with 25.9 kg/d. In Narela and Mangolpuri, it is 15 kg/d and in other areas like Anand Parbat, Patparganj, Moti Nagar it is less than 10 kg/d. In industrial areas like Rajasthan Udyog Nagar, Small and Medium Industrial area, Small-Scale Industrial Area, Tilak Nagar and Shahdara this sector is absent. Of the various sub-sectors it is seen that pharmaceutical formulations in the main sector causes highest hazardous waste followed by food colours and dyes.

Electronic Components

This industrial sector includes electroplating which causes hazardous waste in the form of etching sludge. This generates a total of 35 kg/d of hazardous wastes, of which highest of 20 kg/d waste is created by Okhla Industrial Area followed by Mayapuri with 10 kg/d and 5 kg/d by Okhla Flatted Factories. This industrial activity is absent in all other industrial areas.

Glass

The industrial sector comprises the sub-sector of glass etching with acids, which cause hazardous wastes in the form of spent acid. This activity is not prevalent in many industrial areas of Delhi. It is concentrated only in Jhilmil generating 25 kg/d of hazardous wastes.

Heat Treatment

This involves the process of hardening of various metals called case hardening which generates hazardous waste in the form of hardening salts and sludge from cleaning water. A total of 110 kg/d of hazardous waste is created, of which maximum of 21.7 kg/d is generated in Jhilmil, followed by Badli with 19.56 kg/d, Mayapuri and Kirti Nagar with 11 kg/d. In Anand Parbat, Najafgarh Road, Wazirpur, G.T.Karnal Road and Okhla Industrial Area less than 10 kg/d of waste is created. This industrial activity is not present in the industrial areas like Lawrence Road, Small and Medium Industrial area, Small-Scale Industrial Area, Udyog Nagar, Nangloi, Okhla Estate, Naraina, Patparganj, Mohan Co-operative and Tilak Nagar.

Leather

In this industrial sector, the dyeing and post-tanning

processes cause hazardous waste as effluent treatment plant sludge. This activity is on small scale in few of the industrial areas generating 19 kg/d of hazardous waste in total, which is concentrated at Okhla Industrial Estate with 13.8 kg/d and Moti Nagar with 5.5 kg/d.

Metal Finishing

This broad industrial sector includes sub-sectors like aluminium, copper, nickel, chrome, silver, gold plating, enameling, anodizing, pickling, metal powder coating, which cause hazardous wastes as various residues and effluent treatment plant sludge. This is the major sector in terms of generating hazardous wastes of more than one lakh kg/d of the total of 151584 kg/d from all sectors. In the metal finishing, maximum of 36143 kg/d of hazardous waste is generated in the process of pickling, followed by annealing of steel plates with 35403 kg/d and wire drawing with 25024 kg/d. Of this more than one lakh kg/d waste, more than 40 per cent is generated alone from Wazirpur, followed by Small-Scale Industrial Area causing 14000 kg/d, Badli with nearly 10,000 kg/d and Narela with 9000 kg/d. G.T.Karnal Road and Mayapuri accounts for more than 5000 kg/d of wastes. Okhla, Udyog Nagar and Anand Parbat generates 2000 to 4000 kg/d, smaller quantities of waste generation are evident from Shahdara, Moti Nagar, Najafgarh Road, Friends Colony, Jhilmil, Naraina, Mangolpuri and Lawrence Road. This activity is absolutely absent in Nangloi, Okhla Flatted Factories, Mohan Co-operatives, Tilak Nagar and Patparganj.

Printing

This industrial sector comprises plate making, printing and printing accessories causing hazardous wastes in the form of developers, fixer residue and ink residue. This sector generates a total of 14393 kg/d of hazardous wastes, of which major share is by Mayapuri with 6512 kg/d of waste, followed by Naraina with 2875 kg/d, Okhla Industrial Area, Wazirpur, G.T.Karnal Road, Okhla Industrial Estate, Patparganj, Jhilmil contributes 100 to 400 kg/d. Conversely, Lawrence Road and Nangloi create small quantities of waste. This activity is not found in Udyog Nagar, Rajasthan Udyog Nagar, Small and Medium Industrial area, Small-Scale Industrial Area, Badli, Friends Colony, Mohan Co-operatives and Tilak Nagar.

Service Stations

Service of heavy and medium vehicles cause hazardous wastes in the form of oil sludge and effluent treatment plant sludge. A total of 1708 kg/d of waste is generated, of which Lawrence Road and Mayapuri cause 500 kg/d, followed by Udyog Nagar with 477 kg/d, Mangolpuri and Okhla Industrial Area with 100 kg/d. The industrial areas like Mohan Co-operative, Patparganj, Udyog Nagar, Wazirpur, and G.T. Karnal Road generate waste of 20 to 50 kg/d. This activity is absent in other industrial areas like Jhandewalan flatted factories, Shahdara, Narela, Tilak Nagar, Jhilmil, Okhla flatted factories and Nangloi.

Textile (Wet Processing)

This industrial sector involves bleaching, dyeing of cotton/ synthetic fabric and yarn which produce hazardous wastes in the form of effluent treatment plant sludge. This sector generates a total of more than 24000 kg/d of hazardous waste, which is second highest after the metal finishing sector. Rajasthan Udyog Nagar generates highest amount of wastes, *i.e.*7925 kg/d, followed by Okhla Industrial Area and Okhla Industrial Estate with more than 6000 kg/d of wastes. The other industrial areas like Wazirpur, Udyog

Nagar, Mayapuri, and Kirti Nagar contribute moderately. Textiles are absent in the industrial areas like Lawrence Road, Nangloi, Mangolpuri, Naraina, Badli, Patparganj, Mohan Co-operatives, Tilak Nagar, Jhandewalan Flatted Factories, Shahdara and Narela.

Recycling

This industrial sector comprises sub-sectors like ferrous and non-ferrous, which cause hazardous waste in the form of residue from gas cleaning and oven debris. Recycling generates a total of 1797 kg/d of hazardous wastes, of which 1656 kg every day owes to ferrous recycling and 141 to non-ferrous. Among the industrial areas maximum ferrous recycling waste is generated at Rajasthan Udyog Nagar, *i.e.* 1650 kg/d, whereas ferrous recycling is not seen in other industrial areas except in Anand Parbat area. Non-ferrous recycling is seen in Friends Colony with 60 kg/d, Mangolpuri with 32 kg/d, Okhla Industrial Area with 25 kg/d, Mayapuri with 12 kg/d, and Small and Medium industries area with 10 kg/d. This activity is absent in the Industrial Areas of Small-Scale Industries Area, Nangloi, Okhla flatted factories, Jhandewalan flatted factories, Badli, Jhilmil, Patparganj, Moti Nagar and Narela.

Pollution Management in Practice

Effluent Treatment Plant

As far as the installation of effluent treatment plant in Delhi's approved industrial areas is concerned, only 38 per cent of the industrial units have installed in their premises treating liquid waste and 22 per cent units require it but do not have. There is almost similar number, *i.e.* 36 per cent units who have no knowledge regarding effluent treatment and nearly 3 per cent units are engaged in such activities that do not fall in the category which need effluent treatment.

Mayapuri has maximum, *i.e.* 70 per cent of its units with effluent treatment plants installed for treating liquid waste and only about 7 per cent with no such provision. Tilak Nagar has also 67 per cent enterprises with installed effluent treatment plants and only 5 per cent without it. Other industrial areas like Wazirpur, G.T.Karnal Road, Udyog Nagar, Naraina, Badli, Friends Colony, Najafgarh Road, Jhandewalan flatted factories, Anand Parbat and Shahdara have 40-50 per cent industrial units with provision of effluent treatment. Other industrial estates have 20-30 per cent units with effluent treatment plants, whereas Nangloi and Narela Industrial Areas have about 10 per cent plants with this facility. Mohan Cooperative has about two per cent with such provision of effluent treatment (Fig. 5.9).

It would be apparent from Fig. 5.9 that Okhla Flatted Factories has maximum number, *i.e.* 66 per cent enterprises with no effluent treatment plants. Other areas where 20-40 per cent units do not have such provisions are Lawrence Road, Okhla Industrial Estate, Anand Parbat, Kirti Nagar, Moti Nagar, Jhilmil and Wazirpur. The awareness among people in these industrial areas regarding effluent treatment shows highest, *i.e.* 86 per cent in Narela, followed by above 70 per cent in Nangloi, Patparganj and Mohan Co-operative. In almost all other industrial areas except Lawrence Road 20 per cent people are ignorant regarding effluent treatment plants (Fig. 5.9).

Solid Waste Handling Practices

Of the solid waste generated by industrial units in various approved industrial areas, about 55 per cent units handle their wastes manually inspite of health hazard. This shows that mechanical handling of industrial waste is not prevalent, as 7 per cent units use mechanical way for handling waste

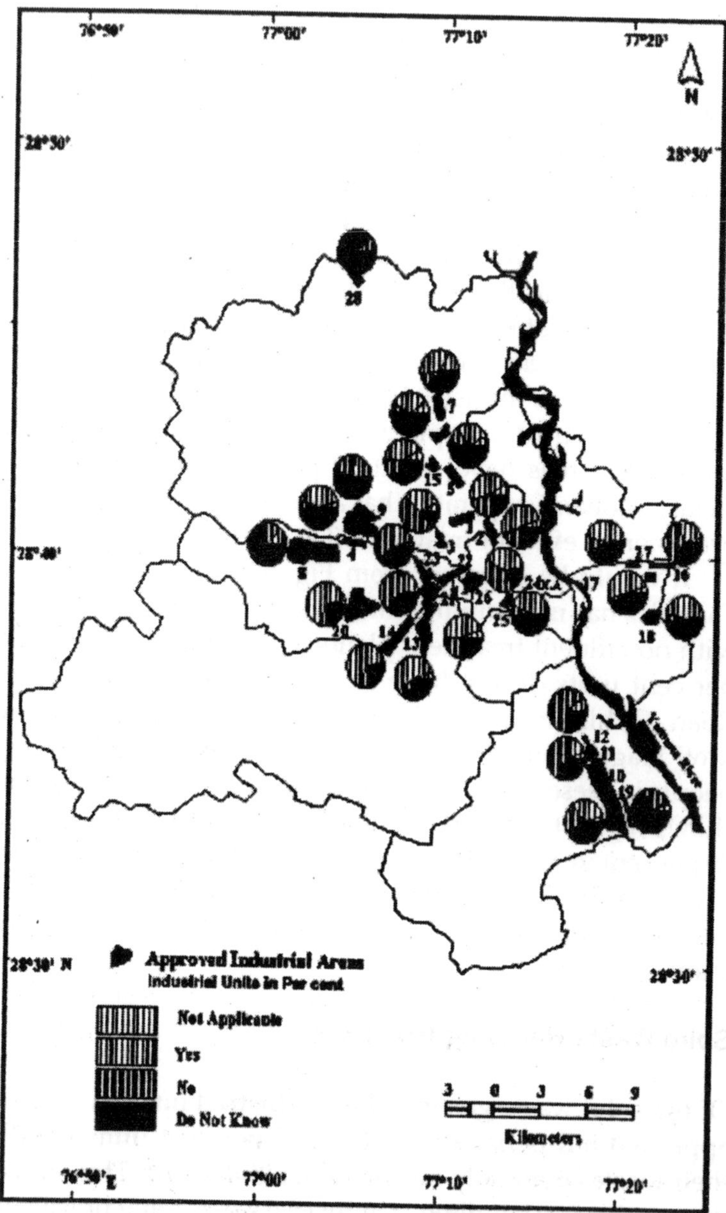

Fig. 5.9 : Effluent Treatment Plants, 2001

and another 7 per cent units use both mechanical as well as manual waste handling methods. If seen in different industrial areas, it is found that in most of the areas more than 90 per cent units use manual waste handling practices. Few industrial areas viz. Mangolpuri, Okhla Industrial Estate, Okhla Flatted Factories, Mohan Co-operative have 60 per cent units handling the solid waste manually. It would be evident from Fig. 5.10 that in Moti Nagar and Jhilmil 70 per cent units are using mechanical practices.

Another few industrial areas like Small-Scale industries, Okhla flatted factories, Mayapuri, Friends Colony, Mohan Co-operative and Narela have 10 per cent units handling their solid waste mechanically, and in the rest other industrial areas have small number of units practicing mechanical handling.

Solid waste handling by both methods of manual and mechanical is mainly done in five industrial areas like Mangolpuri, Okhla flatted factories, Okhla Industrial Estate and Mohan Co-operative. In these areas about 20-30 per cent units are such which use both mechanical and manual practices. In the rest industrial areas very few number of units have these kinds of solid waste handling. Industrial areas like Rajasthan Udyog Nagar, Nangloi, Moti Nagar and Shahdara do not use both ways of handling their wastes rather use manual technique (Fig. 5.10).

Solid Waste Storage

There are a variety of modes which are generally used for storing industrial solid wastes before its disposal, such as drums, gunny bags, pit, platform, open land. Of the solid waste generated in different industrial areas, 40 per cent are stored in gunny bags followed by 23 per cent in drums, another 19 per cent in platforms, 15 per cent in open lands and only 1 per cent in pits.

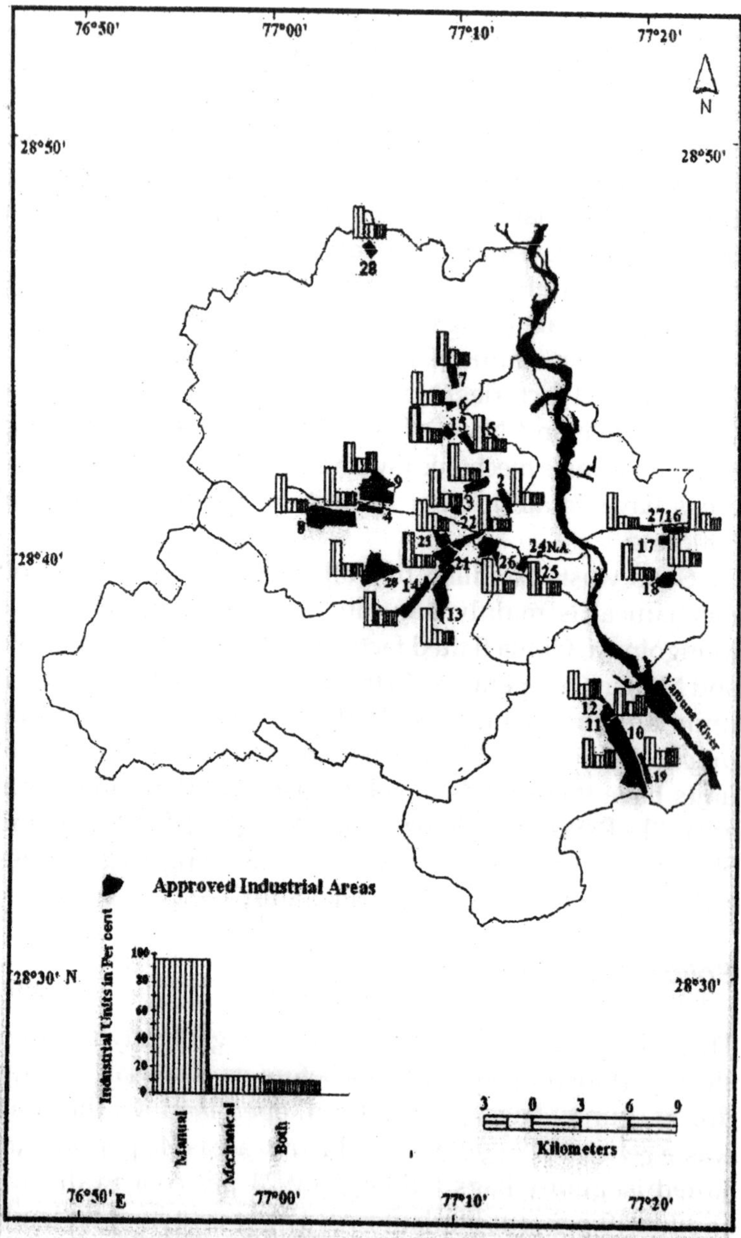

Fig. 5.10 : Solid Waste Handling Practices, 2001

A revealed from Fig. 5.11, different modes of storing solid wastes are prominent in various industrial estates. Gunny bag is used by 60 per cent units in the industrial areas of Small and Medium Industries Area, Rajasthan Udyog Nagar, Udyog Nagar, Nangloi, Okhla Flatted Factories, Patparganj, Jhandewalan Flatted Factories and Shahdara. In all other industrial areas 30 per cent units use gunny bags. Another most prevalent method is drum that is used by 20-40 per cent units in most of the industrial areas. In Lawrence Road, Small-Scale Industries Area, Okhla Industrial Estate and Shahdara this method is used. While in Rajasthan Udyog Nagar, Small and Medium Industrial Area this mode of solid waste storage is not much significant (Fig. 5.11).

About 20-30 per cent units in Anand Parbat, Lawrence Road, Wazirpur, Small-scale Industries Area, Friends Colony and Tilak Nagar use the platform mode of storing solid waste. Only a few industrial units practice this method in industrial areas of Narela, Jhandewalan Flatted Factories, Moti Nagar and Rajasthan Udyog Nagar. In the rest industrial areas 10-20 per cent units use this mode.

As far as the open land as a method for storing industrial solid waste is concerned, it is used in maximum number of units, *i.e.* about 35 per cent in Kirti Nagar followed by Mayapuri and Okhla Industrial Estate with 25 per cent units. In other industrial areas about 10 per cent units use. The industrial areas like Jhandewalan Flatted Factories, Narela, Friends Colony, Badli, Nangloi, Small-Scale Industries Area and Rajasthan Udyog Nagar practice this method minimally (Fig. 5.11).

Pit as a mode for solid waste store is not very popular in any of the twenty-eight approved industrial areas in Delhi, except in Small-Scale Industries Area as only 10 per cent units use this method. Followed by Rajasthan Udyog Nagar with 8 per cent units practice this but in the rest other areas it is less than 5 per cent enterprises that practice this mode (Fig. 5.11).

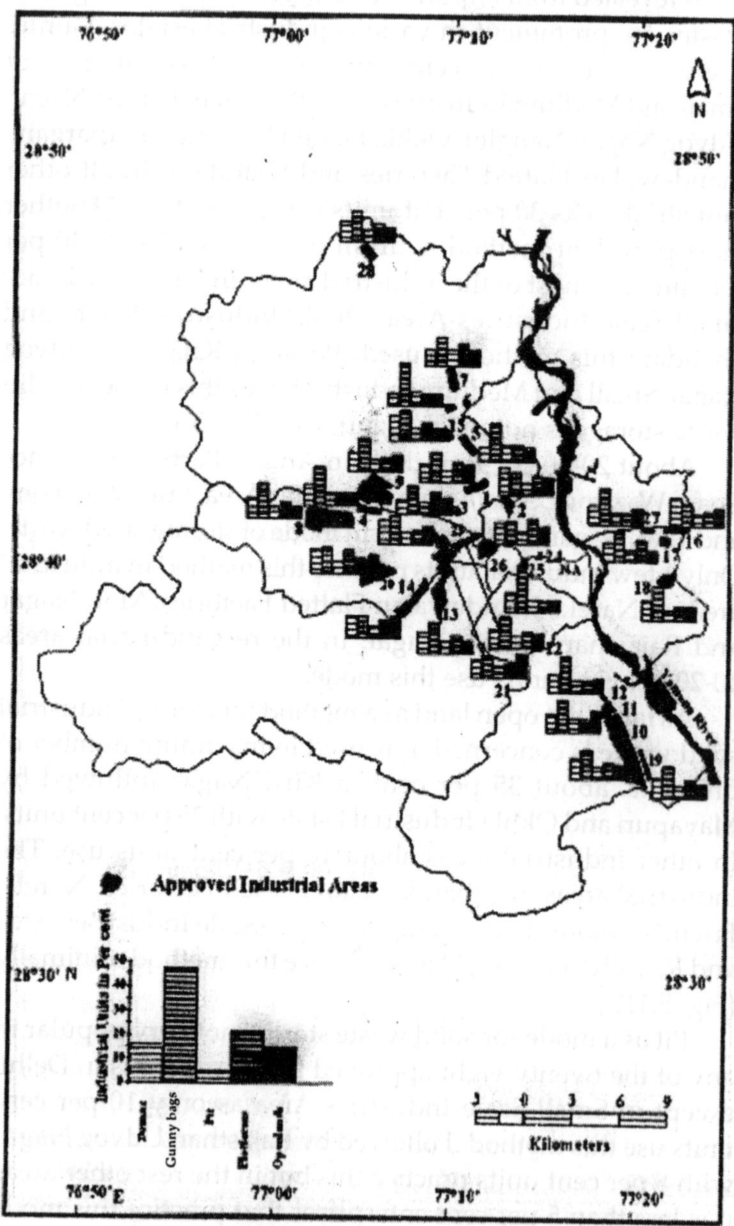

Fig. 5.11 : Mode of Storage of Solid Waste, 2001

Disposal of Solid Waste

Fig. 5.12 on the disposal of solid waste indicates that 60 per cent industrial units dump their wastes within their factory premises and the rest 40 per cent dispose them outside their premises. About 25 per cent industrial units practice roadside dumping of their solid wastes and nearly 15 per cent units use Municipal dump yards and other modes.

The pattern of waste disposing in different industrial estates reveals that in Moti Nagar, 80 per cent enterprises dump their solid wastes within their factory premises, followed by 50 per cent units in Jhilmil, Anand Parbat, Shahdara, Badli, Mayapuri, Mangolpuri, Nangloi, Lawrence Road and Wazirpur. In Rajasthan Udyog Nagar, Okhla Flatted Factories, Mohan Co-operative no industrial units use this method. It is also shown that in Okhla Flatted Factories all the industrial units practice roadside dumping, followed by 30-50 per cent units in Friends Colony, Nangloi, Okhla Industrial estate, Mayapuri, Tilak Nagar, Kirti Nagar and Jhandewalan Flatted Factories. In Wazirpur, Lawrence Road, Rajasthan Udyog Nagar and Mohan Co-operative no industrial unit follow roadside dumping. In Rajasthan Udyog Nagar, Moti Nagar, Tilak Nagar, Naraina and G.T Karnal Road, 30-50 per cent industrial enterprises dispose their solid wastes in municipal dump yard. Another 10-30 per cent units in Wazirpur, G.T. Karnal Road, Mangolpuri, Patparganj, Anand Parbat and Shahdara also use Municipal dump yard (Fig. 5.12).

The areas like Narela, Mohan Co-operative, Najafgarh Road, Small and Medium Industries Area have no industrial units using Municipal dump yard. Around 30-50 per cent units in Shahdara, Kirti Nagar, Okhla Industrial Estate, Small-Scale Industries Area and Rajasthan Udyog Nagar dispose their waste in this manner. Tilak Nagar, Najafgarh Road, Moti Nagar, Okhla Flatted Factories and Nangloi have no units using this method (Fig. 5.12).

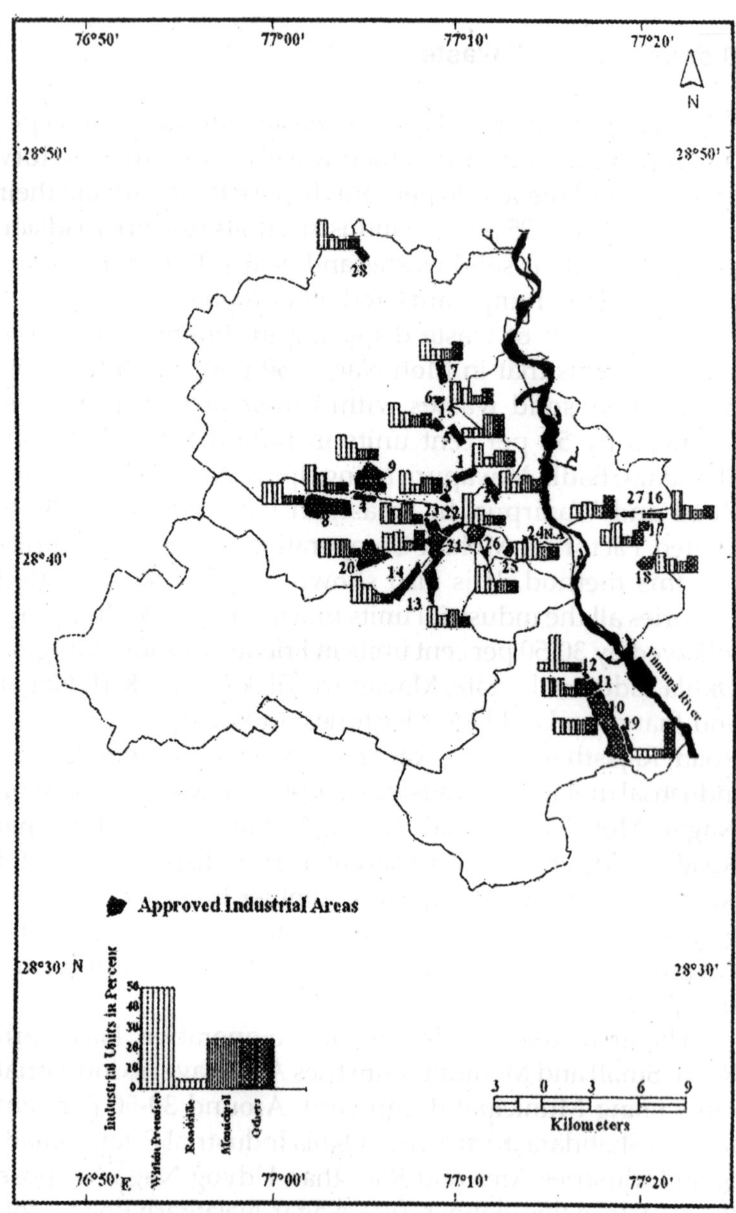

Fig. 5.12 : Disposal of Solid Waste, 2001

Suggestions for Handling Pollution

(i) Hazardous wastes should be handled using protective devices.

(ii) Proper care should be taken for the Common Effluent Treatment Plants (CETP) spillage. The CETP sludge generated from physico-chemical and biological process shall be segregated and stored separately for final disposal.

(iii) Collected waste should have proper labelling. Waste should be stored according to compatibility of one waste with another and clear signs demarcating the storage be used with appropriate warning signs relevant to the hazards of the wastes stored.

(iv) Technically suitable vehicles and trained staff should be provided for transporting the hazardous wastes.

(v) Proper disposal criteria should be there including the pre-treatment methods and potentials of re-use or recycle should be ascertained.

(vi) Industrial units should share the responsibility to maintain data about the quantity and characteristics of pollution generated by them; look for proper collection, handling and storage system and assess the potential of recycle and provide necessary information and data to government bodies.

(vii) Government agencies should work to create and promote awareness among industries and facilitate identification of suitable site for intermediate storage/ common treatment and formation of common waste management facilitating agencies.

(viii) Government agencies should play the role to formulate different pollution management policy; prepare, maintain and update pollution generation data for different industrial areas; approve and notify the sites identified for development of various common uses and monitor the operation of intermediate storage and final disposal sites.

Conclusion

The main objective of this chapter has been to look into spatial-environmental structure of industries in Delhi. The chapter handled pollution scenario in approved industrial areas of Delhi at three levels: first air pollution, wastewater and solid waste generation have been analyzed broadly. Secondly, non-polluting and polluting industries were illustrated. Thirdly, wastewater and solid waste generation were analyzed for different industrial areas and industrial sectors. The chapter also discussed existing pollution management practices besides suggestions were given to meet the challenge. It has been seen that pollution problems are not only the results of rapid industrialization rather unplanned and unorganized industrialization and indifferent attitude of people are equally responsible factors.

The study has revealed that of the total 21627 industrial units, 70 per cent are non-polluting industries and 30 per cent are polluting units. Maximum numbers of non-polluting industrial units were seen in Kirti Nagar (95%), because 40 per cent units here are engaged in trading. Of the 30 per cent polluting units nearly half were located in Lawrence Road, Friends Colony and Small-Scale Industries Area. The industrial areas with few polluting units are Okhla and Jhandewalan Flatted Factories, Udyog Nagar, Mangolpuri and Nangloi. Of the total 5733 polluting industrial units, 12 per cent (717) are air polluting, 16 per cent (900) are generating wastewater and 33 per cent causes hazardous waste. The industrial units creating air pollution and hazardous waste together are 3 per cent, 13 per cent units cause air pollution wastewater and hazardous waste, simultaneously. Maximum air polluting units are located in Lawrence Road, Tilak Nagar, Narela, Najafgarh Road and Moti Nagar. Maximum wastewater is generated at Mohan Co-operative, Anand Parbat and Narela. Hazardous waste has been caused mainly in industrial areas of Jhandewalan and Okhla Flatted Factories, Mayapuri, Naraina and Kirti Nagar. The industrial sectors responsible for water pollution include battery, casting, chemicals, electronic components, food, machining, heat treatment, metal finishing, printing, rubber, textiles, recycling, and service stations. The air polluting sectors are battery, casting, chemicals, heat treatment, food, metal finishing, recycling, rubber and textiles. Hazardous waste is generated by assembly, battery, casting, chemicals, electronic components, machining, leather, printing, textiles, and recycling. The total wastewater generated is 10860kl/d. Maximum wastewater is caused in Lawrence Road, Rajasthan Udyog Nagar, Wazipur and Okhla Industrial Areas. Industrial sector of textile (wet processing), food, metal finishing, and service stations are mainly responsible. Total hazardous waste generated is 151584 kg/d in Delhi, of which maximum is generated in Wazipur, Rajasthan Udyog Nagar, Small-Scale Industries, Okhla Industrial Area, Mayapuri and Badli. Pollution management practices revealed that effluent treatment plants are installed by 38 per cent units, while another 36 per cent units does not know about it. Mayapuri and Tilak Nagar have maximum units with effluent treatment plants. Solid waste is handled by majority (55%) manually and 7 per cent handle mechanically. In Jhilmil and Moti Nagar 70 per cent units use mechanical way. Of the solid waste generated 40 per cent is stored in gunny bags, 23 per cent in drums, 19 per cent in platform and 15 per cent in open land. Solid is disposed of within premises by 60 per cent units, 25 per cent use roadside dumping and 15 per cent units use Municipal yards. For treating wastewater common effluent treatment plants were proposed at 15 locations.

References

1. Annual Report (2001-02), Central Pollution Control Board, Delhi.
2. Study on Hazardous Industries (2001), National Productivity Council, Delhi.

Chapter - 6

Structure of Economy : 1970-71

Introduction

The structure of Delhi's industries and the environmental pollution caused due to the production processes in twenty-eight approved industrial areas are discussed in the previous chapters. Apart from the spatial distribution of industries, their economic and environmental role in economy of Delhi were also studied and interpreted. This chapter describes the basic approach adopted in the compilation of Input-Output Transaction Table (IOTT) for Delhi for 1970-1971 and 2000-2001 and other important issues like the scheme of sector classification, valuation of transaction, overall balancing between total Gross Domestic Product (GDP) and final expenditure and methods of estimation of inputs and outputs of various sectors of the economy. The chapter also includes procedures followed in the preparation of input flow matrix (commodity × industry) also called the absorption matrix; the output flow matrix (industry × commodity) also called the make matrix; and specification of the scheme of detailed sectoral classification (sectors are aggregated from 60 sectors as used in National Accounts Statistics). The chapter contains two sections : (a) approaches and procedures of compilation of IOTT adopted, and (b) analysis and discussion of the economy of Delhi prevalent in 1970-71 based on the input-output table prepared for the year. The inter-sectoral or inter-industry structure is discussed in terms of input-output coefficient, product mix relations, market share relations, backward and forward linkages, multipliers and connectivity matrix.

The word structure indicates that economy like other systems does have a structure where different elements are interacting with each other, and are inter-dependent on each other in terms of either as receiving end or at supplying end of the inputs to the other sector or sectors. These elements of the system in the present economy are industries, which are inter-linked to each other in different degrees or levels of relationships. Some industries are closely inter-connected while some are remotely related. Others are related with many and, still another, have relations with only a few sectors. The structural relations of the economy for 1970-71 are studied through input-output approach. The main thrust is secondary sector, which is analyzed in detail covering the manufacturing industrial sectors, while primary and tertiary sectors are analyzed in broad categories.

Compilation of Input-Output Transaction Table

Sector Classification Adopted

The scheme of sector classification adopted in both IOTT 's, *i.e.*1970-71 and 2000-01 is same for the purpose of comparison. Total of 25 sectors[1] are taken which are actually aggregated sectors prepared from 60 aggregated[2] sectors as followed in National Accounts Statistics. The first five sectors in the sector classification represent primary production, the next 6 to 19 sectors relate to manufacturing industries and the remaining 20 to 25 sectors deal with the tertiary services. In the primary production 1 to 5 sectors belong to agriculture, animal husbandry, forestry/logging, fishing, mining/ quarrying, respectively. The input and output data for the primary sectors are taken from the State Accounts Division (Delhi).

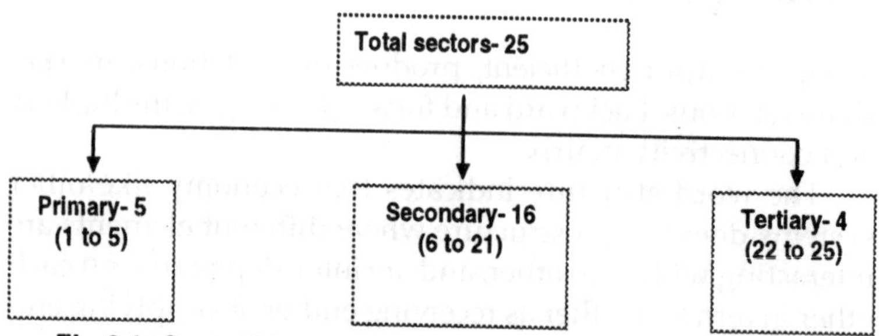

Fig 6.1: Sector Classification for Input-Output Transaction Table

The level of disaggregation adopted for manufacturing industries corresponds to digit level of National Industrial Classification (NIC) 1998. Manufacturing sector, comprising of 6 to 19 sectors in the present IOTT has been prepared separately for both registered and un-registered manufacturing. Data for registered manufacturing for 1970-71 and 2000-01 have been obtained from respective Annual Survey of Industries (ASI), whereas the data for unregistered manufacturing have been taken from surveys conducted by National Sample Survey Organisation (NSSO) 27th round (1972-73) and 56th round (1999-2000). For registered manufacturing the source of data for output and input is ASI. The tables of ASI used for IOTT are Table 4, Table 5 for inputs and Table 6 for output and other outputs for 1970-71. For 2000-01, Table 1 is used for inputs and Table 2 for output and other outputs. The data has been taken at 3 digit level NIC 1970-71 and 2000-01 by considering proper sector concordance for keeping common sector classification (as specified by CSO). The items like (a) other basic materials, (b) other chemical and auxiliary materials, (c) other packing material, and (d) consumable stores are distributed to the relevant conceivable sectors in proportion to their existing values (proportion used by CSO). Similarly, items like other products are proportionally distributed among diagonals and by-products.

For un-registered manufacturing source of data for outputs and inputs is the survey on un-organized manufacturing sector conducted by NSSO during 1972-1973 and 1999-2000. Input/output flows, thus, arrived separately for registered and un-registered manufacturing are clubbed together to arrive at the total flows of the manufacturing sector for both time periods.

Tertiary activities include services like construction, electricity/gas/water supply, railway transport and other transport, storage and warehousing, communication, trade, hotels and restaurant, banking, insurance, ownership of dwelling, education, medical and administration services. The information on input and output for different tertiary sectors are taken from State Accounts Division (Delhi).

Final Demand/Use

The final use/demand of the gross domestic product has been classified into four categories *viz.*

(a) *Private Final Consumption Expenditure (PFCE):* PFCE represents the consumption expenditure of households and non-profit institutions. The data on PFCE was obtained from the report on Consumer Expenditure from Directorate of Economics and Statistics, Delhi for concerned time periods.

(b) *Government Final Consumption Expenditure (GFCE):* GFCE represents current consumption expenditure of the Government. This expenditure comprises of compensation of employees, depreciation and intermediate consumption (purchase of goods and services including repair and maintenance less sales). The total GFCE is divided on the basis of economic classification into sectors of education, medical and health, water supply, construction, other services and public administration and defence. The details of intermediate consumption are available in budget document and report on economic and purpose classification of budget expenditure of Delhi, Statistical Handbook of Delhi, 1970-71, and 2000-01.

(c) *Gross Fixed Capital Formation (GFCF):* The data on GFCF have been taken from economic and purpose classification report, Delhi.

(d) *Others* : This includes Change In Stocks (CIS) exports, (EXP) less imports (IMP). Since data on item-wise export and import for Delhi was not available, therefore crude estimates are used for these parameters on the bases of national level data.

Valuation of Transactions

All the entries in the IOTT are at current market prices, *i.e.* including trade and transport margins and net indirect taxes. In other words, IOTT is prepared at the prices at which actual transactions take place.

Overall Balancing between Total Products and Expenditure

The estimates of GDP and expenditures, used for the present IOTT are from State Accounts Division, Delhi for 1970-71 and 2000-01. For a balanced IOTT, it is essential that adjustments be made for the discrepancies for overall balancing of row and column totals. The overall discrepancy (about 2 to 3 per cent of the total GDP) has been absorbed in various categories of final demand (on the basis of the discrepancies in each of the sectors).

Generation of Matrices

Input Flow Matrix (Absorption Matrix)

The absorption matrix provides basic information for an input-output system in (commodity × industry) flow. The input flows for different sectors are identified in terms of commodities and industries given IOTT sector codes developed for the purpose, as discussed in the earlier paragraphs on sector classification. The input flows for registered and un-registered manufacturing are generated separately on the basis of detailed coded input data. The ASI tables were recorded as per the sector codes used in this study. The data records are then aggregated to IOTT sector codes for both commodities and industries. In each industry sector besides the identified inputs, there are several un-identified input items of the categories of other basic materials, other chemicals, other packing materials etc. The treatment of these un-identified inputs is given in earlier paragraphs. Input flows, thus, arrived at separately for registered and un-registered manufacturing is combined to arrive at the total input flows of the manufacturing sectors.

The single output flow matrix representing the complete manufacturing sector has, then, been combined with input flow matrices of primary and tertiary sector of the economy. The final demand vectors are outside the 25 columns relating to inter-industry transaction. The final demand vectors give row total of utilization of commodities in the final demand column. The input flow at market (purchaser's) prices has been obtained by depicting the inter- industry flows and final uses of the commodities in rows. The sectoral estimates of gross value added have been introduced as a row at the bottom next to the row showing the total inputs by industries. The un-balanced input-output transaction table at market price (purchaser's prices) is thus obtained, where the individual row and column totals show the first result of the exercise in terms of commodity utilization and input structure of industries. The sum of entries along any row shows the total of inter-industry and the final use of the commodity. The sum of the entries in a column of this table shows the output of the industry since the table is (commodity × industry) transaction presentation, the row totals do not tally with the column total even after final balancing though the column and row headings are similar. The balancing here, therefore, refers to an exercise with reference to independent (industry × commodity) classification of output matrix.

Output Matrix (Make Matrix)

The output flow matrix, an industry × commodity classification of outputs, is known as make matrix. A similar procedure is followed for the generation of the output flows relating to registered as well as un-registered manufacturing industries separately on the basis of detailed coded output data and, finally, merged in a single output flow matrix similar to the input flow matrix. The sources of data for the industry-wise details of the output of products and by-products are the same as those utilized for the input flows. These output data are tabulated to obtain the 'industry × commodity matrix' (make matrix) by merging the output flow from manufacturing sectors and output flows from primary and services sectors. The make matrix provides the commodity outputs. The sum of the entries in columns of this table shows the total use of the commodities and the sum of entries along any rows of this table shows total output of that industry.

Input-Output Coefficient Matrix

The input-output coefficient matrix, also called structure matrix, of input-output transactions and its entries are known as input-output coefficient or technical coefficients. The word 'technical' is used because in such a table, the technology of production is clearly displayed while the volume of inter-sectoral transaction is no longer directly visible. This matrix is derived from input flow matrix (absorption matrix), *i.e.* (commodity × industry matrix). The technical coefficients are found by dividing each flow in a particular column of the sectors by the total output of the sector represented by that column.

Product Mix Matrix

This matrix is derived from the output flow or make matrix, by dividing the row entries by the respective industry outputs (matrix is presented as a transpose of this matrix). Product mix relations show the main product and by-products produced by an industry. These relations are analyzed through the product mix matrix, whose column entries show the proportions in which a particular industry produces various commodities in the diagonal elements. They give the proportion of the main products in the output of the industry while the off diagonal elements indicate the subsidiary products and by-products. In all industries whether primary, services and manufacturing industries, the main product of the industry accounts for major part in the total output.

Market Share Matrix

This matrix is also derived from output flow or make matrix by dividing the column entries by the respective commodity outputs. The market relations of economy of Delhi or among various industrial sectors are analyzed through the market share matrix, which represents the proportions in which the various industries produce the total output of particular commodity. The column entries show proportions contributed by different industries in total output of respective commodity. The diagonal elements give the proportions of the output of various commodities produced as main products. The off diagonal elements show the proportions of the commodities as subsidiary products in other industries.

Leontief Inverse Matrix

This matrix is used in the popular open static models for the projection purpose. In the Leontief Inverse, the coefficient matrix used is generated under industry technology assumption.

Input-Output Transactions in 1970 -71

It would be apparent from the absorption matrix[3] that distribution of various components in the total output shows that intermediate demand shared 73.43 per cent, Private Final Consumption Expenditure (PFCE) 17.53 per cent, Government Final Consumption Expenditure (GFCE) 8.5 per cent, Government Fixed Capital Formation (GFCF) 0.54 per cent and others (includes change in stocks, export less import) -2.54 per cent. In total output, major share has been consumed by intermediate demand and private final consumption (Table 6.1).

Table 6.1: Components of Total Output

Items	*Share (%)*
Intermediate demand	73.43
PFCE	17.53
GFCE	8.50
GFCF	0.54
Others	-2.54
Total Output	100

Source : Obtained from absorption matrix prepared in the present research (Appendix IV A).

From the absorption matrix, the entire sectors are divided into commodities (sectors 1 to 21) and services (sectors 22 to 25)[4] to see their share in the total output besides also knowing the total final use. It would be clear from Table 6.2 that 68.46 per cent was the share of intermediate demand and 31.54

per cent was the final use in the total output for 1970-71. This intermediate demand comprised of 41.41 per cent of commodities' share and 27.05 per cent of services. In the case of commodities they contributed 54.18 per cent to self, 25.96 per cent to services and 20.30 per cent to final use of the total output. While, service sector has shared 24.30 per cent of commodities output, 28.88 per cent of self and 46.18 per cent of the final use in the total output. The commodities contributed 50.25 per cent to the gross value added, while service shared 49.75 per cent of it (Table 6.2).

Table 6.2 : Distribution of Outputs (in per cent)

Items	*Commodities*	*Services*	*Intermediate Use*	*Final Use*	*Total Output*
(a)	*(b)*	*(c)*	*(d) (b+c)*	*(e)*	*(f) (d+e)*
Commodities	58.18	25.96	79.87	20.30	100
Services	24.30	28.88	53.19	46.81	100
Sub-total	41.41	27.05	68.46	31.54	100
Gross value added	50.25	49.75	-	-	100

Source : Obtained from absorption matrix prepared in the present research (Appendix IV A).

The input distribution of commodities and services to the total output reveals that in the year 1970-71 for the total output, 68.46 per cent were total inputs with 31.54 per cent of gross value added. In the total final use, commodities shared 36.85 per cent inputs, services shared 63.45 per cent. Of the output, total inputs from commodities were 72.32 per cent and gross value added 27.46 per cent; these inputs consists of 58.18 per cent from the same sector itself and 18.14 per cent from services. In the case of service sector, total inputs contributed towards total output were 63.29 per cent and gross value added 36.71 per cent. These total inputs from services also comprised of 34.41 per cent share from commodities and 28.88 per cent from self-sector (Table 6.3).

Table 6.3 : Distribution of Inputs (In per cent)

Items	*Commodities*	*Services*	*Sub-total*	*Total Final Use*
Commodities	54.18	34.41	45.73	36.85
Services	18.14	28.88	22.73	63.45
Sub-total	72.32	63.29	68.46	-
Gross value added	27.46	36.71	31.54	-
Total output	100	100	100	100

Source : Obtained from absorption matrix prepared in the present research (Appendix IV A).

The inter-industry relations in terms of major sectors *viz.* primary, secondary and tertiary in total intermediate demand show that in the intermediate use primary sector shared 4.05 per cent, secondary sector 48.38 per cent and tertiary sector 47.57 per cent. The primary sector receives 31.52 per cent contribution from self, 28.83 per cent from secondary and 39.65 per cent from tertiary industry in the total intermediate use. Manufacturing sector in its total intermediate use took 1.31 per cent from primary industry, 70.14 per cent from self and 28.55 per cent from service industry. The service sector received 1.41 per cent from primary, 26.31 per cent from manufacturing industry and 72.29 per cent from self in its total intermediate use (Table 6.4).

Table 6.4 : Inter-sectoral Transactions (In per cent)

Sectors	*Primary*	*Secondary*	*Tertiary*	*Total Intermediate Use*
Primary	31.52	28.83	39.65	100
Secondary	1.31	70.14	28.55	100
Tertiary	1.41	26.31	72.29	100
Total Inputs	4.05	48.38	47.57	100

Source : Obtained from absorption matrix prepared in the present research (Appendix IV A).

The distribution of inputs in the total output in terms of primary, secondary and tertiary sectors revealed that in

1970-71, 68.55 per cent were total inputs with 31.53 per cent of gross value added. These inputs included 6.13 per cent from primary industry, 34.12 per cent from secondary and 28.22 per cent from tertiary industry. In the total output of primary industry, it was seen that total inputs used were 62.03 per cent and gross value added 37.96 per cent. In these inputs, the primary sector has taken 43.17 per cent from self-sector, 9.98 per cent from manufacturing and 8.88 per cent from tertiary industry. The total output from secondary sector comprised of total inputs of 72.97 per cent and gross value added of 27.03 per cent. These total inputs by manufacturing sector included contributions of other sectors of economy *viz.* 3.89 per cent, 52.73 per cent, 16.35 per cent from primary, secondary and tertiary industries, respectively. The tertiary sectors' total inputs structure reflected 64.90 per cent of total inputs and 35.04 per cent of gross value added. These total inputs have been contributed by primary sector (4.48 per cent), 19.43 per cent by manufacturing and 40.68 per cent from self-sector (Table 6.5).

Table 6.5 : Distribution of Inputs in Different Sectors (In per cent)

Sectors	*Primary*	*Secondary*	*Tertiary*	*Total Intermediate Use*
Primary	43.17	3.89	4.84	6.13
Secondary	9.98	52.73	19.43	34.12
Tertiary	8.88	16.35	40.68	28.22
Sub-total	62.03	72.97	64.90	68.55
Gross value added	37.96	27.03	35.04	31.53
Total Output	100	100	100	100

Source : Obtained from absorption matrix prepared in the present research (Appendix IV A).

The input-output table has been broadly aggregated into three main sectors of the economy that gives actual level for 1970-71. In Table 6.6 the basic inter-industry matrix consists of columns 2 to 4 and rows 3 to 5. The diagonal cells of the basic inter-industry matrix show the output of goods and services, produced and consumed by the same sector. The sum of column 5 (inter-industry use) and 6 (final use) gives the total supply or output in the economy. It is clear from Table 6.6 that primary sector is very low while tertiary sector is maximum. It is also shown that tertiary sector as most significant sector followed by secondary and primary sectors. In terms of value added same trend has been observed. The total inputs used reveal that secondary sectors utilize maximum inputs. In total final use, primary sector has been almost negligible while secondary and tertiary sectors have been mainly contributing. It is also evident that in the three broad sectors consumed most of the inputs are from self-sectors (Table 6.6).

Table 6.6 : Inter-Sectoral Transactions (In Rs. lakh 1970-71)

Sectors	*Primary*	*Secondary*	*Tertiary*	*Total Inter-mediate Use*	*Total Final Use*	*Total Output*
(1)	*(2)*	*(3)*	*(4)*	*(5)*	*(6)*	*(7)*
Primary	4131	3779	5197	13109	207	13316
Secondary	955	51220	20853	73028	25346	98374
Tertiary	850	15886	43655	60392	42361	102753
Total Inputs	5936	70887	69706	146536	-	-
Gross Value Added	3633	26258	37603 .	67494	-	-
Total Output	9570	97145	107309	214024	67494	281518

Source : Obtained from absorption matrix prepared in the present research (Appendix IV A).

The Gross Value Added (GVA) to total output proportion is considered here as sign for the growth of particular industry indicates that in the primary sectors of agriculture, animal husbandry, forestry and logging, the GVA output ratio is more than 35 per cent while the other two primary sectors of fishing and mining and quarrying have low GVA output-ratio (Fig.6.2).

In the manufacturing sector, plastic/rubber, chemicals, non-metallic products and metal industry are among the significant industries in terms of growth with more than 30 per cent GVA ratio. Wood, food products, industrial machinery, transport equipment industry, miscellaneous manufacturing industry, paper industry and textiles followed these industries with GVA ranging between 20 to 30 per cent. Leather and electric/electronic machinery sector are the only industries in secondary sector with lowest GVA output ratio of less than 20 per cent. The electricity/gas/water supply had the GVA output-ratio of 18.46 per cent and construction with 29.01 per cent. In tertiary sector, other services show the highest GVA ratio of 45.49 per cent, followed by transport/ storage services and banking/insurance with 38.04 per cent, and trade with 21.46 per cent (Fig. 6.2).

The input ratio to the total output of an industry reflects upon the production efficiency or technological efficiency of the production process. It would be evident from the graph that in the primary sector industries, input-ratio ranges between 61 per cent in agriculture and animal husbandry to 69.97 per cent in fishing (Fig. 6.3).

The secondary sector industries witnessed many pictures regarding inputs used. Industries like plastic/ rubber, chemical, non-metallic products, metals have the input proportion about 66 to 68 per cent. Wood products, petroleum products, food products and industrial machinery industries use 70 to 75 per cent inputs, whereas transport equipment, miscellaneous manufacturing, paper and textile industries have their inputs between 75 to 80 per cent to the total output. There are only two industries, *i.e.* leather products and electric/electronic machinery that show input used as high as 81 per cent to their output. Construction industry has the output of about 70 per cent while electricity/gas/water supply show higher input proportion, *i.e.* 81.54 per cent. In the tertiary sector trade has highest input proportion, *i.e.* 78.54 per cent followed by nearly 62 per cent in transport/storage, banking/ insurance industry and 54.51 per cent in other services (Fig. 6.3).

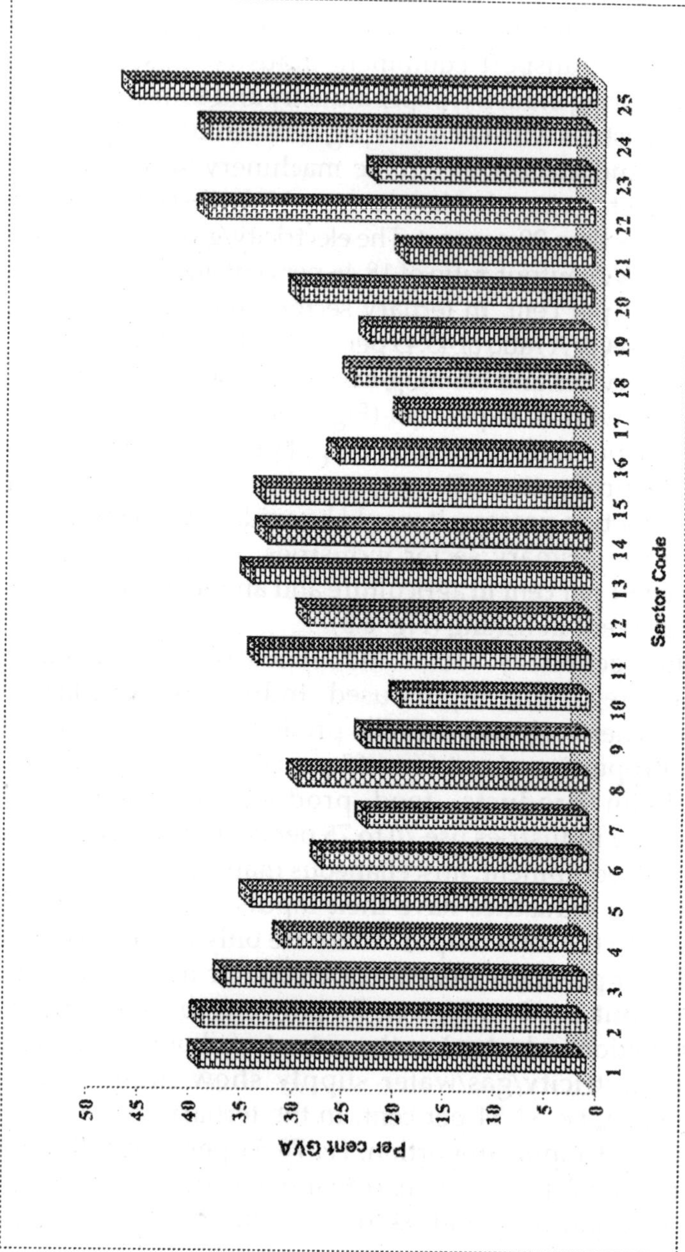

Fig. 6.2 : Gross Value Added-Output Ratios

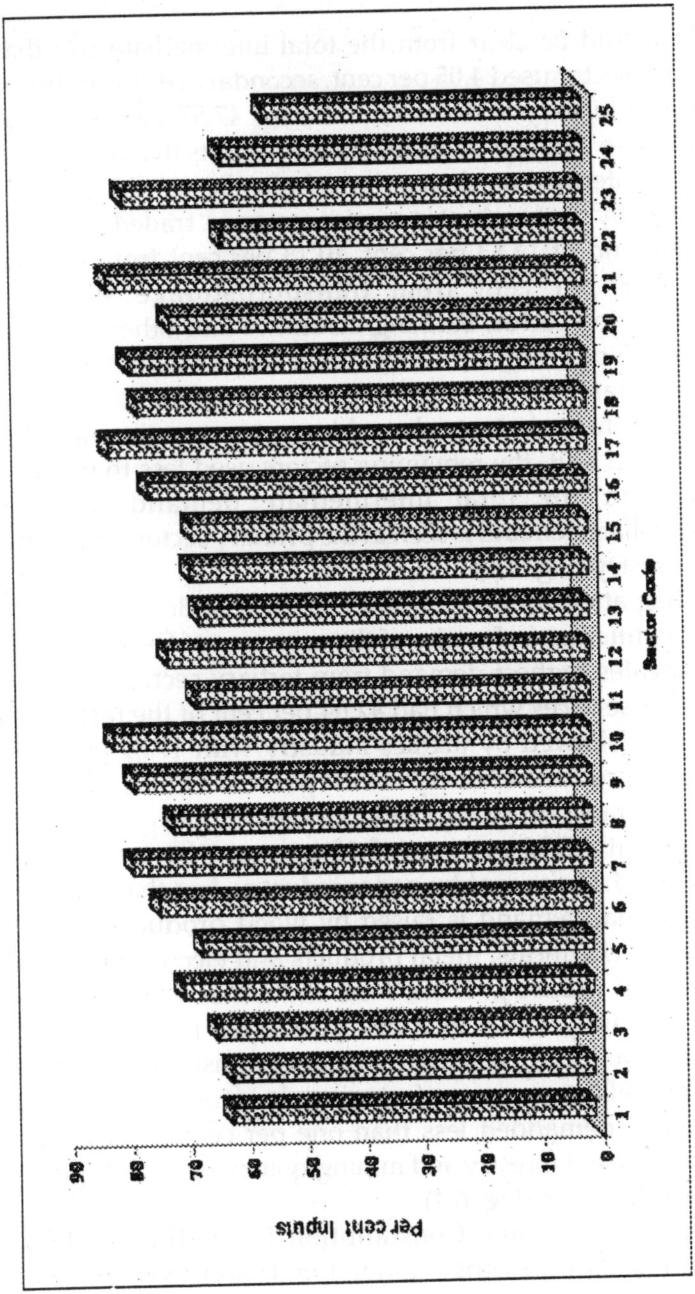

Fig. 6.3 : Input-Output Ratio

It would be clear from the total intermediate use that primary sector used 4.05 per cent, secondary sector 48.38 per cent and tertiary sector accounted for 47.57 per cent. The sector-wise detailed intermediate use reflects that maximum share of intermediate demand was from plastic/rubber sector, followed by next highest in service sector, *i.e.* trade/hotel with the demand of 14.83 per cent, 10.13 per cent from textiles and 7.98 per cent from transport/storage services. Construction sector, banking/insurance and other services demand 5 per cent each. Most other sectors with 3 per cent intermediate use included agriculture, paper, chemicals, metal products, industrial machinery, transport equipment etc. Added to it, the remaining sectors used less than 3 per cent from the total intermediate demand. Lowest intermediate demand is seen in the primary sectors of fishing and forestry (Fig. 6.4).

The pattern of distribution of total final demand or use among different industries of the economy of Delhi in 1970-71 indicates highest demand from tertiary sector industry, *i.e.* other services which had 47.04 per cent of the total final demand followed by textiles industry with 17.59 per cent and food products industry with 11 per cent. Other industries included transport/storage services with 9.67 per cent, plastic/rubber with 6.56 per cent, 5.19 per cent by trade/hotel industry, 4.33 per cent by paper industry, less than one per cent of final demand is raised by wood products, leather products, chemicals, metal products and electric/electronic machinery industry. There were industries with negative final demand, which included petroleum products, non-metallic products, industrial machinery, transport equipment and miscellaneous manufacturing. In primary sector, all industries demanded less than one per cent of total final demand except forestry and mining/quarrying with negative share in final use (Fig. 6.4).

The Private Final Consumption Expenditure (PFCE) pattern reveals the consumption trends and levels in Delhi

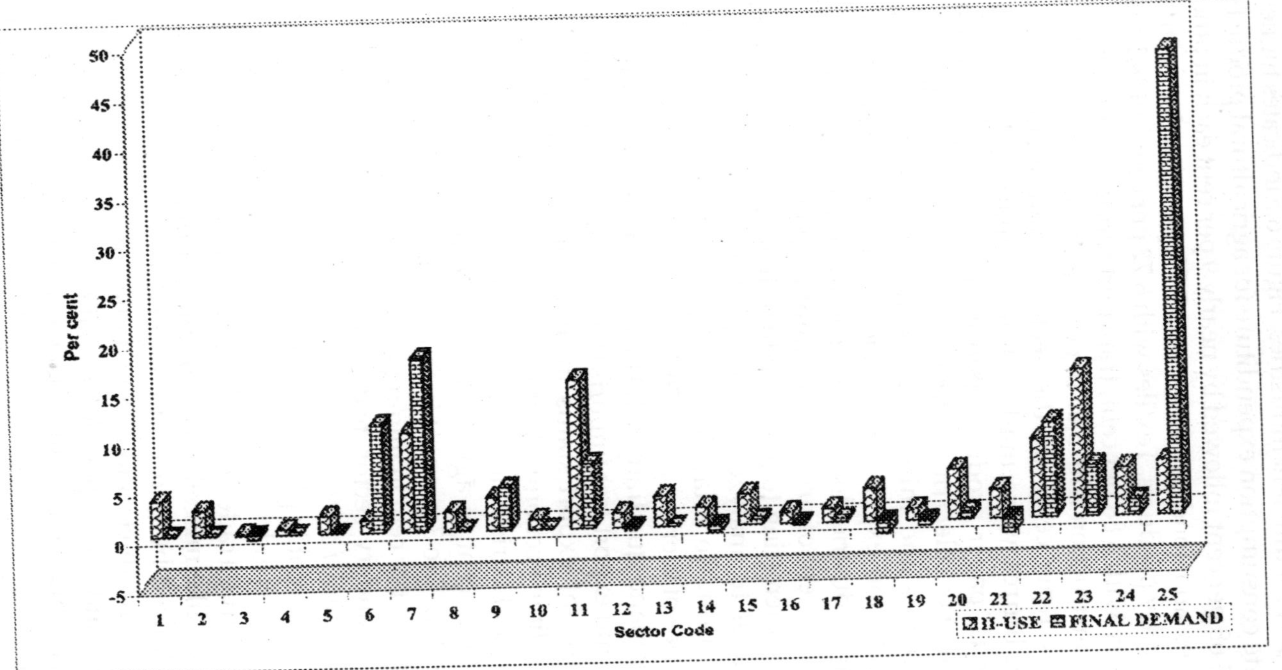

Fig. 6.4 : Intermediate Use and Final Demand

in 1970-71 for different industries. Figure 6.5 indicates highest private consumption expenditure for agricultural products, *i.e.* 45.68 per cent followed by nearly 9 per cent each in other services and food products and 7.77 per cent for animal husbandry products. Textiles with 6.72 per cent, trade/hotel industry with 6.86 per cent, transport services with 5.20 per cent, construction with 3.65 per cent, and banking/insurance with 1.11 per cent, are the sectors where major private expenditures were made. Other industries like wood products, paper products, petroleum products, industrial machinery; electric/electronic machinery, transport equipments and miscellaneous manufacturing have the consumption expenditure of less than 1 per cent. Even primary industries like forestry, fishing and mining have less than 1 per cent of private consumption (Fig.6.5).

It is interesting to point out that there has been no direct parameter to analyze export aspect of the inter-industry transaction. To analyze the export factor in different industries of economy in 1970-71, the column (others) in the final demand quadrant of IOTT that consists of (change in stocks and export less imports) has been used as an indirect indicator for export status in different industries of the metropolitan economy. As it is evident from Fig. 6.6, all the primary industries showed negative figures with highest of -187.23 per cent in agriculture, -37.26 per cent in animal husbandry, -2 to 3 per cent in forestry and fishing, and with less than –1 per cent in mining/quarrying (Fig. 6.6).

In secondary sector, textiles industry had the highest positive value, *i.e.* 92.70 per cent of positive trade, followed by 44.50 per cent in plastic/rubber industry, 39.59 per cent in food products industry and 27.84 per cent in paper industry. The negative trade values have been witnessed in the industries like miscellaneous manufacturing by -17.66 per cent, followed by transport equipment by -11.98 per cent, petroleum products and non-metallic products by -5.76 per cent each and -1 to -3 per cent in leather products, chemicals, industrial machinery and electric/electronic machinery industries. In construction industry, nearly 30 per cent

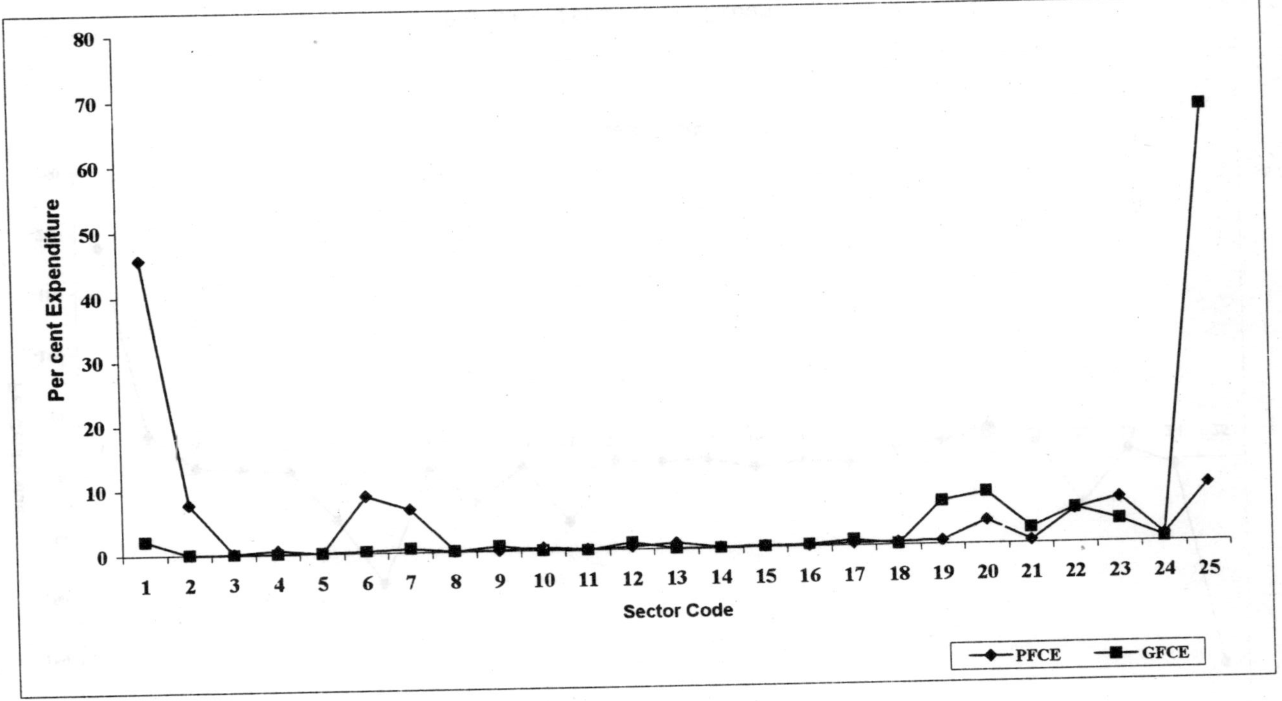

Fig. 6.5 : Final Consumption Expenditure

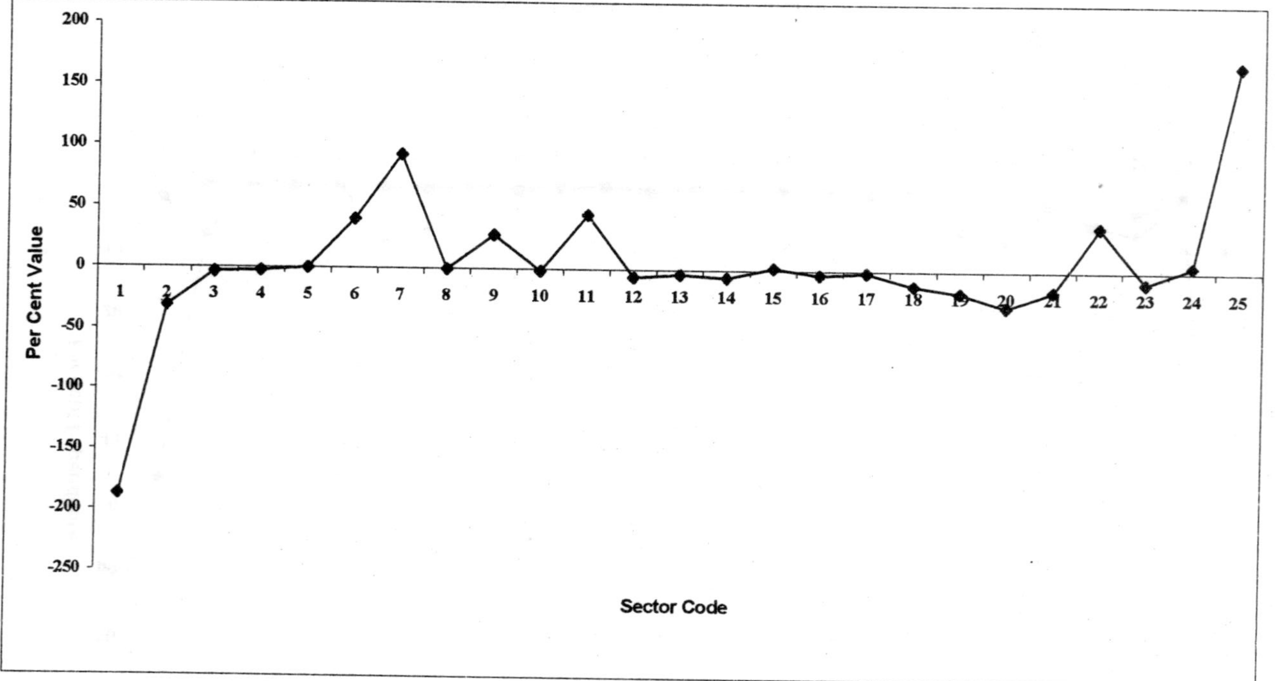

Fig. 6.6 : Distribution of Export

negative export has been registered while in electricity/gas/water supply -15.83 per cent value have been observed (Fig.6.6).

The tertiary sector showed 167.42 per cent of positive export, followed by 36.16 per cent in transport/storage services and 5 per cent in banking/insurance industry while trade/hotel registered -8.83 per cent of negative trade (Fig.6.6).

Input-Output Coefficients

The inter-industry flows can be expressed in the form of input-output coefficient matrix, called structural matrix of technical input-output table and its entries are known as input-output coefficient. This is derived from input flow matrix and these technical coefficients (a_{ij}) are found by dividing each flow in a particular column of the sector by the total output of the sector represented by that column. The principal way in which input-output coefficient is used for analysis, is that they represent the structure of production in the economy. The columns are in effect the production recipes for each sector, in terms of input taken from all the sectors. This shows that to produce one rupee worth good by a sector, how much input does it require putting from other sectors of the economy. In other words, these are inputs required from other productive sectors. These coefficients show only direct purchase among the sectors; however, to know the total input both direct as well as indirect requirements are accounted through inverse matrix. These coefficients are used to explain any change through increase or decrease in the production as well as the demand of various inputs.

Primary Sector

Table 6.7 reveals the production recipes of different industries reflecting that agriculture industry has taken maximum of

26.93 per cent from the same commodity, 16.72 per cent from animal husbandry, 7.05 per cent from chemicals, more than 2 per cent from construction, trade/hotels, more than 1 per cent from electricity/gas/water supply, transport services, banking insurance and petroleum products. It has no intake from fishing, mining/quarrying, leather products, plastic/ rubber, metal/non metal and miscellaneous manufacturing. Animal husbandry industry received 16 per cent inputs from same commodity, 26.95 per cent from agriculture, 7.06 per cent from chemicals, more than 2 per cent from construction and trade, more than 1 per cent from electricity, transport services, trade and petroleum products. This sector showed no relation with fishing, mining, leather products, plastic or rubber and metal/non-metal products. In other words, it showed similar input structure as that of agriculture. Forestry and logging industry has taken major inputs from animal husbandry and agriculture, followed by food products and trade. Fishing industry took inputs of 70 per cent from same commodity in total output. In mining/ quarrying, 19.05 per cent were used from self-commodity, 21.43 per cent from industrial machinery, 16.65 per cent from transport services and 9.52 per cent from electric/ electronic machinery (Table 6.7).

Secondary Sector

Food industry took 22.5 per cent contribution from plastic/ rubber, 16.04 per cent from agriculture, and 7.16 per cent from self, 10.48 per cent from non-metallic products, 6.92 per cent from animal husbandry and 4.13 per cent from transport services. It did not indicate dependence on fishing and leather products. Textile industry received more than 50 per cent from self 5.21 per cent from chemicals, 7.41 per cent from trade, 6.41 per cent from transport and storage services alongwith contribution from many commodities. It has no relation with first three primary sectors, food products and non-metallic products. Wood industry reflects that 13 per cent was shared from self, 15.88 per cent from plastic/rubber, 17.23 per cent from transport/storage services, 5.12 per cent from forestry and 3 per cent each from trade and banking/ insurance. This industry has no input flow from agriculture, animal husbandry, forestry, leather and transport equipments. Paper industry had 31.6 per cent as self, 27.05 per cent from other services, 10.23 per cent from transport/ storage services and 2 per cent each from wood and chemical products. It did not get supplies from first four primary commodities, food products, leather, non-metallic, and transport equipments. Leather industry received 30.79 per cent from plastic/ rubber, 12.38 per cent from chemicals, 11.93 per cent from transport/ storage, 7.75 per cent from trade, 5.43 per cent from wood, 2 per cent each from mining, and same commodity. It indicated no inter-relation with first two primary sectors, non-metallic, metal, transport equipments and other services. Plastic/rubber industry got 43.75 per cent contribution in its output by self, 3 per cent each from wood, leather, banking/insurance and other services. This industry did not show dependence on whole of primary sector, textiles and miscellaneous manufacturing. Petroleum industry got supplies of 27.51 per cent from transport/storage service, 20 per cent from banking/insurance, 12.98 per cent from trade, and 8.30 per cent from textiles. No relation zone covers primary sectors, and other services (Table 6.7).

Chemical industry received 13 per cent from transport/ storage, 10.5 per cent from plastic/rubber and 5 to 7 per cent from metal products, self, paper, textile and trade. This industry got no input from first two primary sectors, fishing, transport equipment and other services. In the production of total output non-metallic industry receive 25 per cent from metal, 19.13 per cent from self, 8.20 per cent from transport/ storage services and 3.98 per cent from banking/insurance. No relationship has been seen with first three primary sectors, leather, and other services. In metal industry, 24.15 per cent are supplied as self-product, 14.86 per cent as plastic/rubber, 9 per cent from non-metallic and 3 per cent from trade. No supplies are observed from primary sectors, leather and transport equipments. The industrial machinery industry has received highest from self, closely followed by 16.98 per cent from electric/electronic machinery, 15.88 per cent from trade, 10.92 from transport/storage services, 3.1 per cent from banking/insurance and 3.25 per cent from chemicals. This industry has no supplies from primary sectors, food products, transport equipment and other services. The electric/electronic machinery industry received mainly from self, *i.e.* 34.94 per cent, 12.97 per cent from trade, 11.54 per cent from metal products, 8.04 per cent from plastic/rubber along with small proportions from many other commodities. It shared nothing from primary products, food products, leather products, and transport equipments. The transport equipment manufacturing industry received 26.7 per cent inputs from self, 18.16 per cent from metal products, 7.24 per cent form plastic/rubber products, 8.36 per cent from chemical, 6.32 per cent from trade and 2.97 per cent from transport/storage services. It has zero supplies from agriculture, animal husbandry, fishing, food products, non-metallic products, and other services. The miscellaneous manufacturing industry took inputs from mining, *i.e.* 21.87 per cent, 11.70 per cent from electric/electronic machinery, 11.31 per cent from self, 14.18 per cent from trade and 4.08 per cent from leather. This industry took no inputs from first four primary commodities, food products, transport equipment, industrial machinery, banking/insurance and other services (Table 6.7).

Construction industry received 27.30 per cent from trade, 20.40 per cent from electricity/water/gas, 7.13 per cent from mining, 5.18 per cent from electric/electronic machinery, 2.25 per cent from self and 6.63 per cent from transport/storage services. Construction industry received no supplies from first four primary, food products, leather, plastic/rubber, and

Table 6.7 : Input-Output Coefficient Matrix (commodity × industry): 1970-71

Sector Code	Industry / Commodity	1	2	3	4	5	6	7	8	9	10	11	12	13
1.	Agriculture	0.2693	0.2695	0.1190	0.0000	0.0000	0.1604	0.0000	0.0000	0.0000	0.0000	0.0000	0.0000	0.0000
2.	Animal Husbandry	0.1672	0.1673	0.3969	0.0000	0.0000	0.0692	0.0000	0.0000	0.0000	0.0000	0.0000	0.0000	0.0000
3.	Forestry and Logging	0.0001	0.0001	0.0000	0.0000	0.0000	0.0004	0.0000	0.0512	0.0000	0.0011	0.0000	0.0000	0.0240
4.	Fishing	0.0000	0.0000	0.0001	0.7000	0.0000	0.0000	0.0000	0.0000	0.0000	0.0000	0.0000	0.0000	0.0000
5.	Mining/Quarrying	0.0000	0.0000	0.0000	0.0000	0.1905	0.0016	0.0253	0.0005	0.0015	0.0288	0.0000	0.0003	0.0063
6.	Food Prod., Beverages and Tobacco Products	0.0001	0.0001	0.0692	-0.0004	0.0000	0.0716	0.0000	0.0000	0.0000	0.0000	0.0037	0.0000	0.0014
7.	Textiles	0.0006	0.0006	0.0100	0.0003	0.0000	0.0015	0.5046	0.0023	0.0051	0.0022	0.0000	0.0830	0.0528
8.	Wood, Wood Prods. and Furniture	0.0002	0.0002	0.0002	0.0003	0.0000	0.0121	0.0065	0.1290	0.0219	0.0543	0.0347	0.0063	0.0039
9.	Paper, Paper Prods., print/Pub.	0.0001	0.0001	0.0009	0.0000	0.0000	0.0040	0.0059	0.0022	0.3160	0.0016	0.0148	0.0038	0.0559
10.	Leather Products	0.0000	0.0000	0.0000	0.0000	0.0000	0.0000	0.0069	0.0000	0.0000	0.0217	0.0378	0.0003	0.0423
11.	Plastic/Rubber Products	0.0000	0.0000	0.0000	0.0000	0.0000	0.2250	0.0044	0.1588	0.0049	0.3079	0.4374	0.0030	0.1050
12.	Coal/Petroleum Products	0.0184	0.0184	0.0004	-0.0002	0.0000	0.0014	0.0061	0.0034	0.0030	0.0407	0.0287	0.0015	0.0035
13.	Chemicals	0.0705	0.0706	0.0036	-0.0003	0.0000	0.0204	0.0521	0.0199	0.0215	0.1238	0.0037	0.0005	0.0608
14.	Non-metallic Products	0.0000	0.0000	0.0000	0.0000	0.0000	0.1048	0.0000	0.0017	0.0000	0.0000	0.0044	0.0001	0.0207
15.	Metal Products	0.0000	0.0000	0.0000	0.0000	0.0000	0.0006	0.0006	0.1723	0.0013	0.0000	0.0052	0.0006	0.0740
16.	Industrial Machinery	0.0050	0.0050	0.0001	0.0000	0.2143	0.0000	0.0013	0.0018	0.0011	0.0005	0.0088	0.0006	0.0004
17.	Electric/Electronic Machinery	0.0001	0.0001	0.0003	0.0000	0.0952	0.0024	0.0041	0.0016	0.0020	0.0011	0.0001	0.0024	0.0016
18.	Rail and other Transport Equipment	0.0001	0.0001	0.0003	-0.0003	0.0000	0.0021	0.0000	0.0000	0.0000	0.0000	0.0001	0.0000	0.0000
19.	Miscellaneous Manufacturing Equipment	0.0000	0.0000	0.0002	0.0000	0.0000	0.0023	0.0005	0.0002	0.0002	0.0005	0.0000	0.0002	0.0003
20.	Construction	0.0201	0.0201	0.0036	0.0000	0.0000	0.0003	0.0001	0.0006	0.0002	0.0003	0.0000	0.0073	0.0001
21.	Electricity/Gas/Water Supply	0.0158	0.0158	0.0001	0.0000	0.0000	0.0003	0.0001	0.0053	0.0014	0.0007	0.0004	0.0050	0.0004
22.	Rail and other Transport / Storage Services	0.0131	0.0131	0.0102	0.0000	0.1665	0.0413	0.0641	0.0889	0.1023	0.1193	0.0024	0.2751	0.1358
23.	Trade/Hotel	0.0252	0.0252	0.0270	0.0003	0.0000	0.0054	0.0741	0.0368	0.0151	0.0775	0.0247	0.1298	0.0551
24.	Banking/Insurance	0.0127	0.0127	0.0002	0.0000	0.0000	0.0105	0.0118	0.0362	0.0117	0.0308	0.0356	0.2005	0.0221
25.	Other services (Edu., Med., Admin., Defence. etc.)	0.0003	0.0003	0.0005	0.0000	0.0000	0.0002	0.0122	0.0002	0.2705	0.0000	0.0302	0.0000	0.0000
	Total Input	0.6190	0.6195	0.6428	0.6997	0.6666	0.7377	0.7806	0.7128	0.7796	0.8130	0.6729	0.7203	0.6664
	Total Output	1.0000	1.0000	1.0000	1.0000	1.0000	1.0000	1.0000	1.0000	1.0000	1.0000	1.0000	1.0000	1.0000
	Gross Value Added	0.3810	0.3805	0.3572	0.3000	0.3334	0.2623	0.2194	0.2872	0.2204	0.1870	0.3271	0.2797	0.3336

Table 6.7 : (Contd...)

Sector Code	Industry Commodity	14	15	16	17	18	19	20	21	22	23	24	25	Total Input
1.	Agriculture	0.0000	0.0000	0.0000	0.0000	0.0000	0.0000	0.0000	0.0000	0.0091	0.0476	0.0000	0.0004	0.8754
2.	Animal Husbandry	0.0000	0.0000	0.0000	0.0000	0.0000	0.0000	0.0000	0.0000	0.0000	0.0647	0.0000	0.0002	0.8655
3.	Forestry and Logging	0.0001	0.0005	0.0001	0.0000	0.0005	0.0000	0.0001	0.0000	0.0000	0.0000	0.0000	0.0005	0.0787
4.	Fishing	0.0000	0.0000	0.0000	0.0000	0.0000	0.0000	0.0000	0.0000	0.0000	0.0336	0.0000	0.0000	0.7337
5.	Mining/Quarrying	0.0273	0.0099	0.0041	0.0009	0.0052	0.2187	0.0713	0.0415	0.0000	0.0118	0.0000	0.0010	0.6467
6.	Food Prod. Beverages and Tobacco Products	0.0000	0.0000	0.0000	0.0000	0.0000	0.0000	0.0000	0.0000	0.0016	0.0443	0.0000	0.0007	0.1923
7.	Textiles	0.0070	0.0030	0.0063	0.0076	0.0087	0.0027	0.0047	0.0000	0.0033	0.0001	0.0000	0.0096	0.7160
8.	Wood, Wood Prods. and Furniture	0.0138	0.0058	0.0151	0.0050	0.0184	0.0062	0.0004	0.0000	0.0019	0.0315	0.0026	0.0002	0.3705
9.	Paper, Paper Prods., Print/Pub.	0.0054	0.0032	0.0071	0.0013	0.0072	0.0065	0.0012	0.0051	0.0038	0.0107	0.0111	0.0259	0.4939
10.	Leather Products	0.0000	0.0000	0.0000	0.0000	0.0000	0.0408	0.0000	0.0000	0.0000	0.0000	0.0000	0.0000	0.1497
11.	Plastic/Rubber Products	0.0050	0.1486	0.0049	0.0804	0.0724	0.0125	0.0000	0.0000	0.0115	0.1070	0.0000	0.0663	1.7551
12.	Coal/Petroleum Products	0.0099	0.0128	0.0066	0.0004	0.0114	0.0009	0.0019	0.0399	0.0155	0.0005	0.0010	0.0073	0.2335
13.	Chemicals	0.0148	0.0103	0.0235	0.0194	0.0836	0.0133	0.0000	0.0006	0.0001	0.0000	0.0000	0.0257	0.6384
14.	Non-metallic Products	0.1913	0.0907	0.0034	0.0013	0.0000	0.0089	0.0000	0.0001	0.0000	0.0030	0.0000	0.0139	0.4444
15.	Metal Products	0.2592	0.2415	0.0131	0.1154	0.1816	0.0602	0.0063	0.0080	0.0016	0.0029	0.0000	0.0144	1.1589
16.	Industrial Machinery	0.0080	0.0006	0.1947	0.0011	0.0000	0.0000	0.0004	0.0194	0.0001	0.0000	0.0000	0.0271	0.4903
17.	Electric/Electronic Machinery	0.0010	0.0013	0.1698	0.3494	0.0011	0.1170	0.0518	0.0674	0.0006	0.0002	0.0000	0.0130	0.8836
18.	Rail and other Transport Equipment	0.0000	0.0000	0.0000	0.0000	0.2670	0.0000	0.0010	0.1273	0.0444	0.0203	0.0450	0.0369	0.5442
19.	Miscellaneous Manufacturing	0.0060	0.0001	0.0004	0.0001	0.0003	0.1131	0.0001	0.0045	0.0036	0.0011	0.0008	0.0349	0.1696
20.	Construction	0.0067	0.0001	0.0005	0.0001	0.0004	0.0005	0.0225	0.0227	0.0870	0.0054	0.4152	0.0425	0.6562
21.	Electricity/Gas/Water Supply	0.0020	0.0013	0.0013	0.0003	0.0008	0.0003	0.2040	0.0416	0.0010	0.0054	0.0084	0.0380	0.3499
22.	Rail and other Transport / Storage Services	0.0820	0.0134	0.1092	0.0810	0.0297	0.0367	0.0663	0.2720	0.1012	0.0066	0.0355,	0.0467	1.9126
23.	Trade/Hotel	0.0008	0.0973	0.1588	0.1297	0.0632	0.1418	0.2720	0.1621	0.2697	0.2167	0.0025	0.0651	2.0758
24.	Banking/Insurance	0.0398	0.0369	0.0310	0.0095	0.0135	0.0000	0.0032	0.0000	0.0592	0.0713	0.0605	0.0295	0.7394
25.	Other services(Edu.,Med., Admin., Defence.etc)	0.0000	0.0000	0.0000	0.0123	0.0000	0.0000	0.0025	0.0033	0.0045	0.1004	0.0369	0.0451	0.5193
	Total Input	0.6800	0.6774	0.7500	0.8154	0.7650	0.7800	0.7099	0.8154	0.6196	0.7854	0.6196	0.5451	0.6846
	Total Output	1.0000	1.0000	1.0000	1.0000	1.0000	1.0000	1.0000	1.0000	1.0000	1.0000	1.0000	1.0000	1.0000
	Gross Value Added	0.3200	0.3226	0.2500	0.1846	0.2350	0.2200	0.2901	0.1846	0.3804	0.2146	0.3804	0.4549	0.3154

Source: Mathematically obtained as part of input-output model (refer page 88-91 and page 299).

chemicals. The electricity/gas/water supply took 27.2 per cent inputs from transport services, 16.21 per cent from trade, 12.73 per cent from transport equipment, 6.7 per cent from self, 4.15 from mining, 3.99 from petroleum product, 2.27 per cent from construction. It got no input from first four primary sectors, food products, leather, and banking/ insurance (Table 6.7).

Tertiary Sector

In transport and storage services, supplies of input were from trade, *i.e.* 26.97 per cent, 10.12 per cent from self, 8.70 per cent from construction, 5.92 per cent from banking/insurance and 4.44 per cent from transport equipment. This service has no relationship with primary sector except agriculture, leather, and non-metallic products. Trade/hotel industry has strong dependence on self commodity by 21.67 per cent followed by 10 per cent each on plastic/rubber and other services, 7.13 per cent from banking/insurance, 4.43 per cent from food products, 3.37 per cent from fishing, 4.76 per cent from agriculture, 4.43 per cent from food products. Trade has no inputs from forestry, leather, chemical and industrial machinery. The banking and insurance industry have shown maximum dependence on construction, *i.e.* 41.52 per cent, 6.05 per cent on self, 4.50 per cent transport equipment, 3 per cent each on transport storage services and other services. This service group has no dependence on first seven sectors, which include primary sectors, food and textile, leather, plastic/rubber, metallic, non-metallic products, industrial machinery, and electric and electronic machinery products. Other services (which include education, medical, research, administration, etc.) reflect inter relationship with all industries of primary, secondary and territory sector except two industries, *i.e.* forestry and leather products. They have received 6 per cent each from plastic/rubber and trade, 4 per cent each from transport/storage, self, construction,

2 to 3 per cent from banking/insurance, electricity/gas/water supply, transport equipment, chemical and small fractions in variety of other industries (Table 6.7).

Industries that have received maximum input from self include fishing with 70 per cent inputs from same sector, textiles with 50.46 per cent, plastic/rubber with 43.74 per cent, electric and electronic machinery with 34.94 per cent, 31 per cent in paper, 26 per cent in transport equipment, agriculture and animal husbandry. On the other hand, industries that received maximum input through trade and transport/storage are petroleum industry, chemicals, industrial machinery, electric/electronic machinery, construction, electricity/gas/water supply and trade. Those industries involved complementary role of transport/ storage, and trade, thus, indicating toward imports (whether domestic or international) in their production process (Table 6.7).

There were also industries that have shown significant inputs from other services *viz.* paper industry (27.05 %), trade (10 %) and banking/insurance (3.69 %). They indicate the important role of public administration with strong inter-dependence (Table 6.7).

Product Mix Relations

Product mix relations show the main product and by-products produced by an industry. These relations are analyzed through the product mix matrix, whose column entries show the proportions in which a particular industry produces various commodities in the diagonal elements. They give the proportion of the main products in the output of the industry, while the off-diagonal elements indicate the subsidiary products and by-products. This matrix is derived from the make matrix by dividing row entries by respective industry output (presented as a transpose of this matrix). In all industries whether primary, secondary and services, the main product of the industry accounts for major part of the total output.

Primary Sector

In the primary industries of agriculture, animal husbandry, forestry, fishing and mining/quarrying main or diagonal output is the total output.

Secondary Sector

In food products industry, 99 per cent outputs are the main products alongwith marginal by-products in agriculture and animal husbandry. Textile industry's 96 per cent output is placed in diagonal cell while by-products are seen for fishing industry. Even the wood industry has 99 per cent of its output as the main product and by-products of very small proportion for metal industry. Paper and leather industry have been seen with full output as their main output. Plastic/rubber industry has 99 per cent as main product and rest by-product for textile industry. Other industries with all their output as main product include, petroleum products, chemicals, industrial machinery, electric/electronic machinery and transport equipments. Non-metallic industry has 91 per cent as main product, 6.36 per cent, and 1.71 per cent of by-products for metal industry and industrial machinery, respectively. The metal industry has 84.05 per cent as the main output that provides subsidiary products to industrial machinery by 16 per cent of its output. The miscellaneous manufacturing has 75.51 per cent in its diagonal cell as output; it provides subsidiary products of 24 per cent to metal industry and very small proportion to electric/electronic machinery industry (Table 6.8).

The construction industry produced 76.26 per cent its main output and 23.74 per cent of subsidiary product for mining/quarrying industry. Electricity/gas/water supply

Table 6.8 : Product Mix Matrix: 1970-71 (Transposed)

Sector Code	Industry / Commodity	1	2	3	4	5	6	7	8	9	10	11	12	13
1.	Agriculture	1.0000	0.0000	0.0000	0.0000	0.0000	0.0008	0.0000	0.0000	0.0000	0.0000	0.0000	0.0000	0.0000
2.	Animal Husbandry	0.0000	1.0000	0.0000	0.0000	0.0000	0.0001	0.0000	0.0000	0.0000	0.0000	0.0000	0.0000	0.0000
3.	Forestry and Logging	0.0000	0.0000	1.0000	0.0000	0.0000	0.0000	0.0000	0.0000	0.0000	0.0000	0.0000	0.0000	0.0000
4.	Fishing	0.0000	0.0000	0.0000	1.0000	0.0000	0.0000	0.0310	0.0000	0.0000	0.0000	0.0000	0.0000	0.0000
5.	Mining/Quarrying	0.0000	0.0000	0.0000	0.0000	1.0000	0.0000	0.0000	0.0000	0.0000	0.0000	0.0000	0.0000	0.0000
6.	Food Prod. Beverages and Tobacco Products	0.0000	0.0000	0.0000	0.0000	0.0000	0.9991	0.0000	0.0000	0.0000	0.0000	0.0000	0.0000	0.0000
7.	Textiles	0.0000	0.0000	0.0000	0.0000	0.0000	0.0000	0.9689	0.0000	0.0000	0.0000	0.0089	0.0000	0.0000
8.	Wood, Wood Prods. and Furniture	0.0000	0.0000	0.0000	0.0000	0.0000	0.0000	0.0000	0.9909	0.0000	0.0000	0.0000	0.0000	0.0000
9.	Paper, Paper Prods., Printing/Publishing	0.0000	0.0000	0.0000	0.0000	0.0000	0.0000	0.0000	0.0000	1.0000	0.0000	0.0000	0.0000	0.0000
10.	Leather Products	0.0000	0.0000	0.0000	0.0000	0.0000	0.0000	0.0000	0.0000	0.0000	1.0000	0.0000	0.0000	0.0000
11.	Plastic/Rubber Products	0.0000	0.0000	0.0000	0.0000	0.0000	0.0000	0.0000	0.0000	0.0000	0.0000	0.9911	0.0000	0.0000
12.	Coal/Petroleum Products	0.0000	0.0000	0.0000	0.0000	0.0000	0.0000	0.0000	0.0000	0.0000	0.0000	0.0000	1.0000	0.0000
13.	Chemicals	0.0000	0.0000	0.0000	0.0000	0.0000	0.0000	0.0000	0.0000	0.0000	0.0000	0.0000	0.0000	1.0000
14.	Non-metallic Products	0.0000	0.0000	0.0000	0.0000	0.0000	0.0000	0.0000	0.0000	0.0000	0.0000	0.0000	0.0000	0.0000
15.	Metal Products	0.0000	0.0000	0.0000	0.0000	0.0000	0.0000	0.0000	0.0091	0.0000	0.0000	0.0000	0.0000	0.0000
16.	Industrial Machinery	0.0000	0.0000	0.0000	0.0000	0.0000	0.0000	0.0000	0.0000	0.0000	0.0000	0.0000	0.0000	0.0000
17.	Electric/Electronic Machinery	0.0000	0.0000	0.0000	0.0000	0.0000	0.0000	0.0000	0.0000	0.0000	0.0000	0.0000	0.0000	0.0000
18	Rail and other Transport Equipment	0.0000	0.0000	0.0000	0.0000	0.0000	0.0000	0.0000	0.0000	0.0000	0.0000	0.0000	0.0000	0.0000
19.	Miscellaneous Manufacturing	0.0000	0.0000	0.0000	0.0000	0.0000	0.0000	0.0000	0.0000	0.0000	0.0000	0.0000	0.0000	0.0000
20.	Construction	0.0000	0.0000	0.0000	0.0000	0.0000	0.0000	0.0000	0.0000	0.0000	0.0000	0.0000	0.0000	0.0000
21	Electricity/Gas/Water Supply	0.0000	0.0000	0.0000	0.0000	0.0000	0.0000	0.0000	0.0000	0.0000	0.0000	0.0000	0.0000	0.0000
22.	Rail and other Transport / Storage Services	0.0000	0.0000	0.0000	0.0000	0.0000	0.0000	0.0000	0.0000	0.0000	0.0000	0.0000	0.0000	0.0000
23.	Trade/Hotel	0.0000	0.0000	0.0000	0.0000	0.0000	0.0000	0.0000	0.0000	0.0000	0.0000	0.0000	0.0000	0.0000
24.	Banking/Insurance	0.0000	0.0000	0.0000	0.0000	0.0000	0.0000	0.0000	0.0000	0.0000	0.0000	0.0000	0.0000	0.0000
25.	Other services (Edu., Med., Admin., Defence.etc)	0.0000	0.0000	0.0000	0.0000	0.0000	0.0000	0.0000	0.0000	0.0000	0.0000	0.0000	0.0000	0.0000
	Total Input	1.0000	1.0000	1.0000	1.0000	1.0000	1.0000	1.0000	1.0000	1.0000	1.0000	1.0000	1.0000	1.0000

Table 6.8 : (Contd...)

Sector Code	Industry Commodity	14	15	16	17	18	19	20	21	22	23	24	25
1.	Agriculture	0.0000	0.0000	0.0000	0.0000	0.0000	0.0000	0.0000	0.0000	0.0000	0.0000	0.0000	0.0000
2.	Animal Husbandry	0.0000	0.0000	0.0000	0.0000	0.0000	0.0000	0.0000	0.0000	0.0000	0.0000	0.0000	0.0000
3.	Forestry and Logging	0.0000	0.0000	0.0000	0.0000	0.0000	0.0000	0.0000	0.0000	0.0000	0.0000	0.0000	0.0000
4.	Fishing	0.0000	0.0000	0.0000	0.0000	0.0000	0.0000	0.0000	0.0000	0.0000	0.0000	0.0000	0.0000
5.	Mining/Quarrying	0.0000	0.0000	0.0000	0.0000	0.0000	0.0000	0.2374	0.0000	0.0000	0.0000	0.0000	0.0000
6.	Food Prod., Beverages and Tobacco Products	0.0000	0.0000	0.0000	0.0000	0.0000	0.0000	0.0000	0.0000	0.0000	0.0000	0.0000	0.0000
7.	Textiles	0.0000	0.0000	0.0000	0.0000	0.0000	0.0000	0.0000	0.0000	0.0000	0.0000	0.0000	0.0000
8.	Wood, Woods Prod. and Furniture	0.0000	0.0000	0.0000	0.0000	0.0000	0.0000	0.0000	0.0000	0.0000	0.0000	0.0000	0.0000
9.	Paper, Paper Prods., ~~Print~~/Pub.	0.0000	0.0000	0.0000	0.0000	0.0000	0.0000	0.0000	0.0000	0.0000	0.0000	0.0000	0.0000
10.	Leather Products	0.0000	0.0000	0.0000	0.0000	0.0000	0.0000	0.0000	0.0000	0.0000	0.0000	0.0000	0.0000
11.	Plastic/Rubber Products	0.0000	0.0000	0.0000	0.0000	0.0000	0.0000	0.0000	0.0000	0.0000	0.0000	0.0000	0.0000
12.	Coal/Petroleum Products	0.0000	0.0000	0.0000	0.0000	0.0000	0.0000	0.0000	0.0000	0.0000	0.0000	0.0000	0.0000
13.	Chemicals	0.0000	0.0000	0.0000	0.0000	0.0000	0.0000	0.0000	0.0000	0.0000	0.0000	0.0000	0.0000
14.	Non-metallic Products	0.9192	0.0000	0.0000	0.0000	0.0000	0.0000	0.0000	0.0000	0.0000	0.0000	0.0000	0.0000
15.	Metal Products	0.0636	0.8405	0.0000	0.0000	0.0000	0.2415	0.0000	0.0000	0.0000	0.0000	0.0000	0.0000
16.	Industrial Machinery	0.0171	0.1595	1.0000	0.0000	0.0000	0.0000	0.0000	0.0000	0.0000	0.0000	0.0000	0.0000
17.	Electric/Electronic Machinery	0.0000	0.0000	0.0000	1.0000	0.0000	0.0033	0.0000	0.3852	0.0000	0.0000	0.0000	0.0000
18.	Rail and other Transport Equipment	0.0000	0.0000	0.0000	0.0000	1.0000	0.0000	0.0000	0.0000	0.0000	0.0000	0.0000	0.0000
19.	Miscellaneous Manufacturing	0.0000	0.0000	0.0000	0.0000	0.0000	0.7551	0.0000	0.0000	0.0000	0.0000	0.0000	0.0000
20.	Construction	0.0000	0.0000	0.0000	0.0000	0.0000	0.0000	0.7626	0.0000	0.0000	0.0000	0.0000	0.0000
21.	Electricity/Gas/Water Supply	0.0000	0.0000	0.0000	0.0000	0.0000	0.0000	0.0000	0.6148	0.0000	0.0000	0.0000	0.0000
22.	Rail and other Transport / Storage Services	0.0000	0.0000	0.0000	0.0000	0.0000	0.0000	0.0000	0.0000	1.0000	0.0000	0.0000	0.0000
23	Trade/Hotel	0.0000	0.0000	0.0000	0.0000	0.0000	0.0000	0.0000	0.0000	0.0000	1.0000	0.0000	0.0000
24	Banking/Insurance	0.0000	0.0000	0.0000	0.0000	0.0000	0.0000	0.0000	0.0000	0.0000	0.0000	1.0000	0.0000
25	Other services (Edu., Med., Admin., Defence.etc)	0.0000	0.0000	0.0000	0.0000	0.0000	0.0000	0.0000	0.0000	0.0000	0.0000	0.0000	1.0000
	Total Input	1.0000	1.0000	1.0000	1.0000	1.0000	1.0000	1.0000	1.0000	1.0000	1.0000	1.0000	1.0000

Source : Mathematically obtained as part of input-output model (refer page 300).

produced 61.48 per cent as main product of its output alongwith 38.52 per cent of subsidiary product for electric/ electronic machinery industry (Table 6.8).

Tertiary Sector

In the service sector, all the service industries of transport/ storage, trade/ hotels, banking/insurance and other services have their total output as their main product. There are no by-products or subsidiary products for other industries (Table 6.8).

Market Share Relations

The market relations of economy of Delhi among various industrial sectors are analyzed through the market share matrix, which represent the proportions in which the various industries produce total output of particular commodity. The column entries show proportions contributed by different industries in total output of respective commodity. The diagonal elements give the proportions of the output of various commodities produced as main products and the off-diagonal elements show proportions of commodities as subsidiary products in other industries.

Primary Sector

The commodities related to primary sector revealed that in agriculture 99 per cent were contributed as main product by same industry and small proportions were added by food products and textile industry. In animal husbandry commodity, 99 per cent was main product and the rest was added by food products industry. In forestry, 99 per cent were the main product with some contribution from wood, non-metallic and transport equipment industries. In case of mining, 92.18 per cent were from construction industry and 7.82 per cent were from the same industry (Table 6.9).

Secondary Sector

In food products commodity, its entire product were contributed by the same industry; while for textile commodity, 99 per cent received as main product and the rest from plastic/rubber industry. Wood products, paper, leather, plastic/rubber, petroleum, chemical and non- metallic commodities all products were supplied by the same industries, respectively. In metal products commodity, 87 per cent were received as main product, whereas 9.25 per cent from miscellaneous manufacturing, 3.19 per cent from non-metallic industry and small proportion from wood industry. In case of industrial machinery commodity, 48.47 per cent were from same industry, 48.98 per cent were contributed by metal industry, 2.55 per cent by non-metallic industry. Electric/electronic machinery as commodity, received 12.78 per cent from the same industry, while 86.96 per cent from electricity/gas/water supply industry and small ratio by miscellaneous manufacturing industry. Transport equipment and miscellaneous manufacturing commodity had all its supplies by the same industry as its main output. In construction and electricity/gas/water supply as commodity, their entire product has been contributed by the same industries as their main output (Table 6.9).

Tertiary Sector

In all industries of tertiary sector including transport/storage services, trade/hotel, banking/insurance and other services, their entire product was supplied by the respective industries as their main output (Table 6.9).

Structural Analysis

The structure of the economy is analyzed and discussed through identifying leading and loosing industries, measuring backward, forward linkages and their coefficients. Output multipliers are computed to find economic structure

Table 6.9 : Market Share Matrix: 1970-71

Sector Code	Industry / Commodity	1	2	3	4	5	6	7	8	9	10	11	12	13
1.	Agriculture	0.9985	0.0000	0.0000	0.0000	0.0000	0.0000	0.0000	0.0000	0.0000	0.0000	0.0000	0.0000	0.0000
2.	Animal Husbandry	0.0000	0.9998	0.0000	0.0000	0.0000	0.0000	0.0000	0.0000	0.0000	0.0000	0.0000	0.0000	0.0000
3.	Forestry and Logging	0.0000	0.0000	0.9997	0.0000	0.0000	0.0000	0.0000	0.0000	0.0000	0.0000	0.0000	0.0000	0.0000
4.	Fishing	0.0000	0.0000	0.0000	0.0117	0.0000	0.0000	0.0000	0.0000	0.0000	0.0000	0.0000	0.0000	0.0000
5.	Mining/Quarrying	0.0000	0.0000	0.0000	0.0000	0.0782	0.0000	0.0000	0.0000	0.0000	0.0000	0.0000	0.0000	0.0000
6.	Food Prod, Beverages and Tobacco Prod.	0.0014	0.0002	0.0000	0.0000	0.0000	1.0000	0.0000	0.0000	0.0000	0.0000	0.0000	0.0000	0.0000
7.	Textiles	0.0001	0.0000	0.0000	0.9883	0.0000	0.0000	0.9911	0.0000	0.0000	0.0000	0.0000	0.0000	0.0000
8.	Wood, Wood Prods and Furniture	0.0000	0.0000	0.0001	0.0000	0.0000	0.0000	0.0000	1.0000	0.0000	0.0000	0.0000	0.0000	0.0000
9.	Paper, Paper Prods., Printing/Publishing	0.0000	0.0000	0.0000	0.0000	0.0000	0.0000	0.0000	0.0000	1.0000	0.0000	0.0000	0.0000	0.0000
10.	Leather Products	0.0000	0.0000	0.0000	0.0000	0.0000	0.0000	0.0000	0.0000	0.0000	1.0000	0.0000	0.0000	0.0000
11.	Plastic/Rubber Products	0.0000	0.0000	0.0000	0.0000	0.0000	0.0000	0.0089	0.0000	0.0000	0.0000	1.0000	0.0000	0.0000
12.	Coal/Petroleum Products	0.0000	0.0000	0.0000	0.0000	0.0000	0.0000	0.0000	0.0000	0.0000	0.0000	0.0000	1.0000	0.0000
13.	Chemicals	0.0000	0.0000	0.0000	0.0000	0.0000	0.0000	0.0000	0.0000	0.0000	0.0000	0.0000	0.0000	1.0000
14.	Non-metallic Products	0.0000	0.0000	0.0001	0.0000	0.0000	0.0000	0.0000	0.0000	0.0000	0.0000	0.0000	0.0000	0.0000
15.	Metal Products	0.0000	0.0000	0.0000	0.0000	0.0000	0.0000	0.0000	0.0000	0.0000	0.0000	0.0000	0.0000	0.0000
16.	Industrial Machinery	0.0000	0.0000	0.0000	0.0000	0.0000	0.0000	0.0000	0.0000	0.0000	0.0000	0.0000	0.0000	0.0000
17.	Electric/Electronic Machinery	0.0000	0.0000	0.0000	0.0000	0.0000	0.0000	0.0000	0.0000	0.0000	0.0000	0.0000	0.0000	0.0000
18.	Rail and other Transport Equipment	0.0000	0.0000	0.0001	0.0000	0.0000	0.0000	0.0000	0.0000	0.0000	0.0000	0.0000	0.0000	0.0000
19.	Miscellaneous Manufacturing	0.0000	0.0000	0.0000	0.0000	0.0000	0.0000	0.0000	0.0000	0.0000	0.0000	0.0000	0.0000	0.0000
20.	Construction	0.0000	0.0000	0.0000	0.0000	0.9218	0.0000	0.0000	0.0000	0.0000	0.0000	0.0000	0.0000	0.0000
21.	Electricity/Gas/Water Supply	0.0000	0.0000	0.0000	0.0000	0.0000	0.0000	0.0000	0.0000	0.0000	0.0000	0.0000	0.0000	0.0000
22.	Rail and other Transport / Storage Services	0.0000	0.0000	0.0000	0.0000	0.0000	0.0000	0.0000	0.0000	0.0000	0.0000	0.0000	0.0000	0.0000
23.	Trade/Hotel	0.0000	0.0000	0.0000	0.0000	0.0000	0.0000	0.0000	0.0000	0.0000	0.0000	0.0000	0.0000	0.0000
24.	Banking/Insurance	0.0000	0.0000	0.0000	0.0000	0.0000	0.0000	0.0000	0.0000	0.0000	0.0000	0.0000	0.0000	0.0000
25.	Other Services (Edu., Med., Admin., Defence.etc)	0.0000	0.0000	0.0000	0.0000	0.0000	0.0000	0.0000	0.0000	0.0000	0.0000	0.0000	0.0000	0.0000
	Total Input	1	1	1	1	1	1	1	1	1	1	1	1	1

Table 6.9 : (Contd...)

Sector Code	Industry Commodity	14	15	16	17	18	19	20	21	22	23	24	25
1.	Agriculture	0.0000	0.0000	0.0000	0.0000	0.0000	0.0000	0.0000	0.0000	0.0000	0.0000	0.0000	0.0000
2.	Animal Husbandry	0.0000	0.0000	0.0000	0.0000	0.0000	0.0000	0.0000	0.0000	0.0000	0.0000	0.0000	0.0000
3.	Forestry and Logging	0.0000	0.0000	0.0000	0.0000	0.0000	0.0000	0.0000	0.0000	0.0000	0.0000	0.0000	0.0000
4.	Fishing	0.0000	0.0000	0.0000	0.0000	0.0000	0.0000	0.0000	0.0000	0.0000	0.0000	0.0000	0.0000
5.	Mining/Quarrying	0.0000	0.0000	0.0000	0.0000	0.0000	0.0000	0.0000	0.0000	0.0000	0.0000	0.0000	0.0000
6.	Food Prod., Beverages and Tobacco Prod.	0.0000	0.0000	0.0000	0.0000	0.0000	0.0000	0.0000	0.0000	0.0000	0.0000	0.0000	0.0000
7.	Textiles	0.0000	0.0000	0.0000	0.0000	0.0000	0.0000	0.0000	0.0000	0.0000	0.0000	0.0000	0.0000
8.	Wood, Wood Prods. and Furniture	0.0000	0.0056	0.0000	0.0000	0.0000	0.0000	0.0000	0.0000	0.0000	0.0000	0.0000	0.0000
9.	Paper, Paper prods., Printing/Publishing	0.0000	0.0000	0.0000	0.0000	0.0000	0.0000	0.0000	0.0000	0.0000	0.0000	0.0000	0.0000
10.	Leather Products	0.0000	0.0000	0.0000	0.0000	0.0000	0.0000	0.0000	0.0000	0.0000	0.0000	0.0000	0.0000
11.	Plastic/Rubber Products	0.0000	0.0000	0.0000	0.0000	0.0000	0.0000	0.0000	0.0000	0.0000	0.0000	0.0000	0.0000
12.	Coal/Petroleum Products	0.0000	0.0000	0.0000	0.0000	0.0000	0.0000	0.0000	0.0000	0.0000	0.0000	0.0000	0.0000
13.	Chemicals	0.0000	0.0000	0.0000	0.0000	0.0000	0.0000	0.0000	0.0000	0.0000	0.0000	0.0000	0.0000
14.	Non-metallic Products	1.0000	0.0319	0.0255	0.0000	0.0000	0.0000	0.0000	0.0000	0.0000	0.0000	0.0000	0.0000
15.	Metal Products	0.0000	0.8700	0.4898	0.0000	0.0000	0.0000	0.0000	0.0000	0.0000	0.0000	0.0000	0.0000
16.	Industrial Machinery	0.0000	0.0000	0.4847	0.0000	0.0000	0.0000	0.0000	0.0000	0.0000	0.0000	0.0000	0.0000
17.	Electric/Electronic Machinery	0.0000	0.0000	0.0000	0.1278	0.0000	0.0000	0.0000	0.0000	0.0000	0.0000	0.0000	0.0000
18.	Rail and other Transport Equipment	0.0000	0.0000	0.0000	0.0000	1.0000	0.0000	0.0000	0.0000	0.0000	0.0000	0.0000	0.0000
19.	Miscellaneous Manufacturing	0.0000	0.0925	0.0000	0.0026	0.0000	1.0000	0.0000	0.0000	0.0000	0.0000	0.0000	0.0000
20.	Construction	0.0000	0.0000	0.0000	0.0000	0.0000	0.0000	1.0000	0.0000	0.0000	0.0000	0.0000	0.0000
21.	Electricity/Gas/Water Supply	0.0000	0.0000	0.0000	0.8696	0.0000	0.0000	0.0000	1.0000	0.0000	0.0000	0.0000	0.0000
22.	Rail and other Transport / Storage Services	0.0000	0.0000	0.0000	0.0000	0.0000	0.0000	0.0000	0.0000	1.0000	0.0000	0.0000	0.0000
23.	Trade/Hotel	0.0000	0.0000	0.0000	0.0000	0.0000	0.0000	0.0000	0.0000	0.0000	1.0000	0.0000	0.0000
24.	Banking/Insurance	0.0000	0.0000	0.0000	0.0000	0.0000	0.0000	0.0000	0.0000	0.0000	0.0000	1.0000	0.0000
25.	Other Services (Edu., Med., Admin., Defence.etc)	0.0000	0.0000	0.0000	0.0000	0.0000	0.0000	0.0000	0.0000	0.0000	0.0000	0.0000	1.0000
	Total Input	1	1	1	1	1	1	1	1	1	1	1	1

Source : Mathematically obtained as part of input-output model (refer page 300).

in terms of significant industrial sector that have potential multiplying effect on self-sector and economy. The connectivity of different industrial sectors is studied through connectivity matrix and graph.

Leading and Loosing Industries

The leading and loosing industrial sectors of the economy are identified through ranking of output multipliers. The industries ranked as top ten are here considered as leading industrial sectors in economy and the rest are loosing industries. As evident from Table 6.10 in 1970-71, textiles

Table 6.10 : Leading and Loosing Sectors of Economy (In terms of output multipliers)

Ranks	*Leading Industries*	*1970-71*
1.	Textiles	5.8979
2.	Electric/Electronic Machinery	5.4412
3.	Plastic/Rubber	5.0981
4.	Paper and Publishing	4.9937
5.	Trade	4.9719
6.	Transport Equipments	4.9703
7.	Industrial Machinery	4.9118
8.	Electricity/Gas/Water Supply	4.866
9.	Miscellaneous Manufacturing	4.8532
10.	Leather Products	4.6887
	Loosing industries	
11.	Construction	4.6294
12.	Metal Products	4.6047
13.	Non-metallic Products	4.4797
14.	Wood, Wood Products and Furniture	4.4644
15.	Petroleum and Coal Products	4.3923
16.	Food Products, Beverages, and Tobacco Products	4.3717
17.	Agriculture	4.3621
18.	Forestry and Logging	4.3469
19.	Rail and other Transport Services/Storage	4.3095
20.	Chemicals	4.2995
21.	Banking/Insurance	4.249
22.	Animal Husbandry	4.1801
23.	Other services (Education, Medical, Admn., Defence, etc.)	3.9535
24.	Fishing	3.9073
25.	Mining and Quarrying	3.3318

Source : These ranks are found after adding direct and indirect output multipliers of 1970-71.

and electric/electronic machinery were the two industrial sectors at the top. The third leading industrial sector was plastic/rubber followed by paper/publishing. Trade was on fifth rank in leading group of industries. Transport equipment sector stood at sixth rank of importance followed by industrial machinery, electricity/gas/water supply, miscellaneous manufacturing and leather products, respectively. It is important to note that in the top ten industries, secondary sector mainly holds the scenario. Surprisingly, from tertiary industries only trade occupies a place of significance among the leading industries.

Interestingly, in loosing group of industries whole of primary sector and tertiary sector occupies the lower ranks while secondary sector was positioned in upper ranks. It seems that these tertiary sectors were not as developed as to reach a prominent rank of influence the economy.

Linkages

Almost every industry producing goods or services takes inputs from other sectors of the economy and, in turn, provides inputs to the latter in the respective production process. These relationships define an industry's backward and forward linkages, respectively. Backward linkage refers to relative purchases of inputs by a sector while forward linkage refers to the downstream industries that use the output of the specified industry or commodity as input in producing their own goods and services or, in other words, relative sales by a sector to other sectors.

The strong backward linkage reflects that each new industrial investment will offer opportunities for suppliers. In terms of selecting 'key sectors' of an economy, backward linkages are very useful. High backward linkage occurs when a sector uses output of many other sectors as an input; thus, by expanding capacity in such a sector 'inducement' or stimuli are provided to supplier industries;

which will have an incentive to supplier industries to expand to take advantage of the increased demand of its output by that sector. The basic idea of backward linkage is to trace the output increase that occurs in supplying sectors when there is change in the sector using their output as inputs.

The strong forward linkages explain that each new industrial investment will offer inducement to user industries by providing more inputs. Forward linkages are also significant in terms of selecting key sectors of an economy, *i.e.* higher the forward linkage stronger the impact area or stronger the chain effect of linkages. The basic idea of forward linkage is to trace the output increase that occurs or might occur in using industries when there is change in the sector supplying inputs. A measure of the overall strength of backward or forward linkages is called the linkage coefficient. This coefficient measures strength of the linkages of the sector under consideration as defined by Rasmussen.[5]

Backward Linkages[6]

Primary Sector

Agriculture purchased maximum of 43.51 per cent from self-sector, 27 per cent from animal husbandry, 11 per cent from chemicals and small per cent of inputs from trade and transport, animal husbandry has similar input relations. Forestry received 61 per cent from animal husbandry, 18 per cent from agriculture, 10.76 per cent from food products and 5 per cent from trade and transport. Fishing industry had full inputs from self-sector, mining took 28 per cent from self sector, 32.15 per cent from industrial machinery, 14.29 per cent from electric/electronic machinery and 24 per cent from transport services (Table 6.11).

Table 6.11 : Backward Linkage (Commodity purchased as inputs by industries in per cent): 1970-71

Sector Code	Industry / Commodity	1	2	3	4	5	6	7	8	9	10	11	12	13
1.	Agriculture	43.51	41.45	18.52	0.00	0.00	21.74	0.00	0.00	0.00	0.00	0.00	0.00	0.00
2.	Animal Husbandry	27.00	25.23	61.75	0.00	0.00	9.38	0.00	0.00	0.00	0.00	0.00	0.00	0.00
3.	Forestry and Logging	0.01	0.03	0.00	0.00	0.00	0.05	0.00	7.19	0.00	0.13	0.00	0.00	3.60
4.	Fishing	0.00	0.00	0.02	100.05	0.00	0.00	0.00	0.00	0.00	0.00	0.00	0.00	0.00
5.	Mining/Quarrying	0.00	0.00	0.00	0.00	28.58	0.21	3.24	0.07	0.19	3.54	0.00	0.05	0.95
6.	Food Prod. , Beverages and Tobacco Prod.	0.02	0.34	10.76	-0.05	0.00	9.71	0.00	0.00	0.00	0.00	0.56	0.00	0.21
7.	Textiles	0.10	0.16	1.55	0.04	0.00	0.21	64.64	0.32	0.65	0.27	0.00	11.53	7.92
8.	Wood, Wood Prod. and Furniture	0.03	0.06	0.03	0.04	0.00	1.63	0.83	18.10	2.80	6.68	5.16	0.88	0.58
9.	Paper, Paper Prods., Printing/Publishing	0.02	0.01	0.14	0.00	0.00	0.55	0.76	0.31	40.53	0.20	2.21	0.53	8.39
10.	Leather Products	0.00	0.00	0.00	0.00	0.00	0.00	0.88	0.00	0.00	2.67	5.61	0.04	6.34
11.	Plastic/Rubber Products	0.00	0.00	0.00	0.00	0.00	30.50	0.56	22.28	0.63	37.87	65.01	0.42	15.76
12.	Coal/Petroleum Products	2.97	3.05	0.07	-0.03	0.00	0.20	0.78	0.47	0.39	5.01	4.27	0.22	0.52
13.	Chemicals	11.40	13.65	0.56	-0.04	0.00	2.76	6.68	2.79	2.76	15.23	0.55	0.07	9.12
14.	Non-metallic Products	0.00	0.00	0.00	0.00	0.00	14.20	0.00	0.24	0.00	0.00	0.65	0.01	3.11
15.	Metal Products	0.00	0.00	0.00	0.00	0.00	0.08	0.07	24.17	0.17	0.00	0.78	0.08	11.10
16.	Industrial Machinery	0.80	0.58	0.01	0.00	32.15	0.00	0.17	0.25	0.14	0.07	1.30	0.09	0.06
17.	Electric/Electronic Machinery	0.02	0.02	0.04	0.00	14.29	0.32	0.53	0.22	0.25	0.13	0.01	0.33	0.24
18.	Rail and other Transport Equipment	0.01	0.01	0.05	-0.05	0.00	0.28	0.00	0.00	0.00	0.00	0.02	0.00	0.00
19.	Miscellaneous Manufacturing	0.00	0.00	0.02	0.00	0.00	0.31	0.06	0.03	0.03	0.07	0.00	0.02	0.05
20.	Construction	3.25	4.39	0.56	0.00	0.00	0.04	0.01	0.08	0.02	0.04	0.00	1.02	0.02
21.	Electricity/Gas/Water Supply	2.56	2.33	0.01	0.00	0.00	0.05	0.01	0.74	0.18	0.09	0.06	0.69	0.06
22.	Rail and other Transport / Storage Services	2.12	2.56	1.58	0.00	24.98	5.60	8.21	12.47	13.12	14.67	0.35	38.19	20.38
23.	Trade/Hotel	4.06	5.06	4.19	0.05	0.00	0.73	9.50	5.16	1.94	9.54	3.68	18.02	8.27
24.	Banking/Insurance	2.06	1.06	0.04	0.00	0.00	1.42	1.52	5.08	1.50	3.79	5.29	27.83	3.31
25.	Other Services (Edu., Med., Admin., Defence. etc)	0.05	0.05	0.07	0.00	0.00	0.02	1.56	0.03	34.69	0.00	4.49	0.00	0.00
	Total Input	100.00	100.00	100.00	100.00	100.00	100.00	100.00	100.00	100.00	100.00	100.00	100.00	100.00

Table 6.11 : (Contd...)

Sector Code	Industry / Commodity	14	15	16	17	18	19	20	21	22	23	24	25
1.	Agriculture	0.00	0.00	0.00	0.00	0.00	0.00	0.00	0.00	1.47	6.06	0.00	0.07
2.	Animal Husbandry	0.00	0.00	0.00	0.00	0.00	0.00	0.00	0.00	0.00	8.24	0.00	0.04
3.	Forestry and Logging	0.01	0.07	0.02	0.00	0.06	0.01	0.01	0.00	0.00	0.00	0.00	0.09
4.	Fishing	0.00	0.00	0.00	0.00	0.00	0.00	0.00	0.00	0.00	4.27	0.00	0.00
5.	Mining/Quarrying	4.01	1.47	0.55	0.11	0.68	28.04	10.05	5.09	0.00	1.51	0.00	0.19
6.	Food Prod., Beverages and Tobacco Prod.	0.00	0.00	0.00	0.00	0.00	0.00	0.00	0.00	0.26	5.64	0.00	0.13
7.	Textiles	1:03	0.44	0.84	0.94	1.14	0.34	0.67	0.00	0.53	0.01	0.01	1.77
8.	Wood, Wood Prod., and Furniture	2.03	0.85	2.02	0.61	2.40	0.79	0.06	0.00	0.30	4.01	0.43	0.05
9.	Paper, Paper Prods., Printing/Publishing	0.79	0.48	0.94	0.17	0.94	0.83	0.17	0.63	0.61	1.36	1.78	4.75
10.	Leather Products	0.00	0.00	0.00	0.00	0.00	5.23	0.00	0.00	0.00	0.00	0.00	0.00
11.	Plastic/Rubber Products	0.74	21.94	0.65	9.86	9.47	1.60	0.00	0.00	1.86	13.62	0.00	12.16
12.	Coal/Petroleum Products	1.45	1.90	0.88	0.05	1.49	0.11	0.27	4.89	2.51	0.07	0.15	1.34
13.	Chemicals	2.17	1.52	3.14	2.38	10.93	1.71	0.00	0.08	0.02	0.00	0.00	4.71
14.	Non-metallic Products	28.14	13.39	0.45	0.16	0.00	1.15	0.00	0.01	0.00	0.38	0.00	2.55
15.	Metal Products	38.11	35.65	1.75	14.16	23.74	7.71	0.89	0.98	0.26	0.38	0.00	2.65
16.	Industrial Machinery	1.17	0.09	25.96	0.13	0.00	0.00	0.06	2.38	0.02	0.00	0.00	4.96
17.	Electric/electronic Machinery	0.15	0.19	22.64	42.86	0.14	15.00	7.30	8.26	0.10	0.03	0.00	2.39
18.	Rail & other Transport Equipment	0.00	0.00	0.00	0.00	34.90	0.00	0.14	15.61	7.17	2.59	7.26	6.77
19.	Miscellaneous Manufacturing	0.88	0.02	0.05	0.02	0.04	14.50	0.02	0.55	0.57	0.14	0.14	6.40
20.	Construction	0.98	0.01	0.06	0.01	0.05	0.06	3.17	2.78	14.04	0.69	67.01	7.80
21.	Electricity/Gas/Water Supply	0.30	0.20	0.17	0.04	0.11	0.03	28.74	5.10	0.16	0.69	1.35	6.98
22.	Rail and other Transport/ Storage Services	12.06	1.97	14.57	9.93	3.89	4.71	9.34	33.36	16.34	0.85	5.73	8.58
23.	Trade/Hotel	0.12	14.36	21.17	15.91	8.26	18.17	38.31	19.88	43.53	27.59	0.41	11.95
24.	Banking/Insurance	5.86	5.45	4.14	1.16	1.76	0.00	0.45	0.00	9.55	9.08	9.77	5.42
25.	Other Services (Edu., Med., Admin., Defence, etc.)	0.00	0.00	0.00	1.51	0.00	0.00	0.36	0.40	0.72	12.79	5.95	8.27
Total Input		100.00	100.00	100.00	100.00	100.00	100.00	100.00	100.00	100.00	100.00	100.00	100.00

Source: Mathematically obtained by dividing industry column entries by total input of that industry.

Secondary Sector

Food industry purchased 21.74 per cent inputs from self-sector, 30.50 per cent from plastic-rubber products, 14.20 per cent from metal products, while textile industry received 64.64 per cent from self-sector and 17 per cent from trade and transport. Wood industry received 18.1 per cent from self-sector, 22 percent from plastic/rubber products, 24 per cent from metal products and 17 per cent from trade and transport services. Paper industry got 40.53 per cent from self sector, 13 per cent from transport and 34.69 per cent from other services, while leather industry took 37.87 per cent from plastic/rubber, 15.23 per cent from chemical, 23 per cent from trade and transport services. Plastic/rubber industry purchased 65 per cent inputs from self-sector, 5 per cent each from wood and leather products and 8 per cent from trade and transport. Petroleum industry received 52 per cent inputs through trade and transport, 27.83 per cent from banking/ insurance and 11.53 per cent from textiles. Chemical industry received 28 per cent from trade and transport services, 15.76 per cent from plastic/rubber, 11 per cent from metal products and 7 per cent from textiles. Non-metallic industry purchased 28.14 per cent from self-sector, 38.11 per cent from metal product, 12 per cent from transport and 4 per cent from mining (Table 6.11).

Metal industry had received 35.65 per cent from self-sector, 13.39 per cent from non-metallic product, 21.94 per cent from plastic/rubber products and 14.36 per cent from trade services. Industrial machinery industry received 48 per cent from electric/electronic machinery products and 35 per cent from trade and transport services. Electric/electronic machinery industry took 42.86 per cent from self, 14.16 per cent from metal products and 23 per cent from trade and transport services. Transport equipment industry got 34.90 per cent from self sector, 23.74 per cent from metal products, 10 per cent from chemical, 9 per cent from plastic/rubber products and 11 per cent from trade and transport services. Miscellaneous manufacturing industry got 28 per cent from mining, 15 per cent from electric/electronic machinery, 14.5 per cent from self-sector and 22 per cent from trade and transport. Construction industry had taken 47 per cent input from trade and transport, 28.74 per cent from electricity group and 10 per cent from mining. For electricity/gas/water supply, 52 per cent has come from trade and transport services, 15.61 per cent from transport services, and 15.61 per cent from transport equipment products, 5 per cent from mining, and 5 per cent from petroleum/coal products (Table 6.11).

Tertiary Sector

Transport/storage services had taken 43 per cent from trade, 16 per cent from self, 14 per cent from construction and 9 per cent from banking and insurance. Trade industry had received 27.59 per cent from self-sector, 12.79 per cent from other services, 13.62 per cent from plastic/rubber products, 8 per cent from animal husbandry, 67 per cent from agriculture, 4 per cent from fishing, 5 per cent from food products and wood products. Banking/insurance industry had received 67 per cent of input from construction, 7.16 per cent from transport equipment, 9 per cent from trade and 6 per cent from self. Other services industry received inputs in small proportion from almost all the sectors except fishing (Table 6.11).

In manufacturing industry, maximum inputs through trade and transport were received by petroleum/coal products industry (52 per cent), followed by industrial machinery (35 per cent), electric/electronic machinery (24 per cent) and miscellaneous manufacturing (22 per cent). In the rest all industries less than 20 per cent inputs are received through this and food products industry is with least (5 per cent) (Table 6.11).

Forward Linkages[7]

Each commodity provides some kind of input to one or other industry. Some commodities are used by many industries while others have a small circumference. This is analyzed by finding out the input share proportion in the total intermediate use.

Primary Sector

In primary sector, agriculture as commodity contributed 27.14 per cent to itself, 19.39 per cent to animal husbandry, while in manufacturing sector it provided inputs only to food products industry, *i.e.* 27.88 per cent, and 22.22 per cent to trade industry, 3.07 per cent to transport and storage industry of tertiary sector. Similarly, animal husbandry as commodity to agriculture industry contributed 23.59 per cent, to self 16.86 per cent and in manufacturing it contributed only to food products industry by 16.84 per cent, while in service sector it provided input only to trade industry by 32.33 per cent. Forestry and logging commodity shared very marginal proportion to the same sector, while share maximum to wood products industry by 52.16 per cent and chemical by 35.17 per cent and marginal share to industrial machinery, transport equipment, miscellaneous construction etc. The tertiary sector provided 6.04 per cent to other service industry only (Table 6.12).

Fishing commodity did not contribute even to self-industry but only to trade industry. The mining and quarrying commodity only 1.52 per cent to self industry; in manufacturing sector, it gave inputs to textiles by 26 per cent, marginal inputs to leather, chemical, metal products, non-metallic products, transport equipment and 15.52 per cent to miscellaneous industry. It contributed 28.01 per cent to construction, 8.45 per cent to electricity and gas. In tertiary sector, it provided inputs only to trade by 11.25 per cent of the total.

Paper and publishing commodity has almost negligible share for primary sector. In manufacturing sector, maximum share of 50 per cent to self, 5.80 per cent to chemicals, 3.64 per cent to textiles, 8.92 per cent to plastic and rubber and smaller proportion with most industries of secondary sector. In tertiary sector, the contributions were 11.08 per cent to other services and small quantities to all other industries. Leather commodity shared nothing with primary sector industries; in secondary sector, it contributed maximum to plastic/rubber industry by 67.18 per cent, 12 per cent each to textile and chemical and 5 per cent to miscellaneous manufacturing and 2.25 per cent to self-industry. The plastic/rubber as commodity has no relation with primary industries, while in manufacturing it shared maximum to self, *i.e.* 54.84 per cent followed nearly 10 per cent to food products, 2 per cent each to wood, leather and chemical industries, 3.55 per cent to metal products besides small quantities to others; whereas in tertiary sector, it mainly contributed to trade by 12.66 per cent and other services by 8.85 per cent (Table 6.12).

Secondary Sector

It would be evident from Table 6.12 that food products sector as commodity sold maximum output to trade industry, *i.e.* 57.15 per cent and marginal to other tertiary industries. In the secondary sector, it provided 34.43 per cent to self-industry and small quantities to rubber/plastic industry and chemical industry. For primary sector, it shared very negligible with all primary industry except mining and quarrying. It is also shown that textile commodity shared 92.89 per cent inputs of self industry besides sharing very small proportion in almost all industries except forestry and logging of primary sector, plastic and rubber of secondary, and electricity/gas/ water supply and banking/insurance of tertiary sector. Wood products commodity, provide negligible proportion to the primary sector industries, except,

Table 6.12 : Forward Linkage (Commodity sales to different industries in percent): 1970-71

Sector Code	Industry / Commodity	1	2	3	4	5	6	7	8	9	10	11	12	13
1.	Agriculture	27.14	19.39	0.03	0.00	0.00	27.88	0.00	0.00	0.00	0.00	0.00	0.00	0.00
2.	Animal Husbandry	23.59	16.86	0.14	0.00	0.00	16.84	0.00	0.00	0.00	0.00	0.00	0.00	0.00
3.	Forestry and Logging	0.17	0.12	0.00	0.00	0.00	1.26	0.00	52.16	0.06	0.57	0.00	0.00	37.17
4.	Fishing	0.00	0.00	0.00	0.00	0.00	0.00	0.00	0.00	0.00	0.00	0.05	0.00	0.00
5.	Mining/Quarrying	0.01	0.00	0.00	0.00	1.52	0.56	26.00	0.06	0.43	1.69	0.00	0.03	1.10
6.	Food Prod., Beverages and Tobacco Prod.	0.03	0.02	0.05	0.39	0.00	34.43	0.00	0.00	0.00	0.00	5.12	0.00	0.33
7.	Textiles	0.02	0.02	0.00	2.18	0.27	0.10	92.89	0.05	0.27	0.02	0.00	1.12	1.63
8.	Wood, Wood Prod., and Furniture	0.04	0.03	0.00	0.13	0.00	3.87	6.02	13.31	5.87	2.89	31.75	0.43	0.61
9.	Paper, Paper Prods., Printing/ Publishing	0.01	0.01	0.00	0.00	0.90	0.85	3.64	0.15	56.01	0.06	8.96	0.17	5.80
10.	Leather Products	0.00	0.00	0.00	0.00	0.00	0.00	12.52	0.00	0.00	2.25	67.18	0.04	12.91
11.	Plastic/Rubber Products	0.00	0.00	0.00	0.00	0.00	9.91	0.56	2.25	0.18	2.25	54.84	0.03	2.26
12.	Coal/Petroleum Products	5.12	3.66	0.00	4.06	0.56	0.69	8.48	0.52	1.21	3.24	39.20	0.16	0.81
13.	Chemicals	8.38	5.99	0.00	0.16	4.83	4.17	31.08	1.31	3.69	10.32	2.16	0.02	16.99
14.	Non-metallic Products	0.00	0.00	0.00	0.00	0.00	44.05	0.00	0.23	0.00	0.00	5.22	0.01	4.26
15.	Metal Products	0.00	0.00	0.00	0.13	0.00	0.14	0.37	12.87	0.26	0.00	3.46	0.03	8.41
16.	Industrial Machinery	1.81	1.29	0.00	0.00	45.41	0.00	2.41	0.35	0.58	0.06	15.67	0.08	0.13
17.	Electric/Electronic Machinery	0.04	0.03	0.00	0.00	0.00	1.40	7.02	0.30	0.96	0.11	0.10	0.29	0.45
18.	Rail and other Transport Equipment	0.01	0.01	0.00	8.59	0.00	29.43	0.00	0.00	0.00	0.00	0.08	0.00	0.00
19.	Miscellaneous Manufacturing	0.01	0.01	0.00	0.00	1.05	2.45	1.55	0.08	0.22	0.10	0.00	0.04	0.17
20.	Construction	1.69	1.21	0.00	0.00	2.98	0.04	0.03	0.03	0.02	0.01	0.01	0.23	0.01
21.	Electricity/Gas/Water Supply	2.60	1.86	0.00	0.00	13.93	0.10	0.07	0.48	0.33	0.03	0.34	0.30	0.06
22.	Rail and other Transport / Storage Services	0.63	0.45	0.00	0.25	0.60	3.44	24.36	2.38	7.12	1.65	0.56	4.88	5.52
23.	Trade/Hotel	0.59	0.42	0.00	0.38	0.50	3.03	26.06	4.16	4.84	0.52	18.00	3.55	5.42
24.	Banking/Insurance	0.84	0.60	0.00	0.18	0.29	1.19	3.93	1.33	1.12	0.58	72.30	4.88	1.23
25	Other Services (Edu., Med., Admin., Defence, etc.)	0.01	0.01	0.00	0.00	5.39	0.01	2.53	0.00	21.43	0.00	6.14	0.00	0.00
	Total Input	2.31	1.65	0.01	0.59	1.79	5.88	18.04	2.06	5.36	1.06	18.16	1.37	3.13

Table 6.12 : (Contd...)

Sector Code	Industry Commodity	14	15	16	17	18	19	20	21	22	23	24	25
1.	Agriculture	0.00	0.00	0.00	0.00	0.00	0.00	0.00	0.00	3.07	22.22	0.00	0.27
2.	Animal Husbandry	0.00	0.00	0.00	0.00	0.00	0.00	0.00	0.00	0.00	42.3	0.00	0.23
3.	Forestry and Logging	0.06	0.80	0.03	0.00	0.64	0.03	0.23	0.06	0.00	0.00	0.00	6.64
4.	Fishing	0.00	0.00	0.00	0.00	0.00	0.00	0.00	0.00	0.00	99.95	0.00	0.00
5.	Mining/Quarrying	2.53	1.90	0.12	0.01	0.80	15.52	28.01	8.45	0.00	11.25	0.00	0.00
6.	Food Prod., Beverages and Tobacco Prod	0.00	0.00	0.00	0.00	0.00	0.00	0.00	0.00	1.47	57.15	0.00	1.01
7,	Textiles	0.12	0.10	0.03	0.02	0.24	0.03	0.33	0.00	0.40	0.01	0.00	0.14
8.	Wood, Wood Prod., and Furniture	1.16	1.00	0.42	0.05	2.58	0.40	0.16	0.00	1.16	27.18	0.74	0.20
9.	Paper, Paper Prods., Printing/Publishing	0.30	0.37	0.13	0.01	0.67	0.27	0.29	0.62	1.54	6.10	2.06	11.08
10.	Leather Products	0.00	0.00	. 0.00	0.00	0.00	5.10	0.00	0.00	0.00	0.00	0.00	0.00
11.	Plastic/Rubber Products	0.06	3.55	0.02	0.12	1.39	0.11	0.00	0.00	0.98	12.66	0.00	8.85
12.	Coal/Petroleum Products	1.24	3.34	0.27	0.01	2.39	0.09	1.01	11.00	10.40	0.69	0.40	1.47
13.	Chemicals	0.79	1.14	0.41	0.13	7.48	0.55	0.00	0.07	0.04	0.00	0.00	0.28
14.	Non-metallic Products	21.10	20.66	0.12	0.02	0.00	0.75	0.00	0.01	0.00	3.38	0.00	0.18
15.	Metal Products	15.81	30.42	0.26	0.87	18.44	2.80	1.63	1.06	0.71	1.84	0.00	0.47
16.	Industrial Machinery	1.31	0.20	23.03	0.02	0.00	0.00	0.31	6.99	0.17	0.04	0.00	0.15
17.	Electric/Electronic Machinery	0.16	0.41	8.49	6.64	0.28	13.71	33.60	22.63	0.72	0.31	0.00	2.35
18	Rail and other Transport Equipment	0.00	0.00	0.00	0.00	31.63	0.00	0.30	19.85	8.93	0.38	0.22	0.57
19.	Miscellaneous Manufacturing	1.67	0.07	0.03	0.00	0.16	24.11	0.13	2.74	7.33	3.16	0.79	54.12
20.	Construction	0.25	0.00	0.01	0.00	0.02	0.01	3.63	17.36	1.31	2.12	68.41	0.61
21.	Electricity/Gas/Water Supply	0.15	0.21	0.03	0.00	0.10	0.01	64.27	6.78	0.55	4.13	2.09	1.5
22.	Rail and other Transport / Storage Services	1.79	5.03	0.78	0.22	1.08	0.61	6.13	8.59	7.48	10.34	2.59	3.52
23.	Trade/Hotel	3.40	6.77	0.55	0.17	5.23	2.87	1.56	1.63	1.73	5.87	0.09	2.65
24.	Banking/Insurance	1.19	2.28	0.30	0.04	0.67	0.00	0.40	0.00	2.06	3.80	0.15	0.62
25	Other Services (Edu., Med., Admin., Defence, etc.)	0.00	0.00	0.00	0.03	0.00	0.00	0.20	0.13	0.61	57.91	1.17	4.43
Total Input		1.69	3.44	0.54	0.17	2.80	1.28	3.38	3.02	1.91	13.58	3.50	3.29

Source: Mathematically obtained by dividing commodity row cntries by total inputs.

forestry, mining/quarrying; it the secondary sector provides 13.31 per cent self, 31.75 per cent to plastic and rubber, 6.02 per cent to textile, 5.87 per cent to paper/publishing industry, 4 per cent to food product industry and 2 per cent to transport equipment industry (Table 6.12).

Petroleum/coal commodity sold small quantities to all primary sector industries, *i.e.* 3 to 5 per cent except forestry. In secondary sector, it contributed maximum to plastic/ rubber by 39 per cent, followed by 8.48 per cent to textile, 2.26 per cent to chemicals, 3.55 per cent to metal products and in small fraction to all secondary industries and tertiary industries. It shared 11 per cent each to electricity/gas/water supply and transport services. Chemical as commodity has contributed 8.38 per cent to agriculture industry, 5.99 per cent to animal husbandry and 4.38 per cent to mining the primary sector.

In manufacturing sector, chemical commodity shared inputs with all industries maximum to textiles, *i.e.* 31 per cent, 4 per cent to food industry, 10 per cent to leather, 16.99 per cent to self and 7.48 per cent to transport equipment; while in tertiary industries, small fraction to trade and other services. Non-metallic commodity, did not share inputs to primary industries, whereas in secondary sector it contributed maximum to food industry by 44 per cent, more than 20 per cent each self and metal industry, 5 per cent to plastic/rubber industry and 4 per cent to chemicals. In tertiary industry, it shares 3.38 per cent to trade. Metal commodity shares nil with primary industries. In secondary industries, it provides 30 per cent to self, 18 per cent to transport equipment, 15 per cent to non-metal industry, 12.87 per cent to wood industry and 2.80 to miscellaneous manufacturing, and small quantities to tertiary industries (Table 6.12).

The industrial machinery commodity, shared maximum with mining/quarrying, *i.e.* 45 per cent, small shares with agriculture and animal husbandry, while nothing to forestry and fishing. In manufacturing, it shared 23 per cent to self,

16 per cent to plastic/rubber and 2.41 per cent to textiles. It contributed 7 per cent to construction industry, whereas little fraction to tertiary industries except banking/insurance. Electric/electronic machinery had nil relationship with primary industries; in secondary industries, it contributed 13.71 per cent to miscellaneous manufacturing, 8.49 per cent to industrial machinery, 7 per cent to self, 7 per cent textile and 1.4 per cent to food industry. This commodity shared maximum of 33.60 per cent with construction and 23 per cent to electricity/gas/water supply industry. Surprisingly, tertiary industries shared very small fractions. Transport equipment commodity, shared only with forestry industry in primary sector. In secondary, it shared 31.68 per cent to self and 30 per cent to food industry. This commodity had provided 20 per cent inputs to electricity/gas/water supply industry. At the same time, in service sector, it provides only 9 per cent to transport services and small share to others. If anything, miscellaneous manufacturing commodity has no relation with primary industries. As shown in Table 6.12, in secondary sector, it shares 24 per cent to self, 2.45 per cent to food industry, more than 1 per cent each in textiles and non-metallic industry with the rest other industries very small amounts were shared. Similarly, in service industry, it shared 7.33 per cent to transport services and 3.16 per cent to trade and maximum of 54 per cent to other services. Finally, construction as commodity has been seen as input in almost all industries with maximum of 68.41 per cent in banking/insurance followed by 17 per cent of electricity/gas/water supply and 3.36 per cent self. Taking the results at face value, it has been seen that the electricity/gas/water supply has been purchased by almost all industries with maximum of 64 per cent to construction, 13 per cent to mining, 6 per cent to self, 4.13 per cent to trade and 2 per cent each to other services, banking/insurance (Table 6.12).

Tertiary Sector

Transport and storage services were used in all industries.

In textiles, maximum of 24.36 per cent services were used, followed by 7 per cent in paper industry, 5 per cent each in chemical and metal industry and 6 to 8 per cent in construction and electricity. It is shown that trade/hotels provided inputs to the whole economy. It is important to acknowledge that maximum contribution of 26 per cent went to textiles, 18 per cent to plastic/rubber, 7 per cent to metallic and 5 per cent each to transport equipment and trade nearly 3 per cent each to miscellaneous manufacturing. Basically, other services, non-metallic products, petroleum products and about 1 per cent to many industries followed at the same time, banking/insurance sector as commodity sold its outputs to all primary industries except forestry. For secondary sector, in particular, it provided maximum of 72 per cent to plastic/rubber, 5 per cent to petroleum products, 4 per cent to textiles, more than 1 per cent to food products, wood products, paper products, chemicals, 2 to 4 per cent inputs to transport services and trade and slight quantity to others. In transport equipment and miscellaneous manufacturing and electricity/gas/water, no inputs were sold from banking/insurance. Clearly then, other services provided 5.39 per cent to mining and quarrying in the primary industry, 21.43 per cent to paper industry, 6 per cent to plastic/rubber, 2.5 per cent to textile, 57.91 per cent to trade, 4.43 per cent to self and 1.17 per cent to banking/insurance (Table 6.12).

Backward Linkage Coefficient[8]

Backward linkage coefficient of various sectors derived through input-output table reflects that in 1970-71 the industrial sectors with high backward coefficient than the economy as a whole, *i.e.* more than 1 included textiles, paper and publishing, leather products, petroleum and coal products, industrial machinery, electric/electronic machinery, rail and other transport equipments, construction, electricity/gas/water supply and trading. This signifies that these industrial sectors are very well linked or strongly related to the rest of the economy as an input receiver. This implies that the above industrial sector depends strongly on the other sectors of the economy for producing their output. Thereby, any unit change in these industrial sectors would have a direct positive or negative impact on the related sectors and, thus, on the economy as a whole. Of the twenty-five sectors, 11 sectors show the strong backward linkage coefficient while rest 14 has the backward coefficient of less than '1', *i.e.* a weak relationship. These industrial sectors with less than average economy linkage include all primary sectors, food products, wood products, plastic/ rubber products, chemicals, non-metallic products, metal products, transport/storage services, banking/insurance and other services. The strong backward linkage explains that each new industrial investment will offer opportunities for suppliers. In terms of selecting 'key sectors' of an economy, backward linkages are very vital and significant. High backward linkages occur when a sector uses output of many other sectors as an input, thus, by expanding capacity in such a sector inducement or stimuli are provided to supplier industries; which will have an incentive to expand output to take advantage of the increased demand of its output by that sector. The basic idea of backward linkage is to trace the output increase that occurs in supplying sectors when there is change in the sector using their output as input (Table 6.13).

Forward Linkage Coefficient[9]

Forward linkage coefficient values reflect that ten industrial sectors of the total of twenty-five industrial sectors have shown higher forward linkage coefficients, which are greater than whole economy's average. These industries include agriculture, animal husbandry among the primary sector; textile, rubber and plastic, metal products, electric/electronic

Table 6.13 : Linkage Coefficients

Sector Code	Industrial Sectors	Backward	Forward
1.	Agriculture	0.8547	1.1453
2.	Animal Husbandry	0.8551	1.0087
3.	Forestry and Logging	0.8677	0.3558
4.	Fishing	0.9992	1.2974
5.	Mining and Quarrying	0.9855	0.7476
6.	Food Products, Beverages and Tobacco Products	0.9811	0.4928
7.	Textiles	1.1511	0.9061
8.	Wood, Wood Products and Furniture	0.9797	0.6794
9.	Paper, Paper Products, Printing/Publishing	1.0441	0.7246
10.	Leather and Leather Products	1.0844	0.4651
11.	Plastic and Rubber Products	0.9457	2.6244
12.	Petroleum and Coal Products	1.0070	0.5509
13.	Chemicals	0.9553	0.8142
14.	Non-metallic Products	0.9513	0.6529
15.	Metal Products	0.9551	1.3153
16.	Industrial Machinery	1.0916	0.6751
17.	Electric/Electronic Machinery	1.1595	1.0137
18.	Rail and other Transport Equipment	1.0681	0.8264
19.	Miscellaneous Manufacturing	1.1117	0.3983
20.	Construction	1.0539	1.0719
21.	Electricity/Gas/Water Supply	1.1309	0.6559
22.	Rail and other Transport Services/Storage	0.9283	1.7921
23.	Trade/Hotels	1.0546	2.6921
24.	Banking/Insurance	0.9335	1.1258
25.	Other services (Education, Medical, Administration, Defence, etc.)	0.8499	0.9670

Source : Mathematically calculated from inverse matrix. (For inverse refer Appendix VII A)

products, construction from secondary sector; and transport/storage services, trade and banking/insurance from tertiary sector. The high forward linkage coefficient explains that these above industries are very strongly connected with the rest sectors of the economy of Delhi as an input supplier to various sectors. The rest of the 15 industrial sectors have shown forward linkage coefficient of less than one, which include forestry and logging, fishing and mining of primary sector; food products, wood products, paper and publishing, leather products, petroleum and coal products, chemicals, non-metallic products, industrial machinery, transport equipment, miscellaneous manufacturing of secondary sector; and electricity/gas/water supply and other services of tertiary sector. These forward linkages reflect that of the 14 secondary sectors only four sectors show high forward linkages thereby it makes clear that in 1970-71 in the economy of Delhi manufacturing sectors were not very strong and significant. The higher linkage coefficients of tertiary sector clearly emphasize the nature and structure of Delhi's economy (Table 6.13).

The high forward linkage occurs when a sector's output is or could be used by many other sectors as an input. By expanding the capacity in such a sector, inducements are provided to use industries that now have an incentive to expand output to take advantage of the increased availability of inputs. The strong forward linkage explains that even new industrial investment will affect to inducement to user industries by providing more inputs. Forward linkages are also significant in terms of selecting key sectors of an economy, *i.e.* high forward linkages would have stronger impact area or stronger chain effect of linkages. The basic idea of forward linkage is to trace the output increase that occurs or might occur in using industries when there is a change in the sector supplying inputs (Table 6.13).

Output Multipliers[10]

Output multiplier of a commodity-producing sector is the factor by which a unit increases in the demand for and, consequently, production of the commodity in that sector leads to expansion of, output in the whole economy. This multiplier is the sum of the factors by which individual sector of the economy get expanded for unit increase in the demand for product in one sector. Output coefficients are of three types; one measuring only the direct, the second the sum of the direct and indirect impacts, and third the total (including the induced effect) of an increase in the final demand.

In the present work, the first two types of output coefficients have been computed. In general, the direct output multipliers are a little over '1', signifying the fact that to meet the unit increase in the final demand for its own product an industry will have produced slightly more than that of increase in demand, which is likely to be caused by linkage effect. In other words, '1' represents, '1' unit to satisfy the original new unit of final demand plus an additional for intra- and inter-industry uses. The direct plus indirect multipliers vary from industry to industry depending on the strength of industry's linkages with other industries, but grossly ranging between 2.5 to 3.6.

The direct output multipliers reveal that in 1970-71, textile, showed the highest multiplying potential of the self-sector with the coefficient value of 2.0455 and for the direct plus indirect multiplying impact it has the second highest coefficient values very close to the first highest, *i.e.* 3.8524 for the total economy's output. Plastic/rubber products sector ranks second in terms of direct coefficient, *i.e.* with one unit increase in final demand the sector produces one unit and 1.9328 for the inter-industry transaction, while for the total economy's output it ranks at 19th rank. This implies that for self-sector it has high potential but for the economy as a whole the multiplying factor is lower as compared to other sectors. Electric/electronic machinery sector with coefficient value of 1.5606 has third rank in case of direct multipliers whereas the coefficient for the total output of the economy, *i.e.* indirect multiplier, this sector has maximum multiplying factor. Paper and publishing industry that scoring fourth position as regard the output multiplication for the self-sector but for total economy's output it has sixth rank (Table 6.14).

Trade/hotels sector holds fifth position in terms of direct multiplier and among tertiary sector it has highest coefficient value. As regards the total impact for the economy as a whole its ranks were quite low. Metal products sector was with sixth position as regard the multiplier for self-sector, *i.e.* with 1.4082

Table 6.14 : Output Multipliers

Sectors Code	Industrial Sectors	Direct	Rank	Indirect	Rank
1.	Agriculture	1.5016	4	2.8605	24
2.	Animal Husbandry	1.3183	9	2.8618	22
3.	Forestry and Logging	1.0031	23	2.9042	23
4.	Fishing	1.0029	24	3.3440	12
5.	Mining and Quarrying	0.0334	25	3.2984	13
6.	Food Products, Beverages, and Tobacco Products	1.0880	19	3.2837	14
7.	Textiles	2.0455	1	3.8524	2
8.	Wood, Wood Products and Furniture	1.1856	14	3.2788	15
9.	Paper, Paper Products, Printing/Publishing	1.4992	5	3.4945	10
10.	Leather and Leather Products	1.0593	21	3.6294	6
11.	Plastic and Rubber Products	1.9328	2	3.1653	19
12.	Petroleum and Coal Products	1.0220	22	3.3703	11
13.	Chemicals	1.1024	17	3.1971	16
14.	Non-metallic Products	1.2960	10	3.1837	18
15.	Metal Products	1.4082	7	3.1965	17
16.	Industrial Machinery	1.2584	11	3.6534	5
17.	Electric/Electronic Machinery	1.5606	3	3.8806	1
18.	Rail and other Transport Equipment	1.3956	8	3.5747	7
19.	Miscellaneous Manufacturing	1.1326	14	3.7206	4
20.	Construction	1.1021	18	3.5273	9
21.	Electricity/Gas/Water Supply	1.0810	20	3.7850	3
22.	Rail and other Transport Services/Storage	1.2027	12	3.1068	21
23.	Trade/Hotels	1.4424	6	3.5295	8
24.	Banking/ Insurance	1.1247	15	3.1243	20
25.	Other Services (Education, Medical, Administration, Defence, etc.)	1.1088	16	2.8447	25

Source : Mathematically calculated from inverse matrix. (For inverse refer Appendix VII A)

coefficient value, whereas for the economy as whole it ranks low at 17th position. Transport equipment sector had 7th rank for multiplying potential for self-sector and for whole economy. Similarly, wood products and non-metallic products have 8th and 10th rank for direct multiplier while for total multipliers the rank was 15th and 17th, respectively. Industrial machinery sector stands with ninth position for the direct multiplier has much higher rank of multiplying potential of the total output of the economy (Table 6.14).

The other manufacturing sectors with low direct as well as indirect output multipliers include food products, leather products, coal/petroleum products, chemicals and miscellaneous manufacturing. In tertiary sector, except trade other sectors have low coefficients; in fact, other services sectors have the lowest coefficient among tertiary sectors. Primary sector has low multipliers in terms of both direct and indirect coefficient values (Table 6.14).

Connectivity Matrix and Graph

In order to investigate the structure of relationship and structure of linkages among different sectors of the economy of Delhi, a connectivity matrix is derived from input-output coefficient matrix. The connectivity matrix qualifies all connections by three indices, *i.e.* 0,1,2. The indices value of '0' indicate no relationship between sector i and sector j. In other words, i and j sectors are isolated from each other. The index value of '1' implies a unidirectional flow from sector i to sector j. The unilateral flow is clearly specified whether it is a forward connection or a backward connection. The index value of '2' denotes a bilateral (mutual) or two-way linkage existing between sector i and j.

The connectivity matrix is displayed in the form of a graph where all connections are denoted through the network of flows. Figure 6.7 shows graph associated with connectivity matrix derived from technology coefficient matrix for internal transactions of the economy of Delhi in 1970-71 aggregated into 25 sectors. These matrices and diagrams show every liaison between industries as defined by $a_{ij} > 0$. With this approach industrial complexes or clusters can be identified in an input-output matrix. In this context industrial complexes are defined in terms of relative intensities of inter-industry liaisons, *i.e.* those industries that are closely interlinked through relationships defined in the technology coefficient matrix. The connectivity matrix and its graphical representation is very useful for analyzing an economic structure. Indeed, one can think of Hirschman's[11] concept of linkage and find an industrial complex; those sectors interlinked both through their distribution and supply networks. Thus, it provides a clear picture of city's economic dynamics.

The connectivity matrix is presented in the form of graph that displays inter-sectoral linkages through flow of networks signifying unidirectional and mutual, *i.e.* two-way linkages among different sectors. In 1970-71, this flow of networks of inter-sectoral relationships has been showing a complex web of flows among different sectors of the economy but no distinguishable pattern has emerged. It has been observed from the connectivity graph that most primary sectors including agriculture, animal husbandry, fishing, and forestry are at receiving end of the inputs. These sectors are not supplying inputs to other sectors. Only one primary sector, *i.e.* mining/quarrying shared mutual, backward and forward relations with some sectors of economy. Thus, among the primary sectors mining/quarrying had been the industry with better linkage with the economy rather than others. Agriculture, animal husbandry and forestry showed relationship among each other and also with other sectors as well but fishing sector appears to be isolated from rest of the economy except trade (Table 6.15).

In manufacturing sector as Table 6.15 indicates that food products, textiles, chemicals, miscellaneous manufacturing, industrial machinery and transport equipment have been the industrial sectors with their prominent positions in economy as revealed from their backward, forward and mutual linkages. These industries shared relationship with 15 and more other industrial sectors of the economy. The industries like plastic/rubber with their least connections with rest of the economy had appeared in its infancy stage of development and growth. Whereas the industries as wood products, leather products, coal/petroleum products, non-metallic products, metal products, paper and publishing and

Table 6.15 : Connectivity Matrix: 1970-71

Sector Code	*1*	*2*	*3*	*4*	*5*	*6*	*7*	*8*	*9*	*10*	*11*	*12*	*13*	*14*	*15*	*16*	*17*	*18*	*19*	*20*	*21*	*22*	*23*	*24*	*25*
1.	*	2	2	0	0	2	1F	1F	1F	0	0	1F	1F	0	0	1F	0	0	0	1F	1F	2	2	1F	0
2.	2	*	2	0	0	2	1F	1F	1F	0	0	1F	1F	0	0	1F	0	0	0	1F	1F	1F	2	1F	2
3.	2	2	*	0	0	2	1F	2	2	1B	0	1F	2	1B	1B	2	0	2	2	2	2	1F	1F	0	2
4.	0	0	0	*	0	0	0	0	0	0	0	0	0	0	0	0	0	0	0	0	0	0	2	0	0
5.	0	0	0	0	*	2	0	0	1B	1B	0	0	1B	1B	2	2	1F	1B	1B	1B	1B	1F	1B	0	0
6.	2	2	2	0	2	*	1F	1F	1F	0	2	1F	2	1F	0	0	1F	1F	1F	1F	1F	2	2	1F	1F
7.	1B	1B	1B	0	0	1B	*	2	2	2	1F	2	2	1B	2	2	2	1B	2	2	1F	2	2	1F	2
8.	1B	1B	2	0	0	1B	2	*	2	0	2	2	2	2	2	2	2	1B	2	2	1F	2	2	2	2
9.	1B	1B	2	0	1F	1B	2	2	*	1B	2	2	2	1B	2	2	2	1B	2	2	2	2	2	2	2
10.	0	0	1F	0	1F	0	2	0	1F	*	2	2	2	0	0	0	1F	1B	2	1F	1F	1F	1F	1F	1F
11.	0	0	0	0	0	2	1B	2	2	2	*	2	2	2	2	2	2	2	1B	0	1B	2	2	1F	2
12.	1B	1B	1B	0	0	1B	2	2	2	2	2	*	2	2	2	2	2	1B	2	2	2	2	2	1B	2
13.	1B	1B	2	0	1F	2	2	2	2	2	2	2	*	2	2	2	2	1B	2	1F	2	1F	2	1F	2
14.	0	0	1F	0	1F	1B	1F	2	1F	0	2	2	2	*	2	2	2	0	2	1F	1F	1F	2	1B	1B
15.	0	0	1F	0	2	0	2	2	2	0	2	2	2	2	*	2	2	1B	1B	1B	2	2	2	0	1B
16.	1B	1B	2	0	2	0	2	2	2	0	2	2	2	2	2	*	2	0	2	2	2	2	2	1F	1B
17.	0	0	0	0	1B	1B	2	2	2	1B	2	2	2	2	2	2	*	1B	2	2	2	2	2	1F	2
18.	0	0	2	0	1F	1B	1F	1F	1F	1F	2	1F	1F	0	1F	0	1F	*	1F	1F	2	2	2	2	1B
19.	0	0	2	0	1F	1B	2	2	2	2	1F	2	2	2	1F	2	2	1B	*	2	2	2	2	1B	1B
20.	1B	1B	2	0	1F	1B	2	2	2	1B	0	2	1B	1B	1F	2	2	1B	2	*	2	2	2	2	2
21.	1B	1B	2	0	1F	1B	1B	1B	2	1B	1F	2	2	1B	2	2	2	2	2	2	*	2	2	1B	2
22.	2	1B	1B	0	1B	2	2	2	2	1B	2	2	1B	1B	2	2	2	2	2	2	2	*	2	2	2
23.	2	2	1B	2	1F	2	2	2	2	1B	2	2	2	2	2	2	2	2	2	2	2	2	*	2	2
24.	1B	1B	0	0	0	1B	1B	2	2	1B	1B	1F	1B	1B	0	1B	1B	2	1F	2	1F	2	2	*	2
25.	0	2	2	0	0	1B	2	2	2	1B	2	2	2	1F	1F	1F	2	1F	1F	2	2	2	2	2	*

Source : Obtained from coefficient matrix, backward linkage matrix and forward linkage matrix (refer Appendix IX A, V A and VI A, respectively). F—implies forward, B—implies backward. '0' says no relationship, '1' implies one-way relation and '2' indicates two-way flow. For sector codes refer Table 6.13.

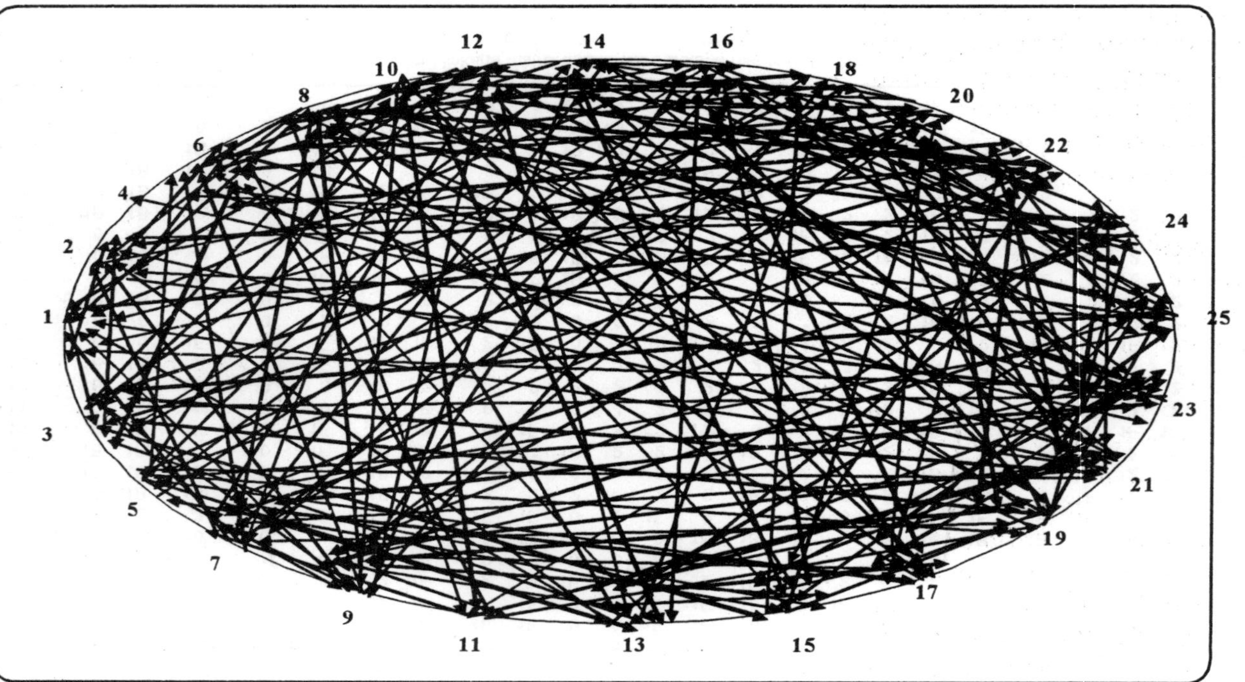

Fig. 6.7: The Web of Economy: 1970-71

Note: 1 to 25 are industrial sectors. For sector code refer Table 6.13. The flow arrows are based on Table 6.15

electric/electronic machinery have been moderate level of industries in economy of Delhi, which are developed and share medium level of interaction with rest of the economy. The whole of secondary sector does not share much interaction with primary sector industries. Construction sector and electricity/gas/water supply sector fall in the category of medium linkage sectors (Table 6.15).

Tertiary sectors were very significant in the economy of Delhi in 1970-71. Among these service industries, trade/hotel and other services sectors were at much prominent level as it is clearly observed from Fig. 6.7 that these two sectors share relationship with most other sectors whether backward, forward or mutual linkages. Transport/storage industry followed the previous two service sectors in terms of stronger interaction with the economy. The only service sector which was found in its developing stage was banking/ insurance industry which had not shared stronger linkages with other sectors (Table 6.15).

Conclusion

The structural relationships of Delhi's economy is analyzed and discussed through different levels of summarization of input-output transaction tables prepared for 1970-71. Distribution of commodities and service in total output, input and primary/secondary/tertiary sectors were illustrated. Inter-sectoral distribution of gross value added, inputs, intermediate use, final uses and private final consumption were also dealt with. The structure of economy was studied through linkages, multipliers and connectivity analysis.

It is found that in 1970-71, commodities constituted 45.73 per cent while 22.73 per cent was service sector in total output. The final use shows 36 per cent commodities and 63.45 per cent service in the total inputs. While in the total output, commodities share had been 80 per cent and final use of 20.3 per cent and for service the intermediate use was

53.19 per cent and final use of 46.18 per cent. In terms of broad sector of the economy in intermediate use, primary sector has least share (6.13 %) followed by secondary sector with 34.12 per cent and tertiary sector share 58.22 per cent. It is to be added that in inter-sectoral transactions primary sector shared lowest but, surprisingly, secondary sector and tertiary sector shared same proportions. This indicates an absolute insignificant primary sector and a prominent position of tertiary sector. In manufacturing sector, highest gross value added to output ratio has been seen in chemical, plastic/ubber, metal and non-metallic industry, thus, these were leading industries in 1970-71. While leather and electric/ electronic machinery had shown lowest. As regards the technological efficiency, the industries *viz.* plastic/rubber, chemical, non-metallic and metallic product had lower input-ratio as compared with other industries indicating towards higher efficiency; but leather, electric/electronic machinery showed highest input ratios, thus, not considered technologically efficient. The private consump-tion trend reflected towards higher private expenditure on agricultural products, animal husbandry product, service sector, construction, food products and textile products. The final demand has been highest in food products, textile, plastic/ rubber and all service sectors.

Trade and transport has not shown much significant role, *i.e.* only upto 20 per cent in the total output with maximum in petroleum industry (37 per cent) and minimum 2 per cent in plastic and rubber industry. The backward linkages or relative purchases showed food industry with well spread connectivity with 22 sectors while leather, paper, plastic/ rubber and miscellaneous sector have lowest backward linkages. The forward linkage reflects sale to maximum number of industries by petroleum industry, *i.e.* 24 industries, whereas lowest number of sales by leather sector to only 6 industries. The products-mix relation explained that most of the secondary industries got 90-100 per cent inputs from same products. While miscellaneous manufacturing and metal products received less than 80 per cent from same products. The market-share relations revealed most commodities got the products from same industries while electric/electronic machinery products received lowest inputs (12.78 per cent) from same industry and industrial machinery got 48 per cent inputs from same industry. The connectivity flow of networks of inter-sectoral relationships shows a complex web of flows among different sectors of the economy but no distinguishable pattern has emerged. It has been observed from the connectivity graph that most primary sectors are at receiving end of the inputs. The tertiary sectors were most significant in the economy.

References

1. See Appendix III.
2. See Appendix II.
3. See Appendix IVA.
4. For sectors refer Appendix II and III.
5. Rasmussen, P.N. (1956) Studies in Inter-Sectoral Relations, *op. cit.*
6. Refer p. 111.
7. Refer p. 112.
8. Refer p. 113.
9. Refer p. 113.
10. For details refer pp. 107-108.
11. Hirschman, A. (1958) *The Strategy of Economic Development,* New Haven and London: Yale University Press.

Chapter - 7

Inter-Industry Relations : 2000-01

Introduction

The previous chapter discussed structure of economy of Delhi for the year 1970-71 in terms of inter-industry relations measured by input-output coefficients, product mix relations, market share relations, backward and forward linkages, output multipliers and connectivity matrix. In the present chapter the inter-sector or inter-industrial structure is analyzed for the year 2000-01 in the same pattern, *i.e.* with reference to input-output coefficients, product mix matrix, market share matrix, backward and forward linkages, output multipliers and connectivity matrix. This chapter also analyzes pollution aspect accounted in input-output transaction table. A comparative analysis is made for coefficients, linkages and output multipliers between non-pollution and pollution accounted input-output transaction tables.

Inter-Industry Transactions

The distribution of various components in the total output shows that total intermediate demands share was 67.37 per cent, Private Final Consumption Expenditure (PFCE) 12.42 per cent, Government Final Consumption Expenditure (GFCE) 4.17 per cent, Government Fixed Capital Formation (GFCF) 0.31 per cent and others [including Change In Stock

(CIS) export less imports] 15.73 per cent. Table 7.1 shows that in total output major share was consumed by intermediate demand, export and private final consumption.

Table 7.1 : Distribution of Outputs (In per cent)

Components	*Distribution*
Intermediate demand	67.37
PFCE	12.42
GFCE	4.17
GFCF	0.31
Others	15.73
Total output	100

Source : Obtained from absorption matrix prepared in the present research (*See* Appendix VIB).

As revealed from the analysis of inter-industry structural relations, the role of commodities (Sectors 1 to 21) and services (Sectors 22 to 25)[1] and consumption for final use in the total output shows that in totality commodities shared 17.21 per cent, services 50.16 per cent, whereas final use was 32.63 per cent of the total output. The total gross value added comprised of 20.44 per cent of commodities and 79.56 per cent of services share in the economy of Delhi. Commodities contributed to the total intermediate use by 76.39 per cent, which included 27.34 per cent to commodities itself, and 49.06 per cent to services and 23.39 per cent to final use. Whereas the service shared 64.77 per cent of intermediate use which included 14.29 per cent to commodities, 50.48 per cent to itself and 35.32 per cent towards final use into total output during the year 2000-01 (Table 7.2).

The analysis of inputs used for the production recipes indicates that in the total output by commodities, 70.97 per cent were total inputs and 27.50 per cent of gross value added. The total inputs of commodities included 26.74 per cent from commodities alongwith 45.76 per cent from service. The service industry used 65.76 per cent of total input with 34.27

Table 7.2 : Distribution of Outputs (In per cent)

Items *(a)*	*Commodities* *(b)*	*Services* *(c)*	*Intermediate Use* *(d):(b+c)*	*Final Use* *(f)*	*Total Output* *(g): (d+f)*
Commodities	27.34	49.06	76.39	21.39	100
Services	14.29	50.48	64.77	35.23	100
Sub-total	17.21	50.16	67.37	32.63	100
Gross Value Added	20.44	79.56	—	—	100

Source : Obtained from absorption matrix prepared in the present research (*See* Appendix IVB).

of gross value added. This total input comprised 14.48 per cent inputs from commodities and 51.78 per cent from self. The economy of Delhi, as a whole, used total inputs of 67.9 per cent with 32.63 per cent gross value added. Commodities and services in the proportion of 17.58 per cent and 50.29 per cent contributed to the inputs, respectively. In the case of final use commodities share, 16.17 per cent and services provided 83.83 per cent (Table 7.3).

Table 7.3 : Distribution of Inputs (In per cent)

Items	*Commodities*	*Services*	*Sub-total*	*Final Use*
Commodities	26.74	14.48	17.58	16.17
Services	45.76	51.78	50.29	83.83
Sub-total	70.97	65.76	67.37	—
Gross Value Added	27.50	34.27	32.63	—
Total Output	100	100	100	100

Source: Obtained from absorption matrix prepared in the present research (*See* Appendix IVB).

The inter-industry transactions in terms of inputs from different sectors to total intermediate use indicated that primary sector gave 1.38 per cent; secondary sector provided 11.98 per cent and 74.43 per cent by service sector. The primary sector supplied 20.26 per cent to same industry, 7.59 per cent to secondary and 72.15 per cent to tertiary sector.

Of the total intermediate use by secondary sector, it supplied 3.52 per cent to primary sector industries, 58.98 per cent to the same industry and 37.51 per cent to service industry. The tertiary sector from its contribution to intermediate use provided 0.98 per cent to primary industry, 9.58 per cent to secondary industry and 77.93 per cent to the same industry (Table 7.4).

Table 7.4 : Inter-Industry Transactions (In per cent)

Items	*Primary*	*Secondary*	*Tertiary*	*Intermediate Use*
Primary	20.26	7.59	72.15	100
Secondary	3.52	58.98	37.51	100
Tertiary	0.98	9.58	77.93	100
Total Input	1.38	11.98	74.43	100

Source : Obtained from absorption matrix prepared in the present research (*See* Appendix IVB).

The analysis in terms of the three main sectors of the economy and their share to the total output reveals that in primary sector inputs used were 58.34 per cent and gross value added was 41.66 per cent of the total output. In secondary sector, it was 74.59 per cent and 26.75 per cent of inputs and gross value added, respectively. In tertiary sector, 64.33 per cent was input and 34.27 per cent was gross value added to the total output produced. In the total output produced by primary sector, it took 15.46 per cent from same commodity, 23.27 per cent from manufacturing sector and 37.08 per cent from services to the total inputs used. The manufacturing industry in its total input for products received from primary sector (7.58 per cent), 35.15 from self and 35.50 per cent from services. Tertiary (services industry) sector got 0.79 per cent from primary sector, 3.56 per cent from secondary sector and 52.83 per cent from main sector in its input structure (Table 7.5).

Table 7.5 : Distribution of Inputs in Total Output (In per cent)

Items	*Primary*	*Secondary*	*Tertiary*	*Intermediate Use*
Primary	15.46	7.58	0.79	0.93
Secondary	23.27	35.15	3.56	16.12
Tertiary	37.08	35.50	52.83	50.29
Gross Value Added	41.66	26.75	34.27	—
Total Output	100	100	100	100

Source : Obtained from absorption matrix prepared in the present research (*See* Appendix IVB).

The input-output transaction table has been broadly aggregated into three main sectors of the economy that gives actual levels for the year 2000-01.In Table 7.6, the basic inter-industry matrix consists of columns 2 to 4 and rows 3 to 5. The diagonal cells of the basic inter-industry matrix show the output of goods and services, produced and consumed by the same sector. The sum of column 5 (Inter-industry use) and 6 (Final use) gives the total supply or output in the economy. It has been visible from data that primary sector very low while tertiary sector has been maximum (Table 7.6).

Table 7.6 : Inter-Industry Transactions (In lakh Rs)

Items (1)	*Primary* (2)	*Secondary* (3)	*Tertiary* (4)	*Intermediate Use* (5)	*Total Final Use* (6)	*Total Output* (7)
Primary	33332	12478	118677	164488	45639	210128
Secondary	50187	841638	535240	1427066	648783	3733037
Tertiary	86623	852243	9382931	10321798	5060257	13691541
Total Input	170143	1706361	10036849	11913353	—	—
Gross Value Added	89835	588201	5076644	5754680	—	—
Total Output	215651	2394062	15024993	17634707	5754680	17634707

Source : Obtained from absorption matrix prepared in the present research (*See* Appendix IVB).

Gross Value Added Output Ratio

The Gross Value Added (GVA) output ratio indicates the growth or profit margins of a particular industry. It has been revealed that in the whole of primary sector in Delhi is around 30-40 per cent. In the manufacturing sector, different industries show different ratios as indicated by Fig. 7.1. Plastic/rubber and chemicals industries were with more than 50 per cent GVA in total output reflecting that these industries were flourishing in Delhi's economy in 2000-01. Food products and non-metallic industries had nearly 40 per cent GVA in the total output. Wood products and non-metallic industries had little more than 30 per cent GVA in their total output, followed by leather and industrial machinery industries with their GVA about less than 30 per cent. Other industries like textile, paper, metallic products, electric/ electronic machinery, transport equipment and miscellaneous manufacturing had GVA proportion upto 25 per cent. Construction sector had the GVA output ratio of 28.96 per cent, whereas electric/water supply had lower ratio of 21.38 per cent (Fig. 7.1).

In the service sector, the ratio was between 30-40 per cent of GVA for trade, transport and storage. Banking/insurance had the highest of 40.63 per cent and other services had lowest of 28.84 per cent (Fig.7.1).

Input Ratio

The input ratio to the total output produced shows the technological efficiency of particular industry. Fig. 7.2 exhibits that in the whole of the primary sector the ratio of inputs is between 60 to 65 per cent.

While in the secondary sector different industries show different proportions. Maximum input ratios are seen in textile, miscellaneous manufacturing and metal products with 79.3 per cent, 78.67 per cent and 79.88 per cent, respectively. They are followed by electric/electronic

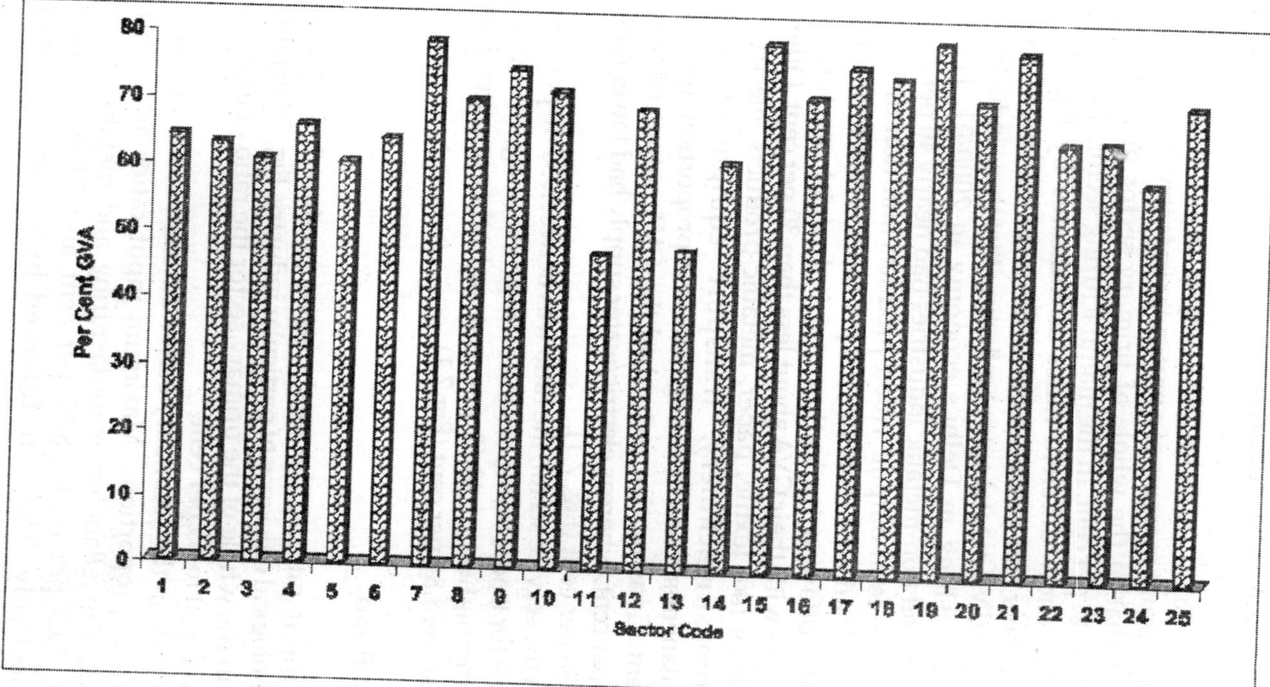

Fig. 7.1 : Proportion of Gross Value Added to Output

machinery, transport equipment, industrial machinery, leather products, paper with more than 70 per cent inputs used for producing a particular output. Wood products and petroleum products used nearly 70 per cent inputs, while non-metallic industry used input ratio of 61.19 per cent. Plastic/rubber and chemical industries had the lowest input ratio of 47.14 and 48.03 per cent, respectively. Construction and electricity/gas/water supply accounted for input use of 70 to 78 per cent. In the service sector, transport/storage, trade and banking/insurance had 60 to 65 per cent input ratios while other services had 67 to 70 per cent (Fig. 7.2).

Final Demand

The pattern of total final demand as indicated by different sectors of Delhi's economy during 2000-2001 reflects that highest demand is seen in banking insurance sector by 44.81 per cent of the total final demand, other services with 14.32 per cent, followed by trade and transport/storage services with 12 per cent of the final demand (Fig. 7.3).

In the manufacturing sector, food product industry with 8.89 per cent, textiles, chemicals, metal industry with more than 2 per cent shared the total final demand. Paper and miscellaneous manufacturing industry had more than 1 per cent of final demand. It is to be added that wood products, plastic, rubber, coal/petroleum products, non-metallic products and transport equipment had less that 1 per cent of final demand. Leather products, industrial machinery, and electric/electronic machinery had negative final demand of less 1 per cent. In the primary sector industries in all the sectors had less than 1 per cent of final demand between 0.01 to 0.48 per cent; while forestry/logging had no share in final demand (Fig.7.3).

Private Consumption

Figure 7.4 depicts private consumption levels in different

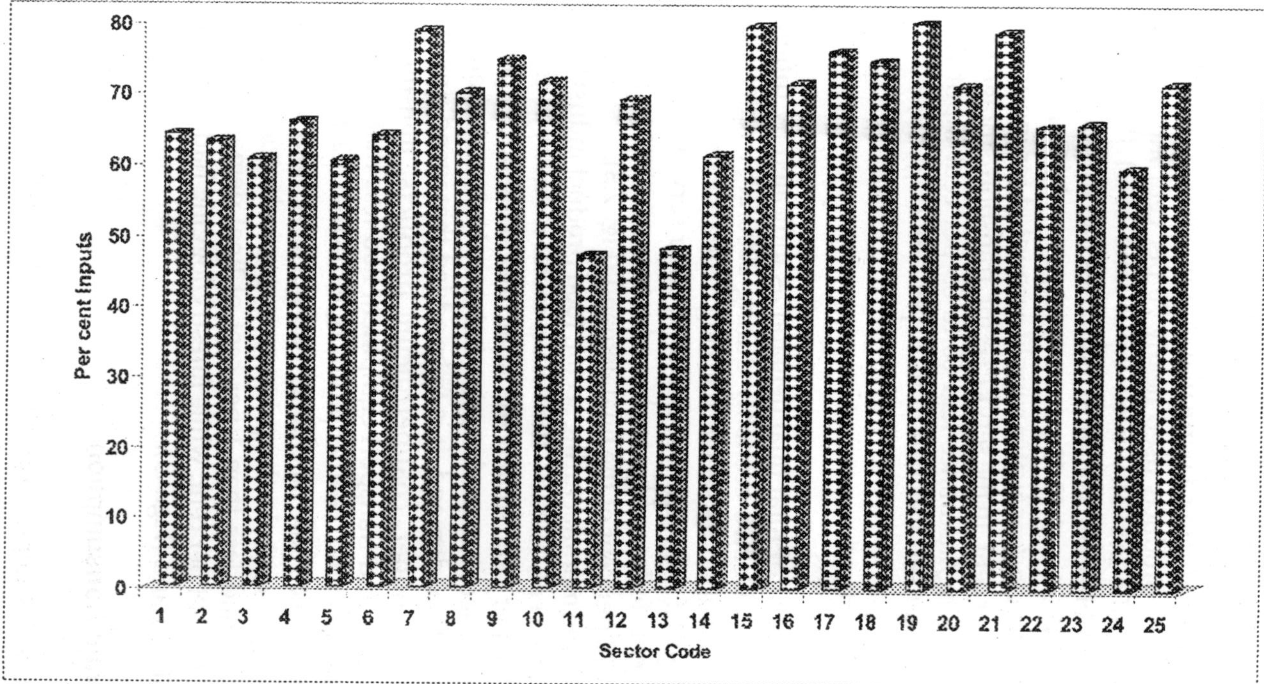

Fig. 7.2 : Proportion of Inputs to Output

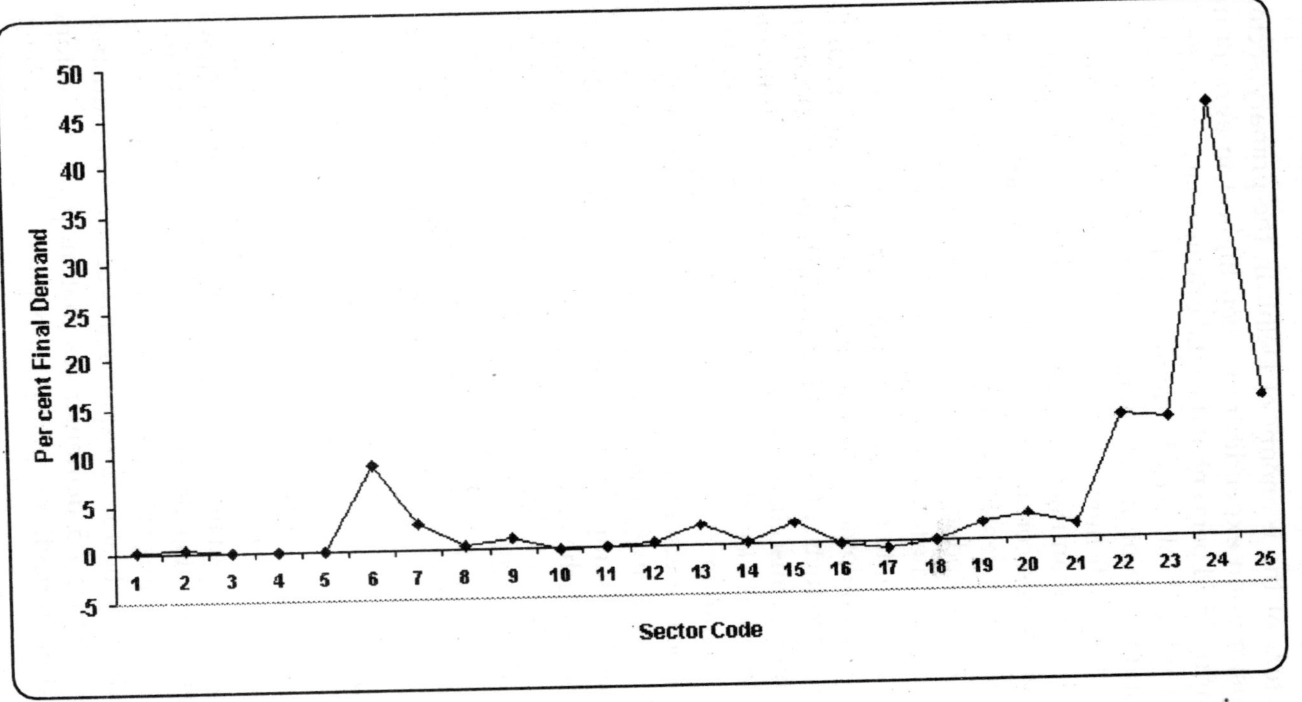

Fig. 7.3 : Distribution of Final Demand

sectors of the economy of Delhi. In the primary sector, consumption expenditure is seen highest in agriculture sharing 25.74 per cent of the total private final consumption expenditure followed by animal husbandry with 9.64 per cent, and minimum in mining/quarrying more than 1 cent in forestry and fishing.

In the manufacturing sector, food products industry shows highest consumption of 9 per cent of the total followed by 5.91 per cent consumption expenditure in textiles. Petroleum products and chemical products show more than 1 per cent of the total consumption, followed by nearly 1 per cent consumption of paper products, metal products, and transport equipments. In other industries *viz.* wood products, leather products, plastic/rubber products, electric/electronic machinery, miscellaneous manufacturing and non-metallic products have less than 0.5 per cent of the total consumption with minimum 0.09 per cent in industrial machinery. The construction sector had 7.75 per cent of the total expenditure while electricity/gas/water supply had nearly 1 per cent of the total consumption. In the service sector, trade and other services had the consumption level of 12.42 and 10.70 per cent, respectively. Transport and storage had 7.72 per cent of private expenditure while banking/insurance with only 7.14 per cent of the total private final consumption expenditure (Fig. 7.4).

Export

To assess the export factors in different sectors of urban economy of Delhi for the year 2000-01, there is no direct parameter to analyze this aspect. However, the column (others) in the final demand quadrant in Absorption Matrix[2] including (change in stocks and export less imports) is taken as indirect indicator for export status of different industrial sector. Figure 7.5 demonstrates that all primary sectors including agriculture, animal husbandry, forestry, fishing

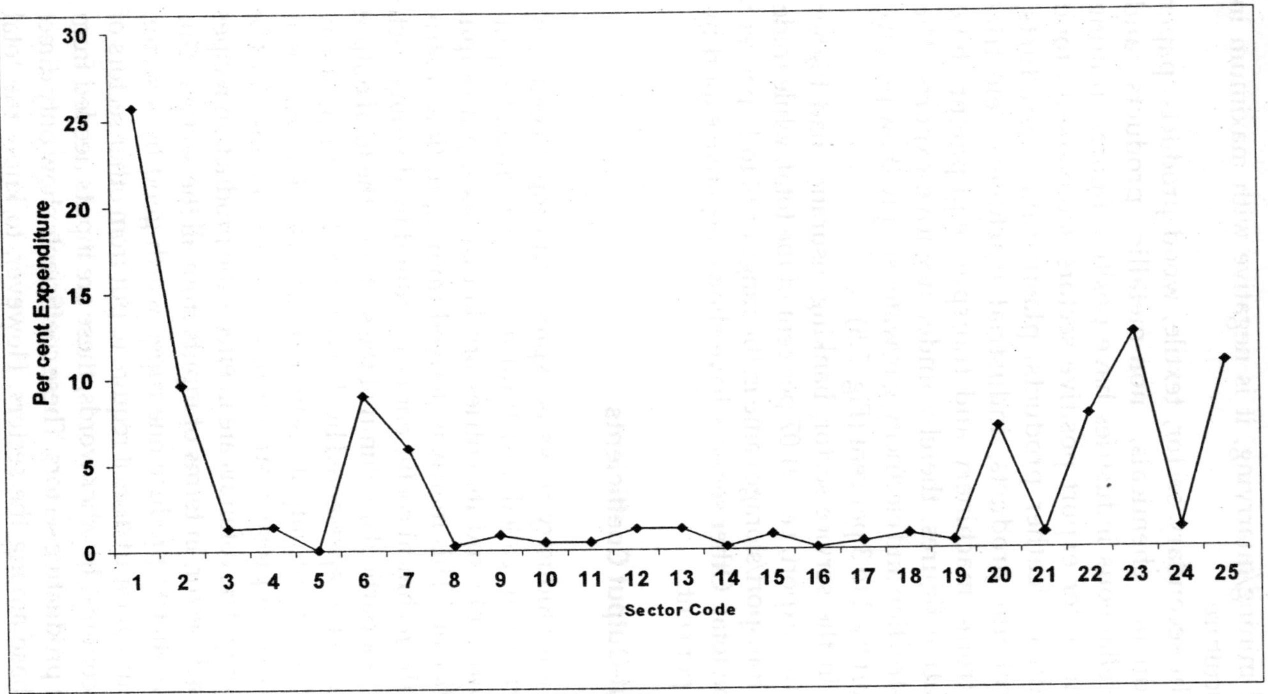

Fig. 7.4 : Distribution of Private Final Consumption Expenditure

and mining/quarrying, it is negative with maximum in agriculture.

In secondary sector, textile, wood products, paper products, chemicals, non-metallic products and miscellaneous industries have positive figures, putting them under export positive sectors. Conversely, food products, leather products, plastic/rubber products, petroleum products, industrial machinery, electric/ electronic machinery and transport equipment show negative figures, thereby under negative exports. The construction and electricity/gas/water supply show positive export by 2 to 3 per cent (Fig. 7.5).

In the service sector, banking/insurance had higher positive export, *i.e.* , 91.07 per cent of the total, while trade and transport/storage came in the range of 14 to 18 per cent of the total. Other services have shown negative export by 2.54 per cent.

Input-Output Coefficients

The inter-industry flows is expressed in input coefficient matrix form, called structural matrix of technical input-output table and its entries are known as input-output coefficients. This matrix is derived from input flow matrix and the technical coefficient (a_{ij}) is found by dividing each flow in a particular column of the sector by the total output of the sector represented by that column. The principal way in which input-output coefficients are used for analysis is that they represent structure of the production in the economy. The columns are in effects the production recipes for each sector, in terms of inputs from all the sectors. This shows that to produce one rupee worth good by a sector, how much input does it require to put from other sectors of the economy. In other words, these are inputs needed from other productive sectors. These coefficients show only direct purchase among the sectors. However, to know the total

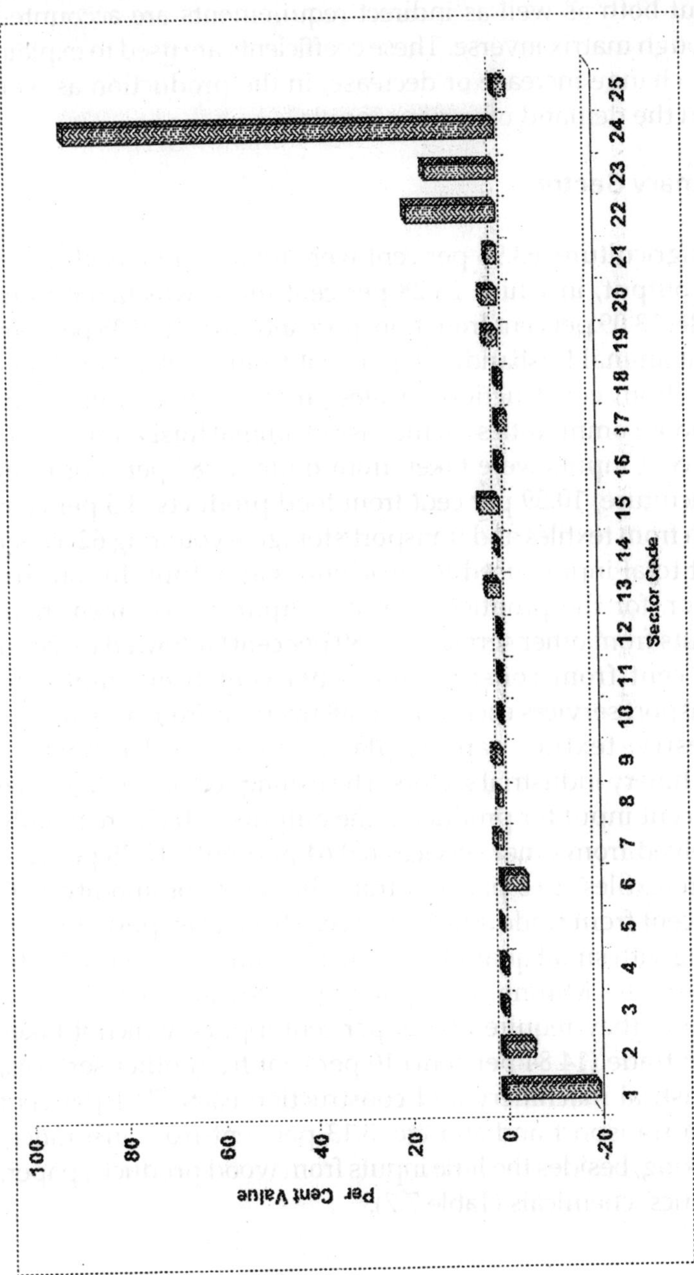

Fig. 7.5 : Distribution of Export

input both as well as indirect requirements are accounted through matrix inverse. These coefficients are used to explain any change increase or decrease, in the production as well as in the demand of various inputs.

Primary Sector

In agriculture, 63.96 per cent were total inputs used to get the output, in which 23.28 per cent input was taken from trade, 13.09 per cent from transport and storage, 9.35 per cent from animal husbandry, 8 per cent from itself and 5.63 per cent from construction besides small fraction from other various commodities. In the case of animal husbandry, 30.87 per cent inputs were taken from trade, 13.84 per cent from agriculture, 10.29 per cent from food products, 3.5 per cent each from textiles and transport/storage accounting 62.89 per cent total inputs used for reaching that output. In forestry sector, for the production of its output it has taken main inputs from other services (26.80 per cent) followed by 20.44 per cent from construction, 5 per cent from trade and transport services each, and small fractions from agriculture, forestry, textile, papers, plastic, metal and industrial machinery industrial sectors. The fishing sector needed 65.76 per cent input for producing the outputs, which are mainly received from other services (20.64 per cent), 15.25 per cent from textiles, 8.68 per cent from the same commodity, 9.97 per cent from trade and 3.5 per cent from transport/storage, alongwith small quantities from agriculture, food products, paper, etc. Mining and quarrying indicate that for total output, they required 60.29 per cent inputs, which it takes from trade (14.84 per cent) 10 per cent from other services, industrial machinery and construction each, 7.91 per cent from transport and storage, 3.13 per cent from insurance/ banking, besides the little inputs from wood products, paper, plastics, chemicals (Table 7.7).

Manufacturing Sector

Table 7.7 demonstrates that food products (Sector 6) show that for producing this output, 63.89 per cent total inputs were supplied by various sectors including 50 per cent from itself, followed by 3 per cent by transport services and trade each, 2.66 per cent from animal husbandry, 1.3 per cent from textiles, and small fractions from banking/insurance, agriculture, wood products, paper, plastics, chemicals and industrial machinery. No relation was seen with forestry, fishing, mining, leather, petroleum products, non-metallic products, transport equipment. Textiles (Sector 7) had main input of 41.74 per cent from itself, followed by 24.13 per cent from trade, 8.54 per cent from transport/storage services, more than 1 per cent from leather and other services each, and small proportion from various other sectors to make the total input of 78.67 per cent. It has taken no inputs from all primary sectors, food products, petroleum products, non-metallic products, miscellaneous manufacturing, and transport equipments. The wood and wood products (Sector 8) received main input 31.8 per cent from trade (as most wood as raw material comes to the city from trade), followed by 15.07 per cent from other services, 8.88 per cent from transport/storage, 7.56 per cent from itself, 3.62 per cent from banking/insurance, besides very little proportion from variety of other sectors. No relationship is seen with sectors like agriculture, animal husbandry, mining, food products, plastic, miscellaneous manufacturing. In the case of paper products, printing and publishing (Sector 9), total inputs of 74.58 per cent included highest input from trade of 27.26 per cent, followed by 19.59 per cent form transport and storage services, 17.65 per cent from itself, 5.66 per cent from textiles, 2.55 per cent from banking and insurance alongwith other inputs. No inputs were taken from sectors including all primary, food products, petroleum products, transport equipments etc. The leather and leather products (Sector 10) main inputs, *i.e.* 40.69 per cent came from itself, 11.70 per cent from transport/storage, 7.62 per cent from trade, 3.03 per cent from banking and insurance 7.25 per cent from textiles alongwith other inputs in the total input of 71.51 per cent. This sector has not received any inputs from primary sector, food products, petroleum products, transport equipments and other services. The rubber and plastic products (Sector 11) have main input from trade, *i.e.* 21.97 per cent, followed by 10.48 per cent from transport and storage, 9.65 per cent from itself, 2.68 per cent from banking and insurance, 1.58 per cent from textiles and other inputs in the total input of 47.11 per cent. This sector has no structural relationship with agriculture, animal husbandry, fishing, mining, food products, leather, petroleum products, non-metallic products and transport equipments. Petroleum products (Sector 12), of the total inputs of 69.03 per cent, had its main input from transport/storage, *i.e.* 24.2 per cent, followed by 23.11 per cent from banking and insurance, 21.08 per cent from trade, besides other inputs. What is true is that it has no dependence on first four primary sectors, transport equipments and other services. Chemicals (Sector 13) received main input for production from trade, *i.e.* 24.98 per cent, 10.73 per cent from transport and storage, 5.63 per cent from textiles, 2.41 per cent from itself with small inputs from other sectors in the total inputs of 48.03 per cent. It generally means sharing no relationship in its production with four of the five primary sectors, leather, petroleum products, non-metallic products, miscellaneous manufacturing, construction and other services (Table 7.7).

The non-metallic products (Sector 14), main inputs were from transport/storage (37.98 per cent), followed by 21.37 per cent from trade, besides other inputs in its total inputs of 61.19 per cent. Interestingly, no inputs were received from first four primary sectors, food products, transport equipment and other services. Metal industry (Sector 15) received its main input of 46.05 per cent from trade, 17.99

per cent from transport and storage, 10.75 per cent from itself, 2.44 per cent from banking/insurance, 1.40 per cent from textile and other inputs. This suggests that this has taken no intakes from petroleum products, transport equipments and other services. The industrial machinery (Sector 16) has required inputs from itself upto 36.83 per cent, followed by 16.37 per cent from trade, 11.26 per cent from transport and storage, 3.20 per cent from banking and insurance, 1.95 per cent from electric/electronic machinery, besides small inputs from other sectors to make the total requirement of inputs of 71.25 per cent. It is, therefore, evident that no structural relation is visible with first six sectors, petroleum products, transport equipments and other services. The manufacture of electric/electronic machinery (Sector 17) had total inputs of 75.83 per cent, where major input of 43.02 per cent was contributed by self, 16.82 per cent from trade, 10.5 per cent from transport and storage, 1.6 per cent from other services, 1.23 per cent each from textile and banking/insurance, besides other inputs. This industry received no input from first six sectors, and petroleum products and transport equipments. Manufacture of rail and other transport equipments (Sector 18) received almost similar per cent of input from self and trade, *i.e.* more than 30 per cent from each, 3.33 per cent from transport/storage, 2.25 per cent from electric/electronic machinery, 1.51 per cent from banking/insurance and other inputs are part of its total input of 74.49 per cent. It has no dependence on first six sectors and other services. The miscellaneous manufacturing (Sector 19) had the production recipe of the total input of 79.88 per cent which included 50.18 per cent from trade, 16.32 per cent from itself, 4 per cent from textile and transport/storage each, 1.34 per cent, 1.27 per cent, 1.20 per cent from plastics/rubber, electric/ electronic machinery, metal products, respectively, besides other inputs. Above all, no inputs are seen from first six sectors and other services (Table 7.7).

The construction sector (Sector 20) in its total inputs of 71.08 per cent, had main input from trade, *i.e.* 39.32 per cent, 10.77 per cent from transport and storage, 9.44 per cent from other services, 1.88 per cent from banking/insurance, 3.02 per cent form itself, 1.21 per cent from non-metallic products, 1.04 per cent from metallic products, besides other inputs. Interestingly, this sector takes no input from fishing, food products, leather, and petroleum products. The electricity/gas/water supply sector (Sector 21) did receive most input of 31.75 per cent from trade, 17.23 per cent from transport and storage, 13.42 per cent from other services, 6.08 per cent from construction, 3.31 per cent from electric/electronic machinery, 2.34 per cent from banking/insurance, 1.15 per cent from industrial machinery alongwith other inputs. More specifically, no inputs were received from agriculture, fishing, forestry, food products, leather and non-metallic products (Table 7.7).

Service Sector

Rail and other transport services/storage (Sector 22) got maximum inputs from other services, *i.e.* , 28.58 per cent followed by 15.36 per cent from trade, 6.49 per cent from construction, 3.37 per cent from banking and insurance, 4.9 per cent from itself, 2.58 per cent from transport equipment, besides other inputs in the total input of 65.28 per cent. This service sector had no role of the four of the primary sectors, chemicals, and non-metallic products. The trade/hotel (Sector 23) got most of its inputs from other services, *i.e.* 41.26 per cent, 5.32 per cent from itself, 4.65 per cent from construction, 4.76 per cent from transport and storage services, 3.28 per cent from banking/insurance, 2.8 per cent from food products, 1.01 per cent from textiles alongwith input in smaller proportion from other sectors to total input of 65.58 per cent. Trading/hotels sector were not dependent on sectors like forestry, mining, leather, petroleum products and chemicals.

Table 7.7 : Input-Output Coefficient Matrix (commodity × industry): 2000-01

Sector Code	*Industry / Commodity*	*1*	*2*	*3*	*4*	*5*	*6*	*7*	*8*	*9*	*10*	*11*	*12*	*13*
1.	Agriculture	0.0806	0.1384	0.0001	0.0003	-	0.0090	-	-	-	-	-	-	0.0002
2.	Animal Husbandry	0.0935	0.0029	-	-	-	0.0266	-	-	-	-	-	-	-
3.	Forestry and Logging	0.0000	-	0.0004	-	-	-	0.0000	0.0011	-	-	0.0013	-	-
4.	Fishing	-	-	-	0.0868	-	-	-	-	-	-	-	-	-
5.	Mining/Quarrying	0.0000	-	-	-	0.0004	0.0000	0.0000	0.0000	-	-	0.0000	0.0000	0.0000
6.	Food Prod., Beverages and Tobacco Products	0.0006	0.1029	-	0.0250	-	0.5090	-	-	-	-	-	-	0.0144
7.	Textiles	0.0028	0.0305	0.0071	0.1525	-	0.0130	0.4174	0.0149	0.0566	0.0725	0.0158	0.0046	0.0563
8.	Wood, Wood Prods. and Furniture	0.0000	-	0.0000	0.0015	0.0011	0.0009	0.0004	0.0756	0.0014	0.0018	0.0011	0.0004	0.0039
9.	Paper, Paper Prods., Print/Pub.	0.0001	-	0.0012	0.0001	0.0006	0.0006	0.0002	0.0007	0.1765	0.0012	0.0007	0.0002	0.0026
10.	Leather Products	0.0000	-	-	-	-	0.0000	0.0174	0.0025	0.0003	0.4069	0.0000	0.0000	0.0000
11.	Plastic/Rubber Products	0.0000	-	0.0011	-	0.0012	0.0005	0.0011	0.0000	0.0055	0.0069	0.0965	0.0002	0.0020
12.	Coal/Petroleum Products	0.0000	-	0.0001	0.0000	0.0000	0.0000	0.0000	0.0000	0.0000	0.0000	0.0000	0.0001	0.0000
13.	Chemicals	0.0048	0.0001	0.0000	0.0003	0.0028	0.0002	0.0000	0.0008	0.0051	0.0007	0.0005	0.0000	0.0241
14.	Non-metallic Products	-	-	0.0000	0.0000	0.0007	0.0000	0.0000	0.0004	0.0002	0.0000	0.0000	0.0000	0.0000
15.	Metal Products	0.0000	0.0001	0.0002	0.0010	0.0028	0.0000	0.0002	0.0018	0.0013	0.0001	0.0001	0.0000	0.0001
16.	Industrial Machinery	0.0043	0.0002	0.0014	0.0000	0.1048	0.0001	0.0001	0.0012	0.0016	0.0001	0.0000	0.0000	0.0016
17.	Electric/Electronic Machinery	0.0001	-	0.0010	0.0000	0.0001	0.0001	0.0004	0.0011	0.0031	0.0002	0.0001	0.0001	0.0002
18.	Rail and other Transport Equip.	0.0008	-	0.0067	0.0444	0.0160	-	-	0.0001	-	-	-	-	-
19.	Miscellaneous Manufacturing	0.0001	-	0.0025	0.0000	0.0089	0.0000	0.0000	-	0.0002	0.0000	0.0000	0.0000	0.0000
20.	Construction	0.0563	0.0041	0.2044	-	0.0955	0.0002	0.0001	0.0006	0.0004	0.0003	0.0003	0.0004	0.0001
21	Electricity/Gas/Water Supply	0.0020	-	0.0001	0.0001	0.0057	0.0003	0.0001	0.0053	0.0026	0.0007	0.0016	0.0003	0.0003
22	Rail and other Transport / Storage Services	0.1309	0.0332	0.0518	0.0350	0.0791	0.0336	0.0854	0.0888	0.1959	0.1170	0.1048	0.2420	0.1073
23.	Trade/Hotel	0.2328	0.3087	0.0519	0.0997	0.1484	0.0362	0.2413	0.3180	0.2726	0.0761	0.2197	0.2108	0.2498
24.	Banking/Insurance	0.0105	0.0078	0.0067	0.0043	0.0313	0.0085	0.0096	0.0362	0.0225	0.0303	0.0286	0.2311	0.0174
25	Other Services (Edu., Med., Admin., Defence, etc.)	0.0195	-	0.2680	0.2064	0.1034	0.0001	0.0130	0.1507	0.0001	-	0.0002	-	-
	Total Input	0.6396	0.6289	0.6049	0.6576	0.6029	0.6389	0.7867	0.6997	0.7458	0.7151	0.4714	0.6903	0.4803
	Total Output	1.0000	1.0000	1.0000	1.0000	1.0000	1.0000	1.0000	1.0000	1.0000	1.0000	1.0000	1.0000	1.0000
	Gross Value Added	0.3604	0.3711	0.3951	0.3424	0.3971	0.3611	0.2133	0.3003	0.2542	0.2849	0.5286	0.3097	0.5197

Table 7.7 : (Contd...)

Sector	Industry / Commodity	14	15	16	17	18	19	20	21	22	23	24	25	Total
1.	Agriculture	-	-	-	-	-	-	0.0085	0.0000	0.0076	0.0060	-	0.0021	0.0047
2.	Animal Husbandry	-	-	-	-	-	-	0.0013	0.0052	0.0000	0.0113	-	0.0038	0.0044
3.	Forestry and Logging	-	-	-	-	-	-	0.0002	-	0.0000	0.0000	-	-	0.0000
4.	Fishing	-	-	-	-	-	-	-	0.0000	-	0.0009	-	-	0.0002
5.	Mining/Quarrying	0.0000	0.0000	0.0000	0.0000	-	-	0.0002	0.0036	0.0000	0.0000	-	0.0000	0.0000
6.	Food Prod., Beverages and Tobacco Products	-	-	-	-	-	-	-	0.0000	0.0004	0.0280	-	0.0001	0.0158
7.	Textiles	0.0030	0.0140	0.0060	0.0123	0.0076	0.0452	0.0054	0.0003	0.0059	0.0101	0.0007	0.0036	0.0234
8.	Wood, Wood Prods., and Furniture	0.0002	0.0010	0.0004	0.0010	0.0017	0.0032	0.0047	0.0001	0.0001	0.0006	0.0001	0.0005	0.0010
9.	Paper, Paper Prods., Print/ Publ.	0.0002	0.0005	0.0003	0.0007	0.0001	0.0021	0.0002	0.0012	0.0013	0.0019	0.0021	0.0014	0.0026
10.	Leather Products	0.0008	0.0001	0.0001	0.0001	0.0009	0.0001	-	-	0.0001	-	0.0025	0.0000	0.0027
11.	Plastic/Rubber Products	0.0001	0.0010	0.0003	0.0020	0.0012	0.0134	0.0000	0.0000	0.0057	0.0003	0.0001	0.0000	0.0015
12.	Coal/Petroleum Products	0.0000	0.0000	0.0000	0.0000	0.0000	0.0000	0.0000	0.0000	0.0000	0.0000	0.0000	0.0000	0.0000
13.	Chemicals	0.0001	0.0004	0.0002	0.0006	0.0009	0.0007	0.0007	0.0002	0.0000	0.0000	0.0000	0.0026	0.0012
14.	Non-metallic Products	0.0074	0.0005	0.0001	0.0004	0.0002	0.0002	0.0121	0.0000	0.0000	0.0000	0.0000	0.0000	0.0011
15.	Metal Products	0.0000	0.1075	0.0070	0.0075	0.0036	0.0120	0.0104	0.0001	0.0002	0.0004	0.0001	0.0002	0.0029
16.	Industrial Machinery	0.0006	0.0007	0.3683	0.0013	0.0021	0.0004	0.0002	0.0099	0.0020	0.0008	0.0007	0.0008	0.0022
17.	Electric/Electronic Machinery	0.0001	0.0003	0.0195	0.4302	0.0225	0.0127	0.0203	0.0331	0.0081	0.0001	0.0007	0.0043	0.0127
18.	Rail and other Transport Equip.	-	-	-	-	0.3240	-	0.0004	0.0013	0.0258	0.0000	0.0022	0.0002	0.0046
19.	Miscellaneous Manufacturing	0.0000	0.0001	0.0001	0.0001	0.0001	0.1632	0.0008	0.0038	0.0060	0.0016	0.0034	0.0185	0.0075
20.	Construction	0.0008	0.0001	0.0005	0.0001	0.0004	0.0006	0.0302	0.0608	0.0649	0.0465	0.0486	0.1836	0.0815
21.	Electricity/Gas/ Water Supply	0.0002	0.0022	0.0013	0.0004	0.0009	0.0003	0.0008	0.0193	0.0026	0.0007	0.0008	0.0005	0.0010
22.	Rail and other Transport / Storage Services	0.3798	0.1799	0.1126	0.1050	0.0333	0.0433	0.1077	0.1723	0.0490	0.0476	0.0381	0.0326	0.0554
23.	Trade/Hotel	0.2137	0.4605	0.1637	0.1682	0.3302	0.5018	0.3932	0.3175	0.1536	0.0532	0.0511	0.1249	0.1417
24.	Banking/Insurance	0.0047	0.0244	0.0320	0.0123	0.0151	-	0.0188	0.0234	0.0337	0.0328	0.1028	0.0196	0.0382
25.	Other Services (Edu., Med., Admin., Defence, etc.)	-	-	-	0.0160	-	-	0.0944	0.1342	0.2858	0.4126	0.3397	0.3123	0.2675
	Total Input	0.6119	0.7932	0.7125	0.7583	0.7449	0.7988	0.7104	0.7862	0.6528	0.6558	0.5937	0.7116	0.6737
	Total Output	1.000	1.000	1.000	1.000	1.000	1.000	1.000	1.000	1.000	1.000	1.000	1.000	1.000
	Gross Value Added	0.3881	0.2068	0.2875	0.2417	0.2551	0.2012	0.2896	0.2138	0.3472	0.3442	0.4063	0.2884	0.3263

Source: Input-output coefficient matrix is obtained from commodity × industry matrix (input flow matrix) by dividing the column entry by the respective industry output.

The service sector of banking/insurance (Sector 24) had strong relation with other services, *i.e.* 53.97 per cent of the total inputs, followed by10.28 per cent from self, 4.86 per cent from construction, 5.11 per cent from trade, 3.81 per cent from transport and storage services with little inputs from other sector of the economy to complete its input requirements of 59.37 per cent. The sectors, with no relationship with banking/insurance were primary sector, food products, leather, petroleum products, chemicals, and non-metallic products. Other services (including education, medical, research, public administration, defence, etc.) (Sector 25) took maximum inputs from self, *i.e.* 31.23 per cent, 18.36 per cent from construction, 12.49 per cent from trade, 3.26 per cent from transport and storage, 1.96 per cent from banking/insurance, 1.85 per cent from miscellaneous manufacture alongwith other inputs to its total inputs of 71.16 per cent. This sector did not share structural relation with forestry, fishing, mining, leather, plastic, petroleum products and non-metallic products (Table 7.7).

It would be further apparent from Table 7.7 that on average other services contributed 26.75 per cent as input, 14.17 per cent from trade, 8.15 per cent from construction, 3.82 per cent from banking/insurance, 5.54 per cent from transport/storage, 2.34 per cent from textiles, 1.58 per cent from food products, 1.27 per cent from electric/electronic machinery, and less than 1 per cent output from most sectors. Thus, in other words, all sectors of the economy are interrelated, inter-dependent and are part of the production process of one or the other sector; though in different proportions, some sectors are strongly related and complementary to each other, while the others are loosely related. Further, other sectors share no relationship or dependence at all (Table 7.7).

The industries or sectors which take maximum inputs from self are food products (50.9 per cent), textiles (41.74 per cent), leather (40.69 per cent), industrial machinery (36.83

per cent), electric/electronic machinery (43.02 per cent), transport equipment (32.4 per cent) and other services (31.23 per cent). Industries or sectors receiving maximum inputs from trade, transport and storage are agriculture, animal husbandry wood/wood products, paper/printing, petroleum products, metallic products, miscellaneous manufacturing, construction and electricity / gas / water supply. These are the sectors that received basic raw materials through trade, which involves the complementary role of transport, and storage sector as well. Thus, in other words, these sectors have shown the dependence on import (whether domestic or international) in their production of recipe. There are also sectors which had maximum inputs from services *viz.* trade/ hotel 63.47 per cent banking and insurance 58.35 per cent, transport and storage 44.18 per cent, forestry 44.31 per cent and mining 44.22 per cent. These are the sectors where the role of public administration becomes very significant, where, thus the strong relationship is witnessed (Table 7.7).

Product Mix Relations

Product mix relations show the main product and by-products produced by an industry. These relations are analyzed through the product mix matrix, whose column entries show the proportion in which a particular industry produces various commodities in the diagonal elements giving the proportion of the main products in the output of the industry; while the off-diagonal elements indicate the subsidiary products and by-products. This matrix is derived from the make matrix by dividing the row entries by the respective industry output (presented as a transpose of this matrix). In all industries, whether primary services and manufacturing, the main product of the industry accounts for major part in the total output.

Primary Sector

The agricultural sector is producing 95 to 98 per cent as its diagonal product or, in other words, its main products in the total output, the other subsidiary products are in transport/ storage and construction. Similarly, animal husbandry in Delhi contributes 98.51 per cent as main output of the total and 1.49 per cent of food products as a subsidiary product. As regards the forestry/logging, all the output is seen in main diagonal and no other outputs; even in fishing sector 98.68 per cent is main output with marginal products in trade and other services. Mining/quarrying, too, had its total output in the main diagonal. Thus, the whole of primary sector was not very significant in Delhi in 2000-01, as it did not provide subsidiary output to other commodities (Table 7.8).

Manufacturing Sector

In manufacturing, the industrial sector having more than 90 per cent as its main outputs were food products, paper/ publishing and petroleum products. Paper/publishing had by-products for plastic/rubber commodity and metal products. The manufacturing sector that had 70-80 per cent as main output includes textiles, wood products. Other products comprise for other services followed by trade and construction, textiles and paper products (Table 7.8).

The secondary sector with 60-70 per cent as its main output or diagonal outputs were chemicals, transport equipments, non-metallic products and miscellaneous manufacturing. The subsidiary output of common nature comprised of construction, gas/electricity/water supply, trade, transport/storage and other services in small proportions. The major subsidiary output was miscellaneous manufacturing (23.48 per cent) in case of chemicals; 30.35 per cent of other services as regards transport equipments and miscellaneous manufacturing. Even in non-metallic product, 29.29 per cent subsidiary output was for miscellaneous manufacturing. Other manufacturing sectors with 50-60 per cent output in their main diagonals included leather products, metal products and electric/electronic machinery. In these industries the common other output comprised of other services, trade, construction in small quantities. The major subsidiary output in metallic industry included 11.33 per cent in miscellaneous manufacturing, 8.26 per cent in wood products, 2.69 per cent in electric/electronic machinery, 2.66 per cent in construction and also in transport equipments, non-metallic product, chemicals, paper/publishing and plastic/rubber. In the case of electric/electronic machinery, 29.17 per cent subsidiary output was of miscellaneous manufacturing, 7.30 per cent of metal products, 2.32 per cent of industrial machinery and 1.41 per cent of transport equipments. The leather industries major subsidiary outputs were of textiles (32.76 per cent) and 4.24 per cent of chemicals. Industrial sector with less than 50 per cent output in their main diagonal were industrial machinery and plastic/rubber industry with main output of 45.49 per cent and 24.58 per cent, respectively. The subsidiary output of industrial machinery included 29.30 per cent of other services, 16.51 per cent of non-metallic products, 4.11 per cent of metal products, 1.79 per cent of transport equipments, 2.46 per cent of trade, and small proportion of construction and electric/electronic machinery. In the case of plastic/rubber industry, 30.98 per cent subsidiary output were of miscellaneous manufacturing, 14.36 per cent of chemicals, 8.99 per cent of leather products, 4.31 per cent of construction, marginal outputs of textile products, paper/printing products, metal production, electricity/gas/water supply, trade and services (Table 7.8).

Of the 14 manufacturing sectors in Delhi, it is apparent that some of the sectors produced variety of by-products and subsidiary products, thus, maintaining a stronghold or inter-dependence in the production recipes of many other industrial sectors. For instance, plastic/rubber industry and industrial machinery have the most significant role as they have subsidiary product for twelve other industries besides

Table 7.8 : Product Mix Matrix: 2000-01

Sector Code	Industry / Commodity	1	2	3	4	5	6	7	8	9	10	11	12	13
1.	Agriculture	0.9548	0.0000	0.0000	0.0000	0.0000	0.0012	0.0000	0.0000	0.0000	0.0000	0.0000	0.0000	0.0000
2.	Animal Husbandry	0.0000	0.9851	0.0000	0.0000	0.0000	0.0000	0.0000	0.0000	0.0000	0.0000	0.0000	0.0000	0.0000
3.	Forestry and Logging	0.0000	0.0000	1.0000	0.0000	0.0000	0.0000	0.0000	0.0000	0.0000	0.0000	0.0000	0.0000	0.0000
4.	Fishing	0.0000	0.0000	0.0000	0.9868	0.0000	0.0000	0.0000	0.0000	0.0000	0.0000	0.0000	0.0000	0.0000\
5.	Mining/Quarrying	0.0000	0.0000	0.0000	0.0000	1.0000	0.0000	0.0000	0.0000	0.0000	0.0000	0.0000	0.0000	0.0000
6.	Food Prod., Beverages and Tobacco Products	0.0000	0.0149	0.0000	0.0000	0.0000	0.9546	0.0000	0.0000	0.0000	0.0000	0.0000	0.0000	0.0000
7.	Textiles	0.0000	0.0000	0.0000	0.0000	0.0000	0.0000	0.7767	0.0000	0.0000	0.3276	0.0027	0.0000	0.0000
8.	Wood, Wood Prods. and Furniture	0.0000	0.0000	0.0000	0.0000	0.0000	0.0000	0.0000	0.8341	0.0000	0.0000	0.0000	0.0000	0.0000
9.	Paper, Paper Prods., Print/Pub.	0.0000	0.0000	0.0000	0.0000	0.0000	0.0000	0.0007	0.0000	0.9038	0.0000	0.0009	0.0000	0.0000
10.	Leather Products	0.0000	0.0000	0.0000	0.0000	0.0000	0.0000	0.0000	0.0000	0.0000	0.5064	0.0899	0.0000	0.0000
11.	Plastic/Rubber Products	0.0000	0.0000	0.0000	0.0000	0.0000	0.0000	0.0000	0.0000	0.0003	0.0000	0.2458	0.0000	0.0000
12.	Coal/Petroleum Products	0.0000	0.0000	0.0000	0.0000	0.0000	0.0000	0.0000	0.0000	0.0000	0.0000	0.0000	0.9299	0.0000
13.	Chemicals	0.0000	0.0000	0.0000	0.0000	0.0000	0.0000	0.0000	0.0000	0.0000	0.0424	0.1188	0.0000	0.6963
14.	Non-metallic Products	0.0000	0.0000	0.0000	0.0000	0.0000	0.0000	0.0000	0.0000	0.0000	0.0000	0.0000	0.0000	0.0000
15.	Metal Products	0.0000	0.0000	0.0000	0.0000	0.0000	0.0000	0.0000	0.0000	0.0009	0.0000	0.0002	0.0000	0.0000
16.	Industrial Machinery	0.0000	0.0000	0.0000	0.0000	0.0000	0.0000	0.0000	0.0000	0.0000	0.0000	0.0000	0.0000	0.0000
17.	Electric/Electronic Machinery	0.0000	0.0000	0.0000	0.0000	0.0000	0.0000	0.0000	0.0000	0.0000	0.0000	0.0000	0.0000	0.0000
18.	Rail and other Transport Equip.	0.0000	0.0000	0.0000	0.0000	0.0000	0.0000	0.0000	0.0000	0.0000	0.0000	0.1436	0.0000	0.0000
19.	Miscellaneous Manufacturing	0.0000	0.0000	0.0000	0.0000	0.0000	0.0000	0.0000	0.0000	0.0000	0.0000	0.3098	0.0000	0.2348
20.	Construction	0.0003	0.0000	0.0000	0.0000	0.0000	0.0007	0.0039	0.0006	0.0026	0.0031	0.0431	0.0008	0.0027
21.	Electricity/Gas/Water Supply	0.0000	0.0000	0.0000	0.0000	0.0000	0.0000	0.0002	0.0000	0.0002	0.0000	0.0096	0.0001	0.0003
22.	Rail and other Transport / Storage Services	0.0000	0.0000	0.0000	0.0000	0.0000	0.0000	0.0000	0.0000	0.0000	0.0000	0.0000	0.0000	0.0000
23.	Trade/Hotel	0.0028	0.0000	0.0000	0.0004	0.0000	0.0032	0.0110	0.0098	0.0043	0.0128	0.0058	0.0002	0.0120
24.	Banking/Insurance	0.0000	0.0000	0.0000	0.0000	0.0000	0.0000	0.0000	0.0000	0.0000	0.0000	0.0000	0.0000	0.0000
25.	Other Services (Edu., Med., Admin., Defence, etc.)	0.0421	0.0000	0.0000	0.0129	0.0000	0.0404	0.2075	0.1555	0.0879	0.1076	0.0298	0.0690	0.0539
Total Input		1.0000	1.0000	1.0000	1.0000	1.0000	1.0000	1.0000	1.0000	1.0000	1.0000	:.0000	1.0000	1.0000

Table 7.8 : (Contd...)

Sector Code	Industry Commodity	14	15	16	17	18	19	20	21	22	23	24	25	Total
1.	Agriculture	0.0000	0.0000	0.0000	0.0000	0.0000	0.0000	0.0000	0.0000	0.0000	0.0000	0.0000	0.0000	0.9560
2.	Animal Husbandry	0.0000	0.0000	0.0000	0.0000	0.0000	0.0000	0.0000	0.0034	0.0000	0.0000	0.0000	0.0000	0.9886
3.	Forestry and Logging	0.0000	0.0000	0.0000	0.0000	0.0000	0.0000	0.0000	0.0000	0.0000	0.0000	0.0000	0.0000	1.0000
4.	Fishing	0.0000	0.0000	0.0000	0.0000	0.0000	0.0000	0.0000	0.0000	0.0000	0.0000	0.0000	0.0000	0.9868
5.	Mining/Quarrying	0.0000	0.0000	0.0000	0.0000	0.0000	0.0000	0.0000	0.0000	0.0000	0.0000	0.0000	0.0000	1.0000
6.	Food Prod., Beverages and Tobacco Products	0.0000	0.0000	0.0000	0.0000	0.0000	0.0000	0.0000	0.0000	0.0000	0.0000	0.0000	0.0000	0.9695
7.	Textiles	0.0000	0.0000	0.0000	0.0000	0.0000	0.0000	0.0000	0.0000	0.0000	0.0000	0.0000	0.0000	1.1071
8.	Wood, Wood prods. and Furniture	0.0026	0.0826	0.0000	0.0000	0.0000	0.0000	0.0000	0.0000	0.0000	0.0000	0.0000	0.0000	0.9194
9.	Paper, Paper prods., Print/Pub.	0.0000	0.0109	0.0000	0.0000	0.0000	0.0000	0.0000	0.0000	0.0000	0.0000	0.0000	0.0000	0.9163
10.	Leather Products	0.0000	0.0000	0.0000	0.0000	0.0000	0.0000	0.0000	0.0000	0.0000	0.0000	0.0000	0.0000	0.5963
11.	Plastic/Rubber Products	0.0007	0.0017	0.0000	0.0000	0.0000	0.0054	0.0000	0.0000	0.0000	0.0000	0.0000	0.0000	0.2539
12.	Coal/Petroleum Products	0.0000	0.0000	0.0000	0.0000	0.0000	0.0000	0.0000	0.0000	0.0000	0.0000	0.0000	0.0000	0.9299
13.	Chemicals	0.0000	0.0006	0.0000	0.0000	0.0000	0.0000	0.0000	0.0000	0.0000	0.0000	0.0000	0.0000	0.8581
14.	Non-metallic Products	0.6034	0.0031	0.1651	0.0054	0.0000	0.0000	0.0000	0.0000	0.0000	0.0000	0.0000	0.0000	0.7770
15.	Metal Products	0.0237	0.5736	0.0411	0.0730	0.0011	0.0006	0.0000	0.0000	0.0000	0.0000	0.0000	0.0000	0.7143
16.	Industrial Machinery	0.0000	0.0000	0.4549	0.0232	0.0000	0.0033	0.0000	0.0000	0.0000	0.0000	0.0000	0.0000	0.4815
17.	Electric/Electronic Machinery	0.0113	0.0269	0.0008	0.5322	0.0000	0.0104	0.0000	0.0000	0.0000	0.0000	0.0000	0.0000	0.5816
18.	Rail and other Transport Equipment	0.0000	0.0078	0.0179	0.0191	0.6552	0.0000	0.0000	0.0000	0.0000	0.0000	0.0000	0.0000	0.8435
19.	Miscellaneous Manufacturing	0.2929	0.1133	0.0000	0.2917	0.0000	0.6024	0.0000	0.0000	0.0000	0.0000	0.0000	0.0000	1.8448
20.	Construction	0.0079	0.0266	0.0024	0.0013	0.0186	0.0023	1.0000	0.0000	0.0000	0.0000	0.0000	0.0000	1.1167
21.	Electricity/Gas/Water Supply	0.0001	0.0155	0.0000	0.0000	0.0003	0.0000	0.0000	0.9966	0.0000	0.0000	0.0000	0.0000	1.0228
22.	Rail and other Transport / Storage Services	0.0000	0.0000	0.0000	0.0000	0.0000	0.0000	0.0000	0.0000	1.0000	0.0000	0.0000	0.0000	1.0000
23.	Trade/Hotel	0.0068	0.0128	0.0246	0.0033	0.0151	0.0254	0.0000	0.0000	0.0000	1.0000	0.0000	0.0000	1.1502
24.	Banking/Insurance	0.0000	0.0000	0.0000	0.0000	0.0000	0.0000	0.0000	0.0000	0.0000	0.0000	1.0000	0.0000	1.0000
25.	Other Services (Edu., Med., Admin., Defence, etc.)	0.0506	0.1246	0.2931	0.0509	0.3098	0.3503	0.0000	0.0000	0.0000	0.0000	0.0000	1.0000	2.9858
Total Input		1.0000	1.0000	1.0000	1.0000	1.0000	1.0000	1.0000	1.0000	1.0000	1.0000	1.0000	1.0000	25.000

Source : Mathematically obtained as a part of Input-Output model (refer page 300 and 382)

its main output. Thus, they are significantly inter-dependent and complementary to many industries, whereas sectors like miscellaneous manufacturing, non-metallic products and industrial machinery has by-products for 8-10 commodities. The rest other industrial sectors shared by-products with 4-6 industrial sectors. Construction and electricity/gas/water supply had almost all outputs as their main output (Table 7.8).

Tertiary Sector

All the industries included in the tertiary sector show their outputs in the respective diagonals or as their main output cell, since they are providing services to all other sectors of the economy. Thus, they have nothing as a by-product or subsidiary product.

Market Share Relations

The market share relations of the economy of Delhi or among various industrial sectors are analyzed through the market share matrix. They represent the proportions in which the various industries produce the total output of particular commodity. The column entries show proportions contributed by different industries in total outputs of respective commodity. The diagonal elements give proportion of the output of various commodities produced as main product and the off-diagonal elements show proportion of the commodities as subsidiary products in other industries.

Primary Sector

The commodity group relating to primary sector indicates that most of the output was produced as the main product in all cases except agriculture and animal husbandry where 0.42 per cent and 0.33 per cent, respectively, was produced as a subsidiary product or by-product by the industries of food products, and textiles in former commodity and by the food products and electricity/gas/water supply in case of later commodity. This indicates that the primary sector commodity does not take much from different industrial sectors (Table 7.9).

Manufacturing Sector

The manufacturing sector commodities indicate much dependence on different industries for their total output; in other words, reflect stronger structural relationships, though even in manufacturing sector, some commodities took products from many industries, while in others, output was produced as main product only. The commodity sectors, like food products, textiles, paper/publishing, plastic/rubber and electric/electronic machinery, 95 to 100 per cent outputs were produced as main products. In the case of chemicals, 87.50 per cent were received as main product while 10.41 per cent from plastic and rubber industry, 1.98 per cent from leather industry; industrial machinery and leather commodities sectors received more than 75 per cent as main product and 21.18 per cent from electric/electronic machinery industry by former commodity, and 24.99 per cent from plastic/rubber industry by later commodity. Transport equipment commodity got 67.14 per cent as main product, 21.26 per cent as subsidiary product from plastic and rubber industry, 7.84 per cent from electric/electronic machinery industry and another nearly 4 per cent from metallic industry and industrial machinery industry. The commodities sector of non-metallic products and wood products took more than 50 per cent as main product. Subsidiary products of 48.78 per cent from metal industry were received by wood products and in case of later commodity 34 per cent from industrial machinery, 6.5 per cent from electric/electronic machinery and 2.66 per cent from metallic industries. The miscellaneous manufacturing commodity received minimum as main product, *i.e.* 10.23 per cent and subsidiary products from electric/electronic machinery (41.23 per cent), chemicals (17.14 per cent), 15.78 per cent from plastic and rubber, 12.16 per cent from metal industry, and 3.48 per cent from non-metallic industry. Construction and electricity/gas/water supply commodities sector took more than 90 per cent as main product and these commodities took subsidiary product in smaller proportions from metallic industry, plastic/rubber industry, textiles and paper industry (Table 7.9).

Service Sector

Table 7.9 elucidates that rail/other transport service; storage and banking/insurance had their output products received as the main or diagonal products; whereas in trade/hotels and other services commodity sector, 99.31 per cent and 94.38 per cent inputs were received as main products, respectively. The subsidiary products for former commodity were from food products, textiles, wood products, paper, plastic/rubber and many other industries with very small proportions. The other services took 2.67 per cent from textile industry and in small proportion from variety of other industries (Table 7.9).

Structural Analysis

The structure of the economy is analyzed and discussed through identifying leading and loosing industries, measuring backward/forward linkages and their coefficients. Output multipliers are computed to find economic structure in terms of significant industrial sector that has potential multiplying effect on self-sector and economy. The connectivity of different industrial sectors is studied through connectivity matrix and graph.

Leading and Loosing Industries

The leading and loosing industrial sector of the economy are

Table 7.9 : Market Share Matrix: 2000-01

Sector Code	Industry / Commodity	1	2	3	4	5	6	7	8	9	10	11	12	13
1.	Agriculture	0.9957	0.0000	0.0000	0.0000	0.0000	0.0000	0.0000	0.0000	0.0000	0.0000	0.0000	0.0000	0.0000
2.	Animal Husbandry	0.0000	0.9967	0.0000	0.0000	0.0000	0.0048	0.0000	0.0000	0.0000	0.0000	0.0000	0.0000	0.0000
3.	Forestry and Logging	0.0000	0.0000	1.0000	0.0000	0.0000	0.0000	0.0000	0.0000	0.0000	0.0000	0.0000	0.0000	0.0000
4.	Fishing	0.0000	0.0000	0.0000	1.0000	0.0000	0.0000	0.0000	0.0000	0.0000	0.0000	0.0000	0.0000	0.0000
5.	Mining/Quarrying	0.0000	0.0000	0.0000	0.0000	1.0000	0.0000	0.0000	0.0000	0.0000	0.0000	0.0000	0.0000	0.0000
6.	Food Prod., Beverages and Tobacco Products	0.0040	0.0001	0.0000	0.0000	0.0000	0.9952	0.0000	0.0000	0.0000	0.0000	0.0000	0.0000	0.0000
7.	Textiles	0.0002	0.0000	0.0000	0.0000	0.0000	0.0000	0.9626	0.0000	0.0047	0.0000	0.0000	0.0000	0.0000
8.	Wood, Wood Prods., and Furniture	0.0000	0.0000	0.0000	0.0000	0.0000	0.0000	0.0000	0.5105	0.0000	0.0000	0.0000	0.0000	0.0000
9.	Paper, Paper Prods., Printing/Publishing	0.0000	0.0000	0.0000	0.0000	0.0000	0.0000	0.0000	0.0000	0.9686	0.0000	0.0011	0.0000	0.0000
10.	Leather Products	0.0000	0.0000	0.0000	0.0000	0.0000	0.0000	0.0369	0.0000	0.0000	0.7501	0.0000	0.0000	0.0198
11.	Plastic/Rubber Products	0.0000	0.0000	0.0000	0.0000	0.0000	0.0000	0.0006	0.0000	0.0010	0.2499	0.9765	0.0000	0.1041
12.	Coal/Petroleum Products	0.0000	0.0000	0.0000	0.0000	0.0000	0.0000	0.0000	0.0000	0.0000	0.0000	0.0000	1.0000	0.0000
13.	Chemicals	0.0000	0.0000	0.0000	0.0000	0.0000	0.0000	0.0000	0.0000	0.0000	0.0000	0.0000	0.0000	0.8750
14.	Non-metallic Products	0.0000	0.0000	0.0000	0.0000	0.0000	0.0000	0.0000	0.0017	0.0000	0.0000	0.0006	0.0000	0.0000
15.	Metal Products	0.0000	0.0000	0.0000	0.0000	0.0000	0.0000	0.0000	0.4878	0.0257	0.0000	0.0145	0.0000	0.0010
16.	Industrial Machinery	0.0000	0.0000	0.0000	0.0000	0.0000	0.0000	0.0000	0.0000	0.0000	0.0000	0.0000	0.0000	0.0000
17.	Electric/Electronic Machinery	0.0000	0.0000	0.0000	0.0000	0.0000	0.0000	0.0000	0.0000	0.0000	0.0000	0.0000	0.0000	0.0000
18.	Rail and other Transport Equipment	0.0000	0.0000	0.0000	0.0000	0.0000	0.0000	0.0000	0.0000	0.0000	0.0000	0.0000	0.0000	0.0000
19.	Miscellaneous Manufacturing	0.0000	0.0000	0.0000	0.0000	0.0000	0.0000	0.0000	0.0000	0.0000	0.0000	0.0072	0.0000	0.0000
20.	Construction	0.0000	0.0000	0.0000	0.0000	0.0000	0.0000	0.0000	0.0000	0.0000	0.0000	0.0000	0.0000	0.0000
21.	Electricity/Gas/Water Supply	0.0000	0.0032	0.0000	0.0000	0.0000	0.0000	0.0000	0.0000	0.0000	0.0000	0.0000	0.0000	0.0000
22.	Rail and other Transport / Storage Services	0.0000	0.0000	0.0000	0.0000	0.0000	0.0000	0.0000	0.0000	0.0000	0.0000	0.0000	0.0000	0.0000
23.	Trade/Hotel	0.0000	0.0000	0.0000	0.0000	0.0000	0.0000	0.0000	0.0000	0.0000	0.0000	0.0000	0.0000	0.0000
24.	Banking/Insurance	0.0000	0.0000	0.0000	0.0000	0.0000	0.0000	0.0000	0.0000	0.0000	0.0000	0.0000	0.0000	0.0000
25.	Other Services (Edu., Med., Admin., Defence, etc.)	0.0000	0.0000	0.0000	0.0000	0.0000	0.0000	0.0000	0.0000	0.0000	0.0000	0.0000	0.0000	0.0000
Total Input		1.0000	1.0000	1.0000	1.0000	1.0000	1.0000	1.0000	1.0000	1.0000	1.0000	1.0000	1.0000	1.0000

Table 7.9 : (Contd...)

Sector Code	Industry Commodity	14	15	16	17	18	19	20	21	22	23	24	25	Total
1.	Agriculture	0.0000	0.0000	0.0000	0.0000	0.0000	0.0000	0.0000	0.0000	0.0000	0.0001	0.0000	0.0008	0.9966
2.	Animal Husbandry	0.0000	0.0000	0.0000	0.0000	0.0000	0.0000	0.0000	0.0000	0.0000	0.0000	0.0000	0.0000	1.0015
3.	Forestry and Logging	0.0000	0.0000	0.0000	0.0000	0.0000	0.0000	0.0000	0.0000	0.0000	0.0000	0.0000	0.0000	1.0000
4.	Fishing	0.0000	0.0000	0.0000	0.0000	0.0000	0.0000	0.0000	0.0000	0.0000	0.0000	0.0000	0.0000	1.0000
5.	Mining/Quarrying	0.0000	0.0000	0.0000	0.0000	0.0000	0.0000	0.0000	0.0000	0.0000	0.0000	0.0000	0.0000	1.0000
6.	Food Prod., Beverages and Tobacco Products	0.0000	0.0000	0.0000	0.0000	0.0000	0.0000	0.0001	0.0001	0.0000	0.0003	0.0000	0.0025	1.0024
7.	Textiles	0.0000	0.0000	0.0000	0.0000	0.0000	0.0000	0.0017	0.0012	0.0000	0.0025	0.0000	0.0267	0.9996
8	Wood, Wood Prods., and Furniture	0.0000	0.0000	0.0000	0.0000	0.0000	0.0000	0.0000	0.0000	0.0000	0.0001	0.0000	0.0007	0.5113
9.	Paper, Paper Prods., Printing/Publishing	0.0000	0.0006	0.0000	0.0000	0.0000	0.0000	0.0002	0.0002	0.0000	0.0002	0.0000	0.0018	0.9728
10.	Leather Products	0.0000	0.0000	0.0000	0.0000	0.0000	0.0000	0.0001	0.0000	0.0000	0.0003	0.0000	0.0013	0.8085
11.	Plastic/Rubber Products	0.0000	0.0001	0.0001	0.0000	0.2126	0.1578	0.0033	0.0112	0.0000	0.0002	0.0000	0.0007	1.7181
12.	Coal/Petroleum Products	0.0000	0.0000	0.0000	0.0000	0.0000	0.0000	0.0000	0.0000	0.0000	0.0000	0.0000	0.0003	1.0003
13.	Chemicals	0.0000	0.0000	0.0000	0.0000	0.0000	0.1714	0.0003	0.0005	0.0000	0.0007	0.0000	0.0017	1.0496
14.	Non-metallic Products	0.5729	0.0038	0.0000	0.0017	0.0000	0.0348	0.0001	0.0000	0.0000	0.0001	0.0000	0.0003	0.6161
15.	Metal Products	0.0266	0.8396	0.0000	0.0369	0.0243	0.1216	0.0043	0.0381	0.0000	0.0010	0.0000	0.0058	1.6273
16.	Industrial Machinery	0.3400	0.0144	0.7781	0.0003	0.0134	0.0000	0.0001	0.0000	0.0000	0.0005	0.0000	0.0033	1.1501
17.	Electric/Electronic Machinery	0.0605	0.1407	0.2181	0.9589	0.0784	0.4120	0.0003	0.0000	0.0000	0.0003	0.0000	0.0031	1.8722
18.	Rail and other Transport Equipment	0.0000	0.0005	0.0000	0.0000	0.6714	0.0000	0.0010	0.0002	0.0000	0.0004	0.0000	0.0047	0.6782
19.	Miscellaneous Manufacturing	0.0000	0.0001	0.0037	0.0023	0.0000	0.1023	0.0001	0.0000	0.0000	0.0003	0.0000	0.0026	0.1186
20.	Construction	0.0000	0.0000	0.0000	0.0000	0.0000	0.0000	0.9883	0.0000	0.0000	0.0000	0.0000	0.0000	0.9883
21.	Electricity/Gas/Water Supply	0.0000	0.0000	0.0000	0.0000	0.0000	0.0000	0.0000	0.9485	0.0000	0.0000	0.0000	0.0000	0.9517
22.	Rail & other Transport / Storage Services	0.0000	0.0000	0.0000	0.0000	0.0000	0.0000	0.0000	0.0000	1.0000	0.0000	0.0000	0.0000	1.0000
23.	Trade/Hotel	0.0000	0.0000	0.0000	0.0000	0.0000	0.0000	0.0000	0.0000	0.0000	0.9931	0.0000	0.0000	0.9931
24.	Banking/Insurance	0.0000	0.0000	0.0000	0.0000	0.0000	0.0000	0.0000	0.0000	0.0000	0.0000	1.0000	0.0000	1.0000
25.	Other Services (Edu., Med., Admin., Defence, etc.)	0.0000	0.0000	0.0000	0.0000	0.0000	0.0000	0.0000	0.0000	0.0000	0.0000	0.0000	0.9438	0.9438
Total Input		1.0000	1.0000	1.0000	1.0000	1.0000	1.0000	1.0000	1.0000	1.0000	1.0000	1.0000	1.0000	25.0000

Source : Market share matrix is obtained from the make matrix by dividing column entries by the respective commodity output.

identified through ranking of output multipliers. The industries ranked as top ten are here considered as leading industrial sectors in economy and the rest are loosing industries. Table 7.10 that textiles and electric/electronic machinery were the two industrial sectors at the top in 2000-01.The third leading sectors were other services, which reflects the importance of tertiary sector in economy. Leather and transport equipments sector follows on fourth and fifth rank, respectively. Food products and industrial machinery ranked on sixth and seventh positions, respectively. Miscellaneous manufacturing was on eighth rank, and was closely followed by metal and paper/publishing. The list of top ten leading industries comprised of mainly secondary and one of tertiary sector but primary sector had no place.

The lower position in loosing group of industries mainly includes whole of primary sector and those secondary sectors that are associated with pollution norm problems like plastic/rubber and chemicals. In 2000-01, it has been observed that non-metallic products sector, chemicals sector and plastic/rubber industries are at lowest ranks in loosing group of industries. This behaviour of these secondary industries may be explained to the fact that under Master Plan norms certain category of polluting industries has been shifted from the economy of Delhi to National Capital Region or closed down.

Linkages

Almost every industry producing goods or services takes inputs from other sectors of the economy and, in turn, provides inputs to the latter in the respective production process. These relationships define industry's backward and forward linkage, respectively. Backward linkage refers to relative purchase of inputs by a sector, while forward linkage refers to the downstream industries that use the output of the specified industry or commodity as input in producing

Table 7.10 : Leading and Loosing Sectors of Economy (In terms of output multipliers)

Ranks	*Leading Industries*	*2000-01*
1.	Textiles	5.4458
2.	Electric/Electronic Machinery	5.3348
3.	Other Services	5.2353
4.	Leather Products .	5.0498
5.	Transport Equipments	4.925
6.	Food Products	4.9206
7.	Industrial Machinery	4.8791
8.	Miscellaneous Machinery	4.8105
9.	Metal Products	4.6413
10.	Paper and Publishing	4.6148
	Loosing Industries	
11.	Electricity/Gas/Water Supply	4.5245
12.	Trade	4.4996
13.	Construction	4.4705
14.	Wood, Wood Products and Furniture	4.3058
15.	Banking/Insurance	4.3625
16.	Rail and other Transport Services/ Storage	4.2646
17.	Petroleum and Coal Products	4.1031
18.	Agriculture	4.0867
19.	Fishing	4.0023
20.	Animal Husbandry	3.9690
21.	Forestry and Logging	3.9634
22.	Mining and Quarrying	3.9330
23.	Non-metallic Products	3.9123
24.	Chemicals	3.5332
25.	Plastic/Rubber	3.5117

Source : These ranks are found after adding direct and indirect output multipliers.

their own goods and services or, in other words, relative sales by a sector to other sectors.

The strong backward linkage reflects that each new industrial investment will offer opportunities for suppliers. In terms of selecting 'key sectors' of an economy, backward linkages are very useful. High backward linkage occurs when a sector uses output of many other sectors as an input. Thus, by expanding capacity in such a sector 'inducement' or stimuli are provided to supplier industries; which provides an incentive to expand in order to take advantage of the increased demand. The basic idea of backward linkage is to trace the increase in output that occurs in supplying sectors when there is change in the sector using their output as inputs.

The high forward linkage occurs when a sector's output is used by many other sectors as an input. By expanding capacity of such a sector, 'inducements' are provided to use industries that have an incentive to expand output to take advantage of the increased availability of inputs. The strong forward linkage indicates that each new industrial investment will offer inducement to user industries by providing more inputs. Forward linkages are also significant in terms of selecting key sectors of an economy, *i.e.* higher the forward linkage, stronger the impact area or the stronger the chain effect of linkage. The basic idea of forward linkage is to trace the increase in output that occurs in using industries when there is change in the sector supplying inputs. A measure of strength of the backward or forward linkages is called the linkage coefficient. The coefficient measures the strength of the linkage of the sector under consideration compared to other sectors of the economy as defined by Rasmussen. [3]

Backward Linkage[4]

Primary Sector

The backward linkage reveals that in the whole of primary sector relative purchases from trade and transport/storage services have been significant. In agriculture, 56 per cent of inputs have been from trade and transport, 12.6 per cent from same sector, 14.62 per cent from animal husbandry, 54 per cent from trade and transport, 22 per cent from agriculture, and 16.36 per cent from food products. Table 7.11 further indicates that maximum of 44 per cent were purchased from other services, 31 per cent from fishing industry, 20 per cent from other services, 23 per cent from textiles, and 13.12 per cent from same sector, while mining received more than 60 per cent inputs from service sector, 15.34 per cent from construction, and 17.39 per cent from industrial machinery (Table 7.11).

Secondary Sector

An important observation made from Table 7.11 is that food industry purchased nearly 80 per cent from same sector, 10 per cent from trade and transport, 4.16 per cent from animal husbandry, and 1.41 per cent from agriculture. Also, textile industry got 53 per cent inputs from the same sector and 40 per cent from trade and transport services. Likewise, wood products industry purchased 57 per cent from trade and transport services, more than 20 per cent from other services and 10.81 per cent from the same sector. Paper industry, too, has taken 62 per cent inputs from trade and transport, 23.67 per cent from the same sector and 7.58 per cent from textiles. Leather industry purchased 56.91 per cent from self-sector, 26 per cent from trade and transport and 10.41 per cent from textiles. Lastly, it is to be seen that plastic/rubber industry received 68 per cent inputs through trade and transport and 20.47 per cent from self-sector (Table 7.11).

Petroleum industry has the backward relation with mainly trade, transport and banking/insurance sectors, while chemical industry received 74 per cent inputs from trade and transport, 11.71 per cent from textile and 5 per cent from self sector. Surprisingly, non-metallic industry purchased mainly from trade and transport. Metal industry purchased 13.56 per cent from self-sector and nearly 80 per cent from trade and transport. Industrial machinery industry purchased 51.7 per cent from self-sector and 37 per cent from trade and transport. Similarly, electric/electronic machinery industry took 56.74 per cent inputs from self-sector and 35 per cent from trade and transport. Transport equipment manufacturing industry took 43.5 per cent inputs from self-sector and 48 per cent from trade and transport services, miscellaneous manufacturing industry purchased 67 per cent

Table 7.11: Backward Linkage (purchased as inputs by industries in per cent): 2000-01

Sector Code	*Industry / Commodity*	*1*	*2*	*3*	*4*	*5*	*6*	*7*	*8*	*9*	*10*	*11*	*12*	*13*
1.	Agriculture	12.60	22.00	0.02	0.04	0.00	1.41	0.00	0.00	0.00	0.00	0.00	0.00	0.04
2.	Animal Husbandry	14.62	0.46	0.00	0.00	0.00	4.16	0.00	0.00	0.00	0.00	0.00	0.00	0.00
3.	Forestry and Logging	0.00	0.00	0.07	0.00	0.00	0.00	0.00	0.16	0.00	0.00	0.28	0.00	0.00
4.	Fishing	0.00	0.00	0.00	13.21	0.00	0.00	0.00	0.00	0.00	0.00	0.00	0.00	0.00
5.	Mining/Quarrying	0.00	0.00	0.00	0.00	0.07	0.00	0.00	0.00	0.00	0.00	0.00	0.00	0.00
6.	Food Prod., Beverages and Tobacco Products	0.10	16.36	0.00	3.80	0.00	79.66	0.00	0.00	0.00	0.00	0.00	0.00	3.00
7.	Textiles	0.44	4.86	1.18	23.20	0.00	2.03	53.06	2.13	7.58	10.14	3.36	0.67	11.71
8.	Wood, Wood Prods. and Furniture	0.00	0.00	0.00	0.23	0.18	0.14	0.05	10.81	0.19	0.26	0.24	0.05	0.81
9.	Paper, Paper Prods., Printing/ Publishing	0.01	0.00	0.19	0.01	0.10	0.09	0.03	0.09	23.67	0.17	0.15	0.03	0.54
10.	Leather Products	0.00	0.00	0.00	0.00	0.00	0.00	2.21	0.36	0.04	56.91	0.00	0.00	0.00
11.	Plastic/Rubber Products	0.00	0.00	0.18	0.00	0.19	0.07	0.14	0.00	0.73	0.97	20.47	0.02	0.41
12.	Coal/Petroleum Products	0.00	0.00	0.02	0.00	0.01	0.00	0.00	0.01	0.00	0.00	0.00	0.01	0.00
13.	Chemicals	0.75	0.01	0.00	0.05	0.46	0.04	0.00	0.11	0.68	0.10	0.11	0.00	5.01
14.	Non-metallic Products	0.00	0.00	0.00	0.00	0.12	0.00	0.00	0.05	0.03	0.00	0.00	0.00	0.00
15.	Metal Products	0.00	0.01	0.04	0.16	0.46	0.01	0.02	0.26	0.18	0.02	0.03	0.00	0.03
16.	Industrial Machinery	0.67	0.03	0.23	0.00	17.39	0.01	0.01	0.17	0.22	0.02	0.01	0.00	0.33
17.	Electric/Electronic Machinery	0.02	0.00	0.17	0.01	0.02	0.01	0.05	0.16	0.41	0.03	0.02	0.02	0.04
18.	Rail and other Transport Equipment	0.12	0.00	1.10	6.76	2.65	0.00	0.00	0.02	0.00	0.00	0.00	0.00	0.00
19.	Miscellaneous Manufacturing	0.01	0.00	0.42	0.00	1.47	0.00	0.00	0.00	0.02	0.00	0.00	0.00	0.00
20.	Construction	8.80	0.65	33.80	0.00	15.84	0.04	0.01	0.08	0.05	0.04	0.06	0.06	0.02
21.	Electricity/Gas/Water Supply	0.32	0.00	0.01	0.02	0.94	0.04	0.02	0.75	0.35	0.10	0.34	0.04	0.07
22.	Rail and other Transport / Storage Services	20.47	5.28	8.57	5.32	13.12	5.26	10.85	12.69	26.26	16.37	22.23	35.05	22.33
23.	Trade/Hotel	36.39	49.09	8.58	15.16	24.62	5.67	30.67	45.44	36.55	10.64	46.61	30.54	52.02
24.	Banking/Insurance	1.64	1.24	1.12	0.65	5.20	1.33	1.22	5.17	3.01	4.23	6.06	33.48	3.63
25.	Other Services (Edu., Med., Admin., Defence, etc.)	3.05	0.00	44.31	31.39	17.15	0.01	1.65	21.53	0.02	0.00	0.03	0.00	0.00
Total Input		100.00	100.00	100.00	100.00	100.00	100.00	100.00	100.00	100.00	100.00	100.00	100.00	100.00

Table 7.11 : (Contd...)

Sector Code	Industry / Commodity	14	15	16	17	18	19	20	21	22	23	24	25	Total
1.	Agriculture	0.00	0.00a	0.00	0.00	0.00	0.00	1.19	0.00	1.17	0.91	0.00	0.30	0.69
2.	Animal Husbandry	0.00	0.00	0.00	0.00	0.00	0.00	0.18	0.66	0.00	1.72	0.00	0.53	0.65
3.	Forestry and Logging	0.00	0.00	0.00	0.00	0.00	0.00	0.02	0.00	0.00	0.00	0.00	0.00	0.00
4.	Fishing	0.00	0.00	0.00	0.00	0.00	0.00	0.00	0.00	0.00	0.14	0.00	0.00	0.03
5.	Mining/Quarrying	0.01	0.00	0.00	0.00	0.00	0.00	0.02	0.45	0.00	0.00	0.00	0.00	0.01
6.	Food Prod., Beverages and Tobacco Products	0.00	0.00	0.00	0.00	0.00	0.00	0.00	0.00	0.06	4.27	0.00	0.01	2.35
7.	Textiles	0.49	1.77	0.84	1.63	1.02	5.66	0.76	0.03	0.90	1.54	0.11	0.50	3.47
8.	Wood, Wood Prods., and Furniture	0.04	0.13	0.06	0.13	0.23	0.40	0.66	0.01	0.01	0.09	0.02	0.06	0.14
9.	Paper, Paper Prods., Printing/ Publishing	0.04	0.06	0.04	0.09	0.02	0.26	0.02	0.15	0.20	0.29	0.36	0.20	0.38
10.	Leather Products	0.13	0.01	0.02	0.01	0.13	0.01	0.00	0.00	0.02	0.00	0.41	0.00	0.40
11.	Plastic/Rubber Products	0.02	0.13	0.05	0.27	0.16	1.67	0.01	0.01	0.87	0.04	0.01	0.00	0.22
12.	Coal/Petroleum Products	0.00	0.00	0.00	0.00	0.01	0.00	0.00	0.00	0.00	0.00	0.00	0.00	0.00
13.	Chemicals	0.02	0.06	0.02	0.08	0.12	0.08	0.10	0.02	0.01	0.00	0.00	0.37	0.18
14.	Non-metallic Products	1.21	0.06	0.01	0.05	0.02	0.02	1.71	0.00	0.01	0.00	0.00	0.00	0.17
15.	Metal Products	0.01	13.56	0.99	0.99	0.48	1.50	1.46	0.01	0.03	0.06	0.02	0.03	0.43
16.	Industrial Machinery	0.10	0.08	51.70	0.17	0.29	0.05	0.02	1.26	0.31	0.13	0.12	0.12	0.33
17.	Electric/Electronic Machinery	0.01	0.04	2.74	56.74	3.02	1.59	2.85	4.22	1.25	0.02	0.12	0.60	1.88
18.	Rail and other Transport Equipment	0.00	0.00	0.00	0.00	43.50	0.00	0.06	0.16	3.95	0.01	0.37	0.03	0.68
19.	Miscellaneous Manufacturing	0.00	0.01	0.01	0.01	0.01	20.43	0.12	0.48	0.92	0.25	0.57	2.61	1.11
20.	Construction	0.13	0.01	0.07	0.02	0.06	0.07	4.25	7.73	9.94	7.10	8.19	25.80	12.10
21.	Electricity/Gas/Water Supply	0.04	0.27	0.19	0.05	0.12	0.04	0.12	2.45	0.39	0.11	0.14	0.07	0.14
22.	Rail and other Transport / Storage Services	62.06	22.68	15.81	13.85	4.47	5.42	15.16	21.91	7.50	7.26	6.41	4.58	8.23
23.	Trade/Hotel	34.92	58.06	22.98	22.19	44.33	62.82	55.35	40.39	23.52	8.11	8.61	17.55	21.03
24.	Banking/Insurance	0.76	3.08	4.49	1.62	2.03	0.00	2.65	2.98	5.16	5.00	17.31	2.76	5.66
25.	Other Services (Edu, Med., Admin., Defence, etc.)	0.00	0.00	0.00	2.11	0.00	0.00	13.28	17.07	43.78	62.92	57.22	43.89	39.72
	Total Input	100.00	100.00	100.00	100.00	100.00	100.00	100.00	100.00	100.00	100.00	100.00	100.00	100.00

Source : Mathematically obtained by dividing industry column entries by total input of that industry.

from trade and transport 20.4 per cent from same sector and 5.66 per cent from textiles. In the case of construction and electricity/gas/water supply, 60 to 70 per cent were purchased from trade and transport, while construction received 13.28 per cent from other services, 4.25 per cent from same sector and electricity group took 7.73 per cent from construction, 2.45 per cent from self sector and 4.22 per cent from electric/ electronic machinery (Table 7.11).

Tertiary Sector

It would be further clear from Table 7.11 that transport/ storage industry purchased 23.75 per cent inputs from trade, 43.78 per cent from other services, 9.94 per cent from construction and 3.95 per cent from rail and other transport equipment. Trade industry received 62.92 per cent inputs from other services, 8 per cent from self-sector, 7.26 per cent from transport/storage, 7.10 per cent from construction and 4.27 per cent from food products. Banking/insurance purchased 57 per cent inputs from other services, 14 per cent from trade and transport, 8 per cent from construction, while other services industry received 43.89 per cent inputs from same sector, 20 per cent from trade and transport and 25.80 per cent from construction (Table 7.11).

In manufacturing industries, non-metallic industry (97 per cent), metal industry (80 per cent) received maximum inputs from trade and transport. Chemicals, petroleum, received 60 to 70 per cent inputs through trade and transport. Paper, leather, textiles, industrial machinery and electric/ electronic machinery received 20 to 40 per cent.

Forward Linkage[5]

Primary Sector

The inter-industry transaction makes clear that in total intermediate use, the primary sector commodity contributed

1.38 per cent, secondary sector 11.98 per cent and tertiary sector 74.43 per cent. The primary sector commodity is totally provided 20.26 per cent to itself, 7.59 per cent manufacturing and 72.15 per cent to tertiary industries. The secondary sector commodities gave 3.52 per cent to primary, 58.98 per cent to itself and 37.51 per cent to service industries, whereas service sector commodity shared in the total intermediate use by providing 0.98 per cent to primary, 9.58 per cent to secondary and 74.43 per cent to itself (Table 7.12).

On the contrary, among different sectors it is seen that in the total intermediate use, agriculture contributed highest of 23.09 per cent to trade industry, 17.82 per cent to animal husbandry, 15.73 per cent to transport services and storage, 13.36 per cent to other services, 10.07 to agriculture industry and 3.76 per cent to food products. In particular, as shown in Table 7.11, the animal husbandry commodity sector shows maximum for trade industry (46.46 per cent), 25.62 per cent to other services, 12.44 per cent to agriculture industry and 11.82 per cent to food products industry. At the same time, forestry and logging commodity contributed highest to construction industry by 50.20 per cent, 29.72 per cent to plastic/rubber industry and 5.55 per cent to wood industry. Clearly enough, the fishing commodity contributed 87.86 per cent to trade and 12.14 to its own industry in the total intermediate use; mining and quarrying shared the total intermediate use by 49.61 percent to electricity/gas/water supply, 35.93 per cent to construction, 7.75 per cent to trade and 4.96 per cent to transport and storage (Table 7.12).

Manufacturing Sector

Manufacturing sector commodities share in the total intermediate use differs with secondary commodity sectors. In other words, as seen from the inter-industry relations, food products commodity contributed maximum to itself (62.80 per cent), 31.96 per cent to trade and very marginal chemicals, other services and transport service industry; textile commodity provided 72.30 to textile industry, 7.76 per cent to trade industry, 4.55 per cent to other services and 2.41 per cent to transport and storage industry. Similarly, wood and wood products commodity shared in the total intermediate use by giving 44.08 per cent to construction, 14.35 per cent to other services, 11.51 per cent to trade, 11.99 per cent to itself, 4.06 per cent to chemicals and smaller proportions to various other industries. This becomes clear that the paper products commodity contributed to the total intermediate use through 45.71 per cent to the same industry, 16.53 per cent to other services, 15.4 per cent to banking/insurance, 13.46 per cent to trade and 4.81 per cent to transport and storage industry. The textile product commodity provided 72.30 per cent to the same industry, 7.76 per cent to trade, 4.55 per cent to other services and 2.5 to transport/storage. On the other hand, plastic/rubber commodity supplied 44 per cent to own industry, 36.29 per cent to transport/storage industry, 2.04 per cent to miscellaneous manufacturing and 3.33 per cent to trade industry. Finally, it is worth pointing out that petroleum products commodity as visible from the Table 7.12 that it shared in the intermediate use by contributing to almost all the industries in various proportions, maximum of 41.84 per cent to banking/insurance, 33.48 per cent to transport/storage, nearly 2 per cent each to trade and other services. In the case of chemicals products commodity, it contributed 65.44 per cent to other services, 20 per cent to same industry and 5.52 per cent to construction. In short, non-metallic commodity supplied 96.18 per cent to construction industry besides small fractions to metal industries, electric/electronic machinery. Even more dramatically, the metal products commodity supplied 54.15 per cent to the same industry, 31.93 per cent to construction, 4.99 per cent to electric/electronic machinery, and 2.62 per cent to trade. The industrial machinery commodity provided 58.36 per cent to the same industry, 11.43 per cent to other services, 6 per cent each to trade and banking/insurance, 8.84 per cent to transport/storage and 2.53 per cent to electricity/gas/water supply industry. The electric / electronic machinery supplied 64.96 per cent to the same industry, 14.21 per cent to construction, 9.95 per cent to other services, 6.18 per cent to transport and storage. Transport equipments commodity absolutely not providing anything to 1 to 17 industry groups, it supplied maximum of 54.31 per cent to transport and storage industry, 33.86 per cent to the same industry, 8.84 per cent to banking and insurance. Miscellaneous manufacturing provided 73.63 per cent to other services, 8.83 per cent to banking/insurance, 7.73 per cent to transport/storage and only 5 per cent to the same industry. Construction as a commodity supplied, 66.84 per cent to other services, more than 10 per cent each to trade and banking/insurance, 7.66 per cent to transport/storage and 3.29 per cent to the same industry. Electricity/gas/water supply contributed 25.40 per cent to transport/storage, 16 per cent each to other services and banking/insurance, 11.18 per cent to the same industry and 7.68 per cent to construction (Table 7.12).

Service Sector

In service sector, transport/storage contributed in almost all industrial sectors *viz.* 17 per cent in each construction and other service industry, nearly, 15.48 per cent to trade and 12.65 per cent to banking/insurance, 8.50 per cent to the same industry and in marginal proportion to many sectors. Trade is also significant as it contributed towards all industries with 26.14 per cent to other services, 24.46 per cent to construction, 10.43 per cent to the transport/storage industry, more than 5 per cent each to same industry and banking/insurance, metal industry and 6.90 per cent to textile. Banking/insurance supplied nearly 50 per cent to the same industry, 15 per cent each to trade and other services, 8.49 per cent to transport/

storage, 4.39 per cent to construction and 2 per cent each to metal and textile industry. Other services shared 34.62 per cent to same industry, 27 per cent to trade, 23.41 per cent to banking/insurance and 28 per cent to transport/storage industry (Table 7.12).

Backward Linkage Coefficient[6]

Backward linkage coefficient of various sectors derived from input-output tables reveals that textiles, wood and wood products, paper and publishing, leather products, metal products, industrial machinery, electronic and electric machinery, rail and other transport equipments, miscellaneous manufacturing, construction, electricity/water/gas supply, trade/hotels and other services have backward linkage coefficients of more than '1', *i.e.* greater than unity, which signify that these industrial sectors are linked strongly to the rest of the economy as an input receiver. In fact, 12 of the 25 sectors have strong backward linkages while the rest thirteen have the coefficient value of less than one, which imply a weak or less than average backward linkage coefficient. These include all primary sectors, food and beverage, plastic and rubber, chemicals, non-metallic products, rail and other transport services, and banking and insurance. The strong backward linkage reflects that each new industrial investment will offer opportunities for suppliers. In terms of selecting 'key sectors' of an economy, backward linkages are very useful. High backward linkage occurs when a sectors uses output of many other sector as an input, thus, by expanding capacity in such a sector 'inducement' or stimuli are provided to supplier industries; which will have an incentive to expand output to take advantage of the increased demand of its output by that sector. The basic idea of backward linkage is to trace the increase in output that occurs in supplying sectors when there is change in the sector using their output as inputs. In

Table 7.12 : Forward Linkage (sales to different industries in per cent): 2000-01

Sector Code	Industry / Commodity	1	2	3	4	5	6	7	8	9	10	11	12	13
1.	Agriculture	10.07	17.82	0.00	0.00	0.00	3.76	0.00	0.00	0.00	0.00	0.00	0.00	0.04
2.	Animal Husbandry	12.44	0.40	0.00	0.00	0.00	11.82	0.00	0.00	0.00	0.00	0.00	0.00	0.00
3.	Forestry and Logging	0.01	0.00	0.03	0.00	0.00	0.00	0.02	5.55	0.00	0.00	29.72	0.00	0.00
4.	Fishing	0.00	0.00	0.00	12.14	0.00	0.00	0.00	0.00	0.00	0.00	0.00	0.00	0.00
5.	Mining/Quarrying	0.02	0.00	0.00	0.00	0.08	0.03	0.14	0.01	0.00	0.00	0.01	0.06	0.16
6.	Food Prod., Beverages and Tobacco Products	0.02	3.92	0.00	0.04	0.00	62.80	0.00	0.00	0.00	0.00	0.00	0.00	0.90
7.	Textiles	0.07	0.79	0.00	0.18	0.00	1.08	72.30	0.10	1.60	1.14	0.47	0.02	2.38
8.	Wood, Wood Prods., and Furniture	0.02	0.00	0.00	0.04	0.01	1.87	1.59	11.99	0.99	0.71	0.81	0.05	4.06
9.	Paper, Paper Prods., Printing/ Publishing	0.02	0.00	0.00	0.00	0.00	0.45	0.38	0.04	45.71	0.18	0.20	0.01	1.00
10.	Leather Products	0.00	0.00	0.00	0.00	0.00	0.01	26.23	0.14	0.07	55.84	0.00	0.00	0.01
11.	Plastic/Rubber Products	0.01	0.00	0.00	0.00	0.01	0.61	2.90	0.00	2.40	1.69	44.09	0.01	1.29
12.	Coal/Petroleum Products	1.21	0.00	0.04	0.10	0.05	1.08	0.92	0.84	1.60	0.17	0.94	1.44	0.87
13.	Chemicals	2.34	0.03	0.00	0.01	0.02	0.41	0.08	0.10	2.81	0.23	0.29	0.00	20.04
14.	Non-metallic Products	0.00	0.00	0.00	0.00	0.00	0.01	0.09	0.05	0.11	0.00	0.00	0.00	0.01
15.	Metal Products	0.00	0.01	0.00	0.01	0.01	0.03	0.22	0.09	0.30	0.01	0.03	0.00	0.05
16.	Industrial Machinery	1.13	0.05	0.00	0.00	0.37	0.06	0.21	0.08	0.49	0.02	0.01	0.00	0.72
17.	Electric/Electronic Machinery	0.01	0.00	0.00	0.00	0.00	0.01	0.12	0.01	0.16	0.01	0.00	0.00	0.02
18.	Rail and other Transport Equipment	0.10	0.00	0.00	0.26	0.03	0.00	0.00	0.00	0.00	0.00	0.00	0.00	0.00
19.	Miscellaneous Manufacturing	0.00	0.00	0.00	0.00	0.01	0.00	0.01	0.00	0.01	0.00	0.00	0.00	0.00
20.	Construction	0.40	0.03	0.01	0.00	0.01	0.01	0.01	0.00	0.00	0.00	0.00	0.00	0.00
21.	Electricity/Gas/Water Supply	1.23	0.00	0.00	0.00	0.05	0.55	0.57	0.82	1.78	0.27	1.13	0.04	0.34
22.	Rail and other Transport/ Storage Services	1.38	0.36	0.00	0.02	0.01	1.18	6.24	0.24	2.33	0.78	1.31	0.55	1.92
23.	Trade/Hotel	0.96	1.31	0.00	0.02	0.01	0.50	6.90	0.34	1.27	0.20	1.07	0.19	1.75
24.	Banking/Insurance	0.16	0.12	0.00	0.00	0.01	0.43	1.02	0.14	0.39	0.29	0.52	0.76	0.45
25.	Other Services (Edu., Med., Admin., Defence, etc.)	0.04	0.00	0.00	0.02	0.00	0.00	0.20	0.08	0.00	0.00	0.00	0.00	0.00
	Total Input	0.55	0.56	0.00	0.03	0.01	1.85	4.73	0.16	0.73	0.39	0.48	0.13	0.71

Table 7.12 : (Contd...)

Sector Code	*Industry / Commodity*	14	15	16	17	18	19	20	21	22	23	24	25	Total
1.	Agriculture	0.00	0.00	0.00	0.00	0.00	0.00	16.14	0.00	15.73	23.09	0.00	13.36	100.00
2.	Animal Husbandry	0.00	0.00	0.00	0.00	0.00	0.00	2.59	0.66	0.00	46.46	0.00	25.62	100.00
3.	Forestry and Logging	0.00	0.00	0.00	0.00	0.00	0.00	50.20	0.00	0.08	14.39	0.00	0.00	100.00
4.	Fishing	0.00	0.00	0.00	0.00	0.00	0.00	0.00	0.00	0.00	87.86	0.00	0.00	100.00
5.	Mining/Quarrying	0.18	0.42	0.02	0.01	0.00	0.00	35.93	49.61	4.96	7.75	0.00	0.62	100.00
6.	Food Prod., Beverages and Tobacco Products	0.00	0.00	0.00	0.00	0.00	0.00	0.00	0.00	0.25	31.96	0.00	0.11	100.00
7.	Textiles	0.02	0.87	0.09	1.01	0.16	0.44	2.04	0.01	2.41	7.76	0.51	4.55	100.00
8.	Wood, Wood Prods., and Furniture	0.04	1.53	0.14	2.06	0.85	0.77	44.08	0.04	0.52	11.51	1.98	14.35	100.00
9.	Paper, Paper Prods., Printing/ Publishing	0.01	0.27	0.04	0.49	0.02	0.19	0.53	0.26	4.81	13.46	15.40	16.53	100.00
10.	Leather Products	0.05	0.06	0.02	0.08	0.17	0.01	0.00	0.00	0.40	0.00	16.92	0.00	100.00
11.	Plastic/Rubber Products	0.02	0.97	0.08	2.56	0.38	2.04	0.24	0.02	36.29	3.33	0.79	0.27	100.00
12.	Coal/Petroleum Products	0.41	0.17	0.11	1.67	2.51	0.33	2.60	2.52	33.48	2.60	41.84	2.51	100.00
13.	Chemicals	0.01	0.54	0.05	0.92	0.35	0.13	5.52	0.09	0.35	0.26	0.00	65.44	100.00
14.	Non-metallic Products	1.07	0.60	0.03	0.70	0.07	0.04	96.18	0.01	0.36	0.13	0.00	0.54	100.00
15.	Metal Products	0.00	54.15	0.85	4.99	0.59	0.95	31.93	0.02	0.58	2.62	0.66	1.88	100.00
16.	Industrial Machinery	0.05	0.45	58.36	1.10	0.46	0.04	0.64	2.53	8.84	6.93	6.02	11.43	100.00
17.	Electric/Electronic Machinery	0.00	0.04	0.54	64.96	0.85	0.23	14.21	1.47	6.18	0.21	1.02	9.95	100.00
18.	Rail and other Transport Equipment	0.00	0.00	0.00	0.00	33.86	0.00	0.78	0.15	54.31	0.18	8.84	1.48	100.00
19.	Miscellaneous Manufacturing	0.00	0.01	0.00	0.01	0.00	5.03	0.98	0.29	7.73	3.89	8.38	73.63	100.00
20.	Construction	0.00	0.00	0.00	0.00	0.00	0.00	3.29	0.42	7.66	10.30	11.01	66.84	100.00
21.	Electricity/Gas/Water Supply	0.04	3.24	0.48	0.80	0.45	0.07	7.68	11.18	25.40	13.48	15.99	14.40	100.00
22.	Rail and other Transport / Storage Services	1.10	4.72	0.71	3.63	0.29	0.18	17.26	1.75	8.50	15.48	12.65	17.42	100.00
23.	Trade/Hotel	0.24	4.73	0.40	2.27	1.11	0.82	24.66	1.26	10.43	6.77	6.65	26.14	100.00
24.	Banking/Insurance	0.02	0.93	0.29	0.62	0.19	0.00	4.39	0.35	8.49	15.50	49.67	15.26	100.00
25.	Other Services (Edu., Med., Admin., Defence, etc.)	0.00	0.00	0.00	0.11	0.00	0.00	3.13	0.28	10.28	27.80	23.41	34.62	100.00
	Total Input	0.15	1.71	0.37	2.16	0.53	0.27	9.37	0.66	9.33	17.55	16.25	31.33	100.00

Source : Mathematically obtained by dividing commodity row entries by total inputs.

the case of the economy of Delhi, trading sector and other services have shown very high backward linkage coefficient much higher than greater than unity, thereby highlighting the significance of these industries (Table 7.13).

Table 7.13 : Linkage Coefficients

Sector Code	*Industrial Sectors*	*Backward*	*Forward*
1.	Agriculture	0.9402	0.5019
2.	Animal Husbandry	0.9268	0.4683
3.	Forestry and Logging	0.9390	0.3178
4.	Fishing	0.9235	0.3511
5.	Mining and Quarrying	0.9276	0.3181
6.	Food products, Beverages, and Tobacco Products	0.9044	1.0348
7.	Textiles	1.1699	1.0918
8.	Wood, Wood Products and Furniture	1.0191	0.3686
9.	Paper, Paper Products, Printing/Publishing	1.0744	0.4177
10.	Leather and Leather Products	1.0617	0.5735
11.	Plastic and Rubber Products	0.7602	0.3865
12.	Petroleum and Coal Products	0.9814	0.3165
13.	Chemicals	0.7930	0.3486
14.	Non-metallic Products	0.9181	0.3433
15.	Metal Products	1.1125	0.4043
16.	Industrial Machinery	1.0416	0.5925
17.	Electric/Electronic Machinery	1.1275	0.7759
18.	Rail and other Transport Equipments	1.0878	0.5898
19.	Miscellaneous Manufacturing	1.1376	0.5320
20.	Construction	1.0263	1.8989
21.	Electricity/Gas/Water Supply	1.1079	0.3470
22.	Rail and other Transport /Storage Services	0.9821	2.1070
23.	Trade/Hotels	1.0094	4.5801
24.	Banking/Insurance	0.9186	1.0107
25.	Other Services (Education, Medical, Administration, Defence, etc.)	1.0463	5.3223

Source : Mathematically calculated from inverse matrix (refer Appendix VIIB).

Forward Linkage Coefficient[7]

Forward linkage coefficient indicates that only seven industrial sectors of the twenty-five have shown the above average, *i.e.* greater than one. These include food products, textiles, construction, transport services, trade, banking/

insurance and other services. The higher forward linkage coefficient shows that these industrial sectors are very strongly linked with the rest sectors of the economy of Delhi as an input supplier to various sectors. The rest eighteen industrial sectors have shown the forward linkage coefficient of less than one, including whole of primary sectors, most of secondary sectors excluding food products and textiles, while the complete tertiary sectors have shown the forward linkage coefficient of greater than unity. This clearly reflects the structure and nature of the economy of Delhi where significance of tertiary sector is corroborated with the strong forward linkages as well. The high forward linkage occurs when a sector's output is or could be used by many other sectors as an input; by expanding capacity such a sector, 'inducements' are provided to using industries that now have an incentive to expand output to take advantage of the increased availability of inputs. The strong forward linkage elucidates that each new industrial investment will offer inducement to user industries by providing more inputs. Forward linkage is also significant in terms of selecting key sectors of an economy, *i.e.* higher the forward linkage stronger the impact area or the stronger the chain effect of linkages. The basic idea of forward linkage is to trace the increase in output that occurs or might occur in using industries when there is change in the sector supplying inputs (Table 7.13).

Output Multipliers[8]

Output multiplier of a commodity-producing sector is the factor by which a unit increases in the demand for and, consequently, production of the commodity in that sector leads to expansion of, output in the whole economy. This multiplier is he sum of the factors by which individual sectors of the economy get expanded for unit increase in the demand for product in one sector. Output coefficients are of three types; one measuring only the direct, the second the sum of the direct and indirect impacts, and third the total (including the induced effect) of an increase in the final demand.

In the present work the first two types of output coefficients are computed for various sectors. In general, the direct output multipliers are a little over '1', signifying the fact that to meet the unit increase in the final demand for its own product an industry will have produced slightly more than that of increase in demand, which is likely to be caused by linkage effect. In other words, '1' represents, '1' unit to satisfy the original new unit of final demand plus an additional for intra- and inter-industry uses. The direct-plus-indirect multipliers vary from industry to industry depending on the strength of industry's linkages with other industries, but grossly ranging between 2.5 to 3.6.

The direct output multipliers are arranged in ascending ranks. The highest direct output multiplier is witnessed for food products sector, *i.e.* 2.0611, but in terms of indirect and direct multiplier it is only 2.8594 with 23rd rank. This implies that every unit increase in demand from food products sector, *i.e.* every rupee of food products expenditure would result in an output of Rs.2.0611 in food products sector itself and Rs.2.8594 in the total output in the economy. Similarly, in the case of other services which shows second rank in terms of direct multiplier of 1.9273, whereas the direct- plus-indirect multipliers show 2.9042, *i.e.* 21st rank. The textiles sector with 4th rank in case of direct multiplier, *i.e.* 1.7469 witness 1st rank as the direct-plus-indirect multiplier with 3.6988 which implies that with every rupee of textile expenditure, *i.e.* demand would result in an output of Rs.1.7469 in textile sector itself and Rs.3.6988 in other total output in this economy (Table 7.14).

The miscellaneous manufacturing ranked second in terms of total direct and indirect multipliers with 3.5966 and the direct multiplier was 1.2139 with 10 ranks. In this case, any additional demand was nearly three times more impact

Table 7.14: Output Multipliers

Sectors Code	Industrial Sectors	Direct	Rank	Indirect	Rank
1.	Agriculture	1.1141	15	2.9726	17
2.	Animal Husbandry	1.0334	19	2.9300	20
3.	Forestry and Logging	1.0004	23	2.9686	18
4.	Fishing	1.0955	17	3.1914	13
5.	Mining and Quarrying	1.0004	24	2.9326	19
6.	Food Products, Beverages, and Tobacco Products	2.0611	1	2.8594	23
7.	Textiles	1.7469	4	3.6988	1
8.	Wood, Wood Products and Furniture	1.0839	18	3.2219	12
9.	Paper, Paper Products, Printing/Publishing	1.2179	10	3.3969	7
10.	Leather and Leather Products	1.6933	5	3.3565	8
11.	Plastic and Rubber Products	1.1083	16	2.4034	25
12.	Petroleum and Coal Products	1.0001	25	3.1029	16
13.	Chemicals	1.0259	20	2.5073	24
14.	Non-metallic Products	1.0095	22	2.9028	22
15.	Metal Products	1.1240	14	3.5173	4
16.	Industrial Machinery	1.5857	6	3.2932	10
17.	Electric/Electronic Machinery	1.7701	3	3.5647	3
18.	Rail and other Transport Equipment	1.4858	7	3.4391	6
19.	Miscellaneous Manufacturing	1.2139	11	3.5966	2
20.	Construction	1.2256	9	3.2448	11
21.	Electricity/Gas/Water Supply	1.0219	21	3.5026	5
22.	Rail and other Transport/ Storage Services	1.1596	12	3.1049	15
23.	Trade/Hotels	1.3805	8	3.1190	14
24.	Banking/ Insurance	1.1583	13	2.9042	21
25.	Other Services (Education, Medical, Administration, Defence, etc.)	1.9273	2	3.3080	9

Source : Mathematically calculated from inverse matrix (Appendix VIIB).

on total output of the economy than the sector itself. Electric/ electronic machinery also witnessed quite high multiplying potential for the total economy ranks 3rd with 3.5647 multiplier value and its own sector the direct coefficient was 1.7701. Metal products, transport equipment, electricity/ water/gas supply, paper and publishing, leather products and industrial machinery had the direct and indirect multiplier of more than 3.2 and among the direct coefficient, leather products, industrial machinery, transport equipment had higher direct coefficient than paper and publishing, electricity/gas/ water supply, metal products (Table 7.14).

Among the manufacturing sector, plastic and rubber, chemical products, non-metallic products, food products had lower multiplier effect for the total economy as well as self-sector; while textiles, electric/electronic machinery, miscellaneous manufacturing, metal products, paper and publishing transport equipment, industrial machinery and leather had higher multipliers (Table 7.14).

Connectivity Matrix and Graph

The connectivity matrix (Table 7.15) presented in diagrammatic form through connectivity graph (web of economy) displays inter-sectoral linkages through flows of networks signifying uni-directional and mutual linkages among different sectors of the economy. In 2000-01, there has been complex web of networks of flows in the economy of Delhi as seen in the graph (Fig. 7.6) besides, a distinguishable pattern is also observed. The pattern emerged from flows of network reveals a left to right intensification of flows. The industries placed on the left side of the diagram shared a week relationship with rest of the economy. These poorly connected industries include agriculture, animal husbandry, forestry, fishing and mining/quarrying. The whole of the primary sector did not share bond among them. These industries have been seen in the diagram (Fig. 7.6) as input receivers, and not as suppliers to other industries. Thus, it appears that primary sector does not hold much significance in Delhi's economy. In primary sector, agriculture shared mutual linkages with animal husbandry, forestry, food products, chemicals, construction, trade, transport and other services no relation with other sectors of the economy. Forestry had two-way linkage with agriculture, food products, construction trade and other services. Fishing was related with only wood products, construction and trade. Mining and quarrying were connected with non-metallic products, construction and trade (Table 7.15 and Fig. 7.6).

Table 7.15: Connectivity Matrix: 2000-01

Sector Code	*1*	*2*	*3*	*4*	*5*	*6*	*7*	*8*	*9*	*10*	*11*	*12*	*13*	*14*	*15*	*16*	*17*	*18*	*19*	*20*	*21*	*22*	*23*	*24*	*25*
1.	*	2	2	1B	0	2	0	0	0	0	0	0	2	0	0	0	0	0	0	2	0	2	2	0	2
2.	2	*	0	0	0	2	0	0	0	0	0	0	0	0	0	0	0	0	0	2	1B	0	2	0	2
3.	0	0	*	0	0	0	0	2	0	0	1F	0	0	0	0	0	0	0	0	2	0	1F	2	0	0
4.	0	0	0	*	0	0	0	0	0	0	0	0	0	0	0	0	0	0	0	0	0	0	0	0	0
5.	0	0	0	0	*	0	0	0	0	0	0	0	0	2	0	0	0	0	0	2	2	0	2	0	0
6.	2	2	0	0	0	*	1F	1F	1F	0	0	0	2	0	1F	2	2	1B	0	1F	1F	2	2	1F	0
7.	1B	0	0	1B	0	1B	*	2	2	2	2	2	2	2	2	2	2	1B	2	2	2	2	2	2	2
8.	0	0	2	0	2	1B	2	*	2	2	2	2	2	2	2	2	2	2	1B	1B	2	2	2	2	2
9.	1B	0	0	0	1B	1B	2	2	*	2	2	1B	2	2	2	2	2	2	1B	1B	2	2	2	2	2
10.	0	0	0	0	0	0	2	2	2	*	1F	0	2	2	2	2	2	1B	1B	0	1F	2	2	2	0
11.	0	0	1B	0	0	2	2	2	2	1B	*	2	2	2	2	2	2	1B	1B	0	2	2	2	2	0
12.	0	0	0	0	0	0	1F	2	1F	0	2	*	1B	0	1B	1B	2	1B	0	0	0	1F	1B	1F	0
13.	2	0	0	0	0	1B	1F	2	2	2	2	1F	*	2	2	2	2	1B	1B	1B	2	2	1B	2	1B
14.	0	0	0	0	2	0	1F	2	2	1F	1F	1F	2	*	2	2	2	1B	1B	1B	2	2	1B	2	1B
15.	0	0	0	0	0	1B	2	2	2	2	2	1F	2	2	*	2	2	2	2	2	2	2	2	2	2
16.	1B	0	0	0	0	2	2	2	2	2	2	1F	2	2	2	*	2	2	2	1B	2	2	2	2	2
17.	0	0	0	0	0	1B	2	2	2	2	2	2	2	2	2	2	*	2	2	2	2	2	2	1B	2
18.	1B	0	0	0	1B	0	1F	2	2	1F	1F'	1F	1F	2	2	2	2	*	1F	1B	2	2	2	2	1B
19.	0	0	0	0	1B	0	2	1F	1F	1F	1F	0	1F	1F	2	2	2	1B	*	2	2	2	2	2	1B
20.	2	2	2	0	2	1B	2	1F	2	0	2	2	1F	1F	2	2	2	2	2	*	2	2	2	2	2
21.	1B	1F	1B	0	2	1B	2	2	2	1B	2	2	2	2	2	2	2	2	2	2	*	2	2	2	2
22.	2	1B	1B	1B	0	2	2	2	2	2	2	2	2	2	2	2	2	2	2	2	2	*	2	2	2
23.	2	2	2	2	2	2	2	2	2	1B	2	2	1F	1F	2	2	2	2	2	2	2	2	*	2	2
24.	1B	0	0	1B	0	1B	2	2	2	2	2	1B	1B	1B	2	2	2	2	1F	2	2	2	2	*	2
25.	2	2	0	1B	0	2	2	2	2	0	0	0	1F	1F	2	2	2	1F	1F	2	2	2	2	2	*

Source: Obtained from coefficient matrix, backward linkage matrix and forward linkage matrix (refer Appendix, IX B, VB, VI B, respectively). F—implies forward, B—implies backward. '0'—implies no relationship, '1'—refers to one-way flow and '2'—indicates two-way flow. For sector code refer Table 7. 13.

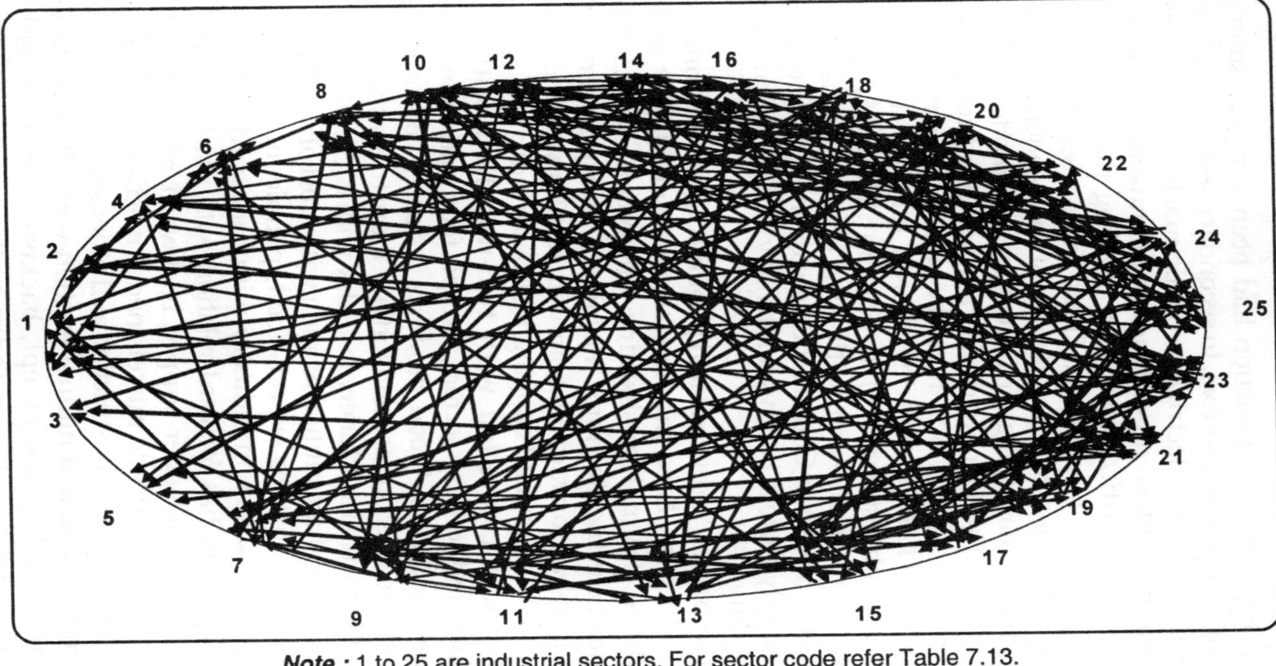

Note : 1 to 25 are industrial sectors. For sector code refer Table 7.13.
The flow arrows are based on Table 7.15.

Fig. 7.6 : Connectivity Graph, 2000-01

The intensity of interaction had been stronger among secondary and tertiary sectors. In secondary sector, industries as metal products, electric/electronic machinery, textiles, industrial machinery, miscellaneous manufacturing, wood products and plastic/rubber were holding the prominent position in Delhi's economy. These industries have been strongly connected to most sectors of the economy. Thus, level of impact may be higher. Industries with moderate level of impact included chemicals, leather products, coal/ petroleum products, non-metallic products, paper and publishing. These industries shared medium range of interaction with rest sectors of the economy. The food product industry had been seen with low level of linkage in manufacturing sector. Construction sector and electricity/gas/ water supply sectors had high intensity of interaction with the economy.

All secondary industries had poor linkages with primary sector industries. Food industry shared mutual flow with agriculture, animal husbandry, chemicals, industrial machinery, electric/electronic machinery, transport services and trade. It had forward relations with textiles, wood, paper, metal, construction, and banking/insurance industry. Textile industry was connected with two-way flow with all secondary and tertiary sectors, except, food and industrial machinery industry. Wood products industry had mutual links with most secondary and tertiary industries other than food and industrial machinery industry with backward links. Paper industry share mutual relation with most of secondary and tertiary industries expects food, petroleum, miscellaneous, and construction industry with backward linkages. Leather industry has forward relation with plastic/rubber, and electricity/gas/water supply, backward relation with industrial machinery and miscellaneous machinery but zero links with petroleum, construction and other services. Plastic/ rubber industry shared mutual relation with all secondary and tertiary industries, except, backward relation with leather, industrial machinery and miscellaneous machinery, and zero link with other services. Petroleum industry shared backward links with chemical, metal, industrial machinery, and trade. It had forward link with textiles, paper, transport/storage, banking/insurance and no relation was seen with food, leather, non-metallic products, miscellaneous, construction and electricity/gas/water supply sectors. Chemical industry had forward link with textile, petroleum and backward link with food, industrial machinery, miscellaneous machinery trade and other services. It shared mutual relation with rest of the sectors (Table 7.15 and Fig. 7.6).

Non-metallic products shared mutual linkage with wood, paper, chemical, metal, industrial machinery, electric/electronic machinery, transport/storage and banking/insurance. The backward relation included transport equipment, miscellaneous machinery, construction, trade and other services, and forward with textile, leather and plastic/rubber. Metal products had most of the mutual relations with all secondary/tertiary sectors, except, backward with food and forward with petroleum products. Industrial machinery also had two-way relations with most industries, except, forward with petroleum and backward with construction industry. Electric/electronic machinery shared mutual linkage with most sectors, except, backward with food and banking/insurance. Transport equipment sector had forward relation with textiles, leather, petroleum, plastic/rubber, chemical and miscellaneous machinery, and backward with construction and other services. With other sectors it share mutual linkages. Electric/electronic machinery shows a mix of forward, backward and mutual linkages. Construction industry shared mutual links with almost the whole economy including primary sectors, except, forward with wood, chemical, non-metallic and backward with food. Electricity / gas / water supply had no links with mining, backward with food, leather, agriculture, animal husbandry and with all others it had two-way relations (Table 7.15 and Fig. 7.6).

The service sector industries had been very well connected with most sectors of the economy. Transport/storage, trade/hotel had higher level of interaction followed by banking/insurance and other services. Transport/storage had mutual relation with all secondary and tertiary sectors, backward with animal husbandry, fishing, and zero with mining. Trade sector had two-way relation with whole economy, except, backward with leather and forward with chemical. Banking/insurance and other services had stronger linkage with all secondary and tertiary sectors than with primary sectors (Table 7.15 and Fig. 7.6).

Pollution Accounting in Input-Output Table

In this section, pollution associated with manufacturing or secondary sector is analyzed. Data on expenditure made on pollution abatement is used as an indicator of pollution. Data has been obtained from Annual Survey of Industries (ASI), 1997-98. Information on pollution was collected only once in 1997-98 by ASI. From this data, it is statistically estimated for 2000-01. In the original input-output data the pollution data was internalized by adding one row and one column on pollution. Pollution industry is treated as an input provider to other industries of the economy, but, it has no output of its own. Thus, inputs and outputs are considered the same. The pollution data is appropriately adjusted in the table for manufacturing industries that includes sectors from 6 to 19. After the addition of pollution data in the original absorption matrix, a new absorption matrix is prepared. Coefficient matrix and inverse matrix are computed for the new input-output table.

The inter-industry flows are expressed in coefficient matrix form, called structural matrix of technical input-output table, and each cell entries are known as input-output coefficient. This matrix is derived from absorption matrix and these technical coefficients (a_{ij}) are found by dividing each flow in a particular industry or column by the total output of that industry. These input-output coefficients represent the structure of the production in the economy; the columns or, in fact, the production recipes for each sector in terms of import from all other sectors. This shows that to produce one rupee worth good by a sector how much input does it require to put from other sectors of the economy. These coefficients show direct purchase among the sectors. However, to know the total input both direct as well as indirect requirement inverse are required. These coefficients are used to explain any increase or decrease in the production as well as demand of various inputs.

In this coefficient matrix, the structural relationships of the primary and tertiary sectors have remained unchanged, as pollution has been accounted only in the secondary sector. In 14 sectors of manufacturing activity, it is seen that miscellaneous manufacturing and industrial machinery sector have the lowest input from pollution sector and main inputs from self, and transport storage and trade sectors. Transport equipment manufacturing and electric/electronic products also have very low per cent of inputs coming from the pollution sector. Wood products, coal and petroleum products, plastic and rubber products used pollution inputs from 0.2 per cent to 0.3 per cent. While in leather products and food products the coefficient values of pollution ranged from 0.35 to 0.45 per cent. Metal products demonstrated the pollution inputs of 0.69 to 1 per cent. Chemical products and textiles used the inputs of pollution sector nearly 2 per cent, whereas non-metallic products sector had shown the highest input of 3 per cent from the pollution sector, *i.e.* for producing one unit of output there is 0.3 units of pollution factor involved (Appendix X B).

Linkages

Backward Linkage in New Input-Output Scenario

With the accounting of pollution in the original input-output, the structure of backward linkage has changed. To trace the change in backward linkage of different sectors, backward linkage of this table is computed. In the five primary sectors no change in backward linkage has been observed. Similarly, in the tertiary sector no change in the structure of backward linkage has happened since in these two categories no pollution data has been accounted.

Conversely, in the secondary sector, backward linkages have changed. In the food products industry, it purchased 79.66 per cent from self, but now it is 78.97 per cent and 0.70 per cent is spent on pollution aspect, while the other purchases are same. In textile products, the self-sector purchases have reduced from 53 to 52.25 per cent. This decrease has shown a gain in pollution abatement expenses. In wood products industry, major purchases were made from trade, transport and other services, *i.e.* 45.44 per cent, 12.69 per cent and 21.53 per cent, respectively. The self-sector purchases got reduced marginally and only 0.35 per cent was spent on pollution abatement. In the paper and publishing industry, 2.30 per cent expenditure was made on pollution abatement and a slight decrease has occurred in self-sector purchases, with 62 per cent inputs from trade and transport. Leather industry spent 0.53 per cent on pollution aspects with a decline from purchases of self-sector marginally. The plastic and rubber industry spent 0.68 per cent of the total inputs as pollution expenses and the self-sector purchases got reduced to 19.78 per cent from 20.47 per cent and 68 per cent inputs came from trade and transport sector. Coal and petroleum industry mainly depending on trade and transport sector for its inputs, spent 0.47 per cent inputs on pollution. Slight decrease in transport and storage sector inputs had been seen. Chemical industry incurred second highest, *i.e.* 3.43 per cent on pollution expenses, with a slight decrease in inputs from textiles and self-sector. Other major sources of inputs were trade and transport. In the case of non-metallic industry, 4.19 per cent, *i.e.* highest expenditure among the secondary sector was made on pollution expenses. However, there was a decline in inputs from 62 to 57 per cent from transport sector, while the other was remained the same as in the original input-output table. In the metal products industry, the input got reduced from 13.56 per cent to 12.46 per cent from the self-sector, while 1.20 per cent of the inputs were used for pollution abatement. The industrial machinery sector and electric/electronic machinery sector used only 0.3 and 0.21 per cent on the pollution abatement, with a slight decline in their input from self-sector and 35 to 38 per cent from trade and transport sectors. The manufacturing of transport equipments industry spent only 0.18 per cent on pollution problems and a marginal decline in self-sector. The trade sector appeared quite significant as it contributed more than 40 per cent of the total inputs. Miscellaneous manufacturing showed the least expenditure on pollution aspects. This sector registered a slight decline in the input supplied by self-sector. Here, trade was very vital as it supplied 63 per cent of the inputs. With the addition of pollution as row and column slight changes in backward linkages has happened (Appendix X D).

Forward Linkage

Forward linkage shows the sells by individual sectors to different industries. The present inter-industry transactions show that in the total intermediate use, the changes are evident in the sells by different sectors as compared to the earlier scenario. Agricultural sale to self-sector was 10.07 per cent and now 11.19 per cent, to animal husbandry from 17.82 to 19.81 per cent, to food products from 3.76 to 4.18 per cent, to transport/storage from 15.73 to 17.49 per cent, to trade from 23 per cent to 25.68 per cent and to other services from 13.36 per cent to 14.85 per cent. The animal husbandry sector's sales were increased from 12.4 per cent to 14.21 per cent to self-sector, from 11.82 to 13.50 per cent to food products, from 46.46 to 53.06 per cent to trade and hotels, from 25.62 to 29.26

per cent to other services. Forestry and logging sector showed no change in its forward linkage, as it sold same proportion to construction sector, trade, plastic and rubber and wood products. Fishing, mining/quarrying sector also exhibited no change in their respective sells to other sectors of the economy (Appendix X C).

In secondary sector, food products sold little higher to self-sector and has marginally declined its sales to trade and hotels sector. Textiles reduced sale very slightly to the self-sector, leather, chemicals, while minor increase of sales has been noticed to electric/electronic machinery, construction, transport/storage and other services. The wood products forward linkages showed minor decline with self-sector, construction, trade, whereas small increase in forward linkages has been witnessed with sectors of food products, chemicals, industrial machinery and other services, with rest of the sectors it remained the same. Paper and publishing sector's forward linkages have come down with the industries of self, trade and hotel, while improved linkages are seen with other services, banking and insurance, trade and hotels, transport and storage, construction and miscellaneous manufacturing. Leather products sector registered positive direction of linkage with textiles, banking and insurance, while slight decrease has been noticed in self, and with rest of the sectors it has remained unchanged. Plastic and rubber sectors have improved forward relationship with textiles, paper and publishing, leather, self, chemicals, electric/electronic machinery, miscellaneous manufacturing, transport and storage and other services, while it has not decreased with any of the sector. Petroleum and coal products sector have improved relations with textiles, wood products, paper and publishing, miscellaneous manufacturing, transport, equipment, construction, transport and storage, banking and insurance, while other services marginal decrease had been visible in trade and hotel, electricity and nature supply. The chemical sector has enhanced forward linkage with agriculture, textiles, paper and publishing, leather, plastic and rubber, self, metal products, electric/ electronic machinery, other services and construction while it has come down in case of self-sector only. Non-metallic sector has not shown any change in its forward linkage, it sold more than 95 per cent to the construction industry. Metal products sector marginal increase in sales was seen in industries of textile, wood, paper and publishing, industrial machinery, transport equipments, miscellaneous manufacturing, construction while decrease was observed in self-sector and other services (Appendix X C).

In general, the industrial machinery sector has improved the relationship with textiles, paper and publishing, electric and electronic machinery, transport equipment, miscellaneous manufacturing, transport/storage, trade/hotels and other tertiary industries, though there was decline in the case of self sector. Electric and electronic machinery sector has reduced its sales to self-sector and increased to construction, transport/storage, and other services while with rest of the economy it has remained the same. In contrast, rail and other transport equipment sectors had reduced its sales to self-sector slightly while increased to the transport and storage sector, banking/insurance, while with others it was the same. As regards miscellaneous manufacturing sector, the forward linkage remained same with more than 70 per cent sales to other services sector. The other major aspect that has changed was that the construction sector showed increase in the forward linkage with self-sector, transport/storage, trade/ hotels, and other services while with other sectors of the economy same relationship existed. Electricity/water/gas supply sector has shown marginal increase of sales to all sectors of the economy except the primary sector where it has remained the same. Rail and other transport services and storage sector had improved forward linkage with agriculture, animal husbandry, food products, textiles, and all other secondary and tertiary industries. Trade and hotels sector's relationship remained the same with primary sector except slight improvement in the case of animal husbandry. In secondary and tertiary sectors, it has improved with the entire sector except miscellaneous manufacturing, leather and petroleum/coal products industries, which remained the same. Banking and insurance sector's forward linkages existed unchanged with the whole of primary sector, also the same with secondary sector industries, while it has enhanced slightly in all tertiary sector industries. The other services sectors' (including education, medical, administrative defence etc.) forward linkage with the economy remained unchanged with whole of primary and secondary sector industries, only marginal rise was noticed in trade/hotels, banking/insurance and self-sector. The pollution abatement expenditure sectors were addition to the original input-output table to observe the change in the forward and backward relationship of different industries in the economy. This sector's forward linkage shows that in the manufacturing sector maximum of 28.95 per cent contribution witnessed for textiles industry followed by chemical industry with 18.20 per cent, metal products with 15.53 per cent, paper and publishing with 12.65 per cent, food products with 7.73 per cent and 2 to 5 per cent in non-metallic products, electric/electronic machinery and plastic/rubber industries. A minimum sale of this sector was observed in miscellaneous manufacturing and industrial machinery products (Appendix X C).

Backward Linkage Coefficient

Backward linkage coefficients of different sectors of the economy were derived through input-output table in which pollution aspect is also accounted as a part of the production recipe of different manufacturing industries. The coefficient values reflects that the whole of primary sector industries had the coefficient value of less than unity which implies that these industries had a weaker or less than average linkage with the rest of the economy.

Table 7.16 : Linkage Coefficients

Sector Code	Industrial Sectors	Without Pollution		With Pollution	
		Backward	Forward	Backward	Forward
1.	Agriculture	0.9403	0.5019	0.8123	0.2988
2.	Animal Husbandry	0.9268	0.4684	0.8024	0.2369
3.	Forestry and Logging	0.9391	0.3178	0.8517	0.2087
4.	Fishing	0.9235	0.3511	0.9032	0.2334
5.	Mining and Quarrying	0.9276	0.3181	0.9876	0.4956
6.	Food Products, Beverages, and Tobacco Products	0.9044	1.0348	0.9654	0.5056
7.	Textiles	1.1699	1.0919	1.1612	0.2836
8.	Wood, Wood Products and Furniture	1.0191	0.3686	1.0665	0.2789
9.	Paper, Paper Products, Printing/Publishing	1.0744	0.4177	1.1575	0.3280
10.	Leather and Leather Products	1.0616	0.5735	1.1561	0.2629
11.	Plastic and Rubber Products	0.7602	0.3866	0.8101	0.2081
12.	Petroleum and Coal Products	0.9814	0.3166	1.0813	0.2185
13.	Chemicals	0.7930	0.3486	0.8095	0.2164
14.	Non-metallic Products	0.9185	0.3433	1.0161	0.2792
15.	Metal Products	1.1125	0.4043	1.2002	0.4737
16.	Industrial Machinery	1.0416	0.5926	1.1656	0.5077
17.	Electric/Electronic Machinery	1.1275	0.7759	1.2129	0.4312
18.	Rail and other Transport Equipment	1.0878	0.5899	1.1849	0.3974
19.	Miscellaneous Manufacturing	1.1376	0.5321	1.2116	0.8067
20.	Construction	1.0264	1.8989	1.0754	0.3159
21.	Electricity/Gas/Water Supply	1.1079	0.3471	1.1982	1.4426
22.	Rail and other Transport/ Storage Services	0.9821	2.1070	0.9939	3.0453
23.	Trade/Hotels	1.0095	4.5801	0.9729	1.0177
24.	Banking/Insurance	0.9186	1.0108	0.9111	2.9408
25.	Other Services (Education, Medical, Administration, Defence, etc.)	1.0463	5.3223	1.0850	0.3489
26.	Pollution Abatement			0.2076	10.2173

Source : Mathematically calculated from inverse matrix (Appendix XE).

In manufacturing sector, except, food products, chemicals and plastic/rubber industry, the rest industries had the coefficient value greater than unity that emphasize the fact that these industries had stronger relationship with the rest of the economy in terms of input receiver. These include textile, paper/publishing, wood, leather, metal products, petroleum/coal, products, non-metallic products, industrial machinery, electronic/electric machinery, transport equipments and miscellaneous manufacturing. The construction and electricity/water/gas supply also shows strong backward relationship with the various sectors of the economy. In the tertiary sector, only other services sector appeared as an industry with good backward connectivity with whole economy. The pollution abatement industry showed very poor connectivity, which indicates that it is not such an industry to have an output to produce (Table 7.16).

Backward Linkage Coefficient

The backward linkage coefficient compared with the backward linkage coefficients derived from the original input-output table reveals that in the primary sector industries the coefficient values are less than unity in both cases. In fact, the values further reduced when pollution is added except for mining/quarrying. In manufacturing sector industries, the status of food products, plastic/rubber and chemicals remained same with less than unity of coefficient values. Petroleum/coal products and non-metallic products industries which had less than '1' coefficient value have now gained more than 1 coefficient value. The position of other industries with more than unity of coefficient maintained the same. The construction and electricity/water/gas supply also maintained strong connectivity in both cases. In tertiary industries, trade/hotel changed their position from more the unity of coefficient value to less than unity, while the other services sector maintained strong linkages (Table 7.16)..

Forward Linkage Coefficient

Forward linkage coefficients show the relationship as an input provider. After addition of pollution in the input-output table, it is seen that forward linkage coefficient shows more than unity in case of electricity/water/gas supply, transport/storage, trade/hotels, banking/insurance, *i.e.* these sectors provided inputs to most sectors of the economy. Transport and trade industries displayed quite high coefficients. Pollution abatement sector appears as the most strongly connected sector with rest of the economy as high values of coefficients are observed.

The forward linkage coefficient compared with the originally derived coefficient values indicated that forward linkage coefficients have changed when pollution sector is added. Food products, textiles and constructions and other industries that had higher more than unit of the coefficient value have now quite low value of coefficient, thus, changing their level of significance in the economy. Only one industry, *i.e.* electricity/water/gas supply emerged with more than one coefficient value with low value in earlier case. The position of transport/storage, trade/hotels, banking/insurance has remained the same with the coefficient values of greater than unity, *i.e.* strong forward linkage, although their values have changed. In the case of transport/storage, earlier it was 2.1, which is now 3.04, while trade/hotels has the coefficient value of 4.58 is now 1.01 and banking/insurance from 1.01 increased to 2.94. In other industries, which had less than one coefficient, the values of coefficient have further come down. The only sector emerged with highest coefficient value is pollution abatement sector which seems to be strongly connected with rest of the economy (Table 7.16).

Output Multipliers

The pattern of multipliers after pollution accounting in input-output table reveals that the values of coefficients in all sectors have increased and the ranks in terms of direct and indirect multipliers have also changed. The multiplying coefficients, which earlier ranged between 2.40 to 3.69, have now increased to 3.00 to 5.84. In terms of ranks it has been observed that electric/electronic machinery sector had the highest multiplicity potential as this sector has the lowest pollution among the manufacturing industries, with the coefficient of 5.8422, while in the input-output table with the accounting of pollution aspect this sector had third rank. Miscellaneous manufacturing retained its rank at second order in both cases, though, with higher values of multipliers in later case. Metal products sector moved its rank up from 4th to 3rd alongwith rise in the coefficient value in case of pollution added to the scenario. Transport equipment sector also gained one rank up from 6th to 5th and coefficient value of 5.7072 from 3.4391. In the case of industrial machinery a big jump was witnessed from 10th rank earlier to 6th rank now with the coefficient value of 5.6139 from 3.2932. It might be due to lower pollution expenditure associated with it. Interestingly, an absolute contrast occurred with textile sector which has shown highest multiplying potential earlier but ranks 7th in later case, because textile industry had higher levels of pollution expenditures, which made its output multiplier lower in later case. Paper and publishing sector and leather products have also declined in terms of their rank order by one level, due to comparatively higher pollution expenditures in the production process. The other industries, which enhanced their rank included food products, plastic products, non-metallic products, and coal/petroleum products. Although primary and tertiary sectors have also shown changes in their coefficient values and rank orders but these changes have occurred due to linkage effects because for these sector pollution data were not accounted in the input-output table (Table 7.17).

Accounting pollution in input-output table also influences the direct multipliers. All the twenty-five sectors of the economy have witnessed a decline in their multiplying factor for the self-sector. The primary and tertiary sectors' multipliers got affected due to linkage effects. All the tertiary sectors including trade, transport, banking/insurance and other services displayed high coefficient values and ranks than the manufacturing sector. Among secondary sector, electric/electronic machinery ranked first followed by industrial machinery, non-metallic products, metal products, transport equipment, leather products, and non-metallic sector. The secondary sector with low direct coefficient included textiles, chemicals, paper/publishing plastic/rubber and coal/petroleum products. The secondary sectors' direct multipliers got reduced in their production recipes. The rank order of direct multiplier also changed for example, food products sector earlier with first rank changed into third rank (Table 7.17).

It would be quite apparent from Table 7.17 that both types of output multipliers are relatively higher in case of secondary sector industries mainly textiles, miscellaneous manufacturing, electric/electronic machinery, metal products, transport equipments, industrial machinery, paper/publishing, leather and other services which ranked among first 10 sectors according to their output multiplying potentials. Primary sector comprising agriculture, animal husbandry, mining etc. had low output multipliers of both natures. In the case of tertiary sector, except, other services, the other sectors like transport, storage, trade and banking/insurance had low output multipliers, though trade and transport has relatively higher multiplier than banking/insurance.

Thus, for example, if Government agency would like to determine in which sector of the economy to spend an additional rupee (or Rs.100 or Rs. 1 lakh or whatever amount), the comparison of multipliers may show where this spending would have the greatest impact in terms of total rupee value of output generated throughout the economy. Besides these output multipliers that are absolute economic in nature, there might well be other factors as trade-balance and socio-ecological factors to be taken into consideration.

Table 7.17 : Output Multipliers

Sector Code	Industrial Sectors	Without Pollution				With Pollution			
		Direct	*Rank*	*Indirect*	*Rank*	*Direct*	*Rank*	*Indirect*	Rank
1.	Agriculture	1.11410	15	2.9726	17	1.1094	6	3.9124	22
2.	Animal Husbandry	1.03340	19	2.9300	20	1.0182	14	3.8645	25
3.	Forestry and Logging	1.00049	23	2.9686	18	1.0005	22	4.1022	21
4.	Fishing	1.09557	17	3.1914	13	1.0956	8	4.3502	20
5.	Mining and Quarrying	1.00048	24	2.9326	19	1.0125	16	4.7567	16
6.	Food Products, Beverages, and Tobacco Products	2.06115	1	2.8594	23	1.0252	10	4.6498	18
7.	Textiles	1.74697	4	3.6988	1	1.0024	21	5.5929	7
8.	Wood, Wood Products and Furniture	1.08390	18	3.2219	12	1.0050	19	5.1370	13
9.	Paper, Paper Products, Printing/Publishing	1.21794	10	3.3969	7	1.0069	18	5.5753	8
10.	Leather and Leather Products	1.69334	5	3.3565	8	1.0137	15	5.5683	9
11.	Plastic and Rubber Products	1.10838	16	2.4034	25	1.0000	25	3.9014	23
12.	Petroleum and Coal Products	1.00010	25	3.1029	16	1.0004	23	5.2082	11
13.	Chemicals	1.02598	20	2.5073	24	1.0002	24	3.8988	24
14.	Non-metallic Products	1.00954	22	2.9028	22	1.0043	20	4.8936	14
15.	Metal Products	1.12402	14	3.5173	4	1.0230	12	5.7807	3
16.	Industrial Machinery	1.58576	6	3.2932	10	1.0509	9	5.6139	6
17.	Electric/Electronic Machinery	1.77010	3	3.5647	3	1.0251	11	5.8422	1
18.	Rail and other Transport Equipment	1.48586	7	3.4391	6	1.0222	13	5.7072	5
19.	Miscellaneous Manufacturing	1.21390	11	3.5966	2	1.1071	7	5.8355	2
20.	Construction	1.22568	9	3.2448	11	1.0088	17	5.1792	12
21.	Electricity/Gas/Water Supply	1.02191	21	3.5026	5	1.3389	4	5.7711	4
22.	Rail and other Transport /Storage Services	1.15969	12	3.1049	15	1.4465	3	4.7866	15
23.	Trade/Hotels	1.38059	8	3.1190	14	1.1523	5	4.6856	17
24.	Banking/Insurance	1.15834	13	2.9042	21	1.8005	2	4.3883	19
25.	Other Services (Education, Medical, Administration, Defence, etc.)	1.92733	2	3.3080	9	2.1136	1	5.2260	10
26.	Pollution Abatement					1.0000	26	1.0000	26

Source : Mathematically calculated from inverse matrix (Appendix X E).

Conclusion

It has been elucidated that in 2000-01, intermediate demand constituted 67 per cent, while final use accounted for 32 per cent of the total output. In terms of broad sector of the economy, tertiary sector comprised 75 per cent in the intermediate use, secondary sector 12 per cent and primary sector only one per cent. The highest gross value added ratios were recorded for plastic/rubber industry and chemical industry, *i.e.* more than followed by food products and non-metallic industry. The highest technological efficiency was observed with miscellaneous manufacturing and textile industry. Agricultural products had highest private final consumption expenditure followed by trade, other services, food products and animal husbandry products. The highest final demand was observed for banking/insurance followed by other tertiary sectors, food products and textile products. The closest factor relating to export indicated that in manufacturing sectors, textile, paper, wood, chemical, metal, non-metal and miscellaneous manufacturing showed positive trade results. But, leather, plastic/rubber, petroleum, industrial machinery, electronics/electric machinery have shown negative trade. The structural coefficient as revealed from coefficient matrix reflected that in Delhi trade and transport sectors played significant role in the production recipes. In miscellaneous manufacturing, metal and petroleum 40-50 per cent of the total output has been received from trade and transport services. The product mix relation reflected that plastic/rubber and industrial machinery have most significant role as they have subsidiary products for 12 other industries, besides, its main output. Thus, they are very significantly inter-dependent and complementary to many industries. The market-share relations showed that food, paper, textile, plastic/rubber and electric/electronic contribute 95-100 per cent as their main product, while the other industries like non-metallic, miscellaneous manufacturing and wood 20-30 per cent produced as other products. The forward linkage or relative sales elucidated that industries like petroleum products sold its products to almost all other sectors, while food products and textile's relative sales to other industries has been small. Textiles, wood, paper/publishing, metal, non-metallic, electric/electronic machinery, transport equipments and miscellaneous manufacturing were strongly connected as revealed by high backward linkage coefficient. Food, textiles, construction, transport/storage, trade/hotels, banking/insurance and other services have strong forward linkage exhibited from forward linkage coefficient. Output multipliers were high in textiles, miscellaneous manufacturing, electric/electronic machinery, metal, paper/publishing, electricity/gas/water supply and transport equipments. The connectivity matrix showed the service sector industries have been very well connected with most sectors of the economy. Transport/storage and trade/hotel have higher level of interaction followed by banking/insurance and other services. The web of economy has shown a distinguishable pattern of inter-sectoral linkage with intensity of linkages intensifying in secondary and tertiary sectors and sparse in primary sectors.

The objective of internalizing the pollution levels (production externalities) into the input-output transaction table has been achieved at broad levels. With the accounting of pollution in the original input-output table, the structures of backward linkages have changed. Textile, paper/publishing, wood, leather, metal products, petroleum/coal products, non-metallic products, industrial machinery, electronic/electric machinery, transport equipments, and miscellaneous manufacturing have shown stronger relationship. Forward linkage indicated that the primary sector industries' coefficient values were less than unity in both cases; in fact, the values have further reduced when pollution is added except for mining/quarrying. In manufacturing sector industries, the status of food products, plastic/rubber and chemicals have remained same with less than unity of coefficient values. The construction and electricity/water/gas supply also maintained strong connectivity in both cases. In tertiary industries, trade/hotel changed its position from more the unity of coefficient value to less than unity, while the other services sector maintained strong linkage. The multiplying coefficients, which were earlier ranging between 2.40 to 3.69 per cent, have now increased to 3.00 to 5.84 per cent. Electric/electronic machinery, miscellaneous manufacturing, industrial machinery have higher multiplying potential. Textiles, paper/publishing, chemicals, plastic/rubber and coal/petroleum products have shown low multiplying potentials because these sectors are associated with pollution generation.

References

1. For sectors refer Appendix II and III.
2. Refer Appendix IB for Absorption matrix.
3. Rasmussen, P.N. (1956) Studies in Inter-Sectoral Relations, *op. cit.*, p. 84.
4. Refer p. 111.
5. Refer p. 112.
6. Refer p. 112.
7. Refer p. 113.
8. For details refer pp. 107-108.

Chapter -8

Comparative Inter-Industry Transactions

Introduction

The analysis and discussion of the inter-industrial structure for 2000-01 with reference to input-output coefficients, product mix matrix, market share matrix, backward and forward linkages, output multipliers and connectivity matrix are presented in he previous chapter. This chapter also analyzed pollution aspect accounted in input-output transaction tables. Comparative analysis was made for coefficients, linkages and output multipliers between non-pollution and pollution accounting input-output transaction tables. The present chapter demonstrates a comparative analysis and description of the structure of Delhi's economy for the years 1970-71 and 2000-01 emphasizing inter-industry transactions. The analysis may reveal the structure of economy, its linkages, multipliers and connectivity relations.

Input-Output Transaction : Comparative Scenario

The IOTT can be viewed as an extensive disaggregation of the production account of an economy. In the open input-output system, the components of the final demand are exogenous to the basic inter-industry matrix. The analysis technique is useful only under the assumption of consistency of the technical coefficients. This assumption is justified unless there are major changes in the technology of the production. For the purpose of comparison the sector groups are aggregated to common 25-sector classification (Appendix II and III).

The intermediate demand of industries accounted for nearly three-fourth of the total domestic output in 1970-71, whereas it has come down to about two-third in 2000-01. The contribution of Private Final Consumption Expenditure (PFCE) has come down from 17 per cent in 1970-71 to 12 per cent in 2000-01, while Government Final Consumption Expenditure (GFCE) has declined to almost half from 8 per cent in 1970-71 to 4 per cent in 2000-01. Similarly, the decrease in Government fixed capital formation is seen from 0.54 in 1970-71 to 0.31 in 2000-01, though it has very insignificant share even in 1970-71 to 2000-01. The category of others (which includes change in stocks, import and exports) shows a major change from -2.54 per cent in 1970-71 to 15.73 per cent in 2000-01 (Fig. 8.1).

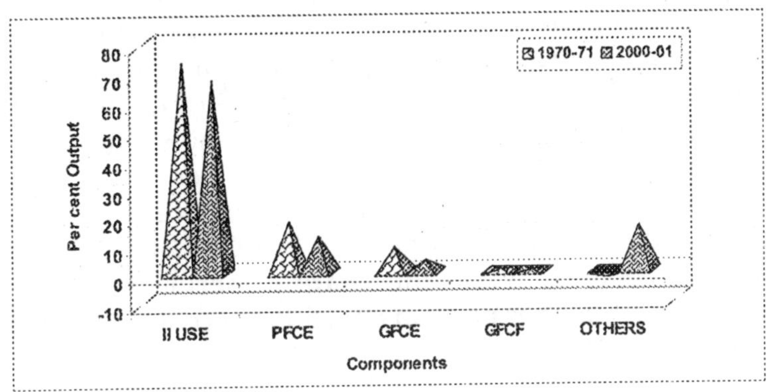

Fig. 8.1: Components of Total Output

To analyze the situation prevailing in respective years, the 25-sector commodity×industry table has been summarized to show only two sectors in the economy *viz.* 'commodity' comprising sectors 1 to 21 and 'service' comprising sectors 22 to 25. These tables provide a comparative picture of percentage distribution of output distributions and input structure of commodities and services for 1970-71 and 2000-01(Table 8.1).

The IOTT's compilation reveals some deviation in the inter-industry utilization of output of various commodities and services. The commodities have utilized 27.34 per cent of the commodity output in 2000-01 as against 54.18 per cent in 1970-71. The services have utilized 49.06 per cent of service output for intermediate consumption in 2000-01 as against of only 25.96 per cent in 1970-71. Here, the significance of service sector in the total output has increased more than 150 per cent in the three decades, in other words, the gross structure in terms of commodities and services has drastically changed over the time period. The intermediate use of services in commodities have changed markedly from 27.05 per cent in 1970-71 to 50.16 per cent in 2000-01, whereas the intermediate use of commodities in services has shown decline from 41.41 per cent in 1970-71 to only 17.21 per cent in 2000-01 (Table 8.1).

The component of final use in the output shows the corresponding marginal increase in commodities from 20 per cent in 1970-71 to 21 per cent in 2000-01; and total intermediate use of commodities has shown marginal decrease from 79 per cent in 1970-71 to 76 per cent in 2000-01. The final use of the total output of service has shown slight decrease from 46.81 per cent in 1970-71 to 35.32 per cent in 2000-01, while the share of services in total intermediate use has gone up from 5.19 per cent to 64.77 per cent in 2000-01 (Table 8.1).

The contribution of commodities in the gross value added has gone down from 50.25 per cent in 1970-71 to 20.44 per cent in 2000-01, whereas services contribution has gone up from 49.75 per cent in 1970-71 to 79.56 per cent in 2000-01 (Table 8.1).

In the year 2000-01, 27 per cent of the total outputs of industries producing commodities form gross value added and 73 per cent intermediate inputs (Table 8.2). On the other

Table 8.1: Distribution of Outputs (In per cent)

Items	*Years*	*Commodities*	*Services*	*Inter-mediate Use*	*Final Use*	*Total Output*
		(a)	*(b)*	*a+b (c)*	*(d)*	*c+d (e)*
Commodities	1970-71	54.18	25.96	79.87	20.3	100
	2000-01	27.34	49.06	76.39	21.39	100
Services	1970-71	24.3	28.88	53.19	46.81	100
	2000-01	14.29	50.48	64.77	35.23	100
Sub-Total	1970-71	41.41	27.05	68.46	31.54	100
	2000-01	17.21	50.16	67.37	32.63	100
Gross Value Added	1970-71	50.25	49.75	-	-	100
	2000-01	20.44	79.56	-	-	100

Source : Obtained from absorption matrix prepared in the present research (Appendix IVA and IVB).

hand, in case of service industries, intermediate inputs formed 65 per cent and gross value added comprised of 35 per cent. The material inputs of commodities have declined from 54 per cent in 1970-71 to 26 per cent in 2000-01. It is reverse in case of services, while inputs have increased from 18 per cent share in commodities to 45 per cent in 2000-01. The component of commodities in service as an input has shown a decline from 34 per cent in 1970-71 to 28 per cent in 2000-01 and there is a tremendous change in service as an input in the service producing industries from 28 per cent in 1970-71 to 51 per cent in 2000-01. Thus, the GVA output ratio in case of commodity producing industries has remained the same; on the other hand, share of services has gone down from 36 per cent in 1970-71 to 34 per cent in 2000-01 (Table 8.2).

It is observed that of the total final use, 16 per cent relate to commodities and 83 per cent to service sector in 2000-01. In 1970-71, it was 36 per cent from commodities and 63 per cent from services, showing drastic increase in services and decrease in commodities (Table 8.2).

The IOTT is aggregated broadly to correspond to the classification of gross domestic product by industry of origin

Table 8.2 : Distribution of Inputs (In per cent)

Items	*Year*	*Commodities*	*Services*	*Sub-Total*	*Final Use*
Commodities	1970-71	54.18	34.41	45.73	36.85
	2000-01	26.74	14.48	17.58	16.17
Services	1970-71	18.14	28.88	22.73	63.45
	2000-01	45.76	51.78	50.29	83.83
Sub-Total	1970-71	72.32	63.29	68.45	—
	2000-01	70.97	65.76	67.37	
Gross Value Added	1970-71	27.67	36.71		—
	2000-01	27.50	34.27	32.63	
Total Output	1970-71	100	100	100	100
	2000-01	100	100	100	100

Source : Obtained from absorption matrix prepared in the present research (Appendix IVA and IVB).

in Table 8.3.This table gives a comparative picture of the first quadrant of inter-industry transaction for the year 1970-71 and 2000-01. Here, sectors 1 to 5 of the IOTT are considered as belonging to primary sector, secondary sector corresponds to sectors 6 to 21 and tertiary sector relates to sectors 22 to 25. During 2000-01, the consumption of the sectors own output is 20 per cent in case of primary sector, 7.59 per cent for secondary sector and 72.15 per cent for the tertiary sector. The corresponding figures for 1970-71 were 31.52 per cent, 28 per cent and 39 per cent, respectively. The rest of the industrial use of primary sector is shared by the secondary sector (20 per cent) and tertiary sector (72 per cent) in 2000-01, whereas in 1970-71, the share by secondary sector was (28 per cent) and tertiary sector (32 per cent) reflecting that intermediate use of primary sector has an almost equal sharing among other services. The use of secondary sector products by primary and tertiary sectors in 2000-01 has been 3.52 per cent and 58.98 per cent, respectively. This was 1.31 per cent and 28.55 per cent, respectively in 1970-71. The intermediate supply of tertiary sector has declined from 26.36 per cent to 9.58 per cent to secondary sector and 1.41 per cent to 0.98 per cent to primary sector in three decades. The total inputs used by the sector reflect decline in primary sector from 4.05 per cent to 1.38 per cent, from 48.38 per cent to 11.98 per cent in secondary sector, whereas tertiary sector consumption has increased remarkably from 47.57 per cent to 74.57 per cent in two time periods, *i.e.* 1970-71 to 2000-01 (Table 8.3).

Table 8.3 : Inter-Industry Transactions (In per cent)

Items	*Year*	*Primary*	*Secondary*	*Tertiary*	*Intermediate Use*
Primary	1970-71	35.52	28.83	39.65	100
	2000-01	20.26	7.59	72.15	100
Secondary	1970-71	1.31	70.14	28.55	100
	2000-01	3.52	58.98	37.51	100
Tertiary	1970-71	1.41	26.31	72.29	100
	2000-01	0.98	9.58	77.93	100
Total Input	1970-71	4.05	48.38	47.57	100
	2000-01	1.38	11.98	74.43	100

Source : Obtained from absorption matrix prepared in the present research (Appendix IVA and IVB).

Table 8.4 indicates the input structure of different sectors. The input requirement of primary sector from itself has gone down from 43.17 per cent in 1970-71 to 15.46 per cent in 2000-01; from secondary sector it has increased from 9.98 per cent to 23.27 in respective years, whereas input requirement from tertiary sector has gone up from 8.88 per cent in 1970-71 to 37.08 per cent in 2000-01. In case of secondary sector the input requirement from itself has come down from 52.73 per cent to 35.15 per cent, from primary sector it has increased from 3.89 per cent to 7.58 per cent, whereas input from tertiary sector has increased from 16.35 per cent to 35.50 per cent from 1970-71 to 2000-01. The composition of input requirement of tertiary sector reveals that its own role has improved from 40.68 per cent to 52.83 per cent; from primary and secondary sectors it has reduced from 54.84 per cent to 0.79 per cent and 19.43 per cent to 3.56 per cent, respectively from 1970-71 to 2000-01. The proportion of Gross Value

Added (GVA) to the total output trends reflects that in primary sector it has increased from 37.66 per cent to 41.66 per cent; in secondary sector from 27.03 to 24.56 per cent, and in tertiary sector it has come down from 35.04 per cent to 33.79 per cent from 1970-71 to 2000-01, respectively (Table 8.4).

Table 8.4 : Distribution of Inputs in the Total Output (In per cent)

Items	*Year*	*Primary*	*Secondary*	*Tertiary*	*Inter-mediate Use*
Primary	1970-71	43.17	3.89	4.84	6.13
	2000-01	15.46	7.58	0.79	0.93
Secondary	1970-71	9.98	52.73	19.43	34.12
	2000-01	23.27	35.15	3.56	16.12
Tertiary	1970-71	8.88	16.35	40.68	28.22
	2000-01	37.08	35.50	52.83	50.29
Gross Value Added	1970-71	37.96	27.03	35.04	31.53
	2000-01	41.66	26.75	34.27	32.63
Total	1970-71	100	100	100	100
	2000-01	100	100	100	100

Source : Obtained from absorption matrix prepared in the present research (Appendix IVA and IVB).

Gross Value Added Output (GVA) Ratio

The GVA to output ratio indicates that in the primary sector, agriculture has registered a decrease from 38.1 per cent to 36.04 per cent, with a small decline in animal husbandry and a minor increase in forestry and logging, whereas tremendous increase is noticed in fishing. In addition, mining/quarrying has also registered some increase from 1970-71 to 2000-01 (Fig. 8.2).

In the case of secondary sector industries it is evident that most industries have shown increasing trend, except metal products with slight decline. Rubber and plastic products show increase from 32 to 52 per cent; closely followed by chemical products and leather with increase from 33 to 51 per cent and 18 to 28 per cent, respectively. Sectors 6 and 17, which are food products and electric/ electronic machinery show an increase in the GVA to output ratio from 26 to 36 per cent and 18 to 24 per cent, respectively. The industries with decline in their GVA ratio are industrial machinery which have come down from 32 to 20 per cent, miscellaneous manufacturing from 22 to 20 per cent and textiles from 21.94 to 21.33 per cent. The construction (Sector Code 20) GVA to output ratio has come down marginally from 29.01 to 28.96 per cent, against the gas, electricity/water supply (Sector Code 21) that has registered increase from 18 to 21 per cent (Fig. 8.2).

In the tertiary sector, trade (Sector Code 23) has noticed maximum increase from 21 to 34 per cent, followed by banking and insurance from 38 to 40.63 per cent, as against decline in transport/storage (Sector Code 23) from 38 to 34 per cent and education, medical/public administration etc. (Sector Code 25) from 45 to 28 per cent (Fig. 8.2).

It is further seen that in the primary sector a negative growth of 5.41 per cent and 2.47 per cent is registered in agriculture and animal husbandry with the average growth rate of 0.19 per cent and 0.08 per cent, respectively. Forestry, fishing and mining/quarrying show a positive trend of 10.61 per cent, 14.13 per cent, 19.11 per cent, respectively; the average annual growth rate is maximum in mining/quarrying, *i.e.* 0.58 per cent, 0.44 per cent and 0.34 per cent in fishing and forestry, respectively. The secondary sector reflects a mixed picture, where in most cases there is positive growth while in some industries negative trend. Industries showing negative growth are textiles with marginal negative trend, *i.e.* by -2.78 per cent and -0.09 per cent of annual average. Miscellaneous manufacturing industry also displayed negative growth of -0.03 per cent. In the manufacturing sector highest negative growth is visible in metal industry -35.90 per cent with the annual average of -1.47 per cent (Fig. 8.2).

The secondary sector with positive growth rate includes plastic/rubber industry with 61.60 per cent increase in its GVA output ratio, chemical industry with average growth rate of 55.79 per cent, followed by leather industry with 52.35

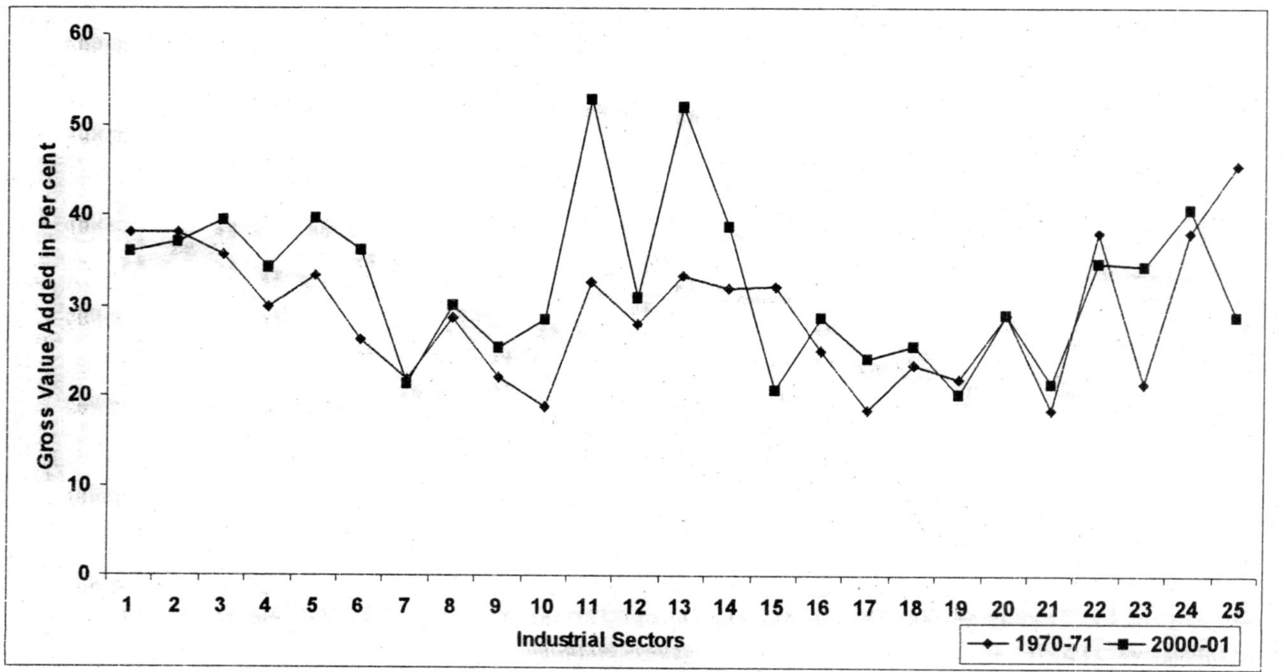

Fig. 8.2 : Proportion of Gross Value Added to Output

per cent growth in its GVA output ratio. The following is food products and electric/electronic machinery with more than 30 per cent growth in terms of GVA. Non-metallic industry is seen with more than 20 per cent. Similarly, paper and industrial machinery industries have registered 15 per cent growth during the three decades. The industries of transport equipments manufacturing, petroleum products and wood have less than 10 per cent increase in their GVA (Fig. 8.2).

The service sector shows a marginal decrease in the GVA output ratio of transport/storage services, while other services have registered a decline in the GVA output ratio by 36.60 per cent. Trade has registered phenomenal increase in their GVA by 60.39 per cent followed by banking insurance with positive trend by an increase of 6.81 per cent (Fig. 8.2).

Inputs

The proportion of inputs used for the production of particular total output is the ratio of input to output or, in other words, also called as technological ratio, which reflects the change in technology used with the change in the respective ratio. Table 8.6 shows the inputs used in primary sector industries with more than 60 per cent in all the five primary industries, though a slight change is seen in average growth trend. It further shows that in agriculture and animal husbandry the efficiency has decreased by 3.3 per cent and 1.52 per cent, respectively. In the case of forestry, fishing and mining/quarrying, the decline in inputs shows increased efficiency by 5.90 per cent, 6.02 per cent and 9.56 per cent, respectively (Fig. 8.3).

In the manufacturing sector, plastic/rubber industry and chemical industry show 30 per cent enhancement in the technological efficiency, respectively, followed by metal industry with 17.09 per cent decline in inputs. The food product industry and leather industry have declined the

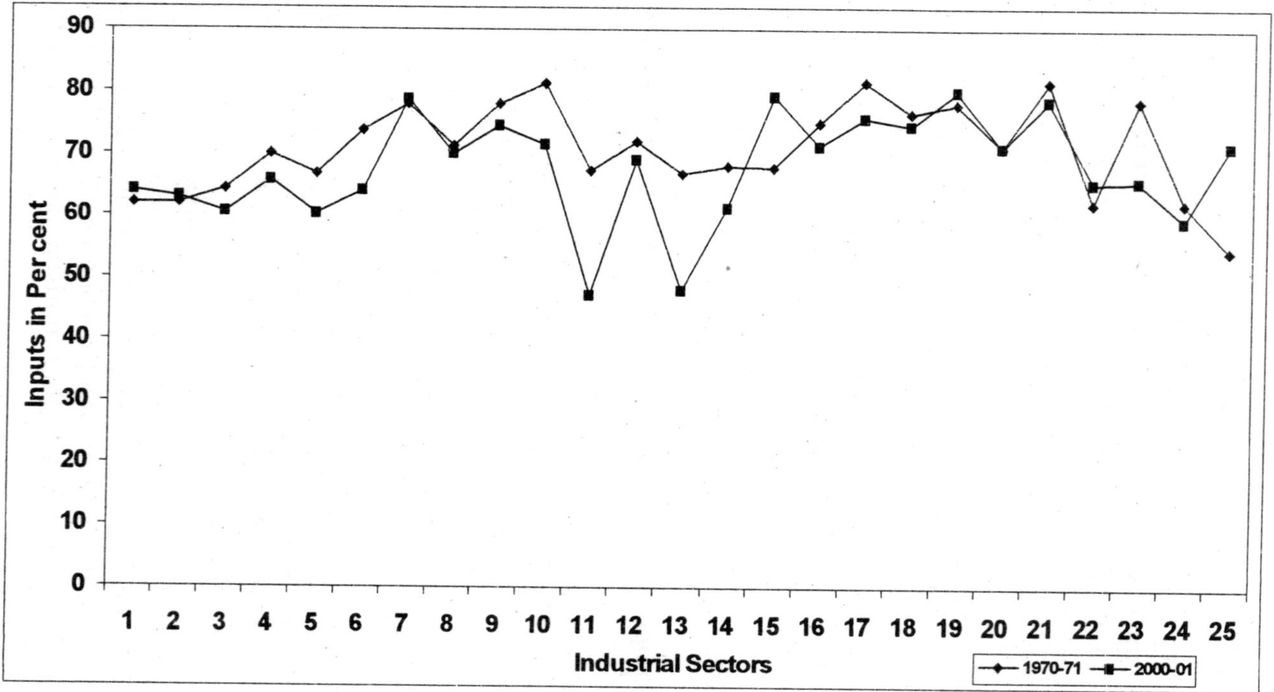

Fig. 8.3 : Proportion of Inputs to Output

input used for production by more than 12 per cent. Non-metallic industry has also improved its production technology by about 10 per cent with annual average of 0.35 per cent in three decades. In other industries like electric/electronic machinery, industrial machinery, petroleum products, paper, transport equipments and wood products, the decline in inputs is found between 2 to 7 per cent. Textile industry has registered slight increase in inputs in the production process by 0.78 per cent. Miscellaneous manufacturing industry has also seen increased inputs by 2.41 per cent. The construction industry inputs used pattern has almost remained the same, whereas electricity/gas/water supply industry has declined in inputs used by 3.58 per cent (Fig. 8.3).

In the service sector, maximum efficiency is seen in trade with 16.50 per cent decline in inputs used and 90.6 per cent annual average followed by banking/insurance with increased efficiency of 4.18 per cent and annual average of 0.14 per cent. Transport and other services have registered increased inputs of 5.36 per çent and 30.54 per cent, respectively. This increase in inputs of service sectors might be because of multifold increase in the users (Fig. 8.3).

Private Consumption

The pattern of the private final consumption expenditure during the three decades in different industrial sectors of the economy of Delhi reveals the trends in private consumption. In the primary sector, agricultural commodity faces a decline in the private expenditure by 43.65 per cent. The other primary sectors show increase with maximum in forestry followed by fishing. But at the same time mining/quarrying does not show any change (Fig.8.4).

The private expenditure trend in manufacturing sector reflects maximum increase in paper products by 453.33 per cent, followed by metal products with an increase of

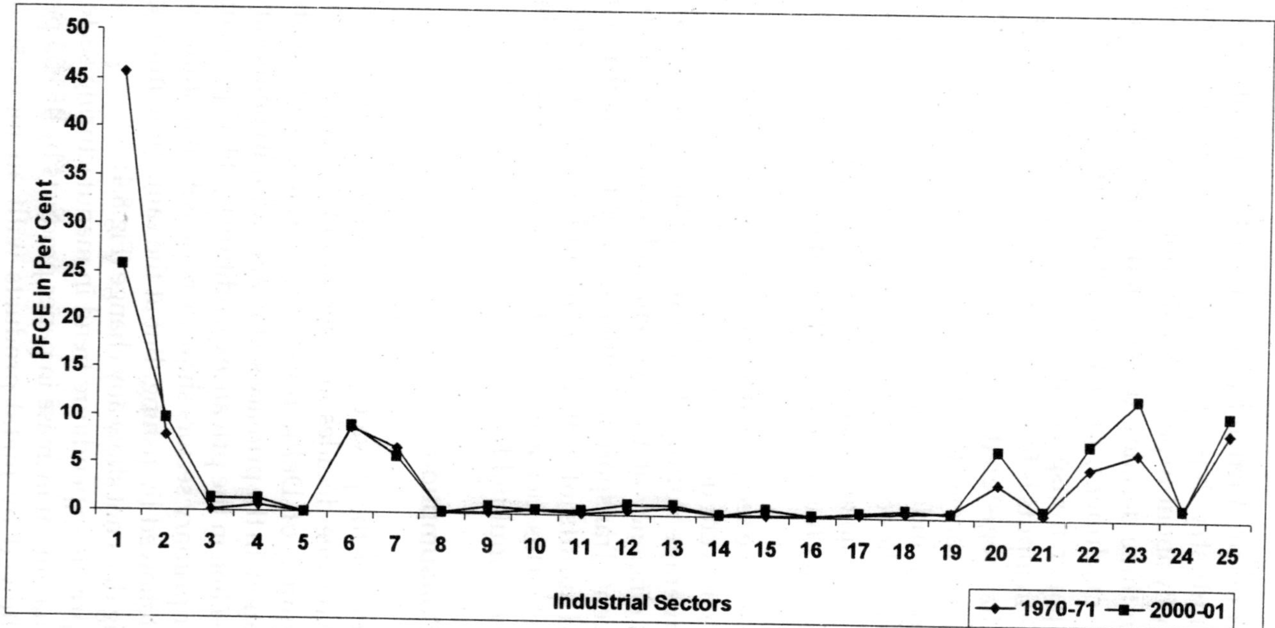

Fig. 8.4 : Distribution of Private Final Consumption Expenditure

331.58 per cent. Meanwhile, petroleum products have shown an escalation by 168.18 per cent and plastic/rubber products with 147.06 per cent. In non-metallic products and transport equipments manufacturing, the expenditure has increased by 70-80 per cent. Private expenditure of chemical products has increased by 42.86 per cent and wood products consumption has risen by 22.22 per cent. Conversely, a negative trend is noticed in industrial machinery and miscellaneous manufacturing by about 30 per cent with the annual rate of more than 1 per cent. Added to this, the construction sector expenditure has increased by 93.15 per cent and in case of electricity/gas/water supply the consumption has increased by 117.07 per cent at an annual rate of 2.62 per cent (Fig. 8.4).

In the service sector, trade has maximum increase in private consumption, *i.e.* by 81.05 per cent, transport services show 48.46 per cent increase and banking/insurance showing slight increase while other services indicate a rise of 20.50 per cent (Fig. 8.4).

Final Demand

The trend in total final demand or use of total GVA as shown in Fig. 8.5 shows that in the economy of Delhi, agriculture sector has registered 3 per cent increase from 0.07 to 0.28 per cent followed by animal husbandry with an increase of 8.60 per cent from 0.05 to 0.48 per cent and for forestry and mining/quarrying it has gone down by 1 to 2 per cent (Fig.8.5).

In the secondary sector, maximum escalation in final demand is seen in chemical industry with 204 per cent from 0.01 to 205 per cent, for metal products and wood products there is also increase in final demand by more than 3 per cent. In the other secondary industries the final demand has declined *viz.* 2 to 4 per cent in sectors like, miscellaneous manufacturing, electric/electronic machinery, petroleum products. Similarly, in leather products, non-metallic products and transport equipments less than 2 per cent decline in final demand is seen, whereas food products, textiles, paper products, plastic/rubber, industrial machinery have a decline of less than 1 per cent. Construction has an increase in final demand by 2 per cent; electricity/gas/water supply has a decline of about 2 per cent. In the service industry, all sectors show an increase in final demand except other services that show slight decline with maximum of 27.91 per cent increase in banking/insurance, 1.35 per cent in trade, 0.29 per cent in transport services (Fig. 8.5).

Structural Analysis

The comparative analysis of structure of economy for 1970-71 and 2000-01 has been done through identifying leading and loosing industries, measuring backward and forward linkages, and their coefficients. Output multipliers are computed to find economic structure in terms of significant industrial sectors that have potential multiplying effect on self-sector and economy. The connectivity of different industrial sector has been studied through connectivity matrix and connectivity graph.

Leading and Loosing Industries

As far as the significance of different industries in Delhi's economy is concerned it has been discussed through ranking industrial sectors according to output multipliers for the years 1970-71 and 2000-01. The results are also compared with location quotient calculated in a study by Department of Industries of Government of Delhi.

In Table 8.5 value of location quotient above '1' indicates that the particular industrial activity is getting specialized in the economy over years. As witnessed from Table 8.5, food products, textile, paper/publishing, leather products, metal

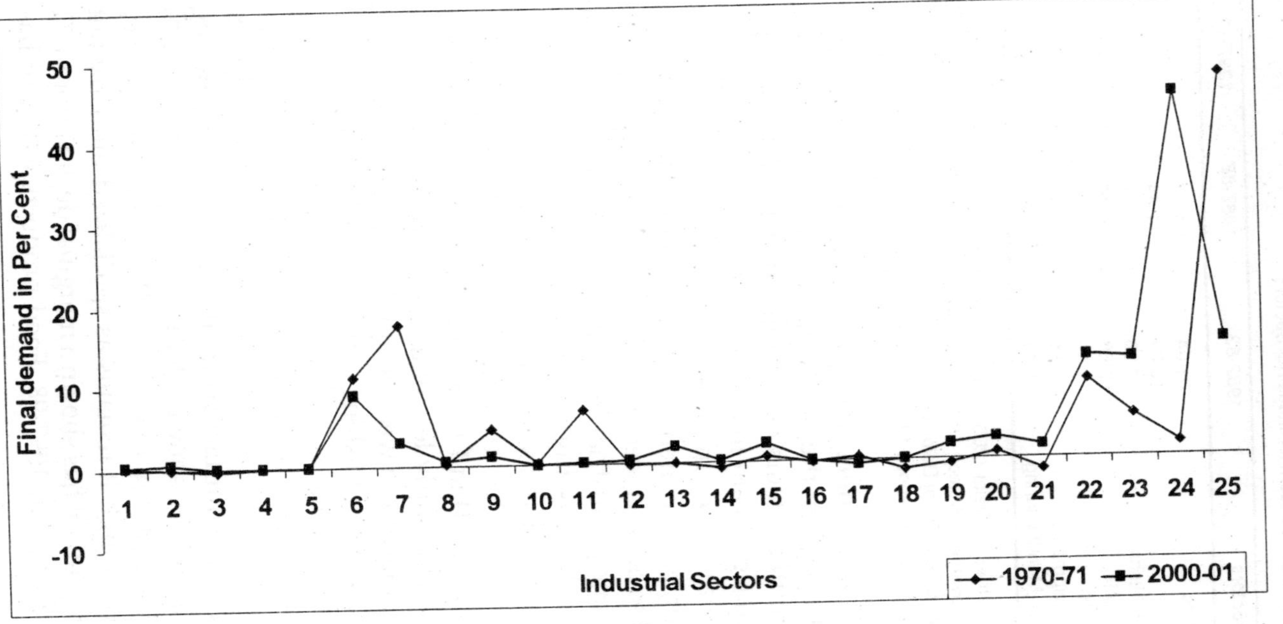

Fig. 8.5 : Distribution of Final Demand

Table 8.5 : Location Quotient for Industrial Sectors

Industrial Sectors	*1982-83*	*1987-88*	*1997-98*
Food Products	1.04	1.17	1.1
Textiles	10.04	11.34	11.13
Paper and Publishing	3.36	3.11	3.6
Leather Products	0.58	0.76	1.17
Metal Products	1.39	1.47	2.57
Machinery Equipments	1.71	1.6	1.24
Miscellaneous Manufacturing	1.79	1.54	1.83

Source : Industries in Delhi (2001) Delhi Urban Environment and Infrastructure Improvement Project, Department of Industries, Government of National Capital Territory of Delhi, Delhi.

Note : Location Quotient above 1.00 indicates activity getting specialized.

products, machinery equipments and miscellaneous manufacturing are the industrial activities that are more specialized than others in economy of Delhi. These are also considered significant industries that influence economy in various ways, *i.e.* in terms of output, value added, investment, employment, location, consumption of energy, trade and so on. It is seen from Table 8.5 that textiles in Delhi is a very major industrial sector with 10.04 value of location quotient, which is highest among all sectors. Textiles appeared as the activity getting more and more specialized over time as is evident from the increasing value of location quotient from 10.04 in 1982-83 to 11.13 in 1997-98. Although textiles in Delhi imply less of textile processing rather it is mainly manufacture of wearing apparel. The next specialized industry is paper/publishing with location quotient value of 3.36 in 1982-83 that has increased to 3.6 in 1997-98. Metal products sector is seen as following industry with the location quotient value of 1.39 in 1982-83 to 2.57 in 1997-98. Miscellaneous manufacturing also seems to be among important industries showing location quotient value of 1.79 in 1982-83 to 1.83 in 1997-98. In the case of machinery equipments though it remains as specialized industry but its value of quotient has shown a marginal decline from 1.71 in 1982-83 to 1.24 in 1997-98. Food products industry has been appearing as consistent important activity. Leather products sector has come up very significantly from 0.58 in 1982-83, *i.e.* the non-specialized activity to specialized activity in 1997-98 with location quotient value of 1.17 (Table 8.5).

The leading and loosing industrial sectors of the economy have also been identified through ranking of output multipliers. The industries ranked as top ten are here considered as leading industrial sectors in economy and the rest are loosing industries. As evident from Table 8.6 in 1970-71, textiles and electric/electronic machinery have been the two industrial sectors at the top. These two industrial sectors have been able to maintain their same positions of dominance in the year 2000-01.The third leading industrial sector in 1970-71 has been plastic/rubber but this industry could not retain its position in 2000-01 and has gone to the list of loosing industries. This also reflects towards closure of plastic/rubber processing industries from the economy of Delhi under pollution norms of Master Plan. Paper/publishing has been the fourth leading industry and has remained in the list of top ten leading industries although it has gone to tenth level in 2000-01.Trade sector being on fifth rank in 1970-71 among leading group of industries in 1970-71 has been shifted to loosing industries group in 2000-01. This decline of position of trade sector does not indicate actual fall of the sector rather some other sectors have grown at much faster rate to reach to top ten category. Transport equipments sector has up-graded itself from sixth level in 1970-71 to fifth in 2000-01.Industrial machinery has maintained itself on the same rank in both points of time. Electricity/gas/water supply sector has gone down to loosing group of industries in 2000-01 from its eighth level in 1970-71. Miscellaneous manufacturing has gone up by one step from ninth rank in 1970-71 to eighth rank 2000-01. In the case of leather products there has been major jump from tenth level in 1970-71 to fourth level in 2000-01. It is evident from Table 8.6 that other services sector which were there in loosing industries group in 1970-71 have made spectacular growth by placing itself to third position in 2000-01. Similarly, food products industry has been among loosing industries in 1970-71 has reached to sixth level in leading industries group in 2000-01. Metal products sector has also grown from loosing industries group to leading industries group (Table 8.6).

Table 8.6 : Leading and Loosing Sectors of Economy (In terms of output multipliers)

Ranks	*Leading Industries*	*1970-71*	*Leading Industries*	*2000-01*
1.	Textiles	5.8979	Textiles	5.4458
2.	Electric/electronic machinery	5.4412	Electric/electronic machinery	5.3348
3.	Plastic/rubber	5.0981	Other services	5.2353
4.	Paper and publishing	4.9937	Leather products	5.0498
5.	Trade	4.9719	Transport equipments	4.925
6.	Transport equipments	4.9703	Food products	4.9206
7.	Industrial machinery	4.9118	Industrial machinery	4.879
8.	Electricity/gas/water supply	4.866	Miscellaneous machinery	4.8105
9.	Miscellaneous manufac-turing	4.8532	Metal products	4.6413
10.	Leather products	4.6887	Paper and publishing	4.6148
	Loosing industries		**Loosing industries**	
11.	Construction	4.6294	Electricity/gas/water supply	4.52451
12.	Metal products	4.6047	Trade	4.49959
13.	Non-metallic products	4.4797	Construction	4.47048
14.	Wood, wood products and furniture	4.4644	Wood, wood products and furniture	4.3058
15.	Petroleum and coal products	4.3923	Banking/ insurance	4.36254
16.	Food products, beverages, and tobacco products	4.3717	Rail/other transport services/storage	4.26459
17.	Agriculture	4.3621	Petroleum and coal products	4.103
18.	Forestry and logging	4.3469	Agriculture	4.0867
19.	Rail and other transport services/ storage	4.3095	Fishing	4.0023
20.	Chemicals	4.2995	Animal husbandry	3.9690
21.	Banking/insurance	4.249	Forestry/logging	3.9634
22.	Animal husbandry	4.1801	Mining/quarrying	3.9330
23.	Other services (education, medical, admn., defence, etc.)	3.9535	Non-metallic products	3.9123
24.	Fishing	3.9073	Chemicals	3.5332
25.	Mining/quarrying	3.3318	Plastic/rubber	3.5117

Source: These ranks are found after adding direct and indirect output multipliers for each sector for respective year.

From the list of loosing industries in 1970-71 other services sector, food products sector and metal products sector have joined as members of top ten leading industries in 2000-01. Whereas plastic/rubber sector, trade and electricity/gas/water supply sector has shifted down from leading industries of 1970-71 to loosing industries in 2000-01. The loosing group of industries mainly includes whole of primary sector and tertiary sector from sixteenth rank downwards in 1970-71. In 2000-01, it is observed that non-metallic products sector, chemicals sector and plastic/rubber industries are at lowest ranks in loosing group of industries. This behaviour of these secondary industries may be explained by the fact that under Master Plan norms certain category of polluting industries has been shifted from the economy of Delhi to National Capital Region or closed down (Table 8.6).

Linkages

Almost every industry producing goods or services takes inputs from other sectors of the economy and, in turn, provides inputs to the latter in the respective production process. These relationships define an industry's backward and forward linkage, respectively. Backward linkage refers to relative purchase of inputs by a sector while, forward linkage refers to the downstream industries that use the output of the specified industry or commodity as input in producing their own goods and services or, in other words, relative sales by a sector to other sectors.

The strong backward linkage reflects that each new industrial investment will offer opportunities for suppliers. In terms of selecting 'key sectors' of an economy, backward linkages are very useful. High backward linkage occurs when a sector uses output of many other sectors as an input. Thus, expanding capacity in such a sector provide 'inducement' or stimuli to supplier industries; which have an incentive to expand output to take advantage of the increased demand of its output by that sector. The basic idea of backward linkage is to trace the output increase that occurs in supplying sectors when there is change in the sector using their output as inputs.

The high forward linkage occurs when a sector's output is or could be used by many other sectors as an input; by expanding capacity such a sector, 'inducements' are provided to using industries that now have an incentive to expand output to take advantage of the increased availability of inputs. The strong forward linkage explains that each new industrial investment will offer inducement to user industries by providing more inputs. Forward linkages are also significant in terms of selecting key sectors of an economy, *i.e.* higher the forward linkage stronger the impact area or the stronger the chain effect of linkage. The basic idea of forward linkage is to trace the output increase that occurs or might occur in using industries when there is change in the sector supplying inputs.

Backward Linkage [1]

Primary Sector

In primary sector in 1970-71, agriculture and animal husbandry sectors purchased almost 70 per cent inputs from the two same sectors only and 11.40 per cent from chemicals besides the rest from various other sectors; while in 2000-01, the purchases from two respective have come down to only 22 to 26 per cent and purchases from trade and transport/ storage services have increased from 6 per cent to more than 50 per cent. In forestry/logging, construction and other services sector became major input provider in 2000-01. In mining/quarrying, 30 per cent purchases were made from self-sector in 1970-71 but in 2000-01, it was almost nil (Appendix VA and VB).

Secondary Sector

The food products industry used to take 21 per cent input from agriculture but it is now only 1.41 per cent while the self-sector purchase increased from 9.71 per cent to 80 per cent. The textiles purchased 64 per cent inputs from self in 1970-71 but now buy 52.5 per cent, the contribution of trade as input provider increased in 2000-01. The wood products industry purchased from self-sector, plastic/rubber, chemicals, and metal products, in 2000-01 purchases have increased from the trade sector. The input structures of paper and publishing have also changed. The self-sector inputs have reduced, whereas trade and transport/storage inputs have increased. The leather industry has increased purchase of inputs from self-sector and textile in 2000-01 as compared to 1970-71. Plastic/rubber industry has maximum purchase from self-sector in 1970-71, but in 2000-01, it is from self-sector, transport/storage and trade sectors. Coal/petroleum products sector's input structure has remained same over the three decades. Chemicals industry's production recipe included input from self-sector, textile, plastic/rubber, metal products and transport/storage in 1970-71, while in 2000-01, the main purchases belonged to transport/storage and trade sectors. The non-metallic products used to take inputs from self and metal products, and in 2000-01, transport/storage and trade became important. Metal product industry's self-sector inputs have remained unchanged and trade sector inputs have increased. In industrial machinery sector in 1970-71, self-sector, electronic machinery, and trade were significant input providers, whereas in 2000-01, trades' position remained same but self-sector inputs increased in electronic/electric machinery in 2000-01 (*see* Appendix VA and VB).

Transport equipment manufacturing sector has increased in inputs from self-sector and trade. The miscellaneous manufacturing has been taking inputs from different sectors as self-sector, leather, plastic/rubber, metal products, electric/electronic, transport services and trade in 1970-71, while in 2000-01, the input from these sectors went up in some cases and down in others. The self-sector and trade input have increased. In the construction sector, inputs were received from mining/quarrying, electric/electronic machinery, self-sector, transport, trade in 1970-71, but in 2000-01, inputs from mining/quarrying became almost negligible, and increase has been seen in other sectors. In electricity/gas/water supply, input has been purchased from coal/petroleum products, industrial machinery, electric/electronic machinery, transport/storage services and trade mainly in 1970-71, whereas in 2000-01, self-sector purchases decreased (Appendix VA and VB).

Tertiary Sector

In tertiary sector, transport/storage services purchased from transport equipments, self-sector, trade, banking/insurance and other services in 1970-71, while in 2000-01, electric/electronic machinery in miscellaneous manufacturing increased along with the other services. Trade sector in 1970-71 purchased inputs from agriculture, animal husbandry, food products, self-sector, banking/insurance and other services. In 2000-01, textiles inputs were added and other services increased. Banking/insurance sector in 1970-71 showed inputs from construction and other service sectors, while in 2000-01, construction sector inputs came down and other services went up. The other services sector have shown the backward linkage with most sectors in different ratios in 1970-71, while in 2000-01 as well it received inputs from many sectors with maximum from self-sector (Appendix VA and VB).

Forward Linkage[2]

Primary Sector

The forward linkage of primary sector has undergone substantial changes in the last three decades. Agriculture sector provided inputs to self, animal husbandry, food products and trade in 1970-71, while in 2000-01, its sales to self, animal husbandry, and food products declined and for trade, transport/storage services and other services increased. In the case of animal husbandry maximum sales were to agriculture, self, food products and trade in 1970-71, while in 2000-01, the self-sector, agriculture and food products sales reduced but increased in trade and other services. Forestry/ logging had main sales to wood products sector, chemicals and other services in 1970-71, but now they got reduced to wood products and increased to plastic/rubber sector, construction sector and trade sector in 2000-01. Fishing had sales to only trade sector in 1970-71, while 2000-01, it has sales to self-sector and trade. Mining /quarrying in 1970-71 had sales to self-sector, textiles, non-metallic sector, miscellaneous manufacturing, construction and trade. This has changed to reduced supplies to self, miscellaneous manufacturing and increased supplies to construction, electricity/gas/waster supply, transport/storage service and trade in 2000-01 (Appendix VIA and VIB).

Secondary Sector

Food products industry's supplies to other industries reveal that it had sales to self-sector, plastic/rubber, transport/ storage services and trade in 1970-71, while in 2000-01, the self-sector and trade sales increased and others declined. Textiles industry in 1970-71 supplied inputs to fishing, self-sector, and small sales to others, while in 2000-01, it supplied in small quantities to most other sectors. Wood products industry had sales to food products, textiles, self, paper and publishing, leather, plastic/rubber, non-metallic products, transport equipments, trade and small quantities to other sectors in 1970-71. It has been seen after three decades that small quantities of sales increased to construction, trade and other services. Paper and publishing industry in 1970-71 supplied inputs to self sector, plastic/rubber, chemicals and other services along with other sectors, while in 2000-01, the main sales got induced to self sector, other services, banking/insurance, trade and transport services. Leather industry had supplies to textile, self, plastic/rubber, chemicals, miscellaneous manufacturing in 1970-71, however, in the next three decades it has supplied to textiles, increase in supplies to self-sector and trade (Appendix VIA and VIB).

Plastic/rubber industry was an input provider to food products, wood products, leather products, self-sectors, industrial machinery, transport equipments, trade and other services in 1970-71, whereas in 2000-01, it supplied inputs to textiles, paper/publishing, self-sector, miscellaneous manufacturing, transport/storage services and trade. Petroleum/coal industry supplied inputs to primary sector, textiles, paper/ publishing, leather products, plastic/rubber sector, industrial machinery, transport equipment, electricity/gas/water supply, transport/storage services and other services in 1970-71, whereas in 2000-01, it supplied to primary sector and many other sectors in small quantities. The major supply included trade, banking/insurance, transport equipments, construction and electricity/gas/water supply. Chemical industry had sales in 1970-71 to primary sector, food products, textiles, paper/publishing, leather, self-sector, transport equipments and other services, while in 2000-01, it supplied to primary sector and other many sectors in small amount and main supplies included self-sector, paper/publishing, construction, trade and other services. The non-metallic industry had sales to food products sector, plastic/rubber, chemicals, self-sector, industrial machinery, miscellaneous manufacturing and other services in 1970-71, while in 2000-01, sales to food products reduced and increased mainly to construction sector (Appendix VIA and VIB).

The metal industry had sales to wood products, plastic/rubber, chemicals, non-metallic products, self-sector, electric/electronic machinery, transport equipments and miscellaneous manufacturing in 1970-71, whereas in 2000-01, sales to wood products reduced and increased for self-sector, electric/electronic machinery and construction sector. The industrial machinery supplied inputs/quarrying of primary sector to textiles, plastic/rubber, self-sector, electricity/gas/ water supply in 1970-71, while in 2000-01, the supplies to primary sector declined and self-sector, transport/storage services, electricity/gas/water supply, trade, banking/ insurance and other services increased. Electric/electronic machinery had sales to food products, textiles, industrial machinery, self-sector, miscellaneous manufacturing, construction, electricity/gas/ water supply and other services in 1970-71, whereas in 2000-01, maximum supplies included self-sector and to many other sectors. The transport equipment sector's supplies to other sectors in 1970-71 included small supplies to primary sector and to food products, self-sector, electricity/gas/water supply, transport/ storage services, banking/insurance and other services, while in 2000-01, its sales included mainly self-sector, trade and banking/insurance. The miscellaneous manufacturing has sales to food products, textiles, non-metallic products, self-sector and other services in 1970-71, whereas in 2000-01, supplies to food products and textiles have declined. On the other hand, it has increased to construction, transport/storage services, trade, banking/insurance and mainly to other services (Appendix VIA and VIB).

Construction sector supplied inputs to primary sector, self-sector, electricity/gas/water supply, transport/storage services, and banking/ insurance in 1970-71, while in 2000-01, sales to primary sector declined. It mainly included self-sector, banking/insurance, trade, other services, and small quantities to many sectors in 1970-71, whereas in 2000-01, the primary sector supplies have declined and major supplies included construction, transport storage services, banking/ insurance, trade and other services (Appendix VIA and VIB).

Tertiary ector

Transport/storage services have major sales to textiles, food products, wood products, paper/publishing, petroleum/coal products, chemicals, industrial machinery, electricity /gas/ water supply, self-sector and, in fact, to all sectors of the economy in 1970-71, while in 2000-01 also, it sold to all sectors of the economy in different proportions. Trade/hotels industry supplied to primary sector, textiles, plastic/rubber, electric/electronic machinery, miscellaneous machinery, electricity/gas/water supply and in small proportions to most sectors in 1970-71, while in 2000-01, it supplied to whole economy with major supplies to construction, transport/ storage and other services. Banking/insurance industry supplied to all sectors with major supplies to plastic/rubber and tertiary sector in 1970-71, whereas in 2000-01, alongwith self-sector, trade and other services. The other services industry had supplied to next sector with main supplies in tertiary sector in 1970-71, while in 2000-01, its supplies were mainly directed to tertiary sector only (Appendix VIA and VIB).

Backward Linkage Coefficient[3]

The comparison of the backward linkage coefficient between two time periods, *i.e.* 1970-71 and 2000-01 shows that the whole of primary sector including agriculture, animal husbandry, forestry and logging, fishing and mining have less than 1 coefficient, *i.e.* a weak coefficient than the coefficient of the economy as a whole. It is, therefore, clear that the primary sector was not significant in terms of taking inputs from other sectors of the economy or as an input receiver it has no strong linkages with rest of the sectors of the economy during 1970-71 and 2000-01. Thus, it reflects that primary sector does not occupy a significant place in the structure of Delhi's economy (Table 8.7).

The manufacturing sector shows that industrial sectors like wood products and metal products had weak backward linkage in 1970-71, which shows more than unity of the backward linkage coefficient in 2000-01. This demonstrates that these sectors have gained stronger relationship or connectivity as an input receiver during three decades while petroleum and coal products sectors have shown a reverse trend, *i.e.* in 1970-71 this sector had shown strong backward linkage coefficient implying that this sector utilizes inputs from many sectors of the economy. But, in 2000-01, its coefficient has become less than unity, which means now as an input receiver sector it does not share a strong connection with other sectors of the economy. The other industrial sectors *viz.* textiles, paper and publishing, leather products, industrial machinery, electric/electric machinery, transport equipments and miscellaneous manufacturing have the coefficient values greater than unity in both points of time. Thus, it reflects that these industrial sectors were strongly related to other sectors of the economy in 1970-71 and in 2000-01 as well. However, some industrial sectors like as food products, plastic and rubber, chemicals, non-metallic products have shown weaker coefficients in 1970-71 and 2000-01, *i.e.* this sector does not receive inputs from many sectors (Table 8.7).

Forward Linkage Coefficient[4]

In the primary sector, agriculture and animal husbandry have shown higher forward linkage in 1970-71 as an input supplier to other industries of the economy, while the other three, *i.e.* forestry/logging, fishing and mining have lower linkage coefficients. In 2000-01, the whole primary sector has shown weaker forward linkage coefficient values, which implies that the agriculture and animal husbandry, earlier suppliers to many sectors of the economy are not holding the same position as supplier of input to many other industries in the economy.

Table 8.7 : Linkage Coefficient

Sector Code	Industrial Sectors	Backward Linkage 1970-71	Backward Linkage 2000-01	Forward Linkage 1970-71	Forward Linkage 2000-01
1.	Agriculture	0.8547	0.9402	1.1454	0.5019
2.	Animal Husbandry	0.8551	0.9268	1.0088	0.4683
3.	Forestry and Logging	0.8678	0.9390	0.3558	0.3178
4.	Fishing	0.9992	1.0094	1.2975	0.3511
5.	Mining and Quarrying	0.9856	0.9276	0.7476	0.3181
6.	Food Products, Beverages, and Tobacco Products	0.9812	0.9044	0.4928	1.0348
7.	Textiles	1.1511	1.1699	0.9062	1.0919
8.	Wood, Wood Products and Furniture	0.9797	1.0191	0.6795	0.3686
9.	Paper, Paper Products, Printing/ Publishing	1.0442	1.0744	0.7246	0.4177
10.	Leather and Leather Products	1.0845	1.0617	0.4651	0.5735
11.	Plastic and Rubber Products	0.9458	0.7602	2.6245	0.3865
12.	Petroleum and Coal Products	1.0070	0.9814	0.5510	0.3166
13.	Chemicals	0.9553	0.7930	0.8142	0.3486
14.	Non- metallic Products	0.9513	0.9181	0.6530	0.3433
15.	Metal Products	0.9551	1.1125	1.3153	0.4043
16.	Industrial Machinery	1.0916	1.0416	0.6752	0.5926
17.	Electric/Electronic Machinery	1.1595	1.1275	1.0138	0.7759
18.	Rail and other Transport Equipment	1.0681	1.0878	0.8264	0.5899
19.	Miscellaneous Manufacturing	1.1117	1.1376	0.3983	0.5321
20.	Construction	1.0540	10263	1.0719	1.8990
21.	Electricity/Gas/Water Supply	1.1310	1.1079	0.6559	0.3471
22.	Rail and other Transport. Services/ Storage	09283	0.9821	1.7921	2.1070
23.	Trade/ Hotels	1.0546	0.9865	2.6922	4.5801
24.	Banking/ Insurance	0.9335	09186	1.1258	1.0108
25.	Other Services (Education, Medical, Administration, Defence, etc.)	0.8500	1.0463	0.9671	5.3223

Source : Obtained from inverse matrix computed in the present research (Appendix VIIA and VIIB).

The manufacturing sector shows that food products industry has gained its position as an input supplier to many sectors of the economy as its coefficient value has become greater than 1 in 2000-01 as compared to lower values in 1970-71. While it has reversed with other sector including plastic and rubber, metal products and electric/electronic products. They have shown strong forward linkage coefficients in 1970-71 but now in 2000-01 have shown inputs from many sectors of the economy and not related to many of them, thus the coefficient values are low. On the other hand, construction and electricity/gas/water supply sectors have shown strong linkages in both time periods indicating that these sectors are significant as input receiver (Table 8.7).

In tertiary sector, trade appears to be important sector as it has strong linkage with higher coefficient values which indicates that trading has always been vital sector in the economy of Delhi and its place has remained unchanged in the last three decades. The other service sector has shown improvement in terms of higher values of forward linkages. Thus, this sector has changed its position as it has shown better or linkages with other sectors of the economy in 2000-01 than in 1970-71. Transport/storage services and banking/insurance sectors have remained same with weak backward linkage coefficients showing lower values of coefficients. Thus, it indicates a weaker forward relation with other sectors of the economy. These results ascertain that this reversal of linkage of these sectors may be because of Supreme Court ruling on industries in Delhi, whereby polluting industries have been asked to relocate outside Delhi. Only textile industry has maintained higher forward linkage from 1970-71 to 2000-01 possibly because in Delhi textile industry involves more of readymade garments and trading than the processing of textiles. The other sectors as wood products, paper and publishing, leather products, petroleum and coal products, chemicals, non-metallic products, industrial machinery, transport equipments and miscellaneous manufacturing have shown lower coefficient values in both the time periods, though in some sectors the value has further declined. Conversely, construction sector has higher forward linkage in both the time periods as it shares strong linkage with many other sectors of the economy (Table 8.7).

In tertiary sector, transport/storage services, trade, banking/insurance had higher coefficient value in 1970-71 and 2000-01. But the values of the coefficients have shown increase in trade and transport/storage that emphasize that these sectors are very strongly connected to other sectors of the economy. The other services sectors have shown a lower coefficient value in 1970-71 and a very high forward linkage coefficient in 2000-01. In terms of forward linkage coefficients, the structure of economy of Delhi clearly indicates the significance of tertiary sector or service sector (Table 8.7).

Output Multipliers[5]

Output multiplier of a commodity-producing sector is the factor by which a unit increases in the demand for and, consequently, production of the commodity in that sector leads to expansion of, output in the whole economy. This multiplier is the sum of the factors by which individual sectors of the economy get expanded for unit increase in the demand for product in one sector. Output coefficients are of three types; one measuring only the direct, the second the sum of the direct and indirect impacts, and third the total (including the induced effect) of an increase in the final demand.

In the present work, the first two types of output coefficients are computed for various sectors. In general, the direct output multipliers are a little over 1, signifying the fact that to meet the unit increase in the final demand for its own product an industry will have to produce slightly more than that of increase in demand, which is likely to be caused by linkage effect. In other words, 1 represents, 1 unit to satisfy the original new unit of final demand plus an additional for intra-and inter-industry uses. The direct plus indirect multipliers vary from industry to industry depending on the strength of industry's linkage with other industries.

The direct plus indirect output multipliers reveal that among the first ten ranking sectors, textile that was at second position has gone up to first rank as multiplying potential industry. Miscellaneous manufacturing has, too, up-graded its importance from fourth to second level in influencing the economies total output. Metal products sector has emerged as another leading sector which was nowhere among the first ten industries, has now occupied the fourth rank. Thus, it indicates the significance and strong linkages that the metal industry has gained in the previous decades. The other sector that has emerged is other services sector that was, in fact, the last ranking sector, *i.e.* at 25th rank in the economy in 1970-71 in terms of its linkages with other sectors and influencing the output of the economy as a whole. In 2000-01, it has reached to the 9th rank of output multipliers. Paper and publishing industry has also jumped from tenth order to seventh in 2000-01. Thus, the sector has been able to develop strong links with the sector of the economy. Similarly, transport equipments manufacturing industry has also improved its rank order of output multiplier from seventh to sixth in 2001 (Table 8.8).

While the industries that have downgraded their position of output multiplier include electric/electronic machinery which has come down from first position in 1971 to third in 2001, but holds very strong position in the economy of Delhi in 2001 as well. Electricity/gas/water supply and leather products have also come down relatively in their position from 3rd and 6th in 1971 to 5th and 8th in 2001. Industrial machinery sector has declined from fifth order in output multiplier in 1971 to tenth place in 2001. Trade and construction sector's position has been replaced from 8th and 9th in 1971 to 10th and 11th in 2001, respectively. Thus, of first ten important sectors, grossly sectors have changed their rank orders both ways, *i.e.* changed downward and upward alongwith some new sectors emerged among the first ten sectors in 2001, while some sectors from the first ten sectors of 1971 have gone down beyond the first ten positions (Table 8.8).

The total output multiplier analyzed broadly categories reflects that the primary sector industries were among the 21st to 24th rank in 1971, while in 2001, these positions have been between 17th to 20th which clearly indicates that

Table 8.8 : Output Multipliers

Sector Code	Industrial Sectors	1970-71 Direct	1970-71 Rank	2000-01 Direct	2000-01 Rank	1970-71 Indirect	1970-71 Rank	2000-01 Indirect	2000-01 Rank
1.	Agriculture	1.5016	4	1.1141	15	2.8605	24	2.9726	17
2.	Animal Husbandry	1.3183	9	1.0334	19	2.8618	22	2.9311	20
3.	Forestry and Logging	1.0031	23	1.0005	23	2.9042	23	2.9686	18
4.	Fishing	1.0029	24	1.0956	17	3.3441	12	3.1914	13
5.	Mining and Quarrying	0.0334	25	1.0005	24	3.2984	13	2.9326	19
6.	Food Products, Beverages, and Tobacco Products	1.088	19	2.0611	1	3.2837	14	2.8594	23
7.	Textiles	2.0455	1	1.7469	4	3.8524	2	3.6988	1
8.	Wood, Wood Products and Furniture	1.1856	14	1.084	18	3.2788	15	3.2219	12
9.	Paper, Paper Products, Printing/Publishing	1.4992	5	1.2179	10	3.4945	10	3.3969	7
10.	Leather and Leather Products	1.0593	21	1.6933	5	3.6294	6	3.3565	8
11.	Plastic and Rubber Products	1.9328	2	1.1084	16	3.1653	19	2.4034	25
12.	Petroleum and Coal Products	1.022	22	1.0001	25	3.3703	11	3.1029	16
13.	Chemicals	1.1024	17	1.0259	20	3.1971	16	2.5073	24
14.	Non-metallic Products	1.296	10	1.0095	22	3.1837	18	2.9028	22
15.	Metal Products	1.4082	7	1.1240	14	3.1965	17	3.5173	4
16.	Industrial Machinery	1.2584	11	1.5857	6	3.6534	5	3.2932	10
17.	Electric/Electronic Machinery	1.5606	3	1.7701	3	3.8806	1	3.5647	3
18.	Rail and other Transport Equipment	1.3956	8	1.4858	7	3.5747	7	3.4391	6
19.	Miscellaneous Manufacturing	1.1326	14	1.2139	11	3.7206	4	3.5966	2
20.	Electricity/Gas/Water Supply	1.1021	18	1.2256	9	3.5273	9	3.2448	11
21.	Rail and other Transport. Services/Storage	1.081	20	1.0219	21	3.785	3	3.5026	5
22.	Trade/Hotels	1.2027	12	1.15969	12	3.1068	21	3.1049	15
23.	Banking/Insurance	1.4424	6	1.3806	8	3.5295	8	3.1190	14
24.	Other Services (Education, Medical, Administration, Defence, etc.)	1.1247	15	1.1583	13	3.1243	20	2.9042	21
25.*	Pollution Abatement	1.1088	16	1.9273	2	2.8447	25	3.3081	9

Source: Obtained from inverse matrix computed in the present research (Appendix VIIA and VIIB).

primary sectors are not of much significance as regard the linkage with other industries and the output of economy in totality. In manufacturing sector, industries with coefficient values of low multiplying potential in 1971 include non-metallic products, metal products, chemicals, coal/petroleum products, wood products, food products with less than 10th rank. Industries with high multiplying potential in 1971 include textiles, plastic/ rubber, electronic/electric machinery, and paper/publishing. In 2001, the low potential industries include plastic/rubber, chemicals, non-metallic products and food products. Among the tertiary sector except trade, transport/storage services, banking/insurance and other services have low multipliers in 1971, while in 2001 other services emerged as the sector with high multiplying potential. Banking/insurance and trade have moved up in their positions from 20th and 21st in 1971 to 21st and 15th in 2001 (Table 8.8).

It would be evident from Table 8.8 that in 1971 textile sector has been the leading sector with highest multiplier for the self, while in 2001 this position has been taken over by food products industry and textile has reached to 4th rank. The plastic/rubber sector had the 2nd position as a multiplying factor for self-industry in 1971, whereas in 2001, this sector has been surpassed by the tertiary category's other services sector that had attained its position and plastic/ rubber sector was pushed to 16th order. Electric/electronic machinery sector with 3rd position in 1971 has remained at the same rank during three decades. In fact, this sector has become more significant as direct multiplier is concerned (Table 8.8).

Paper and publishing sector was at 5th position in 1971, but in 2001, it came down to 10th position and is replaced by leather sector to this rank. Similarly, trade/hotels sector with 6th rank in 1971 has been pushed down to 8th position in 2001 and by industrial machinery manufacturing, which with 9th rank in 1971. Metal products industry with 7th rank in terms of direct output multiplier has been pulled down to 14th rank by transport equipment sector. The seventh order sector, *i.e.* transport equipment has changed its rank and is replaced by trade/hotels in 2001. Non-metallic sector was positioned at 10th rank in 1971, while in 2001 it was pushed to 22nd position. Industrial machinery sector with its 11th rank has gone up to 6th order and 9th order has been filled by miscellaneous manufacturing which has up-graded itself to this rank. The wood product sector was at 14th rank in 1971 while it has replaced by metal products sector in 2001 and the wood products sector has come down to 18th rank (Table 8.8).

In totality, the sectors that have gone up in terms of direct output multipliers from 1970-71 to 2000-01 include leather products, industrial machinery, transport equipment, miscellaneous manufacturing, construction, banking/ insurance and other services. The sectors that have come down in terms of direct output multipliers from 1970-71 to 2000-01 include primary sectors, textiles, wood products, paper and publishing, plastic and rubber and non-metallic products. And the sectors that have remained nearly same for direct multipliers are coal/petroleum products, chemicals, electricity/gas/water supply and transport/ storage services etc.

It is quite clear that in primary sector all industries including agriculture, animal husbandry, fishing, mining and forestry, the multipliers were low in 1971. In other words, primary sector was not significant in 1971. In manufacturing sector, all the fourteen categorized industries except coal/ petroleum have changed their positions of importance as multipliers from one to another. In the tertiary sector, four industries, *i.e.* transport/ storage services, trade/hotels, banking/insurance and other services have gained much importance in the previous decades. These industries have up-graded their rank in order of significance. Thus, it reflects that the tertiary component of Delhi's economy has increased and is significant (Table 8.8).

Connectivity Matrix and Graph

In order to investigate the structure of relationship and structure of linkages among different sectors of the economy of Delhi, a connectivity matrix is derived from input-output coefficient matrix. The connectivity matrix qualifies all connections by three indices, *i.e.* 0, 1, 2. The index value of '0' indicates no relationship between sector *i* and sector *j*, in other words, *i* and *j* sectors are isolated from each other. The index value of '1' implies a unidirectional flow from sector *i* to sector *j*. The unilateral flow has been clearly specified whether it is a forward connection or a backward connection. The index value of '2' denotes a bilateral (mutual) linkage which exists between sector *i* and *j*.

The connectivity matrix is displayed in the form of a graph where all connections have been denoted through the network of flows. Figures 8.6 and 8.7 show graph associated with connectivity matrix derived from technology coefficient matrix for internal transactions for the economy of Delhi in 1970-71[6] and 2000-01[7] aggregated into 25 sectors. These matrices and diagrams show every liaison between industries as defined by $a_{ij} > 0$. With this approach industrial complexes or clusters can be identified in an input-output matrix. In this context industrial complexes are defined in terms of relative intensities of inter-industry liaisons, *i.e.* those industries that are closely inter-linked through relationships defined in the technology coefficient matrix. This connectivity matrix and its graphical representation is very useful for analyzing an economic structure. Indeed, one can think of Hirschman's[8] concept of linkages and find in a complex, those sectors interlinked both through their distribution and supply networks. Thus, they provide a clear picture of city's economic dynamics.

Figures 8.6 and 8.7 represent the economic web of Delhi for the year 1970-71 and 2000-01, respectively. The economic structure in terms of technology coefficient matrix, *i.e.* flows of input towards and outputs to among different sectors of economy reveal that during the period of three decades economic structure has gone under tremendous change. There are few industrial sectors that were not significant in 1970-71 that has emerged as important industries in 2000-01. In contrast to this, industries were holding significant positions in the economy of Delhi in 1970-71 but have come down in 2000-01. As it is clearly observed from the diagram that in 1970-71 the network of flows was showing existing pattern of economic structure but no distinct pattern was visible. In 2000-01, Delhi's economic web has taken a distinguishable pattern of network of flows. This pattern reveals a gradation in the intensity of linkages among different sectors. Intensity of interactions has been more complex as one moves from left to right in the diagram, *i.e.* industrial sectors placed in left side of the diagram are weakly connected to the rest of the economy. These sectors include primary industries of agriculture, animal husbandry, forestry, fishing and mining/quarrying. These primary sectors do not share relationship among themselves. Whole of the primary sector is mainly seen as input receiver from the economy and they do not contribute or supply to rest of the economy. Thus, the primary sector is isolated and is not well connected. Although the significance of these sectors has been low in both time periods, it has come further down in the previous decades. In fact, in 1970-71, these sectors were connected to a number of sectors to receive inputs. But in 2000-01, the consumption of inputs from different sectors has been reduced many times; corroborating that importance of primary sector industries in the economy of Delhi is not significant. Agricultural industry used to receive inputs from 14 sectors, which now receives from 12 sectors. Animal husbandry used to receive inputs from 11 sectors that now receive only from 6 sectors. Forestry shared unidirectional linkage as receiver from 14 sectors in 1970-71 but had linkages with only three sectors in 2000-01. In case of mining/

quarrying, though number of input suppliers remained same, but this sector was a supplier to other sectors as well in 1970-71, which is nil in 2000-01. In the fishing sector, the numbers of input suppliers have increased, because of increase in fish consumption and creation of fishpond in some areas of Delhi.

The secondary sector industries' structures of linkages have also gone through tremendous change in the last three decades. The intensity of linkages among secondary sector itself and rest of the economy has intensified as observed from the increase in networks among different sectors. The level of interactions is stronger among secondary and tertiary sectors. The emerging important industrial sectors from 1970-71 to 2000-01 include plastic/rubber, which now share much stronger relations with rest of the economy. Metal products, electric/electronic machinery, transport equipments, industrial machinery and wood products have strengthened their linkages with economy. In contrast to this, there are industries that have come down or, in other words, they are loosing ground in terms of interaction with rest of the economy. These include mainly food products, textiles, and chemicals and marginal decline has been seen in leather products. Non-metallic products and coal/ petroleum products remained the same. The construction and electricity/gas/water supply sector have enforced their vital role in economic set-up of Delhi within three decades. Their linkages have grown stronger with different sectors of the economy.

It would be quite apparent from the connectivity matrix and Figures 8.6 and 8.7 that tertiary sector has developed strong interactions with rest of the economy and also among themselves. Transport/storage services and trade/hotels sector have stronger and wider interactions in 2000-01 as compared to 1970-71. In case of banking/ insurance the level of interaction has increased multi-fold in three decades. Other services sectors have remained almost the same as earlier.

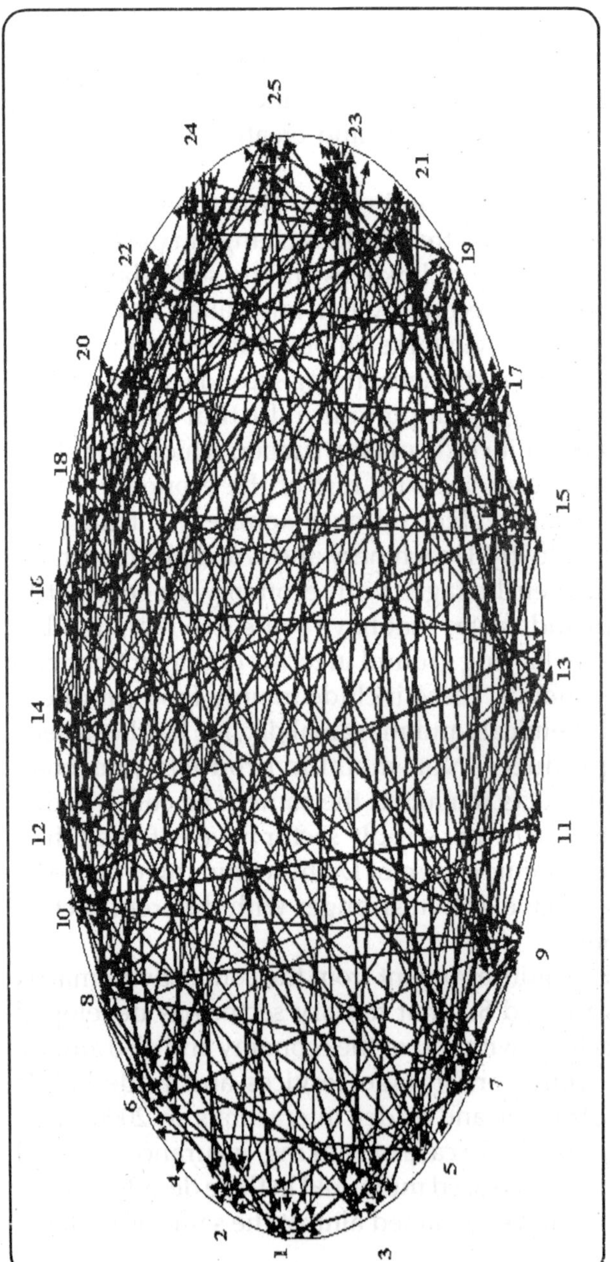

Note: 1 to 25 are industrial sectors codes. For industrial sectors refer Table 8.6. The flow arrows are based on connectivity matrix (Appendix VIIIA)

Fig. 8.6 : Web of Economy, 1970-71

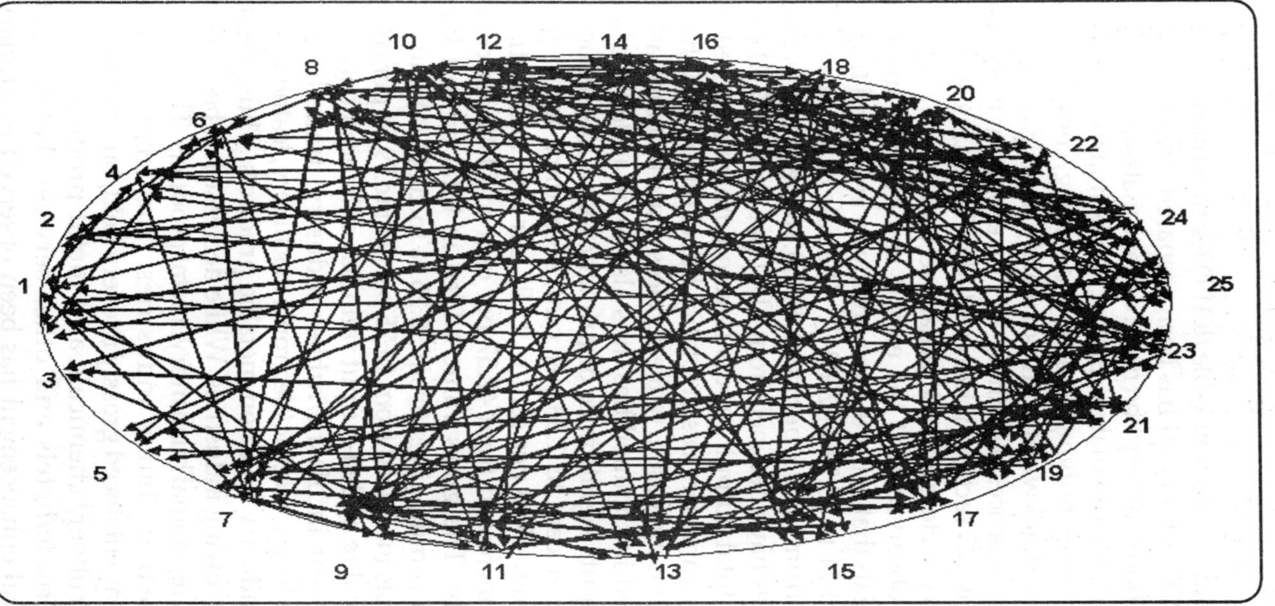

Note: 1 to 25 are industrial sectors codes. For industrial sectors refer Table 8.6. The flow arrows are based on connectivity matrix (Appendix VIIIB)

Fig. 8.7 : Web of Economy, 2000-01

Conclusion

Input-Output Transaction Table (IOTT) for two-time periods, *i.e.* 1970-1971 and 2000-01 has been prepared. These include the preparation of absorption matrix, make matrix, coefficient matrix, market share matrix, products-mix matrix, Leontief inverse matrix, identifying leading and loosing, computation of linkages (backward and forward) multipliers and connectivity matrices. For these IOTT's economy has been classified into 25 sectors, which includes 5 primary sectors, 14 secondary sectors and six tertiary sectors.

It was observed that the export components in total output reveals that exports have positively enhanced from – 2.54 in 1970-71 to 15.73 in 2000-01. The role of services has increased from 27.05 per cent to 50.16 per cent while commodities have declined from 41.41 per cent to 17.21 per cent in the total output. Inputs have not much changed in commodities and services in totality, but commodities share in services has increased, while services share in it increased and declined in commodities. It is also to be added that in the total inputs significance of primary sector has reduced from 4.05 per cent to 1.38 per cent, secondary sector has declined from 48.38 per cent to 11.98 per cent and tertiary sector has increased from 47.57 per cent to 74.43 per cent, respectively. The gross value added in total output has declined in commodities (from 50.25 % to 20.44 %) and for services it has increased from 49.75 per cent to 79.56 per cent. The gross value added-output ratio has enhanced between 20-60 per cent in plastic/rubber industry, trade/hotels, chemical industry, electric/electronic machinery, leather, food products industry and non-metallic products. Thus, these appear as growing industries. While decrease has been seen in agriculture, animal husbandry, metal products. Therefore, these appear declining industries. The technological efficiency has enhanced grossly in every field, but maximum in plastic/rubber, chemicals and metal products, food products, trade/hotels and other services. While least technological enhancement has been observed in primary sectors, transport equipments, wood industry and paper/ printing. The private consumption trends showed high expenditure on animal products, paper products, metal products, petroleum products and plastic/rubber products, and electricity/gas/water. Linkage coefficient values show that primary sector has less than 1, *i.e.* weak backward linkage in both time periods. Wood, metal products have improved backward linkages in 2000-01, while textiles, paper/ publishing, leather products, industrial machinery, electric/ electronic machinery and miscellaneous manufacturing maintained same higher backward linkages. Non-metallic products and chemicals have shown a decline in their backward linkages. Output multipliers reveal that textiles, miscellaneous manufacturing, metal products, other services, paper /publishing, electric/electronic machinery, transport equipment and electricity/gas/water supply have high multipliers. Whereas, primary sectors, chemicals, plastic/ rubber, non-metallic products have a declined output multiplier from 1970-71 to 2000-01. The connectivity matrix has shown a distinguishable pattern of inter-sectoral linkages in 2000-01, which shows intensity of linkages intensifying in secondary and tertiary sectors and sparse in primary sectors. Such pattern has not clearly developed in economy in the year 1970-71.

References

1. For details refer p. 110.
2. For details refer p. 110.
3. Refer p.111.
4. Refer p. 14.
5. For details refer pp. 107-108.
6 See Appendix VIII A
7 See Appendix VIII B
8 Hirschman, A. (1958) The Strategy of Economic Development, *op. cit.*

Chapter - 9

Summary and Conclusions

The city is in a constant process of evolution. The economic base of the city continues in the process of change, in its location within city and rejuvenation to perform different city functions. In addition to spatial motion within city, there is temporal motion as well. Functions of city are altered through time and their importance within the regional systems. The temporal dynamics of the city generates changes in structure and function by social, demographic, economic and technological changes. To understand the temporal and spatial dynamics of city, various aspects are needed to be examined, such as economic functions, production, role of city as consumption factor of production and its geographical location. There is a need to investigate and explore the woven web of economic inter-dependence, both theoretically and empirically for planning and forecasting purpose.

Metropolitan cities and city systems play a major role in the modern national as well as global economy. They do so by virtue of their functions as the agglomerated growth centers of the world capitalism, continually reinforcing their practical importance. Metropolitan cities tend to deepen and widen their competitive advantages over time. A steep rise in the role of knowledge as a factor of production and enhanced information technologies, the production, distribution and exchange became important element in the economic system. The economic dynamics of cities and city systems can be understood in relation to the dynamics of urban enterprises that are distributed across space, consume resources, enter into forms of cooperation or competition and transact with one another intra-and inter-regionally.

The present work has been an attempt to study the spatial and temporal industrial structure of Delhi and their linkage. The temporal study has included the period of three decades, *i.e.* 1971-2001. For analyzing spatial structure of industries, approved industrial areas were selected. Since, industries are functionally related, the input-output analysis has highlighted the demand by one industry for the product of other, *i.e.* backward and forward linkages. The technical inter-dependence between the levels of desirable and undesirable outputs can be described in terms of structural coefficients similar to those among all the regular branches of production and consumption. This research has been an endeavour to explain how such externalities (pollution) are associated with modern technology and uncontrolled and unplanned economic growth. In order to assess the economic structure, the main objectives of the study were to identify spatial-economic structure of industries, looking into spatial-environmental structure of industries, preparing inter-industry tables of Delhi for 1970-71 and 2000-01, identifying leading and loosing industries, finding temporal and horizontal structure, *i.e.* linkages and inter-dependence of industries and, finally, to internalize the pollution levels (production externalities) into the input-output transaction table.

Delhi is spread over an area of 1483 sq. kms. of land consisting of 9 districts and 27 tehsils, alongwith Delhi Municipal Corporation, New Delhi Municipal Corporation (NDMC), Delhi Cantonment and 59 census towns. Delhi had grown at rapid pace during the past few decades from mere 14.5 lakhs populations in 1951, it has reached to 137 lakhs by 2001. Each year approximately two lakh people migrate to the city from neighbouring states. The impact of in-migration is immediately reflected in changing ratios of rural-urban population. Rural component was 10.30 per cent in 1971, which decreased to 7.21 per cent in 1981. But, in 1991, the rural population to the total population increased to 10.07

per cent, mainly due to the new migrants settled in rural areas. Shortage of housing facilities has forced people to settle in rural areas where land prices and rent are comparatively lower. Delhi has witnessed rapid industrial growth in last decade and half. During the period 1981-1991 the increase was from about 60000 to 80000, and in 2001 it reached to 1.29 lakhs. The investment rose from Rs.18.3 crores in 1951 to Rs. 700 crores in 1981, and reached to Rs. 2524 crores in 2001. The production increased from Rs. 35.35 crores in 1951 to Rs. 6310 crores in 2001. The industries employed about 0.95 lakh persons in 1951, which rose to 14.40 lakhs in 2001. Industries in Delhi form a complex group, comprising textiles, chemicals, leather, metals and alloys, machinery and equipments, transport equipments, food products and activities associated with to manufacturing process, repair services, personal services, generation and transmission of electricity/gas and cold storage etc. Industrial sector occupies an important position in Delhi's economy and plays a pivotal role in its rapid economic growth. With such a broad and rapidly expanding industrial base and also with globalization and liberalization of economy several multinational companies have entered into the economic web of the city, making Delhi an integral part of the global economy. Delhi's industrial and commercial structure has been undergoing rapid change. New technologies, management techniques and products are generating new inter-sectoral relations.

There are several approaches and techniques, which are used by regional scientists to analyze the underlying inter-dependence among the sectors of an urban economy. Input-output analysis is one of them; it is a technique of looking at the existing inter-firm, inter-industry and inter-regional transactions, and of determining the impact of various sectoral and regional changes in an economy. This technique can be fruitfully used in planning and forecasting purposes of an urban area or region. The present study has analyzed and discussed the structure of the economy of Delhi using input-output analysis with a view to find out the ensuing changes.

The present research has been totally based on secondary data source. The required data has been collected from different Government departments, Ministries and bodies as Central Statistical Organization, Planning Commission, National Sample Survey Organization, Central Pollution Control Board, Delhi Development Authority, Directorate of Economics and Statistics, Directorate of Industries, Delhi Pollution Control Committee, and different reports of various Departments of Delhi Administration. The Chapters 4 and 5, where spatial, economic and environmental structure of industries of Delhi have been analyzed, are based on data obtained from the Census of Industries published from Delhi Pollution Control Committee, Profile of Industries published from Department of Industries, unpublished information on industrial areas/estate, investment, production and employment from Department of Industries. Master Plan document of 1962, 1981, 2001 and Master Plan 2021 under preparation (partial information) is used. Economic Survey of Delhi from Department of Planning, Statistical Handbook of Delhi, Quarterly Digest of Delhi and Economic Census of Delhi from Directorate of Economics and Statistics, Census on Hazardous Industries of Delhi from Delhi Pollution Control Committee, Census Reports on Delhi, and Supreme Court orders regarding industrial pollution in Delhi were used and referred. The Chapters 6, 7 and 8 are based on input-output transaction tables prepared as a part of study of the present research work. For the preparation of these input-output tables for two points of time, *i.e.* 1970-71 and 2000-01, data has been collected from Annual Survey of Industries (ASI) which provided data for item-wise inputs and outputs for respective years alongwith data on fuel use for registered manufacturing. As regards the unregistered manufacturing, concerned data were obtained from National Sample Survey Organization (NSSO) for the required years. For the primary and tertiary sectors data were obtained from State Accounts Division. Data for demand vectors were obtained from report on Household Consumer Expenditure, Economic Purpose Classification Report and Delhi Budget

Document. Also, reports from Central Statistical Organization on National Industrial Classification, report on Concordance Tables, and National Input-Output Transaction tables for the year 1973-74 and 1993-94 were used.

There are certain constraints and limitations that have been felt regarding data. For instance, the Leontief model is considered at its best, or in other words, most stable at factor cost, and for reaching at factor cost, one need item-wise data on trade and transport and also item-wise indirect taxes. These two sets of matrices, i.e., TTMM (Trade and Transport Margins Matrix) and ITM (Indirect Tax Matrix) are required to be subtracted from the absorption matrix to bring the absorption matrix from purchaser's price to factor cost. Since these two sets of detailed data were not available in the present work, Leontief model has been prepared on purchasers' price. Similarly, in the final demand quadrant, vector/column on change in stocks required in detail for all sectors, but change in stock for un-registered manufacturing, private sector, primary and tertiary industries were not available. Another vector of net export needed detailed item-wise data on trade for all sectors of the economy and was not available (because trade data is collected at Central Government level for the country as whole and broad information for states are prepared and states have no role in data collection for trade). Thus, these two vectors of change in stock and net export are clubbed together.

The secondary data used in the present research were obtained from the most authentic, reliable and the only source of data generation. Although at some places constraints and limitations were felt. For instance, data on industries were collected for two types of categories, one, industries were classified according to their investment slabs where they were considered as small, medium and large scale industries. This pattern was followed by Department of Industries where most of the data were for registered small-scale industries. While, Annual Survey of Industries collects the data for industries which are registered under Sections 2m(i) and 2m(ii) of the Factories Act, 1948. The Sections 2m(i) and 2m(ii) refers to any premises (a) where ten or more workers are working, or were working on any day of the preceding twelve months, and in any part of which a manufacturing process is being carried on with the aid of power or in ordinarily so carried on, or (b) where twenty or more workers are working or were working on any day of the preceding twelve months and in any part of which a manufacturing process is being carried on without the aid of power. In this context, it has been felt that there might be overlapping of industries in the surveys conducted by the two data generating agencies. Another limitation regarding data that has been faced was that environmental problems in relation to industries has been very significant but there is only one census conducted on hazardous industries of Delhi in the year 2001 by Delhi Pollution Control Committee, no such secondary data for earlier years is available.

Input-output technique has been found very appropriate for such an analysis. It represents a fruitful technique for depicting and investigating the underlying process, which binds together the sectors of a system and all the separate facets of their sub-systems. Input-output tables as descriptive devices are extremely useful. Its strength lies in: (a) detailed presentation of the production and distribution characteristics of individual industries. The checkerboard table describes a system that is operating, in other words, a regional economic system with its inter-connections and links with various parts, (b) input-output analysis is a powerful tool for town planning and development, (c) the technique imposes a desirable statistical discipline on data collection and empirical investigations. The technique reveals gaps in data and may help filling them, and (d) this technique is used extensively for projections.

There are limitations of this technique as well. The most significant problem with the input-output technique is the validity of constant production coefficients largely reflecting technological relations. These coefficients were derived from transactions of a base year, which must reflect technological structure of that year. But in situations, where technology advances and introduction of new products is unpredictable it is not very relevant. A general objection to projection based on constant coefficient is that such projections are centered on rather a mechanical concept of a regional economy, an engineering type relationship, where other factors like resource limitation, time lags, choice of firms and consumers etc., have little role. The preparation of input-output table requires voluminous data. The availability or collection of huge data has been the most significant limitation.

There are other techniques, which are used for analysis in urban and regional studies. These include: (a) location quotient, a device for gauging the relative specialization of a region in selected industries, (b) mix and share analysis provides a descriptive explanation of the change in regional employment over a period. It does this by isolating the individual components of change reflecting the national growth effect, the industry-mix effect and regional share effect, (c) the economic base theory is the proposition that the rate and direction of growth of a region or a city is determined by its function as an exporter to the rest of the region. The export industries constitute the economic base of the region, (d) factor analysis provides some objective basis for synthetically condensing measurement of a number of characteristics, more so because the characteristics are closely related and, (e) besides the above techniques, other methods like gravity model, linear programming, spatial interaction models, and industrial complex approach are used to study various aspects of urban economies. The further researchers can also apply them.

To achieve the objectives of present research, data were processed using different approaches and methodology. In order to identify spatial economic structure of industries in Delhi, the first objective analyzed the economic aspect of manufacturing sectors in relation to different economic parameters. These included growth of industries, employment, size of plot and area, type of manufacturing, investment in plant and machinery and capacity utilization of machinery. Besides these other commercial establishments, slums and non-slum residences were also considered. It has been indicated that in most of the industrial areas, maximum industrial units came up only in last decade, *i.e.* 1990-2001 as compared to previous two decades between 1970-1990. This clearly indicates the relevance of open economy and globalization, thus, elucidates impact of policies. It is also shown that in the industrial unit of small investment expenses on raw material were more, while as the investment slab increases, the expenditure on wage becomes significant. It has been observed that nearly two-thirds of all industrial units are located in six large industrial areas, namely, Anand Parbat (17.23 %), Mayapuri (15.10 %), Okhla Industrial Area (11.34 %), Narela (9.59 %), Wazirpur (7.7 %), and Kirti Nagar (6.82 %). Only one-third of the units are located in remaining 22 industrial areas. Conversely, another six areas account for less than 1 per cent of the total industrial units each. These include Tilak Nagar, Small-Scale Industries Area, Rajasthan Udyog Nagar, Small and Medium Industries Area, Okhla Industrial Estate and Mohan Co-operatives Industrial Area. In addition to it, on an average 8.8 per cent of the units employ upto 20 workers, 37 per cent units employ between 1-5 workers, and 37 per cent industrial units employ between 6 to 10 workers. Further, maximum firms of Mohan Co-operatives employ more than 50 workers. The main industrial activities are manufacture of fabricated metal products being pursued by more than 15 per cent industrial units, plastic products, parts and accessories of motor vehicles accounts for 5 per cent each. While furniture, general purpose machinery, special purpose machinery, iron, steel, weaving apparel account for more than 3 per cent each. Others like, printing, manufacture of footwears, business activities, transport activities, wholesale of household goods, retails of goods in specialized stores and chemical products engaged less than 3 per cent each. Interestingly, 92 per cent of industrial units fall in the category of tiny sectors in terms of value of plant and machinery and 5 per cent belong to Small-scale. Industries having plant and machinery over Rs. 1 crore comprise 3 per cent of the total units. The ownership pattern reveals that single proprietor owns 69 per cent industrial units and partnership accounts for 19 per cent of units. In addition, private limited firms are 10 per cent while public limited are 2 per cent of the total industrial units. Further, maximum public limited firms are located in Mohan Co-operatives and Okhla Industrial Area while maximum private limited are found in Small-Scale Industries Area. The capacity-utilization exhibits that one-fourth of the units has been utilizing less than 50 per cent of their installed capacity and 30 per cent unit work on upto 75 per cent of their capacity. In Kirti Nagar Industrial Area more than 80 per cent units use more than 75 per cent capacity. It is apparent that 60 per cent of the industrial units owned industrial plots, and others operate in rented plots. Added to it, 57 per cent of the total industrial units have been operating in plot size of less than 200 sq. m. Surprisingly, Okhla and Jhandewalan flattered factories have more than 90 per cent units in rented premises. While maximum owned plots are seen in Nangloi (95 %). In both the cases the size of plots is 100 sq. m. The plots of biggest size, *i.e.* more than 500 sq. m are owned maximum in Mohan Co-operatives Industrial Area while rented plots of the size are seen maximum in Okhla Industrial Area. In almost all industrial areas, there are establishments other than industrial enterprises, maximum are concentrated in Wazirpur, Mangolpuri and Okhla Industrial Area. Maximum slums and other residences are in Wazirpur and G.T.Karnal Road, respectively.

Another objective has been to analyse the spatio-environmental structure of industries in Delhi. The study has revealed that of the total 21627 industrial units, 70 per cent are non-polluting industries and 30 per cent are polluting units. It is shown that maximum numbers of non-polluting industrial units are seen in Kirti Nagar (95%), because 40 units here are engaged in trading. In addition, of the 30 per cent polluting units, nearly half are located in Lawrence Road, Friends Colony and Small-Scale Industries Area. The industrial areas with few polluting units are Okhla and Jhandewalan flatted factories, Udyog Nagar, Mangolpuri and Nangloi. It is suggested that of the total 5733 polluting units,

12 per cent (717) are air polluting, 16 per cent (900) are generating wastewater and 33 per cent cause hazardous waste. It is also important to note that maximum air polluting units are located in Lawrence Road, Tilak Nagar, Narela, Najafgarh Road and Moti Nagar and maximum wastewater is generated in Mohan Co-operatives, Anand Parbat and Narela areas. Further, hazardous waste is caused mainly in Jhandewalan and Okhla flatted factories, Mayapuri, Naraina and Kirti Nagar. It is shown that industrial sectors responsible for pollution include battery, casting, chemicals, electronic components, food, machining, heat treatment, metal finishing, printing, rubber, textiles, recycling, and service stations. Interestingly, maximum wastewater is caused in Lawrence Road, Rajasthan Udyog Nagar, Wazipur and Okhla Industrial Area. Wazipur, Rajasthan Udyog Nagar, Small-Scale Industries, Okhla Industrial Area, Mayapuri, Badli are main areas for hazardous waste generation. Pollution management practices revealed that 38 per cent units install effluent treatment plants, while another 36 per cent units do not know about it. Mayapuri and Tilak Nagar have maximum units with effluent treatment plants. For treating wastewater common effluent treatment plants are proposed at 15 locations. Solid waste is handled by majority (55%) manually and 7 per cent are handled mechanically. In Jhilmil and Moti Nagar 70 per cent units use mechanical way. Of the solid waste generated, 40 per cent are stored in gunny bags, 23 per cent in drums, 19 per cent in platform and 15 per cent in open land. Solid is disposed within premises by 60 per cent units, 25 per cent use roadside dumping and 15 per cent units use Municipal Yards.

Another objective was preparation of input-output transaction table, which has been successfully achieved. Input-Output Transaction Tables (IOTT) were prepared for two time periods, *i.e.* 1970-1971 and 2000-01. For these IOTT's, economy has been classified into 25 sectors, which include 5 primary sectors, 14 secondary sectors and 6 tertiary sectors. The exercise included the preparation of absorption matrix, make matrix, coefficient matrix, market share matrix, products mix matrix, Leontief inverse matrix, computation of linkages (backward and forward), multipliers and connectivity matrix. These IOTT's have become the basis for analyzing the further objectives of the study. It has been observed that in 1970-71, commodities constituted 45.73 per cent and service sector comprised of 22.73 per cent in total output. In broad sector of the economy in intermediate use, primary sector has the least share (6.13 per cent) followed by secondary sector with 34.12 per cent and tertiary sector share 58.22 per cent. It is to be added that in inter-sectoral transactions primary sector shared lowest but, surprisingly, secondary sector and tertiary sector shared same proportions. This indicates an absolute insignificant primary sector and a prominent position of tertiary sector. In manufacturing sector, highest gross value added to output ratio had been seen in chemical, plastic/rubber, metal and non-metallic industry, but leather and electric/electronic machinery had shown the lowest. The technological efficiency of plastic/rubber, chemical, non-metallic and metallic product had high efficiency, but leather, electric/electronic machinery was not considered technologically efficient. The private consumption trend reflected higher private expenditure on agricultural products, animal husbandry products, service sector, construction, food products and textile products. The final demand has been highest in food products, textile, plastic/rubber and all service sectors. The backward linkages or relative purchases showed food industry with well spread connectivity with 22 sectors, while leather, paper, plastic/rubber and miscellaneous sector have lowest backward linkage. The forward linkage reflected sales to maximum number of industries by petroleum industry, *i.e.* 24 industries, whereas lowest number of sales by leather sector to only 6 industries. The products-mix relation indicated that most of the secondary industries get 90-100 per cent inputs from the same products. The market share relations revealed most commodities have got the products from same industries, whereas electric/electronic machinery products received lowest inputs. The connectivity flow of networks of inter-sectoral relationships showed a complex web of flows among different sectors of the economy but no distinguishable pattern had emerged.

It has been elucidated that in 2000-01, intermediate demand constituted 67 per cent, while final use accounted for 32 per cent of the total output. In terms of broad sector of the economy, tertiary sector comprised 75 per cent in the intermediate use, secondary sector 12 per cent and primary sector only 1 per cent. The highest gross value added ratios were recorded for plastic/rubber industry and chemical industry, *i.e.* more than followed by food products and non-metallic industry. The highest technological efficiency was observed with miscellaneous manufacturing and textile industry. Agricultural products had highest private final consumption expenditure followed by trade, other services, food products and animal husbandry products. The highest final demand was observed for banking/insurance followed by other tertiary sectors, food products and textile products. The closest factor relating to export indicated that in manufacturing sectors, textile, paper, wood, chemical, metal, non-metal and miscellaneous manufacturing showed positive trade results. But, leather, plastic/rubber, petroleum, industrial machinery, electronic/electric machinery have shown negative trade. The structural coefficient as revealed from coefficient matrix reflected that in Delhi trade and transport sectors plays significant role in the production recipes. In miscellaneous manufacturing, metal and petroleum 40-50 per cent of the total output has been received from trade and transport services. The product mix relation reflected that plastic/rubber and industrial machinery have most significant role as they have subsidiary products for 12 other industries, besides, its main output. Thus, they are very significantly inter-dependent and complementary to many industries. The market-share relations showed that food, paper, textile, plastic/rubber and electric/electronic contribute 95-100 per cent as their main product, while the other industries like non-metallic, miscellaneous manufacturing and wood 20-30 per cent produced as other products. The forward linkage or relative sales elucidated that industries like petroleum products sold its products to almost all other sectors, while food products and textile's relative sales to other industries has been small. Textiles, wood, paper/publishing, metal, non-metallic, electric/ electronic machinery, transport equipments and miscellaneous manufacturing were strongly connected as revealed by high backward linkage coefficient. Food, textiles, construction, transport/storage, trade/hotels, banking/insurance and other services have strong forward linkage exhibited from forward linkage coefficient. Output multipliers were high in textiles, miscellaneous manufacturing, electric/electronic machinery, metal, paper/ publishing, electricity/gas/water supply and transport equipments. The connectivity matrix showed the service sector industries have been very well connected with most sectors of the economy. Transport/storage and trade/hotel have higher level of interaction followed by banking/ insurance and other services. The web of economy has shown a distinguishable pattern of inter-sectoral linkage with intensity of linkages intensifying in secondary and tertiary sectors and sparse in primary sectors.

The objective of internalizing the pollution levels (production externalities) into the input-output transaction table has been achieved at broad levels. With the accounting of pollution in the original input-output table, the structures of backward linkages have changed. Textile, paper/ publishing, wood, leather, metal products, petroleum/coal products, non-metallic products, industrial machinery, electronic/electric machinery, transport equipments, and miscellaneous manufacturing have shown stronger relationship. Forward linkage indicated that the primary sector industries' coefficient values are less than unity in both cases; in fact, the values have further reduced when pollution is added except for mining/quarrying. In manufacturing sector industries, the status of food products, plastic/rubber and chemicals have remained same with less than unity of coefficient values. The construction and electricity/water/gas supply also maintained strong connectivity in both cases. In tertiary industries, trade/hotels changed its position from more the unity of coefficient value to less than unity, while the other services sector maintained strong linkage. The multiplying coefficients, which were earlier ranging between 2.40 to 3.69 per cent, have now increased to 3.00 to 5.84 per cent. Electric/electronic machinery, miscellaneous manufacturing, industrial machinery have higher multiplying potential. Textiles, paper/publishing, chemicals, plastic/rubber and coal/petroleum products have shown low multiplying potentials because these sectors are associated with pollution generation.

The objective of identifying leading and loosing industries revealed that textiles and electric/electronic machinery were top industries in both points of time, followed by transport equipments, food products, leather, industrial machinery and miscellaneous manufacturing. Tertiary sector industries have emerged but primary sector industries have an insignificant role to play in the economy of Delhi.

The objective of finding temporal and horizontal economic structure, *i.e.* linkages, inter-dependence and multipliers of industries has been achieved through the analysis of input-output transactions tables for 1970-71 and 2000-01. The export components in total output reveals that exports have positively enhanced in thirty years, from –2.54 in 1970-71 to 15.73 in 2000-01. The role of services has increased from 27.05 per cent to 50.16 per cent, while commodities have declined from 41.41 per cent to 17.21 per cent in the total output. Inputs have not much changed in commodities and services in totality, but commodities share in services have increased. As regards the inter-industry transactions, it has been found that in the total inputs used the significance of primary sector has reduced from 4.05 per cent to 1.38 per cent, secondary sector has declined from 48.38 to 11.98 per cent and tertiary sector has increased from 47.57 per cent to 74.43 per cent. In plastic/rubber industry, trade/hotels, chemical industry, electric/electronic machinery, leather, food products industry and non-metallic products gross value added-output ratio have enhanced between 20-60 per cent during three decades. Thus, these appear as growing industries, while decrease has been observed in agriculture, animal husbandry, and metal products. The technological efficiency has enhanced grossly in every field, but maximum is in plastic/rubber, chemicals, metal products, food products, trade/hotels and other service industries, whereas least technological enhancement has been observed in primary sector, transport equipment, wood industry and paper/printing. The private consumption trends showed high expenditure on animal products, paper products, metal products, petroleum products and plastic/rubber products and electricity/gas/water. Linkage coefficient values show that primary sector has less than '1', *i.e.* weak backward linkage in both time periods. While textiles, paper/publishing, leather products, industrial machinery, electric/electronic machinery and miscellaneous manufacturing maintained high backward linkages. Non-metallic products and chemicals have shown a decline in their backward linkages. Output multipliers revealed that textiles, miscellaneous manufacturing, metal products, other services, paper /publishing, electric/electronic machinery, transport equipments and electricity/gas/water supply have high multipliers. Whereas, primary sectors, chemicals, plastic/rubber, non-metallic products have declined output multiplier from 1970-71 to 2000-01. The decline in linkages and multipliers in secondary sector industries is associated with Master Plan pollution regulations that enforced shifting of polluting industries from the city. The connectivity matrix has shown a distinguishable pattern of inter-sectoral linkages in 2000-01, which shows intensity of linkages intensifying in secondary and tertiary sectors and sparse in primary sectors. Such pattern has not clearly developed in economy in the year 1970-71.

As regards the testing of hypothesis is concerned, the first hypothesis, inter-industry linkages in Delhi have undergone substantial changes during the last three decades, has been accepted. Figures 8.6 and 8.7 explains this hypothesis in nutshell. The second hypothesis that basic component (export orientation) of production has increased, has been proved by the results that show exports have positively enhanced in total output from –2.54 in 1970-71 to 15.73 in 2000-01. The third hypothesis that economic liberalization leads to technological obsolescence of traditional firms and plants has been accepted. The input-output ratio of different industries that revealed technological efficiency has enhanced grossly in every field. The fourth hypothesis, rapid industrialization increases the output of externalities (pollution) has not been accepted in true sense. It is found that rapid industrialization is not the only reason rather un-planned, unregulated, un-accounted industrialization, besides, lack of awareness, indifferent attitude, lack of coordination among concerned people and agencies, poor implementation of policies are equally important factors in pollution generation and its handling.

In the present research work attempts were made to analyse and discuss the economic structure, changing role of different sectors in the economy, besides, also the structural changes occurring among different industries in the economy of Delhi during three decades of 1970-71 and 2000-01. The manufacturing sector has been studied considering both angles, economic as well as environmental aspect, where descriptive analysis of various issues has been covered comprising growth of manufacturing industries, their investment in plant and machinery, capacity of plant and machinery used, number of persons employed by these industrial units, size and type of ownership of plots, nature of corporate ownership, major heads of expenditures and main industrial activities. The environmental factors studied for manufacturing industries comprised number of industrial units responsible for air, wastewater, hazardous waste and nature of economic activities associated with various types of production externalities. Some light has been also thrown on the industries operating in the non-conforming areas and relocation of these industries in new industrial areas as well as the issue of *in-situ* regularization of some of the non-conforming industrial areas by making certain land use changes in the Master Plan of Delhi 2021. The structural change, inter-dependence, connectivity and linkages among different sectors have been analyzed through input-output tables for two-time periods, i.e.1970-71 and 2000-01. Using this method the structural or technological change occurring in the three decades in the production recipes of various industries have been discussed. The backward and forward linkages or, in other words, relative purchases and relative sales of various industries, the production mix relations, market share relation of industries has been highlighted for 1970-71 and 2000-01. It has been seen that the industries like plastic/rubber, chemical, non-metallic products, food products, electric/electronic machinery have shown significant role in the economy of Delhi. Another important point is that trade and transport services have been found vital in terms of relationships and linkages with various sectors of the economy.

The present research has contributed in understanding the changing structure of metropolitan economy of Delhi. It is found that the export components in total output have positively enhanced in the thirty years, from -2.54 in 1970-71 to 15.73 in 2000-01. The significance of primary sector has reduced from 4.05 per cent to 1.38 per cent. The role of secondary and services sector has increased. The gross value added in total output has declined for commodities (from 50.25 % to 20.44%) and for services it has increased from 49.75 per cent to 79.56 per cent. In manufacturing sector, highest gross value added to output ratio has been seen in chemicals, plastic/rubber, metal, non-metallic industry and food products. The technological efficiency has enhanced grossly in every field, but maximum has been seen in plastic/ rubber, chemical and metal products, food products, trade/ hotels and other service industries. Industries with high backward linkage include textiles, paper/publishing, leather products, industrial machinery, electric/electronic machinery and miscellaneous manufacturing. Output multipliers revealed that textiles, miscellaneous manufacturing, metal products, other services, paper/publishing, electric/electronic machinery, transport equipments and electricity/gas/water supply maintained high multipliers. The connectivity matrix has shown a distinguishable pattern of inter-sectoral linkages in 2000-01, which shows intensity of linkages intensifying in secondary and tertiary sectors and sparse in primary sectors. Such pattern has not been clearly developed in economy in 1970-71. Nearly two-third of all industrial units are located in six large industrial areas, namely, Anand Parbat, Mayapuri, Okhla Industrial Area, Narela, Wazirpur and Kirti Nagar. It is apparent that 92 per cent of industrial units fall in the category of tiny sectors, 5 per cent belong to small-scale and over only 3 per cent units have more than Rs. one crore.

The present research is significant in terms of the use of input-output approach for analyzing an urban economy, particularly, a metropolitan economy. The Leontief model prepared in the present work, is a nearly operational model which may be used for projections, impact analysis and advance studies regarding the metropolitan economy by adding some of the essential features to the model which could not be furnished in the present work. This work is important, as no such studies on Delhi's economy were done earlier. Another feature is that it is an inter-disciplinary research integrating concept of region and methods of applied economics. Thus, the present research has contributed to the field of urban economy, firstly, by demonstrating the use of input-output method in geographical research, secondly, by preparing nearly operational model (needs some essential features to be added) for projections and further analysis.

Further research needs to be carried on in the following directions. Once the basic input-output transaction tables have been prepared, they may be utilized for variety of further analysis and studies. Firstly, in the present research input-output transaction table has been prepared at purchasers price because of data constraints and, in fact, the

Leontief model is considered at its best, or in other words, most stable at factor cost. This model can be made functional for projections by converting it at factor-cost. Secondly, economic and ecological analysis where ecological aspects are studied within input-output model, the ecology may include a particular kind of pollution to a particular kind of ecological setting in a regional system. Although internalizing pollution in input-output transaction table was one of the objectives in the present research, but it has been studied only at broad level because detailed data were not available. The data constraints forced to curtail the scope of pollution study in the present research. Thirdly, impact analysis may be carried on, for instance, impact of particular industry as tourism, horticulture, petrochemical, plastic/ rubber or export/import on economy. In the present work impact analysis of service industry (Delhi as a center of global/national administration, educational and medical services) on economy of Delhi could not be studied in order to demarcate the limit of the research.

APPENDIX - I

Classification of Industries

(Master Plan Delhi - 2001)

Group A

1. Agarbati and similar products
2. Assembly and repair of electrical gadgets.
3. Assembly and repair of electronic goods.
4. Assembly and repair of sewing machines.
5. Batic works.
6. Block making and photo enlarging.
7. Biscuit, pappey, cakes and cookies making.
8. Button making, fixing of button and hooks.
9. Calico and textile products.
10. Cane and bamboo products.
11. Clay and modelling.
12. Coir and jute products.
13. Cardboard boxes.
14. Candles.
15. Copper and brass art wares.
16. Cordage, rope and twine making.
17. Carpentry
18. Contact lens.
19. Canvas bags and holdalls making.
20. Candles, sweets, rasmalai etc. (when not canned).
21. Cotton/silk printing (by hand).
22. Dari and carpet weaving.
23. Detergent (without bhatti).
24. Embroidery

25. Framing of pictures and mirrors.
26. Fountain pens, ball pens and felt pens.
27. Gold and silver thread, *kalabattu*.
28. Hosiery products (without dyeing and bleaching).
29. Hats, caps, turbans including embroideries.
30. Ivory carving
31. Ink making for fountain pens.
32. Jewellery items.
33. Khadi and handloom.
34. Lace products.
35. Leather footwear.
36. Leather and rexine made ups.
37. Production of following items:
    (i) Blanco cakes.
    (ii) Brushes.
    (iii) Kulfi and confectionery.
    (iv) Crayons.
    (v) Jam, jellies and fruit preserves.
    (vi) Musical instruments (including repairs).
    (vii) Lace work and like.
    (viii) Ornamental leather goods like purses, handbags.
    (ix) Small electronic components.
38. Name plate making.
39. Paper stationery items and book binding.
40. Pith hat, garlands of flowers and pith.
41. P.V.C. products (with one molding machine).
42. Paper machine.
43. Perfumery and cosmetics.
44. Photo setting.
45. Photostat and cyclostyling.
46. Preparation of vadi, papad etc.
47. Processing of condiments, spices, groundnuts and dal etc.
48. Pan masala.
49. Repair of watches and clocks.
50. Rakhee making.

51. Stone engraving.
52. Sports goods.
53. Surgical bandage rolling and cutting.
54. Stove pipe, safety pins and aluminum buttons (by hand press).
55. Silver foil making.
56. Saree fall making.
57. Tailoring.
58. Thread balls and cotton fillings.
59. Toys and dolls.
60. Umbrella assembly.
61. Velvet embroidered shoe/shawls.
62. Vermicelli and macaroni.
63. Wood carving and decorative wood wares.
64. Wool balling and lachee making.
65. Wooden/cardboard jewellery boxes (subject to no objection certificate from the department).
66. Wool knitting (with machine).
67. Zari zardozi.

Group A-1

68. Blacksmithy.
69. Village pottery industry (without *bhatti*).
70. Village oil ghani.

Group B

71. Air conditioner's parts.
72. Aluminum doors/windows/fittings/furniture.
73. Assembly and repair of cycles.
74. Atta chakki, spices (except chillies).
75. Auto parts.
76. Belts and buckles.
77. Bulbs (battery).
78. Bread and bakeries.

79. Cloth dying.
80. Cotton ginning.
81. Cotton and silk screen printing.
82. Cycle chain.
83. Cycle locks.
84. Dal mills.
85. Diamond cutting and polishing work.
86. Electric fittings (switch, plug, pin, etc.).
87. Electroplating, engraving.
88. Elastic products.
89. Electric motor and parts.
90. Electric press assembling.
91. Engineering works.
92. Foundry (small job works).
93. Ice-cream.
94. Ice boxes and body of the coolers.
95. Iron grills and door making.
96. Jute products.
97. Key rings.
98. Knife making.
99. Marbles stone items.
100. Metal letter cutting.
101. Motor winding works.
102. Oil industry.
103. Powerlooms.
104. Photographs, printing (including sign-board painting).
105. Printing press (provided not creating problem).
106. Repair of small domestic appliances and gadgets (like room heater, room coolers, hot plates etc.).
107. Rubber stamps.
108. Sanitary goods.
109. Screw and nails.
110. Screen printing.
111. Scissors making.
112. Shoe-laces.
113. Soap making.

114. Spectacles and optical frames.
115. Steel furniture.
116. Steel lockers.
117. Steel springs.
118. Steel almirahs.
119. Stamp pads.
120. Surgical instruments and equipments.
121. Table lamps and shades.
122. Tin box making.
123. Transformer covers.
124. T.V., radio, cassette recorders etc.
125. T.V./radio/ transistor cabinets.
126. Typewriter parts manufacturing and assembling.
127. Water meters repairing.
128. Water tanks.
129. Welding works.
130. Wire knitting.
131. Wooden furniture works.

Group C

132. Brass fittings.
133. Copper metal pats.
134. Dies for plastic moldings.
135. Glass work (assembly type).
136. Hinges and hardware.
137. Locks.
138. Lamps and burners.
139. Milk creams separators and mixers.
140. Polishing of plastic parts.
141. Utensils.

Group D

142. Brief cases and bags.
143. Decorative goods.

144. Denting and painting of vehicles.
145. Ice-factory.
146. Metal containers.
147. Rolling shutters.
148. Tyre retreating.

Group E

149. Aerated water and fruit beverages.
150. Agricultural equipments repairing.
151. Arms parts.
152. Aluminum-wares, moulds of cakes and pastry.
153. Attachee, suitcases, brief case.
154. Automobile service and repair workshop.
155. Battery charging.
156. Blower fans.
157. Brushes and brooms.
158. Brass work (pipes).
159. Builders hardware.
160. Button clips and hooks.
161. Buckets.
162. Cold storage and refrigeration and ice.
163. Cement products.
164. Copper-ware and utensils.
165. Cutlery.
166. Conduit pipes.
167. Drugs and medicines.
168. Door shutters and windows.
169. Electric lamp shades, fixtures.
170. Electrical appliances (room heaters, lamps etc.).
171. Fabrication (like trusses and frames).
172. Fluorescent light fitting (including neon-signs).
173. Fruit canning.
174. Grinding works.
175. Household utensils (welding, soldering, patching and polishing).
176. Household/kitchen appliances.

177. Hand tools.
178. Helmets..
179. Iron foundries.
180. Industrial fasteners.
181. Interlocking and buttoning.
182. Ink making.
183. Laboratory porcelain, dental porcelain wares.
184. Laundry, dry-cleaning and dyeing.
185. Lantern, torches and flashlights.
186. Manufacturing of trunks and metal boxes.
187. Metal polishing.
188. Milk cream machines.
189. Milk testing equipments.
190. Miscellaneous machines parts.
191. Nuts, bolts, pulleys, chains and gears.
192. Optical instruments.
193. Oil stoves, pressure lamps and accessories.
194. Printing, bookbinding, embossing and photograms etc.
195. Padlock and pressed locks.
196. Precision instruments of all kinds.
197. Plastic jigs, fixtures and metal embossing.
198. Photography goods.
199. Paper cutting machines.
200. Pressure cookers.
201. Rings and eyelets.
202. Razor blades.
203. Stationary items (including educational and school drawing instruments).
204. Steel wire products.
205. Sheet metal works.
206. Shoe making and repairing.
207. Show grindery.
208. Safety pins.
209. Stapler pins.
210. Tobacco products (cigarette and bidies).
211. Tin products.

212. Tailoring materials.
213. Truck and bus (body building).
214. Telephone parts.
215. Thermometers.
216. Upholstery springs and other springs.
217. Wax polishing.
218. Watch and clock parts.
219. Washing soap.
220. Water meters.
221. Zip fasteners.

Group F

222. Automobile part and casting.
223. Acids and chemicals small-scale.
224. Agricultural appliances and implements.
225. Aluminum products.
226. Aluminum anodizing.
227. Ancillary industries of the slaughter house.
228. Auto electroplated accessories.
229. Automobile leaf springs.
230. Battery boxes.
231. Batteries and accessories.
232. Cattle feed.
233. Centrifugal pumps and small turbines.
234. Concrete and mosaic products.
235. Collapsible gates, railing and grills.
236. Cotton ginning (large scale).
237. Duree and carpets (large scale).
238. Dyeing, bleaching, finishing, processing cloth (including mercerizing, calendaring, glazing etc.)
239. Electrical motors, transformers and generators.
240. Electroplating (large scale).
241. Enamel ware.
242. Expanded metals.
243. Fire fighting equipments.

244. Fluorescence lights.
245. Flourmills.
246. Foot wears.
247. Foam piles.
248. Fuel gases (including by-products).
249. Galvanized buckets.
250. Glass products.
251. Grease, oil etc.
252. C.I., malleable pipe fittings.
253. Hand Press.
254. Reinforced cement concrete pipes (small scale).
255. Hydraulic press.
256. Iron foundries.
257. Iron pipes.
258. Iron hammers.
259. Lathe machines.
260. Leather upholstery and other leather goods.
261. Nickel polishing.
262. Paints and varnishes.
263. Plastic products.
264. Plastic dye.
265. Polish work.
266. Paper products.
267. Processing of clay and other earths.
268. P.V.C. compounds.
269. Polythene gas.
270. Refrigerators and air-conditioners.
271. Rail coupling parts.
272. Rubber products.
273. Electric Fans.
274. Saw mills and wood work.
275. Small machine and machine tools.
276. Sprayers (hand and foot).
277. Structural steel fabrications.
278. Sheet bending press.
279. Speedometers.

280. Steel re-rolling mills (small scale).
281. Steel casting.
282. Steel wire drawings.
283. Stone crusher parts.
284. Scissors making.
285. Spice factory.
286. Surgical goods.
287. Tarpaulin and tent cloth.
288. Textiles mills (medium scale).
289. Toilet soap.
290. Tractor parts.
291. Typewriters.
292. Umbrella ribs.
293. Utensils.
294. Vacuum flasks.
295. Veneer of plywood.
296. Water proof textile products.
297. Wire drawing, coating and electric cables.
298. Wire netting.
299. Wooden structural goods.
300. Writing and making ink.
301. X-ray machines.
302. Zinc polishing.

Group G

1. Activated carbon.
2. Barley malt and extract.
3. Bar candy and guava fruit bar.
4. Cattle feed.
5. Citrus fruit concentrate.
6. Confectionery.
7. Dal milling.
8. Dehydrated vegetables.
9. Eucalyptus oil.
10. Flour milling.

11. Fuel briquettes.
12. Grading, waxing and polishing of malta.
13. Grape vinegar and juice.
14. Groundnut oil.
15. Guar split.
16. Gur and *khandsari*.
17. Handmade paper.
18. Ice-cream.
19. Lactic and oxalic acids.
20. Milling pulses.
21. Mustard oil and powder.
22. Pasteurized milk and its products.
23. Pickles, chutneys and murabba.
24. Poultry feed.
25. Processed fruit and vegetables products.
26. Pyrolysed glucose and starch.
27. Rapeseed oil.
28. Red chilies oleoresin.
29. Rice milling.
30. Sesame oil.
31. Spice grinding.
32. Sugarcane wax.
33. Straw boards.
34. Surgical bandage.
35. Tomato ketchup and vegetable sauce.
36. Weaning food.
37. The industrial units given in serial numbers 1 to 70 shall also be permitted.

Group G-1

1. Biscuit, pappey, cakes and cookies making.
2. Candles, sweets, rasmalai etc.
3. Agarbati and similar products.
4. Assembly and repair of electrical gadgets.
5. Assembly and repair of electronic goods.

6. Batic works.
7. Embroidery.
8. Gold and silver thread, *kalabattu*.
9. Hats, caps, turbans including embroideries.
10. Product of following items:
    (i) Blanco cakes.
    (ii) Brushes.
    (iii) Crayons.
    (iv) Kulfi and confectionery.
    (v) Jam, jellies and fruit preserves.
    (vi) Musical instruments (including repairs).
    (vii) Lace work and like.
    (viii) Ornamental leather goods like purses, handbags.
    (ix) Small electronic components.
11. Name plate making.
12. Pith hat, garlands of flowers and pith.
13. Perfumery and cosmetics.
14. Photo setting.
15. Photostat and cyclostyling.
16. Preparation of vadi, papad etc.
17. Processing of condiments, spices, groundnuts and dal etc.
18. Pan masala.
19. Repair of watches and clocks.
20. Rakhee making.
21. Saree fall making.
22. Tailoring.
23. Vermicelli and macaroni.
24. Wool balling and lachee making.
25. Wool knitting.
26. Zari zardozi.
27. Atta chakki, spices, and dal grinding.
28. Bread and bakeries.
29. Dal mills.
30. Electronic goods manufacturing.
31. Ice-cream.
32. Screen printing

33. Water meter repairing.
34. Milk cream separators.
35. Decorator goods.
36. Ice-factory.
37. Aerated water and fruit beverages.
38. Confectionery candies and sweets.
39. Cold storage and refrigeration.
40. Electric lamp shades, fixtures.
41. Fruit canning.
42. Grinding works.
43. Laundry, dry-cleaning and dyeing.
44. Milk cream machines.
45. Milk testing equipments.
46. Printing bookbinding, embossing and photograms etc.
47. Tobacco products (cigarette and bidies).
48. Cattle feed.
49. Flourmill.
50. Paper products.
51. Polythene bags.
52. Spice factory.
53. Barley malt and extract.
54. Beer candy and guava fruit bar.
55. Citrus fruit concentrate.
56. Dehydrated vegetables.
57. Vinegar and juice.
58. Groundnut oil.
59. Guar split.
60. Gur and *khandsari*.
61. Lactic and oxalic acids.
62. Pasteurized milk and it products.
63. Pickles, chutneys and murabba.
64. Poultry feed.
65. Processed fruit and vegetables products.
66. Tomato ketchup and vegetable sauce.
67. Containers lids.
68. Juicer (only assembling).
69. Readymade garments.
70. Labels/stickers.

Group H

Industries prohibited within Union Territory of Delhi

(a) Hazardous/Noxious Industrial Units

Cellulosic Products	*Characteristics*
1. Carbon black and carbon black of all kind	Fire hazards.
2. Crude oil refining, processing and cracking, petroleum jellies, naphtha cracking including gas packing etc.	Inflammable fumes and noise.
3. Fuel oils, illuminating oils and other oil.	Fire hazards.
4. Industrial alcohol.	Unpleasant smell.
5. Matches.	Fire hazard.
6. Newsprint.	Unpleasant smell, contaminated waste water, fire hazard.
7. Paints, enamels, colours, varnish. (other than litho varnish) varnish. removers, turpentine and turpentine substitutes.	Fire hazard.
8. Petroleum-coke, graphite production.	Fire hazard.
9. Printing ink.	Fire hazard.
10. Rayon fiber, waste products, mayophane paper etc. Cellulose nitrate, celluloid articles, scraps and solution.	Fire hazard.
Cement and Refractories	
1. Enameling vitreous.	Smoke.
2. Glass furnaces (more than 3 ton capacity).	Fire hazard.
3. Heavy metal forging (using steam and power hammer).	Noise, smoke vibration.
4. Mechanical stone crushing.	Dust, slurry, noise.
5. Portland cement.	Dust.
6. Refractories.	Smoke.
Explosive and Ammunition	
1. Explosives or their ingredients such as fire-works, gunpowder, gun cotton etc.	Fire hazard.
2. Industrial gelatins nitro glycerin and fulminate.	Fire hazard.
Fertilizers	
1. Nitrogenous and phosphate fertilizers, except mixing of fertilizers for compounding (large scale).	Fire, noise, noxious gases and dust.

Fruits

1.	Abattoirs	Obnoxious smell-waste water
2.	Alcohol distillery, braveries and potable spirits.	Noise, fire hazard, unpleasant smell due to oxygen.
3.	Sewer refining.	Unpleasant smell, fire hazard.
4.	Vegetable oil.	Noise, unpleasant smell.

Inorganic Chemical Industries

1.	Acid-sulphuric acid, nitric acid, acetic boric acid, rochloric acid, phosphoric acid, battery acid, bengeic acid, carbolic acid, chloro-suluphic acid etc.	Fire hazard, offensive fumes and smoke.
2.	Alkalies — caustic soda, caustics potash, soda-ash etc.	Fire hazard corrosive.
3.	Carbon-disulphide, ultramarine blue, chlorine-fumes.	Fire hazard, dust and hydrogen etc.
4.	Mineral salts (which involves use of acids).	Fire hazard, fumes and smoke.

Leather and other Animal Products

1.	Animal and fish oils.	Fire hazard.
2.	Bone-grist, bone-meal, bone powder or storages of bones in open and Glandular extraction.	Obnoxious smell.
3.	Glue and gelatins from bones and flesh	Obnoxious.
4.	Leather tanning.	Obnoxious smell.

Metallurgical Industries

1.	Blast furnaces oxides of mixtures.	Noise dust smoke and fire hazard.
2.	Reacting of ore sulphide, oxides of mixtures.	Noise dust smoke and fire hazard.
3.	Sintering, smelting.	Noise dust smoke and fire hazard.

Organic Chemical Industries

1.	Acetylides, phridines iodofarm, chloroform, *e*-nepthol etc.	Fire hazard.
2.	Compressed permanent liquefied and dissolved industrial passes.	Fire hazard.
3.	Dyes and dye-stuff intermediates.	Acidic liquid effluent.
4.	Insecticides, pesticides, fungicides and fire hazard.	Unpleasant smell, dusty.
5.	Organic solvent, chlorinated minerals, methanol aldehydes, methylated spirits.	Fire hazard, unpleasant smell.

6.	Phenols and related industries based on coalta distillation.	Fire hazard.
7.	Polyethylene, P.V.C., resin, nylon.	Fire hazard.
8.	Synthetic detergents.	
9.	Synthetic rubber.	Liquid effluent with unpleasant smell.

Paper and Paper Products

Manufacturing of paper pulp, paper board and straw boards (large scale).

Poisons

•	Ammonium sulpho ajanide, arsenic and its compounds, barium carbonate, barium cyanide, barium, ethyl sulphate, barium acetate cinnabar, copper sulphocyanide, Ferro cyanide, hydro-cyanmide, hydro-cyanic acid, potassium bioccelate, potassium-cyanide, prusslate of potash, pynogallic acid Silver cyanide.	Contamination of food if stored on same floor or on floors or on floors above, fire hazard.

Radioactive Elements

•	Thorium, radium and similar isotopes and recovery of rare-earth.	Radiation hazard.

Rubber Industries

•	Reclamation of rubber and production of tyres, rubber solutions containing mineral neptha, rubber waste.	Unpleasant smell, dust, fire.

Wood and Wood Products

•	Distillation of wood, seasoning and curing gases readily ignitable.	Fire hazard, obnoxious.

Miscellaneous

•	Calcium carbide, phosphorous, aluminum dust paste and powderly, copper, zinc etc. (electro thermal industries).	Fire hazard

(b) Heavy and Large Industries

1. Agricultural implements (large-scale).
2. Air and gas compressor.
3. Aircraft building.
4. Automobiles and coach building.
5. Bicycles (large scale).

6. Conveyors and conveying equipments.
7. Cotton textile (large scale).
8. Cranes and hoists.
9. Diesel engines.
10. Earth moving machinery.
11. Electrical steel sheets and stampings.
12. Electric wires and cables (large-scale).
13. Foundries (heavy).
14. Central industrial machinery (such as hydraulic equipments, drilling equipments boilers etc.)
15. Heavy iron and steel forcing
16. Reinforced cement concrete pipes (large-scale)
17. Industrial trucks, trailers, stakers etc.
18. Lifts
19. Locomotives and wagons.
20. Motor cycles and scooters.
21. Optical glass.
22. Other primary metal industries (*e.g.* Cold rolled sheet, alloy sheet etc.)
23. Power driven pump and pumping equipments.
24. Sewing machines (large scale).
25. Sluice gates and gearings.
26. Special industrial machinery.
27. Steam engines.
28. Steel pipes and tubes.
29. Steel chains.
30. Steel works, rolling and re-rolling mills.
31. Structural steel fabrication (large-scale).
32. Sugar.
33. Telephone equipments.
34. Tractors and agricultural machinery (power drive).
35. Under frames and chassis.
36. Water turbines.
37. Wire ropes.
38. Woollen textiles (large-scale).

APPENDIX - II

Sector Specification for Input-Output Table*

IOTT Sector No.	*Name*
1.	Food Crops
2.	Cash Crops
3.	Plantation Crops
4.	Other Crops
5.	Animal Husbandry
6.	Forestry and Logging
7.	Fishing
8.	Coal and Lignite
9.	Crude Petroleum and Natural gas
10.	Iron Ore
11.	Other Minerals
12.	Sugar
13.	Food Products excluding Sugar
14.	Beverages
15.	Tobacco Products
16.	Cotton Textiles
17.	Wool, Silk and Synthetic Fiber Textiles
18.	Jute, Hemp Textiles
19.	Textile Products including Wearing Apparel
20.	Wood and Wood Products except Furniture

* Aggregated sectors specification used by Central Statistical Organization.

IOTT Sector No.	Name
21.	Furniture and Fixtures
22.	Paper and Paper Products
23.	Printing, Publishing and Allied Activities
24.	Leather and Leather Products
25.	Plastic and Rubber Products
26.	Petroleum Products
27.	Coal Tar Products
28.	Inorganic Heavy Products
29.	Organic Heavy Chemicals
30.	Fertilizers
31.	Paints, Varnishes and Lacquers
32.	Pesticides, Drugs and other Chemicals
33.	Cement
34.	Non-metallic Mineral Products
35.	Iron and Steel Industries and Foundries
36.	Other Basic Metal Industry
37.	Metal Products except Machinery and Transport Equipment
38.	Agricultural Machinery
39.	Industrial Machinery for Food and Textiles
40.	Other Machinery
41.	Electrical, Electronic Machinery and Appliances
42.	Railway Transport Equipment
43.	Other Transport Equipment
44.	Miscellaneous Manufacturing Industries
45.	Construction
46.	Electricity
47.	Gas and Water Supply
48.	Railway Transport Services
49.	Other Transport Services
50.	Storage and Warehousing
51.	Communication
52.	Trade
53.	Hotels and Restaurants

IOTT Sector No.	*Name*
54.	Banking
55.	Insurance
56.	Ownership of Dwellings
57.	Education Research
58.	Medical and Health
59.	Other Services
60.	Public Administration and Defence

APPENDIX - III

Aggregated Sector Classification for Input-Output Transactions*

Sector Code	*Description of Aggregated Sector*	*Sectors in Appendix II*
1.	Agriculture	1, 2, 3, 4
2.	Animal Husbandry	5
3.	Forestry and Logging	6
4.	Fishing	7
5.	Mining and Quarrying	8, 9, 10, 11
6.	Food Products, Beverages and Tobacco Products	12, 13, 14, 15
7.	Textiles	16, 17, 18, 19
8.	Wood, Wood Products and Furniture	20, 21
9.	Paper, Paper Products, Printing/ Publishing	22, 23
10.	Leather and Leather Products	24
11.	Plastic and Rubber Products	25
12.	Petroleum and Coal Products	26, 27
13.	Chemicals	28, 29, 30, 31, 32
14.	Non-metallic Products	33, 34
15.	Metal Products	35, 36, 37
16.	Industrial Machinery	38, 39, 40

* These 25 Aggregated Sectors are used for input-output transaction table in the present study.

Sector Code	*Description of Aggregated Sector*	*Sectors in Appendix II*
17.	Electric/Electronic Machinery	41
18.	Rail and other Transport Equipment	42, 43
19.	Miscellaneous Manufacturing	44
20.	Construction	45
21.	Electricity/Gas/Water Supply	46, 47
22.	Rail and other Transport Services/Storage	48, 49, 50, 51
23.	Trade/Hotels	52, 53
24.	Banking/ Insurance	54, 55
25.	Other services (Education, Medical, Administration, Defence, etc.)	56, 57, 58, 59, 60

Appendix - IVA : Input- Output Transactions Matrix (Commodity × Industry), 1970-71, Absorption Matrix (Value in Rs.000)

Sector Code	Industry / Commodity	1	2	3	4	5	6	7	8	9	10	11	12	13
1.	Agriculture	146692	104829	167	0	0	150698	0	0	0	0	0	0	0
2.	Animal Husbandry	91047	65064	556	0	0	64999	0	0	0	0	0	0	0
3.	Forestry and Logging	50	36	0	0	0	373	0	15476	19	169	0	0	11027
4.	Fishing	0	0	0	700	0	0	0	0	0	0	41	0	0
5.	Mining/Quarrying	15	11	0	0	4000	1487	69012	161	1142	4484	0	66	2916
6.	Food Prod., Beverages and Tobacoo Prod.	56	40	97	0	0	67297	0	0	0	0	10007	0	646
7.	Textiles	337	241	14	0	0	1429	1378665	691	3977	338	0	16638	24238
8.	Wood,Wood Prod. and Furniture	114	82	0	0	0	11328	17624	38970	17170	8461	92920	1264	1776
9.	Paper,Paper Prod., Printing/ Publishing	61	43	1	0	0	3780	16119	668	248199	254	39700	763	25682
10.	Leather Products	2	2	0	0	0	0	18833	0	0	3384	101038	57	19413
11.	Plastic/Rubber Products	0	0	0	0	0	211377	11946	47969	3874	47971	1170000	600	48216
12.	Coal/Petroleum Prod.	10018	7159	1	0	0	1360	16601	1013	2367	6345	76786	310	1586
13.	Chemicals	38423	27458	5	0	0	19129	142481	6011	16894	19294	9884	95	27905
14.	Non-metallic Prod.	2	2	0	0	0	98449	0	507	0	0	11671	19	9526
15.	Metal Products	8	6	0	0	0	565	1512	52025	1043	0	13969	120	33974
16.	Industrial Machinery	2714	1939	0	0	4500	0	3605	530	866	85	23485	123	190
17.	Electric/Electronic Machinery	56	40	0	0	2000	2252	11292	484	1544	169	163	474	722
18.	Rail and Other Transport Equipment	37	26	0	0	0	1929	0	0	0	0	286	0	0
19.	Miscellaneous Manufacturing	9	7	0	0	0	2164	1374	69	192	85	0	35	152
20.	Construction	10952	7827	5	0	0	276	183	173	152	46	82	1466	61
21.	Electricity/Gas/Water Supply	8620	6160	0	0	0	317	245	1592	1077	114	1123	1001	197
22.	Rail and Other Transport / Storage Services	7155	5113	14	0	3496	38818	175035	26842	80370	18580	6346	55122	62381
23.	Trade/Hotels	13700	9790	38	0	0	5055	202526	11100	11851	12078	66175	26015	25294
24.	Banking/Insurance	6935	4956	0	0	0	9831	32353	10932	9214	4802	95273	40180	10127
25.	Other Services(Edu., Med., Admin., Defence, etc.)	152	109	1	0	0	170	33321	61	212472	0	80890	0	0
	Total Input	337155	240939	900	700	13997	693082	2132727	215274	612422	126659	1799839	144349	306029
	Total Output	544655	388939	1400	1000	20998	939458	2732275	302010	785550	155791	2674816	200404	459241
	Gross Value Added	207500	148000	500	300	7000	246376	599548	86736	173128	29132	874977	56055	153212

Appendix- IVA : (Contd..)

Sector Code	Industry Commodity	14	15	16	17	18	19	20	21	22	23	24	25
1.	Agriculture	0	0	0	0	0	0	0	0	16580	120116	0	1444
2.	Animal Husbandry	0	0	0	0	0	0	0	0	0	163335	0	880
3.	Forestry and Logging	19	236	10	1	190	8	68	17	0	0	0	1971
4.	Fishing	0	0	0	0	0	0	0	0	0	84681	0	0
5.	Mining/Quarrying	6720	5053	330	29	2122	41183	74359	22441	0	29874	0	4032
6.	Food Prod., Beverages and Tobaco Prod.	0	0	0	0	0	0	0	0	2880	111717	0	2734
7.	Textiles	1722	1530	506	233	3577	505	4925	0	5960	207	29	38379
8.	Wood,Wood Prod. and Furniture	3407	2939	1216	152	7543	1160	468	0	3387	79569	2177	976
9.	Paper, Paper Prod., Printing/ Publishing	1322	1641	568	41	2950	1218	1278	2766	6845	27023	9116	103112
10.	Leather Products	0	0	0	0	0	7675	0	0	0	0	0	0
11.	Plastic/Rubber Products	1234	75651	393	2457	29719	2354	0	0	20942	270000	0	263796
12.	Coal/Petroleum Prod.	2436	6538	532	12	4684	168	1970	21550	28323	1346	784	28969
13.	Chemicals	3639	5237	1889	592	34308	2504	0	333	188	0	0	102138
14.	Non-metallic Prod.	47162	46181	272	40	0	1683	0	33	0	7543	0	55400
15.	Metal Products	63879	122931	1053	3528	74527	11329	6592	4298	2887	7440	0	57433
16.	Industrial Machinery	1960	306	15646	33	0	0	468	10471	248	59	0	107627
17.	Electric/Electronic Machinery	251	657	13643	10682	455	22034	54007	36386	1156	503	0	51785
18.	Rail and Other Transport Equipment	0	0	0	0	109546	0	1024	68765	80913	51331	37086	146737
19.	Miscellaneous Manufacturing	1478	59	31	4	141	21295	117	2424	6476	2796	697	138737
20	Construction	1647	29	38	3	154	92	23463	12241	158454	13682	342283	169217
21.	Electricity/Gas/Water Supply	496	685	105	10	339	48	212740	22448	1829	13667	6910	151290
22.	Rail and Other Transport/ Storage Services	20220	6809	8777	2475	12196	6911	69161	146937	184412	16776	29294	185984
23.	Trade/Hotels	195	49518	12756	3965	25920	26692	283592	87577	491341	546840	2090	259076
24.	Banking/Insurance	9816	18783	2494	290	5524	0	3316	0	107771	179933	49917	117472
25.	Other Services(Edu., Med., Admin., Defence, etc.)	0	0	0	376	0	0	2653	1774	8107	253463	30416	179411
	Total Input	167603	344783	60260	24925	313894	146860	740200	440461	1128700	1981900	510800	2168600
	Total Output	246475	508997	80343	30568	410331	188281	1042700	540161	1821700	2523400	824400	3978600
	Gross Value Added	78872	164214	20083	5643	96437	41421	302500	99700	693000	541500	313600	1810000

Appendix- IVA : (Contd..)

Sector Code Industry Commodity	Total Input	PFCE	GFCE	GFCF	Others	Total Final Use	Total Output
1. Agriculture	540526	1814837	26931	0	-1836794	4974	545500
2. Animal Husbandry	385881	308559	423	782	-306645	3119	389000
3. Forestry and Logging	29670	6208	0	0	-34478	-28270	1400
4. Fishing	85422	22940	47	0	-22609	378	85800
5. Mining/Quarrying	269435	1658	1060	0	-3653	-935	268500
6. Food Prod., Beverages and Tobaco Prod.	195473	349841	4894	0	388407	743143	938616
7. Textiles	1484142	267005	10658	0	909404	1187066	2671208
8. Wood, Wood Prod., and Furniture	292706	7170	2415	372	-3391	6566	299272
9. Paper, Paper Prod., Printing/Publishing	493150	5814	13489	0	273097	292400	785550
10. Leather Products	150405	18869	1120	0	-14604	5386	155791
11. Plastic/Rubber Products	2208499	6856	138	975	434566	442535	2651034
12. Coal/Petroleum Prod.	220861	17558	18484	0	-56499	-20457	200404
13. Chemicals	458409	33334	403	0	-32921	816	459225
14. Non-metallic Prod.	278490	4511	0	59	-56493	-51923	226567
15. Metal Products	459120	7582	2107	1757	21153	32598	491718
16. Industrial Machinery	174856	5101	5123	14801	-34140	-9115	165741
17. Electric/Electronic Machinery	210754	15240	15636	10617	-12987	28505	239259
18. Rail and Other Transport Equipment	497681	18728	3210	8261	-117549	-87350	410331
19. Miscellaneous Manufacturing	178340	24146	112196	744	-173251	-36164	142176
20. Construction	742527	145000	134709	61853	-288889	52673	795200
21. Electricity/Gas/Water Supply	431013	16349	40068	0	-155329	-98913	332100
22. Rail and Other Transport /Storage Services	1169224	206434	89992	1346	354704	652476	1821700
23. Trade/Hotels	2173182	272485	59012	5334	13387	350218	2523400
24. Banking/Insurance	719920	44189	11245	0	49046	104480	824400
25. Other Services(Edu., Med., Admin., Defence, etc.)	803376	352890	1134821	0	1687513	3175224	3978600
Total Input	14653059	3973305	1688181	106900	981047	6749433	21402492
Total Output	21402492						
Gross Value Added	6749433						

Source : Endeavour present research (see chapter 3 and chapter 6).

Appendix- IV B : Input-Output Transactions Matrix (Commodity×Industry) , 2000-01. Absorption Matrix

(Value in Rs. 000)

Sector Code	Industry / Commodity	1	2	3	4	5	6	7	8	9	10	11	12	13
1.	Agriculture	829501	1468244	6	130	0	309735	0	0	0	0	0	0	2984
2.	Animal Husbandry	962724	30957	0	0	0	915216	0	0	0	0	0	0	0
3.	Forestry and Logging	6	0	18	0	0	0	13	3018	0	0	16155	0	0
4.	Fishing	0	0	0	41593	0	0	0	0	0	0	0	0	0
5.	Mining/Quarrying	14	0	0	0	55	25	103	9	0	0	7	41	113
6.	Food Prod.Beverages and Tobaco Prod.	6281	1091536	0	11979	0	17507147	0	0	0	0	0	0	251383
7.	Textiles	28955	324039	319	73046	0	446342	29829659	39574	659231	470721	192842	10249	982013
8.	Wood,Wood Prod., and Furniture	275	0	1	716	150	31419	26712	201086	16646	11973	13590	778	68086
9.	Paper, Paper Prod., Printing/ Publishing	919	0	53	33	86	20383	17174	1746	2057981	7881	8823	470	44931
10.	Leather Products	90	0	0	0	0	345	1240243	6749	3494	2640655	102	35	353
11.	Plastic/Rubber Products	261	0	48	0	160	16268	77406	29	63822	44941	1174887	370	34371
12.	Coal/Petroleum Prod.	160	0	5	13	6	144	122	112	213	23	125	191	115
13.	Chemicals	49089	609	0	161	381	8555	1730	2043	58956	4783	6068	59	420293
14.	Non-metallic Prod.	0	0	0	1	96	222	1723	987	2249	94	35	12	227
15.	Metal Products	137	566	11	494	382	1436	11265	4752	15404	744	1583	74	2529
16.	Industrial Machinery	43810	2067	61	10	14337	2216	8337	3187	19101	799	474	76	27775
17.	Electric/Electronic Machinery	1174	0	46	23	17	3008	27431	2992	35812	1498	886	292	3620
18.	Rail and Other Transport Equipment	7803	0	299	21275	2188	0	0	281	0	0	0	0	0
19.	Miscellaneous Manufacturing	571	0	113	11	1211	316	1363	0	1781	77	80	22	104
20.	Construction	579141	43484	9159	0	13055	8223	7300	1523	4316	1878	3444	903	1845
21.	Electricity/Gas/Water Supply	21081	0	3	50	774	9441	9775	14002	30603	4648	19465	617	5920
22.	Rail and Other Transport / Storage Services	1347802	352459	2323	16745	10820	1154942	6101836	236123	2283198	759535	1276457	533957	1872604
23.	Trade/Hotels	2396208	3275730	2326	47746	20297	1246230	17242446	845373	3177522	493713	2675772	465161	4361200
24.	Banking/Insurance	107812	83035	302	2038	4285	292500	688292	96168	261761	196314	348097	509901	304006
25.	Other Services (Edu., Med., Admin., Defence, etc)	200641	0	12007	98850	14142	1892	926851	400535	1418	0	1940	0	0
	Total Input	6584454	6672725	27099	314913	82442	21976005	56219780	1860290	8693508	4640277	5740830	1523208	8384472
	Total Output	10294054	10610625	44799	478913	136742	34397415	71459074	2658666	11656692	6489151	12178107	2206575	17456116
	Gross Value Added	4809600	3937900	17700	204000	14300	12421410	2639293	1198376	2963184	1048873	7387276	2083367	9671644

Appendix- IVB : (Contd.)

Sector Code	Industry Commodity	14	15	16	17	18	19	20	21	22	23	24	25
1.	Agriculture	0	0	0	0	0	0	1330123	83	1296088	1902705	0	1100520
2.	Animal Husbandry	0	0	0	0	0	0	200641	51365	0	3596136	0	1983025
3	Forestry and Logging	0	0	0	0	0	0	27289	0	42	7821	0	0
4.	Fishing	0	0	0	0	0	0	0	1	0	301074	0	0
5.	Mining/Quarrying	126	300	12	5	0	0	25756	35566	3556	5556	0	444
6.	Food Prod., Beverages and Tobaco Prod.	0	0	0	0	0	0	0	0	69196	8911372	0	29717
7.	Textiles	8584	359393	36790	416591	64222	183565	841997	2722	993526	3202638	212437	1877730
8.	Wood,Wood Prod., and Furniture	696	25693	2418	34473	14244	12883	739365	655	8661	193041	33152	240715
9.	Paper, Paper Prod., Printing/ Publishing	653	12009	1824	22082	1040	8347	24060	11641	216388	606026	693189	744189
10.	Leather Products	2307	2814	745	3704	7958	279	0	0	18688	0	800003	1
11.	Plastic/Rubber Products	403	25927	2091	68270	10064	54236	6366	478	967024	88840	21079	7304
12.	Coal/Petroleum Prod.	55	23	14	222	333	44	345	334	4445	345	5555	333
13.	Chemicals	266	11239	975	19372	7304	2647	115828	1837	7284	5479	0	1372435
14.	Non-metallic Prod.	21082	11763	544	13900	1338	746	1899953	163	7043	2628	2	10646
15.	Metal Products	96	2759432	43182	254237	30221	48585	1627108	803	29609	133478	33498	95945
16.	Industrial Machinery	1753	17296	2265741	42829	17930	1523	25003	98193	343062	269063	233692	443794
17.	Electric/Electronic Machinery	235	7996	119939	14526655	189584	51423	3176647	329646	1382298	47325	228829	2224194
18.	Rail and Other Transport Equipment	0	0	0	0	2730751	0	63100	12471	4379514	14594	713082	119048
19.	Miscellaneous Manufacturing	12	1433	379	1901	506	662755	128837	37917	1018623	512590	1104157	9701027
20.	Construction	2225	2333	3008	4899	3553	2334	4730682	604345	11013226	14797839	15814241	96042508
21.	Electricity/Gas/Water Supply	670	55642	8301	13695	7792	1228	131809	191850	435966	231446	274412	247230
22.	Rail and Other Transport / Storage Services	1077318	4616130	692893	3545697	280701	175695	16880660	1713530	8314413	15134268	12371528	17031348
23.	Trade/Hotel	606137	11818176	1007040	5680250	2783076	2037940	61631118	3157927	26060869	16910255	16627553	65315328
24.	Banking/Insurance	13261	626233	196923	415258	127140	0	2952251	232691	5711124	10430327	33417894	10266166
25.	Other Services (Edu., Med., Admin., Defence, etc.)	0	0	0	539195	0	0	14791178	1334986	48504377	131169601	110459700	163358511
	Total Input	1735879	20353831	4382817	25603234	6277757	3244230	111350116	7819204	110785023	208474444	193044005	372212157
	Total Output	2836812	25661637	6151690	33765508	8427445	4061331	156745616	9945303	169711323	317897445	325132605	523067058
	Gross Value Added	2650933	3507806	1768874	8162274	2149689	1167100	48395500	1426100	59926300	111223000	135838600	150854900

Appendix- IVB : (Contd.)

Sector Code	*Industry Commodity*	*Total Input*	*PFCE*	*GFCE*	*GFCF*	*Others*	*Total Final Use*	*Total Output*
1.	Agriculture	8240118	56359390	228838	0	-54957477	1630751	987086
2.	Animal Husbandry	7740065	21114027	861421	37962	-19265627	2747783	10487847
3.	Forestry and Logging	54362	2871788	855	0	-2882205	-9562	44799
4.	Fishing	342667	3022314	3095	0	-2895499	129910	472577
5.	Mining/Quarrying	71688	83035	26423	0	-44404	65054	136742
6.	Food Prod., Beverages and Tobaco Prod.	27878611	19705999	81684	0	-14671492	5116191	32994802
7.	Textiles	41257185	12936863	10656	826	3457962	16406307	57663492
8.	Wood, Wood Prod.and Furniture	1677427	480000	75395	14309	2097393	2667096	4344524
9.	Paper, Paper Prod., Printing/Publishing	4501928	1809571	667843	0	3897354	6374768	10876695
10.	Leather Products	4728565	958528	1	0	-1306171	-347643	4380922
11.	Plastic/Rubber Products	2664646	915697	545394	92205	-1152901	400395	3065041
12.	Coal/Petroleum Prod.	13277	2582167	796759	0	-1340334	2038592	2051869
13.	Chemicals	2097392	2619914	1966758	0	7207642	11794314	13891706
14.	Non-metallic Prod.	1975455	442716	21	694	568771	1012202	2987656
15.	Metal Products	5095571	1784580	32002	193475	10425961	12436018	17531589
16.	Industrial Machinery	3882130	201082	1313209	692623	-2492445	-285530	3596599
17.	Electric/Eiectronic Machinery	22361568	967929	287411	622616	-5500481	-3622524	18739044
18.	Rail and Other Transport Equipment	8064405	1792329	591540	700113	-2924030	159952	8224357
19.	Miscellaneous Manufacturing	13175784	887412	3055390	188006	6597373	10728180	23903964
20.	Construction	143695463	15432876	4153717	2574874	-7255090	14906377	158601840
21.	Electricity/Gas/Water Supply	1716420	1956618	1395070	0	5381520	8733207	10449627
22.	Rail and Other Transport /Storage Services	97782981	16898725	2559621	139613	52330384	71928343	169711323
23.	Trade/Hotels	249885391	27191815	1705202	222685	41097141	70216843	320102234
24.	Banking/Insurance	67283781	2500488	2705485	0	252642852	257848824	325132605
25.	Other Services (Edu., Med., Admin., Defence. etc)	471815824	23437666	50559011	0	8395476	82392153	554207977
Total Input		1188002704	218953528	73622800	5480000	27741672	575468000	1763470704
Total Output		1763470704						
Gross Value Added		575468000						

Source : Endeavour present research (refer chapter 3 and chapter 7).

APPENDIX- V A : Backward Linkages (commodity purchased as inputs by industries in per cent): 1970- 71

Sector Code	Industry / Commodity	1	2	3	4	5	6	7	8	9	10	11	12	13
1.	Agriculture	43.51	41.45	18.52	0.00	0.00	21.74	0.00	0.00	0.00	0.00	0.00	0.00	0.00
2.	Animal Husbandry	27.00	25.23	61.75	0.00	0.00	9.38	0.00	0.00	0.00	0.00	0.00	0.00	0.00
3.	Forestry and Logging	0.01	0.03	0.00	0.00	0.00	0.05	0.00	7.19	0.00	0.13	0.00	0.00	3.60
4.	Fishing	0.00	0.00	0.02	100.05	0.00	0.00	0.00	0.00	0.00	0.00	0.00	0.00	0.00
5.	Mining/Quarrying	0.00	0.00	0.00	0.00	28.58	0.21	3.24	0.07	0.19	3.54	0.00	0.05	0.95
6.	Food Prod., Beverages and Tobacco Products	0.02	0.34	10.76	-0.05	0.00	9.71	0.00	0.00	0.00	0.00	0.56	0.00	0.21
7.	Textiles	0.10	0.16	1.55	0.04	0.00	0.21	64.64	0.32	0.65	0.27	0.00	11.53	7.92
8.	Wood, Wood Prods., and Furniture	0.03	0.06	0.03	0.04	0.00	1.63	0.83	18.10	2.80	6.68	5.16	0.88	0.58
9.	Paper, Paper Prods., Printing/ Publishing	0.02	0.01	0.14	0.00	0.00	0.55	0.76	0.31	40.53	0.20	2.21	0.53	8.39
10.	Leather Products	0.00	0.00	0.00	0.00	0.00	0.00	0.88	0.00	0.00	2.67	5.61	0.04	6.34
11.	Plastic/Rubber Products	0.00	0.00	0.00	0.00	0.00	30.50	0.56	22.28	0.63	37.87	65.01	0.42	15.76
12.	Coal/Petroleum Products	2.97	3.05	0.07	-0.03	0.00	0.20	0.78	0.47	0.39	5.01	4.27	0.22	0.52
13.	Chemicals	11.40	13.65	0.56	-0.04	0.00	2.76	6.68	2.79	2.76	15.23	0.55	0.07	9.12
14.	Non-metallic Products	0.00	0.00	0.00	0.00	0.00	14.20	0.00	0.24	0.00	0.00	0.65	0.01	3.11
15.	Metal Products	0.00	0.00	0.00	0.00	0.00	0.08	0.07	24.17	0.17	0.00	0.78	0.08	11.10
16.	Industrial Machinery	0.80	0.58	0.01	0.00	32.15	0.00	0.17	0.25	0.14	0.07	1.30	0.09	0.06
17.	Electric/Electronic Machinery	0.02	0.02	0.04	0.00	14.29	0.32	0.53	0.22	0.25	0.13	0.01	0.33	0.24
18.	Rail and other Transport Equipment	0.01	0.01	0.05	-0.05	0.00	0.28	0.00	0.00	0.00	0.00	0.02	0.00	0.00
19.	Miscellaneous Manufacturing	0.00	0.00	0.02	0.00	0.00	0.31	0.06	0.03	0.03	0.07	0.00	0.02	0.05
20.	Construction	3.25	4.39	0.56	0.00	0.00	0.04	0.01	0.08	0.02	0.04	0.00	1.02	0.02
21.	Electricity/Gas/Water Supply	2.56	2.33	0.01	0.00	0.00	0.05	0.01	0.74	0.18	0.09	0.06	0.69	0.06
22.	Rail and other Transport / Storage Services	2.12	2.56	1.58	0.00	24.98	5.60	8.21	12.47	13.12	14.67	0.35	38.19	20.38
23.	Trade/Hotels	4.06	5.06	4.19	0.05	0.00	0.73	9.50	5.16	1.94	9.54	3.68	18.02	8.27
24.	Banking/Insurance	2.06	1.06	0.04	0.00	0.00	1.42	1.52	5.08	1.50	3.79	5.29	27.83	3.31
25.	Other services (Edu., Med., Admin., Defence, etc.)	0.05	0.05	0.07	0.00	0.00	0.02	1.56	0.03	34.69	0.00	4.49	0.00	0.00
	Total Input	100.00	100.00	100.00	100.00	100.00	100.00	100.00	100.00	100.00	100.00	100.00	100.00	100.00

Appendix-V A : (Contd.)

Sector Code	Industry / Commodity	14	15	16	17	18	19	20	21	22	23	24	25
1.	Agriculture	0.00	0.00	0.00	0.00	0.00	0.00	0.00	0.00	1.47	6.06	0.00	0.07
2.	Animal Husbandry	0.00	0.00	0.00	0.00	0.00	0.00	0.00	0.00	0.00	8.24	0.00	0.04
3.	Forestry and Logging	0.01	0.07	0.02	0.00	0.06	0.01	0.01	0.00	0.00	0.00	0.00	0.09
4.	Fishing	0.00	0.00	0.00	0.00	0.00	0.00	0.00	0.00	0.00	4.27	0.00	0.00
5.	Mining/Quarrying	4.01	1.47	0.55	0.11	0.68	28.04	10.05	5.09	0.00	1.51	0.00	0.19
6.	Food Prod. Beverages and Tobacco Prod.	0.00	0.00	0.00	0.00	0.00	0.00	0.00	0.00	0.26	5.64	0.00	0.13
7.	Textiles	1.03	0.44	0.84	0.94	1.14	0.34	0.67	0.00	0.53	0.01	0.01	1.77
8.	Wood, Wood Prods., and Furniture	2.03	0.85	2.02	0.61	2.40	0.79	0.06	0.00	0.30	4.01	0.43	0.05
9.	Paper, Paper Prods., Printing/Publishing	0.79	0.48	0.94	0.17	0.94	0.83	0.17	0.63	0.61	1.36	1.78	4.75
10.	Leather Products	0.00	0.00	0.00	0.00	0.00	5.23	0.00	0.00	0.00	0.00	0.00	0.00
11.	Plastic/Rubber Products	0.74	21.94	0.65	9.86	9.47	1.60	0.00	0.00	1.86	13.62	0.00	12.16
12.	Coal/Petroleum Products	1.45	1.90	0.88	0.05	1.49	0.11	0.27	4.89	2.51	0.07	0.15	1.34
13.	Chemicals	2.17	1.52	3.14	2.38	10.93	1.71	0.00	0.08	0.02	0.00	0.00	4.71
14.	Non-metallic Products	28.14	13.39	0.45	0.16	0.00	1.15	0.00	0.01	0.00	0.38	0.00	2.55
15.	Metal Products	38.11	35.65	1.75	14.16	23.74	7.71	0.89	0.98	0.26	0.38	0.00	2.65
16.	Industrial Machinery	1.17	0.09	25.96	0.13	0.00	0.00	0.06	2.38	0.02	0.00	0.00	4.96
17.	Electric/Electronic Machinery	0.15	0.19	22.64	42.86	0.14	15.00	7.30	8.26	0.10	0.03	0.00	2.39
18.	Rail and other Transport Equipment	0.00	0.00	0.00	0.00	34.90	0.00	0.14	15.61	7.17	2.59	7.26	6.77
19.	Miscellaneous Manufacturing	0.88	0.02	0.05	0.02	0.04	14.50	0.02	0.55	0.57	0.14	0.14	6.40
20.	Construction	0.98	0.01	0.06	0.01	0.05	0.06	3.17	2.78	14.04	0.69	67.01	7.80
21.	Electricity/Gas/Water Supply	0.30	0.20	0.17	0.04	0.11	0.03	28.74	5.10	0.16	0.69	1.35	6.98
22.	Rail and other Transport/Storage Services	12.06	1.97	14.57	9.93	3.89	4.71	9.34	33.36	16.34	0.85	5.73	8.58
23.	Trade/Hotels	0.12	14.36	21.17	15.91	8.26	18.17	38.31	19.88	43.53	27.59	0.41	11.95
24.	Banking/Insurance	5.86	5.45	4.14	1.16	1.76	0.00	0.45	0.00	9.55	9.08	9.77	5.42
25.	Other Services (Edu., Med., Admin., Defence, etc.)	0.00	0.00	0.00	1.51	0.00	0.00	0.36	0.40	0.72	12.79	5.95	8.27
	Total Input	100.00	100.00	100.00	100.00	100.00	100.00	100.00	100.00	100.00	100.00	100.00	100.00

Source : Mathematically obtained by dividing industry column entries by total input of that industry.

Appendix – VB : Backward Linkages (Per cent purchased as inputs by industries in per cent): 2000-01

Sector Code	Industry / Commodity	1	2	3	4	5	6	7	8	9	10	11	12	13
1.	Agriculture	12.60	22.00	0.02	0.04	0.00	1.41	0.00	0.00	0.00	0.00	0.00	0.00	0.04
2.	Animal Husbandry	14.62	0.46	0.00	0.00	0.00	4.16	0.00	0.00	0.00	0.00	0.00	0.00	0.00
3.	Forestry and Logging	0.00	0.00	0.07	0.00	0.00	0.00	0.00	0.16	0.00	0.00	0.28	0.00	0.00
4.	Fishing	0.00	0.00	0.00	13.21	0.00	0.00	0.00	0.00	0.00	0.00	0.00	0.00	0.00
5.	Mining/Quarrying	0.00	0.00	0.00	0.00	0.07	0.00	0.00	0.00	0.00	0.00	0.00	0.00	0.00
6.	Food Prod. Beverages and Tobacco Products	0.10	16.36	0.00	3.80	0.00	79.66	0.00	0.00	0.00	0.00	0.00	0.00	3.00
7.	Textiles	0.44	4.86	1.18	23.20	0.00	2.03	53.06	2.13	7.58	10.14	3.36	0.67	11.71
8.	Wood, Wood Prods., and Furniture	0.00	0.00	0.00	0.23	0.18	0.14	0.05	10.81	0.19	0.26	0.24	0.05	0.81
9.	Paper, Paper Prods. , Printing/ Publishing	0.01	0.00	0.19	0.01	0.10	0.09	0.03	0.09	23.67	0.17	0.15	0.03	0.54
10.	Leather Products	0.00	0.00	0.00	0.00	0.00	0.00	2.21	0.36	0.04	56.91	0.00	0.00	0.00
11.	Plastic/Rubber Products	0.00	0.00	0.18	0.00	0.19	0.07	0.14	0.00	0.73	0.97	20.47	0.02	0.41
12.	Coal/Petroleum Products	0.00	0.00	0.02	0.00	0.01	0.00	0.00	0.01	0.00	0.00	0.00	0.01	0.00
13.	Chemicals	0.75	0.01	0.00	0.05	0.46	0.04	0.00	0.11	0.68	0.10	0.11	0.00	5.01
14.	Non-metallic Products	0.00	0.00	0.00	0.00	0.12	0.00	0.00	0.05	0.03	0.00	0.00	0.00	0.00
15.	Metal Products	0.00	0.01	0.04	0.16	0.46	0.01	0.02	0.26	0.18	0.02	0.03	0.00	0.03
16.	Industrial Machinery	0.67	0.03	0.23	0.00	17.39	0.01	0.01	0.17	0.22	0.02	0.01	0.00	0.33
17.	Electric/Electronic Machinery	0.02	0.00	0.17	0.01	0.02	0.01	0.05	0.16	0.41	0.03	0.02	0.02	0.04
18.	Rail and other Transport Equipment	0.12	0.00	1.10	6.76	2.65	0.00	0.00	0.02	0.00	0.00	0.00	0.00	0.00
19.	Miscellaneous Manufacturing	0.01	0.00	0.42	0.00	1.47	0.00	0.00	0.00	0.02	0.00	0.00	0.00	0.00
20.	Construction	8.80	0.65	33.80	0.00	15.84	0.04	0.01	0.08	0.05	0.04	0.06	0.06	0.0ct2
21.	Electricity/Gas/Water Supply	0.32	0.00	0.01	0.02	0.94	0.04	0.02	0.75	0.35	0.10	0.34	0.04	0.07
22.	Rail and other Transport / Storage Services	20.47	5.28	8.57	5.32	13.12	5.26	10.85	12.69	26.26	16.37	22.23	35.05	22.33
23.	Trade/Hotels	36.39	49.09	8.58	15.16	24.62	5.67	30.67	45.44	36.55	10.64	46.61	30.54	52.02
24.	Banking/Insurance	1.64	1.24	1.12	0.65	5.20	1.33	1.22	5.17	3.01	4.23	6.06	33.48	3.63
25.	Other Services (Edu., Med., Admin., Defence, etc.)	3.05	0.00	44.31	31.39	17.15	0.01	1.65	21.53	0.02	0.00	0.03	0.00	0.00
	Total Input	100.00	100.00	100.00	100.00	100.00	100.00	100.00	100.00	100.00	100.00	100.00	100.00	100.00

Appendix – VB : (Contd.)

Sector Code	Industry / Commodity	14	15	16	17	18	19	20	21	22	23	24	25	Total
1.	Agriculture	0.00	0.00a	0.00	0.00	0.00	0.00	1.19	0.00	1.17	0.91	0.00	0.30	0.69
2.	Animal Husbandry	0.00	0.00	0.00	0.00	0.00	0.00	0.18	0.66	0.00	1.72	0.00	0.53	0.65
3.	Forestry and Logging	0.00	0.00	0.00	0.00	0.00	0.00	0.02	0.00	0.00	0.00	0.00	0.00	0.00
4.	Fishing	0.00	0.00	0.00	0.00	0.00	0.00	0.00	0.00	0.00	0.14	0.00	0.00	0.03
5.	Mining/Quarrying	0.01	0.00	0.00	0.00	0.00	0.00	0.02	0.45	0.00	0.00	0.00	0.00	0.01
6.	Food Prod. Beverages and Tobacco Prod.	0.00	0.00	0.00	0.00	0.00	0.00	0.00	0.00	0.06	4.27	0.00	0.01	2.35
7.	Textiles	0.49	1.77	0.84	1.63	1.02	5.66	0.76	0.03	0.90	1.54	0.11	0.50	3.47
8.	Wood, Wood Prods., and Furniture	0.04	0.13	0.06	0.13	0.23	0.40	0.66	0.01	0.01	0.09	0.02	0.06	0.14
9.	Paper, Paper Prods. Printing/Publishing	0.04	0.06	0.04	0.09	0.02	0.26	0.02	0.15	0.20	0.29	0.36	0.20	0.38
10.	Leather Products	0.13	0.01	0.02	0.01	0.13	0.01	0.00	0.00	0.02	0.00	0.41	0.00	0.40
11.	Plastic/Rubber Products	0.02	0.13	0.05	0.27	0.16	1.67	0.01	0.01	0.87	0.04	0.01	0.00	0.22
12.	Coal/Petroleum Products	0.00	0.00	0.00	0.00	0.01	0.00	0.00	0.00	0.00	0.00	0.00	0.00	0.00
13.	Chemicals	0.02	0.06	0.02	0.08	0.12	0.08	0.10	0.02	0.01	0.00	0.00	0.37	0.18
14.	Non-metallic Products	1.21	0.06	0.01	0.05	0.02	0.02	1.71	0.00	0.01	0.00	0.00	0.00	0.17
15.	Metal Products	0.01	13.56	0.99	0.99	0.48	1.50	1.46	0.01	0.03	0.06	0.02	0.03	0.43
16.	Industrial Machinery	0.10	0.08	51.70	0.17	0.29	0.05	0.02	1.26	0.31	0.13	0.12	0.12	0.33
17.	Electric/Electronic Machinery	0.01	0.04	2.74	56.74	3.02	1.59	2.85	4.22	1.25	0.02	0.12	0.60	1.88
18.	Rail and other Transport Equipment	0.00	0.00	0.00	0.00	43.50	0.00	0.06	0.16	3.95	0.01	0.37	0.03	0.68
19.	Miscellaneous Manufacturing	0.00	0.01	0.01	0.01	0.01	20.43	0.12	0.48	0.92	0.25	0.57	2.61	1.11
20.	Construction	0.13	0.01	0.07	0.02	0.06	0.07	4.25	7.73	9.94	7.10	8.19	25.80	12.10
21.	Electricity/Gas/Water Supply	0.04	0.27	0.19	0.05	0.12	0.04	0.12	2.45	0.39	0.11	0.14	0.07	0.14
22.	Rail and other Transport / Storage Services	62.06	22.68	15.81	13.85	4.47	5.42	15.16	21.91	7.50	7.26	6.41	4.58	8.23
23.	Trade/Hotels	34.92	58.06	22.98	22.19	44.33	62.82	55.35	40.39	23.52	8.11	8.61	17.55	21.03
24.	Banking/Insurance	0.76	3.08	4.49	1.62	2.03	0.00	2.65	2.98	5.16	5.00	17.31	2.76	5.66
25.	Other services (Edu, Med., Admin., Defence, etc.)	0.00	0.00	0.00	2.11	0.00	0.00	13.28	17.07	43.78	62.92	57.22	43.89	39.72
	Total Input	100.00	100.00	100.00	100.00	100.00	100.00	100.00	100.00	100.00	100.00	100.00	100.00	100.00

Source: Mathematically obtained by dividing industry column entries by total input of that industry.

Appendix-VI A : Forward Linkages (commodity sales to different industries): 1970-71

Sector Code	Industry / Commodity	1	2	3	4	5	6	7	8	9	10	11	12	13
1.	Agriculture	27.14	19.39	0.03	0.00	0.00	27.88	0.00	0.00	0.00	0.00	0.00	0.00	0.00
2.	Animal Husbandry	23.59	16.86	0.14	0.00	0.00	16.84	0.00	0.00	0.00	0.00	0.00	0.00	0.00
3.	Forestry and Logging	0.17	0.12	0.00	0.00	0.00	1.26	0.00	52.16	0.06	0.57	0.00	0.00	37.17
4.	Fishing	0.00	0.00	0.00	0.00	0.00	0.00	0.00	0.00	0.00	0.00	0.05	0.00	0.00
5.	Mining/Quarrying	0.01	0.00	0.00	0.00	1.52	0.56	26.00	0.06	0.43	1.69	0.00	0.03	1.10
6.	Food Prod., Beverages and Tobacco Prod.	0.03	0.02	0.05	0.39	0.00	34.43	0.00	0.00	0.00	0.00	5.12	0.00	0.33
7.	Textiles	0.02	0.02	0.00	2.18	0.27	0.10	92.89	0.05	0.27	0.02	0.00	1.12	1.63
8.	Wood, Wood Prod., and Furniture	0.04	0.03	0.00	0.13	0.00	3.87	6.02	13.31	5.87	2.89	31.75	0.43	0.61
9.	Paper, Paper Prod., Printing/ Publishing	0.01	0.01	0.00	0.00	0.90	0.85	3.64	0.15	56.01	0.06	8.96	0.17	5.80
10.	Leather Products	0.00	0.00	0.00	0.00	0.00	0.00	12.52	0.00	0.00	2.25	67.18	0.04	12.91
11.	Plastic/Rubber Products	0.00	0.00	0.00	0.00	0.00	9.91	0.56	2.25	0.18	2.25	54.84	0.03	2.26
12.	Coal/Petroleum Products	5.12	3.66	0.00	4.06	0.56	0.69	8.48	0.52	1.21	3.24	39.20	0.16	0.81
13.	Chemicals	8.38	5.99	0.00	0.16	4.83	4.17	31.08	1.31	3.69	10.32	2.16	0.02	16.99
14.	Non-metallic Products	0.00	0.00	0.00	0.00	0.00	44.05	0.00	0.23	0.00	0.00	5.22	0.01	4.26
15.	Metal Products	0.00	0.00	0.00	0.13	0.00	0.14	0.37	12.87	0.26	0.00	3.46	0.03	8.41
16.	Industrial Machinery	1.81	1.29	0.00	0.00	45.41	0.00	2.41	0.35	0.58	0.06	15.67	0.08	0.13
17.	Electric/Electronic Machinery	0.04	0.03	0.00	0.00	0.00	1.40	7.02	0.30	0.96	0.11	0.10	0.29	0.45
18.	Rail and other Transport Equipment	0.01	0.01	0.00	8.59	0.00	29.43	0.00	0.00	0.00	0.00	0.08	0.00	0.00
19.	Miscellaneous Manufacturing	0.01	0.01	0.00	0.00	1.05	2.45	1.55	0.08	0.22	0.10	0.00	0.04	0.17
20.	Construction	1.69	1.21	0.00	0.00	2.98	0.04	0.03	0.03	0.02	0.01	0.01	0.23	0.01
21.	Electricity/Gas/Water Supply	2.60	1.86	0.00	0.00	13.93	0.10	0.07	0.48	0.33	0.03	0.34	0.30	0.06
22.	Rail and other Transport / Storage Services	0.63	0.45	0.00	0.25	0.60	3.44	24.36	2.38	7.12	1.65	0.56	4.88	5.52
23.	Trade/Hotels	0.59	0.42	0.00	0.38	0.50	3.03	26.06	4.16	4.84	0.52	18.00	3.55	5.42
24.	Banking/Insurance	0.84	0.60	0.00	0.18	0.29	1.19	3.93	1.33	1.12	0.58	72.30	4.88	1.23
25.	Other services (Edu., Med., Admin., Defence, etc.)	0.01	0.01	0.00	0.00	5.39	0.01	2.53	0.00	21.43	0.00	6.14	0.00	0.00
Total Input		2.31	1.65	0.01	0.59	1.79	5.88	18.04	2.06	5.36	1.06	18.16	1.37	3.13

Appendix-VI A : (Condt.)

Sector Code	*Industry / Commodity*	14	15	16	17	18	19	20	21	22	23	24	25
1.	Agriculture	0.00	0.00	0.00	0.00	0.00	0.00	0.00	0.00	3.07	22.22	0.00	0.27
2.	Animal Husbandry	0.00	0.00	0.00	0.00	0.00	0.00	0.00	0.00	0.00	42.3	0.00	0.23
3.	Forestry and Logging	0.06	0.80	0.03	0.00	0.64	0.03	0.23	0.06	0.00	0.00	0.00	6.64
4.	Fishing	0.00	0.00	0.00	0.00	0.00	0.00	0.00	0.00	0.00	99.95	0.00	0.00
5.	Mining/Quarrying	2.53	1.90	0.12	0.01	0.80	15.52	28.01	8.45	0.00	11.25	0.00	0.00
6.	Food Prod., Beverages and Tobacco Prod.	0.00	0.00	0.00	0.00	0.00	0.00	0.00	0.00	1.47	57.15	0.00	1.01
7.	Textiles	0.12	0.10	0.03	0.02	0.24	0.03	0.33	0.00	0.40	0.01	0.00	0.14
8.	Wood, Wood Prod and Furniture	1.16	1.00	0.42	0.05	2.58	0.40	0.16	0.00	1.16	27.18	0.74	0.20
9.	Paper, Paper Prod., Printing/Publishing	0.30	0.37	0.13	0.01	0.67	0.27	0.29	0.62	1.54	6.10	2.06	11.08
10.	Leather Products	0.00	0.00	0.00	0.00	0.00	5.10	0.00	0.00	0.00	0.00	0.00	0.00
11.	Plastic/Rubber Products	0.06	3.55	0.02	0.12	1.39	0.11	0.00	0.00	0.98	12.66	0.00	8.85
12.	Coal/Petroleum Products	1.24	3.34	0.27	0.01	2.39	0.09	1.01	11.00	10.40	0.69	0.40	1.47
13.	Chemicals	0.79	1.14	0.41	0.13	7.48	0.55	0.00	0.07	0.04	0.00	0.00	0.28
14.	Non-metallic Products	21.10	20.66	0.12	0.02	0.00	0.75	0.00	0.01	0.00	3.38	0.00	0.18
15.	Metal Products	15.81	30.42	0.26	0.87	18.44	2.80	1.63	1.06	0.71	1.84	0.00	0.47
16.	Industrial Machinery	1.31	0.20	23.03	0.02	0.00	0.00	0.31	6.99	0.17	0.04	0.00	0.15
17.	Electric/Electronic Machinery	0.16	0.41	8.49	6.64	0.28	13.71	33.60	22.63	0.72	0.31	0.00	2.35
18.	Rail and other Transport Equipment	0.00	0.00	0.00	0.00	31.63	0.00	0.30	19.85	8.93	0.38	0.22	0.57
19.	Miscellaneous Manufacturing	1.67	0.07	0.03	0.00	0.16	24.11	0.13	2.74	7.33	3.16	0.79	54.12
20.	Construction	0.25	0.00	0.01	0.00	0.02	0.01	3.63	17.36	1.31	2.12	68.41	0.61
21.	Electricity/Gas/Water Supply	0.15	0.21	0.03	0.00	0.10	0.01	64.27	6.78	0.55	4.13	2.09	1.5
22.	Rail and other Transport/Storage Services	1.79	5.03	0.78	0.22	1.08	0.61	6.13	8.59	7.48	10.34	2.59	3.52
23.	Trade/Hotels	3.40	6.77	0.55	0.17	5.23	2.87	1.56	1.63	1.73	5.87	0.09	2.65
24.	Banking/Insurance	1.19	2.28	0.30	0.04	0.67	0.00	0.40	0.00	2.06	3.80	0.15	0.62
25.	Other services (Edu., Med., Admin., Defence, etc.)	0.00	0.00	0.00	0.03	0.00	0.00	0.20	0.13	0.61	57.91	1.17	4.43
	Total Input	1.69	3.44	0.54	0.17	2.80	1.28	3.38	3.02	1.91	13.58	3.50	3.29

Source: Mathematically obtained by dividing commodity row entries by total inputs.

Appendix – VI B : Forward Linkages (Per cent sales to different industries): 2000-01

Sector Code	Industry / Commodity	1	2	3	4	5	6	7	8	9	10	11	12	13
1.	Agriculture	10.07	17.82	0.00	0.00	0.00	3.76	0.00	0.00	0.00	0.00	0.00	0.00	0.04
2.	Animal Husbandry	12.44	0.40	0.00	0.00	0.00	11.82	0.00	0.00	0.00	0.00	0.00	0.00	0.00
3.	Forestry and Logging	0.01	0.00	0.03	0.00	0.00	0.00	0.02	5.55	0.00	0.00	29.72	0.00	0.00
4.	Fishing	0.00	0.00	0.00	12.14	0.00	0.00	0.00	0.00	0.00	0.00	0.00	0.00	0.00
5.	Mining/Quarrying	0.02	0.00	0.00	0.00	0.08	0.03	0.14	0.01	0.00	0.00	0.01	0.06	0.16
6.	Food Prod., Beverages and Tobacco prods	0.02	3.92	0.00	0.04	0.00	62.80	0.00	0.00	0.00	0.00	0.00	0.00	0.90
7.	Textiles	0.07	0.79	0.00	0.18	0.00	1.08	72.30	0.10	1.60	1.14	0.47	0.02	2.38
8.	Wood, Wood Prods. and Furniture	0.02	0.00	0.00	0.04	0.01	1.87	1.59	11.99	0.99	0.71	0.81	0.05	4.06
9.	Paper, Paper Prods., Printing/ Publishing	0.02	0.00	0.00	0.00	0.00	0.45	0.38	0.04	45.71	0.18	0.20	0.01	1.00
10.	Leather Products	0.00	0.00	0.00	0.00	0.00	0.01	26.23	0.14	0.07	55.84	0.00	0.00	0.01
11.	Plastic/Rubber Products	0.01	0.00	0.00	0.00	0.01	0.61	2.90	0.00	2.40	1.69	44.09	0.01	1.29
12.	Coal/Petroleum Products	1.21	0.00	0.04	0.10	0.05	1.08	0.92	0.84	1.60	0.17	0.94	1.44	0.87
13.	Chemicals	2.34	0.03	0.00	0.01	0.02	0.41	0.08	0.10	2.81	0.23	0.29	0.00	20.04
14.	Non-metallic Products	0.00	0.00	0.00	0.00	0.00	0.01	0.09	0.05	0.11	0.00	0.00	0.00	0.01
15.	Metal Products	0.00	0.01	0.00	0.01	0.01	0.03	0.22	0.09	0.30	0.01	0.03	0.00	0.05
16.	Industrial Machinery	1.13	0.05	0.00	0.00	0.37	0.06	0.21	0.08	0.49	0.02	0.01	0.00	0.72
17.	Electric/Electronic Machinery	0.01	0.00	0.00	0.00	0.00	0.01	0.12	0.01	0.16	0.01	0.00	0.00	0.02
18.	Rail and other Transport Equipment	0.10	0.00	0.00	0.26	0.03	0.00	0.00	0.00	0.00	0.00	0.00	0.00	0.00
19.	Miscellaneous Manufacturing	0.00	0.00	0.00	0.00	0.01	0.00	0.01	0.00	0.01	0.00	0.00	0.00	0.00
20.	Construction	0.40	0.03	0.01	0.00	0.01	0.01	0.01	0.00	0.00	0.00	0.00	0.00	0.00
21.	Electricity/Gas/Water Supply	1.23	0.00	0.00	0.00	0.05	0.55	0.57	0.82	1.78	0.27	1.13	0.04	0.34
22.	Rail and other Transport /Storage Services	1.38	0.36	0.00	0.02	0.01	1.18	6.24	0.24	2.33	0.78	1.31	0.55	1.92
23.	Trade/Hotels	0.96	1.31	0.00	0.02	0.01	0.50	6.90	0.34	1.27	0.20	1.07	0.19	1.75
24.	Banking/Insurance	0.16	0.12	0.00	0.00	0.01	0.43	1.02	0.14	0.39	0.29	0.52	0.76	0.45
25.	Other services (Edu., Med., Admin., Defence, etc.)	0.04	0.00	0.00	0.02	0.00	0.00	0.20	0.08	0.00	0.00	0.00	0.00	0.00
Total Input		0.55	0.56	0.00	0.03	0.01	1.85	4.73	0.16	0.73	0.39	0.48	0.13	0.71

Appendix – VI B : (Contd.)

Sector Code	Industry / Commodity	14	15	16	17	18	19	20	21	22	23	24	25	Total
1.	Agriculture	0.00	0.00	0.00	0.00	0.00	0.00	16.14	0.00	15.73	23.09	0.00	13.36	100.00
2.	Animal Husbandry	0.00	0.00	0.00	0.00	0.00	0.00	2.59	0.66	0.00	46.46	0.00	25.62	100.00
3.	Forestry and Logging	0.00	0.00	0.00	0.00	0.00	0.00	50.20	0.00	0.08	14.39	0.00	0.00	100.00
4.	Fishing	0.00	0.00	0.00	0.00	0.00	0.00	0.00	0.00	0.00	87.86	0.00	0.00	100.00
5.	Mining/Quarrying	0.18	0.42	0.02	0.01	0.00	0.00	35.93	49.61	4.96	7.75	0.00	0.62	100.00
6.	Food Prod., Beverages and	0.00	0.00	0.00	0.00	0.00	0.00	0.00	0.00	0.25	31.96	0.00	0.11	100.00
	Tobacco Products											0.00		100.00
7.	Textiles	0.02	0.87	0.09	1.01	0.16	0.44	2.04	0.01	2.41	7.76	0.51	4.55	100.0
8.	Wood, Wood Prods., and Furniture	0.04	1.53	0.14	2.06	0.85	0.77	44.08	0.04	0.52	11.51	1.98	14.35	100.00
9.	Paper, Paper Prods., Printing/ Publishing	0.01	0.27	0.04	0.49	0.02	0.19	0.53	0.26	4.81	13.46	15.40	16.53	100.00
10.	Leather Products	0.05	0.06	0.02	0.08	0.17	0.01	0.00	0.00	0.40	0.00	16.92	0.00	100.00
11.	Plastic/Rubber Products	0.02	0.97	0.08	2.56	0.38	2.04	0.24	0.02	36.29	3.33	0.79	0.27	100.00
12.	Coal/Petroleum Products	0.41	0.17	0.11	1.67	2.51	0.33	2.60	2.52	33.48	2.60	41.84	2.51	100.00
13.	Chemicals	0.01	0.54	0.05	0.92	0.35	0.13	5.52	0.09	0.35	0.26	0.00	65.44	100.00
14.	Non-metallic Products	1.07	0.60	0.03	0.70	0.07	0.04	96.18	0.01	0.36	0.13	0.00	0.54	100.00
15.	Metal Products	0.00	54.15	0.85	4.99	0.59	0.95	31.93	0.02	0.58	2.62	0.66	1.88	100.00
16.	Industrial Machinery	0.05	0.45	58.36	1.10	0.46	0.04	0.64	2.53	8.84	6.93	6.02	11.43	100.00
17.	Electric/Electronic Machinery	0.00	0.04	0.54	64.96	0.85	0.23	14.21	1.47	6.18	0.21	1.02	9.95	100.00
18.	Rail and other Transport Equipment	0.00	0.00	0.00	0.00	33.86	0.00	0.78	0.15	54.31	0.18	8.84	1.48	100.00
19.	Miscellaneous Manufacturing	0.00	0.01	0.00	0.01	0.00	5.03	0.98	0.29	7.73	3.89	8.38	73.63	100.00
20.	Construction	0.00	0.00	0.00	0.00	0.00	0.00	3.29	0.42	7.66	10.30	11.01	66.84	100.00
21.	Electricity/Gas/Water Supply	0.04	3.24	0.48	0.80	0.45	0.07	7.68	11.18	25.40	13.48	15.99	14.40	100.00
22.	Rail and other Transport / Storage Services	1.10	4.72	0.71	3.63	0.29	0.18	17.26	1.75	8.50	15.48	12.65	17.42	100.00
23.	Trade/Hotels	0.24	4.73	0.40	2.27	1.11	0.82	24.66	1.26	10.43	6.77	6.65	26.14	100.00
24.	Banking/Insurance	0.02	0.93	0.29	0.62	0.19	0.00	4.39	0.35	8.49	15.50	49.67	15.26	100.00
25.	Other services (Edu., Med., Admin., Defence, etc.)	0.00	0.00	0.00	0.11	0.00	0.00	3.13	0.28	10.28	27.80	23.41	34.62	100.00
	Total Input	0.15	1.71	0.37	2.16	0.53	0.27	9.37	0.66	9.33	17.55	16.25	31.33	100.00

Source : Mathematically obtained by dividing commodity row entries by total inputs.

Appendix-VII A : Leontief Inverse-1970-71

Sector Code	Industry / Commodity	1	2	3	4	5	6	7	8	9	10	11	12	13
1.	Agriculture	1.5016	0.5020	0.4062	-0.0002	0.0400	0.3144	0.0481	0.0555	0.0354	0.0465	0.0268	0.0581	0.0477
2.	Animal Husbandry	0.3181	1.3183	0.5786	-0.0001	0.0337	0.1687	0.0427	0.0616	0.0307	0.0419	0.0239	0.0497	0.0468
3.	Forestry and Logging	0.0045	0.0045	1.0031	0.0000	0.0024	0.0051	0.0056	0.0622	0.0051	0.0111	0.0058	0.0029	0.0289
4.	Fishing	0.0197	0.0197	0.0178	3.3335	0.0334	0.0184	0.0414	0.0277	0.0285	0.0368	0.0206	0.0500	0.0314
5.	Mining/Quarrying	0.0165	0.0165	0.0131	0.0000	1.2534	0.0228	0.0827	0.0220	0.0271	0.0589	0.0174	0.0356	0.0332
6.	Food Prod., Beverages and Tobacco Prod.	0.0097	0.0098	0.0829	-0.0013	0.0157	1.0880	0.0195	0.0189	0.0142	0.0203	0.0173	0.0230	0.0192
7.	Textiles	0.0290	0.0290	0.0387	0.0014	0.0210	0.0254	2.0455	0.0252	0.0416	0.0431	0.0215	0.1843	0.1319
8.	Wood, Wood Prod., and Furniture	0.0151	0.0151	0.0149	0.0012	0.0293	0.0512	0.0434	1.1856	0.0604	0.1150	0.0937	0.0381	0.0427
9.	Paper, Paper Prod., Printing/ Publishing	0.0219	0.0219	0.0178	-0.0001	0.0217	0.0347	0.0471	0.0318	1.4992	0.0475	0.0567	0.0331	0.1129
10.	Leather Products	0.0104	0.0104	0.0083	-0.0001	0.0080	0.0251	0.0279	0.0224	0.0116	1.0593	0.0765	0.0098	0.0635
11.	Plastic/Rubber Products	0.0973	0.0973	0.1062	-0.0005	0.1647	0.5518	0.1897	0.5130	0.1959	0.7607	1.9328	0.1689	0.3815
12.	Coal/Petroleum Prod.	0.0428	0.0428	0.0266	-0.0008	0.0178	0.0352	0.0289	0.0323	0.0242	0.0764	0.0655	1.0220	0.0296
13.	Chemicals	0.1459	0.1460	0.0880	-0.0012	0.0305	0.0773	0.1360	0.0515	0.0666	0.1645	0.0341	0.0333	1.1024
14.	Non-metallic Prod.	0.0109	0.0109	0.0180	-0.0002	0.0166	0.1581	0.0164	0.0458	0.0215	0.0226	0.0233	0.0136	0.0531
15.	Metal Products	0.0350	0.0350	0.0288	-0.0002	0.0791	0.0922	0.0539	0.3097	0.0662	0.0762	0.0610	0.0482	0.1564
16.	Industrial Machinery	0.0195	0.0195	0.0130	0.0000	0.3390	0.0194	0.0322	0.0184	0.0291	0.0296	0.0308	0.0176	0.0188
17.	Electric/Electronic Machinery	0.0216	0.0216	0.0158	0.0000	0.2829	0.0242	0.0462	0.0241	0.0421	0.0335	0.0232	0.0386	0.0262
18.	Rail and Other Transport Equipment	0.0262	0.0262	0.0202	-0.0015	0.0405	0.0290	0.0400	0.0348	0.0603	0.0433	0.0283	0.0693	0.0386
19.	Miscellaneous Manufacturing	0.0025	0.0025	0.0025	0.0000	0.0044	0.0070	0.0067	0.0045	0.0207	0.0060	0.0053	0.0064	0.0059
20.	Construction	0.0794	0.0795	0.0555	-0.0001	0.0703	0.0651	0.0724	0.0787	0.0886	0.0924	0.0694	0.1805	0.0762
21.	Electricity/Gas/Water Supply	0.0505	0.0506	0.0312	0.0000	0.0221	0.0274	0.0247	0.0313	0.0439	0.0303	0.0240	0.0548	0.0255
22.	Rail and Other Transport/ Storage Services	0.1066	0.1067	0.0850	-0.0005	0.3432	0.1414	0.2428	0.1916	0.2685	0.2636	0.0966	0.4087	0.2574
23.	Trade/Hotel	0.1761	0.1762	0.1547	0.0011	0.2986	0.1644	0.3699	0.2470	0.2550	0.3287	0.1836	0.4466	0.2809
24.	Banking/Insurance	0.0670	0.0671	0.0488	-0.0002	0.0785	0.0873	0.0983	0.1249	0.0941	0.1410	0.1246	0.2987	0.1051
25.	Other Services (Edu., Med., Admin., Defence, etc)	0.0325	0.0325	0.0287	0.0001	0.0516	0.0499	0.0902	0.0582	0.4640	0.0802	0.1027	0.0787	0.0812

Appendix-VII A : (Contd.)

Sector Code	Industry Commodity	14	15	16	17	18	19	20	21	22	23	24	25
1.	Agriculture	0.0289	0.0372	0.0629	0.0577	0.0399	0.0548	0.0738	0.0689	0.0806	0.1689	0.0408	0.0361
2.	Animal Husbandry	0.0251	0.0336	0.0559	0.0514	0.0365	0.0488	0.0657	0.0594	0.0625	0.1545	0.0360	0.0318
3.	Forestry and Logging	0.0037	0.0041	0.0049	0.0044	0.0079	0.0040	0.0030	0.0036	0.0028	0.0053	0.0022	0.0036
4.	Fishing	0.0239	0.0329	0.0559	0.0513	0.0335	0.0489	0.0675	0.0598	0.0612	0.1614	0.0364	0.0306
5.	Mining/Quarrying	0.0674	0.0385	0.0307	0.0269	0.0325	0.3279	0.1248	0.0838	0.0329	0.0399	0.0610	0.0365
6.	Food Prod., Beverages and Tobacco Prod.	0.0118	0.0166	0.0258	0.0246	0.0171	0.0228	0.0304	0.0276	0.0293	0.0712	0.0167	0.0156
7.	Textiles	0.0368	0.0264	0.0404	0.0440	0.0553	0.0285	0.0284	0.0317	0.0247	0.0200	0.0189	0.0399
8.	Wood, Wood Prod.and Furniture	0.0455	0.0469	0.0586	0.0520	0.0662	0.0476	0.0389	0.0419	0.0372	0.0763	0.0276	0.0297
9.	Paper, Paper Prod., Printing / Publishing	0.0311	0.0328	0.0418	0.0357	0.0497	0.0377	0.0300	0.0388	0.0312	0.0489	0.0376	0.0633
10.	Leather Products	0.0115	0.0208	0.0132	0.0209	0.0234	0.0606	0.0104	0.0124	0.0100	0.0182	0.0071	0.0149
11.	Plastic/Rubber Products	0.2301	0.4856	0.2569	0.4575	0.4226	0.2829	0.2204	0.2475	0.2083	0.4015	0.1434	0.2663
12.	Coal/Petroleum Prod.	0.0333	0.0405	0.0284	0.0281	0.0415	0.0234	0.0293	0.0670	0.0340	0.0272	0.0194	0.0270
13.	Chemicals	0.0422	0.0372	0.0639	0.0609	0.1487	0.0534	0.0323	0.0475	0.0309	0.0481	0.0264	0.0561
14.	Non-metallic Prod.	1.2960	0.1662	0.0295	0.0460	0.0550	0.0426	0.0195	0.0244	0.0162	0.0294	0.0140	0.0357
15.	Metal Products	0.4772	1.4082	0.1234	0.2905	0.3935	0.1815	0.0812	0.1246	0.0597	0.0697	0.0636	0.0872
16.	Industrial Machinery	0.0365	0.0217	1.2584	0.0200	0.0179	0.0954	0.0468	0.0558	0.0168	0.0252	0.0253	0.0529
17.	Electric/Electronic Machinery	0.0363	0.0258	0.3480	1.5606	0.0242	0.2875	0.1483	0.1547	0.0347	0.0328	0.0730	0.0670
18.	Rail and Other Transport Equipment	0.0332	0.0301	0.0479	0.0432	1.3956	0.0384	0.0863	0.2410	0.1105	0.0741	0.1160	0.0914
19.	Miscellaneous Manufacturing	0.0121	0.0049	0.0063	0.0064	0.0049	1.1326	0.0071	0.0120	0.0096	0.0105	0.0069	0.0455
20.	Construction	0.0861	0.0716	0.0904	0.0783	0.0666	0.0658	1.1021	0.1232	0.1807	0.1023	0.5042	0.1079
21.	Electricity/Gas/Water Supply	0.0276	0.0249	0.0316	0.0280	0.0236	0.0237	0.2459	1.0810	0.0507	0.0453	0.1250	0.0716
22.	Rail and Other Transport / Storage Services	0.2016	0.1068	0.2631	0.2224	0.1470	0.2126	0.2456	0.4421	1.2027	0.1096	0.1757	0.1559
23.	Trade/Hotel	0.2131	0.2940	0.4992	0.4580	0.2995	0.4369	0.6033	0.5341	0.5472	1.4424	0.3257	0.2739
24.	Banking/Insurance	0.1270	0.1273	0.1322	0.1128	0.1071	0.0879	0.0963	0.1141	0.1467	0.1605	1.1247	0.0957
25.	Other Services (Edu., Med., Admin., Defence, etc)	0.0457	0.0620	0.0842	0.0992	0.0651	0.0744	0.0899	0.0880	0.0857	0.1862	0.0967	1.1088

Source : Mathematically obtained as part of input-output model (refer chapter 3).

Appendix-VII B : Leontief Inverse-1970-71

Sector Code	Industry / Commodity	1	2	3	4	5	6	7	8	9	10	11	12	13
1.	Agriculture	1.1141	0.1652	0.0112	0.0102	0.0099	0.0327	0.0117	0.0118	0.0123	0.0084	0.0075	0.0110	0.0087
2.	Animal Husbandry	0.1145	1.0334	0.0097	0.0112	0.0095	0.0612	0.0124	0.0127	0.0121	0.0076	0.0077	0.0100	0.0093
3.	Forestry and Logging	0.0001	0.0000	1.0005	0.0000	0.0001	0.0000	0.0001	0.0013	0.0001	0.0001	0.0015	0.0001	0.0000
4.	Fishing	0.0006	0.0006	0.0004	1.0956	0.0005	0.0002	0.0007	0.0007	0.0007	0.0004	0.0004	0.0005	0.0005
5.	Mining/Quarrying	0.0001	0.0000	0.0001	0.0000	1.0005	0.0000	0.0001	0.0001	0.0001	0.0000	0.0000	0.0001	0.0000
6.	Food Prod., Beverages and Tobacco Prod.	0.0569	0.2493	0.0251	0.0838	0.0285	2.0611	0.0414	0.0396	0.0398	0.0238	0.0258	0.0306	0.0586
7.	Textiles	0.0329	0.0783	0.0342	0.3094	0.0233	0.0572	1.7470	0.0534	0.1442	0.2281	0.0458	0.0303	0.1171
8.	Wood, Wood Prod., and Furniture	0.0019	0.0017	0.0029	0.0038	0.0034	0.0027	0.0026	1.0839	0.0038	0.0047	0.0025	0.0022	0.0056
9.	Paper, Paper Prod., Printing/ Publishing	0.0030	0.0028	0.0043	0.0030	0.0036	0.0026	0.0039	0.0045	1.2179	0.0050	0.0032	0.0039	0.0056
10.	Leather Products	0.0013	0.0026	0.0013	0.0095	0.0012	0.0019	0.0515	0.0067	0.0053	1.6933	0.0017	0.0023	0.0038
11.	Plastic/Rubber Products	0.0021	0.0016	0.0029	0.0020	0.0033	0.0021	0.0047	0.0021	0.0104	0.0155	1.1084	0.0030	0.0040
12.	Coal/Petroleum Prod.	0.0000	0.0000	0.0001	0.0000	0.0001	0.0000	0.0000	0.0001	0.0000	0.0000	0.0000	1.0001	0.0000
13.	Chemicals	0.0071	0.0023	0.0026	0.0026	0.0048	0.0013	0.0020	0.0033	0.0082	0.0026	0.0018	0.0020	1.0260
14.	Non-metallic Prod.	0.0026	0.0017	0.0048	0.0021	0.0038	0.0008	0.0021	0.0029	0.0024	0.0016	0.0014	0.0023	0.0015
15.	Metal Products	0.0034	0.0024	0.0059	0.0044	0.0085	0.0011	0.0032	0.0056	0.0049	0.0024	0.0021	0.0031	0.0022
16.	Industrial Machinery	0.0101	0.0035	0.0047	0.0027	0.1686	0.0015	0.0032	0.0051	0.0065	0.0027	0.0020	0.0033	0.0047
17.	Electric/Electronic Machinery	0.0166	0.0114	0.0256	0.0178	0.0246	0.0062	0.0165	0.0199	0.0243	0.0138	0.0105	0.0180	0.0113
18.	Rail and Other Transport Equipment	0.0111	0.0061	0.0169	0.0783	0.0318	0.0046	0.0102	0.0088	0.0142	0.0117	0.0075	0.0146	0.0077
19.	Miscellaneous Manufacturing	0.0149	0.0125	0.0229	0.0182	0.0265	0.0059	0.0170	0.0208	0.0180	0.0128	0.0110	0.0186	0.0116
20.	Construction	0.2092	0.1391	0.3925	0.1705	0.2499	0.0599	0.1678	0.2005	0.1754	0.1241	0.1090	0.1806	0.1150
21.	Electricity/Gas/Water Supply	0.0039	0.0016	0.0017	0.0016	0.0076	0.0013	0.0020	0.0076	0.0053	0.0028	0.0030	0.0024	0.0017
22.	Rail and Other Transport/ Storage Services	0.2420	0.1418	0.1641	0.1515	0.1944	0.1134	0.2499	0.2052	0.3544	0.2907	0.1826	0.3462	0.1886
23.	Trade/Hotel	0.5438	0.5664	0.3977	0.4441	0.4571	0.2031	0.6739	0.6396	0.6420	0.3831	0.4185	0.4917	0.4612
24.	Banking/Insurance	0.0610	0.0538	0.0558	0.0532	0.0856	0.0390	0.0729	0.0989	0.0883	0.0982	0.0697	0.3079	0.0583
25.	Other Services (Edu., Med., Admin., Defence, etc)	0.5197	0.4518	0.7808	0.7156	0.5858	0.1996	0.6021	0.7869	0.6061	0.4228	0.3798	0.6182	0.4042
		2.9726	2.9300	2.9686	3.1914	2.9326	2.8594	3.6988	3.2219	3.3969	3.3565	2.4034	3.1029	2.5073

Appendix-VII B : (Contd.)

Sector Code	Industry Commodity	14	15	16	17	18	19	20	21	22	23	24	25	Total
1.	Agriculture	0.0117	0.0144	0.0096	0.0105	0.0113	0.0138	0.0223	0.0149	0.0193	0.0194	0.0092	0.0156	1.5867
2.	Animal Husbandry	0.0097	0.0152	0.0094	0.0104	0.0131	0.0162	0.0157	0.0192	0.0118	0.0238	0.0090	0.0161	1.4807
3.	Forestry and Logging	0.0000	0.0001	0.0000	0.0001	0.0001	0.0001	0.0002	0.0001	0.0001	0.0001	0.0001	0.0001	1.0048
4.	Fishing	0.0005	0.0009	0.0005	0.0006	0.0008	0.0010	0.0007	0.0007	0.0005	0.0014	0.0004	0.0005	1.1101
5.	Mining/Quarrying	0.0001	0.0001	0.0001	0.0001	0.0001	0.0001	0.0002	0.0037	0.0001	0.0001	0.0001	0.0001	1.0058
6.	Food Prod., Beverages and Tobacco Prod.	0.0305	0.0513	0.0307	0.0340	0.0455	0.0564	0.0444	0.0438	0.0313	0 0842	0.0218	0 0333	3.2717
7.	Textiles	0.0279	0.0568	0.0373	0.0593	0.0453	0.1242	0.0372	0.0311	0.0345	0.0415	0.0216	0.0340	3 4520
8.	Wood, Wood Prod., and Furniture	0.0019	0.0034	0.0022	0.0036	0.0046	0.0064	0.0074	0.0027	0.0025	0.0030	0.0023	0.0037	1 1654
9.	Paper, Paper Prod., Printing / Publishing	0.0034	0.0047	0.0034	0.0044	0.0036	0.0070	0.0039	0.0055	0.0049	0.0056	0.0057	0.0053	1.3206
10.	Leather Products	0.0026	0.0024	0.0019	0.0025	0.0041	0.0041	0.0016	0.0014	0.0017	0.0016	0.0055	0.0014	1.8132
11.	Plastic/Rubber Products	0.0038	0.0041	0.0030	0.0063	0.0037	0.0198	0.0023	0.0030	0.0082	0.0020	0.0016	0.0021	1.2221
12.	Coal/Petroleum Prod.	0.0000	0.0000	0.0000	0.0000	0.0001	0.0000	0.0000	0.0000	0.0000	0.0000	0.0000	0.0000	1 0009
13.	Chemicals	0.0018	0.0028	0.0018	0.0028	0.0032	0.0030	0.0031	0.0029	0.0028	0 0030	0.0027	0.0057	1 1022
14.	Non-metallic Prod.	1.0095	0.0031	0.0019	0.0027	0.0023	0.0026	0.0150	0.0035	0 0034	0.0033	0.0031	0.0050	1 0855
15.	Metal Products	0.0029	1.1240	0.0153	0.0175	0.0092	0.0196	0.0156	0.0052	0.0047	0.0046	0.0040	0.0064	1.2784
16.	Industrial Machinery	0.0043	0.0048	1.5858	0.0063	0.0077	0.0039	0.0035	0.0202	0.0062	0.0041	0.0037	0.0043	1.8735
17.	Electric/Electronic Machinery	0.0186	0.0196	0.0680	1.7701	0.0720	0.0426	0.0539	0.0823	0 0357	0.0207	0.0201	0.0330	2.4532
18.	Rail and Other Transport Equipment	0.0189	0.0132	0.0110	0.0113	1.4859	0.0076	0.0102	0.0146	0.0451	0.0069	0.0094	0.0074	1.8649
19.	Miscellaneous Manufacturing	0.0169	0.0205	0.0143	0.0158	0.0159	1.2139	0.0209	0.0273	0.0289	0.0260	0.0259	0.0456	1.6822
20.	Construction	0.1635	0.2031	0.1403	0.1536	0.1601	0.1925	1.2257	0.2807	0.2691	0.2672	0.2492	0.4055	6.0038
21.	Electricity/Gas/Water Supply	0.0024	0.0047	0.0038	0.0025	0.0030	0.0023	0.0028	1.0219	0.0043	0.0024	0.0023	0.0023	1.0973
22.	Rail and Other Transport / Storage Services	0.4795	0.3237	0.2699	0.2797	0.1531	0.1808	0.2308	0.3087	1.1597	0.1555	0 1350	0 1604	6.6616
23.	Trade/Hotel	0.4880	0.8344	0.4974	0.5505	0.7431	0.9217	0.7116	0.6888	0.4843	1.3806	0.3429	0.5151	14.4804
24.	Banking/Insurance	0.0586	0.0958	0.1013	0.0728	0.0772	0.0646	0.0799	0 0914	0 0889	0 0862	1 1583	0 0780	3.1957
25.	Other Services (Edu., Med., Admin., Defence, etc.)	0.5458	0.7143	0.4839	0.5476	0.5743	0.6924	0.7357	0.8291	0.8570	0.9756	0.8705	1.9273	16.8269
		2.926	3 5173	3.2932	3.5647	3.4391	3.5966	3.2448	3.5026	3.1049	3.1190	2.9042	3.3080	79.0397

Source : Mathematically obtained as part of input-output model.

Appendix- VIII A : Connectivity Matrix:2000-01

Sectors	*1*	*2*	*3*	*4*	*5*	*6*	*7*	*8*	*9*	*10*	*11*	*12*	*13*	*14*	*15*	*16*	*17*	*18*	*19*	*20*	*21*	*22*	*23*	*24*	*25*
1.	*	2	2	0	0	2	1F	1F	1F	0	0	1F	1F	0	0	1F	0	0	0	1F	1F	2	2	1F	0
2.	2	*	2	0	0	2	1F	1F	1F	0	0	1F	1F	0	0	1F	0	0	0	1F	1F	1F	2	1F	2
3.	2	2	*	0	0	2	1F	2	2	1B	0	1F	2	1B	1B	2	0	2	2	2	2	1F	1F	0	2
4.	0	0	0		0	0	0	0	0	0	0	0	0	0	0	0	0	0	0	0	0	0	2	0	0
5.	0	0	0	0		2	0	0	1B	1B	0	0	1B	1B	2	2	1F	1B	1B	1B	1B	1F	1B	0	0
6.	2	2	2	0	2	*	1F	1F	1F	0	2	1F	2	1F	0	0	1F	1F	1F	1F	1F	2	2	1F	1F
7.	1B	1B	1B	0	0	1B	*	2	2	2	1F	2	2	1B	2	2	2	1B	2	2	1F	2	2	1F	2
8.	1B	1B	2	0	0	1B	2	*	2	0	2	2	2	2	2	2	2	1B	2	2	1F	2	2	2	2
9.	1B	16	2	· 0	1F	1B	2	2	*	1B	2	2	2	1B	2	2	2	1B	2	2	2	2	2	2	2
10.	0	0	1F	0	1F	0	2	0	1F	*	2	2	2	0	0	0	1F	1B	2	1F	1F	1F	1F	1F	1F
11.	0	0	0	0	0	2	1B	2	2	2	*	2	2	2	2	2	2	2	1B	0	1B	‘2	2	1F	2
12.	1B	1B	1B	0	0	1B	2	2	2	2	2	*	2	2	2	2	2	1B	2	2	2	2	2	1B	2
13.	1B	1B	2	0	1F	2	2	2	2	2	2	2	*	2	2	2	2	1B	2	1F	2	1F	2	1F	2
14.	0	0	1F	0	1F	1B	1F	2	1F	0	2	2	2	*	2	2	2	0	2	1F	1F	1F	2	1B	1B
15.	0	0	1F	0	2	0	2	2	2	0	2	2	2	2	*	2	2	1B	1B	1B	2	2	2	0	1B
16.	1B	1B	2	0	2	0	2	2	2	0	2	2	2	2	2	*	2	0	2	2	2	2	2	1F	1B
17.	0	0	0	0	1B	1B	2	2	2	1B	2	2	2	2	2	2	*	1B	2	2	2	2	2	1F	2
18.	0	0	2	0	1F	1B	1F	1F	1F	1F	2	1F	1F	0	1F	0	1F	*	1F	1F	2	2	2	2	1B
19.	0	0	2	0	1F	1B	2	2	2	2	1F	2	2	2	1F	2	2	1B	*	2	2	2	2	1B	1B
20.	1B	1B	2	0	1F	1B	2	2	2	1B	0	2	1B	1B	1F	2	2	1B	2	‘~	2	2	2	2	2
21.	1B	1B	2	0	1F	1B	1B	1B	2	1B	1F	2	2	1B	2	2	2	2	2	2	*	2	2	1B	2
22.	2	1B	1B	0	1B	2	2	2	2	1B	2	2	1B	1B	2	2	2	2	2	2	2	*	2	2	2
23.	2	2	1B	2	1F	2	2	2	2	1B	2	2	2	2	2	2	2	2	2	2	2	2	*	2	2
24.	1B	1B	0	0	0	1B	1B	2	2	1B	1B	1F	1B	1B	0	1B	1B	2	1F	2	1F	2	2	*	2
25.	0	2	2	0	0	1B	2	2	2	1B	2	2	2	1F	1F	1F	2	1F	1F	2	2	2	2	2	*

Source : Obtained from Coefficient Matrix. Backward Linkage Matrix and Forward Linkage Matrix. (Refer Chapter-6)

Appendix- VIII B : Connectivity Matrix:2000-01

Sectors	*1*	*2*	*3*	*4*	*5*	*6*	*7*	*8*	*9*	*10*	*11*	*12*	*13*	*14*	*15*	*16*	*17*	*18*	*19*	*20*	*21*	*22*	*23*	*24*	*25*
1.	*	2	2	1B	0	2	0	0	0	0	0	0	2	0	0	0	0	0	0	2	0	2	2	0	2
2.	2	*	0	0	0	2	0	0	0	0	0	0	0	0	0	0	0	0	0	2	1B	0	2	0	2
3.	0	0	*	0	0	0	0	2	0	0	1F	0	0	0	0	0	0	0	0	2	0	1F	2	0	0
4.	0	0	0	*	0	0	0	0	0	0	0	0	0	0	0	0	0	0	0	0	0	0	0	0	0
5.	0	0	0	0	*	0	0	0	0	0	0	0	0	2	0	0	0	0	0	2	2	0	2	0	0
6.	2	2	0	0	0	*	1F	1F	1F	0	0	0	2	0	1F	2	2	1B	0	1F	1F	2	2	1F	0
7.	1B	0	0	1B	0	1B	*	2	2	2	2	2	2	2	2	2	2	1B	2	2	2	2	2	2	2
8.	0	0	2	0	2	1B	2	*	2	2	2	2	2	2	2	2	2	2	1B	1B	2	2	2	2	2
9.	1B	0	0	0	1B	1B	2	2	*	2	2	1B	2	2	2	2	2	2	1B	1B	2	2	2	2	2
10.	0	0	0	0	0	0	2	2	2	*	1F	0	2	2	2	2	2	1B	1B	0	1F	2	2	2	0
11.	0	0	1B	0	0	2	2	2	2	1B	*	2	2	2	2	2	2	1B	1B	0	2	2	2	2	0
12.	0	0	0	0	0	0	1F	2	1F	0	2	*	1B	0	1B	1B	2	1B	0	0	0	1F	1B	1F	0
13.	2	0	0	0	0	1B	1F	2	2	2	2	1F	*	2	2	2	2	1B	1B	1B	2	2	1B	2	1B
14.	0	0	0	0	2	0	1F	2	2	1F	1F	1F	2	*	2	2	2	1B	1B	1B	2	2	1B	2	1B
15.	0	0	0	0	0	1B	2	2	2	2	2	1F	2	2	*	2	2	2	2	2	2	2	2	2	2
16.	1B	0	0	0	0	2	2	2	2	2	2	1F	2	2	2	*	2	2	2	1B	2	2	2	2	2
17.	0	0	0	0	0	1B	2	2	2	2	2	2	2	2	2	2	*	2	2	2	2	2	2	1B	2
18.	1B	0	0	0	1B	0	1F	2	2	1F	1F	1F	1F	2	2	2	2	*	1F	1B	2	2	2	2	1B
19.	0	0	0	0	1B	0	2	1F	1F	1F	1F	0	1F	1F	2	2	2	1B	*	2	2	2	2	2	1B
20.	2	2	2	0	2	1B	2	1F	2	0	2	2	1F	1F	2	2	2	2	2	*	2	2	2	2	2
21.	1B	1F	1B	0	2	1B	2	2	2	1B	2	2	2	2	2	2	2	2	2	2	*	2	2	2	2
22.	2	1B	1B	1B	0	2	2	2	2	2	2	2	2	2	2	2	2	2	2	2	2	*	2	2	2
23.	2	2	2	2	2	2	2	2	2	1B	2	2	1F	1F	2	2	2	2	2	2	2	2	*	2	2
24.	1B	0	0	1B	0	1B	2	2	2	2	2	1B	1B	1B	2	2	2	2	1F	2	2	2	2	*	2
25.	2	2	0	1B	0	2	2	2	2	0	0	0	1F	1F	2	2	2	1F	1F	2	2	2	2	2	*

Source: Obtained from Coefficient Matrix, Backward Linkage Matrix and Forward Linkage Matrix. (*Refer Chaper-7*)

Appendix –IXA : Input-Output Coefficient Matrix (commodity × industry): 1970-71

Sector Code	Industry / Commodity	1	2	3	4	5	6	7	8	9	10	11	12	13
1.	Agriculture	0.2693	0.2695	0.1190	0.0000	0.0000	0.1604	0.0000	0.0000	0.0000	0.0000	0.0000	0.0000	0.0000
2.	Animal Husbandry	0.1672	0.1673	0.3969	0.0000	0.0000	0.0692	0.0000	0.0000	0.0000	0.0000	0.0000	0.0000	0.0000
3.	Forestry and Logging	0.0001	0.0001	0.0000	0.0000	0.0000	0.0004	0.0000	0.0512	0.0000	0.0011	0.0000	0.0000	0.0240
4.	Fishing	0.0000	0.0000	0.0001	0.7000	0.0000	0.0000	0.0000	0.0000	0.0000	0.0000	0.0000	0.0000	0.0000
5.	Mining/Quarrying	0.0000	0.0000	0.0000	0.0000	0.1905	0.0016	0.0253	0.0005	0.0015	0.0288	0.0000	0.0003	0.0063
6.	Food Prod., Beverages and Tobacco Products	0.0001	0.0001	0.0692	-0.0004	0.0000	0.0716	0.0000	0.0000	0.0000	0.0000	0.0037	0.0000	0.0014
7.	Textiles	0.0006	0.0006	0.0100	0.0003	0.0000	0.0015	0.5046	0.0023	0.0051	0.0022	0.0000	0.0830	0.0528
8.	Wood, Wood Prods., and Furniture	0.0002	0.0002	0.0002	0.0003	0.0000	0.0121	0.0065	0.1290	0.0219	0.0543	0.0347	0.0063	0.0039
9.	Paper, Paper Prods., Printing/ Publishing	0.0001	0.0001	0.0009	0.0000	0.0000	0.0040	0.0059	0.0022	0.3160	0.0016	0.0148	0.0038	0.0559
10.	Leather Products	0.0000	0.0000	0.0000	0.0000	0.0000	0.0000	0.0069	0.0000	0.0000	0.0217	0.0378	0.0003	0.0423
11.	Plastic/Rubber Products	0.0000	0.0000	0.0000	0.0000	0.0000	0.2250	0.0044	0.1588	0.0049	0.3079	0.4374	0.0030	0.1050
12.	Coal/Petroleum Products	0.0184	0.0184	0.0004	-0.0002	0.0000	0.0014	0.0061	0.0034	0.0030	0.0407	0.0287	0.0015	0.0035
13.	Chemicals	0.0705	0.0706	0.0036	-0.0003	0.0000	0.0204	0.0521	0.0199	0.0215	0.1238	0.0037	0.0005	0.0608
14.	Non-metallic Products	0.0000	0.0000	0.0000	0.0000	0.0000	0.1048	0.0000	0.0017	0.0000	0.0000	0.0044	0.0001	0.0207
15.	Metal Products	0.0000	0.0000	0.0000	0.0000	0.0000	0.0006	0.0006	0.1723	0.0013	0.0000	0.0052	0.0006	0.0740
16.	Industrial Machinery	0.0050	0.0050	0.0001	0.0000	0.2143	0.0000	0.0013	0.0018	0.0011	0.0005	0.0088	0.0006	0.0004
17.	Electric/Electronic Machinery	0.0001	0.0001	0.0003	0.0000	0.0952	0.0024	0.0041	0.0016	0.0020	0.0011	0.0001	0.0024	0.0016
18.	Rail and other Transport Equipment	0.0001	0.0001	0.0003	-0.0003	0.0000	0.0021	0.0000	0.0000	0.0000	0.0000	0.0001	0.0000	0.0000
19.	Miscellaneous Manufacturing	0.0000	0.0000	0.0002	0.0000	0.0000	0.0023	0.0005	0.0002	0.0002	0.0005	0.0000	0.0002	0.0003
20.	Construction	0.0201	0.0201	0.0036	0.0000	0.0000	0.0003	0.0001	0.0006	0.0002	0.0003	0.0000	0.0073	0.0001
21.	Electricity/Gas/Water Supply	0.0158	0.0158	0.0001	0.0000	0.0000	0.0003	0.0001	0.0053	0.0014	0.0007	0.0004	0.0050	0.0004
22.	Rail and other Transport / Storage Services	0.0131	0.0131	0.0102	0.0000	0.1665	0.0413	0.0641	0.0889	0.1023	0.1193	0.0024	0.2751	0.1358
23.	Trade/Hotels	0.0252	0.0252	0.0270	0.0003	0.0000	0.0054	0.0741	0.0368	0.0151	0.0775	0.0247	0.1298	0.0551
24.	Banking/Insurance	0.0127	0.0127	0.0002	0.0000	0.0000	0.0105	0.0118	0.0362	0.0117	0.0308	0.0356	0.2005	0.0221
25	Other services (Edu., Med., Admin., Defence, etc.)	0.0003	0.0003	0.0005	0.0000	0.0000	0.0002	0.0122	0.0002	0.2705	0.0000	0.0302	0.0000	0.0000
Total Input		0.6190	0.6195	0.6428	0.6997	0.6666	0.7377	0.7806	0.7128	0.7796	0.8130	0.6729	0.7203	0.6664
Total Output		1.0000	1.0000	1.0000	1.0000	1.0000	1.0000	1.0000	1.0000	1.0000	1.0000	1.0000	1.0000	1.0000
Gross Value Added		0.3810	0.3805	0.3572	0.3000	0.3334	0.2623	0.2194	0.2872	0.2204	0.1870	0.3271	0.2797	0.3336

Appendix –IXA : (Contd.)

Sector Code	Industry Commodity	14	15	16	17	18	19	20	21	22	23	24	25
1.	Agriculture	0.0000	0.0000	0.0000	0.0000	0.0000	0.0000	0.0000	0.0000	0.0091	0.0476	0.0000	0.0004
2.	Animal Husbandry	0.0000	0.0000	0.0000	0.0000	0.0000	0.0000	0.0000	0.0000	0.0000	0.0647	0.0000	0.0002
3.	Forestry and Logging	0.0001	0.0005	0.0001	0.0000	0.0005	0.0000	0.0001	0.0000	0.0000	0.0000	0.0000	0.0005
4.	Fishing	0.0000	0.0000	0.0000	0.0000	0.0000	0.0000	0.0000	0.0000	0.0000	0.0336	0.0000	0.0000
5.	Mining/Quarrying	0.0273	0.0099	0.0041	0.0009	0.0052	0.2187	0.0713	0.0415	0.0000	0.0118	0.0000	0.0010
6.	Food Prod., Beverages and Tobacco Products	0.0000	0.0000	0.0000	0.0000	0.0000	0.0000	0.0000	0.0000	0.0016	0.0443	0.0000	0.0007
7.	Textiles	0.0070	0.0030	0.0063	0.0076	0.0087	0.0027	0.0047	0.0000	0.0033	0.0001	0.0000	0.0096
8.	Wood, Wood Prod. and Furniture	0.0138	0.0058	0.0151	0.0050	0.0184	0.0062	0.0004	0.0000	0.0019	0.0315	0.0026	0.0002
9.	Paper, Paper Prod., Printing/ Publishing	0.0054	0.0032	0.0071	0.0013	0.0072	0.0065	0.0012	0.0051	0.0038	0.0107	0.0111	0.0259
10.	Leather Products	0.0000	0.0000	0.0000	0.0000	0.0000	0.0408	0.0000	0.0000	0.0000	0.0000	0.0000	0.0000
11.	Plastic/Rubber Products	0.0050	0.1486	0.0049	0.0804	0.0724	0.0125	0.0000	0.0000	0.0115	0.1070	0.0000	0.0663
12.	Coal/Petroleum Products	0.0099	0.0128	0.0066	0.0004	0.0114	0.0009	0.0019	0.0399	0.0155	0.0005	0.0010	0.0073
13.	Chemicals	0.0148	0.0103	0.0235	0.0194	0.0836	0.0133	0.0000	0.0006	0.0001	0.0000	0.0000	0.0257
14.	Non-metallic Products	0.1913	0.0907	0.0034	0.0013	0.0000	0.0089	0.0000	0.0001	0.0000	0.0030	0.0000	0.0139
15.	Metal Products	0.2592	0.2415	0.0131	0.1154	0.1816	0.0602	0.0063	0.0080	0.0016	0.0029	0.0000	0.0144
16.	Industrial Machinery	0.0080	0.0006	0.1947	0.0011	0.0000	0.0000	0.0004	0.0194	0.0001	0.0000	0.0000	0.0271
17.	Electric/Electronic Machinery	0.0010	0.0013	0.1698	0.3494	0.0011	0.1170	0.0518	0.0674	0.0006	0.0002	0.0000	0.0130
18.	Rail and other Transport Equipment	0.0000	0.0000	0.0000	0.0000	0.2670	0.0000	0.0010	0.1273	0.0444	0.0203	0.0450	0.0369
19.	Miscellaneous Manufacturing	0.0060	0.0001	0.0004	0.0001	0.0003	0.1131	0.0001	0.0045	0.0036	0.0011	0.0008	0.0349
20.	Construction	0.0067	0.0001	0.0005	0.0001	0.0004	0.0005	0.0225	0.0227	0.0870	0.0054	0.4152	0.0425
21.	Electricity/Gas/Water Supply	0.0020	0.0013	0.0013	0.0003	0.0008	0.0003	0.2040	0.0416	0.0010	0.0054	0.0084	0.0380
22.	Rail and other Transport / Storage Services	0.0820	0.0134	0.1092	0.0810	0.0297	0.0367	0.0663	0.2720	0.1012	0.0066	0.0355	0.0467
23.	Trade/Hotels	0.0008	0.0973	0.1588	0.1297	0.0632	0.1418	0.2720	0.1621	0.2697	0.2167	0.0025	0.0651
24.	Banking/Insurance	0.0398	0.0369	0.0310	0.0095	0.0135	0.0000	0.0032	0.0000	0.0592	0.0713	0.0605	0.0295
25.	Other services(Edu., Med., Admin., Defence, etc.)	0.0000	0.0000	0.0000	0.0123	0.0000	0.0000	0.0025	0.0033	0.0045	0.1004	0.0369	0.0451
	Total Input	0.6800	0.6774	0.7500	0.8154	0.7650	0.7800	0.7099	0.8154	0.6196	0.7854	0.6196	0.5451
	Total Output	1.0000	1.0000	1.0000	1.0000	1.0000	1.0000	1.0000	1.0000	1.0000	1.0000	1.0000	1.0000
	Gross Value Added	0.3200	0.3226	0.2500	0.1846	0.2350	0.2200	0.2901	0.1846	0.3804	0.2146	0.3804	0.4549

Source: Mathematically obtained as part of input-output model (refer chapter 3 and chapter 6).

Appendix- IX B : Input-Output Coefficient Matrix (commodity × industry): 2000-01

Sector Code	*Industry / Commodity*	*1*	*2*	*3*	*4*	*5*	*6*	*7*	*8*	*9*	*10*	*11*	*12*	*13*
1.	Agriculture	0.0806	0.1384	0.0001	0.0003	-	0.0090	-	-	-	-	-	-	0.0002
2.	Animal Husbandry	0.0935	0.0029	-	-	-	0.0266	-	-	-	-	-	-	-
3.	Forestry and Logging	0.0000	-	0.0004	-	-	-	0.0000	0.0011	-	-	0.0013	-	-
4.	Fishing	-	-	-	0.0868	-	-	-	-	-	-	-	-	-
5.	Mining/Quarrying	0.0000	-	-	-	0.0004	0.0000	0.0000	0.0000	-	-	0.0000	0.0000	0.0000
6.	Food Prod., Beverages and Tobacco Prod.	0.0006	0.1029	-	0.0250	-	0.5090	-	-	-	-	-	-	0.0144
7.	Textiles	0.0028	0.0305	0.0071	0.1525	-	0.0130	0.4174	0.0149	0.0566	0.0725	0.0158	0.0046	0.0563
8.	Wood, Wood Prods., and Furniture	0.0000	-	0.0000	0.0015	0.0011	0.0009	0.0004	0.0756	0.0014	0.0018	0.0011	0.0004	0.0039
9.	Paper, Paper Prods., Printing/ Publishing	0.0001	-	0.0012	0.0001	0.0006	0.0006	0.0002	0.0007	0.1765	0.0012	0.0007	0.0002	0.0026
10.	Leather Products	0.0000	-	-	-	-	0.0000	0.0174	0.0025	0.0003	0.4069	0.0000	0.0000	0.0000
11.	Plastic/Rubber Products	0.0000	-	0.0011	-	0.0012	0.0005	0.0011	0.0000	0.0055	0.0069	0.0965	0.0002	0.0020
12.	Coal/Petroleum Products	0.0000	-	0.0001	0.0000	0.0000	0.0000	0.0000	0.0000	0.0000	0.0000	0.0000	0.0001	0.0000
13.	Chemicals	0.0048	0.0001	0.0000	0.0003	0.0028	0.0002	0.0000	0.0008	0.0051	0.0007	0.0005	0.0000	0.0241
14.	Non-metallic Products	-	-	0.0000	0.0000	0.0007	0.0000	0.0000	0.0004	0.0002	0.0000	0.0000	0.0000	0.0000
15.	Metal Products	0.0000	0.0001	0.0002	0.0010	0.0028	0.0000	0.0002	0.0018	0.0013	0.0001	0.0001	0.0000	0.0001
16.	Industrial Machinery	0.0043	0.0002	0.0014	0.0000	0.1048	0.0001	0.0001	0.0012	0.0016	0.0001	0.0000	0.0000	0.0016
17.	Electric/Electronic Machinery	0.0001	-	0.0010	0.0000	0.0001	0.0001	0.0004	0.0011	0.0031	0.0002	0.0001	0.0001	0.0002
18.	Rail and other Transport Equipment	0.0008	-	0.0067	0.0444	0.0160	-	-	0.0001	-	-	-	-	-
19.	Miscellaneous Manufacturing	0.0001	-	0.0025	0.0000	0.0089	0.0000	0.0000	-	0.0002	0.0000	0.0000	0.0000	0.0000
20.	Construction	0.0563	0.0041	0.2044	-	0.0955	0.0002	0.0001	0.0006	0.0004	0.0003	0.0003	0.0004	0.0001
21.	Electricity/Gas/Water Supply	0.0020	-	0.0001	0.0001	0.0057	0.0003	0.0001	0.0053	0.0026	0.0007	0.0016	0.0003	0.0003
22.	Rail and other Transport / Storage Services	0.1309	0.0332	0.0518	0.0350	0.0791	0.0336	0.0854	0.0888	0.1959	0.1170	0.1048	0.2420	0.1073
23.	Trade/Hotels	0.2328	0.3087	0.0519	0.0997	0.1484	0.0362	0.2413	0.3180	0.2726	0.0761	0.2197	0.2108	0.2498
24.	Banking/Insurance	0.0105	0.0078	0.0067	0.0043	0.0313	0.0085	0.0096	0.0362	0.0225	0.0303	0.0286	0.2311	0.0174
25.	Other services (Edu., Med., Admin., Defense, etc.)	0.0195	-	0.2680	0.2064	0.1034	0.0001	0.0130	0.1507	0.0001	-	0.0002	-	-
	Total Input	0.6396	0.6289	0.6049	0.6576	0.6029	0.6389	0.7867	0.6997	0.7458	0.7151	0.4714	0.6903	0.4803
	Total Output	1.0000	1.0000	1.0000	1.0000	1.0000	1.0000	1.0000	1.0000	1.0000	1.0000	1.0000	1.0000	1.0000
	Value Added	0.3604	0.3711	0.3951	0.3424	0.3971	0.3611	0.2133	0.3003	0.2542	0.2849	0.5286	0.3097	0.5197

Appendix- IX B : (Contd.)

Sector Code	Industry / Commodity	14	15	16	17	18	19	20	21	22	23	24	25	Total
1.	Agriculture	-	-	-	-	-	-	0.0085	0.0000	0.0076	0.0060	-	0.0021	0.0047
2.	Animal Husbandry	-	-	-	-	-	-	0.0013	0.0052	0.0000	0.0113	-	0.0038	0.0044
3.	Forestry and Logging	-	-	-	-	-	-	0.0002	-	0.0000	0.0000	-	-	0.0000
4.	Fishing	-	-	-	-	-	-	-	0.0000	-	0.0009	-	-	0.0002
5.	Mining/Quarrying	0.0000	0.0000	0.0000	0.0000	-	-	0.0002	0.0036	0.0000	0.0000	-	0.0000	0.0000
6.	Food Prod., Beverages and Tobacco Prod.	-	-	-	-	-	-	-	0.0000	0.0004	0.0280	-	0.0001	0.0158
7.	Textiles	0.0030	0.0140	0.0060	0.0123	0.0076	0.0452	0.0054	0.0003	0.0059	0.0101	0.0007	0.0036	0.0234
8.	Wood, Wood Prods., and Furniture	0.0002	0.0010	0.0004	0.0010	0.0017	0.0032	0.0047	0.0001	0.0001	0.0006	0.0001	0.0005	0.0010
9.	Paper, Paper Prods., Printing/Publishing	0.0002	0.0005	0.0003	0.0007	0.0001	0.0021	0.0002	0.0012	0.0013	0.0019	0.0021	0.0014	0.0026
10.	Leather Products	0.0008	0.0001	0.0001	0.0001	0.0009	0.0001	-	-	0.0001	-	0.0025	0.0000	0.0027
11.	Plastic/Rubber Products	0.0001	0.0010	0.0003	0.0020	0.0012	0.0134	0.0000	0.0000	0.0057	0.0003	0.0001	0.0000	0.0015
12.	Coal/Petroleum Products	0.0000	0.0000	0.0000	0.0000	0.0000	0.0000	0.0000	0.0000	0.0000	0.0000	0.0000	0.0000	0.0000
13.	Chemicals	0.0001	0.0004	0.0002	0.0006	0.0009	0.0007	0.0007	0.0002	0.0000	0.0000	0.0000	0.0026	0.0012
14.	Non-metallic Products	0.0074	0.0005	0.0001	0.0004	0.0002	0.0002	0.0121	0.0000	0.0000	0.0000	0.0000	0.0000	0.0011
15.	Metal Products	0.0000	0.1075	0.0070	0.0075	0.0036	0.0120	0.0104	0.0001	0.0002	0.0004	0.0001	0.0002	0.0029
16.	Industrial Machinery	0.0006	0.0007	0.3683	0.0013	0.0021	0.0004	0.0002	0.0099	0.0020	0.0008	0.0007	0.0008	0.0022
17.	Electric/Electronic Machinery	0.0001	0.0003	0.0195	0.4302	0.0225	0.0127	0.0203	0.0331	0.0081	0.0001	0.0007	0.0043	0.0127
18.	Rail and other Transport Equipment	-	-	-	-	0.3240	-	0.0004	0.0013	0.0258	0.0000	0.0022	0.0002	0.0046
19.	Miscellaneous Manufacturing	0.0000	0.0001	0.0001	0.0001	0.0001	0.1632	0.0008	0.0038	0.0060	0.0016	0.0034	0.0185	0.0075
20.	Construction	0.0008	0.0001	0.0005	0.0001	0.0004	0.0006	0.0302	0.0608	0.0649	0.0465	0.0486	0.1836	0.0815
21.	Electricity/Gas/Water Supply	0.0002	0.0022	0.0013	0.0004	0.0009	0.0003	0.0008	0.0193	0.0026	0.0007	0.0008	0.0005	0.0010
22.	Rail and other Transport / Storage Services	0.3798	0.1799	0.1126	0.1050	0.0333	0.0433	0.1077	0.1723	0.0490	0.0476	0.0381	0.0326	0.0554
23.	Trade/Hotels	0.2137	0.4605	0.1637	0.1682	0.3302	0.5018	0.3932	0.3175	0.1536	0.0532	0.0511	0.1249	0.1417
24.	Banking/Insurance	0.0047	0.0244	0.0320	0.0123	0.0151	-	0.0188	0.0234	0.0337	0.0328	0.1028	0.0196	0.0382
25.	Other services (Edu., Med., Admin., Defence, etc.)	-	-	-	0.0160	-	-	0.0944	0.1342	0.2858	0.4126	0.3397	0.3123	0.2675
	Total Input	0.6119	0.7932	0.7125	0.7583	0.7449	0.7988	0.7104	0.7862	0.6528	0.6558	0.5937	0.7116	0.6737
	Total Output	1.000	1.000	1.000	1.000	1.000	1.000	1.000	1.000	1.000	1.000	1.000	1.000	1.000
	Value Added	0.3881	0.2068	0.2875	0.2417	0.2551	0.2012	0.2896	0.2138	0.3472	0.3442	0.4063	0.2884	0.3263

Source: Input output coefficient matrix is obtained from commodity × industry matrix (input flow matrix) by dividing the column entry by the respective industry output.

Appendix-X A : Input-Output Absorption Matrix (Commodity × Industry) 2000-01 (Pollution Accounted)

Sector Code	Industry / Commodity	1	2	3	4	5	6	7	8	9	10
1.	Agriculture	829501	1468244	6	130	0	309735	0	0	0	0
2.	Animal Husbandry	962724	30957	0	0	0	915216	0	0	0	0
3.	Forestry and Logging	6	0	18	0	0	0	13	3018	0	0
4.	Fishing	0	0	0	41593	0	0	0	0	0	0
5.	Mining/Quarrying	14	0	0	0	55	25	103	9	0	0
6.	Food Prod., Beverages and . Tobacco Prod.	6281	1091536	0	11979	0	17353442	0	0	0	0
7.	Textiles	28955	324039	319	73046	0	446342	29376507	39574	659231	470721
8.	Wood, Wood Prod., and Furniture	275	0	1	716	150	31419	26712	194502	16646	11973
9.	Paper, Paper Prod. Printing/Publishing	919	0	53	33	86	20383	17174	1746	1858205	7881
10.	Leather Products	90	0	0	0	0	345	1240243	6749	3494	2615840
11.	Plastic/Rubber Products	261	0	48	0		16268	77406	29	63822	44941
12.	Coal/Petroleum Prod.	160	0	5	13	6	144	122	112	213	23
13.	Chemicals	49089	609	0	161	381	8555	1730	2043	58956	4783
14.	Non-metallic Prod.	0	0	0	1	96	222	1723	987	2249	94
15.	Metal Products	137	566	11	494	382	1436	11265	4752	15404	744
16.	Industrial Machinery	43810	2067	61	10	14337	2216	8337	3187	19101	799
17.	Electric/Electronic Machinery	1174	0	46	23	17	3008	27431	2992	35812	1498
18.	Rail and Other Transport Equipment	7803	0	299	21275	2188	0	0	281	0	0
19.	Miscellaneous Manufacturing	571	0	113	11	1211	316	1363	0	1781	77
20.	Construction	579141	43484	9159	0	13055	8223	7300	1523	4316	1878
21.	Electricity/Gas/Water Supply	21081	0	3	50	774	9441	9775	14002	30603	4648
22.	Rail and Other Transport / Storage Services	1347802	352459	2323	16745	10820	1154942	6101836	236123	2283198	759535
23.	Trade/Hotels	2396208	3275730	2326	47746	20297	1246230	17242446	845373	3177522	493713
24.	Banking/Insurance	107812	83035	302	2038	4285	292500	688292	96168	261761	196314
25.	Other Services (Edu., Med., Admin., Defence, etc.)	200641	0	12007	98850	14142	1892	926851	400535	1418	0
26.	Pollution Abatement	0	0	0	0	0	153705	457152	6584	199776	24815
	Total Input	6584454	6672725	27099	314913	82442	21976005	56219780	1860290	8693508	4640277
	Total Output	10294054	10610625	44799	478913	136742	34397415	71459074	2658666	11656692	6489151
	Gross Value Added	4809600	3937900	17700	204000	14300	12421410	2639293	1198376	2963184	1048873

Appendix-X A : (Contd.)

Sector Code	Industry / Commodity	11	12	13	14	15	16	17	18	19	20
1.	Agriculture	0	0	2984	0	0	0	0	0	0	1330123
2.	Animal Husbandry	0	0	0	0	0	0	0	0	0	200641
3.	Forestry and Logging	16155	0	0	0	0	0	0	0	0	27289
4.	Fishing	0	0	0	0	0	0	0	0	0	0
5.	Mining/Quarrying	7	41	113	126	300	12	5	0	0	25756
6.	Food Prod., Beverages and Tobacco Prod.	0	0	251383	0	0	0	0	0	0	0
7.	Textiles	192842	10249	782013	8584	359393	36790	416591	64222	183565	841997
8.	Wood, Wood Prod. and Furniture	13590	778	68086	696	25693	2418	34473	14244	12883	739365
9.	Paper, Paper Prod., Printing /	470	44931	653	12009	1824	22082	1040	8347	24060	
	Publishing	8823									
10.	Leather Products	102	35	353	2307	2814	745	3704	7958	279	0
11.	Plastic/Rubber Products	1135789	370	34371	403	25927	2091	68270	10064	54236	6366
12.	Coal/Petroleum Prod.	125	191	115	55	23	14	222	333	44	345
13.	Chemicals	6068	59	332903	266	11239	975	19372	7304	2647	115828
14.	Non-metallic Prod.	35	12	227	21082	11763	544	13900	1338	746	1899953
15.	Metal Products	1583	74	2529	96	2514216	43182	254237	30221	48585	1627108
16.	Industrial Machinery	474	76	27775	1753	17296	2260166	42829	17930	1523	25003
17.	Electric/Electronic Machinery	886	292	3620	235	7996	119939	14473028	189584	51423	3176647
18.	Rail and Other Transport Equipment	0	0	0	0	0	0	0	2719244	0	63100
19.	Miscellaneous Manufacturing	80	22	104	12	1433	379	1901	506	660202	128837
20.	Construction	3444	903	1845	2225	2333	3008	4899	3553	2334	4730682
21.	Electricity/Gas/Water Supply	19465	617	5920	670	55642	8301	13695	7792	1228	131809
22.	Rail and Other Transport/ Storage Services	1276457	526873	1872604	992076	4616130	692893	3545697	280701	175695	16880660
23.	Trade/Hotels	2675772	465161	4361200	606137	11818176	1007040	5680250	2783076	2037940	61631118
24.	Banking/Insurance	348097	509901	304006	13261	626233	196923	415258	127140	0	2952251
25.	Other Services (Edu., Med., Admin., Defence, etc.)	1940	0	0	0	0	0	539195	0	0	14791178
26.	Pollution Abatement	39098	7084	287390	85242	245216	5575	53627	11507	2553	
	Total Input	5740830	1523208	8384472	1735879	20353831	4382817	25603234	6277757	3244230	111350116
	Total Output	12178107	2206575	17456116	2836812	25661637	6151690	33765508	8427445	4061331	156745616
	Gross Value Added	7387276	2083367	9671644	2650933	3507806	1768874	8162274	2149689	1167100	48395500

Appendix-X A : (Contd.)

Sector Code	Industry Commodity	21	22	23	24	25 II use	26 II use	Total use	Total Final out put	Total
1.	Agriculture	83	1296088	1902705	0	1100520	0	7410617	2460252	9870869
2.	Animal Husbandry	51365	0	3596136	0	1983025	0	6777341	3710507	10487847
3.	Forestry and Logging	0	42	7821	0	0	0	54355	-9556	44799
4.	Fishing	1	0	301074	0	0	0	342667	129910	472577
5.	Mining/Quarrying	35566	3556	5556	0	444	0	71674	65068	136742
6.	Food Prod., Beverages and Tobacco Prod.	0	69196	8911372	0	29717	0	27718625	5276177	32994802
7.	Textiles	2722	993526	3202638	212437	1877730	0	40575078	17088414	57663492
8.	Wood, Wood Prod. and Furniture	655	8661	193041	33152	240715	0	1670568	2673956	4344524
9.	Paper, Paper Prod., Printing / Publishing	11641	216388	606026	693189	744189	0	4301233	6575462	10876695
10.	Leather Products	0	18688	0	800003	1	0	4703660	-322737	4380922
11.	Plastic/Rubber Products	478	967024	88840	21079	7304	0	2625287	439753	3065041
12.	Coal/Petroleum Prod.	334	4445	345	5555	333	0	13117	2038752	2051869
13.	Chemicals	1837	7284	5479	0	1372435	0	1960913	11930793	13891706
14.	Non-metallic Prod.	163	7043	2628	2	10646	0	1975455	1012202	2987656
15.	Metal Products	803	29609	133478	33498	95945	0	4850218	12681372	17531589
16.	Industrial Machinery	98193	343062	269063	233692	443794	0	3832744	-236145	3596599
17.	Electric/Electronic Machinery	329646	1382298	47325	228829	2224194	0	22306768	-3567724	18739044
18.	Rail and Other Transport Equipment	12471	4379514	14594	713082	119048	0	8045095	179261	8224357
19.	Miscellaneous Manufacturing	37917	1018623	512590	1104157	9701027	0	13172660	10731304	23903964
20.	Construction	604345	11013226	14797839	15814241	96042508	0	143116323	15485518	158601840
21.	Electricity/Gas/Water Supply	191850	435966	231446	274412	247230	0	1695339	8754288	10449627
22.	Rail and Other Transport / Storage Services	1713530	8314413	15134268	12371528	17031348	0	96342852	73368471	169711323
23.	Trade/Hotel	3157927	26060869	16910255	16627553	65315328	0	247489184	72613050	320102234
24.	Banking/Insurance	232691	5711124	10430327	33417894	10266166	0	67175969	257956636	325132605
25.	Other Services (Edu., Med., Admin., Defence, etc.)	1334986	48504377	131169601	110459700	163358511	0	471615183	82592794	554207977
26.	Pollution Abatement						0	1579324	0	1579324
	Total Input	7819204	110785023	208474444	193044005	372212157	1579324	1181422250	583627778	1763470704
	Total Output	9945303	169711323	317897445	325132605	523067058	1579324	1754755974		

Source : In sector 13 adjustment for pollution data has been done from 7 and 13 sector. In Sec. 12 from Sec. 22 because in Delhi petroleum use as max in tpt

Appendix-X B : Input-Output Coefficient Matrix (Commodity × Industry) , 2000-01 (Pollution Accounted)

Sector Code	Industry / Commodity	1	2	3	4	5	6	7	8	9	10	11	12	13
1.	Agriculture	8.06%	13.84%	0.01%	0.03%	0.00%	0.90%	0.00%	0.00%	0.00%	0.00%	0.00%	0.00%	0.02%
2.	Animal Husbandry	9.35%	0.29%	0.00%	0.00%	0.00%	2.66%	0.00%	0.00%	0.00%	0.00%	0.00%	0.00%	0.00%
3.	Forestry and Logging	0.00%	0.00%	0.04%	0.00%	0.00%	0.00%	0.00%	0.11%	0.00%	0.00%	0.13%	0.00%	0.00%
4.	Fishing	0.00%	0.00%	0.00%	8.68%	0.00%	0.00%	0.00%	0.00%	0.00%	0.00%	0.00%	0.00%	0.00%
5.	Mining/Quarrying	0.00%	0.00%	0.00%	0.00%	0.04%	0.00%	0.00%	0.00%	0.00%	0.00%	0.00%	0.00%	0.00%
6.	Food Prod., Beverages and Tobacco Prod.	0.06%	10.29%	0.00%	2.50%	0.00%	50.45%	0.00%	0.00%	0.00%	0.00%	0.00%	0.00%	1.44%
7.	Textiles	0.28%	3.05%	0.71%	15.25%	0.00%	1.30%	41.11%	1.49%	5.66%	7.25%	1.58%	0.46%	4.48%
8.	Wood, Wood Prod.and Furniture	0.00%	0.00%	0.00%	0.15%	0.11%	0.09%	0.04%	7.32%	0.14%	0.18%	0.11%	0.04%	0.39%
9.	Paper, Paper Prod., Printing/ Publishing	0.01%	0.00%	0.12%	0.01%	0.06%	0.06%	0.02%	0.07%	15.94%	0.12%	0.07%	0.02%	0.26%
10.	Leather Products	0.00%	0.00%	0.00%	0.00%	0.00%	0.00%	1.74%	0.25%	0.03%	40.31%	0.00%	0.00%	0.00%
11.	Plastic/Rubber Products	0.00%	0.00%	0.11%	0.00%	0.12%	0.05%	0.11%	0.00%	0.55%	0.69%	9.33%	0.02%	0.20%
12.	Coal/Petroleum Prod.	0.00%	0.00%	0.01%	0.00%	0.00%	0.00%	0.00%	0.00%	0.00%	0.00%	0.00%	0.01%	0.00%
13.	Chemicals	0.48%	0.01%	0.00%	0.03%	0.28%	0.02%	0.00%	0.08%	0.51%	0.07%	0.05%	0.00%	1.91%
14.	Non-metallic Prod.	0.00%	0.00%	0.00%	0.00%	0.07%	0.00%	0.00%	0.04%	0.02%	0.00%	0.00%	0.00%	0.00%
15.	Metal Products	0.00%	0.01%	0.02%	0.10%	0.28%	0.00%	0.02%	0.18%	0.13%	0.01%	0.01%	0.00%	0.01%
16.	Industrial Machinery	0.43%	0.02%	0.14%	0.00%	10.48%	0.01%	0.01%	0.12%	0.16%	0.01%	0.00%	0.00%	0.16%
17.	Electric/Electronic Machinery	0.01%	0.00%	0.10%	0.00%	0.01%	0.01%	0.04%	0.11%	0.31%	0.02%	0.01%	0.01%	0.02%
18.	Rail and Other Transport Equipment	0.08%	0.00%	0.67%	4.44%	1.60%	0.00%	0.00%	0.01%	0.00%	0.00%	0.00%	0.00%	0.00%
19.	Miscellaneous Manufacturing	0.01%	0.00%	0.25%	0.00%	0.89%	0.00%	0.00%	0.00%	0.02%	0.00%	0.00%	0.00%	0.00%
20.	Construction	5.63%	0.41%	20.44%	0.00%	9.55%	0.02%	0.01%	0.06%	0.04%	0.03%	0.03%	0.04%	0.01%
21.	Electricity/Gas/Water Supply	0.20%	0.00%	0.01%	0.01%	0.57%	0.03%	0.01%	0.53%	0.26%	0.07%	0.16%	0.03%	0.03%
22.	Rail and Other Transport/ Storage Services	13.09%	3.32%	5.18%	3.50%	7.91%	3.36%	8.54%	8.88%	19.59%	11.70%	10.48%	23.88%	10.73%
23.	Trade/Hotel	23.28%	30.87%	5.19%	9.97%	14.84%	3.62%	24.13%	31.80%	27.26%	7.61%	21.97%	21.08%	24.98%
24.	Banking/Insurance	1.05%	0.78%	0.67%	0.43%	3.13%	0.85%	0.96%	3.62%	2.25%	3.03%	2.86%	23.11%	1.74%
25.	Other Services (Edu., Med., Admin., Defence, etc.)	1.95%	0.00%	26.80%	20.64%	10.34%	0.01%	1.30%	15.07%	0.01%	0.00%	0.02%	0.00%	0.00%
26.	Pollution Abatement	0.00%	0.00%	0.00%	0.00%	0.00%	0.45%	0.64%	0.25%	1.71%	0.38%	0.32%	0.32%	1.65%
	Total Input	63.96%	62.89%	60.49%	65.76%	60.29%	63.89%	78.67%	69.97%	74.58%	71.51%	47.14%	69.03%	48.03%
	Total Output	100.00%	100.00%	100.00%	100.00%	100.00%	100.00%	100.00%	100.00%	100.00%	100.00%	100.00%	100.00%	100.00%
	Gross Value Added	46.72%	37.11%	39.51%	42.60%	10.46%	36.11%	3.69%	45.07%	25.42%	16.16%	60.66%	94.42%	55.41%
		0.00%	0.00%	0.00%	0.00%	0.00%	0.00%	0.00%	0.00%	0.00%	0.00%	0.00%	0.00%	0.00%

Appendix-X B : (Contd.)

Sector Code	Industry Commodity	14	15	16	17	18	19	20	21	22	23	24	25	26	Total
1.	Agriculture	0.00%	0.00%	0.00%	0.00%	0.00%	0.00%	0.85%	0.00%	0.76%	0.60%	0.00%	0.21%	0.00%	0.42%
2.	Animal Husbandry	0.00%	0.00%	0.00%	0.00%	0.00%	0.00%	0.13%	0.52%	0.00%	1.13%	0.00%	0.38%	0.00%	0.39%
3.	Forestry and Logging	0.00%	0.00%	0.00%	0.00%	0.00%	0.00%	0.02%	0.00%	0.00%	0.00%	0.00%	0.00%	0.00%	0.00%
4.	Fishing	0.00%	0.00%	0.00%	0.00%	0.00%	0.00%	0.00%	0.00%	0.00%	0.09%	0.00%	0.00%	0.00%	0.02%
5.	Mining/Quarrying	0.00%	0.00%	0.00%	0.00%	0.00%	0.00%	0.02%	0.36%	0.00%	0.00%	0.00%	0.00%	0.00%	0.00%
6.	Food Prod., Beverages and Tobacco Prod.	0.00%	0.00%	0.00%	0.00%	0.00%	0.00%	0.00%	0.00%	0.04%	2.80%	0.00%	0.01%	0.00%	1.58%
7.	Textiles	0.30%	1.40%	0.60%	1.23%	0.76%	4.52%	0.54%	0.03%	0.59%	1.01%	0.07%	0.36%	0.00%	2.31%
8.	Wood, Wood Prod. and Furniture	0.02%	0.10%	0.04%	0.10%	0.17%	0.32%	0.47%	0.01%	0.01%	0.06%	0.01%	0.05%	0.00%	0.10%
9.	Paper, Paper Prod., Printing / Publishing	0.02%	0.05%	0.03%	0.07%	0.01%	0.21%	0.02%	0.12%	0.13%	0.19%	0.21%	0.14%	0.00%	0.25%
10.	Leather Products	0.08%	0.01%	0.01%	0.01%	0.09%	0.01%	0.00%	0.00%	0.01%	0.00%	0.25%	0.00%	0.00%	0.27%
11.	Plastic/Rubber Products	0.01%	0.10%	0.03%	0.20%	0.12%	1.34%	0.00%	0.00%	0.57%	0.03%	0.01%	0.00%	0.00%	0.15%
12.	Coal/Petroleum Prod.	0.00%	0.00%	0.00%	0.00%	0.00%	0.00%	0.00%	0.00%	0.00%	0.00%	0.00%	0.00%	0.00%	0.00%13
	Chemicals	0.01%	0.04%	0.02%	0.06%	0.09%	0.07%	0.07%	0.02%	0.00%	0.00%	0.00%	0.26%	0.00%	0.11%
14.	Non-metallic Prod.	0.74%	0.05%	0.01%	0.04%	0.02%	0.02%	1.21%	0.00%	0.00%	0.00%	0.00%	0.00%	0.00%	0.11%
15.	Metal Products	0.00%	9.80%	0.70%	0.75%	0.36%	1.20%	1.04%	0.01%	0.02%	0.04%	0.01%	0.02%	0.00%	0.28%
16.	Industrial Machinery	0.06%	0.07%	36.74%	0.13%	0.21%	0.04%	0.02%	0.99%	0.20%	0.08%	0.07%	0.08%	0.00%	0.22%
17.	Electric/Electronic Machinery	0.01%	0.03%	1.95%	42.86%	2.25%	1.27%	2.03%	3.31%	0.81%	0.01%	0.07%	0.43%	0.00%	1.27%
18.	Rail and Other Transport Equipment	0.00%	0.00%	0.00%	0.00%	32.27%	0.00%	0.04%	0.13%	2.58%	0.00%	0.22%	0.02%	0.00%	0.46%
19.	Miscellaneous Manufacturing	0.00%	0.01%	0.01%	0.01%	0.01%	16.26%	0.08%	0.38%	0.60%	0.16%	0.34%	1.85%	0.00%	0.75%
20.	Construction	0.08%	0.01%	0.05%	0.01%	0.04%	0.06%	3.02%	6.08%	6.49%	4.65%	4.86%	18.36%	0.00%	8.16%
21.	Electricity/Gas/Water supply	0.02%	0.22%	0.13%	0.04%	0.09%	0.03%	0.08%	1.93%	0.26%	0.07%	0.08%	0.05%	0.00%	0.10%
22.	Rail and other Transport/ Storage Services	34.97%	17.99%	11.26%	10.50%	3.33%	4.33%	10.77%	17.23%	4.90%	4.76%	3.81%	3.26%	0.00%	5.49%
23.	Trade/Hotel	21.37%	46.05%	16.37%	16.82%	33.02%	50.18%	39.32%	31.75%	15.36%	5.32%	5.11%	12.49%	0.00%	14.10%
24.	Banking/Insurance	0.47%	2.44%	3.20%	1.23%	1.51%	0.00%	1.88%	2.34%	3.37%	3.28%	10.28%	1.96%	0.00%	3.83%
25.	Other Services (Edu., Med., Admin., Defence, etc.)	0.00%	0.00%	0.00%	1.60%	0.00%	0.00%	9.44%	13.42%	28.58%	41.26%	33.97%	31.23%	0.00%	26.88%
26.	Pollution Abatement	3.00%	0.96%	0.09%	0.16%	0.14%	0.06%	0.00%	0.00%	0.00%	0.00%	0.00%	0.00%	0.00%	0.09%
	Total Input	61.19%	79.32%	71.25%	75.83%	74.49%	79.88%	71.04%	78.62%	65.28%	65.58%	59.37%	71.16%	100.00%	67.33%
	Total Output	100.00%	100.00%	100.00%	100.00%	100.00%	100.00%	100.00%	100.00%	100.00%	100.00%	100.00%	100.00%	100.00%	100.00%
	Gross Value Added	93.45%	13.67%	28.75%	24.17%	25.51%	28.74%	30.88%	14.34%	35.31%	34.99%	41.78%	28.84%	0.00%	32.52%
		0.00%	0.00%	0.00%	0.00%	0.00%	0.00%	0.00%	0.00%	0.00%	0.00%	0.00%	0.00%	0.00%	0.00%

Appendix-X C : Forward Linkages (commodity sales to different industries in per cent): 2000-01 (Pollution Accounted)

Sector Code	*Industry* / *Commodity*	*1*	*2*	*3*	*4*	*5*	*6*	*7*	*8*	*9*	*10*	*11*	*12*	*13*
1.	Agriculture	11.19	19.81	0.00	0.00	0.00	4.18	0.00	0.00	0.00	0.00	0.00	0.00	0.04
2.	Animal Husbandry	14.21	0.46	0.00	0.00	0.00	13.50	0.00	0.00	0.00	0.00	0.00	0.00	0.00
3.	Forestry and Logging	0.01	0.00	0.03	0.00	0.00	0.00	0.02	5.55	0.00	0.00	29.72	0.00	0.00
4.	Fishing	0.00	0.00	0.00	12.14	0.00	0.00	0.00	0.00	0.00	0.00	0.00	0.00	0.00
5.	Mining/Quarrying	0.02	0.00	0.00	0.00	0.08	0.03	0.14	0.01	0.00	0.00	0.01	0.06	0.16
6.	Food Prod., Beverages and Tobacco Prods	0.02	3.94	0.00	0.04	0.00	62.61	0.00	0.00	0.00	0.00	0.00	0.00	0.91
7.	Textiles	0.07	0.80	0.00	0.18	0.00	1.10	72.40	0.10	1.62	1.16	0.48	0.03	1.93
8.	Wood, Wood Prods., and Furniture	0.02	0.00	0.00	0.04	0.01	1.88	1.60	11.64	1.00	0.72	0.81	0.05	4.08
9.	Paper, Paper Prods., Printing/ Publishing	0.02	0.00	0.00	0.00	0.00	0.47	0.40	0.04	43.20	0.18	0.21	0.01	1.04
10.	Leather Products	0.00	0.00	0.00	0.00	0.00	0.01	26.37	0.14	0.07	55.61	0.00	0.00	0.01
11.	Plastic/Rubber Products	0.01	0.00	0.00	0.00	0.01	0.62	2.95	0.00	2.43	1.71	43.26	0.01	1.31
12.	Coal/Petroleum Products	1.22	0.00	0.04	0.10	0.05	1.10	0.93	0.85	1.62	0.18	0.95	1.46	0.88
13.	Chemicals	2.50	0.03	0.00	0.01	0.02	0.44	0.09	0.10	3.01	0.24	0.31	0.00	16.98
14.	Non-metallic Products	0.00	0.00	0.00	0.00	0.00	0.01	0.09	0.05	0.11	0.00	0.00	0.00	0.01
15.	Metal Products	0.00	0.01	0.00	0.01	0.01	0.03	0.23	0.10	0.32	0.02	0.03	0.00	0.05
16.	Industrial Machinery	1.14	0.05	0.00	0.00	0.37	0.06	0.22	0.08	0.50	0.02	0.01	0.00	0.72
17.	Electric/Electronic Machinery	0.01	0.00	0.00	0.00	0.00	0.01	0.12	0.01	0.16	0.01	0.00	0.00	0.02
18.	Rail and other Transport Equipment	0.10	0.00	0.00	0.26	0.03	0.00	0.00	0.00	0.00	0.00	0.00	0.00	0.00
19.	Miscellaneous Manufacturing	0.00	0.00	0.00	0.00	0.01	0.00	0.01	0.00	0.01	0.00	0.00	0.00	0.00
20.	Construction	0.40	0.03	0.01	0.00	0.01	0.01	0.01	0.00	0.00	0.00	0.00	0.00	0.00
21.	Electricity/Gas/Water Supply	1.24	0.00	0.00	0.00	0.05	0.56	0.58	0.83	1.81	0.27	1.15	0.04	0.35
22.	Rail and other Transport/ Storage Services	1.40	0.37	0.00	0.02	0.01	1.20	6.33	0.25	2.37	0.79	1.32	0.55	1.94
23.	Trade/Hotels	0.97	1.32	0.00	0.02	0.01	0.50	6.97	0.34	1.28	0.20	1.08	0.19	1.76
24.	Banking/Insurance	0.16	0.12	0.00	0.00	0.01	0.44	1.02	0.14	0.39	0.29	0.52	0.76	0.45
25.	Other services (Edu., Med., Admin., Defence, etc.)	0.04	0.00	0.00	0.02	0.00	0.00	0.20	0.08	0.00	0.00	0.00	0.00	0.00
Total Input		0.00	0.00	0.00	0.00	0.00	9.73	28.95	0.42	12.65	1.57	2.48	0.45	18.20

Appendix-X C :(Contd..)

Sector Code	Industry Commodity	14	15	16	17	18	19	20	21	22	23	24	25	26	Total
1.	Agriculture	0.00	0.00	0.00	0.00	0.00	0.00	17.95	0.00	17.49	25.68	0.00	14.85	0.00	100.00
2.	Animal Husbandry	0.00	0.00	0.00	0.00	0.00	0.00	2.96	0.76	0.00	53.06	0.00	29.26	0.00	100.00
3.	Forestry and Logging	0.00	0.00	0.00	0.00	0.00	0.00	50.20	0.00	0.08	14.39	0.00	0.00	0.00	100.00
4.	Fishing	0.00	0.00	0.00	0.00	0.00	0.00	0.00	0.00	0.00	87.86	0.00	0.00	0.00	100.00
5.	Mining/Quarrying	0.18	0.42	0.02	0.01	0.00	0.00	35.93	49.62	4.96	7.75	0.00	0.62	0.00	100.00
6.	Food Prod., Beverages and Tobacco Products	0.00	0.00	0.00	0.00	0.00	0.00	0.00	0.00	0.25	32.15	0.00	0.11	0.00	100.00
7.	Textiles	0.02	0.89	0.09	1.03	0.16	0.45	2.08	0.01	2.45	7.89	0.52	4.63	0.00	100.00
8.	Wood, Wood Prods., and Furniture	0.04	1.54	0.14	2.06	0.85	0.77	44.26	0.04	0.52	11.56	1.98	14.41	0.00	100.00
9.	Paper, Paper Prods., Printing/Publishing	0.02	0.28	0.04	0.51	0.02	0.19	0.56	0.27	5.03	14.09	16.12	17.30	0.00	100.00
10.	Leather Products	0.05	0.06	0.02	0.08	0.17	0.01	0.00	0.00	0.40	0.00	17.01	0.00	0.00	100.00
11.	Plastic/Rubber Products	0.02	0.99	0.08	2.60	0.38	2.07	0.24	0.02	36.83	3.38	0.80	0.28	0.00	100.00
12.	Coal/Petroleum Products	0.42	0.18	0.11	1.69	2.54	0.34	2.63	2.55	33.89	2.63	42.35	2.54	0.00	100.00
13.	Chemicals	0.01	0.57	0.05	0.99	0.37	0.13	5.91	0.09	0.37	0.28	0.00	69.99	0.00	100.00
14.	Non-metallic Products	1.07	0.60	0.03	0.70	0.07	0.04	96.18	0.01	0.36	0.13	0.00	0.54	0.00	100.00
15.	Metal Products	0.00	51.84	0.89	5.24	0.62	1.00	33.55	0.02	0.61	2.75	0.69	1.98	0.00	100.00
16.	Industrial Machinery	0.05	0.45	58.97	1.12	0.47	0.04	0.65	2.56	8.95	7.02	6.10	11.58	0.00	100.00
17.	Electric/Electronic Machinery	0.00	0.04	0.54	64.88	0.85	0.23	14.24	1.48	6.20	0.21	1.03	9.97	0.00	100.00
18.	Rail and other Transport Equipment	0.00	0.00	0.00	0.00	33.80	0.00	0.78	0.16	54.44	0.18	8.86	1.48	0.00	100.00
19.	Miscellaneous Manufacturing	0.00	0.01	0.00	0.01	0.00	5.01	0.98	0.29	7.73	3.89	8.38	73.65	0.00	100.00
20.	Construction	0.00	0.00	0.00	0.00	0.00	0.00	3.31	0.42	7.70	10.34	11.05	67.11	0.00	100.00
21.	Electricity/Gas/Water Supply	0.04	3.28	0.49	0.81	0.46	0.07	7.77	11.32	25.72	13.65	16.19	14.58	0.00	100.00
22.	Rail and other Transport /Storage Services	1.03	4.79	0.72	3.68	0.29	0.18	17.52	1.78	8.63	15.71	12.84	17.68	0.00	100.00
23.	Trade/Hotels	0.24	4.78	0.41	2.30	1.12	0.82	24.90	1.28	10.53	6.83	6.72	26.39	0.00	100.00
24.	Banking/Insurance	0.02	0.93	0.29	0.62	0.19	0.00	4.39	0.35	8.50	15.53	49.75	15.28	0.00	100.00
25.	Other Services (Edu., Med., Admin., Defence, etc.)	0.00	0.00	0.00	0.11	0.00	0.00	3.14	0.28	10.28	27.81	23.42	34.64	0.00	100.00
26.	Pollution Abatement	5.40	15.53	0.35	3.40	0.73	0.16	0.00	0.00	0.00	0.00	0.00	0.00	0.00	100.00

Source: Mathematically obtained by dividing commodity row entries by total inputs.

Appendix-X D : Backward Linkages (commodity purchased as inputs by industries in percent): 2000-01. (Pollution Accounted)

Sector Code	Industry / Commodity	1	2	3	4	5	6	7	8	9	10	11	12	13
1.	Agriculture	12.60	22.00	0.02	0.04	0.00	1.41	0.00	0.00	0.00	0.00	0.00	0.00	0.04
2.	Animal Husbandry	14.62	0.46	0.00	0.00	0.00	4.16	0.00	0.00	0.00	0.00	0.00	0.00	0.00
3.	Forestry and Logging	0.00	0.00	0.07	0.00	0.00	0.00	0.00	0.16	0.00	0.00	0.28	0.00	0.00
4.	Fishing	0.00	0.00	0.00	13.21	0.00	0.00	0.00	0.00	0.00	0.00	0.00	0.00	0.00
5.	Mining/Quarrying	0.00	0.00	0.00	0.00	0.07	0.00	0.00	0.00	0.00	0.00	0.00	0.00	0.00
6.	Food Prod., Beverages and Tobacco Prods.	0.10	16.36	0.00	3.80	0.00	78.97	0.00	0.00	0.00	0.00	0.00	0.00	3.00
7.	Textiles	0.44	4.86	1.18	23.20	0.00	2.03	52.25	2.13	7.58	10.14	3.36	0.67	9.33
8.	Wood, Wood Prods., and Furniture	0.00	0.00	0.00	0.23	0.18	0.14	0.05	10.46	0.19	0.26	0.24	0.05	0.81
9.	Paper, Paper Prods. Printing/Publishing	0.01	0.00	0.19	0.01	0.10	0.09	0.03	0.09	21.37	0.17	0.15	0.03	0.54
10.	Leather Products	0.00	0.00	0.00	0.00	0.00	0.00	2.21	0.36	0.04	56.37	0.00	0.00	0.00
11.	Plastic/Rubber Products	0.00	0.00	0.18	0.00	0.19	0.07	0.14	0.00	0.73	0.97	19.78	0.02	0.41
12.	Coal/Petroleum Products	0.00	0.00	0.02	0.00	0.01	0.00	0.00	0.01	0.00	0.00	0.00	0.01	0.00
13.	Chemicals	0.75	0.01	0.00	0.05	0.46	0.04	0.00	0.11	0.68	0.10	0.11	0.00	3.97
14.	Non-metallic Products	0.00	0.00	0.00	0.00	0.12	0.00	0.00	0.05	0.03	0.00	0.00	0.00	0.00
15.	Metal Products	0.00	0.01	0.04	0.16	0.46	0.01	0.02	0.26	0.18	0.02	0.03	0.00	0.03
16.	Industrial Machinery	0.67	0.03	0.23	0.00	17.39	0.01	0.01	0.17	0.22	0.02	0.01	0.00	0.33
17.	Electric/Electronic Machinery	0.02	0.00	0.17	0.01	0.02	0.01	0.05	0.16	0.41	0.03	0.02	0.02	0.04
18.	Rail and other Transport Equipment	0.12	0.00	1.10	6.76	2.65	0.00	0.00	0.02	0.00	0.00	0.00	0.00	0.00
19.	Miscellaneous Manufacturing	0.01	0.00	0.42	0.00	1.47	0.00	0.00	0.00	0.02	0.00	0.00	0.00	0.00
20.	Construction	8.80	0.65	33.80	0.00	15.84	0.04	0.01	0.08	0.05	0.04	0.06	0.06	0.02
21.	Electricity/Gas/Water Supply	0.32	0.00	0.01	0.02	0.94	0.04	0.02	0.75	0.35	0.10	0.34	0.04	0.07
22.	Rail and other Transport / Storage Services	20.47	5.28	8.57	5.32	13.12	5.26	10.85	12.69	26.26	16.37	22.23	34.59	22.33
23.	Trade/Hotels	36.39	49.09	8.58	15.16	24.62	5.67	30.67	45.44	36.55	10.64	46.61	30.54	52.02
24.	Banking/Insurance	1.64	1.24	1.12	0.65	5.20	1.33	1.22	5.17	3.01	4.23	6.06	33.48	3.63
25.	Other services (Edu., Med., Admin., Defence, etc.)	3.05	0.00	44.31	31.39	17.15	0.01	1.65	21.53	0.02	0.00	0.03	0.00	0.00
26.	Pollution Abatement	0.00	0.00	0.00	0.00	0.00	0.70	0.81	0.35	2.30	0.53	0.68	0.47	3.43
	Total Input	100.00	100.00	100.00	100.00	100.00	100.00	100.00	100.00	100.00	100.00	100.00	100.00	100.00

Appendix-X D : (Contd.)

Sector Code	Industry / Commodity	14	15	16	17	18	19	20	21	22	23	24	25	26	Total
1.	Agriculture	0.00	0.00	0.00	0.00	0.00	0.00	1.19	0.00	1.17	0.91	0.00	0.30	0.00	0.63
2.	Animal Husbandry	0.00	0.00	0.00	0.00	0.00	0.00	0.18	0.66	0.00	1.72	0.00	0.53	0.00	0.57
3.	Forestry and Logging	0.00	0.00	0.00	0.00	0.00	0.00	0.02	0.00	0.00	0.00	0.00	0.00	0.00	0.00
4.	Fishing	0.00	0.00	0.00	0.00	0.00	0.00	0.00	0.00	0.00	0.14	0.00	0.00	0.00	0.03
5.	Mining/Quarrying	0.01	0.00	0.00	0.00	0.00	0.00	0.02	0.45	0.00	0.00	0.00	0.00	0.00	0.01
6.	Food Prod., Beverages and Tobacco Products	0.00	0.00	0.00	0.00	0.00	0.00	0.00	0.00	0.06	4.27	0.00	0.01	0.00	2.35
7.	Textiles	0.49	1.77	0.84	1.63	1.02	5.66	0.76	0.03	0.90	1.54	0.11	0.50	0.00	3.43
8.	Wood, Wood Prods., and Furniture	0.04	0.13	0.06	0.13	0.23	0.40	0.66	0.01	0.01	0.09	0.02	0.06	0.00	0.14
9.	Paper, Paper Prods., Printing/ Publishing	0.04	0.06	0.04	0.09	0.02	0.26	0.02	0.15	0.20	0.29	0.36	0.20	0.00	0.36
10.	Leather Products	0.13	0.01	0.02	0.01	0.13	0.01	0.00	0.00	0.02	0.00	0.41	0.00	0.00	0.40
11.	Plastic/Rubber Products	0.02	0.13	0.05	0.27	0.16	1.67	0.01	0.01	0.87	0.04	0.01	0.00	0.00	0.22
12.	Coal/Petroleum Products	0.00	0.00	0.00	0.00	0.01	0.00	0.00	0.00	0.00	0.00	0.00	0.00	0.00	0.00
13.	Chemicals	0.02	0.06	0.02	0.08	0.12	0.08	0.10	0.02	0.01	0.00	0.00	0.37	0.00	0.17
14.	Non-metallic Products	1.21	0.06	0.01	0.05	0.02	0.02	1.71	0.00	0.01	0.00	0.00	0.00	0.00	0.17
15.	Metal Products	0.01	12.35	0.99	0.99	0.48	1.50	1.46	0.01	0.03	0.06	0.02	0.03	0.00	0.41
16.	Industrial Machinery	0.10	0.08	51.57	0.17	0.29	0.05	0.02	1.26	0.31	0.13	0.12	0.12	0.00	0.32
17.	Electric/Electronic Machinery	0.01	0.04	2.74	56.53	3.02	1.59	2.85	4.22	1.25	0.02	0.12	0.60	0.00	1.89
18.	Rail and other Transport Equipment	0.00	0.00	0.00	0.00	43.32	0.00	0.06	0.16	3.95	0.01	0.37	0.03	0.00	0.68
19.	Miscellaneous Manufacturing	0.00	0.01	0.01	0.01	0.01	20.35	0.12	0.48	0.92	0.25	0.57	2.61	0.00	1.11
20.	Construction	0.13	0.01	0.07	0.02	0.06	0.07	4.25	7.73	9.94	7.10	8.19	25.80	0.00	12.11
21.	Electricity/Gas/Water Supply	0.04	0.27	0.19	0.05	0.12	0.04	0.12	2.45	0.39	0.11	0.14	0.07	0.00	0.14
22.	Rail and other Transport / Storage Services	57.15	22.68	15.81	13.85	4.47	5.42	15.16	21.91	7.50	7.26	6.41	4.58	0.00	8.15
23.	Trade/Hotels	34.92	58.06	22.98	22.19	44.33	62.82	55.35	40.39	23.52	8.11	8.61	17.55	0.00	20.95
24.	Banking/Insurance	0.76	3.08	4.49	1.62	2.03	0.00	2.65	2.98	5.16	5.00	17.31	2.76	0.00	5.69
25.	Other services (Edu., Med., Admin., Defence, etc.)	0.00	0.00	0.00	2.11	0.00	0.00	13.28	17.07	43.78	62.92	57.22	43.89	0.00	39.92
26.	Pollution Abatement	4.91	1.20	0.13	0.21	0.18	0.08	0.00	0.00	0.00	0.00	0.00	0.00	0.00	0.13
	Total Input	100.00	100.00	100.00	100.00	100.00	100.00	100.00	100.00	100.00	100.00	100.00	100.00	100.00	100.00

Source: Mathematically obtained by dividing industry column entries by total input of that industry.

Appendix-XI A : Distribution of Non-Polluting Industrial Units According to Sectors in 28 Industrial Area

Industrial Sectors	*1*	*2*	*3*	*4*	*5*	*6*	*7*	*8*	*9*	*10*	*11*	*12*	*13*	*14*	*15*	*16*	*17*	*18*	*19*	*20*	*21*	*22*	*23*	*24*	*25*	*26*	*27*	*28*
Assembly	50	-	-		-		-		-	160	-	-	50	100	-	-	-	-	-	-	-	-	-	-	-	100	-	-
Chemicals	43	20		-		-		-		30	-	-	10	60	10	20	-	-	-	-	-	10	-	-	10	-	-	10
Glass	05	10	-	-	-	-	-	-	-	20	-	-	-	18	12	-	-	-	-	-	05	-	-	-		10	-	-
Leather	-	-	-	10	-	-		-		30	-	-	08	20	07	-	-	-	-	-	-	08	06	-	20	08	-	-
Services		-	Y	-	-	-	-	-	-	200	-	-	Y	Y	-	-	-	-	-	-	-	Y	-	-	Y	Y	-	-
Textile (wet processing)	Y	Y	-	Y	-	-	-	-	Y	300	-	-	Y	Y	-	-	-	Y	-	-	-		-	-	Y	Y	-	-
Machining	-	200	-	-	-	-	-	-	-	700	-	-		100	150	-	-	-	-	-	180	200	-	-	-	-	-	-
Plastic	Y	Y	-	Y	-	-	-	-	Y	-	-	-	-	300	-	-	-	-	-	-	Y	Y		-		Y	-	Y
Paper	Y	Y	-	-		-		-	Y	-	-	-	-	-	-	-	-	-	-	-	Y	Y	-	-	-	Y	-	-
Molding																												
Trading	-	Y	-	-	-	-	-	-	Y	Y	-	-	-	Y	-	-	-	-	-	-	-	-	-	-	Y	Y	-	.

Note : Y implies Yes i.e. existence of Polluting units. Refer Chapter-5 for name of 1-28 industrial areas.

Appendix-XI B : Distribution of Polluting Industrial Units According to Sectors

Industrial Sectors	*1*	*2*	*3*	*4*	*5*	*6*	*7*	*8*	*9*	*10*	*11*	*12*	*13*	*14*	*15*	*16*	*17*	*18*	*19*	*20*	*21*	*22*	*23*	*24*	*25*	*26*	*27*	*28*
Assembly	-	-	-	-	-	-	-	-	-	-	-	-	-	Y	-	-	-		-		-		-	-	Y	-	-	-
Battery	-	-	Y	-	-	-	-	-	-	-	-	-	-	Y	-	-		-		-		-		-		-	-	-
Casting	Y	Y	-	-		-	Y	-	-	Y	-	-	-	Y	Y	Y	-	-	-	-	Y	Y	-	-	-	Y	-	-
Chemicals	Y	Y	Y	Y	-	-	-	-	Y	Y	-	-	-	Y	Y	-	-	Y	Y	-	Y	Y	-	-	-	Y	-	Y
Electronic Components	-	-	-	-	-	-	-	-	-	Y	Y	-		Y	-	-	-	-	-	-	-	-	-	-	-	-	-	-
Glass	-	-	-	-	-	-	-	-	-	Y	-	-		-		Y	-	-	-	-	-	-	-	-	Y	-	-	-
Heat Treatment	Y	Y	-	-		-	Y	-	-	Y	-	-	Y	Y	-	Y	-	-	-	-	Y	Y	-	-	-	Y	-	-
Leather	-	-	-	-	-	-	-	-	-	-	-	Y	-	-		-		-		-		-	Y	-	-	-	-	-
Metal Finishing	Y	Y	-	Y	-	Y	-	-	Y	Y	-	-	Y	Y	Y	Y	Y	Y	Y	-	Y	Y	Y	-	-	Y	Y	
Printing	Y	Y	-	-		-		-	Y	Y	-	-	Y	Y	-	Y	-	Y	-	-	-	Y	-	-	-	Y	-	Y
Service Station	Y	Y	Y	-	-	-	-	-	-	Y	Y	-	-	Y	-	-	-	Y	-	-	Y	Y	-	-		Y	-	-
Textile (wet processing)	Y	-	-	Y	-	Y	Y	-	-	Y	-	-	Y	Y	-	-	-	Y	-	-	Y	Y	-	-	-	-	-	-
Recycling	Y	-	-		Y	-	-	-	Y	-	-	-	-	Y	-	-	-	-	-	-	-	Y	-	-	-	Y	-	Y
Machining	Y	Y	-	Y	Y	-	-	-	Y	Y	-	-	Y	Y	-	-	-	Y	Y	-	-	-	Y	-	Y	Y	-	-
Rubber	Y	Y	-	Y	Y	Y	Y	-	Y	Y	-	-	Y	Y	Y	-	-	-	-	-	-	Y	Y		-	Y	-	Y
Food	-	-	Y	-	-	-	-	-		Y	-	-	-	Y	Y	-	-	Y	-	-	-	-	-	-	-	-	-	-
Tobacco Blending	-	-	Y	-	-	Y	-	-	-	-	-	-	Y	-	-	-	-	Y	-	-	-	Y	-	-	-	-	Y	-

Note : Y implies Yes i.e. existence of Polluting units. Refer Chapter-5 for name of 1-28 industrial areas.

Appendix-XI C : Wastewater Generation from Industrial Sectors

Industrial Sectors	*1*	*2*	*3*	*4*	*5*	*6*	*7*	*8*	*9*	*10*	*11*	*12*	*13*	*14*	*15*	*16*	*17*	*18*	*19*	*20*	*21*	*22*	*23*	*24*	*25*	*26*	*27*	*28*
Battery	-	-	-	-	-	-	-	-	-	-	-	-	Y	Y	-	-	-	-	-	-	-	-	-	-	-	-	-	-
Machining (with cutting oil)	Y		-		-		-		-		-	-	-	Y	-	-	Y	-	Y	-	-	-	-	-	-	-	-	-
Chemicals	-	-	Y	-	-	-	-	-	-	Y	-	-	-	Y	Y	-	-	-		-		Y	-	-	-	-	-	-
Electronic Component	-	-	-	-	-	-	-	-	-	Y	-	-	-	Y	-	-	-	-	-	-	-	-	-	-	Y	-	-	
Heat Treatment	Y	Y	-	-	Y	-	Y	-	-	-	-	-	-	-	Y	Y		-		-	Y	Y	-	-	-	Y	-	-
Leather	-	-	-	-	-	-	-	-	-	-	Y	-	Y	-	-	-	-	-	-	-	-	-	Y	-	-	-	-	
Metal Finishing	Y	Y	-	Y	Y	-	Y	-	-	-	-	-	Y	Y	Y	Y	Y	-	-	-	-	-	Y	-	Y	Y	Y	-
Rubber	-	Y	-	-	-	-	-	-	-	-	-	-	-	Y	Y		-		-		-	-	-	-	-	Y	-	-
Service Station	-	-	Y	Y	-	Y	-	-	-	Y	-	-		Y	-	-	Y	Y	-	-	Y	Y	Y	-	-	Y	-	Y
Textile (wet processing)	Y	-	-	-	Y	-	-	-	-	Y	Y	-	-	Y	-	-	Y	-	-	-	Y	-	-	-	-	-	-	-
Wood	-	-	-	-	-	-	-	-	-	-	-	-	-	-	-	-	-	-	Y	-	-	-	-		-		-	
Food	-	-	Y	-	-	-	-	-	-	-	-	-	-	-	-	-	-	-	Y	-	-	-	-	-		-		-
Plastic Recycling	Y	-	-	-	Y	-	-	-	Y	-	-	-	-	Y	Y		-		-		-	Y	Y	-	-	-	-	-

Note : Y implies Yes i.e. existence of Polluting units. Refer Chapter-5 for name of 1-28 industrial areas.

Appendix-XI D : Hazardous Waste Generation

Industrial Sectors	*1*	*2*	*3*	*4*	*5*	*6*	*7*	*8*	*9*	*10*	*11*	*12*	*13*	*14*	*15*	*16*	*17*	*18*	*19*	*20*	*21*	*22*	*23*	*24*	*25*	*26*	*27*	*28*
Assembly	-	-	-	-	-	-	-	-	-	-	-	-	-	-	-	-	-	-		-		-		-	Y	-	-	-
Battery	-	-	Y	-	-	-	-	-		-		-	Y	Y	-	-	-	-	-	-	-	-	-	-	-	-	-	-
Casting	-	-	-	-	-	Y	-	-	-	Y	-	-	-	Y	Y	Y	-	-	-	-	-	Y	-	-	-	Y	Y	-
Chemicals	-	-	Y	-	-	-	-	-	Y	Y	-		-		Y	-	-	Y	-	-	Y	-	Y	-	-	Y	-	Y
Electronic components	-	-	-	-	-	-	-	-	-	Y	-	-	-	Y	-	-	-	-	-	-	-	-	-	-	-	-	-	-
Glass	-	-	-	-	-	-	-	-	-	-	-	-	-	-	-	-	-	Y	-	-	-	-	-	-	-	-	-	-
Heat Treatment	Y	Y	-	-		-		-		Y	-	-	-	Y	Y	-	-	Y	-	-	Y	Y	-	-	-	Y	-	-
Leather	-	-	-	-	-	-	-	-	-	-	Y	-	-		-		-		-		-		Y	-	-	-	-	-
Metal Finishing	Y	Y	Y	Y	-	Y	-	-	Y	Y	-	-	Y	Y	Y	-	Y	Y	-	-	-	Y	Y	-	-	Y	Y	Y
Printing	Y	Y	-	-		-		-		Y	Y	-	Y	Y	-	Y	-	Y	-	-	-	-	-	-	-	-	-	-
Service Station	Y	Y	Y	Y	-	-	-	-	Y	Y	-	-	-	Y	-	-	-	Y	Y	-	-	-		-		-		-
Textile (wet processing)	Y	-	-	Y	Y	-	-	-	-	Y	Y	-	-	Y	-	-	-	-	-	-	Y	-	-	-		-		-
Recycling	-	-	-	-	Y	-	Y	-	Y	Y	-	-	-	Y	-	-	Y	-	-	-	-	-	-	-	-	Y	-	-

Note : Y implies Yes i.e. existence of Polluting units. Refer Chapter-5 for name of 1-28 industrial areas.

Bibliography

Alagh, Y.K. and Kashyap, S.P. (1972) "A consistent forecasting model of Gujarat's economy", *Anvesak*, 2:127-37.

Albino, V. and Dietzenbacher, E. (2003) "Analyzing materials and energy flows in industrial district using an enterprise model", *Economic Systems Research*, 15: 457-80.

Alcantara, V. and Radilla E. (2000) "CO_2 emission from production perspective in Spain", Papers in 13th *International Conference on Input-Output Techniques*, Italy.

Alfred, L.E. and Graham, A.K. (1976) *Introduction to Urban Dynamics*, Cambridge: Wright Hillen Press.

Algera, S.B. and Tuinen, H.K.V.C. (1983) "Problems in the compilation of input-output tables in the Netherlands", *Review of Income and Wealth*, 89: 67-87.

Allen, J.K. and Reid, B. (2004) "Material flow analysis in industrial system", *Journal of Industrial Ecology*, 8: 69-91.

Almon, C. and Atkinson, L.C. (1972) "Dynamic inter-industry forecasting for business planning", in A.P. Carter and A. Brody (eds.) *Input-Output Techniques*, Amsterdam: North Holland Publishing Company, 518-530.

Annual Survey of Industries (1970-71) Central Statistical Organisation, Ministry of Statistics and Programme Implementation, Government of India.

Annual Survey of Industries (1997-98) Central Statistical Organisation, Ministry of Statistics and Programme Implementation, Government of India.

Annual Survey of Industries (2000-01) Central Statistical Organisation, Ministry of Statistics and Programme Implementation, Government of India.

Anselin, L. and Madden, M. (eds.) (1990) *New Directions in Regional Analysis: Integrated and Multi-Regional Approach,* London: Belhaven Press.

Ara, K. (1959) "The aggregation problem in input-output analysis", *Econometrica,* 27: 257-262.

Artle, R. (1959) *Studies in the Structure of Stockholm Economy,* Stockholm: Stockholm School of Economics.

Augustinovics, M. (1971) "A twin pair of model of long-term planning", in A. P. Carter and A. Brody (eds.) *Input-Output Techniques,* Amsterdam: North Holland Publishing Company, 502-578.

Ayres, R. and Knees, A. (1969) "Production, consumption and externalities", *American Economic Review,* 59:282-97.

Balaz, V. (2004) "Knowledge-intensive business services in transition economies", *Business Industries Journal,* 24:83-100.

Banerjee, B. (1975) "Shahjahanabad and the Master Plan for Delhi: A Critical Appraisal", *Economic and Political Weekly,* 15: 1779-84.

Barker, T.S. (1973) "Foreign trade in multi-sectoral models", in A.P. Carter and A. Brody, (eds.) *Input-Output Techniques,* Amsterdam: North Holland Publishing Company, 111-126.

Barna, T. (1975) "Quesnay's tableau in modern guise", *The Economic Journal,* 85: 485-496.

Barna, T. (1952) "The inter-dependence of the British Economy", *Journal of the Royal Statistical Society,* 115(A): 29-81.

Batey, P.W.J. and Weeks, M. J. (1989) "The effects of household disaggregation in extended input-output models", in R.E. Miller and K.R. Polenske (eds.) *Frontiers in Input-Output Analysis,* New York: Oxford University Press, 119-131.

Batten, D.F. (1983) *Spatial Analysis of Interacting Economics: The Role of Entropy and Information Theory and Spatial Input-Output Modelling,* Boston: Kluwer Nijhoff.

Baumol, W.S. and Wolff, E.N. (1994) "A key role of input-output analysis in policy design", *Regional Science and Urban Economics*, 24: 93-113.

Bawa, U.S. and Gupta, T.R. (1967) "Purchasers prices, producers prices and margins in the organized industries in India", in P.N. Mathur (ed.) *Economic Analysis in Input-Output Framework*, Poona: Gokhale Institute of Political Economy, 34-41.

Beckmann, M.J. (1971) "An input-output model of a Von-Thunen Economy", *The Annals of Regional Science*, 5 : 6-10.

Bedzek, R.H. (1984) "Test of three hypotheses relating to the Leontief Input-Output Model", *Journal of Royal Statistical Society*, 147:499-509.

Bedzek, R.H. and Wendling, R.M. (1976) "Disaggregation of structure change in the American Economy: 1947-1966", *Review of Income and Wealth*, 22: 167-182.

Berry, B.J.L. (1973) *Human Consequences of Urbanization: Divergent Paths in the Urban Experience of the Twentieth Century*, London: Macmillan.

Berry, B.J.L. and Horton, F.E (1970) *Geographic Perspectives on Urban Systems with Integrated Readings*, New Jersey: Englewood Cliffs N.J.: Prentice Hall.

Berry, B.J.L. and Horton, F.E. (1974) *Urban Environmental Management: Planning for Pollution Control*, Englewood Cliff N.J.: Prentice Hall.

Bhalla, G.S. (1971) "Sectoral income multipliers in Punjab and India", *Anvesak*, 1: 210-229.

Bharadwaj, R. (1969) "Methodological survey of the application of input-output in developing countries", *Artha Vijnana*, 11: 148-165.

Bhatia, S.S. (1956) "Historical geography of Delhi" *The Indian Geographer*, 2: 17-43.

Blin, J.M. (1977) "Technological similarity and aggregation in input-output system", *Review of Economics and Statistics*, 59: 82-91.

Boer, P.M.C. (1982) *Input-Output Relations: A Theoretical and Empirical Study for the Netherlands: 1949-67*, Berlin: Springer-Verlag.

Bon, R. (1988) "Qualitative Input-Output Analysis", *Journal of Regional Science*, 28: 41-50.

Bon, R. (1988) "Supply-side multi-regional input-output models", *Journal of Regional Science*, 29: 41-52.

Bose, A. (1967) *Delhi's Urban Sprawl, Land Development and Land Prices*, Institute of Economic Growth, Delhi.

Bruno, M. (1971) "Optimal pattern of trade and development", in H. Chenery (ed.) *Studies in Development Planning*, Cambridge: Harvard University Press.

Buford, R.L. (1977) "Regional input-output multipliers within a full input-output table", *Annals of Regional Science*, 11: 21-38.

Bulmer-Thomas, V. (1978) "Trade, structure and linkages in Costa Rica", *Journal of Development Economics*, 5: 73-86.

Bulmer-Thomas, V. (1979) "Export promotion *vs.* import substitution in Central American Common Market", *Journal of Economic Studies*, 6:182-203.

Byrd, B. (1972) "The crude oil industry in USA and Leontief dynamic inverse", in A.P. Carter and A. Brody (eds.), *Input-Output Techniques*, Amsterdam: North Holland Publishing Company, 531-561.

Cai, J. and Leung, P. (2004) "Linkage Measures: A revisit and a suggested alternative", *Economic Systems Research*, 16:35-64.

Carter, A.P. (1986) "Energy, environment and economic growth", *Bell Journal of Economics and Management*, 5: 587-92.

Carter, H.O. and Ireri, D. (1970) "Linkage of California-Arizona input-output models to analyze water transfer patterns", in A. P. Carter and A. Brody (eds.) *Applications of Input-Output Analysis*, Amsterdam: North-Holland Publishing Company, 119-137.

Census on Hazardous Industries in Delhi (2001) Delhi Pollution Control Committee, Government of National Capital Territory of Delhi, Delhi.

Census on Industries of Delhi (2001) Delhi Pollution Control Committee Government National Capital Territory of Delhi, Delhi.

Central Statistical Organisation (1981) *Input-Output Transaction Table: 1973-74*, Ministry of Statistics and Programme Implementation, Government of India, Delhi.

Central Statistical Organisation (1989) *Input-Output Transaction Table: 1978-79*, Ministry of Statistics and Programme Implementation, Government of India, Delhi.

Central Statistical Organisation (1990) *Input-Output Transaction Table: 1983-84*, Ministry of Statistics and Programme Implementation, Government of India, Delhi.

Central Statistical Organisation (1997) *Input-Output Transaction Table: 1989-90*, Ministry of Statistics and Programme Implementation, Government of India, Delhi.

Central Statistical Organisation (2000) *Input-Output Transaction Table: 1993-94*, Ministry of Statistics and Programme Implementation, Government of India, Delhi.

Central Statistical Organization (1978) *Input-Output Transaction Table: 1968-69*, Ministry of Statistics and Programme Implementation, Government of India, Delhi.

Chakravorti, A.K (1969) "Some aspects of the structural characteristics of the Turkish Economy", *Vijnana*, 11: 236-255.

Chakravorti, D. and Raa, T. (1981) "Aggregation problem in input-output analysis: A survey", *Artha Vijnana*, 23: 326-344.

Chandel, H. (1991) "Inter-temporal, inter-industry linkage pattern of Gujarat manufacturing industries", *Anvesak*, 21:19-40.

Chenery, H.B. and Clark, P.G. (1958) "Structure and Growth of Italian Economy", *Econometrics*, 26 (4): 481-521.

Chenery, H.B. and Clark, P. (1959) Inter-Industry Economics, New York: Wiley.

Chowdhary, C. (1985) "Delhi Master Plan-2001 A.D; Need for Pragmatic Approach", *Delhi Vikas Yatra*, 3: 30-33.

Cohen, S.I. (1989) "Multipliers analysis in social accounting and input-output framework", in R.E. Miller and K.R. Polenske (eds.) *Frontiers in Input-Output Analysis*, New York: Oxford University Press, 79-102.

Collado, J.C. and Sancho, F. (2002) "Recovering hidden indirect tax rates for improved calibrations in multi-sectoral modelling", *Economic Systems Research*, 14:81-88.

Costa, A.M. (1984) "U.N. global modelling: Experimental projection on the basis of alternative procedures", in Proceedings of the *Seventh International Conference on Input-Output Techniques*, New York, 7-32.

Costanza, R. (1986) "Embodied energy and economic valuation", in I. Sohn (ed.) *Readings in Input-Output Analysis*, New York: Oxford University Press, 432-444.

Cripps, E.L. (ed.) (1974) Space-Time Concept in Urban and Regional Models, London: Pion Ltd.

Cumberland, J.H. and Korbach, J.K. (1973) "A regional inter-industry environmental model", *Papers and Proceedings of Regional Science Association*, 30: 61-75.

Cumberland, J.H. and Stram, B.M. (1974) "Empirical application of input-output models to environmental problems", in K.R. Polenske and J.U. Skolka (eds.) *Advances in Input-Output Analysis*, Cambridge: Ballinger Publishing Company, 365-383

Czayka, L. (1972) "Qualitative Input-Output Analysis", Berlin: Verlag Anton Hain.

Daly, H.E. and Isard, W. (1968) "On economics of life science", *Journal of Political Economy*, 76: 392-406.

Das, N. and Sardesai, D.D. (1976) "Location of industries in India and transport cost minimization", in P.N. Mathur (ed.) *Economic Analysis in Input-Output Framework*, Poona: Gokhale Institute of Political Economy, 177-183.

David, G. (1970) "Regional impact of inter-regional trade in input-output analysis", Papers of the *Regional Science Association*, 25:203-220.

Day, R.H. (1970) "Recursive programming model of industrial development and technological change", in A. P. Carter and A. Brody (eds.) *Contribution to Input-Output Analysis*, Amsterdam: North Holland Publishing Economy, 99-118.

De Mesnard, L. (2004) "Understanding the shortcomings of commodity based technology in input-output models", *Journal of Regional Science*, 44:125-43.

Delhi Census Altus (1981) Census of India, Directorate of Census Operations, Delhi.

Delhi Census Altus (1991) Census of India, Directorate of Census Operations, Delhi.

Delhi Development Authority (1961) Some Salient Features of the Draft Master Plan for Delhi, *Journal of Institute of Town Planners*, Jan-April 104-110.

Delhi District Gazetteer (1976) Delhi Administration, Delhi.

Delhi Master Plan-2001 (1990) Revised and Updated, Perspective Planning Wing, Delhi Development Authority, Delhi.

Delhi Master Plan-2021, Guidelines (2003), Perspective Planning Wing, Delhi Development Authority, Delhi.

Development Plan Delhi-2001 (1982), Perspective Planning Wing, Delhi Development Authority, Delhi.

Dhar, R. (1967) "The study of inter-regional relations of the Indian Economy-1953-54", in P.N. Mathur (ed.) *Economic Analysis in Input-Output Framework*, Poona: Gokhale Institute of Political Economy, 155-166.

Dietrich, M. (1999) "Explaining economic restructuring: An input-output analyses of organizational change in

European Union", *International Review of Applied Economics*, 13: 219-40.

Dietzenbacher, E. (1990) "The sensitivity of input-output multipliers", *Journal of Regional Science*, 30: 239-58.

Directory for National Studies Concerned Urban-Regional Research (1968) New York: United Nations.

Diwakar, A. and Qureshi, M.H. (1996) "Growth of a legendary city: Delhi through the Ages", *National Geographical Journal of India*, 42:184-190.

Dorfman, R. (1954) "The nature and significance of input-output technique", *Review of Economics and Statistics*, 36:121-33.

Drake, R.L. (1976) "A short cut to estimate regional input-output multipliers", *International Regional Science Review*, 1: 1-18.

Dridi, C. and Hewings G. J. D. (2003) "Sector associations and similarities in input-output system: An application to Canada and U.S.", *Annals of Regional Science*, 37: 629-56.

Duer, F. (1976) Urban Economy, Scarton: Intext Educational Publications.

Dupont, V. (ed.) (2000) Delhi: Urban Space and Human Densities, Delhi: Manohar Publications.

Dutta, U. (1954) A Preliminary Study of Inter-industry Relations in India, Indian Statistical Institute, Working Paper, No. 7.

Dwyer, P.S. and Waugh, F.U. (1953) "On errors in matrix inversion", *Journal of American Statistical Association*, 6 8: 289-319.

Economic Census Report (1977) Directorate of Economics and Statistics, Government of National Capital, Territory of Delhi, Delhi.

Economic Census Report (1988) Directorate of Economics and Statistics, Government of National Capital Territory of Delhi, Delhi.

Economic Census Reports (1998) Directorate of Economics

and Statistics, Government of National Capital Territory of Delhi, Delhi.

Economic Survey (2000-01) Department of Planning, Government of National Capital Territory of Delhi, Delhi.

Economic Survey (2002-03) Department of Planning, Government of National Capital Territory of Delhi, Delhi.

Economic Survey of Delhi (1973) National Council of Applied Economic Research, Delhi.

Economic-*cum*-purpose classification of the Budget Expenditure of Delhi Government (2000-01) Directorate of Economics and Statistics, Government of National Capital Territory of Delhi, Delhi.

Edel, M. and Rothenbergi, J. (1972) Readings in Urban Economics, New York: McMillan.

Eder, P. and Narodoslawsky, M. (1999) "What environmental pressures are a region's industries responsible for? An input-output model", *Ecological Economics*, 29: 359-74.

Eicher City Guide (1988) Delhi Eicher, New Delhi: Good Earth.

Emerson, M.J. (1969) "Towards dynamic regional export model", *Annals of Regional Science*, 3: 127-138.

Eskelinen, H. (1983) "Core and periphery in a three region input-output framework", '*The Annals of Regional Science*, 17: 41-56.

Estevao, M. and Tevlin, S. (2003) "Do firms share their success with workers? The response of wages to product market conditions: Use of input-output tables", *Economica*, 46:367-85.

Estimates of State Domestic Products (1980) Directorate of Economics and Statistics Government of National Capital Territory of Delhi, Delhi.

Estimates of State Domestic Products (2001) Directorate of Economics and Statistics, Government of National Capital Territory of Delhi, Delhi.

Evan, W.D. and Hoffenberg, P. M. (1952) "Inter-industry relations study", *The Review of Economics and Statistics*, 34:74 -89.

Evans, M. and Baxter, J. (1980) "Regionalizing national projections with a multi-regional input-output model linked to demographic model", *Annals of Regional Science*, 14: 57-71.

Evans, W.D. (1954) "The effect of structural matrix errors on inter-industry relations estimate", *Econometrica*, 22: 461-480.

Faden, A.M. (1977) *Economics of Space and Time: Theoretical Foundations of Social Sciences*, Iowa: Iowa State University.

Ferng, J. (2003) "Allocating the responsibility of CO_2 over emissions from perspective benefit principle and ecological deficit", *Ecological Economics*, 46:121-145.

Fingleton, B. (2003) "Externalities, economic geography and spatial econometrics: Conceptual and modelling Development", *International Regional Science Review*, 26:197-207.

Forsell, O. (1988) "Growth and Change in Finish Economy", in M. Giaschini (ed.) *Input-Output Analysis*, New York: Chapman and Hall Ltd., 287-302.

Forsund, F.R. (1985) "Input-output Model and the Environment", in A.V. Kneese and J.L. Sweeney (eds.) *Handbook of Natural Resources and Energy Economics*, Vol.1, New York: Economics Science Publishers, 325-41.

Frankel, J.A. and Stein, E. (1998), "Continental trading blocks: Are they natural or supernatural?" in J. A. Frankel (ed.) *The Rationalization of the World Economy*, Chicago: University of Chicago Press.

Fritz, O. and Sonis, M. (1998) "Analysis of interaction between polluting and non-polluting sectors", *Structural Change and Economic Dynamics*, 9: 289-305.

Frykenberg, R.E. (1986) *Delhi Through Ages: Essays in Urban History, Culture and Society*, Delhi: Oxford University Press.

Fujikawa, K. and Milana, L. (2002) "Input-output decomposition analysis of sectoral price gaps between Japan and China", *Economic Systems Research*, 14:59-79.

Fujita, N. (1989) "Input-output analysis of agricultural production quotas", *Annals of Regional Science,* 23: 40-50.

Furukawa, S. (1986) *International Input-Output Analysis: Case Studies,* Tokyo: Institute of Developing Economics.

Garhart, R.E. Jr. (1985) "The role of error structure in simulations on regional input-output analysis", *Journal of Regional Science,* 25: 353-366.

Ghosh, A. (1967) "An inter-regional progressing model for production and transportation of commodities for different regions of India", *Artha Vijnana,* 9: 210-227.

Ghosh, S. and Roy, J. (1998) "Qualitative input-output analyses of Indian Economic Structure", *Economic Systems Research,* 10: 263-73.

Giarratani, F. (1974) "Air pollution abatement: Output and relative price effects", *Environment and Planning,* 6: 307-12.

Gigantes, T. and Hoffman, R. (1972) "A price output nucleus for simulation models", in A.P. Carter and A. Brody (eds.) *Input-Output Techniques,* Amsterdam: North Holland Publishing Company, 319-342.

Giljum, S. and Hubacek, K. (2004) "Alternative approaches of physical input-output analysis to estimate primary material input of production and consumption activities", *Economic Systems Research,* 16:301-310.

Goodall, B. (1972) *The Economics of Urban Areas,* Oxford: Pergamon Press.

Goodwin, R.R. and Chowdhary, T.P. (1955) *Transaction Matrices for the Indian Union, 1950-51,* Indian Statistical Institute (Mimeographed Paper), No. 17.

Gosh, A. (1964) *Experiments with Input-Output Models,* Cambridge: Cambridge University Press.

Granberg, A.G. (1991) "The SYRENA (synthesis of regional and national model) complex", in W. Peterson, (ed.) *Advances in Input-Output Analysis,* New York: Oxford University Press, 161-172.

Greytak, D. (1970) "Regional impact of inter-regional trade", *Papers and Proceedings of the Regional Science Association*, 25: 203-17.

Guncavdi,O. and Mckay, A. (2003) "Adjustments, stabilizations and the analysis of the employment in Turkey: An input-output approach", *Ecological Economics*, 50: 49-67.

Gupta, N. (1986) Delhi Between Two Empires: Society, Government and Urban Growth, New Delhi: Oxford University Press.

Hadded, P.R. (1973) "Experiments with input-output analysis at regional and local level", *Annals of Regional Science*, 7: 23-46.

Hammada, F. (1991) "A long -term projection of the industrial and environment aspects of the Hokkaido Economy: 1985-2005", in W. Peterson (eds.) *Advances in Input-Output Analysis*, New York: Oxford University Press, 223-235.

Hansen, N.M. (1975) Challenges of Urban Growth: The Basic Economic Size of City Size and Structure, London: Lexington Books.

Hashim, S.R. and Dadi, M. (1967) "Leontief capital-output ratio for large-scale manufacturing industries", in P.N. Mathur (ed.) *Economic Analysis and Input-Output Framework*, Vol. 3, Poona: Gokhale Institute of Political Economy, 220-229.

Hazari, B.R (1970) "Empirical identification of key sectors in Indian Economy", *Review of Economics and Statistics*, 53: 301-305.

Hearn, G.R. (1974) *Seven Cities of Delhi*, New Delhi: S.B.W. Publishers.

Heppel, L. (2000) "Input-output analysis" in R.J. Johnston, D. Gregory, G. Pratt and M. Watts (eds.) *Dictionary of Human Geography*, Oxford: Blackwell Publishers Ltd., 397.

Hewings, G. J D. (1977) "Evaluating the possibilities for exchanging regional input-output coefficients", *Environment and Planning*, 9: 927-44.

Hewings, G.J.D. (1984) "Updating regional input-output tables", *Socio-Economic Planning Science*, 18: 319-336.

Hewings, G.J.D. (1993) "The development and use of inter-regional models for Indonesia", *Review of Urban and Regional Development Studies*, 5:135-153.

Hewings, G.J.D. and Munroe, D.K. (2000) "The role of inter-industry trade in inter-regional trade in Midwest of US", Papers, *13th International Conference on Input-Output Techniques*, Italy.

Hirsch, W.Z. (1959) "Inter-industry relations of a metropolitan area", The *Review of Economics and Statistics*, 41: 360-67.

Hoffenberg, P.M. and Lees, L.H. (1985) *The Making of Urban Europe*, Cambridge: Harvard University Press.

Hoglund, B. and Werin, L. (1964) *The Production System of the Swedish Economy: An Input-Output Study*, Uppsala: Almquist and Wiksells.

Holub, H.W. and Schnabl, H. (1985) "Qualitative input-output analysis and structural information", *Economic Modelling*, 2: 67-73.

Hoover, E. (1971) *An Introduction to Regional Economics*, New York: Alfred A. Knopl.

Household Consumer Expenditure (1970) National Sample Survey Organisation, Ministry of Statistics and Programme Implementation, Government of India, Delhi.

Hubacek, K. and Sun, L. (2001) "A scenario analysis of China's land use and landcover change: Incorporating biophysical information into input-output modelling", *Structural Change and Economic Dynamics*, 12:367-97.

Immanuel, N. (1999) "Delhi", in *Encyclopedia of World Cities*, Chicago: Fitzroy Dearborn Publishers, 198.

Isard, W. (1951) "Regional input-output analysis: A model of space economy", *Review of Economics and Statistics*, 34:318-28.

Isard, W. (1956) *Location and Space Economy: A General Theory*

Relating to Industrial Location and Urban Structure, Cambridge: MIT Press.

Isard, W. (1967) "On linkages of socio-economic and ecological systems", *Papers and Proceedings of Regional Science Association*, 21: 79-99.

Isard, W. and Kuenne, R. E. (1953) "The impact of steel upon the Greater New York —Philadelphia Industrial Region", Review *of Economics and Statistics*, 35: 289-301.

Isard, W. and Longford, T.W. (1971) *Regional Input-Output Study: Recollections, Reflections and Diverse Notes on Philadelphia Experience*, New York: MIT Press.

Isard, W., Choghuill C. and Kissin, J. (eds.) (1971) *Ecological and Economic Analysis for Regional Planning*, New York: The Free Press.

Isserman, A.M. (1977) "A bracketing approach for estimating regional economic impact multipliers" *Environment and Planning*, 9: 1003-11.

Jagmohan (1975) *Rebuilding Shahajahanabad: The Walled City of Delhi*, Delhi: Vikas Publishing House.

Jain, A.K. (1990) *The Making of a Metropolis: Planning and Growth of Delhi*, New Delhi: National Book Organi-zation.

Jalili, A. R. (2000) "Comparisons of two methods of identifying input-output coefficients for exogenous estimation", *Economic Systems Research*, 12: 113-29.

Jensen, R.C. (1979) *Regional Economic Planning: Generation of Regional Input-Output Analysis*, London: Croom Helm.

Jensen, R.C. (1980) "The effect of relative coefficient size on input-output multipliers", *Environment and Planning*, 12: 654-670.

Jensen, R.C. and Hewings, G.J.D. (1987) "The study of regional economic structure: Using input-output tables", *Urban Studies*, 22: 207-220.

Jha, G. (1978) "Growing under the Master Plan: A study of Delhi", *Nagarlok*, 10: 61-74.

Jin, D. and Hoagland, P. (2003) "Linking economic and ecological model for a marine ecosystem", *Ecological Economics*, 46: 457-80.

John, A.S. (1972) "Import forecasts for input-output models", *Review of Income and Wealth,* 18: 303-12.

Johnson, M.H. and Bennett, J.T. (1981) "Regional environmental and economic impact evaluation", *Regional Science and Urban Economics,* 11: 215-230.

Johonsen, L. (1978) "On the theory of dynamic input-output models with different time profiles of capital construction", *Journal of Economic Theory,* 19: 573-33.

Jorgenson, D.W. (1960) "Dynamic Input-Output System", *Review of Economic Studies,* 28: 105-116.

Jun, M. (2004) A metropolitan input-output model: Multi-sectoral and multi-spatial relations of production, consumption and income", *Annals of Regional Science,* 38:131-47.

Kagawa, S. and Inamura, H. (2001) "A structural decomposition based on a hybrid rectangular input-output framework: A Case of Japan", *Economic Systems Research,* 13:339-64.

Kalmbach, P. and Kurz, H.D. (1990) "A dynamic input-output study of West Germany", *Structural Change and Economic Dynamics,* 1: 371-86.

Karaska, G. (1968) "Variation of input-output coefficients for different levels of aggregation", Journal *of Regional Science,* 8: 215-27.

Kashyap, S.P. (1984) *Facts of an Urban Economy: Economic Base Study of Ahemedabad:* Sardar Patel Institute of Economic and Social Research.

Keuning, S. (1988) "Guidelines for the construction of a social accounting matrix", *Review of Income and Wealth,* 34: 71-100.

Kogiku, K.C. and D'Arge, R.C. (1973) "Economic growth and environment", *The Review of Economic Studies,* 4: 61-76.

Kol, J. (1991) "Comparative advantage and international shifts in employment and trade relation", in W. Peterson (ed.) *Advances in Input-Output Analysis,* New York: Oxford University Press, 199-210.

Koti, R.K. (1967) "Dynamic inverse for the Indian Economy-1963", in P.N. Mathur (ed.) *Economic Analysis in Input-Output Framework,* Poona: Gokhale Institute of Political Economy, 65-86.

Koti, R.K. and Santanam, K.V. (1967) "Capital Coefficient Matrix", in P.N. Mathur and R. Bharadwaj (eds.) *Economic Analysis in Input-Output Framework,* Poona: Gokhale Institute of Political Economy, 65-87.

Kraines, S. and Yoshida, Y. (2004) "Process system modelling of production technology alternatives using input-output tables with sector specifications", *Economic Systems Research,* 16:23-26.

Krishan, G. (1988) "National Capital Region: A case of metropolitan growth management", *Population Geography,* 10: 73-91.

Krishnamurty, J. and Hazari, B.R. (1970) "Employment implications of India's industrialization: An input-output approach", *Review of Economics and Statistics,* 52: 262-71.

Kundu, A. (1992) *Urban Development and Urban Research in India,* New Delhi: Khanna Publishers.

Kurtzweg, L.R (1977) "A comparison of the US and USSR Economies", in V.G. Treml (ed.) *Studies in Soviet Input-Output Analysis,* New York: Praeger Publishers, 369-412.

Kuyenhoven, A. (1974) "Sectoral appraisal where trade opportunities are limited", in K. Polenske and J.V. Skolka (eds.) *Advances in Input-Output Analysis,* Cambridge: Ballinger, 279-293.

Lakhshmanan, T.R. and Nijkamp, P. (eds.) (1980) *Economic-Environmental-Energy Interactions: Modelling and Policy Analysis,* Boston: Martinus Nijhoff.

Lakhshmanan, T.R. and Nijkamp, P. (1993) *Structure and Change in the Space Economy,* Berlin: Springer-Verlag.

Lakhshmanan, T.R. and Nijkamp, P. (eds.)(1993) *Structure and Change in Space Economy,* Berlin: Springer-Verlag.

Lange, G.M. (1998) "Applying integrated environment natural resource accounts and input-output model for development planning in Indonesia", *Economic Systems Research*, 10: 113-34.

Latham, W.R. III and Montgomery, M. (1979) "Method for calculating regional industry impact multiplier", *Growth and Change*, 10: 2-9.

Lawrence, H. (1996) *The Good City,* Bloomington: Indiana University Press.

Leahy, W.H. (1970) *Urban Economics: Theory, Development and Planning*, New York: The Free Press.

Lecomber, J.R.C. (1973) "Input-output and the trading economy", in W.F. Gossling (ed.) *Input-Output in United Kingdom*, London: Frank Cass and Company Ltd., 124-148.

Lee, C. F. and Lewis, C. (2001) "Devising an integrated methodology for analyzing energy use CO_2 emissions from Taiwan's petrochemical industries", *Journal of Environmental Management*, 63:377-85.

Lee, K.S. (1981) "A generalized model of an economy with environmental protection", *Review of Economics and Statistics*, 64: 466-73.

Leontief, W.W. (1936) "Quantitative input and output relations in the economic system of the United States", *Review of Economic and Statistics*, 18: 93-115.

Leontief, W.W. (1941) *The Structure of United States Economy, 1919-39*, Harvard: Harvard University Press.

Leontief, W. (1970) "Environmental repercussions and the economic structure: An input-output approach", *Review of Economics and Statistics*, 52: 262-71.

Leontief, W. (1986) *Input-Output Economics,* New York: Oxford University Press, 279-94.

Leontief, W. (1986) *Studies of the Structure of American Economy*, New York: Oxford University Press, 94-129.

Lesuis, P. and Nijkamp, P. (1980) "An inter-regional policy model for energy-economic-environmental interactions", *Regional Science and Urban Economics*, 10: 343-70.

Liews, C. J. (1984) "Pollution-related variable input-output model", *Urban Economics*, 15: 327-49.

Linnemann, A. (1966) *An Economic Study of International Trade Flows*, Amsterdam: North Holland Publishing Company.

Lipnowski, I.F. (1976) "An input-output analysis of environmental preservation", *Journal of Environmental Economics and Management*, 3: 205-14.

Los, B. (2000) "Endogenous growth and structural change in a dynamic input-output model', Papers of *13th International Conference on Input-Output Techniques*, Italy.

Louiseek, A.C. (1982) "Industrial cluster analysis: Backward and forward linkages", *Annals of Regional Science*, 65: 36-47.

Lynch, R.G. (1986) "An assessment of methods for updating input-output tables", in I. Sohn (ed.) *Readings in Input-Output Analysis*, Oxford: Oxford University Press, 271-284.

Machado, G.V. (2000) "Ecology use and CO_2 emission: An input-output approach applied to Brazilian case", Papers in *13th International Conference on Input-Output Techniques*, Italy.

Machado, G. and Schaeffer, R. (2001) "Energy and carbon embodied in the international trade of Brazil: An input-output approach", *Ecological Economics*, 39:409-24.

Mahajan, B.M. (1970) "Why regional input-output analysis?", *Artha Vijnana*, 12: 507-522.

Mahmood, A. (1977) *Statistical Methods in Geographical Studies*, Delhi: Rajesh Publications.

Malenbaum, W. (1955) "India's domestic product, 1951-52 to 1953-54", *Indian Economic Journal*, 11(3): 247-253.

Masakova, I.D. and Sokolin, V. L. (1988) "Experience of input-output tables for Russia", Papers in *12th International Conference on Input-Output Techniques*, New York, 18-22.

Mathur, P.N. (1969) "Input-output flow table 1963", *Artha Vijnana*, 11:181-199.

Mathur, P.N. (1975) "Input-output economics", *Anvesak*, 5:1-18.

Matuszewski, T. (1972) "Partly disaggregated rectangular

input-output models and their use for purpose of a large corporation", in A.P. Carter and A. Brody (eds.) *Input-Output Techniques*, Amsterdam: North Holland Publishing Company, 301-318.

McGilvary, J. and Simpson, D.C. (1972) "The pattern of Irish Trade", in A.P. Carter and A. Brody, (eds.) *Input-Output Techniques*, Amsterdam: North Holland Publishing Company, 145-168.

McMenamin, D.G. and Haring, S.E. (1974) "An appraisal of non-survey techniques for estimating regional input-output models", *Journal of Regional Science*, 14: 191-205.

Mehta, B.C. (1971) "Structure of Rajasthan Economy", *Anvesak*, 1: 274-80.

Mentioned by Richard, S. (1986) "Where are we now" in I. Sohn (ed.) *Readings in Input-Output Analysis*, New York: Oxford University Press, 13-31.

Miller, R.E. and Blair, P.D. (1985) *Input-Output Analysis: Foundations and Extensions*, New Jersey: Prentice-Hall, 236-265.

Mills, E.S. (1972) *Studies in the Structure of the Urban Economy*, Baltimore: Johns Hopkins University Press.

Misra, R.P. and Misra, K. (eds.) (1998) *Million Cities of India, Growth Dynamics, Internal Structure, Quality of Life and Planning Perspectives*, New Delhi: Sustainable Development Foundation.

Mitra, A.K. (1970) *Delhi : Capital City*, New Delhi: Thomson Press.

Miyao, C.T. and Kanemoto, Y. (1987) *Urban Dynamics and Urban Externalities*, London: Harwood Academics Publishing.

Moore, F. T. and Peterson, W. (1955) "Regional Analysis: An inter-industry model of Utah", *The Review of Economics and Statistics*, 37: 368-83.

Morimoto, Y. (1970) "On aggregation in input-output analysis", *Review of Economic Studies*, 37: 119-26.

Morley, S. and Smith, G. (1970) "On the measurement of

import substitution", *American Economic Review*, 60: 728-735.

Morrison, W. and Smith, P. (1974) "Non-survey input-output techniques at the small area level", *Journal of Regional Science*, 14:1-29.

Moses, L.N. (1955) "The stability of inter-regional trading patterns and input-output analysis", *The American Economic Review*, 45: 808-32.

Mukherjee, M. (1967) "On the construction and use of inter-industry transactions table in India", in P.N. Mathur (ed.) *Economic Analysis in Input-Output Framework*, Poona: Gokhale Institute of Political Economy, 15-26.

Mukherjee, M. (1967) "On the construction of inter-industry transaction tables in India", in P.N. Mathur and Bharadwaj, R. (eds.) *Economic Analysis in Input-Output Framework*, Poona: Gokhale Institute of Political Economy, 15-26.

Nagia, S. (1976) *Delhi Metropolitan Region: A Study in Settlement Geography*, New Delhi: K.B. Publications.

Nath, R. (1967) "Skill-cost input coefficients in Indian manufacturing", in P.N. Mathur, (ed.) *Economic Analysis and Input-Output Framework*, Vol. 3, Poona: Gokhale Institute of Political Economy, 54-66.

Nester, D.V. and Pasurka, C.A. (1995) "Environmental economic accounting and indicators of economic importance of environmental protection activities", *Review of Income and Wealth*, 41: 46-87.

Nijkamp, P. (1979) *Multi-dimensional Spatial Data and Decision Analysis*, New York: John Wiley.

Nijkamp, P. and Cappellin, R. (eds.) (1990) *Spatial Context of Technological Development*, Aveburg: Aidershot.

Nijkamp, P. and Chatterjee, L. (1981) *Urban Problems and Economic Development*, Berlin: Springer-Verlag.

Nijkamp, P. and Mills, E.S. (eds.) (1986) *Handbook of Regional and Urban Economics*, Amsterdam: North Holland.

Nijkamp, P. and Reggiani, A. (1988) "Analysis of dynamic

spatial interaction models", *Geographical Analysis*, 20: 18-30.

Norton, G.A. and Parlour, J.W. (1972) "The economic philosophy of pollution: A critique", *Environment Planning*, 4: 3-11.

Nyhus, D. (1988) "The international system of macro economic input-output model", in M.Giaschini (ed.) *Input-Output Analysis*, New York: Chapman and Hall Ltd., 391-410.

Ochoa, L. and Mathews, H. S. (2002) "Economic input-output life cycle assessment of U.S. residential buildings", *Journal of Infrastructure Systems*, 8:132-38.

Oosterhaven, J. and Stelder, D. (2001)"Clusters, linkages and inter-regional spillovers: Methodology and Policy Implications for the two Dutch main ports and rural north", *Regional Studies*, 35:809-22.

Ozkam, B. and Kurkle, A. (2004) "An input-output energy analysis in greenhouse vegetable production: A case of Turkey", *Bio-mass and Bio-energy*, 26:89-95.

Paithankar, R.G. (1976) "Inter-industry study of Marathwada Region", in P.N.Mathur (ed.) *Economic Analysis in Input-Output Framework*, Poona: Gokhale Institute of Political Economy, 187-208.

Paithankar, R.V. (1976) "Economic impact of the indigenous purchase by the Government of India during 1961-66", *Anvesak*, 6: 83-92.

Pan, X. (2000) "Social and ecological accounting matrix: An empirical study for China", Papers of *13th International Conference on Input-Output Techniques*, Italy.

Panchmukhi, V.R. (1967) "Planning for import substitution: Some methodological and empirical results", in P.N. Mathur (ed.) *Economic Analysis in Input-Output Framework*, Poona: Gokhale Institute of Political Economy, 184-219.

Panchmukhi, V.R. (1973) "Revealed comparative advantage: Indian trade with East Asian Countries", *Economic and Political Weekly*, 7: 65-74.

Panchmukhi, V.R. (1974) "A multi-sectoral and multi-country planning model for production and trade", in K. R. Polenske and J. V. Skolka (eds.) *Advances in Input-Output Analysis*, Cambridge: Ballinger, 499-527.

Park, S. (1973) "On input-output multipliers with errors in input-output coefficients", *Journal of Economic Theory*, 6: 399-403.

Perloff, H.S. (1968) *Issues in Urban Economics*, Baltimore: Johns Hopkins University Press.

Peschal, K. (1981) "On the impact of geographic distance on factors of production and trade", *Environment and Planning*, 13: 605-622.

Petri, P. (1976) "A multi-lateral model for Japanese-American Trade", in K.R. Polenske, and J. V. Skolka (eds.) *Advances in Input-Output Analysis*, Cambridge: Ballinger, 481-497.

Pfaijfar, L. and Dolinar, L. (2000) "Inter-sectoral linkages in the Slovenian Economy for the years 1990, 1992, 1993 and 1995", Papers in *13th International Conference on Input-Output Techniques*, Italy.

Phibbs, P.J. and Holsman, A.J. (1982) "Estimating input-output multipliers: A hybrid approach", *Environment and Planning*, 14: 335-342.

Phillips, A. (1955) "The tableau economique as a simple Leontief model", *Quarterly Journal of Economics*, 69(1): 137-44.

Pigozzi, B.W. and Hinojosa, R.C. (1985) "Regional input-output inverse coefficients", *Growth and Change*, 16: 8-12.

Piispalla, J. (2000) "On regionalizing input-output tables: regional tables in Finland", Papers in *13th International Conference on Input-Output Techniques*, Italy.

Polenske, K.R (1986) "The implementation of a multi-regional input-output model for United States", in I. Sohn (ed.) *Readings in Input-Output Analysis*, New York: Oxford University Press, 93-106.

Policy for Abatement of Pollution (1992) Ministry of

Environment and Forests Government of India, Delhi.

Prakash, S. and Patnaik, P.K. (1975) "Inter-industry structure of the economy of Madhya Pradesh", *Anvesak*, 5:141-186.

Prasad, K.N. (1967) "Structure of India's trade explorations with natural resources", in P.N. Mathur (ed.) *Economic Analysis and Input-Output Framework*, Vol. 3, Poona: Gokhale Institute of Political Economy, 220-229.

Prasad, K.N. (1969) "Aggregation in input-output analysis", *Artha Vijnana*, 11: 167-179.

Problems in Input-Output Tables and Analysis, Studies in Methods (1966) Series F, No. 14, United Nations Statistical Office, New York: United Nations.

Problems in Input-Output Tables and Analysis, Studies in Methods (1973) Series F, No. 14, United Nations Statistical Office New York: United Nations.

Profile of Industries (1995) Department of Industries, Government of National Capital Territory of Delhi, Delhi.

Profile of Industries (1998) Department of Industries Government of National Capital Territory of Delhi, Delhi.

Profile of Industries (2000) Department of Industries, Government of National Capital Territory of Delhi, Delhi

Proops, J.L. (1999) "International Trade and Sustainability Footprints", *Ecological Economics*, 28: 75-97.

Provisional Population Totals (1981) Delhi-Series-28, Census of India, Directorate of Census Operations, Delhi.

Provisional Population Totals (1991) Delhi-Series-31, Census of India, Directorate of Census Operations, Delhi.

Provisional Population Totals (2001) Delhi-Series-8, Census of India, Directorate of Census Operations, Delhi.

Pyatt, G. and Round, J.I. (1988) "Social accounting matrices for development planning", *Review of Income and Wealth*, 23: 339-64.

Raa, T. (1986) "Dynamic input-output analysis", *Review of Economics and Statistics*, 68: 300-10.

Rampa, G. and Lanza, A. (1988) "A model for assessing the growth opportunities of EEC Countries", in M. Giaschini (ed.) *Input-Output Analysis*, New York: Chapman and Hall Ltd., 367-390.

Rana, L. (2000) *Dynamics of Urban Land Use Planning: A Study of Metropolitan Delhi*, Delhi: Manisha Publications.

Rangarajan, C. and Reddy, K.S. (1981) "Impact of hike in prices of coal and petroleum products on the other sector of the economy", *Artha Vijnana*, 28: 176-181.

Rao, V.K.R.V. and Desai, P.B. (1965) *The City of Greater Delhi: A Study of Urbanization*, Bombay: Asia Publishing House.

Rasul, G. (1964) *Input-Output Relationship in Pakistan in 1954*, Rotterdam: Rotterdam University Press.

Reed, J.D. (1971) "The impact of a dominant industry on a metropolitan area", *Annals of Regional Science*, 5: 62-83.

Reggiani, A. Nijkamp, P. (1992) *Interactions, Evolution and Chaos in Space*, Berlin: Springer-Verlag.

Regional Plan 2001: National Capital Region (1988), Government of India National Capital Region Planning Board, Ministry of Urban Development, Government of India, Delhi.

Report on Household Consumer Expenditures (2001) Directorate of Economics and Statistics, Government of National Capital Territory of Delhi, Delhi.

Report on Un-registered Manufacturing (1972-73) National Sample Survey Organisation, Ministry of Statistics and Programme Implementation, Government of India, Delhi.

Report on Un-registered Manufacturing (2000-01) National Sample Survey Organisation, Ministry of Statistics and Programme Implementation, Government of India, Delhi.

Reshaping the Urban Growth Patterns: Some Options (1988) National Institute of Urban Affair, Delhi.

Rey, S.J. (1998) "The performance of alternative strategies for combining regional econometric input-output models", *International Regional Science Review*, 21: 1-36.

Richardson, H.R. (1985) "Input-output and economic base multipliers", *Journal of Regional Science*, 25: 647-661.

Richardson, H.W. (1972) *Input-Output and Regional Economics*, London: Weidenfeld and Nicolson.

Rickman, D.S. and Miller S.R. (2002) "An evaluation of alternative strategies for incorporating inter-industry relationship into regional employment forecasting model", *Review of Regional Studies*, 32:133-47.

Rickman, D.S. (2001) "Using input-output information for Bayesian forecasting of industry employment in a regional econometric model", *International Regional Science Review*, 24: 226-44.

Riedel, J. (1975) "Factor proportions, linkages and open, developing economy", *The Review of Economics and Statistics*, 57: 484-94.

Rieffer, R. and Tiebout, C.M. (1970) "Inter-regional input-output: An empirical California-Washington Model", *Journal of Regional Science*, 10:135-152.

Roberts, P. (eds.) (1993) *Managing the Metropolis: Metropolitan Renaissance*, Aveburg: Aidershot.

Roepke, H. and Adams, D. (1974) "A new approach to the identification of industrial complexes using input-output data", *Journal of Regional Science*, 14: 15-29.

Rogers A. (1971) *Matrix Methods in Urban and Regional Analysis*, San Francisco: Oldenburg.

Round, J. I. (1978) "On estimating trade flows in inter-regional input-output models", *Regional Science and Urban Economics*, 7: 289-302.

Saenz, G.M. (2000) "A hybrid input-output model of water", Papers of *13th International Conference on Input-Output Techniques*, Italy.

Saigal, O. (ed.) (1994) *Problems and Prospects of Industrial Development in a Metropolitan City: A Case of Delhi*, Delhi: Mittal Publications.

Sakurai N. and Moriizumi, Y. (2000) "Trade pattern and factor use: Evidence for Asia-Pacific Countries", Papers, *13th International Conference on Input-Output Techniques*, Italy.

Saluja, M.R. (1968) "Structure of Indian Economy: Inter-industry flows", *Sankhya,* 30:97-122.

Sarkar, H. (1975) "A model for forecasting of input-output coefficient: An aggregate approach", *Anvesak,* 5: 45-48.

Sastry, M.L. (1992) "Estimating the economic impact of elderly migration: An input-output analysis", *Growth and Change,* 54-65.

Sawyer, J.A. (1991) "Forecasting with input-output matrices", *Economic System Research,* 4: 325-47.

Saxena, K.K. and Bhatnagar, E. (1987) "Comparison of regional input-output tables", *Anvesak,* 17: 77-113.

Schaffer, W.A. (1976) *On the Use of Input-Output Models for Regional Planning,* London: Martinus Nijhoff.

Scherer, F. M. (1982) "Inter-industry technology flows and productivity measurement", *Review of Economics and Statistics,* 64: 627-34.

Sebald, A. V. and Bulbard, C.W. (1977) "Effects of parametric uncertainty and technological change in input-output models", *Review of Economics and Statistics,* 59:75-81.

Selvaldon, P. (1986) "The stability of input-output coefficients", in I. Sohn, (ed.) *Readings in Input-Output Analysis,* Oxford: Oxford University Press, 226-52.

Selvlic, M. and Gradic, G. (1972) "Using input-output analysis for Yugoslavia Price and Currency Reforms", in A.P. Carter and A. Brody (eds.) *Input-Output Techniques,* Amsterdam: North Holland Publishing Company, 233-241.

Sharma, K. R. and Leung, P.S. (1999) "Accounting for the linkages of agriculture in Hawaii's economy within input-output model", *Annals of Regional Science,* 33: 123-40.

Sharma, S.P. and Saxena, K.K. (1998) "Structural reforms and their impact on employment generation in India: An input-output approach", *Economic Systems Research,* 10:263-73

Shestalova, V. (2001) "General equilibrium analysis of

internal total factor productivity growth rates", *Economic Systems Research*, 13:391-404.

Simpson, D. and Tsukui, J. (1965) "The development structures of input-output tables", *The Review of Economics and Statistics*, 47: 434-46.

Singh, B. (1972) "West Bengal's Industrial Economy: An analysis in input-output framework", *Anvesak*, 2: 216-18.

Singh, P. and Dhamija, R. (eds.) (1989) *Delhi : The Developing Urban Crisis*, Delhi: Sterling Publications.

Singh, S. and Joshi, M. (1991) "Structural linkages and key sectors in the Economy of Uttar Pradesh", *Indian Journal of Regional Science*, 23: 89-94.

Smith, P. and Morrison, W.I. (1974) *Simulating the Urban Economy: Experiments with Input-Output Techniques*, London: Pion Ltd.

Socio-Economic Tables (1981) Delhi-Series-28, Census of India, Directorate of Census Operations, Delhi.

Socio-Economic Tables (1991) Delhi-Series-31, Census of India, Directorate of Census Operations, Delhi.

Solo, R. (1953) "Industrial capacity as a concept in input-output analysis", *Review of Economics and Statistics*, 35: 354-57.

Sonis, M. and Hewings, G.J.D. (1995) "The structure of multi-regional trade flows: Hierarchy, feedbacks and spatial linkages", *Annals of Regional Science*, 29: 409-430.

Staglin, P. and Wessels, H. (1971) "Inter-temporal analysis of structural change in the German Economy", in A.P. Carter and A. Brody (eds.) *Input-Output Techniques*, Amsterdam: North Holland Publishing Company, 370-393.

Staglin, R. (1989) "Towards an input-output sub-system for information sector", in R.E. Miller and K R. Polenske (eds.) *Frontiers in Input-Output, Analysis*, New York: Oxford University Press, 65-78.

Stanley, H.M. (1967) "An inter-industry analysis of wages

and plant size", *Review of Economics and Statistics*, 51: 341-45.

Stastry, D.V. (1976) "Import substitution in Indian Economy: a case of automobiles", in P. N. Mathur (ed.) *Economic Analysis in Input-Output Framework*, Poona: Gokhale Institute of Political Economy.

Statistical Handbook of Delhi (1971) Directorate of Economics and Statistics, Government of National Capital Territory of Delhi, Delhi.

Statistical Handbook of Delhi (1975) Directorate of Economics and Statistics, Government of National Capital Territory of Delhi, Delhi.

Statistical Handbook of Delhi (1981) Directorate of Economics and Statistics, Government of National Capital Territory of Delhi, Delhi.

Statistical Handbook of Delhi (2001) Directorate of Economics and Statistics, Government of National Capital Territory of Delhi, Delhi.

Stevens, B. and Glynnis, A.T. (1980) "Error generation in regional input-output analysis", in P. Saul (ed.) *Economic Impact Analysis: Methodology and Application*, Boston: Martinus Nijhoff, 68-84.

Stewart, I.G. (1958) "Input-output tables for the United Kingdom, 1948", *The Review of Industry*, 28: 7-15.

Stone, R. (1972) "The evaluation of pollution balancing gains and losses", *Minerva*, 10: 412-25.

Strassert, G. (2001) "The flow network of a physical input-output table: Theory and applications", in M. Lahr and Dietzenbaher, (eds.) *Input-Output Analysis: Frontiers and Extension*, London: Macmillan, 35-54.

Supreme Court of India (1996) M.C. Mehta *vs*. Union of India and Organisation Write Petition (Civil) No. 4677 of 1985, Supreme Court of India, New Delhi.

Suri, P. (1991) "Critical issues in Delhi Master Plan 2001", *Delhi Vikas Yatra*, 2: 25-31.

Suzuki, K. (1971) "Stability of the structure of the inter-regional flow of goods", *Journal of Regional Science*, 11: 187-209.

Techno-Economic Survey of Delhi (1973) National Council of Applied Economic Research, Delhi.

Thakur, B. and Parai A. (1995) "A review of recent urban geographic studies in India", *Geo-Journal*, 29:187-96.

Theil, H. (1967) "The information approach to the aggregation of input-output tables", *Review of Economics and Statistics*, 53: 451-61.

Thomas, V. (1982) *Input-Output Analysis in Developing Countries*, New York: John Wiley.

Thorbecke, E. and Alfred, J.F. (1974) "A ten-region model of world trade", in W. Sellekaerts (ed.) *International Trade and Finance*, London: Macmillan, 91-112.

Tiebout, C.M. (1969) "An empirical regional input-output projection model: The State of Washington", *The Review of Economics and Statistics*, 51: 334 -40.

Tilanus, C.B. (1966) *Input-Output Experience: The Netherlands 1948-61*, Rotterdam: Rotterdam University Press.

Tohmo, T. (2004) "New developments in the use of location quotients to estimates regional input-output coefficients and multipliers", *Regional Studies*, 38:43-54.

Tokoyama, K. (1976) "Structure of trade, production and development", in K. R. Polenske, and J.V. Skolka (eds.) *Advances in Input-Output Analysis*, Cambridge: Ballinger, 463-478.

Torii, Y. and Akayama, Y. (1989) "Effects of tariff reductions on trade in the Asia-Pacific Region", in R.E. Miller, K.R. Polenske and A. Z. Rose (eds.) *Frontiers of Input-Output Analysis*, New York: Oxford University Press, 165-179.

Torii, Y. and Fukasaku, K. (1984) "Economic development: an input-output analysis of Republic of Korea and Japan", in U.N., *Proceedings of the Seventh International Conference on Input-Output Techniques*, New York, 333-366.

Tyagi, V.K. (1976) *Urban Growth and Urban Villages*, New Delhi: Kalyani Publishers.

U.S.S.R, Central Statistical Board, Balance Sheet of the National Economy of USSR 1923-24, transaction of the Board, 26, Moscow, discussed in G.T.Vladimir (1977) *Studies in Soviet Input-Output Analysis,* New York: Praeger Publishers, 4-12.

Ukidwe, N.U. and Bakshi, B. R. (2004) "Thermodynamic accounting of ecosystem contribution to economic sectors with application to U. S. Economy", *Environmental Science and Technology,* 38: 4810-27.

Urata, S. (1988) "Economic growth and structural change in Soviet Economy: 1959-72", in M. Giaschini (ed.) *Input-Output Analysis,* New York: Chapman and Hall Ltd., 303-324.

Veena, D.R. (1974) "Input-output model for manpower projection and occupation and educational level in Gujarat", *Anvesak,* 4: 119-144.

Venkatramaih, P. and Argade, L. (1979) "Input-output coefficients and their impact on production level", *Artha Vijnana,* 21: 479-56.

Verduras, C.A. (2000) "The estimation of the inter-regional trade in the context of an inter-regional input-output model", Papers, *13th International Conference on Input-Output Techniques,* Italy.

Victor, R. (1968) *Pollution: Economy and Environment,* London: Allen and Unwin.

Waelbraeck, J. and Gupta, S. P. (1984) "World Bank Global Modelling Research", in proceedings of *the Seventh International Conference on Input-Output Techniques,* New York, 102-112.

Walras, L. (1954) *Elements of Pure Economics,* 1874, Translated in English by W.J. Homewood, London: Allen and Unwin Inc.

Watanabe, T. (1970) "Planning application of Leontief Model in Japan", in A.P. Carter and A. Brody (eds.) *Contributions to Input-Output Analysis,* Amsterdam: North Holland Publishing Company, 9-23.

Weiler, S. and Richardson, R. (2002) "Driving regional economic models with a statistical model: Hypothesis testing for economic impact analysis", *Review of Regional Studies*, 32: 97-111.

Weisskoff, R. (1975) "Development and trade dependence: The case of Puerto Rico, 1948-63", *The Review of Economics and Statistics*, 57: 470-77.

West, G. (1981) "An efficient approach to the estimation of regional input-output multipliers", *Environment and Planning*, 13: 857-867.

Wolff, E.W. and Howell, D.R. (1989) "Labour quality and productivity growth in United States: An input-output growth accounting frameworks", in R.E. Miller and K.R. Polenske (eds.) *Frontiers in Input-Output Analysis*, New York: Oxford University Press, 148-164.

Wurtele, W.C. (1958) "A problem encountered in the comparison of technical coefficients", Review *of Economic Studies*, 26:148-152.

Yadav, C.S. (1979) *Land Use in Big Cities: A Study of Delhi*, Delhi: Inter-India Publications.

Yan, C. (1969) Introduction to Input-Output Economics, Holt: Rinehart and Winston.

Index